TAMASIN'S KITCHEN BIBLE

TAMASIN'S KITCHEN BIBLE

THE ONE & ONLY BOOK FOR EVERY COOK

TAMASIN DAY-LEWIS

PHOTOGRAPHY BY DAVID LOFTUS

WEIDENFELD & NICOLSON

CONT

1
2
3

EASY THINGS

16

Learning how to make and bake jam tarts, flapjacks, easy chocolate cakes and cookies, scones, pancakes, fudge and the ultimate Victoria sponge

SIMPLE SKILLS

50

Eggy things, perfect pasta dishes, salads, soups, the definitive Sunday roast with all the trimmings, game and accompaniments, easy puddings and cakes

FRUGAL FOOD

122

Gorgeous grain, pilav, risotto and paella, couscous, polenta, starters and snacks, more pasta, substantial meaty dishes, unfiddly fishy things, pastry and dinner party lore

ENTS

INTRODUCTION

The original Mrs Beeton's *The Book of Household Management* was a Victorian landmark. I can't think of any other cookery book, before or since, that has had more of an impact on our lives and eating habits for over a century. Not only is it a unique record of social history, it is also a highly personal and characterful account of a life, filled with charming and ridiculous archaisms and anecdotes, which we all seize upon with glee when we want to learn about our heritage. In its time it was clearly a bible, without which the new wife of the mid-19th century would have started married life at her peril.

Isabella Mayson was born in 1836 and started her own married life to Sam Beeton at 20. A year later she had started collecting and compiling recipes, which over the next four years of what she termed 'incessant labour', became the original magnum opus. Mrs Beeton copied the style of Eliza Acton, who, in her *Modern Cookery* of 1845, was the first English food writer to go into methodical and minute detail when setting down her recipes, extraordinary though it may seem now.

The Book of Household Management was first published in 1861, when Mrs Beeton was only 25. By 1865, at the age of 28, she was dead. Her husband, Sam, an impecunious publisher, signed her book away to Messrs Ward, Lock and Tyler, who turned her into the great British domestic legend that to some extent she still is. More domestic governess than goddess, her stern tones and strict pronouncements were what made the first edition of this incredible compendium as gripping and compulsive as any good upstairs-downstairs novel.

The problem was, that with each successive revision and re-publication, her original vision was gradually glazed with refinement, extravagance, Frenchification and tinkering. It bore less and less resemblance to the original, to the redoubtable, governessy tones with which she galvanised and educated the clueless young mistresses of middle-class homes all over England. By the time the 1960 edition was published, none of the original recipes remained. Gone were the social observations that define and reveal the character of the author; the advice on the treatment of servants; the social etiquette of paying visits; the duties of everyone in the mid-Victorian household from the dairy maid to the wet-nurse; how the reader should choose their acquaintances. Gone, too, were the chapters on frugality and economy in the kitchen; on the rearing and management of children, from suckling to childhood illnesses; on invalid cookery and suggested 'bills of fare'; and Mrs Beeton's classic treatises on the role of the mistress and the housekeeper.

Originally she had quoted my ancestor Oliver Goldsmith's definition of the ideal mistress of the house: 'the modest virgin, the prudent wife, and the careful matron, are much more serviceable in life than petticoated philosophers, blustering heroines, or virago queens. She who makes her husband and her children happy, who reclaims the one from vice and trains up the other to virtue, is a much greater character than ladies described in romances, whose whole occupation is to murder mankind with shafts from their quiver, or their eyes.' All these gems which would magnetise even the modern reader and disseminate the past have been dispensed with by the band of editors who, over the years, wrote and re-wrote Mrs Beeton out of her own story.

Mrs Beeton was not essentially a food writer. She was an anthologist, who recorded the recipes of an era, of a stratum of society, and set them in their social context. From the wages of the servants to the breeds and rearing of animals and birds for the table, she set down, with encyclopaedic knowledge, the blueprint that would carry the new wife right through her married life without falling prey to the unthinkable: culinary disaster or social faux pas.

Any attempt to replicate such a bible nowadays would automatically be doomed to being remaindered in some cut-price provincial bookshop. How, anyway, could the premise for a modern culinary bible reflect a way of life that finally lurched to a long overdue close between the wars, a time when each family had as large and as formal an infrastructure as in Mrs Beeton's day? Even the word servant is a term so anachronistic as to be used only in parentheses in historical discussion. As for household management, it is a concept that expired on the tide of women's liberation, something as inappropriate to our age as turtle soup or collared pig's face.

But I have long hankered after a book that covers every by-way and boulevard under one roof, like the black cab driver's knowledge; a book in which you can find out how to make a basic biscuit if you're a child who's never cooked, or how to cook a woodcock and spread the trail on toast if you're a little more aspirant than the ingénue; a book that explains how to co-ordinate your first roast, make perfect pastry, poach a salmon, rescue a split sauce, stop a soufflé subsiding, impress a lover – all in something that doesn't feel like an indigestible manual. I have longed for a 'collected works' that feels like the story of a cooking life, with the disasters and triumphs and brave attempts. Something that reflects the gradual enlightenment as the novice cook becomes fledged into the world of good food without being tied to the apron strings of technique that domestic science or food technology would suggest – is there the faintest whiff of pleasure about either of those terms?

In marketing-speak, I guess I mean a look-no-further book, but I see it more as a sort of Shakespearean journey, a seven ages of man adventure, which starts by leading the child by the hand to explore the excitements and the possibilities of that most satisfying of experiences, making something delicious to eat.

The perfect kitchen has everything in the right place, where you need it and know you can find it. So should the perfect cook book, so that the reader isn't led to run before they can walk, braise before they can bake. The tools of the trade, a simple calendar of when things are in season, where you can lay your hands on them, what works with what, how to stock a store cupboard, use leftovers, feed children – these are all things that need to feel integrated but perfectly pitched and placed. The way we cook and eat at different stages of our lives changes as abruptly and as dramatically as the English weather. We wean children onto puréed food, then off it onto solids; we end up cooking two meals in place of one; we cook for wacky diets, to seduce, impress, comfort, console, when we have empty purses, empty fridges; we cook in other people's kitchens, other countries, in the country, in the city, for pleasure, because we have to, for unexpected guests, grand occasions, Christmas, birthdays. Is there any other activity that permeates our very soul to the depth and complexity of food, or that inhabits our memories quite so tenaciously, in so influential and formative a way? I dearly hope not. It only saddens me that in this era of the instant we could so easily lose not just the tradition of which Mrs Beeton was so inexorably a part, but the notion of society having a cuisine, of its being a universal, in which the family is part of that historical truth, that culture, that good cooking and eating are heir to.

In the preface to her first edition, Mrs Beeton admits that what moved her to write *The Book of Household Management*, was 'the discomfort and suffering which I had seen brought upon men and women by household mismanagement. I have always thought that there is no more fruitful source of family discontent than a housewife's badly cooked dinners and untidy ways.' Wonderfully anachronistic though this sounds now, I believe it to be as true at the beginning of the 21st century as it clearly was in the middle of the 19th. The fact that she pitches her prose as strongly as 'suffering' implies is as funny as it is cruelly true. So how sophisticated are we in an era when half our schoolchildren are clinically obese, when fats and sugars and salts are ladled by the food giants into readymade, processed foods, and our children in the inner cities don't even realise that milk doesn't originate in bottles and fish in fingers? A time in which a take-away generation has failed to learn the rudiments of cooking and housekeeping and have never tasted food that tastes how food ought to taste – so industrially produced is it at base level? I have been to schools teaching 'Home Economics' where the children are told to bring readymade pastry and tins of meat to make steak and kidney pies; where they are given pizza bases on which to empty their 'creative' choice of ingredients: hormone-plumped tinned ham, tinned pineapple and mozzarella that's more elastic than your knickers.

Whatever happened to the perfect sponge cake – airy, sandy and as light as dawn, with a seam of clotted strawberry or seeded raspberry jam spread across its middle and a gentle dusting of unrefined icing sugar shaken from above over its rack-etched surface? To damp, dense gingerbread, shortbread and parkin, the oozing dark brownie with its shards of walnut or almond, the jam tart filled to eruption level with the hottest jam that welds itself to the roof of your mouth, the crisply gooey cookie, the deliquescent melting moment?

Fairy cakes, chocolate biscuit cake, rice crispie or cornflake cakes, banana bread, these are all recipes that are so basic and elementary that you don't stop to think – can I cook? They are mud-pie easy, from stir straight to stove, but they are the building blocks that breed confidence, excitement and passion in the kitchen. If as a child you get to roll and cut and fill your mother's tarts with the leftover pastry from her spiced apple pie, you are not going to encounter the fear I'm constantly told about when perfectly competent cooks ask me if they have to make their own pastry. Pastry, soufflés, mayonnaise, bread, it's like running round your backhand. If you don't practise, if fear gets in the way, you are cast adrift without the foundations. No, it simply won't do. Pastry takes a minute in a food processor, five minutes by hand. You rub sifted flour and cold pieces of butter through your fingers until it turns breadcrumby. You add a splosh of icy water. You cohere the whole into a ball, quickly. And that's all there is to it. No mystery, merely the transforming alchemy of cookery.

Mrs Beeton may have been schoolmarmy and uncompromising in her instruction, but she must have given confidence to even the least experienced and talented of cooks. It is to her I turned to when making my first Yorkshire pudding, my first steamed puddings, my first lemon meringue pie and Bakewell tart. Not the most outré or modish of things I know, but fail-safe methods and results are the springboard from which we leap. She made things accessible and clear, and she eliminated doubt by means of the thorough working of her recipes and her detailed social instruction. She wanted the happiness of the household through the harmony of understanding good food and good behaviour. And, actually, I don't think I've ever met a good cook who wasn't bossy; one who didn't understand that the great kitchen, the good dinner is dependent upon order, precision, craft, dedication, attention to detail, clear instruction and timing. Mrs Beeton implies we should all be captains of industry, running the armed forces, the government and the country, and she is probably right!

I have to confess that the undertaking of a book such as this is bound to fill the writer with fears of inadequacy for the task ahead and dread of the sins of omission. For as much as I want people of all levels, ages and skills to be able to turn to these pages and cook up a storm, find the recipe they want, the dish they can't find anywhere else, the method they understand, it can't pretend to be all things to all people. I would rather people read these pages for inspiration, knowing that they might find something they'd never cooked, never heard of or never dared try, and just got cooking. It is not meant to be a manual. I start and finish with one principle where food and eating are concerned, the pleasure principle. The rest is up to you in your kitchen.

TAMASIN DAY-LEWIS

THE KITCHEN

Everything in life can be divided into necessities and luxuries, never more so than in the kitchen. The following is a list of my essentials. I am not a gadget freak, desperate for the newest time-saving kitchen appliance. In fact, I still whisk egg whites by hand with an old-fashioned rotary whisk. I reckon it takes me no longer than it does to get the electric whisk out and put it together, and anyway it's easier to wash up the hand version and it can be fun putting a little elbow grease into your cooking. So feel free to take or leave any of the electrical items I have put in here, though I would be loath to live without my Magimix, KitchenAid and blender, and my Gelato 2000 ice-cream machine.

IN MY KITCHEN DRAWER I HAVE:

Bottle opener/corkscrew
Carving fork
Cheese knives, one for soft, one for hard cheese
Apple corer
Kitchen cutlery
Kitchen scissors
Knife sharpener and steel
Lemon squeezer
Matches, tapers
Rubber stoppers and vacuum pump for wine bottles
Skewers
String
Swivel-bladed potato peeler
Tin opener
Wooden salad servers
Wooden spoons, 4, different sizes
Zester

IN MY PUDDING DRAWER BY MY MARBLE SLAB FOR PASTRY I HAVE:

Balloon whisks (small and large)
Birthday candles and holders
Cherry stoner
Dariole moulds
Funnel
Ice cream scoop
Jam-making sets (waxed circles, labels etc)
Mandolin (Benriner)
Muslin
2 palette knives, 1 bendy, 1 firm
Pastry brush
Pastry-cutting circles and shapes, several sizes
Rolling pin
Rotary whisk
Spatula
Sugar thermometer
Tart slice

POTS AND PANS

2 large heavy-bottomed Le Creuset casseroles (26cm and 28cm)
1 large Le Creuset frying pan with a handle (can be put in the oven so good for tatins)
1 large vegetable steamer
6 stainless-steel saucepans from milk pan size to large, heavy-bottomed
1 griddle, long enough for 6 steaks or lots of vegetables
1 omelette pan, used for nothing else
2 frying pans
1 small frying pan for tempering spices
Wok
Deep-frying pan
Double saucepan (for delicate sauces and for melting chocolate)
Kettle

TINS, TRAYS AND RACKS

2 roasting tins (small and large)
2 baking trays (small and large)
2 x 1 dozen jam tart tins
1 x 1 dozen muffin tin
Individual tart tins
Assorted cake tins, including a
  springform tin, 1 x 20cm/8in
  loose-bottomed tin and
  1 larger tin
2 tart tins with push-out
  bottoms, 1 x 20cm/8in and
  1 x 23cm/9in
2 racks for cooling cakes and
  biscuits
2 metal bread tins
1 pizza, bread stone

KNIVES

Bread: serrated
Carving
Chopper
Filleting
Paring
Poultry
Small serrated (for tomatoes)
Vegetable
2 heavier, larger-bladed knives
The sizes of knife you have are
  a matter of personal choice;
  what feels right in the hand

ELECTRIC GADGETS

Blender
Coffee machine
Coffee/spice grinder
Gelato 2000 ice-cream machine
KitchenAid
Magimix
Toaster
Waring juicer

BOWLS AND BASINS

6 glass bowls of different sizes
1 large mixing bowl
1 large and 1 small terrine
Gratin dishes of different sizes
4 pudding basins of different
  sizes
12 ramekins
Tupperware boxes for storage
  and ice cream

OTHER ESSENTIALS

Kitchen scales
2 measuring jugs
2 metal sieves (small and large)
1 nylon sieve for fruit
1 conical strainer
1 colander
1–3 large metal spoons,
  1 slotted for skimming
1 big flat perforated skimming
  spoon
1 masher
1 ladle
1 microplane
1 box grater
1 nutmeg grater
1 large mezzaluna
Salad spinner
Pepper mill
Mouli-légumes
Pestle and mortar
Carving board with spikes
Cheese board
2 wooden chopping boards
Oven gloves and tea towels

FOR WRAPPING AND LINING

Bakewell paper
Clingfilm
Greaseproof paper
Kitchen foil
Silicone paper
Ziploc bags

STORE CUPBOARD

A store cupboard is as expandable or as contractible as your storage space and budget dictate. I find there is always a row of things at the back of my cupboard or fridge which end up past their sell-by date, the sort of speciality things it looks fun to try but you can never find a way of incorporating into dishes, or you just need once or twice a year.

The following is a comprehensive list that works for me and the way I live. It includes the sort of ingredients I always want to have in the house, so that pasta and rice dishes, puddings, cakes and ice creams can all be made if I suddenly have an influx of starving children or friends, or just want to experiment with a new recipe, or comfort with an old dish. The thing to remember is always to replace each item the moment it has run out or nearly run out. Otherwise you won't remember until it is too late and end up trawling your shelves at the last minute, thinking you have that essential ingredient.

I always keep a selection of alcohol, liqueurs and things like Madeira, port and Marsala on the shelves for use in cooking.

OILS
Olive oil, three kinds —an ordinary one to cook with; a cold pressed extra virgin olive oil for dressings, fish etc; a seriously good extra virgin one you particularly like for special dishes
Nut oil for salads — hazelnut, walnut, whatever you favour
Sesame oil
Vegetable oil for frying

VINEGARS
White wine
Tarragon
Red wine
Cider
Balsamic, an everyday one and an aged, mellow, velvety one

DRIED PASTA
Lasagna
Macaroni
Penne
Spaghetti
And whatever else you like

RICE
Carnarole, Vialone Nano or Arborio rice for risotto
Basmati, brown and white
Jasmine rice
Long-grain rice, brown and white
Short-grain rice such as Calasparra for paella

OTHER GRAINS
Couscous
Bulghur (cracked wheat)
Polenta

PULSES – A SELECTION OF THE FOLLOWING
Borlotti beans
Butter beans

Black-eyed peas
Chickpeas, always
Flageolets
Haricot beans
Puy lentils
Split peas

NUTS AND SEEDS
Almonds (whole blanched almonds and flaked almonds)
Hazelnuts
Pine nuts
Walnuts
Sesame seeds
Poppy seeds
Sunflower seeds

DRIED FRUITS
Apricots, unsulphured
Currants
Figs
Prunes
Raisins
Sultanas

CHOCOLATE

Dark chocolate, 64–70% cocoa
    solids, at least 500g
Good-quality cocoa powder

BAKING THINGS

Baking powder
Bicarbonate of soda
Cream of tartar
Cornflour
Flour – plain, self-raising and
    wholemeal
Leaf gelatine
Vanilla pods
Vanilla extract
Bitter almond extract
Dried yeast

SUGAR

Icing
Caster
Demerara
Granulated
Molasses
Muscovado (light and dark)

EGGS AND DAIRY

Organic free-range eggs
Milk, cream, crème fraîche
Good unpasteurised Cheddar
Good unsalted butter
An aged Parmigiano Reggiano
    (Parmesan cheese)

SPICES

Allspice
Cardamom pods

Cayenne
Dried chillies
Cinnamon sticks
Cloves
Cumin seeds
Fennel seeds
Fenugreek
Garam masala
Ginger, dried root and powdered
    ginger
Whole nutmegs
Paprika and smoked paprika
Peppercorns (black, white and
    green)
Saffron
Sea salt
Star anise
Turmeric

MUSTARDS AND SAUCES

English mustard powder
French mustard like Dijon and
    Moutarde de Meaux
Hellmann's mayonnaise
Horseradish sauce
Soya sauce
Tabasco sauce
Tahini paste
Thai fish sauce
Tomato ketchup and purée
Worcestershire sauce
Rose/orange-flower water

TINS, JARS AND PACKETS

Anchovies, either salted or in
    olive oil
Capers

Chutneys and relishes
Gherkins
Black olive/green olive paste
    from Seggiano or Carluccio
Green olives
Black olives
Stem ginger
Italian plum tomatoes
Tuna (good brand like Ortiz from
    Brindisa)
Baked beans
Tea
Coffee

JAMS, JELLIES, SYRUPS

Blackstrap molasses
Honeys, runny and set
Jams and marmalade
Jellies, like redcurrant, apple and
    rosemary
Golden syrup
Maple syrup

BISCUITS

Cheese biscuits
Boudoir, amaretti, digestives for
    puddings

IN THE FREEZER

However dinky your freezer, try to
fit in a few necessities:
Bread
Ice cream
Homemade stock

VEGETABLE RACK

Onions, garlic, lemons

SEASONAL BRITISH DIARY

I have always found the *Books For Cooks* series from the eponymous cookbook shop to contain the best of the indigenous food calendars. I add and subtract my own list of items to these and write in the things that we don't grow in Britain but couldn't live without, like Seville and blood oranges, truffles and porcini, while I carry in my head the best times to eat certain foods. The season for Vacherin Mont d'Or, for example, is from October-March, but to my mind the late Vacherins, when the cows have fed on the summer grass, have the absolutely best flavour. I never buy lamb at Easter – it is too young, tasteless and anaemic, I prefer hogget in September/October or older lamb at the end of May or in June. It is all very well giving a time for tomatoes, but English tomatoes are rarely worth eating; their seedy acidity and tough-skinned lack of flavour and meatiness will never match a Provençal, Spanish or Italian tomato grown in the sun and picked when fully ripe, succulent and sweet.

There are certain fish that are watery, soft fleshed and 'spent' by spawning, so their flavour and texture are really not as good then as they are the rest of the year. Dover and lemon sole and plaice spring to mind, as do mussels. So, in late spring, talk to your fishmonger and ask him about the quality before buying.

JANUARY
FRUIT: apples (cooking and dessert), stored from the autumn, pears, forced rhubarb
VEGETABLES: artichokes (Jerusalem), beetroot, Brussels sprouts, cabbages of all colours, cardoons, carrots, celeriac, chard, chicory, curly kale, leeks, mushrooms, onions, parsnips, potatoes, salsify, seakale, shallots, spring greens, Swedes, turnips
FISH: cod, Dover sole, grey mullet, haddock, halibut, lemon sole, monkfish (throughout the year), mussels, oysters, scallops, turbot
POULTRY: goose, guinea fowl, turkey
GAME: hare, pheasant, pigeon, rabbit, snipe, venison
PLUS: Seville oranges for marmalade, and blood oranges

FEBRUARY
FRUIT: apples (cooking and dessert), pears, forced rhubarb
VEGETABLES: artichokes (Jerusalem), beetroot, Brussels sprouts, cabbages of all colours, cardoons, carrots, celeriac, chard, chicory, curly kale, leeks, mushrooms, onions, parsnips, potatoes, salsify, seakale, shallots, spring greens, Swedes, turnips, watercress
FISH: cod, Dover sole, grey mullet, haddock, halibut, lemon sole, mussels, oysters, scallops, turbot
POULTRY: goose
MEAT: lamb (hogget)
GAME: pigeon, rabbit, venison

MARCH
FRUIT: apples (cooking and dessert), pears, rhubarb
VEGETABLES: artichokes (Jerusalem), beetroot, broccoli, (sprouting), cabbages, (green), carrots, chicory, cucumbers, leeks, mushrooms, onions, parsnips, potatoes, seakale, shallots, spring greens, Swedes, turnips, watercress
FISH: halibut, lemon sole, mussels, oysters, scallops, shrimp
MEAT: lamb (hogget)

APRIL
FRUIT: apples (cooking), rhubarb
VEGETABLES: broccoli (sprouting), cabbages (spring green), carrots, cucumbers, leeks, mushrooms, potatoes (maincrop and Jersey Royals), radishes, seakale, sorrel, spinach, spring greens, swedes, watercress
FISH: brown trout, crab, halibut, lemon sole, lobster, mussels, prawns, oysters, salmon, sea trout (from the end of April or the beginning of May), shrimp

MAY
FRUIT: apples (cooking), rhubarb
VEGETABLES: asparagus, broccoli (sprouting), cucumbers, kohlrabi, mushrooms, potatoes (maincrop and Jersey Royals), radishes, rocket, sorrel, spinach, spring greens, spring onions, watercress
FISH: brown trout, crab, haddock, lobster, mussels, prawns, salmon, sea trout, shrimp
MEAT: lamb (new season)

JUNE

FRUIT: apples (cooking), cherries, gooseberries, rhubarb, strawberries
VEGETABLES: asparagus, broad beans, broccoli, carrots (new season), celery, courgettes, cucumbers, lettuce, peas, new potatoes, radishes, rocket, sorrel, spinach, spring onions, turnips (new season)
FISH: bass, brown trout, crab, Dover sole, grilse (young salmon), haddock, lobster, prawns, salmon, sea trout, shrimp
POULTRY: duckling
MEAT: lamb (new season)

JULY

FRUIT: bilberries (wortleberries), blackcurrants, blueberries, cherries (morello, sweet), gooseberries, loganberries, raspberries, redcurrants, strawberries, whitecurrants
VEGETABLES: artichokes (globe), beans (broad, French, runner), beetroot, broccoli, carrots, celery, chard, courgettes, cucumbers, kohlrabi, leeks, lettuce, marrows, mushrooms, onions (pickling), peas, potatoes (new), radishes, rocket, shallots, sorrel, spinach, spring onions, tomatoes, turnips
FISH: bass, crab, Dover sole, grey mullet, grilse, haddock, halibut, lobster, prawns, salmon, shrimp, turbot
POULTRY: duckling

AUGUST

FRUIT: apricots, bilberries (wortleberries), blackberries, blackcurrants, blueberries, cherries, gooseberries, loganberries, mulberries, plums, raspberries, redcurrants, strawberries, whitecurrants
VEGETABLES: artichokes (globe), beans (broad, French, runner), beetroot, broccoli, carrots, celery, chard, courgettes, cucumbers, kohlrabi, leeks, lettuce, marrows, mushrooms, onions (pickling), peas, potatoes (new), radishes, rocket, shallots, sorrel, spinach, spring onions, tomatoes, turnips
FISH: bass, crab, Dover sole, grey mullet, haddock, halibut, lobster, mackerel, prawns, salmon, shrimp, turbot
POULTRY: guinea fowl
GAME grouse from the glorious 12th

SEPTEMBER

FRUIT: apples (cooking and dessert), blackberries, blueberries, crab apples, damsons, elderberries, figs, green grapes, mulberries, plums, strawberries
VEGETABLES: artichokes, beans (French, runner), beetroot, broccoli, carrots, celery, chard, chicory, courgettes, cucumber, kohlrabi, leeks, lettuce, marrow, mushrooms, onions (pickling, maincrop), potatoes (maincrop, new), pumpkins, radishes, rocket, shallots, sorrel, spinach, spring onions, Swedes, sweetcorn, tomatoes, turnips, watercress
FISH: bass, cod, Dover sole, grey mullet, haddock, halibut, lobster, mackerel, mussels, prawns, oysters, shrimp, turbot
POULTRY: guinea fowl
MEAT: lamb (hogget)
GAME: grouse, mallard, pigeon, rabbit

OCTOBER

FRUIT: apples (cooking and dessert), blackberries, crab apples, damsons, hazelnuts, medlars, pears, quinces, slows, walnuts
VEGETABLES: beans (French, runner), beetroot, broccoli, cabbages (green, red, Savoy), celeriac, chicory, chard, corn salad, kohlrabi, leeks, lettuce, marrows, mushrooms, (wild, porcini and chanterelles), onions (pickling, maincrop), parsnips, potatoes, pumpkins, radishes, rocket, shallots, spinach, Swedes, sweetcorn, turnips, watercress
FISH: bass, cod, Dover sole, grey mullet, haddock, halibut, mackerel, mussels, prawns, oysters, shrimp, turbot
POULTRY: goose, guinea fowl
MEAT: lamb (hogget)
GAME: grouse, hare, partridge, pheasant, pigeon, rabbit, teal, venison

NOVEMBER

FRUIT: apples (cooking and dessert), chestnuts, filberts, hazelnuts, medlars, pears, quinces, walnuts
VEGETABLES: beetroot, broccoli, Brussels sprouts, cabbages (green, red Savoy), celeriac, chard, chicory, corn salad, kohlrabi, leeks, mushrooms, wild mushrooms, onions, (pickling, maincrop), parsnips, potatoes, pumpkins, shallots, spinach, Swedes, turnips, watercress
FISH: bass, cod, Dover sole, grey mullet, haddock, halibut, mackerel, mussels, oysters, turbot
POULTRY: goose, guinea fowl, turkey
GAME: hare, mallard, partridge, pheasant, pigeon, rabbit, snipe, woodcock, venison

DECEMBER

FRUIT: apples (cooking and dessert), chestnuts, pears, quinces, walnuts
VEGETABLES: artichokes (Jerusalem), beetroot, Brussels sprouts, cabbages of all colours, cardoons, celeriac, chard, chicory, corn salad, curly kale, leeks, mushrooms, onions, parsnips, potatoes, salsify, swedes, turnips
FISH: bass, cod, Dover sole, grey mullet, haddock, halibut, lemon sole, mussels, oysters, scallops, turbot
POULTRY: goose, guinea fowl, turkey
GAME: hare, mallard, pheasant, pigeon, rabbit, snipe, venison, woodcock

EASY

THINGS

1

A CHILD WANTS TO COOK what a child wants to eat, so the first

rolling up of sleeves and scrambling onto a kitchen chair should be met with a recipe that is a cast-iron, dead-cert success every time. You want something that is going to make the child glow with pride at the result and is so simple and quick to prepare that there is no time 'twixt stir, stove and scoff when boredom or, horror of horrors, disaster, has the faintest chance of getting the upper hand.

Obvious though this may sound, my early school experiences of cooking were largely confined to things I hated or that just didn't turn out how they ought to have done, a sure-fire way to propel you as swiftly as a gas flame out of the kitchen and into the sweet shop. There were rock buns that set like granite, melting moments that did just that, only before you could eat them, desert-dry esse biscuits that crumbled to dust in the mouth, sinking sponges whose craterous middles had to be filled to be concealed, but whose inner depths wept anyway when they were cut, biscuits with burnt edges that melded into each other, meringues which I never liked anyway.

I think my domestic science teacher probably despaired of both me and my taste, for the only way to ensure that no one else wanted to eat my hideous creations, was to lash on the food colouring as though everything edible was being entered for an Addams Family Halloween party. So I made emerald green Madeira cakes, Quink ink blue meringues and summoned up the courage to eat the results of my labours only because, as everyone knows, the ravening maw of childhood and teenagedom means being in a semi-permanent state of appetite arousal.

When I reached fifteen, my baking skills still barely rudimentary, we were asked to prepare a main course of our own choosing and cook it without any help from our teacher. My greatest treat when staying with my grandparents, which I also believed to be the nemesis of sophistication, was a dish of rump steak cooked medium rare, served in a wine and cream sauce with mushrooms fried in butter and petit pois laced with more cream, butter, sugar and mint. I put in my ingredients request alongside my classmates' more achievable and affordable million-ways-with-mince recipes and was met with a somewhat stony and quizzical look by the teacher. What could such a dismally maladjusted, cack-handed, no-taste cook be wanting with such a dish and how was she ever going to cook it?

Whatever dormant or budding instincts I possessed somehow steered me through the minefields of technique, mostly, I suspect, because the young taste everything as they go, so eager are they to eat what they are cooking. I may even have rung up my grandmother, but she, as with all ladies in her position, ordered just what she wanted every morning from her cook, knew just how she wanted it cooked, but had never actually been behind the green baize door to cook it.

The steak was as bloodily, rosily pink as it should have been, the confluence of juices from meat and wine as appetising as you could imagine and even the cream, without overwhelming, discretely made the rich amalgam that I was hoping for. The tinned peas, Hero if I remember rightly, were divinely sweet and delicately minted, the field mushrooms had absorbed the butter, their juices had run and the softened black tangle was lightly but firmly peppered. The only thing missing from the dish as served at my grandparents' house, were the rustlingly crisp, salt, hand-cut chips, burnished to a deep mahogany and sent to the dining room like children in a school dinner queue, in endless succession.

But we need our disasters too. The dishes that disappoint, despite their seemingly invincible instruction, that send us to another book, back to the stove, to a more experienced cook, in search of a better quality ingredient, make us think about why we went wrong. There is no cookery lesson from any book that can substitute for watching the thing with your own eyes, seeing technique in action, watching a recipe translate from page or head to dish with the particular imprimatur of a good cook. So, these first recipes are designed as a duet would be, for two. Stirring, weighing, measuring, pouring, rolling and cutting are the earliest of triumphs in the kitchen. At the next stage on, these are the sort of recipes that my children first learned to cook solo once they could read, with just a discreet bit of hand-holding or method explaining from the kitchen chair, tea or stiff drink in hand.

Baking is, to my mind, the foundation of all cooking and the thing that transforms beyond all else the hearth into the home. And there is no child, probably in history, who doesn't want to eat what they have helped to create. When it comes to the food wars that parents constantly engage in with their children, the 'he won't eat any vegetables' or 'she will only eat white food' stuff, I just want to say, get them cooking with you in the kitchen, show them the whiskers on the prawns and how to unfurl the bendy pink carapaces, turn the broccoli into forests, the carrots into coins, the parsnips into witches' fingers. Just don't commit the heinous crime of only allowing children to cook with inferior ingredients or make 'children's food'. There is no such thing as children's food. There is only food that they want to eat and that they'll want you to try and enjoy when they've cooked it, not treat like an experiment from the school chemi lab. Let them melt chocolate, slide pudgy fingers round the bowl, lick the spoon, pour and squeeze the barbecue sauce ingredients into the bowl and slosh the meat around in it, pod the peas and pick the beans. They'll eat anything if they've become part of the plot.

Make sure with each of these recipes that you read the recipe first and lay out the ingredients and the kitchen equipment before you start. That way you won't struggle sticky fingeredly to undo jars, tins, cupboards and packets and you'll know you have everything you need, including the main ingredient!

And there's one more thing, which I promise will make your cooking life easier even though it reeks of organisation. Wash up as you go. Never leave the kitchen looking like a weapon of mass destruction has recently landed. You'll be surprised at not only how virtuous having a ship-shape kitchen makes you feel, but also at how often you need the same mixer, spoon or sieve for the next stage – and need it clean.

SWEET TREATS

CHOCOLATE BISCUIT CAKE

110g/4oz unsalted butter
110g/4oz dark chocolate,
    Valrhona 64% cocoa solids
    is good for this
2 tbsp golden syrup
225g/8oz digestive biscuits

ICING (OPTIONAL)
55g/2oz dark chocolate as before
1 tbsp or a little more full cream milk

This is better known as chocolate fridge cake. You can make it a day or two in advance if you want to keep it for a children's party. It is uncooked and reliant on two joyously untechnical techniques – melting and bashing.

Melt the butter, chocolate and syrup together very gently over a low heat until liquid, making sure they come nowhere near boiling point. Remove from the heat. Put the digestives into a plastic bag, seal it, then smash them around with a rolling pin until they're bashed to crumbs. A few small chunks are fine, as they will add texture. Pour the crumbs into the chocolate mixture and stir together. Press into a shallow tin that you have greased well with butter and leave to set in the fridge. Add icing if you like.

ICING
Melt the chocolate and milk together very gently over a low heat, adding a little more milk if the mixture seems very thick. Spread over the top of the cake and chill. Turn out, slice and serve with cream or crème fraîche.

JAM TARTS

170g/6oz plain flour
85g/3oz unsalted butter
a selection of jams for different
    colours and flavour

These are the first things my children made, joining and pressing, rolling and cutting the remnants of pastry from whatever tart or pie I was in the process of making. They devised their own concoctions with chunks of unpeeled apples and sugar, pushing great clots of strawberry, apricot and raspberry jams and bramble jelly into the pastry cases. If you want to start from scratch, here is the recipe. The rules for good pastry are really very simple: good flour, best unsalted butter and keep everything cold, cold, cold, handling it as little as possible.

Sift the flour into a food processor, then cut in little chunks of fridge-cold butter. Swirl for a few seconds until the mixture is crumbed, then add about a tablespoon of very cold water and wait for the mixture to cohere. The moment it does, stop the processor, press the ball firmly into a circle, cover with clingfilm and refrigerate for at least 30 minutes.

Turn the oven to 200°C/400°F/Gas 6 to heat up. Sprinkle a little flour onto your marble or cold surface and roll the pastry out thinly, making sure the rolling pin is always covered in flour too, so that it doesn't stick to the pastry. Grease your tray of a dozen little tart tins with butter paper, then start cutting out pastry circles and fitting them into the tray. Add a good spoonful of jam to each tart and set the timer for 10 minutes. It is always best to put a baking sheet in the centre of the oven to heat up before putting your tart tin on it as it makes for crisper pastry.

Check the tarts after 10 minutes; they may need up to 5 more minutes. The filling should be bubbling and beginning to erupt, the pastry browned. Remove from the oven, cool on a rack for 5 minutes before turning them out onto the rack with a palate knife to cool further. Eat warm.

Jam Tarts

CHOCOLATE CORNFLAKE CAKES

No children's party is complete without these moreish, crunchy chocolate cornflake cakes. Child's play to make, too.

MAKES ABOUT 20

55g/2oz cornflakes
170g/6oz bitter chocolate such as Valrhona 64% cocoa solids
30g/1oz unsalted butter

Preheat the oven to 150°C/300°F/Gas 2. Spread the cornflakes on a shallow baking tray and put into the oven, on a low shelf, for 10 minutes. Let them cool for a while before bashing them up a little. Warm the chocolate and butter together in a pan over a low heat until just melted, then stir in the cornflakes. Spoon the mixture into paper cases or use teaspoons to shape into little conical hills on a greased baking tray. Leave to set.

GOOEY CHOCOLATE COOKIES

If you prefer gooey chewy to crisp short, these cookies are the business. Use pecans, hazelnuts or almonds according to the state of your larder and your heart's desire.

MAKES ABOUT 18

4 egg whites
340g/12oz unrefined icing sugar
75g/2½ oz Green and Black's cocoa powder, or something similarly dark and dangerous
55g/2oz plain flour
1 tsp Espresso or instant coffee dissolved in 1 tbsp hot water
110g/4oz nuts, chopped finely

Preheat the oven to 180°C/350°F/Gas 4. Line a baking sheet with non-stick baking parchment. Whisk the egg whites until frothy but not stiff, in a KitchenAid if you have one, then pour over the sifted sugar, cocoa and flour and add the coffee. Turn the beaters on again slowly, then when everything has blended, speed them up and let the mixture thicken for 2–3 minutes. Remove the bowl from the KitchenAid and add the chopped nuts, folding them in.

Dollop tablespoons of the mixture onto the baking sheet, leaving about 5cm/2in between each spoonful. Bake for 12–15 minutes. The tops should be firm and cracked like parched earth, the insides delectably gooey. Remove with a palate knife to a wire rack and leave to cool.

CHOCOLATE OATMEAL COOKIES

MAKES ABOUT 2½ DOZEN

140g/5oz unsalted butter, softened
225g/8oz light muscovado sugar
1 egg
a few drops vanilla extract
110g/4oz plain flour
1 tsp baking powder
225g/8oz organic rolled oats
170g/6oz dark chocolate chips

Preheat the oven to 180°C/350°F/Gas 4. Cream the softened butter and sugar together until light and fluffy. Add the egg and the vanilla extract – go easy so that it doesn't overwhelm, a few drops is all you need – and beat together until smooth. Sift the flour and baking powder into the bowl and fold in lightly. Pour in the oats and the chocolate chips and stir to combine.

Grease a baking tray or line with non-stick baking parchment. Using a tablespoon, roll the mixture into balls and plop them down onto the tin, leaving about 5cm/2in between each cookie as they will spread. Flatten each cookie a little with a fork and put in the oven for about 20 minutes or until golden. Cool for a couple of minutes and then put the cookies on a wire rack to cool completely. Store in an airtight container.

CHOCOLATE CHIP COOKIES

MAKES 2–4 DOZEN
depending on the size you prefer

110g/4oz unsalted butter, softened
50g/scant 2oz vanilla caster sugar
55g/2oz light muscovado sugar
1 egg
½ vanilla pod, split, the seeds
    extracted with the point of a
    teaspoon
110g/4oz plain flour
½ tsp bicarbonate of soda
140g/5oz dark chocolate such as
    Valrhona 64%, finely chopped into
    tiny chips

These need no introduction, no hard sell. The commercial kind are a different animal and the satisfaction of these vanilla-ey, biscuity scent-of-baking cookies is one to bottle, it is so good for the soul.

Preheat the oven to 180°C/350°F/Gas 4. Grease several baking sheets. Cream the butter and sugars together until light and fluffy, about 2–3 minutes, then break in the egg and continue to beat until it has amalgamated. Scrape in the vanilla seeds, then sift the flour and bicarbonate of soda in together. Stir it into the mixture, then do likewise with the chocolate chips. Plop teaspoons or dessertspoons of the mixture onto the baking trays, leaving about 5cm/2in between each, and bake for 10–12 minutes until palely browned.

When you remove the cookies to a wire rack with a palate knife they will still feel soft, but never fear, they will firm up as they cool. Keep them in an airtight tin in layers of greaseproof paper when they've cooled.

PEANUT COOKIES

MAKES ABOUT 24

110g/4oz unsalted butter, softened
110g/4oz vanilla caster sugar
1 egg
170g/6oz plain flour
1 tsp baking powder
140g/5oz raw unsalted peanuts

Utterly nutty cookies, the sort of thing you can make when the store cupboard is nearly bare. You can even substitute crunchy peanut butter if you can't lay your hands on the nuts.

Preheat the oven to 180°C/350°F/Gas 4. Cream the butter and sugar in a KitchenAid or with electric beaters until light and fluffy. Add the egg and mix well – you may need to scrape the mixture down the sides of the bowl at some point. Fold in the sifted flour with the baking powder and peanuts.

Line the baking trays with non-stick baking paper and put well spaced dollops of the mixture on the paper with a tablespoon. Bake for 10–12 minutes or until golden. Cool on wire racks. Don't worry if the biscuits aren't hard when you remove them from the oven, they firm up on the racks.

CHOCOLATE AND PEANUT RICE CRISPY CAKES

MAKES ABOUT 30

225g/8oz dark chocolate such as
    Valrhona 64% cocoa solids
1 egg yolk
55g/2oz unsalted peanuts, chopped
55g/2oz rice crispies

Melt the chocolate in a bowl over a pan of simmering water. Make sure the water doesn't touch the bowl. Add the yolk and stir it in, then add the peanuts and rice crispies and stir until everything is well mixed. Spoon little piles of mixture into paper cases and leave them until set.

MUESLI COOKIES

225g/8oz muesli
55g/2oz light or dark muscovado
   sugar, depending on how treacly a
   taste you like
110g/4oz wholemeal or plain flour
85g/3oz Valencia almonds, grind
   them yourself
170g/6oz unsalted butter
3 tbsp flavoured honey like lavender
   or chestnut
½ tsp bicarbonate of soda

A moreish, solid, substantial cookie that you should not shun on the grounds that it might smack of the health food shop. Just make sure you use a good organic muesli, full of fruit and nuts.

Preheat the oven to 190°C/375°F/Gas 5. Put the muesli, sugar, flour and almonds, which you should grind but not over-grind so that they start looking oily, in a bowl and stir together well. Melt the butter and honey together, remove from the heat and stir in the bicarb. Stir this into the dry mixture and mix it all in together well. Plop dessertspoons of the mixture onto greased baking trays or non-stick baking paper, leaving about 5cm/2in between them. Flatten the cookies down with a fork. Bake in the oven for 10–15 minutes or until golden. Cool on a wire tray, then store in an airtight container.

SNICKERDOODLES

MAKES ABOUT 4 DOZEN

340g/12oz plain flour
1 tsp bicarbonate of soda
225g/8oz unsalted butter, softened
255g/9oz unrefined vanilla caster
   sugar
2 eggs
55g/2oz walnuts, very finely chopped
5 tbsp unrefined vanilla caster sugar
1 tbsp ground cinnamon, ground in a
   mortar is best

A thoroughly American cookie which has a light, cakey texture and a crunchy, cinnamon-sugared exterior. Children will want to cook them for the name alone.

Preheat the oven to 190°C/375°F/Gas 5. Sift the flour and bicarb into a bowl. Cream the butter and sugar until light, then gradually beat in the eggs, one at a time. Stir in the flour and bicarb and the nuts. Form the dough into rolls about 2.5cm/1in in diameter, wrap them in clingfilm and refrigerate for about 30 minutes until firm.

   Stir the 5 tablespoons of sugar and the cinnamon together on a plate or pastry marble. Quickly roll walnut-sized lumps of dough into balls in your hands, rolling them in the cinnamon sugar afterwards. Place them on non-stick parchment paper or greased baking sheets, placing them about 5cm/2in apart. Bake for 10–12 minutes until they are golden brown around the edges. Leave them on the baking tray for a minute before transferring to a rack to cool. Great with poached fruit or ice cream.

BLACK AND WHITE CHOCOLATE COOKIES

MAKES ABOUT 24

225g/8oz unsalted butter, softened
200g/7oz light muscovado sugar
255g/9oz unrefined sugar
3 eggs
285g/10oz plain flour
1 tsp baking powder
55g/2oz dark cocoa powder like
   Green and Black's organic
130g/4½oz dark chocolate,
   broken into small chunks
130g/4½oz white chocolate,
   broken into small chunks

Preheat the oven to 150°C/300°F/Gas 2. Beat the butter and sugars together in a KitchenAid or with electric beaters until light and fluffy. Add the eggs, one by one, beating them in well. Sift in the flour, baking powder and cocoa, throw in the chocolate chunks and mix well, folding with a large metal spoon.

   Use about 2 tablespoonfuls of mixture per cookie, putting them on baking trays lined with non-stick baking paper. Place them about 5cm/2in apart as they will spread! Flatten them down a little and bake in the middle of the oven for 20–25 minutes or until their bottoms have darkened to chocolate brown. Cool on wire racks.

Black and White Chocolate Cookies

CHOCOLATE BROWNIES

MAKES 12–16 SQUARES

200g/7oz best bitter chocolate,
    at least 64% cocoa solids
110g/4oz unsalted butter, softened
225g/8oz unrefined vanilla caster
    sugar
2 eggs and 1 egg yolk
4 tbsp strong, freshly made coffee
140g/5oz plain flour
1 tsp baking powder
a handful of whole hazelnuts

Please don't overcook these. You need to push a skewer right through them to check they are done and, unlike a cake where the skewer comes out clean if it's ready, you need a bit of chocolate goo on the skewer. If they tremble in the middle when you wobble the tin, they are still undercooked. Brownies should emerge with what's known as a 'sad' centre and a thin, dry, slightly crunchy crust.

Preheat the oven to 180°C/350°F/Gas 4. Line the bottom and sides of a small roasting tin or gratin dish, about 30 x 22cm/12 x 9in, with foil, then grease it with butter. Gently melt the chocolate in a double boiler, or a bowl placed over a pan of simmering water. The bowl should not touch the water.

Cream the softened butter and sugar until really light and fluffy, by hand or with electric beaters or a KitchenAid. Add the eggs, one at a time, then the extra yolk, with the mixer running. Pour in the melted chocolate and the coffee, amalgamate, then switch off the machine and sift in the flour and baking powder. Fold them in with a metal spoon.

Pour the mixture into the tin, push in hazelnuts at intervals so they just stand proud, and bake for about 25 minutes. Check with a skewer as above. Leave to cool in the tin on a rack, then cut the brownies into squares and remove them from the tin. Serve with crème fraîche and a scattering of Green and Black's organic cocoa powder if you feel particularly indulgent.

CHOCOLATE CHIP AND HAZELNUT BROWNIES

MAKES 12–16 SQUARES

285g/10oz unrefined
    vanilla caster sugar
4 eggs
225g/8oz unsalted butter
85g/3oz Green and Black's
    organic cocoa
85g/3oz plain flour
200g/7oz best bitter chocolate,
    at least 64% cocoa solids
110g/4oz roasted hazelnuts
110g/4oz cooking chocolate chunks
    (The Chocolate Society do them in
    bags, 70% cocoa solids)

Preheat the oven to 180°C/350°F/Gas 4. Prepare the roasting tin as in the previous recipe. Beat the sugar and eggs together really well until they have thickened and the sugar has completely dissolved. Melt the butter in a small pan and pour it into the sugar and egg. Sieve the cocoa and flour together into the mixture, then melt the 200g/7oz of chocolate in a double boiler as in the previous recipe and add it into the mixture. Stir it in.

Put the hazelnuts and chunks of chocolate into a plastic bag and whack as hard as you dare with a rolling pin, keeping things chunky and in shards. The nuts will inevitably be more pulverised than the chocolate. Fold into the mixture and scrape it into the tin.

Bake for about 25 minutes. Test with a skewer, which should not come out completely clean. Leave to cool in the tin on a rack before cutting into squares. Serve warm or cold with crème fraîche and a scant scattering of extra cocoa powder.

FAIRY CAKES

MAKES 1 DOZEN

110g/4oz unsalted butter, softened
110g/4oz unrefined caster sugar
2 eggs
110g/4oz self-raising flour, sifted
½ tsp pure vanilla extract
2–3 tbsp milk

ICING
170g/6oz unrefined icing sugar
2 tbsp water or lemon/orange/lime
    juice and 1 tsp grated zest

The only food colouring allowed in this house is strictly of the turmeric, saffron or blackberry variety, so if you want lividly iced day-glo toppings invent your own or just make a simple icing and stick on silver balls, Smarties, fresh fruit or what you will. Fairy cakes, like musical bumps, are mandatory children's party fare and every bit as necessary for the comfort and well-being of the parents. They are also a one-step, easy-peasy thing for children to do all by themselves.

Preheat the oven to 200°C/400°F/Gas 6. Put all the ingredients bar the milk in a KitchenAid or food processor and whisk until really smooth. Add a little milk at the end until you have what's known as a soft, dropping consistency, which means the mixture slips off the spoon with ease. Spoon the mixture into a dozen little cake papers, which you've put in a tray of muffin or tart tins and bake for 15–20 minutes or until cooked and golden on top. Cool for 10 minutes before putting the cakes on a rack to cool down.

ICING
Sift the icing sugar into a bowl. Mix in the liquid or liquid and zest until smooth. Utterly simple.

FLAPJACKS

MAKES 12

75g/2½ oz unsalted butter
2–3 tbsp golden syrup
75g/2½ oz light muscovado sugar
140g/5oz rolled oats

Melting, stirring and pressing – three things all children enjoy as much as the end result. Real old-fashioned party tea food.

Preheat the oven to 170°C/325°F/Gas 3. Melt together the butter, golden syrup and muscovado sugar, very gently. Pour them over the oats in a bowl and mix together until everything is stickily combined. Press the mixture into a greased 18 x 28cm/7 x 11in shallow baking tin and bake for 15–20 minutes until golden and set. Cool and then cut into squares. They will only harden as they cool, so be patient.

MELTING MOMENTS

MAKES ABOUT 18

170g/6oz unsalted butter, softened
30g/1oz unrefined icing sugar
a few drops pure vanilla extract
135g/4½ oz plain flour
25g/scant oz cornflour
a handful of pecans or almonds

How could I not include these meltingly buttery confections, which defeated me in the school cookery class all those years ago! I must have under-cooked them – they are really terribly easy. In those days we pushed a glacé cherry on the top, but I have always been inordinately anti those waxy sweet baubles. I suggest using a pecan nut or almond instead or leaving the moments plain.

Preheat the oven to 180°C/350°F/Gas 4. Tip the butter, icing sugar and vanilla into the bowl of the KitchenAid or use your electric beater to beat the mixture thoroughly until light and fluffy. Sieve the flour and cornflour into the bowl and stir in until combined. Either plop spoonfuls of the mixture onto a baking tray lined with non-stick baking parchment or scrape the mixture into a piping bag with a fluted nozzle and pipe 2.5cm/1in circles onto the paper. Push a nut onto each summit. Leave room to spread between each moment. Cook for 12–14 minutes or until golden, then cool on a rack.

OVERNIGHT MERINGUES

MAKES 12

110g/4oz egg whites
225g/8oz unrefined caster sugar
30g/1oz flaked almonds

I have been making meringues in this somewhat unorthodox way ever since I tried Baker and Spice meringues, which sit in huge cloudy piles at the entrance to the shop. The recipe I found in their lovely book *Baking with Passion*. You will get a better result if the eggs are not really fresh but at least a week old, and if the whites are at room temperature when you use them.

Preheat the oven to 150°C/300°F/Gas 2. Cover 2 large baking trays with non-stick baking parchment. Put the egg whites and sugar in a bowl set over a pan of simmering water and stir until the sugar has dissolved and the mixture is quite warm to the touch. Whisk in a KitchenAid or with electric beaters until thick and cool, about 15–20 minutes. Spoon 6 large mounds of meringue onto each tray and lightly sprinkle with almonds. Place the trays in the oven, turn off the heat and leave the meringues to dry out overnight.

MUFFINS

Warm, light and buttery with a splurt of fruit bled into them so the sponge is stained like blotting paper, the muffin is a cake for all seasons. You can scent them with spice or spike them with berries blue or black; lace them with cherries, colour them red, white or black with currants, add dried fruit, apples, pears or chocolate. Children love making them and plopping the little turrets out steaming onto a rack. You can sprinkle a little crumble mixture on top of them or just make them plain. The one thing you can't do is make do with only one. Here is the basic mix. The yoghurt is my friend Sally Edwards's touch and she bakes better than almost anyone I know.

170g/6oz self-raising flour
1 tsp baking powder
110g/4oz caster sugar
1 tsp ground cinnamon, best ground in a mortar
75g/2½oz unsalted butter, melted
1 egg
100ml/3½fl oz milk
100ml/3½fl oz live plain yoghurt, cow's, goat's or sheep's
1 tsp pure vanilla extract
140g/5oz blueberries or cherries, raspberries, redcurrants, etc

CRUMBLE TOPPING (OPTIONAL)
30g/1oz butter
30g/1oz light muscovado sugar
45–55g/1½–2oz flour

Preheat the oven to 180°C/325°F/Gas 4. Sieve the flour and baking powder into a bowl and tip in the sugar and cinnamon. Then add the melted butter, egg, milk, yoghurt and vanilla to the bowl and stir everything together well. Tip in the fruit and fold in very gently so it doesn't break up.

Butter 10 muffin tins, put in muffin papers if you have them and plop in the mixture. Place in the middle of the oven on a pre-heated baking sheet for 35–40 minutes. Leave in the tins for 10 minutes, then turn out onto a rack and eat warm.

CRUMBLE TOPPING

If you like the crumble topping idea, rub the butter, sugar and flour together briefly and sprinkle on top of the muffins before putting them in the oven.

GINGERBREAD MEN

MAKES A COUPLE OF DOZEN HUNKY, SPICY GUYS

110g/4oz unsalted butter, softened
100g/3½oz light muscovado sugar
170g/6oz golden syrup
400g/14oz plain flour, sifted
2 tsp ground ginger, use dried ginger root and grind it yourself if you can
1 tsp bicarbonate of soda, sifted

ICING
1 egg white
55g/2oz unrefined icing sugar, sifted
a squeeze of lemon juice

Preheat the oven to 190°C/375°F/Gas 5. Put the butter and brown sugar in the bowl of the KitchenAid or whisk with electric beaters until light and creamy. Add the golden syrup, sifted flour, ginger and sifted bicarb and mix until you have a smooth dough.

Roll out the dough between sheets of non-stick baking parchment to about 4mm/¼in thick. Cut out the gingerbread men with the cutter and place them on baking trays lined with non-stick baking parchment. Bake for 8–10 minutes or until golden. Cool on racks.

ICING

Mix the egg white and sifted icing sugar together thoroughly with a little squeeze of lemon. Pipe buttons onto the gingerbread men. Plunge edible silver balls into their middles if you have some. Leave them to set.

PARKIN

170g/6oz plain flour
340g/12oz medium oatmeal
1 tbsp light muscovado sugar
½ tsp ground ginger
a pinch of sea salt
450g/1lb treacle
110g/4oz unsalted butter
70ml/2½fl oz milk
1 tsp bicarbonate of soda
a handful of flaked almonds
   (optional)

This is a deliciously old-fashioned sticky, treacly version, as good served at lunch, with a hunk of strong, unpasteurised Cheddar like Montgomery's or Keen's, as for pudding or tea. Dollop on crème fraîche if it's for pudding. Make the parkin at least a day before you want to eat it, preferably a week, and store it wrapped in foil in a tin.

Preheat the oven to 180°C/350°F/Gas 4. Sift the flour into the bowl and add the oatmeal, sugar, ginger and salt. Warm the treacle gently with the butter, then remove from the stove. Heat the milk to blood temperature, add the bicarb and pour it into the dry ingredients with the treacle and butter. Fold together. Grease and flour a roasting tin and line it with non-stick baking parchment. Pour in the mixture and bake for about 40 minutes or until firm to the touch. You may sprinkle a handful of flaked almonds over the parkin about 15 minutes into baking if you feel like it. Keep the parkin for a day or two before cutting it into squares and serving as suggested above.

SHORTBREAD

110g/4oz unsalted butter, softened
55g/2oz unrefined caster sugar
110g/4oz fine plain flour
55g/2oz rice flour
more caster sugar for dredging

Shortbread made without butter, best unsalted butter that is, is not worth eating. The butter is the whole point so no false economising, even if it is a child at the helm here. If you are going to teach your children how to cook this simple and deliciously buttery, sugary biscuit, explain the importance of good ingredients. The 'M' word won't do; it is a heinously disgusting fat anyway.

Preheat the oven to 180°C/350°F/Gas 4. This is a hands-on, hands-in thing. You don't want the butter to become broken up, so plonk it in a large bowl or on a board with the sugar and flours and knead everything together into a dough. Then roll it out into a circle or oblong, about 2.5cm/1in thick, on a floured board.

   Slide it onto a baking tray on a piece of non-stick baking parchment. Decorate the edges by marking them with the tines of a fork and the middle by pricking with the fork and bake for 15–20 minutes or until pale biscuit colour. Dredge (don't you love the word?) with caster sugar when cooked. Cool in the baking tray. Great with ice creams and fools too, in which case cut into fingers, which are more elegant than the normal squares or oblongs.

SCONES – THE LOWDOWN

- The lightest scones are made with sour cream or buttermilk.
- Too much baking soda will ruin the mix, so measure it accurately.
- Keep everything cool. Cold air expands with the heat and helps make the scones lighter.
- Use a palette knife to mix with. It really works down into the bottom of the bowl without pressing on the mixture.
- Add all the liquid at once and mix lightly into a spongy dough.
- Handle the scones as little and as lightly as possible, the same as you would for pastry.
- Cook quickly in a hot oven; 10–15 minutes is all they take.
- Cool them on a rack to keep the outside crisp.
- Allow the mixture to stand for 10 minutes before cooking; they just seem to turn out better.

MAKES 24–30

450g/1lb plain flour
½ tsp salt
55–85g/2–3oz unsalted butter
2 level tsp bicarbonate of soda and
    4½ level tsp cream of tartar with
    every 300ml/10fl oz fresh full-
    cream milk
or
2 level tsp bicarbonate of soda and
    2 level tsp cream of tartar with
    300ml/10fl oz sour cream or
    buttermilk
or
4–6 level tsp baking powder with
    300ml/10fl oz fresh full-cream
    milk

BASIC SCONE RECIPE

Preheat the oven to 220°C/425°F/Gas 7. Sift the flour and salt into a bowl. Cut the butter into little pieces and rub into the flour with the tips of your fingers as quickly as you can. Sift in the raising agents and mix well. Add all the liquid at once and mix lightly into a spongy dough. Knead very lightly to make the dough smooth and roll out to 1–2cm/½–¾ in thick. Cut out with a 5cm/2in cutter and leave to stand for 10 minutes. Brush with egg or milk if you wish before placing on a greased baking sheet in the middle of the oven. Cook for about 10 minutes before cooling.

CHEESE SCONES

Add 140g/5oz good strong unpasteurised grated Cheddar such as Montgomery's or Keen's to the mixture and add a sprinkle of grated cheese to each top before the scones go into the oven. You can add a couple of teaspoons of finely chopped thyme or rosemary as well. Delicious with soup.

FRUIT SCONES

Add 55g/2oz vanilla caster sugar and 55–110g/2–4oz currants or sultanas or raisins to the basic recipe.

TREACLE SCONES

Add 30g/1oz sugar, 1 teaspoon of ground cinnamon, 1 teaspoon of mixed spice and 2 tablespoons of black treacle to the basic recipe. Put the treacle in with two-thirds of the milk, then add the rest as required.

WHOLEMEAL SCONES

Use half wholemeal flour and half plain flour for any of the above recipes.

DROP SCONES

SERVES 5

225g/8oz self-raising flour, sifted
½ tsp each bicarbonate of soda,
   baking powder and cream of tartar
1 tbsp sugar
1 tbsp golden syrup
300ml/10fl oz full-cream milk
1 egg
a little butter

Just the thing to do on a boring Sunday afternoon when it's rainy, the children are quarrelling and you want instant results.

Mix all the dry ingredients together and add the syrup. Add half the milk, whisking it in well, then add the egg and beat that in thoroughly. Add the rest of the milk. The mixture should just plop off the spoon. Let it stand for 15 minutes.

Brush a heavy, cast-iron pan with butter. I have a wonderful Swedish pan that feels leaden enough to have been forged by the god Thor. When the butter begins to smoke, drop tablespoons of the mixture into the pan, 2 at a time, with a ladle. Leave until you begin to see bubbles forming on the surface and a skin, about 3 minutes. Turn gently with a palette knife and cook until golden brown on the underside. Keep warm in a napkin or cloth before serving with butter, jam, syrup or what you will.

POTATO SCONES...AND OAK-SMOKED RASHERS

450g/1lb potatoes peeled, steamed
   and put through a mouli-légumes
   or potato ricer
110–140g/4–5oz flour sieved with a
   teaspoon of sea salt
45g/1½ oz unsalted butter

These are deliciously soft, crumbly crumbed and buttery – divine with oak-smoked organic rashers fried until crisped, then draped with their fat running into the scones for breakfast. It must be my Irish blood, but try this for brunch if it defeats you for breakfast. Whatever happens, you must make the scones with hot potato, so réchauffez if it's last night's potato.

Work all the ingredients together with your fingers, then roll out the dough lightly into thin circles, more biscuit than scone depth, with a very well floured rolling pin. Cut with a scone cutter into circles and either cook on an ungreased griddle top or fry until brown in a little butter. Serve hot and buttered with some rashers frazzled in a pan with no additional fat. Richard Corrigan, my favourite Irish chef, has taught me to keep the rind on the rashers, but that may not be to your taste. Pour over the bacon fat if you dare!

SAVOURY SNACKS

CHEESE STRAWS

170g/6oz plain flour
100g/3½ oz unsalted butter, cold
45g/1½ oz Parmesan or mature, unpasteurised Cheddar like Montgomery's or Keen's, freshly grated
a pinch of mustard powder
a pinch of cayenne (optional)
sea salt and black pepper
1 egg yolk

Thick or thin, long or short, cheese straws are as absorbing to cut as they are compulsive to eat. You may sprinkle the tops with onion seeds, cumin seeds or sesame seeds; you may add a teaspoon of chopped fresh thyme or sage to the cheese pastry mixture, or just some cracked black peppercorns or tiny flecks of dry chilli. You may add a teaspoon of seeded mustard, horseradish or beer. Or keep them plain, with nothing save the cheese. Or you could make a bundle of straws in several different flavours. All are delicious.

Preheat the oven to 180°C/350°F/Gas 4. Sieve the flour into a bowl. Add the fridge-cold butter cut into tiny chunks and rub in with your fingertips until you have a breadcrumby texture. Add the grated cheeses and seasoning and bind with the egg yolk and a little extra liquid in the form of cold water if you need.

Roll out and shape into a rectangle. Cut across into strips and bake on a baking sheet lined with non-stick baking parchment. Check after 10 minutes. The straws should be golden but not brown. Cool on a rack and eat warm.

CHEESE FOOTBALLS

110g/4oz plain flour
110g/4oz Parmesan, freshly grated
a good scrunch of black pepper
a pinch each of English mustard powder and cayenne
1 tsp finely chopped thyme or sage (optional)
110g/4oz unsalted butter, melted

My grandmother, ever indulgent, used to let us eat plates of cheese footballs before Sunday lunch, and do you know what? They never seemed to diminish our appetites – wickedly salty things just don't. They're the best of stimulants and utterly compulsive. So none of that parental 'you won't eat your lunch' nonsense.

Preheat the oven to 180°C/350°F/Gas 4. Mix all the dry ingredients together in a bowl, then pour in the melted butter so the mixture becomes breadcrumby, stirring as you go. You may need a little extra butter if the mixture seems too dry. Make walnut-sized balls of mixture and put them on a buttered baking sheet to cook for about 15–20 minutes until lightly browned. Eat warm, or cool and keep in an airtight container.

CHEESE JACKS

MAKES 12

55g/2oz unsalted butter
1 tsp rosemary leaves, very finely chopped
140g/5oz rolled oats
170g/6oz good, unpasteurised mature Cheddar like Montgomery's or Keen's, grated
1 egg, beaten

Sometimes you long for something savoury, not just sweet, at teatime. These are a fantastic alternative to flapjacks that my children have loved ever since they were tiny. You can also serve them at lunchtime with homemade tomato soup.

Preheat the oven to 180°C/350°F/Gas 4. Melt the butter, throwing in the rosemary leaves for 30 seconds if you want to release the rosemary oil fully. Mix the oats and grated cheese together. Pour in the melted butter, add the egg and mix everything together well. Press the mixture into a greased, shallow baking tin and bake for 30–40 minutes or until golden. Cool and cut into slices. Delicious served warm.

Cheese Jacks

STICKY GOOEY THINGS

FUDGE

500g/1lb 2oz vanilla caster sugar
50g/scant 2oz unsalted butter
90ml/3fl oz evaporated milk
a few drops of pure vanilla extract

This is something you either find so tooth-achingly sweet it sends shudders through you of the not so pleasant kind, or you just can't help your sickly-sweet tooth. No confessions here, of course. After all, it's what the children love to make, right?

Put the sugar, butter and milk into the pan and bring to the boil. Continue to boil it gently, stirring from time to time, until the mixture reaches 115°C. Check the temperature with a sugar thermometer, warming it in a pan of hot water before putting it upright into the pan.

If you don't have a sugar thermometer, test to see if little bits of the mixture plopped into cold water harden up immediately. This should take somewhere between 5–10 minutes of boiling.

As soon as the fudge is ready, take the pan off the heat, stir in the vanilla extract and continue beating until the mixture thickens and becomes distinctly grainy. Pour into a greased baking tray and leave it to cool. Cut into squares and remove when cold.

TOFFEE

340g/12oz demerara sugar
225g/8oz unsalted butter
200g/7oz golden syrup
grated zest and juice of half a lemon

Boil everything together in a pan until a tiny quantity of toffee dropped into a bowl of cold water hardens at once, then pour it into an oiled tin. Allow the toffee to cool, then mark off into squares with a knife. Cut into pieces when cold.

CHOCOLATE FUDGE

450g/1lb sugar, loaf sugar is best or
    use granulated
170ml/6fl oz milk
3 tbsp unsweetened cocoa like Green
    and Black's organic cocoa
55g/2oz unsalted butter, cut into
    small chunks
 a few drops of pure vanilla extract

Stir together the sugar, milk and cocoa until the sugar has dissolved. Cook gently, allowing the temperature to rise gradually until it reaches 115°C on a sugar thermometer. Warm the thermometer in a pan of hot water before putting it upright into the pan and then allow the syrup to boil rapidly without shaking or stirring it.

Once the fudge has reached the desired temperature, remove the thermometer and place it back in the pan of hot water. Take the pan off the heat and dip the base in cold water for a minute to stop the mixture boiling. Then drop in the little chunks of the butter off the heat, still without stirring. Cool. When nearly cold add the vanilla extract and beat well. Pour into an oiled tray, mark into squares with a knife blade and cut up when cold.

BUTTERSCOTCH

450g/1lb loaf sugar
300ml/10fl oz milk
pinch of cream of tartar
225g/8oz butter, cut into small
    chunks

Put the sugar and milk in a pan over a low heat and stir occasionally until the sugar is dissolved. Add the cream of tartar and little chunks of butter, a few pieces at a time. Boil the mixture until a little dropped into a bowl of cold water forms a moderately hard ball. Pour into an oiled or greased tin.

As soon as the mixture has firmed up sufficiently, mark it up into squares or whatever shape you fancy. Divide it into sections when cold and wrap each piece in waxed paper and then foil if you feel like giving it as presents.

BANANA SPLIT WITH CHOCOLATE SAUCE

1 ripe organic banana per child,
    split lengthwise
some good vanilla ice cream,
    1 or 2 scoops each

CHOCOLATE SAUCE
110g/4oz best bitter chocolate,
    such as Valrhona 64%, chopped
2 tbsp freshly made black coffee
    (optional)
1 tsp vanilla caster sugar
3–4 tbsp single cream
1 tbsp golden syrup

However awful school and homework have been, this is the pudding of all puddings to appeal to jaded children at the end of a bad day. It is one of those things to suggest in a crisis. Their world will automatically feel sunnier and they can help make the chocolate sauce, then scrape and lick whatever clings to the pan. Watching the hot, dark, velvety depths freeze into submission the moment this sauce hits the ice cream is one of life's enduring pleasures.

Place all the ingredients for the sauce in a pan and heat through gently, stirring all the time, until they are melted and hot. You may like a thinner sauce, in which case keep adding cream or a tablespoon or more of milk at the end and stirring it in until you have arrived at the desired consistency.

Plop scoops of ice cream between the banana halves and pour over the hot sauce. There should be enough sauce for three to four people. You may sprinkle a few coarsely crushed roasted hazelnuts over the top if your children like them. You may even want to eat this yourself!

BUTTERSCOTCH SAUCE

200g/7oz light muscovado sugar
240ml/8fl oz single cream
85g/3oz unsalted butter
a few drops of pure vanilla extract

Try this as an alternative to the chocolate sauce above. It gives you the banoffee effect without its particularly sickly brand of richness.

Pour everything into a small pan and heat gently, stirring constantly until you have a lively, bubbling morass. This sauce is darker and more minerally still if you use dark muscovado or molasses sugar. Pour scorching from the pan onto the ice cream and bananas.

PANCAKES – THE LOWDOWN

- The flour and seasoning are sieved together into a bowl. Sugar is added if it is a sweet batter.
- Make a well in the flour right down to the bottom of the bowl into which you break the eggs and add a little of the milk. Do not stir any of the flour down into the eggs until you have stirred them into the milk.
- Stir everything in until the consistency is like thick cream; only then start whisking thoroughly.
- If butter or oil is being added, add them now, the butter should be melted but not hot.
- Now let the batter rest, anything from 30 minutes to a few hours according to the recipe, so that the starch cells can swell and be broken down more easily in the cooking. During this time the batter will thicken, so you may need to add more liquid to it to get back to the consistency you want.
- Batter for Yorkshire puddings and clafoutis needs less liquid than batter for thin, lacy pancakes.
- You need to cook pancakes and batter puddings in strong heat, which causes a further breaking down of the soaked starch cells and a release of air bubbles within the mixture to produce a light texture.
- You may use a proportion of water as well as milk for the batter, which also helps the lightness.
- Make sure the pan is hot before you plop in the first of your batter. Remember that a tablespoon of mixture should be enough to cover a 12.5cm/5in diameter pan.

BASIC PANCAKES

MAKES 10–12

225g/8oz plain flour
a pinch of salt
2 organic eggs
600ml/1 pint milk
a nut of unsalted butter

Make sure you really whisk the batter well for several minutes when you get to that stage. After the batter has rested for 30 minutes, brush melted butter over the base of a heavy cast-iron frying pan, the kind you never wash but simply clean with an oiled cloth.

Make the batter, following the instructions opposite. Heat the pan thoroughly, then add the first tablespoon of batter and swirl it round the pan. Adjust the batter in the bowl with more milk if it is too thick. The first pancake is always a test and rarely if ever works in my experience. The pancake should be paper thin. Let it cook until it is golden brown on one side, then ease it and flick or toss it over with the help of a palette knife to the other side and continue cooking for about another 30 seconds. When finished, stack the pancakes up on a warm plate covered with a cloth in a warm oven and keep tossing.

If you need to keep the pancakes for several hours, you may brush a baking sheet with melted butter, overlap the pancakes on top of it and brush the tops of them lightly with more melted butter. Then put them in a hot oven for 5 minutes or so. Finish them in the usual way with whatever topping or filling you have chosen.

Children seem to like pancakes best the simple way, so accompany your dish of warm pancakes with wedges of lemon, sugar or honey, a few chopped bananas and perhaps some vanilla ice cream and/or homemade chocolate sauce with a sprinkling of toasted hazelnuts. Or you can macerate a punnet or two of berries according to season in the juice of an orange, a dessertspoon of sieved cornflour and a tablespoon or two of sugar, depending on the sharpness of the berry, for 30 minutes. Heat this mixture through gently in a small pan just until the fruit begins to bleed but not cook, and place a spoonful on each pancake. Add a spoon of crème fraîche and roll them up to serve warm.

WELSH LIGHT CAKES OR PANCAKES

6 rounded tbsp flour
2 rounded tbsp sugar
3 tbsp sour cream
a pinch of salt
3 eggs
½ tsp bicarbonate of soda
1 rounded tbsp cream of tartar
60ml/2fl oz water
about 150ml/5fl oz buttermilk or milk

These Welsh pancakes, originally made on a girdle or bakestone, are piled up on top of each other with butter spread on each, which melts and oozes through the holes. They are particularly light.

Beat together the flour, sugar, sour cream, salt and eggs. Mix the bicarb and cream of tartar with the water – it will froth up – and add it to the batter. Dilute with the milk gradually until the mixture is bubbly and not too thick.

Brush the pan with butter in the normal way and heat. Cook the pancakes on the first side, which will become perforated with tiny holes. Turn over and repeat. Pile the buttered pancakes up and keep them warm. Serve by cutting down like a cake and serving the wedges of pancakes in quarters.

CAKES — THE LOWDOWN

THE MAKING

The more rules given, the more rules forgotten, broken or just not read. Here are a few that you should read before you start to avoid the horrors of the sunken sponge, the leaden sponge, the overcooked sponge, the unrisen biscuit of a sponge...

- Measure accurately according to instructions.

- Cream the fat and sugar very thoroughly with a wooden spoon or electric beaters or in a KitchenAid until light and fluffy. The butter should be soft when you start, so take it out of the fridge in advance. It should not be melted first. Melted butter doesn't hold air.

- The eggs should be lightly beaten and added by degrees to the creamed mixture. The mixture is beaten again after each addition to incorporate everything thoroughly. The batter can curdle at this stage, especially if the eggs are cold, but NEVER FEAR, a spoonful of sifted flour taken from the recipe will correct it. The cake will just not be quite so delicate and will have a coarser texture.

- The mixture should have a soft, dropping consistency when you have creamed it enough. That means it will plop off the spoon if you bang the spoon on the side of the bowl, but it shouldn't slide off independently — if it does, it's too runny — nor should it drop off reluctantly.

- Put the cake directly into the oven to bake once you have made the mixture. This will always give you the best result.

- Don't keep opening the oven door unless you want your cake to sink like a stone in the middle.

- Make sure you put your cake to cool on a rack where there is circulation of air. If you put it on something solid, it will become damp and sodden.

THE READINESS
- Open the oven door carefully and just enough to test the cake quickly.
- The cake should be well risen and evenly browned.
- Touch the surface lightly and, if it seems firm to the touch, the cake is done.
- Insert a warm skewer into the cake — if it comes out dry the cake is ready.
- If the cake is shrinking away from the sides of the tin, it is probably over-cooked.

THE DISASTER AND WHY IT HAPPENS

A COARSE-TEXTURED CAKE is the result of too much raising agent, so never exceed the specified amount.

A DAMP AND HEAVY CAKE could mean
- you've used the wrong proportion of ingredients
- you've added too much orange or lemon juice to the mixture
- the oven is too cool
- the cake has cooled too quickly, making it damp
- the cake has been put in a storage tin too quickly, making it damp.

IF THE FRUIT SINKS TO THE BOTTOM OF THE CAKE it may be because
- you've used the wrong proportion of ingredients, i.e. too much liquefying matter like sugar
- you've used too much baking powder
- the oven is too cool
- you've used wet fruit
- you've not mixed the fruit with some of the flour before stirring it in
- the cake has been exposed to a sudden draught.

A CAKE WHICH HAS SUNK IN THE MIDDLE may be due to
- the wrong proportion of liquefying ingredient
- a sudden draught caused by opening the oven door too soon
- too hot an oven at first
- too much baking powder, which causes the gluten in the flour to over-stretch and the cake to collapse as a result.

A CAKE WITH A PEAKED TOP is due to
- not enough liquid – the mixture was too dry
- too hot an oven
- baking the cake too high up in the oven.

VICTORIA SPONGE

110g/4oz unsalted butter, softened
110g/4oz unrefined caster sugar
2 eggs
110g/4oz self-raising flour, sifted
water
about 2 tbsp of jam, the best,
    whatever flavour you like, damson,
    raspberry, loganberry, strawberry,
    apricot
unrefined icing sugar for dusting

Baking your first Victoria sponge is one of those classic culinary landmarks that should prove a triumph and lead to greater things. There is nothing quite like the satisfaction of assembling the double-decker sponge, golden, light, buttery, smoothing on the best seeded strawberry or raspberry jam, adding fresh fruit and thick, whipped cream if you will, then closing the top lid of sponge upon it until the scarlet stickiness just squishes out. A dusting of unrefined icing sugar and the world is definitely a better place.

Preheat the oven to 180°C/350°F/Gas 4. Grease two 15cm/6in sandwich tins, non-stick if possible, with a butter paper. Line the bottom of each with a circle of non-stick baking parchment to fit the base and grease that with the butter paper.

Cream the butter and sugar together until light and fluffy. Beat the eggs together in a bowl and gradually beat them into the creamed mixture a little at a time, adding a tablespoon of sifted flour if the mixture begins to curdle. Fold in the flour with a metal spoon, lightly and swiftly, adding a little water to bring the mixture to a soft, dropping consistency. Scrape the mixture into the tins immediately and smooth the tops with a rubber spatula.

Bake in the middle of the oven for about 20 minutes, or until the cakes are well risen, golden and feel spongy when touched with a fingertip. Let the cakes cool for about 5 minutes before turning them out onto a wire rack and peeling away the greased paper. Invert them so that they cool right side up. Cool completely.

Spread the jam with a palette knife over the top of the sponge that is going to be your base or add some freshly sliced strawberries or whole raspberries if you feel like it and they are in season. You can, on the other hand, whisk some Jersey or double cream until slackly stiffened, a small carton will do, and spread that over the jam and then proceed with or without the fresh fruit. Place the top sponge on the jammy sponge and sieve over a restrained amount of unrefined icing sugar.

225g/8oz self-raising flour
¾ level tsp ground mixed spice
½ tsp sea salt
100g/3½ oz vanilla caster sugar
100g/3½ oz unsalted butter, cut into
    small pieces
1 tbsp good runny honey
100g/3½ oz sultanas
55g/2oz chopped walnuts (optional)
450g/1lb ripe organic bananas,
    peeled and mashed with a fork
2 eggs
juice of a lemon

285g/10oz self-raising flour
1 tsp baking powder
1 tsp cinnamon, grind your own for
    the best flavour
½ tsp each ground nutmeg and cloves
250ml/8½fl oz vegetable oil
225g/8oz light muscovado sugar
4 eggs
110g/4oz grated organic carrots
55g/2oz sultanas, soaked in warm
    water for 20 minutes and drained.
110g/4oz walnuts, chopped

ICING
140g/5oz unsalted butter, softened
285g/10oz fresh cream cheese
140g/5oz unrefined caster sugar

BANANA BREAD

This is simple to make and my children have always found it one of the great comfort foods they always want to bake. Probably, in part, because it reassuringly always turns out well and there are always bananas about to hit the over-ripe mark that they want to play with.

Preheat the oven to 180°C/350°F/Gas 4. Sift the flour into a bowl and add the mixed spice, salt and sugar. Add the butter, beat in all the remaining ingredients and pour the batter into a greased loaf tin. Bake for an hour then turn the heat down to 170°C/325°F/Gas 3 for a further 15–30 minutes. Check with a skewer, which should come out clean. Cool in the tin on a rack before turning out. Eat warm with crème fraîche or on its own.

CARROT CAKE

This is an American classic, though I prefer to eschew the desiccated coconut, which always reminds me of old toenails. You may add pecans instead of walnuts, make it with sultanas or sultana-free, or even add a cup of homemade apple sauce to the mixture if you feel like it. If you feel the icing is a shade too rich, leave the cake plain, as in the picture opposite.

Preheat the oven to 180°C/350°F/Gas 4. Grease two 23cm/9in cake tins, line them with a circle of non-stick baking parchment and grease the parchment. Shake a little flour inside the tin, then pour away the excess.

   Sift the flour and baking powder into a large bowl, then add the spices. Beat the oil and sugar together thoroughly in a KitchenAid or by hand, then add 2 of the eggs, one at a time, beating in each thoroughly. Separate the remaining 2 eggs and add the final 2 yolks. Remove the bowl and stir in the grated carrots, sultanas and walnuts, or throw the walnuts onto the top of the mixture before cooking each sponge as I did for the cake in the picture. Sift in the flour and baking powder and add the ground spices, then fold everything in together. Whisk the egg whites stiffly in a clean bowl, then fold them quickly into the mixture.

   Divide the mixture equally between the tins. Set the tins on baking trays in the middle of the oven for about 45 minutes, or until a skewer comes out clean. Cool on a rack until the cake has shrunk away from the sides of the tin and can be turned out onto the rack to cool further.

ICING

Beat all the ingredients together thoroughly until they become a thick, smooth cream. Spread a bit of the mixture over the top of one of the cakes, put the other cake on top and spread the rest of the topping all over the top and sides of the cake. Refrigerate for at least 2 hours before serving and in between use so the topping doesn't soften.

Carrot Cake

170g/6oz good dark chocolate,
chopped
170g/6oz unsalted butter, softened
170g/6oz caster sugar
4 eggs, separated
85g/3oz ground almonds
85g/3oz plain flour, sifted

RICH CHOCOLATE ICING
110g/4oz good dark chocolate,
chopped
45g/1½oz butter
55g/2oz caster sugar
90ml/3fl oz double cream

MIRANDA'S BIRTHDAY CAKE

There is nothing like the first cake your daughter – or son – bakes for you, particularly if it has been made almost secretly for your birthday, and the kitchen, which will have been reduced to rubble, with seemingly every implement used, has also, magically, then been cleaned up. It is even better if the recipe isn't one of those moronic apologies for children's cooking that are just as time-consuming and difficult to cook, and disgustingly inedible. This is the wondrously sticky chocolate cake my eldest daughter Miranda cooked for me one birthday. A competent nine- or ten-year-old is well up to it, though my littlest daughter Charissa managed to produce 'a burnt brick because I forgot about it' when she attempted to make one for my birthday!

Preheat the oven to 180°C/350°F/Gas 4. Grease two 18cm/7in sandwich tins or one deeper, 20cm/8in round tin. Melt the chocolate in a bowl over a saucepan of hot water. Cream the butter with the sugar (this is easily done in a food processor), then add the egg yolks one by one, then the almonds, flour and the melted chocolate. Whisk the egg whites until they form soft peaks, then gently fold them into the mixture, little by little.

Divide the mixture between the sandwich tins and cook in the oven for about 20 minutes. If using one deeper tin, cook for slightly longer. Miranda undercooks hers slightly for a damp, sticky centre. Leave to cool slightly in the tin, then turn out on to a wire rack.

RICH CHOCOLATE ICING

For the icing, put all the ingredients into a bowl over a saucepan of hot water and stir gently over the heat. When smooth, leave to cool and then put into the fridge – it thickens as it cools, and becomes much easier to spread. If you have two sponges, sandwich them together with half the icing and spread half on top. If you have one sponge, cover the top and sides copiously with icing.

SIMPLE

SKILLS

2

DIFFERENT AGES REACH

DIFFERENT AGES REACH different stages at different times in the kitchen, but eventually the helping hands are withdrawn and you have to go solo. It doesn't mean you have to pick the most unimaginably complicated recipes now your mother or father or big sister aren't looking over your shoulder and grabbing control like a back seat driver before you can burn the birthday cake. Quite the reverse. Growing confidence comes from cooking the same simple dish a little better each time and that is true throughout your cooking life. What you choose, how you plan your time and your menu and what goes WITH what or AFTER what – these are just as important as the actual cooking.

Timing is probably the most difficult thing to get right, even with a dish you could make one-armed and blindfolded. Ingredients are never quite the same, nor is the way you cook, the temperature of the stove or the kitchen, the speed you work at or the amount, even if you weigh it, so don't ever expect your food to come out tasting the same each time. Far better to consider the little changes you can make, the subtle tweaks that make a good dish, however simple it may be, great. In fact, getting things to taste different is one of the keys, although the supermarkets have tried their utmost to inculcate us with the extraordinary notion that we should want the thing that we bought one week to be the same each time we buy it.

If you are weighed down by the inertia of teenagedom, there will still be things in this chapter to satisfy some pretty instant cravings; if, on the other hand, you want to whack something in the oven and 'chill' for a few hours, surprise your mates or mama with a Sunday roast, or just bake a great cake for a best friend's birthday, it's all here.

Just to make you feel a little better and take the pressure off, let me tell you that when I left home all I could cook was an omelette. Other than the grisly creations of the school 'bug' labs that I told you about in the last chapter, I was really not even a novitiate in the kitchen. My mother's kitchen was small and certainly not large enough for two, and at my grandmother's house in Sussex, her wonderful cook Rhoda Fisher, who was with the family for over 40 years, did it all. I was a far better eater than I was a cook. The assembling and transforming of the ingredients was not a serious hobby and eating raw cake mixture straight from the bowl was more interesting to me than actually baking the cake.

I remember being left to look after my father one weekend when my mother had gone away. She had told how to prepare the aubergines, but telling is not like watching to a learner cook.

Those squeaky, purple hand grenades defeated me utterly. I served them up half raw and swimming in oil and naturally didn't really know why things had gone wrong. My father chomped away at them as though they were one of the delicious dishes my mother had prepared. I hadn't somehow got the courage to burst out laughing, hurl them in the bin and suggest the local fish and chip shop which, surprisingly, every so often he voiced a preference for. Hardinge's rock and chips would have been infinitely preferable to my offering, which you would have had to squeeze dry with all your might.

My father died when I was 18 so never had to suffer much in the way of my early culinary incompetence. A few months after he had died, I decided to cook my first 'dinner party'. My mother was away, again, so I had the run of the stove. It all comes back to me, writing about the dread aubergines, that I decided to make a moussaka, very trendy in those days along with chilli con carne, carbonnade of beef, beef stroganoff and chicken kiev. I invited a bunch of friends including my new friend and model agent Freddie. (I was busy half pursuing a career in that most fickle of businesses while I waited to go up to Cambridge.) I THINK the dish turned out fine. We ate huge amounts of it that's for sure and I don't remember it being awash with oil. I'd probably used a mile or two of kitchen paper sopping it up. Even the béchamel was lump free. The thing I remember most about the dinner is that the men were wholly uninterested in the food. Huge amounts were drunk and at some stage a bottle of ketchup was produced and we all ended up rather short of clothes, soaking wet and covered in ketchup. Like the first hunt, the first dinner had something of being 'blooded' to it!

Moussaka was a dish I cooked many times in those early cooking days. After all, it had worked. Not so the chilli con carne that I attempted from Robert Carrier's bible *Great Dishes of the World*. What had attracted me to it in the first place was the fact that the chilli was made with cubed meat and wasn't yet another of those million-ways-with-mince things that we all cooked throughout our teenage and student years. Inexpert, I was unable to read the runes of a recipe, which I can most often do now so that if there is some gross misprint or failure to explain I can act accordingly. I trustingly added the 4 tablespoons of dried chilli powder to the dish. Remember this. One teaspoon of cayenne is normally sufficient unto the day unless you're a hardball chilli muncher. What Carrier had omitted to say was that the chilli powder he used was the Mexican, mild variety. It's disasters like this that at once are things we'll dine out on forever, but that can also seem like the end at the time, particularly when you don't know enough to know better.

EGGS

Let's start with eggs because you've probably always got them and you can definitely always eat them at whatever time of day or night. Nothing like a late-night breakfast-food feast, or a brunch of oozing fatty smoked bacon in a butty, the soft white bread dribbling butter and a good fried egg sqozen in its middle or ready to pierce on the side. There is no excuse for those leather omelettes you get at motorway service stations or for boiled eggs so hard they've got a foul black planetary ring around their dry as mustard powder yolk. And it's easy to make a sloppily creamy scramble or a perfect poached egg.

First choose your eggs. At the very least they should be free range, at best organic. Battery farms are cruel and the eggs vile and flavourless, with thin, weak albumen and pale, wan yolks. Eggs need to be fresh too, so check the date stamp if you don't happen to live down the road from the farm!

SOFT-BOILED EGGS

Don't start with cold eggs as the shell will crack when it hits the hot water in the pan. Boil a pan of water with enough water in it to cover the eggs as they cook. Put the eggs gently into the boiling water on a large spoon and simmer for 4 minutes before removing. The white should be just set and the yolk creamy. If you like your eggs a little more firmly set, add half a minute to the time.

Michel Roux senior uses a different method. He puts the eggs in a pan of cold water, brings the water to the boil slowly, then cooks the eggs for a further minute. Experiment. Both ways work.

HARD-BOILED EGGS

People used to cook hard-boiled eggs for 10–12 minutes after the water the eggs had been plunged into came back to the boil, but for most recipes I favour a softly hard-boiled egg, so 6–7 minutes is about right. If you need a very firmly set yolk, perhaps for a dish where you are going to separate yolk from white and incorporate the yolk into, say, a dressing or scatter it on top of something, the 10–12 minute rule applies.

FRIED EGGS

Omelette pans (see page 58) are deep enough. Begin by gently heating a walnut-sized piece of butter, or the equivalent splosh of oil or bacon fat, until it begins to smoke. Butter will begin to smell nutty, but do not allow it to brown. If that happens, pour it away and start again. Break each egg into a small saucer or bowl and slide it carefully into the hot fat, then spoon the fat gently over the yolk and white to help cook it through. The white will have firmed up to a sort of blueish opaqueness when it has set and the yolk will look cooked but still runny. If you prefer your eggs better cooked, continue or flip the egg over with a slice. Remove carefully from the pan, draining away a little of the butter if you wish to as you go.

POACHED EGGS

Use an omelette pan filled half full with water, but don't cook more than 2 eggs at a time. They should not touch each other as they cook. Add 1 tablespoon of vinegar to the water before it comes to the boil, then swirl the water into a vortex with a spoon just before you slide the egg in; it will help the white set more closely to the yolk. You should only bring the water just to boiling point, then cook the egg in barely simmering water. It will take about 3 minutes to poach. Remove it with a slice, allowing the water to drain from it before you plonk it on the plate or buttered toast.

POACHED EGGS TO USE LATER

If you want to keep soft-boiled or poached eggs to use later in a salad or eggy dish, keep them in cold water once you've cooked them or they will harden.

OEUFS EN COCOTTE

Heat a tablespoon of thick cream to each egg in a pan and pour it into each warm cocotte or ramekin. Slip in the broken egg and add a couple of tiny blobs of unsalted butter and a scrunch of black pepper. Put the ramekins in a bain marie, or just a small roasting tin into which you pour boiling water to come halfway up the sides of the ramekins, and place in a medium oven, 180°C/350°F/Gas 4 for 6–7 minutes.

EGGY BREAD

SERVES 2

2 eggs
2 slices of bread
nut of butter

A classic breakfast or brunch dish also known as French Toast. The Americans sweeten it with maple syrup or icing sugar and cinnamon, with some berries on the side. We tend just to fry the egg-soaked bread in butter and eat it hot, golden, slightly crisp and with a little frill of egg around the side like a pillow edge.

Crack the eggs onto a large plate and beat them carefully with a fork. Soak the bread on both sides until nearly all the egg mixture has been absorbed. Melt a little nut of butter in a frying pan and when it begins to bubble, put the bread in, pour any spare egg over the top and cook until the underside is beginning to look slightly crisp and nutty brown in places. Flip over and repeat. Turn onto the warm plate and serve the way you like it.

SCRAMBLED EGGS

generous, walnut-sized lump of
unsalted butter, more if you're
cooking more than 6 eggs
2 or 3 eggs per person
2 tbsp milk or cream
black pepper

When they are overcooked scrambled eggs are very, very nasty – granular and watery with a horrid skin on top where they should be soft, buttery, creamy, sloppy. Remember that they go on cooking in the pan after you have taken it off the heat and if you don't continue to stir when you remove the slightly under-set eggs from the pan, the top will be perfect but the bottom dry, crusty and overcooked. Allow 2 or 3 eggs per person depending on appetite. Some scramblers insist on only eggs and butter. I like to add a little rich Jersey milk or cream which, curiously, has the effect of lightening the finished eggs and making them more delicate and digestible. Never salt eggs until they are ready; it has the effect of making them watery.

Melt the butter in a thick-bottomed pan that will conduct the heat evenly and slowly. You may use more if you're cooking, say, 6 eggs for 2 people. Meanwhile, break the eggs into a small ramekin and throw each one into a bowl large enough to whisk them in. (This way, if you should come across one bad egg, you won't ruin the lot.) Whisk well until the white and the yolk are one, then add a splash, about 2 tablespoons, of milk or cream and a good scrunch of black pepper and whisk them in.

Pour the mixture into the foaming butter and stir on a low heat with a wooden spoon. I find that the slower you cook the eggs the better they taste, so every so often I remove them from the direct heat for a minute and continue to stir them. Just as they are beginning to set, add a few little bits of extra butter. This also has a magical effect on the taste and the texture.

When the eggs are sloppy looking but set, remove from the heat and, still stirring, plop onto the warmed plates or onto hot buttered toast. Perfect Sunday night or anytime comfort food.

OMELETTES – THE LOWDOWN

The perfect omelette, my mother always used to tell me, should take as long to cook as it takes to recite a sonnet, which happens to be 55 seconds. Now that may not sound particularly scientific, but Domestic Science was never a sobriquet that particularly endeared me to the art of cooking. I'd rather remember the above than struggle with a scientific explanation any day.

- The pan is as important as the eggs for this sublime, simple dish. You need a heavy-based iron pan, which should never be washed again after its first wash when you buy it. Then cover the base and sides with olive oil and leave it overnight before you wipe it with kitchen paper. Only wipe the pan with a damp cloth or piece of kitchen paper from now on, occasionally adding a little extra olive oil if it doesn't seem oiled, so that it keeps a smooth, slightly greasy surface and an omelette will never stick to it.

- However many people you're cooking for, don't make your omelette with more than 4–6 eggs at a time. It's impossible to cook an omelette perfectly, right the way through, if it's too large, so make several instead. An 18cm/ 7in pan is good for 4 eggs, a 23cm/9in pan for 6.

- Unless the omelette is a Spanish one, it should be cooked in unsalted butter.

- Please don't get me started on the subject of American 'egg white' omelettes. They are NOT omelettes.

BASIC OMELETTE

Beat the eggs in a bowl with a fork. I beat until foamy, but some prefer to beat less so that you have just mixed the yolks and the whites. Melt a walnut of butter in the pan and when it begins to bubble and foam but before it browns, tip the omelette mixture in and season with black pepper. It will begin to bubble immediately if the pan is hot enough. With a palette knife, worry the edges of the omelette, drawing them to the middle of the pan as they begin to form, so you keep the base of the pan covered with egg. When the egg has begun to set, fold the set part over on each side so that you have an omelette shape. The middle should still appear almost liquid. Flip the omelette onto the plate and serve.

HERB OMELETTE

Add a tablespoon of chopped chives, parsley, chervil, tarragon and basil in any combination to the egg mixture while it is still in the bowl.

CHEESE OMELETTE

Sprinkle a handful of thickly grated cheese over the eggs the moment they go into the pan. If you are using Gruyère, you may add it in small cubes to the egg mixture in the bowl.

BACON OR HAM OMELETTE

Dice and cook the meat and throw into the egg mixture in the pan. A couple of crisped rashers will do.

TOMATO OMELETTE

Either slice a tomato and place it into the pan the moment the egg goes in, or skin and seed the tomato, then chop it and add it in the pan. To skin a tomato, put it into a bowl and cover it completely with boiling water. Make a nick in the side with a knife and after a minute remove it from the water and peel. Cut into quarters, remove the seeds and core, and cut into dice or strips.

FRITTATA STUFFED WITH SPRUE OR ASPARAGUS

SERVES 4

6 large organic eggs
1 bunch basil, roughly torn, keep back a few leaves for serving
1 clove of garlic, peeled and finely chopped
2 tbsp freshly grated Parmesan
salt and pepper
225g/8oz sprue, or fine-stemmed asparagus, cut into 5cm/2in chunks
olive oil

Dipping spears of asparagus into runny boiled egg yolks is a real post-nursery delight, as is throwing the violet-tinged tips into a sea of creamy scrambled eggs. But try these little bundles of sprue wrapped in a basil-scented frittata.

Beat the eggs in a bowl then add the basil, garlic, Parmesan and seasoning. Allow the mixture to rest a bit if you have time, so the basil can permeate the eggs.

Steam the sprue or asparagus stalks on their own for a couple of minutes. Add the tips, and steam for another 2 minutes. Drain, season, and dribble over a bit of olive oil. Put a couple of tablespoons of olive oil into a frying pan on a medium heat, then pour in a quarter of the egg mixture and swirl it around as you would for a pancake. When it turns opaque, flip it over and cook the other side briefly. Cook the remaining frittatas. Put a little bundle of sprue at the edge of each frittata and roll up. Sprinkle on the remaining basil and a bit of extra Parmesan and serve.

SPANISH OMELETTE

SERVES 4

1 onion, peeled and sliced
olive oil
handful of cooked, diced potato
cooked spinach, peas (frozen or fresh), tomatoes or roasted piquillo peppers
6 large organic eggs
sea salt
freshly ground pepper
chopped chives

Sauté the sliced onion gently in a little oil until soft and golden, then add the diced potato and whatever vegetables you're using. Cook for a further minute or two before pouring in the eggs. Season and put the pan in the oven, about 180°C/350°F/Gas 4, until all but the surface has set.

Place the pan under a hot grill until the omelette begins to puff up and brown around the edges. Sprinkles with chopped chives and serve warm to cool straight out of the pan. Never eat a Spanish omelette hot – it won't taste!

Spanish Omelette

PASTA – THE LOWDOWN

The best quality durum wheat takes longer to cook and has a much better texture than the cheaper, quick-cook variety and for the sake of saving a few minutes' cooking time, who wants an inferior taste with slimy, sticky pasta? So don't buy dried pasta that says you can cook it in 3–5 minutes. The longer the cooking time on the instructions, the better the pasta quality. When the pasta shapes are extruded through bronze dies and very slowly dried, you will find more nutrients are retained in the pasta and the flavour and texture are far superior. The little channels and indentations in the pasta when it is extruded like this are what your pasta sauce clings to.

- Packets of dried pasta used to suggest 55–85g/2–3oz per person. Ignore that instruction totally unless someone with a bird-sized appetite has come to dine with you. Most people can manage double that quantity, unless the dish is a starter or subsidiary to the vegetables.

- Always use a large pan filled with water for cooking pasta, otherwise the pasta will stick together and end up horribly starchy. The minimum should be 3 litres/6 pints, even for a single portion of pasta.

- Salt well when the water comes to the boil; a tablespoon of salt to each 450g/1lb of pasta.

- Never put olive oil in the pasta cooking water.

- Return the water to a rolling boil after adding the salt and before you put the pasta in.

- Once the pasta is in, stir the pasta with a wooden spoon, then cover the pot with a lid just until the water returns to the boil. Stir frequently during the cooking process.

- Start testing the pasta a minute before the packet instructions tell you to. The pasta should be what the Italians call 'al dente' and retain some bite but not be tough and chewy. I still enjoy hurling a strand of spaghetti at the wall, knowing that if it sticks it's cooked, but taste it too or it could be over-cooked!

- The moment the pasta is al dente drain it in a colander. Don't shake the colander to get rid of all the cooking water. A little water on the pasta will help lubricate your sauce and stop the pasta going sticky after you have hurled it back into the hot pot.

- I have always found that even with the simplest, olive oil-based pasta sauce, a knob of butter added to the cooked pasta at this stage enriches the dish in a seismic way. Try it, even with something like a pesto sauce, and see if you agree.

- You must have your sauce timed to be ready the moment the pasta is ready. Pasta starts to stick very quickly without lubrication and needs to be thrown into a warm serving bowl or to be dressed with the sauce immediately. If there is grated cheese in the recipe, add a little of it at the same time and serve the rest separately. The cheese will melt and begin to marry with the sauce.

- Never serve the sauce in a great blob on top of a pile of pasta. The sauce should be tossed into the pasta with the olive oil and/or butter so that is distributed throughout the pasta evenly and the two become one. Make sure you really toss the whole dish, pasta and sauce, from the bottom of the pan or bowl, so that the amalgamation is complete.

- Pasta doesn't wait. Once you have tossed the sauce and the pasta together, you should serve it and eat it immediately!

SIMPLE PASTA SUPPERS

If you're home alone (without the parents) these are the sorts of dishes you might just feel like cooking. The sheer bliss of nobody to tell you you've overcooked the meat or undercooked the veg, just friends, brothers, sisters or a girl or boyfriend to impress, may get you into the kitchen to do more than the average pangs of hunger would normally drive you to. Yes, a steak sandwich or butter-sodden bacon butty is great for brunch, lunch or dinner; baked beans have their place, which in my case even stretched as far as being eaten cold out of the tin in dorm binges at school, and the full-fry is one of the great treats of the year to be eaten infrequently but with all its accoutrements whenever fresh air and exercise or a serious grease-up for no particular reason is all you crave. An omelette is as good at midnight as it is at midday, but one day you'll just want to see if you can't cook something worth inviting your friends round for. That's when you need a shortcut to a great recipe and all the help you can get, not just the assumption on the part of the recipe writer that you know what blanch and seal and sauté and skim mean.

However experienced we cooks are, the image of willing guinea pigs in the lab never quite fades. We try things out on those we love best and they're either straight with their criticism as only family can be or they demand a repeat performance, second helpings and the recipe all in one breath. YOU have to learn to be critical too. That way you'll learn more quickly and everyone around you will see the critical process involved in trying new recipes as creative rather than destructive. And remember, all your family and friends will admire you just for making them the simplest pasta dish or tart or baking them a cake. It's the deed that counts. It's not about how-clever-am-I with a Michelin-starred recipe. The best bit about cooking for people is their genuine greed and enjoyment over the simplest of dishes. That's what the cook dines out on; it is his or her secret weapon, the mystery ingredient, the knowledge that spurs you on next time.

If you're an organised, think-ahead type you'll get stuck in to the stove-top with a slow-cooked, richly meaty ragù sauce and will never utter the dread word spagbol again. If you want to wing it and do something zingy and fast, you'll head for a tomato sauce, cooked or raw. If you want an edge of sophistication but none of the culinary hurdles that suggest advanced technique is a given, a carbonara will look and taste sensational. If the kitchen is looking rather Mother Hubbardish, search out the mousetrap, the milk and the macaroni and make a macaroni cheese. It may seem like nursery food but then so do treacle tart and Queen's pudding and none of your friends will object to them. They're far more likely to suggest your house than theirs, as I've discovered with my three children, and I wouldn't have it any other way.

SPAGHETTI BOLOGNESE

SERVES 6–8

2–3 tbsp olive oil
a knob of butter
2 large onions, finely chopped
3 sticks celery, chopped
3 carrots, finely diced
3 or 4 cloves of garlic, finely chopped
1kg/2¼ lb minced beef chuck, or
    similar, with plenty of fat (you can
    add ⅓ part pork mince to the beef
    if you wish)
salt and freshly ground black pepper
2 bay leaves
240ml/8fl oz milk
nutmeg
240ml/8fl oz white wine
2 x 400g/14oz tins of plum tomatoes,
    cut up
spaghetti
freshly grated Parmesan cheese

When I first cooked spaghetti Bolognese I had a bog-standard but classic meat sauce recipe that I abided by for two decades. Then I discovered Marcella Hazan's version and was smitten at first taste, so much so that I have never reverted to my original, even from a misplaced sense of nostalgia. A ragù is characterised by its mellow, gentle flavour, so don't blanch at the idea of adding milk to the meat first. It protects the meat from the acidic bite of the tomatoes you add later. Whatever you do, don't ask for lean mince. You need a good marbling of fat for a sweeter, tastier ragù than you will ever get without it.

Preheat the oven to 200°C/400°F/Gas 6. Warm the oil and butter in a heavy cast-iron pot, add the onion, and sauté gently until softened and translucent. Add the celery, carrots and garlic, cook for another couple of minutes, stirring to coat well. Add the beef and a large pinch of salt, and grind over some pepper. Stir until the beef has lost its raw pink look. Add the bay leaves and milk, and simmer gently for about 10 minutes, until the meat has absorbed the milk. Add a suspicion of nutmeg, about ¼ teaspoon. Add the wine, and let it simmer until it has evaporated, then add the cut-up tomatoes with their juice and stir thoroughly.

Cook uncovered at a lazy simmer, with just an intermittent bubble breaking through the surface, for 3 hours or more. Give it a stir whenever you happen to be passing. Eventually the fat will separate from the sauce, but it will not be dry. Taste, and correct the seasoning.

Cook the spaghetti in plenty of boiling, salted water according to the instructions on the packet. Drain unthoroughly, without shaking the colander, so that there is still water on the pasta when you return it to the pan. Stir in a knob of butter with a splosh of good olive oil, then stir in the sauce. Serve freshly grated Parmesan separately.

SPAGHETTI WITH TOMATO SAUCE

A good tomato sauce is the little black dress of sauces. It will see you through all eventualities and constantly remind you of its versatility; all you need to do is vary the accessories from time to time once you've found the perfect model. This is mine for you to add to or subtract from as you wish. If good organic plum tomatoes are not in season, you may wish to use all tinned tomatoes with some good passata from a jar, as our acidic English tomatoes are not really up to the job. This sauce will anoint meatballs, cod, prawns; it can form the base of that most libidinous of dishes, 'puttanesca' – literal meaning tart's pasta since it is hot and feisty – can be served alongside polpettone, a delicious Italian meatloaf, or seamed through pancakes with béchamel sauce and mozzarella. Texture is an individual thing too. You may serve it straight from the pan or push it through the coarse blade of the mouli if you like a smoother, but not baby-food style, texture.

SERVES 6

3 tbsp olive oil
2 onions, finely chopped
2 sticks of celery, finely chopped
6 cloves of garlic, finely chopped
1kg/2¼lb Italian plum tomatoes, skinned, seeded and chopped, otherwise the best tomatoes you can get
1 x 400g/14oz tin Italian plum tomatoes
half a 200g/7oz jar tomato passata, organic if possible
1 tbsp tomato purée
2 bay leaves
generous bunch of fresh thyme, parsley and/or basil, chopped
2 tsp molasses sugar
about 150ml/5fl oz red wine
salt and pepper
spaghetti
butter and olive oil
extra basil leaves
freshly grated Parmesan

Heat the oil in a large, heavy-bottomed frying pan and sauté the onions, celery sticks and garlic until softened and translucent. Add the fresh and tinned tomatoes, tomato passata and purée, and chop the tinned tomatoes down into the liquid. Add the bay leaves and other herbs, simmer for a minute, then stir in the sugar. Simmer, uncovered, until the sauce is beginning to thicken, stirring occasionally, for about 15 minutes. Add a good splash of wine, season and stir. Keep the sauce simmering happily for up to another 30 minutes, giving it the occasional stir and adding a little more wine or tomato passata if it begins to dry out.

Cook the spaghetti in plenty of boiling, salted water according to the instructions on the packet. Drain unthoroughly, without shaking the colander, so that there is still water on the pasta when you return it to the pan. Stir in a knob of butter with a splosh of good olive oil then stir in the tomato sauce on the heat for a minute. Tear a few basil leaves over the top of the sauce if you have some. Serve freshly grated Parmesan separately.

RAW TOMATO SAUCE

Curiously, this is as good in the winter as it is in the summer. The hot pasta brings out all the heady scents of the herbs, oil and garlic and injects at least the hope of summer flavours and ripe tomatoes. If you can't find good basil, tarragon and flat-leaf parsley make an equally pleasing marriage with the tomatoes.

SERVES 4

1 small onion
1 large clove of garlic
675g/1½ lb ripe, well flavoured tomatoes, skinned, seeded and finely chopped
6 tbsp olive oil
1 tbsp each of torn basil leaves, chopped chives and flat-leaf parsley
2 tbsp juice and the zest of an organic lemon
salt and pepper

Mince the onion and garlic together in a liquidiser or food processor. Put in a bowl with the remaining ingredients, stir, then cover and leave in the fridge for about 30 minutes. Stir again, then mix into a steaming hot bowl of pasta, and serve warm or cold.

SPAGHETTI CARBONARA

SERVES 6

2 or 3 cloves of garlic
3 tbsp best olive oil
225g/8oz pancetta, cut into small
    strips, or shredded prosciutto
120ml/4fl oz dry white wine
2 large eggs
55g/2oz each of Parmesan and
    Pecorino, grated
black pepper
spaghetti
flat-leaf parsley, finely chopped

This is one of the great fast suppers that you can make when the fridge is bare of all but the basics. It is really just a glorious Roman version of eggs and bacon served with spaghetti, so if you can, use fat chunks of pancetta, tear up prosciutto or culatello or opt for oak-smoked back rashers, which I buy organic and nitrite free from Swaddles Farm (see the list of suppliers at the back of this book for details). Bathing the pasta in cream is not what it's about. This dish has eggs and white wine that cling to the pasta and is lighter and less rich as a result.

Smash the garlic gloves with the flat of a knife blade. Warm the olive oil and garlic together in a small pan and remove the garlic when it has turned golden brown. Throw in the pancetta, and cook until browned and beginning to crisp. Pour in the wine, let it bubble for a couple of minutes, then turn the heat off.

Break the eggs into the bowl from which you'll serve the pasta, beat them, then throw the cheeses and the pepper in and beat again.

Add the cooked, drained spaghetti — I allow 85–110g/3–4oz per person — and toss well to coat the pasta stickily. Reheat the pancetta quickly, pour it over the pasta, toss thoroughly with the parsley and some more black pepper and serve.

SPAGHETTI WITH CREAM, BACON AND PEAS

SERVES 6

2 or 3 cloves of garlic
3 tbsp best olive oil
225g/8oz pancetta, cut into small
    strips, or shredded prosciutto
butter
300ml/10fl oz double cream
225/8oz cooked peas, fresh or frozen
spaghetti
black pepper
freshly grated Parmesan

If you don't want to make the classic Carbonara, cook the garlic and bacon as above, then add a nut of butter and the double cream and peas. Bubble the mixture for a couple of minutes before pouring it over the cooked and drained pasta. Grind over some black pepper, throw in a handful of Parmesan and serve some extra Parmesan separately.

MOZZARELLA-STUFFED MEATBALLS
WITH TAGLIATELLE AND FRESH TOMATO SAUCE

SERVES 4–6

1 onion
2 cloves of garlic
some fresh flat-leaf parsley
450g/1lb minced beef
1 tsp chopped thyme or marjoram
salt and pepper
1 egg, beaten
half a buffalo mozzarella, cut into
    1cm/½ in cubes
flour
6–7 tbsp olive oil
tomato sauce (see p. 66)
tagliatelle

When my daughter Miranda was nine years old she went in for a Sainsbury's Future Cooks competition and having reached the regional finals, had to cook a two-course lunch in front of a panel of judges. Her hands were too small at this stage even to chop onions without nicking herself, so we devised a way in the Magimix that wasn't wholly successful but was better than drawing blood. Every Saturday for six weeks we dutifully ate the same lunch as Miranda learned to perfect the cooking of both courses. Then came the penultimate test, cooking the lunch to time. On the day, she acquitted herself brilliantly, winning an ice-cream maker and £50. It took me some time to recover, what with the nerves one has for one's children and getting back the appetite for a dish that I, too, could cook and almost taste in my sleep. Now it is a thing of nostalgia and has returned to its rightful place, an occasional and lovely dish that is loved by all ages and is simple to make once your hands are big enough to wield a knife and chop an onion!

Mince the onion, garlic and parsley together in a liquidiser or food processor, then add them to the meat in a large bowl. Sprinkle in the chopped fresh thyme or marjoram, some salt and pepper, and then work in the beaten egg with your fingers or a wooden spoon. Roll into balls the size of an extra-large marble, pushing a cube of mozzarella into the centre of each. Roll very lightly in flour, and cook in a large frying pan in a generous amount of olive oil, turning to brown all over.

Remove from the pan to a warmed gratin dish, and pour over a quantity of tomato sauce (see page 66). Serve with tagliatelle.

BÉCHAMEL DISHES

This is one of the fundamentals, yet there are many who would see the accomplishment of it as a challenge not worthy of them, or would simply not understand that there are no shortcuts to what is, actually, very simple in the first place. You don't want lumpy glop, so always use hot milk, always whisk, and always cook long enough for the floury taste to gently winnow itself away until the complex, more subtle scent of nutmeg and bay have come to the fore. A little cream at the end if you need a richer sauce passes muster, or strong Cheddar or gooey threads of Gruyère and a spike of mustard if the recipe calls for a cheese sauce. The best milk to use is Jersey because of its creaminess. Just don't attempt a béchamel with skimmed milk; it defeats the object. Try to get used to looking and sensing rather than measuring and recipe reading with this sort of cooking. It is something you need to learn to guess a little rather than make to measure and should become part of the battery of cooking instincts that you will build up gradually over the years if you have a mind to.

BASIC BÉCHAMEL SAUCE

600ml/1 pint full-cream milk, Jersey
   if possible
onion, peeled and stuck with a
   couple of cloves
bay leaf
55g/2oz unsalted butter
1 heaped tbsp plain flour
nutmeg
sea salt
black pepper
double cream (optional)

Bring the milk slowly to the boil in a small pan to which you have also added the clove-studded onion and a fresh bay leaf. Then remove the pan from the heat and leave the onion and bay leaf in the milk in a covered pan to infuse for 20–30 minutes.

Melt the butter over a gentle heat in a small, heavy-bottomed pan. Just as the butter begins to foam and bubble, throw in a heaped tablespoon of plain flour and stir it gently for a few seconds. Too much flour and you'll get a thick floury base layer to the pan instead of a thin bubbling one; too little and the butter won't amalgamate with the flour, so scatter in a little more. Let this bubble together for a minute or so until it begins to turn a pale biscuit colour, but don't let it darken and begin to burn. Add about half a cup of the milk, which you have heated to hot again, whereupon the mixture will bubble furiously and you will whisk it furiously with a small balloon whisk until it suddenly thickens beyond easy whisking. Add more milk and repeat; the sauce will take a little longer to thicken each time you add more milk.

Begin to cook the sauce more slowly while stirring it with a wooden spoon – you should have whisked the lumps out by now – and add more milk as the sauce seems to demand it to keep the texture thick enough but not solid. Cook slowly for 20 minutes, remembering to stir frequently to prevent it sticking to the bottom of the pan and burning, which milk has a tendency to do, and to prevent a skin forming on the surface.

I grate a little nutmeg into the sauce about halfway through the cooking time and season it. When it is cooked, I check the seasoning and adjust if necessary. Nutmeg is always best when you add a 'suspicion' of it; you don't want the sauce to become a nutmeg sauce.

MACARONI CHEESE

SERVES 4

up to 850ml/1½ pints Mornay sauce,
    (use the béchamel sauce recipe on
    p. 70 and add about 170g/6oz
    grated Cheddar off the heat)
450g/1lb macaroni or penne
enough butter to grease the dish and
    dot little bits over the gratin
a clove of garlic, finely chopped
    (optional)
a handful each of breadcrumbs and
    grated Parmesan mixed together
    or just Parmesan

This is not the sort of dish you would normally find in a recipe book, probably because cookery writers usually assume a certain level of expertise and try to give you a new take on a classic rather than teach you how to make the sort of food that is still somewhat pejoratively referred to as nursery food. So it is as hard to find a good, basic recipe for macaroni cheese in all the self-consciously modernist pantheons as it is for a simple sponge pudding. I know, as, since beginning this book, I have been referring to earlier culinary bibles and trying to reach certain conclusions about traditional or classic recipes and how they vary and have been adapted and updated over the years. My thoughts on this one are that while you may wish to add some buttered leeks, a little frazzled bacon chopped into dice, some buttery mushrooms, florets of steamed broccoli or merely a little teaspoon of English mustard, this dish should not be tampered with beyond that. It is, at best, just a gratin of macaroni with a strong Cheddared Mornay sauce, the top sprinkled with Parmesan, a little butter and perhaps a few breadcrumbs and the bottom saucy enough for each tube to be able to absorb the cheesy lubricant both inside and out. The most important ingredient in this dish is the Cheddar, so choose a well matured unpasteurised Cheddar such as Montgomery's, Quicke's, Keen's or Daylesford or the dish will be bland and unremarkable. You may make the upscale model of this with the classic Mornay sauce ingredients of half Parmesan to half Gruyère if you would rather. In this case rather less cheese will be needed to come to full strength, say 55g/2oz each, but check the flavour and up it if you need to.

Preheat the oven to 200°C/400°F/Gas 6. Make the Mornay sauce while you are bringing a huge pan of water to the boil for the pasta. Butter a large gratin dish and scatter over the finely chopped garlic if you are including it.

Drain the pasta, not too thoroughly, tip it into the gratin dish and immediately begin pouring the sauce over it, stirring as you go and allowing the tubes to start absorbing the sauce. Sprinkle the top with Parmesan or the Parmesan and breadcrumb mixture, dot with butter and brown in the oven until the top is bubbling and molten, 15–20 minutes.

CAULIFLOWER CHEESE

SERVES 4

1 large organic cauliflower broken
    into florets
1 tbsp grain mustard or 1 tsp English
    mustard powder
85–110g/3–4oz mature farmhouse
    Cheddar, unpasteurised if
    possible, grated
55g/2oz fresh Parmesan, grated
tbsp or so of cream (optional)

BÉCHAMEL SAUCE
850ml/1½ pints milk
1 bay leaf
1 onion, halved
grated nutmeg
55g/2oz butter
55g/2oz plain white flour
salt and pepper

A main course, a side dish, or even something you can turn into a soup, believe it or not, this simple dish really defines home cooking – if you cook it well. You need a really good, unpasteurised Cheddar like Montgomery's, Quicke's, Keen's or Daylesford so the dish hits the palate with a sharp, tangy, farmyardy note, and you want a touch of grain or English mustard for a little heat. You need enough sauce to cover the cauliflower in a silken mantle and conceal it from the world before you sprinkle on some Parmesan and bronze the top. One of the greats.

Make the béchamel as on page 70 and while it is cooking, bring a large pan of salted water to the boil. Hurl in the cauliflower and cook for about 5 minutes or until the stalks are still resistant but not offensively so! A skewer will tell you all you need to know. Drain in a colander. While the cauliflower is cooking finish the sauce. Stir the mustard into the béchamel and begin to add the Cheddar cheese on a very low heat. When you have the strength of flavour you like, stop. Adjust the seasoning or mustard if you need to and add a little cream if you feel like it, no more than a tablespoon or two.

Put the cauliflower in a gratin dish and pour over the unctuous cloak. Scatter a good handful of Parmesan over the top and either put under the grill or in a hot oven until you've got a lovely dark mahogany pattern on top and the sauce is bubbling. Don't go past this stage; you don't want it to split and turn oily

ELIZA ACTON'S MACARONI À LA REINE

SERVES 4

450g/1lb macaroni
285g/10oz strong unpasteurised
    Cheddar like Montgomery's,
    Quicke's, Keen's or Daylesford,
    thinly sliced
450ml/16fl oz double cream
55g/2oz unsalted butter, cut into
    small cubes, plus extra for
    greasing the dish
sea salt, black pepper, freshly ground
    mace or nutmeg, pinch cayenne

When Eliza Acton wrote her influential *Modern Cookery for Private Families* in 1845, this unfloured, richly creamed version of macaroni cheese graced the pages. I have made a few small alterations to update it. This is exceptionally rich and needs no more than a plain green salad to follow.

Cook the pasta as per the instructions. While it is cooking, melt the thinly sliced cheese in the cream over a low heat, stirring constantly. Stir in the cubes of butter and season with the salt, pepper and spices.

Drain the macaroni and put it into a buttered gratin dish. Pour the sauce over it and stir well until it has been properly absorbed. Brown in a hot oven, 200°C/400°F/Gas 6 for about 15 minutes. You may, Eliza suggests, substitute Stilton for half of the Cheddar.

Cauliflower Cheese

PRAWN AND LEEK LASAGNE

SERVES 6

55g/2oz butter or 4 tbsp olive oil
white parts of 12 thick leeks,
    chopped into 1cm/½in chunks
560g/1¼lb lasagne sheets
900g/2lb cooked peeled prawns
110–170g/4–6oz Parmesan cheese,
    grated

BÉCHAMEL SAUCE
850ml/1½ pints milk
1 bay leaf
1 onion, halved
grated nutmeg
55g/2oz butter
55g/2oz plain white flour
salt and pepper

This is one of those gloriously adaptable dishes that you can dress up or down every which way. Clams, mussels, a tad of smoked haddock, some glistening scallops with great commas of coral or just a plain heap of prawns, whose sweetness has a natural affinity with the leeks. Throw in a handful of fresh or frozen peas if you have them, or some slices of steamed fennel with their feathery fronds to further the pink and green theme. This is a simple supper dish which my children have loved since they were tinies. In fact, I conjured it up with them in mind, after years of pulling heads off whiskery little prawns once the contents of the shrimping net have been cooked in an old tin can of boiling sea water on a driftwood fire – a regular part of our summers in the west of Ireland since the children were small. Sweet prawns and sweet leeks make ideal partners and this is a dish that, even in its simplest form, is as comforting and delicious as can be.

Preheat the oven to 190°C/375°F/Gas 5. Heat the butter or oil in a large saucepan, add the leeks and cook over a low heat until softened and translucent.

Boil the lasagne until tender, then drain by spreading the pasta sheets on a clean tea towel. (Alternatively, use the sort of lasagne that does not need precooking, but make sure you use a good brand or the texture is like toasted cardboard.)

Put a thin layer of béchamel sauce in a large greased baking dish and sprinkle about one-third of the grated Parmesan on top. Add a layer of lasagne, and scatter half the leeks and half the prawns on top. Pour over half the remaining béchamel and sprinkle another third of the grated Parmesan on top. Repeat the layers, starting with the lasagne and ending with the Parmesan. Cook in the preheated oven for 30–40 minutes. Test by inserting a knife into the pasta; the top will be golden and bubbling.

Serve with a green salad with some finely sliced fennel.

DRESSING THE SALAD

I would always advise having two or three olive oils on the go if you can afford to, making sure you reserve your best and fruitiest extra virgin one for a dressing. You can cook with a lesser oil. Ravida, Seggiano, Colonna, Nuñez de Prado are some of my favourites. They have the right degree of grassiness, pepperiness and character to make good salad leaves taste great.

Without the garlic, this sort of dressing keeps well in the fridge for a week or so in a screwtop jar, but remove it at least an hour before you want it to give it time to come back to room temperature.

5:1, 4:1, 3:1, the ratio of olive oil to vinegar is your choice – mine is normally 5:1 – as are the other components you may like to add to your dressing, but here are the basics

1 heaped tsp Dijon mustard
black pepper
sea salt
2 tbsp red or white wine vinegar
6 tbsp best extra virgin olive oil

OPTIONAL EXTRAS
pinch of dark sugar
finely crushed clove of garlic
1 tbsp chopped fresh herbs – chives, parsley, tarragon, chervil

FRENCH DRESSING

Put a heaped teaspoon of Dijon mustard, a good scrunch of black pepper and whisper of sea salt in a small bowl, followed by 2 tablespoons of a good red or white wine vinegar or a white wine and tarragon vinegar. Beat with a tiny balloon whisk or a fork until smooth. Add at least 6 tablespoons of best extra virgin olive oil, a spoonful at a time, whisking as you go. When it has all cohered into a smooth liquid, taste with a fingertip and review. Remember you need something with bite but not so sharp it catches the throat. Once turned into the salad leaves the dressing will lose some of its strength.

You may like to add a pinch of dark sugar like molasses or muscovado after the mustard; you may like to finely crush a clove of garlic under a knife blade and add it chopped fine, in which case the dressing will only keep for a couple of days as garlic goes rancid. You may prefer cider vinegar, though I'm sure the French would not allow this to be called a French dressing. You may wish to add a tablespoon of chopped fresh herbs at the end.

SHERRY VINEGAR

Sherry vinegar is not just for when you're cooking Spanish food. A dressing made with olive oil and sherry vinegar and seasoning is particularly good with roasted vegetables, aubergines, onions, courgettes, what you will. Valdespino make the elixir of sherry vinegars and you can find it in good delis and at wine merchants Lea and Sandeman, who also stock Valdespino sherry.

HAZELNUT OIL, WALNUT OIL

These oils are much more temperamental than olive oil and need to be kept in the fridge after opening. They also turn rancid quite quickly, so buy small bottles and sniff before you sprinkle. My advice would be to use half hazelnut or walnut to half olive oil, so that the nuttiness doesn't overwhelm, and to think carefully about what you are serving with it.

If you are serving an endive, blue cheese and walnut salad, the walnut oil will complement beautifully. Likewise, use hazelnut oil on a salad with crushed roasted hazelnuts – lovely with a fresh goat's cheese. Walnut is good with goat's cheese too. If it is a simple cos salad you can afford the luxury of the nut oil. You don't want too many flavours competing with it.

OLIVE OIL AND BALSAMIC DRESSING

Olive oil and balsamic vinegar make a wonderful dressing, though balsamic has become one of those overworked things that doesn't always hit the right note if served with the wrong ingredient or wantonly lashed on by the tablespoon. The other thing to remember about balsamic is that the cheap brands you find on the supermarket shelves are really not good enough to use in a salad dressing. They have all the sharpness that glitches the throat and none of the mellow, soft, velvety grapeyness that a true aged balsamic does. Cheap balsamic is for cooking with.

Expensive though a 12-, 15-, 20- or even 40-year balsamic may be, the intensity is such that a few raindrops of it scattered onto the salad after you have glugged on the tablespoons of olive oil and seasoning will be all you need. Think of it as an investment that will at least pay off in the taste stakes and remember to use it as a treat. It will last six months if you're sparing. Asparagus served warm with a little balsamic dressing is one of the great treats of May. I abjure the shavings of Parmesan as unnecessary gloss and too much flavour, but you may disagree.

OLIVE OIL AND LEMON JUICE

Again, experiment with the ratio until you get what suits you. This is a particularly good dressing for fish that you're going to eat cold or warm, be it charcoaled squid or octopus with perhaps a hit of red chilli or plain baked white fish. It is also good with vegetables like thinly sliced raw fennel or artichokes and helps preserve their colour in the case of the artichokes. It is a useful way of marinading fish for a ceviche, in which the fish is 'cooked' by the acidity of the lemon or lime and then eaten without being introduced to the oven.

ASIAN DRESSING OR DIPPING SAUCE

2 cloves of garlic
1–2 red bird's eye chillies, finely sliced, depending on your love of heat
3 tbsp unrefined caster sugar
4 tbsp fish sauce
4 tbsp freshly squeezed lime juice
4 tbsp rice vinegar

This works as well with a spicy fishcake as it does as a feisty dressing for all manner of noodley prawn, chicken or raw vegetable salads with ribbons of carrot, cucumber and courgette, or grated carrot, radish, mushroom and spinach. If you are using this as a dipping sauce, add a tablespoon of water and you may add either a tablespoon of olive oil or a couple of teaspoons of toasted sesame oil if you feel like it.

Crush the garlic in a mortar or under the blade of a knife and whisk it together with the other ingredients until the sugar has completely dissolved and the dressing no longer feels gritty. Allow the flavours to marry for 30 minutes before serving or mixing into your salad.

CREAM DRESSING

1 tsp Dijon mustard
1 tsp sugar
2 tsp tarragon vinegar
a scrap of crushed garlic
1 hard-boiled egg, yolk and white separated
200–250ml/7–8fl oz double cream
2 dsrtsp chives, chopped small
110–170g/4–6oz Cashel Blue or similar blue cheese

I make this deliciously pungent, salt, cream of a dressing when I really want to gild the lettuce. It is a rich dressing that doesn't need a rich partner but something simple, though not the American combination of protein on protein where it is served with tranches of steak. Just a simple cos lettuce with the added texture of fudgy Cashel Blue, Roquefort, Beenleigh Blue, Berkshire Blue or a similar soft blue cheese and the chopped white of a separated hard-boiled egg is enough.

Stir the mustard, sugar, vinegar and garlic together in a bowl with the egg yolk, then stir in the cream. Thin with a little milk or water if it has thickened too much. Pour the dressing over torn cos lettuce, then scatter over the chopped egg white, chives and crumbled Cashel Blue.

SOUP

Comforting to eat, comforting to cook and infinitely comforting to sniff and savour, soups burble away in the kitchen, scenting the place with the promise of good things. Soups make home feel like home and are one of the easiest and quickest of things to make. Homemade soups are invariably better than the tinned or packet variety with their gluey texture and ubiquitous over-salting, aimed, I hate to say it, at masking their inferior ingredients.

Soups are great as a starter, great as a main course, great as the only course. Scalding hot cream of tomato soup served at a chilly picnic, straight from the thermos, is one of life's great, simple pleasures. Soups can be coarse, lumpy, peasant dishes, nearer a stew than a soup in texture and substance, or they can be refined, delicate, creamed or clear liquids, intensely or delicately flavoured with herbs, vegetables, meat stock, fish, spices or cereals like barley or rice. You don't even have to have chicken stock to hand, just the water you have cooked the vegetables in is enough if you want a more mild-mannered, vegetarian bowlful and the vegetables you're using are really fresh.

I've got a feeling, when I think back, that the first soup I ever made was a wild mushroom one with field mushrooms I'd picked, a little wholemeal bread to thicken it, a pinch of ginger and a splash of cream. Before that came years of Heinz tomato soup that I used to stir into a bowl of macaroni at boarding school, where a craftily hidden primus stove in the dormitory was lit every night when starvation got the upper hand. Amazing that we never set fire to the place; even more amazing that we were never discovered.

Then there are the memories of that great palliative and restorative, chicken soup. Why it should only be wheeled out as some invalid rite I cannot imagine; an intense chicken stock reduced in the proper way, then peppered with a tiny doll's sized dice of leek, carrot, potato and celery, some morsels of chicken and perhaps some dried chopped morels if you want to lift the ladle on something a little more glamorous, the whole thickened imperceptibly so that it is neither clear nor gloop, and seasoned. What could be of greater cheer or more soothing to prepare and scent as it reaches its comforting, enveloping readiness?

If I had to pick my favourite soup of all, it would probably be the late, great, hugely lamented George Perry-Smith's fish soup served with aïoli and a rouille, croutons and Parmesan. George was the silent star of the movie world of chefs before chefs came out of their kitchens and people even knew or cared who they were. He didn't want the modern celebrity circus of publicity and recognition and the ephemeral fame of television. He wanted to cook and to remain firmly in the kitchen. Indeed, when a couple entered the hallowed portals of his famous Hole in the Wall restaurant in Bath and wondered should they genuflect at the altar, George was utterly horrified. He went on to run Riverside in Helford, Cornwall, one of the first restaurants with rooms, where I passed many a happy week. My room was above the kitchen, from whence rose the scent of the morning croissants and the sound of

George quietly admonishing and encouraging the talents of the gap-year girls and boys and would-be disciples, who were eager to learn from the master. I always secretly wished I could be there in the kitchen, learning George's lore and wisdom instead of trying to work everything out as I ate it in the dining room or occasionally venturing through the ever-open kitchen door and asking George just how the walnut treacle tart or the salmon en croûte with currants and ginger was made.

It was here at Riverside where I really learned what good taste meant. George's intensely flavoured fish soup was one of his signature dishes copied by many but never so well. They always short-cut the ingredients or the process. The sweet, red, barely thickened intensification of lobster and crab, fennel and Pernod, tomato and saffron and all the other fish and vegetables that went into the final soup, married with a garlicky aïoli made with the best olive oil and a hot, vibrant vermilion rouille, was as classic and as marvellous a soup as you can serve and brought to the table in a tureen from which you could go on helping yourself. Dining should always be about this sort of generosity and tureens should always be brimming with wonderful soup.

The method for many of our simple, classic, favourite everyday soups like carrot, celery, pea, tomato, spinach, artichoke, broad bean, parsnip, leek and potato is very simple and once you have made a few successfully you can move on to the more esoteric Asian broths, potages, spiced soups and Mediterranean fish or vegetable soups that demand a greater sense of timing, stock reduction, spicing and effort.

Butter or olive oil or a mixture of the two can be used for any vegetable soups, depending on the flavour you prefer. Sweating and softening the vegetable base, be it just onion, leek or a soffritto of them with garlic, carrot and celery, has to be done slowly so that the vegetables reach a melting texture without browning before you add the liquid. Then keep at a gentle simmer with the lid on, until the vegetables have completely cooked through, and the soup is ready to season, purée, add cream, yoghurt or crème fraîche to and serve. You may just be using water or vegetable stock, the water you have cooked your potatoes and vegetables in, or you may be using meat stock, most often chicken stock for an everyday soup, though I frequently have a game or duck stock on the go in the winter and turkey and goose stock at Christmas.

CHICKEN STOCK

MAKES ABOUT 1.5 LITRES/ 3 PINTS

chicken carcass
2 onions
2 cloves
2–3 celery sticks, broken in half
2 carrots
cleaned green tops of leeks and
    mushroom peelings if you have
    some
bouquet of fresh herbs – parsley,
    bay, thyme and rosemary or
    any combination
a few black peppercorns

The best stock comes from poaching a chicken with vegetables that you are then going to sauce and serve, stripping off the meat for the dish and returning the carcass and a fresh lot of vegetables to the pan. This doubles the intensity and flavour of the stock by simmering it all over again so the result, when cooled, will chill to a wondrous jelly, but this isn't something one does every week. The following is a basic stock recipe to make with the bones of your roast chicken.

Break up the carcass of your roast chicken into large pieces and make sure you save all the bones from people's plates to add. Brown the bones in the roasting tin if you can be bothered, then put them in a large, heavy-bottomed pan. Add a couple of onions halved, skins still on for flavour and colour, each stuck with a clove, and the celery and chopped carrots – chopping the vegetables imparts more flavour than leaving them whole. If you have them, throw in some cleaned green tops of leeks that are too tough to cook with, a few mushroom peelings, a small bouquet of fresh herbs – parsley, bay, thyme and rosemary or any combination of these – and a few black peppercorns. You should also add the giblets if you haven't already used them for your gravy.

Cover with cold water, bring slowly to the boil, skim, then simmer three-quarters covered for a couple of hours. Any longer than this and the flavour doesn't improve. I suspect all the goodness has been released by the bones and the vegetables by then. Strain into a bowl and when cold, put in the fridge covered in clingfilm. Take the fat off when you want to use the stock. The fat can be clarified and used as dripping for your roast potatoes so the cycle is complete and without waste.

LEEK AND POTATO SOUP OR CRÈME VICHYSSOISE

SERVES 4–6

45g/1½ oz unsalted butter
4 fat leeks, or rather more if they are
    spindly, the green part removed,
    washed and chopped into rings
3 or 4 small potatoes, peeled and
    cubed
a little chopped parsley
1.2 litres/2 pints well-flavoured
    chicken stock (above) and
    300ml/10fl oz cream or
half and half water and full-cream
    milk and a little cream to finish
a bunch of chives
sea salt and black pepper

This has always been a favourite with my three children and the hot version was one of the first soups Miranda and Charissa attempted to cook. The cold is, I feel, due a comeback. It is one of those delectable dishes that has fallen from fashion, but when the young leeks and early spring chives are in season it is a perfect start to a cold lunch or supper.

Melt the butter in a heavy-bottomed pan over a low heat and add the leeks. Stir and cook them for a few minutes until they are beginning to soften and turn golden before adding the cubed potato. Turn it briefly in the butter, add the chopped parsley, stock and seasoning and bring back to the boil stirring as you do. Simmer until the potatoes are cooked through, about 15–20 minutes.

Liquidise in the blender, adjust the seasoning and add the cream if you are going to use it. Bring back to simmer point before removing from the heat. Ladle into bowls and sprinkle some snipped chives over the top. You may prefer to use the rich milk in making the soup and not add cream, or add a little swirl of it or a blob of crème fraîche into the bowl, onto which you may scatter a teaspoon of chives.

If you are going to serve the soup cold, do not add the cream until the soup has cooled. Refrigerate until properly chilled, then serve with the chives on top.

CARROT SOUP OR POTAGE CRÉCY

SERVES 4–6

45g/1½oz unsalted butter or half and half olive oil and butter
1 onion, peeled and finely chopped
450g/1lb or thereabouts of organic carrots, peeled and either cut into small dice or slim coins
1.2 litres/2 pints vegetable or chicken stock (see p. 80)
1 tbsp parsley
sea salt and black pepper
juice of 1 orange (optional)
coriander leaves, chopped
crème fraîche (optional)

You may add the juice of an orange at the end of the cooking time to give a citrussy sharpness to this sweet vegetable, or scatter over some chopped coriander leaves if you prefer, with or without a blob of crème fraîche.

Heat the butter gently in a heavy-bottomed pan and add the onion, stirring and cooking it until it is softened and golden. Add the diced carrot and turn it in the butter, cooking it for a few minutes until it just begins to soften. Pour over the stock, add the parsley, season and bring it up to the boil. Simmer with a lid on until the carrots are completely soft, then liquidise and return to the pan, adjusting the seasoning before you re-heat it. As it gets to boiling point add the orange juice if you are using it and remove from the heat. Ladle into bowls and sprinkle over coriander and add a dollop of crème fraîche if you want to.

You may also add a finger of grated raw root ginger with the diced carrot to make a carrot and ginger soup.

CREAM OF TOMATO SOUP, HOT OR CHILLED

SERVES 4–6

450g/1lb ripe organic tomatoes
55g/2oz unsalted butter
1 small onion, peeled and diced
1 small carrot, peeled and diced
1 stick celery, diced
1 clove of garlic, peeled and chopped
700ml/1¼ pints vegetable, beef or chicken stock
1 bay leaf
2 tsp tomato purée
1 tsp molasses or dark muscovado sugar
a suspicion of nutmeg, sea salt and black pepper
150ml/5fl oz cream or Jersey full-cream milk
chopped parsley or chives

If you can, buy organic plum tomatoes or at least the organic vine tomatoes that have some flavour to them, albeit the high acidity and sharpness nothing like that of the great Provençal or Italian specimens. You may add some torn leaves of basil at the end, but this is really the nursery not the Mediterranean version, so I like to keep it as close to childhood memories as possible, though without the farinaceous undertones of a certain proprietary brand!

First skin and seed your tomatoes. This is not as difficult or as time consuming as you would imagine. Put the tomatoes in a bowl and pierce them with the blade of a sharp knife somewhere around their middle. Boil a kettle and pour the boiling water over the tomatoes. It MUST cover them for this to work. Count 30 seconds. Tip the scalding water out of the bowl and fill the bowl with cold water for just long enough to cool the tomatoes so you can handle them. The skins should now unpeel as easily as you would unwrap a parcel. Cut each tomato in quarters and push the seeds out with your fingers. Remove the nasty little core that really doesn't do any tomato dish any favours, hot or cold.

Heat the butter in a pan and sauté the diced onion, carrot, celery and garlic together gently for about 10 minutes, making sure they don't start to brown. Add the quartered tomatoes, stock, bay leaf, tomato purée and sugar and simmer briefly and slowly until the carrots are cooked through. Remove the bay leaf, liquidise and season to taste.

If you are serving the soup hot, scald the cream to boiling point in a pan, add it to the soup and reheat it without letting it boil. Sprinkle the parsley or chives over each bowl as you serve it.

If you are serving the soup cold, allow it to cool down before the addition of the cream and chill it in the fridge in a large bowl. Stir in the cold cream, season more highly than you would for a hot soup and cool further. Sprinkle the parsley or some chives over as you serve each bowl.

CURRIED PARSNIP SOUP

SERVES 6–8

1 large parsnip
110g/4oz chopped onion
1 clove of garlic, crushed
85g/3oz unsalted butter
1 tbsp flour
1 tsp each cumin and coriander
    seeds tempered in a frying pan for
    a minute, then ground in a mortar
1 tsp garam masala
a tiny knifepoint of cayenne
1.2 litres/2 pints hot chicken stock
    (see p. 80)
salt and pepper
150ml/5fl oz cream
chopped chives

This is one of the soups that the inspiring food writer Jane Grigson was famous for and is, perhaps surprisingly, one that my children always loved from an early age. It is the perfect winter soup. Grigson stated curry powder in her original, but I make mine with some toasted coriander and cumin and a touch of garam masala and cayenne, warming but not fiery to the soul.

Peel and slice the parsnip. Put the parsnip, onion and garlic into a heavy pan with the butter and cook for 10 minutes slowly with the lid on the pan. The vegetables must not brown, but gently absorb the butter. Add the flour and the spices to take up the fat, and gradually incorporate the hot stock. Simmer until the parsnip is cooked. Liquidise or push through a mouli-légumes.

Return to the pan, correct seasoning with salt and pepper, then add the cream and a sprinkling of chopped chives. Grigson suggests serving the soup with croutons of bread fried in butter and oil, but I prefer it plain. The soup may need further dilution with some extra stock or some creamy milk.

RISI E BISI, OR RICE AND PEAS

SERVES 4

30g/1oz unsalted butter
2 tbsp mild extra virgin olive oil
1 small onion, very finely chopped
3 tbsp flat-leaf parsley, chopped
450g/1lb shelled weight small, fresh
    peas (or frozen petits pois out of
    season)
225g/8oz risotto rice, preferably
    Vialone Nano
up to 1.2 litres/2 pints of chicken
    stock (see p. 80); if you are using
    fresh peas simmer the pea pods
    until tender then drain, reserving
    the stock
½ –1 tbsp fennel seeds, according to
    taste, crushed in a mortar
sugar, sea salt and black pepper
55g/2oz freshly grated Parmesan

This is the kind of dish you can knock up by merely raiding your mother's fridge and store cupboard, so if a bunch of friends show up unexpectedly you can cook something delicious, hearty and impressive. That is, if your mother is the kind to always have chicken stock lurking in the fridge or the freezer like I do. This is a classic Venetian dish which is turned into a soup, if you feel like it, by the addition of hot chicken stock at the end.

Put the butter, oil, onion and a tablespoon of the parsley in a large, heavy-bottomed pot and sauté very gently for 5 minutes or so. Add the peas and cook, stirring all the time, for a couple of minutes. Stir in the rice until all the grains are coated in the butter and oil, then pour in 700ml/1¼ pints of the hot stock. Stir and bring to the boil before adding the fennel seeds and seasoning and boiling, covered, for 15–20 minutes or until the rice is cooked.

Remove from the heat and stir in the Parmesan and the rest of the parsley. Ladle into bowls into which you ladle extra chicken stock to make them more soupy than risotto-like.

Curried Parsnip Soup

PEA SOUP

SERVES 4–6

55g/2oz unsalted butter
1 medium onion, peeled and finely chopped
2 rashers smoked streaky bacon, snipped small (optional)
225g/8oz shelled weight fresh or frozen peas and the pods if you wish to add them
or
110g/4oz dried split peas, soaked in cold water overnight
1.2 litres/2 pints chicken stock (see p. 80) or ham stock with the ham bone left in it and the remains of the meat stripped off it to add to the soup
sea salt, black pepper
2–3 sprigs fresh mint, leaves chopped small at the last minute

Podding the first tiny, squeaky sweet peas of the season for soup and even including the pods in the water to intensify the pea-ishness is something I look forward to every year, but there is another way. In fact, two other ways, neither of which should be sniffed at or seen as inferior; they are just different. You can also make a very good pea soup with frozen peas and a thicker, muskier but delicious soup with dried yellow or green split peas. The addition of a ham bone and little shards of ham to the finished soup are a distinct advantage if you have any, but there is always crisply fried smoked bacon or pancetta if you want to adulterate the purity of the pea.

Melt the butter in a heavy-bottomed pan and sauté the onion gently until it begins to soften and turn golden. Add the bacon or pancetta if you are using it and continue to fry for a couple of minutes, stirring as you go. Tip in the peas, turn them briefly in the butter then pour in half the stock and simmer until the peas are cooked for 5–10 minutes depending on their size and freshness. Simmer the pods in the rest of stock if you are using them. If you are making the soup with dried split peas, they will take up to an hour to cook, but check the peas are soft after 40 minutes, having skimmed the pan when they first come to the boil. Do not season the dried variety with salt until they are cooked or they will toughen. This applies to all dried lentils and beans as well.

Liquidise and dilute with more of the stock until you have the desired texture, season and sprinkle over fresh mint before serving.

You may also add the rind of a hunk of Parmesan to the soup when you are cooking it if you like a whiff of its flavour with the peas.

LENTIL, TOMATO AND PASTA SOUP

SERVES 6

3 tbsp olive oil
2 onions, finely chopped
6 cloves of garlic, finely chopped
2 sticks of celery, finely chopped
110g/4oz smoked streaky bacon, chopped small
225g/8oz Puy lentils
4 tomatoes, skinned, seeded and chopped
400g/14oz tin Italian plum tomatoes
about 1.5 litres/3 pints chicken stock (see p. 80)
3–4 sprigs of thyme
2 bay leaves
225g/8oz macaroni or similar small pasta
salt and pepper
2–3 tbsp chopped fresh parsley
85–110g/3–4oz Parmesan cheese, grated

I like this soup best made with Puy lentils. It has the smoky earthiness of that always harmonising duo of pork and lentil, the acidity of the tomatoes and the pasta that turns it from just a thick soup into a sort of soupy, pasta stew. Serious ballast for a lunch or dinner, you need serve no more than a baguette of garlic bread with it.

Heat the oil in a large, heavy-bottomed casserole, add the onions, garlic, celery and bacon and cook over a low heat until the vegetables are softened and translucent, about 10–15 minutes. Add the lentils and stir to coat them in oil. Add the fresh and tinned tomatoes, chopping the tinned ones into their juice. Bring to a bubble, then add the stock, thyme and bay leaves. Bring to the boil, then cover and simmer until the lentils are cooked, about 40 minutes. If the mixture is absorbing a lot of stock, ladle in some more, keeping the level above the lentils.

Cook the pasta in boiling water, drain and add to the soup with an extra couple of ladles of stock. Season well, and sprinkle with parsley. Serve in bowls, sprinkled with the Parmesan.

You can also make this soup with chickpeas, but cook them first as they need at least 2 hours compared to the 40 minutes for the lentils.

MUSHROOM SOUP, HOT OR CHILLED

SERVES 4

340g/12oz mushrooms, wiped with a
   damp cloth, not washed, and
   sliced
55g/2oz unsalted butter
2 tbsp chopped parsley
2–3 sprigs thyme (optional)
a small clove of garlic, crushed
   under the back of a knife then
   peeled and finely chopped
sea salt and black pepper
nutmeg or mace
1 thick slice of wholemeal bread,
   crusts removed
1 litre/1¾ pints chicken stock
   (see p. 80)
150ml/5fl oz double cream,
   preferably Jersey

Use wild field or horse mushrooms if you can, or, better still, ceps in the autumn. Otherwise, buy organic chestnut or Portobello mushrooms. They have a far stronger and more bosky flavour than the sad, bland, farmed mushrooms the supermarkets sell. Using wholemeal or rye breadcrumbs to thicken the soup, rather than flour or egg yolks and cream, was the normal thing to do for both soups and sauces in the Middle Ages right through to Tudor times, something our bread sauce is also heir to.

Stew the mushrooms gently in the butter in a heavy-bottomed pan and when their juices begin to run, stir in half the parsley, the thyme leaves if you are using them, the garlic and the seasoning. Grate the nutmeg or mace rather than using powdered if possible. Soak the bread in a little hot stock and add it to the mushrooms, then pour over the rest of the stock. Cook for about 15 minutes at a gentle simmer, then liquidise in the blender or push through the coarse disc of a mouli-légumes – I prefer this last option because it gives the soup a better texture. Pour in the cream and just bring the soup up to the boil before testing the seasoning, ladling it into bowls and scattering over the rest of the parsley.

This soup is also very good chilled. Allow the soup to cool. Then stir in the cream and chill further. Serve with a dollop of extra cream plopped into each bowl.

GARLIC BREAD

3 cloves of garlic, skinned and
   crushed to a paste
a handful chopped flat-leaf or curly
   parsley, or you can substitute
   thyme, sage or oregano depending
   on what works best with what the
   bread is accompanying
110g/4oz or so unsalted butter,
   softened until it is workable
black pepper
a spritz of lemon juice (optional)
1 baguette

Even if you're too young to cut a loaf without risking a finger, the moment you can spread you can slather the garlicky parsleyed butter in between the slices for this perfect accompaniment to most soups and pasta dishes. Try to find good bread made with French flour that is not just doughy pap. It may cost a little more but will always be worth it. A slim baguette will be enough for 4, a weightier one for 6.

Preheat the oven to 180°C/350°F/Gas 4. Work the garlic and parsley into the butter on a large flat plate with a fork, season and add a tiny spritz of lemon juice if you like.

Cut the baguette into slices, not quite down to the base of the loaf. Spread the garlic butter generously into the slices and wrap in foil in a baggy but sealed parcel. Place on a shallow roasting tray and bake in the oven for about 20 minutes. Serve in the opened-out foil. I cut my slices about 2.5cm/1in thick so that each one has enough butter soaked right into the bread.

SIMPLE MEAT DISHES

CHICKEN LIVER PÂTÉ

SERVES 8

450g/1lb or thereabouts organic chicken livers
110g/4oz unsalted butter
sea salt and black pepper
1 small clove of garlic, very finely chopped
a sprig of thyme or a few leaves of basil
2 tbsp Cognac
2 tbsp Madeira, Marsala or Port

This is an exceptionally rich but simple dish, which you can either spread on crostini to accompany your pre-supper drink or serve fridge cold with hot granary toast as a starter. It is something I have made since very early on in my cooking life, feeling it had the right degree of sophistication for any occasion and didn't dent the purse too badly. It is sort of dish that your mother could confidently ask you to help with and make if she's concentrating on the other elements of dinner. I only ever use organic chicken livers. Make this 2–3 days before you need it to allow all the flavours to develop.

First clean the livers and remove all the gristly bits from them, especially any little green stained bits as they will make everything taste bitter. Melt the first 30g/1oz of butter in a frying pan and sling in the livers, cooking them for about 5 minutes and turning them as each surface begins to brown. They should still be rosy pink inside.

Plop a further 55g/2oz of softened butter into your food processor or liquidiser with the chicken livers, seasoning, chopped garlic and thyme leaves. Reserve the hot butter in the pan, to which you now add the Cognac. Allow it to bubble furiously before adding the Madeira, Marsala or Port and heating it through for a minute. Pour the buttery liquor into the processor and process until smooth. Scrape the mixture into a small earthenware tureen or bowl.

Melt the remaining butter – or better still, pork, goose or duck fat if you have it. Skim off the white sediment onto kitchen paper with a slotted spoon and pour the butter onto the top of the pâté to form a protective buttery layer. Cover with foil and a lid when it has set and place in the fridge for 2–3 days before you eat it. Eat cold with hot granary, wholemeal or sourdough toast and a few cornichons.

2 tbsp olive oil
1.5kg/3¼lb chuck steak, cut into large
    cubes and trimmed
1 large onion, chopped
450g/1lb carrots, cut into fingers
6 cloves of garlic, peeled but left
    whole
2 tbsp plain flour
1 tbsp tomato purée
700ml/1¼ pints Guinness
1 bouquet garni with 3 bay leaves,
    2 sprigs of rosemary, thyme and
    parsley and 3 strips of orange
    peel, tied together with string
salt and pepper

CARBONNADE OF BEEF OR BRAISED BEEF WITH GUINNESS

Once you can bake a cake, whisk a meringue, roll out pastry and make a mean chocolate brownie, you're about ready to leave the sweet pastures of your early cooking life for the savoury, and roast your first roast or make a great stew.
The first main course I cooked after the famous school rump steak with petit pois and mushrooms (see page 18) was Carbonnade of Beef, which I served plain with mashed potatoes. It is still one of my favourite dishes and I can't say I've altered the ingredients over the years. I've merely upgraded them to the best organic chuck steak and carrots and got rather better at not over-flouring the meat.

Preheat the oven to 150°C/300°F/Gas 2. Heat the oil in a heavy-bottomed casserole and seal the meat briefly on all sides. Remove with a slotted spoon and put to one side. Add the onion, carrots and garlic and let them begin to colour before sprinkling them with the flour. Add the tomato purée, stir and then return the meat to the casserole. Pour in the Guinness slowly, stirring and allowing the liquid to thicken. Bury the bouquet garni in the liquid and bring to boiling point. Season, cover with a sheet of greaseproof paper and a lid, and put into the oven for 1½ hours.

When the meat is tender, remove and discard the bouquet garni and serve hot, with mashed potato or colcannon (see opposite).

MASHED POTATO

SERVES 2

450g/1lb potatoes, peeled and cut
into chunks
55g/2oz best unsalted butter (more if
you like)
120ml/4fl oz Jersey milk
salt
black pepper

First find the flouriest potatoes, for these make the best mash. Maris Piper or King Edwards are more floury than waxy and that is what you want. Mash is the number one comfort food, but you have to get the texture silken smooth; there is a world of difference between lumpen, dry mash, mash that is puréed like gloopy baby food, gluey-textured mash and the ideal buttery, satiny, peppery mash that has been mouléd and whipped into snowy perfection with a wooden spoon. The butter ratio is yours to decide, but use best unsalted butter. You may want to add more depending on how close and dependent your relationship is with butter, but on no account add some inferior spread on the grounds that it may be better for you. It won't taste like mashed potato! I add Jersey milk to enrich and make the texture of the mash creamier.

I favour steaming chunks of peeled potatoes until they are cooked through, then leaving them drained in the top of the steamer for 5 minutes while you gently heat the butter and milk in a pan. When the butter has melted and the milk is hot, mouli your potatoes into them over a gentle heat on the coarse blade of a mouli-légumes. Some people prefer ricers or mashers, but I find the mouli the perfect tool for the right texture. Now take the pan off the heat, add salt and a good scrunch of black pepper and stir the mixture briskly in the pan with a wooden spoon so that you whip it into a glossy amalgam, ready to serve.

There are other kinds of mash, made with olive oil and perhaps a flavouring of a few roasted cloves of garlic, but I think this simple old-fashioned version is the best of all.

CHAMP

SERVES 6

1kg/2¼lb floury potatoes, peeled and
cut into chunks
300ml/10fl oz creamy milk
55–85g/2–3oz butter
6 spring onions, finely chopped
salt and pepper

Simmer the potatoes until tender. Drain off the water, cover the pan and let the potatoes sit for a few minutes. Put the milk and 55g/2oz of the butter in a saucepan and heat to boiling point. Add the chopped spring onions, turn off the heat, and let the onions infuse in the milk.

Mash the potatoes, then add the milk, butter and spring onion mixture, stirring until smooth. Season to taste. You can make a well in the centre and add an extra lump of butter to melt into the champ if you like.

COLCANNON

SERVES 6–8

1kg/2¼lb green cabbage, finely
chopped
2 small leeks, finely chopped
150–300ml/15–10fl oz milk
1kg/2¼lb floury potatoes, peeled and
roughly chopped
salt and pepper
pinch of grated nutmeg
110g/4oz butter, melted

Simmer the cabbage and leeks in just enough milk to cover, until soft. Boil the potatoes until tender, drain and mash them, then season to taste with salt, pepper and nutmeg.

Add the cabbage, leek and milk mixture. Place in a deep, warmed serving dish, make a well in the centre and pour in the melted butter. Serve the vegetables with spoonfuls of the melted butter.

CHICKEN OR SPARE RIBS IN BARBECUE SAUCE

SERVES 6

110g/4oz tomato ketchup
1 tbsp Japanese shoyu sauce or dark
   soy sauce
1 tbsp Worcestershire sauce
2 tsp cider vinegar
1 tbsp olive oil
2 tsp tomato purée or 1 tsp harissa
2 tsp grainy mustard
1 tbsp clear honey
2 tsp molasses sugar
juice of 1 small orange
3 cloves of garlic, crushed
2.5cm/1in square piece of fresh
   ginger, chopped and squeezed
   through a garlic press
salt and pepper
up to 12 pieces of chicken or about
   1.4kg/3lb spare ribs

This is one of the first great success stories for any teenager to cook. It is as foolproof in the making as it is in the eating, bar vegetarianism or an advanced case of food faddism, and really only involves a competent measuring hand and the best ingredients. Organic chicken legs, drumsticks and thighs, or organic spare ribs with plenty of meat on them are what you want. You can take the chicken on a picnic when it's cooked if you like or eat it cold al fresco; the spare ribs would be too fatty for this, so eat them hot. If you really like heat, a heaped teaspoon of harissa instead of the ketchup or a chopped fresh or dried red chilli can be added to the marinade ingredients.

Mix together all the ingredients except for the meat. Put the chicken or ribs in this mixture and marinate for at least 3 hours, turning when you remember. (You can leave it overnight if you want.)

Preheat the oven to 180°C/350°F/Gas 4. Put the chicken or ribs and marinade in a roasting tin and cover with foil. Bake for about 30 minutes. Test by inserting a skewer into the meat: if the juice runs nearly clear, the chicken is almost cooked. Remove the foil for the final 5–10 minutes. Once the foil is off, the sauce will reduce and adhere to the meat. The ribs can be cooked for much longer once the foil is off. Keep turning them every 10–15 minutes as the sauce reduces and coats them – cook for about 1 hour altogether or until they look really sticky.

SPARE RIBS IN CHINESE-STYLE BARBECUE SAUCE

SERVES 4

150ml/5fl oz stout
40ml/1½fl oz molasses
60ml/2fl oz cider vinegar
3 tbsp Dijon mustard
2 tbsp Worcestershire sauce
1 dsrtsp nam pla (Thai fish sauce)
1 tsp cayenne
1kg/2¼lb spare ribs

Mix the stout, molasses, vinegar, mustard and sauces together with the cayenne in a saucepan. Bring to the boil and simmer for 2 minutes. Cool, then pour over the ribs and turn well. Leave to marinate in a cool place for at least 2 hours.

Preheat the oven to 200°C/400°F/Gas 6. Pour off the excess marinade and reserve. Put the ribs in a roasting dish, cover with foil and bake for an hour, turning at least once. Remove the foil and cook for another 30 minutes, basting every 5 minutes. Add some of the extra marinade if necessary and continue basting and turning the ribs until they are wonderfully dark and sticky.

THE SUNDAY ROAST

Cooking your first Sunday roast is as scary as taking your driving test, make no mistake. Both are about co-ordination, control, foresight, planning, keeping your nerve and luck. It's only when you've passed the test that you really begin to learn how to drive and the same applies with the Sunday roast. No book of theory or advance instruction can substitute for just doing it and doing it again and again. It could take you a lifetime to perfect the techniques and variations. But therein lies the pleasure, as much in the ready rehearsed feeling you have when you have done it a thousand times as in the tentative steps of the novice, hoping for a perfect high-rise Yorkshire to accompany a rare rib of beef; a crisped, furrowed roast potato; a nutmeggy bread sauce; a dashingly dark gravy made with caramelised onion and meat juices; a mahogany skinned chicken with juicy, ivory flesh.

Step-by-step instructions are all very well, but to my mind take the pleasure out of the cooking and turn it into a sort of military exercise. Gentle prodding and reminding is what I've gone for as the army-style approach always makes me feel rebellious.

MAKE SURE THAT YOU TAKE ALL MEAT OUT OF THE FRIDGE well in advance of cooking, so that you cook it from room temperature not fridge cold. An hour ahead should do even the heftiest joint or bird.

ROAST CHICKEN

SERVES 4–6

1.5–2kg/3¼–4½ lb organic, free-range
   chicken
2 onions, peeled
1 organic lemon
a few sprigs of thyme, tarragon or
   rosemary
olive oil or butter
sea salt and black pepper
the giblets: neck, heart and liver

I feel I have to start with roast chicken. It is the definitive roast, in many ways the easiest to master and the one you are most likely to cook most often. It is more than just a Sunday roast. Whether you stuff it or sauce it, do both or neither, it is the ultimate roast if you buy a good bird. The timing is not difficult. Just peel your roast potatoes and parsnips before you put the bird in the oven and get them on to parboil when you put the chicken in.

Preheat the oven to 200°C/400°F/Gas 6. A chicken of this size will take between an hour and an hour and a quarter to cook and should then rest for 15 minutes to allow the juices to flood back through the meat.

Slice a large onion and lay it on the bottom of your roasting dish. Cut another smaller onion into quarters and the lemon likewise. Alternately, stuff the cavity of the bird with the lemon and onion, reserving the last lemon quarter to squeeze over the chicken to add zest and freshness to the flavour. Either push the thyme or tarragon into the cavity or finely chop the rosemary leaves ready to sprinkle over the bird later. Season the cavity and place the bird on one side on the onion in the roasting dish. Splosh on about two tablespoons of good olive oil or rub it with butter, then season the skin.

Place on the bottom rack in the oven and cook for 20 minutes. Turn the bird onto its other side, baste with the pan juices, season and return to the oven for a further 20 minutes. Cooking it on each side helps the heat penetrate to the densest part of the bird, its leg, ensuring it cooks through to the same degree as the breast.

Turn the bird upright, baste again, season and sprinkle over the rosemary if you're using it. Add the giblets to the pan and cook for a further 20–35 minutes. If you insert a skewer into the deep part of the leg after an hour and the meat juices run clear rather than

bloody, the bird is cooked. Remove the bird from the roasting tin with the carving knife and fork, holding it upside down as you do so that all the delicious lemony meat juices run out from the cavity into the tin. Leave to rest on the carving board with foil tucked around it and a tea towel on top for 15 minutes before carving. Now make the gravy.

GRAVY

chicken liver
glass of red wine
cooking water from potatoes and
    parsnips

The old school adds flour, the new school doesn't, but it's bound to revert sooner or later. You already have the caramelised onions from under the bird and the giblets and meat juices in the tin. Place the tin over a high heat, add a good splosh of red wine, about a glassful if you have some open, and stir like crazy so that the sticky onions part company with the tin and break down even further, releasing their flavour and dark colour as they do. Use a fork to crush the chicken liver down into the pan, too, so that you have extra intense flavour and texture. Let the wine bubble away merrily for a minute or two so that the alcohol burns off, then add the cooking water from the potatoes and parsnips which will be nice and starchy and any other cooking water from the vegetables you've cooked. You will not want to add all the potato water if there is lots of it, so pour all but the last half pint down the sink first so that what remains has the starch content which thickens the gravy a little. Bubble this over a high heat to reduce it for 5 minutes or so, longer if you are still finishing other things like the bread sauce (see page 95) and vegetables. Place a sieve over a large jug and set it in the sink. Pour in the gravy and force through as much of the delicious debris as you can with a wooden spoon, then pour into two dégraisseurs. These lovely little French gravy jugs have two pouring sides, one that releases the fat with the gravy, the other that pours fat free!

ROAST POTATOES AND PARSNIPS

potatoes
parsnips
dripping, goose or duck fat
    or 3–4 tbsp olive oil

Roast potatoes are a winter thing. New potatoes simply don't roast successfully, so no amount of begging from my children alters that seasonal fact. You need old season's potatoes, preferably floury ones that you can ruffle up with a fork to make a larger surface area to crisp up. Allow one potato large enough to cut into three big chunks per person and a few extra if you have ravening teenagers anywhere in sight.

Two chunks of parsnip should be enough for each person. Peel and cut them thick enough that they don't burn in the roasting tin, which skinny ones tend to. Peel the potatoes, cut them and put them with the parsnips in a large pan. Just cover them with cold water, salted if you wish, and bring to the boil with the lid on. Remove the lid and boil rapidly for about 5 minutes, by which time the potatoes will not be totally resistant when you poke a knife tip into them. Place a colander over a large jug. Drain the potatoes into the colander, keeping the water for cooking further vegetables in or just for the gravy if you're braising or steaming the rest of the veg.

A couple of minutes before you drain the potatoes and parsnips, place a large roasting tin with either a lump of dripping, goose or duck fat (a well heaped tablespoon and a bit extra) or 3–4 tablespoons of olive oil in the top of the oven and wait until you hear it splutter, about 3–4 minutes. Olive oil makes good, crisp roast potatoes but the flavour imparted from the dripping or fat is infinitely superior, so try to keep some in the fridge from your last joint of beef or duck; it keeps for months.

Remove the roasting tin to the top of the stove and slip the drained potatoes into it, standing back as they will begin to splutter madly. Turn each potato in the fat so that they are completely coated, then plough a fork across the surface of each potato until it looks well furrowed.

Return the tin to the top of the oven and roast for about an hour, turning every 20 minutes as each side crisps. After the first 20 minutes, throw the parsnips into the middle of the tin – they cook more quickly than the potatoes and will burn more easily in the greater heat at the edge. Turn them when you turn the potatoes. When they are crisp all over and the rest of the lunch is ready to put on the table, drain the fat into a bowl and plop the potatoes and parsnips into a heated serving dish. You may, if you'd rather, cook the parsnips around the joint. This is particularly successful with beef, pork, goose or duck as they then cook in the incomparably delicious fat and more slowly to boot!

BREAD SAUCE

SERVES 4–6

1 small peeled onion, stuck with 4 cloves
1 bay leaf
600ml/1 pint Jersey or full-cream milk, organic if possible
nutmeg
sea salt and black pepper
1 small white or wholemeal loaf, the crusts removed, torn to smallish shreds into a bowl
a knob of unsalted butter or a couple of tbsp double cream (optional)

I have never understood the scant dessertspoonful that some people clearly feel is the way to serve bread sauce. In fact, it is as incomprehensible to me as not serving gravy, or making so little of it that one cannot have a lake should one want one. So I never make less than a pint of bread sauce even if there are only two or three of us for lunch. It is SO good served cold and slightly solid with cold chicken that you will not waste it.

Until a year or so ago I always made bread sauce with breadcrumbs, but I have now adopted the torn-chunk-of-bread philosophy. It really does give a better texture and stops a tendency to sliminess that the smoother version has. Bread sauce should be made with day-old or stale bread, white or wholemeal according to your taste, though wholemeal can overwhelm with its own nuttier flavour. You will need to cut the crusts off a whole small loaf before tearing it into bits. If you only have a fresh loaf, remove the crusts, slice it into thickish slices and put it in a warm oven until both sides feel dry before proceeding.

Place the cloved onion in a small saucepan with the bay leaf and milk and bring slowly to scald point, just below boiling. The milk surface should have begun to crinkle. Lower the heat and simmer at a bare bubble for 20–30 minutes, grating in a little nutmeg halfway through. Season and add the torn bread by the handful until the milk has absorbed most of it. Allow for some milk to still be visible; the sauce will go on absorbing and stiffening when you put it to one side with the lid on, which you may now do for up to 20 minutes, so make it when you have a gap in the cooking.

Just before you are ready to serve lunch, take the lid off and if the sauce looks too solid add a little more milk. Test the seasoning – you may want a little more nutmeg and pepper – and reheat very gently until it just comes to the bubble. Stir in the butter or cream if you like a richer finish to what are, after all, poor man's ingredients. I serve my bread sauce in a warmed soufflé dish with the onion still in it, as there is always someone who wants to eat the whole cooked orb.

ROAST BEEF AND YORKSHIRE PUDDING

2–2.5kg/4½–5½lb joint of sirloin with the undercut (which is the fillet) on the bone or a rib of beef weighing the same
sea salt, black pepper and English mustard powder
1–2 large onions, peeled and thinly sliced

Beef is all about breeding and about choosing a cut and a size of cut that best lends itself to this oldest of British traditions, the one which even the French agree we excel at, roasting. If you are lucky enough to be able to afford and lay your hands on a good piece of Aberdeen Angus or Shorthorn that has been reared for as long as the breed needs to reach its peak and hung for several weeks, all well and good. Better still, a hunk of Longhorn, an ancient breed I was lucky enough to eat for the first time a few weeks ago, which made me all the angrier that we inhabit a country so obsessed with the industrialisation and swift processing of food that no one wants to preserve and rear this mighty beast for the table. Its handlebar horns and layer of thickly gorgeous yellow fat may make it less attractive to the farmer and the typically fat-phobic generation of cooks we have spawned, but there is no question it is the best beef I have ever eaten, with the flavour of rump and the texture of butter. Rare breed it may be, but as with all rare breeds, the less you eat them the rarer they become until they die out all together.

There is no point in cooking your joint off the bone; on the bone there are minimum sizes it is actually worth cooking. 'The closer the bone, the sweeter the meat' says ancient Chinese proverb, and to my mind it is infinitely preferable in terms of flavour to cook meat on the bone.

Rub salt and pepper over the meat the night before you are going to cook it if you remember and return it to the fridge.

Preheat the oven to 220°C/425°F/Gas 7. Remove the joint from the fridge to bring it to room temperature and rub in a couple of teaspoons of English mustard powder into the fat. Place the meat on top of the sliced onion in the roasting pan and place the joint in the oven. It will take a little more than 30 minutes per kg/15 minutes per lb to cook it to rare and another 20 minutes if you want well-done meat. Baste the meat every 20 minutes or so and insert the tip of a knife blade into the fat all over it when you baste so as to release more of the fat. This you can use to cook the Yorkshire pudding in and save the rest for roast potatoes.

Test the meat with a skewer when you think it should be ready. If it feels too raw in the middle and the blood looks very red and comes to the surface immediately, allow another 5–10 minutes cooking time. Remove to a carving board, shroud tightly in foil with a tea towel loosely placed over it and leave to rest for 20–30 minutes.

Meanwhile make the mustard, horseradish sauce and gravy, and finish the Yorkshire puddings and vegetables.

YORKSHIRE PUDDING

SERVES 6

225g/8oz plain organic flour
a pinch of sea salt
2 large organic eggs
600ml/1 pint milk
enough hot dripping from the beef to
    cover the floor of the roasting tin

Make the batter for your Yorkshire pudding a good half hour before you put the roast in. It is always better when it is left to stand and then whisked again before pouring into the hot dripping to be cooked. You can also make the batter the night before if you like and keep it in the fridge, whisking it up just before you use it. The lightness of the batter depends on the quick formation of steam within the mixture and the quick cooking of the flour. That is why you need a hot oven and why the Yorkshire is best when cooked at the top of the oven. You may make it in individual tins, but if you have the nerve and a hot oven, Yorkshire always looks better swelling in a large roasting tin, the edges brown and puffed up, the middles with a delicious bit of sog to them.

Sift the flour and salt into a large bowl. Make a well in the centre with a wooden spoon and break the eggs into it. Add a little of the milk and whisk with a balloon whisk, gradually drawing down the flour from the sides of the bowl and adding more milk when the mixture becomes too thick to work. You should finally have a stiff batter which you should then whisk for as long as your arm will hold out for – up to 5 minutes. Add the remaining milk, whisk it in and leave to stand.

Now you need to time things. The fat from the joint needs to be poured onto the base of another roasting tin and returned to the top of the oven where it will take a couple of minutes to smoke. Then pour in the batter, which will take about 35–40 minutes to cook. You want to deliver the Yorkshire Pudding puffed up to the table once the beef has been rested and carved, so plan accordingly.

If you do decide to make individual puddings, squirt a little hot fat from the beef into the bottoms of each tart tin with a bulb baster, then place them at the top of the oven for 20–25 minutes. If you are organised, you will cook the first dozen to come to the table with the beef and set another dozen in the oven on their removal so that they are ready for second helpings.

HORSERADISH SAUCE

2 tbsp grated horseradish or a good
    brand like English Provender
    Company
150ml/5fl oz crème fraîche
a little sugar and salt
juice of half a lemon

Plop the horseradish into a small bowl and stir in the crème fraîche. Add a tiny amount of salt and sugar and a spritz of lemon juice, then taste for seasoning and sharpness.

ROAST LEG OF LAMB

SERVES 6

2–2.5kg/4½–5½lb leg of lamb
6 sprigs of rosemary
6 cloves of garlic, peeled and thinly
   sliced
a few halved fillets of anchovy from a
   tin (optional or use instead of the
   rosemary)
olive oil
sea salt and black pepper
1 large onion, peeled and sliced

Roast leg of lamb seems to be what people slaver for around Easter, but to my mind the gambolling babies are just not mature enough flavour-wise to interest me. I prefer hogget, which has had several more months at least and made the best of the summer pastures and flowers, or even the deeply fallen from grace mutton which is making a small but significant comeback. I also go for shoulder more often than leg, not just for the fact that it is much more reasonably priced, but also because the flavour is always better thanks to the thicker coating and marbling of fat. That said, a good, grass-fed, well-hung leg of late summer lamb – its fatty jacket studded with garlic, rosemary and perhaps anchovy fillets, which deepen the lambiness in an extraordinarily unfishy way, the fat crisped, the meat pink and cut in thick tranches, served with a blob of homemade spiced redcurrant jelly – is a darn delicious Sunday lunch.

Preheat the oven to 200°C/400°F/Gas 6. Cut slits in the fat before sliding in sprigs of rosemary with a slim-bladed knife so that you have a little tussock of rosemary needles poking out of each hole. Do likewise with the anchovies, if you are using them, having halved the fillets first. Slip the slices of garlic into the slits too, avoiding the bone and making sure the leg is scored all over. Pour a little olive oil over the fat, season and place on a thinly sliced onion that you have laid on the bottom of the roasting tin.

Place the joint on the bottom shelf of the oven and roast for 1¼–1½ hours, basting with a bulb baster every 20–30 minutes. Check with a skewer and if the flesh is deeply resistant and the blood rises instantly to the surface, leave for a further 15 minutes until you check again. You want there to be pink juices, but the feel of the flesh will tell you as much. It needs to yield right the way through. If you like your meat pink, now is the time to remove it from the oven. Place it on the carving board, covered with well tucked-in foil and a tea towel placed loosely over it, and let it stand for 20 minutes so the juices can flood back through the meat while you make the gravy and finish off the vegetables.

ROAST SHOULDER OF LAMB

Shoulders are usually smaller than legs, so treat in the same way but cook for a little less time. There will be more fatty juices in the roasting pan, but your parsnips will cope with them! If you are 8 people you might wish to buy two slightly smaller shoulders.

MINT SAUCE

enough mint leaves to fill a small
   bowl when stripped from their
   stems and chopped
3 tbsp boiling water
3 tsps unrefined sugar
4 tbsp white wine vinegar

This is a late spring and summer sauce to serve with your lamb and tiny waxy pebbles of Jersey Royal new potatoes. The French think mint sauce is barbaric, but I find the way it cuts the fatty richness of the meat – and sheep fat really does congeal quickly on the plate – with the sweet sharp redcurrant jelly is a glorious triumvirate. Make the sauce 2 hours before you need it.

Pour the boiling water over the leaves and leave to infuse. When it is barely tepid, stir in the sugar, then the vinegar and stir until the sugar has dissolved. Taste and adjust the seasoning before serving. When mint is not in season or in your garden, go without and make do with redcurrant jelly.

ROAST LEG, LOIN OR SHOULDER OF PORK

SERVES 6–8

2–2.5kg/4½–5½lb leg or shoulder or
   pork or a chined loin
sea salt
black pepper
olive oil
1 onion, peeled and sliced
Cox's apples, 1 per person

The most important thing with pork is that it should come from a traditional breed that lays down a good covering of fat, and an animal that has lived a natural lifespan and has had access to the open fields and woods where it can rootle around. So organic or free range are not the only things to look for; the modern, fast-growing, lean breeds of pig are not going to give you the fat that lays down the flavour of both meat and crackling. Middle Whites are, to my mind, the king of the pig world. Indeed, they are the only surviving breed of pig that has been reared purely for pork and not bacon, so see if you can go to the growing army of small producers who rear them. Failing that, try Gloucester Old Spot, Tamworth, Berkshire or Lop Eared.

Next, make sure the fat has been properly scored. If not, your butcher will do it with a Stanley knife. This is the only way of making sure of tooth-threatening crackling. A 2–2.5kg/4½–5½lb leg or shoulder will feed 6–8. A chined loin will weigh less and feed 4–6 people. It is also spectacularly easy to carve as the meat cuts down into thick chops. A smaller joint is not really worth cooking and this applies to lamb and beef too. It will shrink and be impossible to carve, so even if there are only two of you, buy a decent-sized joint and enjoy the leftovers whichever way you wish.

If you remember, season the meat with sea salt and black pepper the night before you're going to cook it. When you've brought it up to room temperature on the day, rub the crackling with a little olive oil with your fingers and sprinkle sea salt all over it.

Preheat the oven to 220°C/425°F/Gas 7. Place the joint on the peeled, sliced onion in a roasting tin and after 30 minutes, turn the heat down to 170°C/325°F/Gas 3. Calculate the overall cooking time of the joint at 1 hour and 10 minutes per kg/35 minutes per lb. About 40–50 minutes before the end of cooking time, score the skin of the apples around their circumference with a knife blade and core them with a corer. Roll them in the fatty meat juices and cook them standing up in the roasting tin until tender when pierced to their middles.

If the crackling hasn't achieved the heights of crackle that you would wish for at the end of the cooking time, remove it with a long, thin-bladed knife all in one piece and place it under a hot grill. Keep an eye on it so that it doesn't burn. Alternatively, turn the oven temperature back up to its original, remove the apples if you are baking them, and place the roasting tin with the joint in it at the top of the oven for a further 10–15 minutes. Remove the joint in the normal way and allow it to rest for 15 minutes while you make the gravy and finish off the vegetables. This is not, however, a joint to cover. The crackling will sog with the condensation if you do, so just keep the meat warm somewhere. You may add cider, Calvados or Kingston Black to the cooking juices for your gravy. Just burn off the alcohol by bubbling it hard for 3–4 minutes before you add the vegetable water.

APPLE SAUCE

Make your apple sauce while the potatoes and parsnips are par-boiling. That way you stand some chance of it cooling in time for lunch. Allow as many medium-sized apples as you have people to feed and either use a sharp eating apple like Cox's or a cooking apple like Bramley.

COX'S APPLE SAUCE, COX'S APPLE SAUCE WITH THYME

6 Cox's apples, peeled, quartered and
    sliced into the pan
3 tbsp apple juice or water
grated zest of an organic orange
30g/1oz unsalted butter
scrunch of black pepper

Simmer the apples, apple juice and orange zest together gently in a covered pan until the apples have softened. Remove from the heat and either mash or sieve, depending on the texture you prefer. Return to the pan with the butter and pepper and stir to amalgamate. For the thyme version, add the leaves you have torn from a couple of sprigs of thyme and bruised in your fingers. Tip into a bowl to cool.

BRAMLEY APPLE SAUCE

6 medium-sized Bramleys, roughly
    chopped, skins on, cores included
4 tbsp apple juice or water
2 level tbsp unrefined sugar
1 strip organic orange rind
30g/1oz unsalted butter
a good scrunch of black pepper

Put the apples, apple juice, sugar and orange rind into a pan and bring to the boil. Simmer gently with a lid on until the apples are soft. Sieve and return to the pan, cooking gently until the sauce isn't too wet and sloppy.

Add the butter and the pepper off the heat and turn into a bowl to cool. You may refrigerate the sauce from tepid if you are short of time. It will keep, covered, in the fridge for your cold roast pork.

ROAST SHIN OF VEAL

SERVES 4

1 shin of organic, free-range veal
4–6 cloves of garlic, sliced
3–4 sprigs of rosemary
sea salt and black pepper
flour
4 tbsp olive oil
55g/2oz unsalted butter
1 onion, sliced
half a bottle or more of dry white
    wine, heated

Make sure the butcher saws through the bone at the base of the shin as for a leg of lamb. This is a wonderful, tender, gluey-fleshed roast, which is all too rare here in England as properly reared veal is hard to come by and there is something of an aversion to cooking it. The Italians and the French use all the bits that we seem too ignorant or too unwilling to use – the shins, breast, sweetbreads, kidneys and liver, the great ossobuco. Veal has a natural affinity with rosemary, garlic and lemon but can withstand strong tastes like capers and cornichons in a salsa verde, or being stewed with tomatoes, peas and white wine.

Preheat the oven to 190°C/375°F/Gas 5. Make incisions right down into the meat with the sharp point of a knife and bury a slice of garlic and a bit of rosemary sprig into each slash so that the rosemary sprouts from the top of the flesh. Season well and rub a little flour into the meat. Heat the olive oil and butter together in the roasting tin and add the shin, turning it to brown all over. Put your sliced onion under the browned shin and put the roasting tin in the oven. After 20 minutes, pull it out of the oven enough to pour over some of the heated white wine, about 300ml/ ½ a pint to start with. Reduce the temperature of the oven to 170°C/325°F/Gas 3 and continue to roast for 1½ hours. Baste the joint every so often as veal is a dry meat, and add more white wine to the pan. Remove the shin to a carving dish and keep warm under foil and a tea towel for 20 minutes.

Scrape the browned onion and all the crusty bits from the floor of the pan and stir into the winey juices over a medium heat. You may wish to add a little more white wine or some of the cooking water from your vegetables. Boil to reduce a little; the colour should be a beautiful mahogany from the caramelised onion. Serve with the usual accompaniments to a roast such as roast potatoes and parsnips (see pages 94–95).

ROAST DUCK

1 organic or free-range duck
    weighing around 2–2.5kg/4½–5½lb
2 onions and 1 organic orange
sea salt and black pepper
olive oil

GRAVY
duck giblets
a sprig of thyme
a glass of red wine
1 sharp, organic orange or 1 sweet
    orange and a spritz of lemon juice

Other than a goose, the duck is the fattiest thing you are ever likely to roast, but that does not mean that it is fatty to eat. If you start the bird off in a pan or casserole and then in the hot blast of the oven so you release the fat throughout the cooking, you will end up with lean, pink breast, burnished, salt-crackled skin and shards of confit-like leg that are as sweet and soft as you could wish for. And the fat is the most divine thing to roast your vegetables in anyway. Seville orange or orange and lemon in the gravy and a sharp apple sauce are all you need to cut the richness. I think fresh peas stewed in a little chicken stock, butter and mint with the addition of a torn cos lettuce are the perfect accompaniment alongside the roast or new potatoes and roast parsnips. Keep the giblets for the gravy. If you want the full, old-fashioned number, make a sage and onion or onion and thyme stuffing.

Preheat the oven to 220°C/425°F/Gas 7. Remove the duck from the fridge a couple of hours before you are going to cook it and rub the skin all over with salt and black pepper. Leave until it is time to cook. Splosh a little olive oil in the bottom of a heavy-bottomed pan the duck will fit into, and brown it all over. This should take about 4–5 minutes. You can miss out this part of the cooking if you like and head straight for the oven, but it does get the fat running and the skin crisping.

Peel the onions, slice one and quarter the other. Put the sliced onion on the bottom of a roasting tin and put the duck on top. Stuff it with alternating quarters of onion and orange and shove a good sprig of thyme inside the cavity at the same time. Put the bird in the oven. After about 25–30 minutes, remove the duck and spike it all over, not far enough in to hit the meat, with the point of a fork or a skewer to release the fat. Return to the oven and lower the temperature to 200°C/400°F/Gas 6. Repeat the pricking of the fat after another 20 minutes and drain the fat that has collected in the bottom of the pan at the same time into a bowl. This is what you can use for your roast potatoes. If you prefer to cook potatoes and parsnips around the duck, turn the oven back up to its previous temperature when the duck has cooked and is resting, and put the roasting tin up to the top of the oven to finish off the veg. Put the duck liver in the tin for the last 10–15 minutes. You can then mash it into the pan juices to flavour the gravy.

The duck should take between 1 hour and 1 hour 15 minutes to cook depending on whether you prefer it pink or better cooked. Duck is not a meat to serve bloody, but the breast should be pink if you like medium-rare meat. When you remove the duck and transfer it to the carving board, cover it lightly so that the crisped skin has no chance of steaming and losing its texture, and leave for 10 minutes before carving.

Duck is notoriously difficult to carve. I favour thinly slicing the breast, then taking the legs off and carving the meat downwards, top to bottom from the meaty tops to the stringy ankles as it were. Then pick your bones!

GRAVY

While the duck is cooking, put the giblets minus the liver in a small pan and just cover with water. Gently simmer for 30–40 minutes, then remove the giblets and keep the liquid for gravy.

While the duck is resting, put the roasting tin on a brisk heat on top of the stove and scrape all the caramelised onion bits into the juices, mashing down the liver into them as you go. You should pour all the juices out from the cavity of the bird into the roasting tin before you rest the duck. Now pull the leaves off a sprig of thyme and add it to the pan followed by the red wine, which should bubble up and cook into the gravy for a few minutes before you add the giblet liquid. Reduce for a few minutes at a brisk simmer before adding the juice of the orange or orange and lemon. Decant into two dégraisseurs so that the fat doesn't land on your plate.

SAGE AND ONION STUFFING

a little butter and a little olive oil
1 large onion, peeled and finely chopped
12–18 fresh sage leaves
1 fennel bulb, outer leaves removed, chopped fine or 3 sticks of celery, strung and chopped small (optional)
the duck liver (optional)
a small bunch of parsley, chopped
half a small stale white loaf, the crusts removed, blitzed into breadcrumbs
a beaten egg
sea salt and black pepper

This is a very simple stuffing but one you can embellish with different herbs or vegetables. Fennel and celery both marry well with duck, for example, so a diced bulb of fennel or 3 sticks of celery, strung with a potato peeler and finely chopped, can be added to the onion and cooked. Thyme and parsley are also good with duck, so use either or both of them instead of sage if it suits you. You may also add the chopped liver of the duck a couple of minutes before you take the cooked part of the stuffing off the heat.

Melt the butter and oil in a heavy-bottomed frying pan and throw in the onion, sage and fennel or celery if you are using them. Sauté gently until soft and translucent but not browned. Add the chopped duck liver if you're using it and sauté for another couple of minutes before sprinkling over the parsley. Turn the hot stuffing mixture into the breadcrumbs in a bowl, season well and stir in the beaten egg. Plop the mixture in spoonfuls into the duck cavity before roasting the bird.

GAME

Game birds should only be roasted when they are young, so you will have to rely on your butcher, game dealer or the superior wisdom of those you've been shooting with if you are not sure whether the bird in question is a scrawny old boiler or a tender young bird. Soft, pliable feet or ears in the case of rabbits or hares is an indication of youth. I never bother to roast a wood pigeon. They are invariably tough and respond much better to the gentle braising of the pot than the fierce heat of the roasting oven. A squab is different, but even then, I prefer to remove the breasts and fry them until ruby-red rare and use the carcass and legs for stock for the gravy.

The problem with hare, rabbit and venison is that they dry out during roasting. All three are too lean and lissom by nature to lay down the fat you need for a good roast. In the case of rabbit and hare, casserole them instead; in the case of venison, there are three cuts you can roast, the haunch, the leg and the saddle, but make sure you cloak them in pork fat or streaky bacon first. I always marinate them first too, on the grounds that the more moisture and oil they absorb before the start of the cooking process, the less dry and the more tender they will become.

Roasting temperature

All roast game birds should be cooked in a high oven, 220–230°C/425–450°F/Gas 7–8. Cook larger birds, like pheasant, at the lower temperature and smaller ones, like snipe and woodcock, at the higher temperature.

What to put inside

Seasoned butter, onions and fruit are all things that can be put inside the carcass of the birds to increase moisture and flavour and inhibit dryness and toughness.

Hanging times

Make sure that the game you are buying has been properly hung. I do not mean hung until it is green and putrid with maggots, as the faint stomached always imply to those of us who are happy to pluck and gut, but hung until the flesh has begun to break down so that you end up with a tender bird or animal. Pheasants need about 7 days in the winter, though 2–3 days more if the weather is really cold. Partridge should be hung for 3–4 days when it is mild and for up to a week if the weather is cold. The wild duck family need 2–3 days and no more, as their fatty flesh begins to deteriorate. Venison needs up to 10 days; wild rabbit and hare around 3–4 days. Woodcock and snipe need 2–4 days, though some people prefer not to hang them at all.

Plucking

If you've drawn the short straw and been ordered to pluck, usually as the result of road-kill in my case, much to the horror of my children, simply hold the bird over a bin liner so that you pluck inside it. Always pull the feathers with the grain so that you don't tear the skin. Keep a bowl of warm water beside you; feathers stick. Cut off the feet and the wing feathers with a heavy-bladed, sharp knife. To take out the guts, make a small incision by the vent and ease the guts out with your fingers. Keep the liver, heart and gizzard, making sure that you remove the green part from the liver which will taste bitter as it is stained by the gall sac. Slit the gizzard open to remove the grain before you use it.

Snipe need skinning, not plucking; chop off the wings and head and ease off the skin and feathers. Do not draw snipe and woodcock. Their innards are known as the 'trail' and are considered to be a real delicacy, so roast them inside the bird and spread them on toast set underneath it.

ROAST GROUSE

The 'glorious twelfth' is the day in August when both grouse and snipe come into season. There is always something of a rush, similar to the Beaujolais race, to get them down from the moors and into the London restaurants, but they do need to be hung, if only for 24 hours in the August heat, so wait, if but a day, for your first brace. I am happy if I eat grouse just once in the season, preferably early on when they are still tender, which I try and do on my birthday in September. My Irish friend Richard Corrigan, legendary chef and owner of London's Lindsay House Restaurant, cooks a whole grouse breast rare en croûte, with a cabbage and foie gras lining to the croûte: a last-supper dish if ever there was one. Grouse are in prime condition from the beginning of the season to the middle of October and only very young birds should be roasted. Pot roasting or turning into a game pie, pudding or pâté should be the fate of those birds who are a little longer in the beak. Young birds are also good grilled or barbecued, as long as you are rigorous with your basting. I have long hungered for the unique, powerful gamey taste of grouse since, as a very young child, I was allowed to stay up to dinner with my grandparents and given my grandfather's grouse bones to pick. A grouse was clearly not considered the right kind of thing to feed one so young and immature of palate, but I was hooked and have been ever since that definitive first-taste memory.

Shooting season: 12 August–10 December

Roasting time: 30–40 minutes depending on size. Cover with a vine leaf if you have a jar of them and a sheet of pork fat or rashers of unsmoked streaky bacon.

Inside the bird: blueberries, raspberries or seedless grapes and seasoned butter.

Serve with: a bunch of watercress, game chips, some breadcrumbs fried in butter, bread sauce, gravy and rowanberry or redcurrant jelly; mashed potato is also good and some runner beans, which are in season at the same time.

ROAST PARTRIDGE

There are two kinds of partridge, the red-legged, or French, partridge and the English grey, or common, partridge considered to be the king of game birds. You need one partridge per person and that is not negotiable!

Shooting Season: 1 September–1 February.

Roasting time: 30 minutes.

Inside the bird: chopped liver or onion with seasoned butter; a sprig of thyme; mushrooms cooked in butter.

Serve with: braised celery; stir-fried cabbage with bacon and chestnuts; bread sauce, watercress and game chips; mashed potato or roast potatoes; rowan jelly.

ROAST PHEASANT

A brace of pheasants will feed 4 people. The cock pheasant is always larger and tougher and you need to make sure the tendons in the legs have been pulled out by the butcher, otherwise the legs are more difficult to eat.

Shooting season: 1 October–1 February.

Roasting time: 40 minutes per kg/20 minutes per lb plus 10 minutes. Either cover the breast of the birds with unsmoked streaky bacon or with softened, seasoned butter. If you use butter, make sure you baste the birds religiously every 10 minutes.

Inside the bird: a knob of thyme or parsley butter and a small quartered onion; some chopped mushrooms or celery cooked in butter with a little ground juniper or black pepper; or a few strips of seasoned fillet steak (extravagant but they add moisture).

Serve with: bread sauce, gravy and game chips; mashed or roasted potatoes and roast parsnips; celeriac and potato purée; spiced red cabbage, breadcrumbs fried in butter.

WILD DUCK

There are a large variety of wild duck, some, like the pintail, gadwall, tufted, pochard and golden eye, are less likely to wind up at the end of the gun barrel and on your plate than others. The ones you are most likely to encounter, depending on where you live and how keen you are to source interesting game, are the mallard, the largest and most frequently eaten duck; widgeon, less strongly flavoured since they graze mainly on grasses but very good stuffed with apricots or oranges and walnuts or hazelnuts; teal, the smallest duck in the British Isles but the most sought after by those in the know; and shoveler ducks, which need to be scalded in boiling water to rid them of their muddy flavour from bottom feeding.

Shooting season:
Inland: 1 September–31 January.
Foreshore: 1 September–20 February.

WIDGEON AND TEAL

Roasting time: 20–25 minutes, allow 1 bird per person.

Inside the bird: a knob of softened parsleyed butter with a squeeze of lemon juice and the liver mashed into it.

Serve with: orange gravy; orange, endive and watercress salad.

WILD DUCK

Roasting time: 30 minutes if you like your wild duck rare, 40 minutes well cooked.

Inside the bird: a stuffing made with sautéed onion, parsley, walnuts or hazelnuts and dried unsulphured apricots. You may use breadcrumbs as with the classic sage and onion stuffing recipe or rice. Wild rice is good instead of breadcrumbs too.

Serve with: new potatoes, peas, a bitter leaf salad, braised endives or fennel.

ROAST WOODCOCK

It would be a very close call if I had to choose between a grouse or a woodcock. In fact I'd rather not have to make up my mind, but woodcock are a bird you really should try at some stage of your life, difficult though they are both to shoot and thus to lay your hands on. Woodcock are waders with long, straight bills, which can be used as a skewer to truss the bird with.

Shooting season:
England and Wales, 1 October–31 January.

Scotland: 1 September–31 January.

Roasting time: 18 minutes for a rare bird. Allow 1 bird per person.

Inside the bird: leave the trail and add a little knob of butter with marjoram mashed into it. Put a rasher of unsmoked streaky bacon over the breast or smother with butter and baste.

Serve with: fried bread spread with the trail; game chips; mashed potato or roasted potatoes; watercress, green vegetables.

ROAST SNIPE

They may be in season from the 'glorious twelfth' but these delicious and delicately flavoured little birds are not at their best until October or November.

Shooting season: 12 August–31 January.

Roasting time: 15 minutes for rare.

Inside the bird: as for woodcock.

Serve with: fried bread spread with the trail and soaked in the cooking juices; redcurrant jelly; game chips; watercress and orange salad.

ROAST VENISON

When roasted right – tender, moist, ineffably gamey and served with a Francatelli sauce and a whiff of juniper – this is one of the great, traditional dishes. I never think that farmed venison, however well it has been fed and hung, has the gameyness of the wild beast or the texture, though some would argue that was a good thing. If farmed is all you can get, marinate it and roast it right and you will still have a great tasting roast. Haunch, leg and saddle are the roasting cuts. The rest you may turn into a pie or stew. Venison steak and kidney pie is one of the great treats and all the more surprising with its depth and intensity of flavour when people are expecting to taste beef.

Shooting season for red deer:
England, stag: 1 August–30 April; hind: 1 November–28 February.
Scotland: stag: 1 July–20 October, hind: 21 October–15 February.

Roasting time: 1 hour per kg/30 minutes per lb after marinating for smaller joints; larger ones will take less time. Cover with a jacket of pork fat or rashers of unsmoked streaky bacon and keep basting. I rub coarsely crushed juniper berries and black pepper and sea salt into the marinaded flesh once it has been dried for the oven with paper towel.

Serve with: Francatelli sauce; cumberland sauce; cherry sauce; cranberry sauce; mushrooms cooked in butter and garlic; spiced red cabbage; Brussels sprouts; pommes dauphinoise; French beans; celery, potato and celeriac purée; orange salad.

MARINADE FOR VENISON

½ bottle red wine
150ml/5fl oz olive oil
2 tbsp red wine vinegar
a bouquet of fresh rosemary, thyme,
    parsley and bay
1 onion, peeled and sliced
a few strips of orange peel
12 slightly bashed up juniper berries
    and the same of peppercorns

Leave the joint or stewing venison in the marinade overnight.

Remove from the marinade, dry the joint and brush it with melted butter before you cover it in bacon to roast. If you are casseroling the venison, keep the marinade to strain over the meat when you have browned it.

FRANCATELLI SAUCE

225g/8oz elderberry or spiced
    redcurrant jelly
150ml/5fl oz pint port
1 tsp muscovado sugar
pared rind of an organic lemon
a small stick of cinnamon
black pepper
2–3 crushed juniper berries

This famous sauce was invented by Queen Victoria's chef, Charles Elme Francatelli, and is one I have been making ever since I first cooked venison over 20 years ago. I have substituted homemade elderberry jelly for the redcurrant jelly and found it breathes a lovely muskiness, instead of the vibrant freshness of the redcurrants, into the sauce. I have also tinkered with the amount of port, adding quite a lot more than the original recipe, and added a little brown sugar and a few crushed juniper berries.

Simmer all the ingredients together for about 5 minutes in a small pan, stirring to melt the jelly, then strain into a gravy jug. Serve with roast venison.

EASY PUDS AND CAKES

VANILLA CHEESECAKE

The first pudding I ever made was a cheesecake. How '60s it all seems, though my elder daughter Miranda has become as impressed with the recipe in her teens as I was back in what my children alarmingly call 'the olden days' when I was growing up. I remember tearing the recipe out from some gruesome, contemporary teen magazine and actually believing that it was what it said, the best cheesecake recipe there was. How extraordinary that my wobbly-of-confidence efforts should then produce the perfectly wobbly, tremulous ungelatined perfection of a vanilla cheesecake that they did. I've gone on doing the same recipe ever since, though adding my own touches like rather a lot of lemon zest and occasionally dispensing with the base altogether and just cooking the unctuously creamy top. If only all recipes one cooked early on were as achievable and as delicious as this there'd be more converts to the joys of the stove. In my case, as the first pudding I attempted, it worked for me in that way too, fuelling my appetite to cook new and different things as a result and helping me believe I could make them work.

SERVES 6–8

BASE
1 packet Dove's organic digestives
55g/2oz unsalted butter

MIDDLE
450g/1lb fresh cream cheese, full fat, the best you can find
2 organic eggs and 1 egg yolk
170ml/6fl oz Jersey or organic double cream
55g/2oz vanilla sugar
1 split vanilla pod, the vanilla scraped out with a sharp teaspoon
the zest of 2 organic lemons

TOP
1 carton, 150ml/5fl oz, sour cream
1 dsrtsp vanilla sugar

Preheat the oven to 190°C/375°F/Gas 5. Put the biscuits in a Ziploc bag, seal it tight and do maximum damage with a rolling pin until the biscuits are turned to crumb. Tip into a 20cm/8in diameter, loose-bottomed cake tin and pour over the melted butter. Stir to amalgamate, then press the mixture down into the bottom of the tin with a wooden spoon. You don't want too thick a base – keep a little back if you want and either decorate the top with it by shaking it all around the edge, or eat it. Bake for 10 minutes.

Meanwhile, put the cream cheese, eggs and yolk, double cream, sugar, vanilla seeds and zest together in a huge bowl and whisk until utterly smooth. Pour into the tin and cook for 25 minutes or until still slightly trembly in the middle when nudged. Cool in the oven with the door ajar.

Remove the sides of the tin. Mix the sour cream and sugar together and spread over the top of the cheesecake with a rubber spatula. You can refrigerate it before serving or eat it with a memory of warmth. Serve with summer or autumn berries.

APPLE CRUMBLE

SERVES 6

CRUMBLE TOP
225g/8oz flour
85g/3oz sugar
170g/6oz unsalted butter

OR
110g/4oz flour
110g/4oz ground almonds
85g/3oz sugar
170g/6oz butter

FILLING
either 5 large Bramley apples or
   about 10 eating apples, Cox's are
   best for flavour
sugar to taste
1 tsp ground cinnamon or cloves
   (optional)

Short of stirring fruit purée into whipped cream – not a fool's paradise but a paradisiacal fool – a crumble has to be the most instant and easy of puddings to make. It is also one you can go on tinkering with, adding almonds or roasted hazelnuts to the mixture, scattering flaked almonds on top, using half muscovado sugar for a more toffeed, treacly taste, adding oats, nibbed walnuts, demerara sugar scattered over the top to add crunch, even shunning the sweet for a savoury, herbed crumble top.

I think the most luscious crumbles of all are the ones that bleed their dark juices in sticky eruptions, staining the crumble and turning the texture from crumbly to gooey in little sunken patches. Victoria plum, rhubarb, damson, apple and blackberry, blueberry or raspberry, cherry and almond, all have the requisite potential. Suit the top to the bottom, dressing apricots, peaches, plums and greengages with almonds; apple with cinnamon and cloves.

Mix the flour and sugar in a large bowl and add small chunks of butter. Work in the butter, rubbing it in with your fingertips until it has turned to crumble. Or put all three ingredients in a food processor and pulse for a few seconds at a time until you have crumb. Don't overdo this or the butter will start to turn globby!

Preheat the oven to 190°C/375°F/Gas 5. Peel, core and slice the apples and put them into a shallow baking dish, scattering sugar and any spicing over them and turning them to get the juices running. A tablespoon is all you'll need for eating apples and probably treble that amount for cooking apples. You want a nice contrast between sharp interior and sweet top. Spread the crumble over the fruit evenly and bake for about 35–40 minutes or until the crumble top has browned and the bubbling juices risen. Do not let the top burn. Crumbles are pretty good-tempered puds, so you can cook them slower and longer. Leave them in a warming oven once they're cooked or eat warm or cold rather than hot if you like.

Clotted cream, crème fraîche, thin cream or custard are de rigeur with crumble, depending on your taste.

QUEEN OF PUDDINGS

SERVES 6

110g/4oz day-old brown bread
  breadcrumbs
1 heaped tbsp unrefined vanilla
  caster sugar
grated zest of an organic lemon
600ml/1 pint Jersey, Guernsey or
  full-cream milk
55g/2oz unsalted butter
4 large eggs, separated
a jar of best-quality apricot or
  raspberry jam or bramble jelly
110g/4oz vanilla caster sugar

The nirvana of nursery puddings, this can be made by child or ancient alike and goes down just as well with both and those of us somewhere in the middle. So is it to be great amber, sticky clots of apricot jam, strawberry, raspberry, peach, plum or damson jam, bramble or blackcurrant jelly? Whichever you choose, there is something about the texture of this pudding, the soothing soft custard spiked with lemon, the sharp, sweet jam, the heavenly light crunch of the meringue on top that is ultimately, terminally, satisfying. My daughter Miranda first made it before her teenage years when my brother Daniel had come to lunch one day when I was away making a documentary. She had done the whole Sunday lunch, chicken, bread sauce, roast potatoes, the works, right down to her first Queen's Pudding. Nothing thrilled her quite so much, other than the accomplishment itself, as my brother's thank-you card, telling her 'the Queen's Pudding was just as good as your mother's'. This is it.

Preheat the oven to 180°C/350°F/Gas 4. Put the breadcrumbs into the deep, buttered dish you intend to cook the pudding in, with the vanilla sugar and lemon zest. Scald the milk with the butter, stir them into the crumbs and leave to cool for 10 minutes. Now beat in the egg yolks one at a time. Bake in the oven for about 25 minutes until the custard has set.

Heat the jam gently with a teaspoon of two of water and pour it over the custard. Whisk the egg whites until stiff, stir in a spoon of sugar, then whisk in half of the remaining sugar until it is satiny. Fold in all but a spoon of the remaining sugar, pile the meringue on top of the pudding, and sprinkle the rest of the sugar over the top. Put back in the oven for about 15–20 minutes or until the meringue is golden and crisp. Serve hot with plenty of cold, thin cream. You may make the pudding up to the meringue stage a few hours earlier if it suits you.

MALT LOAF

MAKES A 900G/2LB LOAF

8 tbsp malt extract
90ml/3fl oz hot tea, I use Jasmine
170g/6oz wholemeal self-raising
    flour
good pinch of ground, mixed spice
85g/3oz raisins
85g/3oz sultanas
1 egg

There was a malt yard opposite us when I was growing up. The smell was as seductive as hot tar, horses, baking bread or frazzling bacon, so I have always had something of a penchant for malt's sticky sweetness and the scent of it baking. I found this recipe in Gary Rhodes' *New British Classics*. The moist richness of this cake, spread with butter if you dare, is dreamy. Just remember to wrap it in greaseproof paper and foil once it's cooled, put it in an airtight container and don't eat it for at least three days if you can contain yourself. Rather like Parkin (see page 30), the flavour develops.

Preheat the oven to 130°C/250°F/Gas 1. Butter a 900g/2lb loaf tin and line it with greaseproof paper. Mix the malt extract with the hot tea and leave to cool. Place the flour with the mixed spice in a bowl along with the fruits, egg and malt tea. Mix well together before spooning into the lined tin. Bake in the oven on the middle shelf for $1\frac{1}{4}$–$1\frac{1}{2}$ hours. Pierce with a skewer and when it comes out clean, the cake is cooked. Leave it to stand for 10 minutes in the tin before turning out onto a wire rack. When it has cooled, wrap, store and WAIT, as the introduction to the recipe suggests.

FRUIT LOAF

MAKES A 900G/2LB LOAF

8 tbsp malt extract
90ml/3fl oz hot tea, I use Jasmine
170g/6oz wholemeal self-raising
    flour
good pinch of ground, mixed spice
85g/3oz raisins
85g/3oz sultanas
1 egg340g/12oz mixed dried fruit and
    peel if you like it
110g/4oz dark muscovado sugar
200ml/7fl oz strained cold tea; I
    favour green gunpowder here, but
    navvies' brew or smoky Lapsang
    Souchong will work just as well
    depending on your preference
225g/8oz wholemeal or plain self-
    raising flour
1 egg

This is another fruit- and tea-based loaf like the malt loaf, perfect for teatime, which also needs keeping for 3 days. Remember to soak the ingredients the night before you want to cook it. You do not have to interpret the dried fruit as just being currants, sultanas and raisins; sprinkle in a few dried unsulphured apricots, dried cherries or cranberries or even a few prunes.

In the mid-19th century we developed our habit, our passion, for taking tea. That was when tea plantations were successfully cultivated in Assam and Sri Lanka. Polite society began to take afternoon tea, at which were served the delicate, crustless sandwiches and delicious cakes and biscuits that so many of us no longer bother to make for ourselves. Shame. Baking is the cornerstone of cooking, the most rewarding and satisfying of accomplishments, and will endear you to friends and family in a way that precious little else will. No harm in doing it for entirely selfish reasons either if you are on your own and feel like the smell of a good cake – one that will also keep well for a week – baking in the oven.

Preheat the oven to 180°C/350°F/Gas 4. Stir together the dried fruits and chopped peel, sugar and tea. Leave overnight. The dried fruit will have plumped up by the time you are ready to make the cake.

Stir in the flour and the beaten egg and beat well together. Grease and line a loaf tin, pile in the mixture and bake for an hour before turning the heat down to 170°C/325°F/Gas 3 for a further 30 minutes. Cool in the tin for 20 minutes or so before turning out onto a wire rack to cool completely. Wrap in greaseproof and foil, put in an airtight tin and keep for 3 days before eating sliced with thick butter. What could be simpler? It's easier than going to the shop to buy one.

CHOCOLATE CHEESECAKE BROWNIES

Here is a wondrously rich, claggy, hedonistic recipe gleaned from the lovely book *Baking With Passion* by Dan Lepard and Richard Whittington. This is something that any sane brownie-loving person will want to experiment with if they also love cheesecake and they feel like a change from the original, basic brownie. Or the original, basic cheesecake!

I have somewhat simplified the original, which was made in piped and swirled layers of chocolate brownie mixture and cheesecake mixture. I think it is every bit as successful if you make it in the same way as the chocolate marble cake, just dolloping the mixture into the tin in alternate spoonfuls or doing a chocolate bottom and a cheesecake top, according to your creative bent. If you have done the latter, then you may swirl the top with a skewer before you put the brownies in the oven to give the top a rippled effect.

CHEESECAKE MIXTURE
340g/12oz full fat fresh cream cheese, softened, so not straight from the fridge
85g/3oz vanilla caster sugar
1 egg yolk
30g/1oz plain flour
grated zest of 1 organic orange
1 tbsp freshly squeezed orange juice

BROWNIE MIXTURE
285g/10oz unrefined vanilla caster sugar
4 eggs
225g/8oz unsalted butter
85g/3oz Green and Black's organic cocoa
85g/3oz plain flour
200g/7oz best bitter chocolate, at least 64 per cent cocoa solids
110g/4oz roasted hazelnuts
110g/4oz cooking chocolate chunks; The Chocolate Society do them in bags, 70% cocoa solids

Preheat the oven to 180°C/375°F/Gas 4. Line the bottom of a 23cm/9in x 5cm/2in deep square tin. First make the cheesecake mixture. Cream together the cream cheese and sugar, then add the egg yolk followed by the flour. Finish by mixing in the orange zest and juice. Set aside.

Then make the brownie mix. Beat the sugar and eggs together really well until they have thickened and the sugar has completely dissolved. Melt the butter in a small pan and pour it into the sugar and egg. Sieve the cocoa and flour together into the mixture, then melt the chocolate in a double boiler, or a bowl over a pan of simmering water, and pour it into the mixture. Stir it in. Put the hazelnuts and chunks of chocolate into a Ziploc bag and whack it as hard as you dare with a rolling pin, keeping things chunky and in shards. The nuts will inevitably be more pulverised than the chocolate.

Spoon alternate dollops of brownie mixture and cheesecake mixture into the tin or do a black bottom and a white top, swirling the mixture with a skewer when you have finished. Bake for 20–25 minutes or until a skewer comes out warm at the tip with slightly sticky crumbs clinging to it. You do not want a dry sponge, which is always a danger with brownies, so err on the side of underdone for this recipe.

100g/3½oz good bitter chocolate,
   chopped
120ml/4fl oz milk
110g/4oz unsalted butter, softened
140g/5oz vanilla caster sugar
2 eggs
225g/8oz self-raising. flour
1 tsp baking powder
55g/2oz sour cream

CHOCOLATE MARBLE CAKE

Marble cakes always seemed magical when I was a child, in the same way that raspberry ripple ice cream did. I couldn't work out how the dapples or ripples could be effected, though it all became abundantly clear decades later. The quality of the chocolate is paramount. Use Valrhona, Callebaut or The Chocolate Society's chocolate drops, which are all around 70 per cent cocoa solids for that lingering, velvety, bittersweet taste. The mixture makes enough for one loaf tin so double up if you've got hordes of people or simply want to freeze one. This is another adaptation from *Baking With Passion* and has become Charissa's number one choice of birthday cake. She has demanded it two years running now and insists that makes it a 'tradition'.

Preheat the oven to 170°C/325°F/Gas 3. Grease and line a loaf tin, then grease the greaseproof paper and shake a little flour inside it all around, getting rid of the excess. Melt the chocolate with 60ml/2fl oz of milk in a double boiler or in a bowl over a pan of simmering water that the bowl doesn't touch. In the KitchenAid or using electric beaters, cream the butter and sugar until pale and fluffy. Beat in the eggs, one at a time, stopping the mixer and scraping the mixture down the sides if you need to.

In another bowl, sift the flour with the baking powder. Stir the sour cream into the remaining milk. Fold one-third of the flour into the creamed butter, sugar and egg mixture, followed by one-third of the sour cream mixture. Fold in another third of the flour, then another third of the sour cream, then repeat with the final third of each. Spoon half of this mixture into another bowl and add the chocolate mixture to one half, folding it in thoroughly. With two separate spoons, spoon the mixtures into the tin alternately so that the result will be marbled. Put the tin on to a heated baking tray in the middle of the oven and bake for 50–55 minutes or until a skewer comes out clean.

Cool in the tin for 10 minutes. Run a knife between the cake and the sides of the tin and gently upturn the cake onto your cloth-covered hand, then place upright to cool on a wire rack to finish cooling.

LEMON AND POPPYSEED YOGHURT CAKE

MAKES A 900G/2LB LOAF

45g/1½oz poppyseeds
150ml/5fl oz sheep's milk or good
   organic yoghurt
200g/7oz unsalted butter, softened
zest of 2 organic lemons
140g/5oz vanilla caster sugar
3 eggs
255g/9oz plain flour
1½tsp baking powder
juice of the 2 organic lemons

This is a gloriously lemony cake with the slight acidity of the yoghurt and the unexpected crunch of zillions of tiny poppyseeds, an underused seed with a lovely nutty flavour. This is so easy to make but so yummy, working well with a fruit ice cream. I've eaten it with a mango and lime ice cream and with an orange and cardamom one. Or just eat it sliced and plain or with a blob of crème fraîche. It is one of the cakes I bake most frequently, adored by children and grown-ups.

Preheat the oven to 170°C/325°F/Gas 3. Put the poppyseeds into the yoghurt and stir to amalgamate. Cream the softened butter, lemon zest and sugar in a KitchenAid or with electric beaters until light and fluffy. Scrape the mixture down the sides of the bowl to incorporate it all as you go and, keeping the beaters switched on, add the eggs one at a time beating in between each addition. Sift the flour and baking powder onto the creamed mixture. Stir with a metal spoon adding the lemon juice and yoghurt and poppyseed mixture, which you must fold in thoroughly.

Grease and line a loaf tin. Scrape in the mixture and bake on a heated baking sheet in the middle of the oven for 55–60 minutes or until a skewer comes out clean. Cool in the tin for 10 minutes or a little longer, then turn out on to a wire rack to cool.

DATE AND WALNUT LOAF

MAKES A 900G/2LB LOAF

225g/8oz pitted dates, chopped
110g/4oz light muscovado sugar
140g/5oz unsalted butter, chopped
   into small pieces
2 level tsp bicarbonate of soda
120ml/4fl oz boiling water
1 egg
400g/14oz plain or wholemeal flour
a pinch of salt
55g/2oz walnuts, chopped
1 tsp vanilla extract

A plain, but good sweet and nutty cake that you may also eat with butter and which you can stir up in a trice. Child's play.

Put the chopped dates, sugar, chopped butter and bicarb in a mixing bowl. Pour over the boiling water and stir thoroughly. Add the beaten egg, sifted flour and salt, walnuts and vanilla extract and beat together well. Grease and line a loaf tin and scrape the mixture into it. Bake for 1–1½ hours. Check with a skewer after an hour — it should come out clean when the cake is ready.

Lemon and Poppyseed Yoghurt Cake

FRUGA

FOOD

3

I DIDN'T LAST LONG on institutional food when I went up to Cambridge.

In fact, if I remember rightly, it was less than a week. I'd already disgraced myself at Bedales where I'd been the premier insurgent and instigator of a whole school meal strike, an act of open rebellion at the horrors of 'purple puke', a nauseatingly livid-hued blancmange of a pudding that had the sickly twang of evaporated milk about it; spam fritters whose thickly battered walls when assaulted by a knife splurted grease all over the plate and housed a day-glo pink spongy hunk of spam; and Sunday night's horror of horrors, bullet-boiled eggs in a thick, floury mantle of béchamel and tinned sweetcorn.

There were other things. Manchester tart, for one. A layer of soggy grey pastry, a layer of turnip jam, then lumpy, wobbly thick custard and a topping of hideous scratchings of desiccated coconut. As for the gluey, gristly lumps of stewed meat in the pies, the grey beef, the oozing fried bread that accompanied baked beans or tinned tomatoes for breakfast, the soups as salt as the briney, and the drenched bedclothes of cabbage with their uniquely arrest-worthy aroma of rot and boil and compost – well, school was a time of hunger that was never satisfied. It never is when the food is stodgy, lumpen and disgusting.

The tuck shop down the road, Pretty's, sold chocolate by the trailer load and if we were in savoury not sweet mood, Ritz crackers, which we smothered with Primula cheese. These near daily trips were occasionally supplemented by the five-bob meal of the day at the Tai Tong, a local Chinese restaurant in Petersfield, which served greasy chicken chop suey and banana fritters. Or there was tea at one of the town's two teashops, the Punch and Judy or The Donkey Cart. I remember the joy of such simple dishes as soft roes on toast and Welsh Rarebit – who on earth serves them for tea nowadays? – followed by sludge-thick chocolate fudge cake. Or an illicit trip to The Good Intent for nothing more immoral than a chocolate nut sundae that came in a mile-high glass with a long spoon, the chocolate sauce freezing stickily to the ice cream, a rare and wonderful treat.

Boarding school children always eat faster than anyone else, on the grounds that there are always limited supplies of seconds, so the day of the strike came as a real shock to the system. After much slogan shouting and trumpet playing in the school quad, we walked to Pretty's and lunched on Mars bars. That evening, a smaller caucus of militants sat outside the dining room intimidating the starving supper goers for the second time. In the end, hunger got the better of us and we relented, despite our outrage at the kitchen staff for the re-hashing of lunch at suppertime; a school food committee was appointed and we attempted to make our mark on the dire school food. I don't think much was accomplished. Thirty years on, I am struggling to do the same for my children, having already got two children through the horrors of prep- and public-school food. While at the former, my children insisted on packed lunches, such was their dim view of the food.

School food is no better in the private sector than in the state, in my experience, and now I only have one child left to suffer the inexcusable inadequacy of school food, with its poor ingredients unimaginatively and badly cooked. Even the simplest and best of ingredients are ruined, though normally the best ingredients aren't bought in the first place. There is no excuse. It is perfectly possible to serve good, delicious, healthy food, properly sourced and properly cooked if there is a will to do so. I have initiated a national competition to find the best school dinner in Britain, which Waitrose have sponsored in its first year. Perhaps it is unrealistic to expect it to shame the worst offenders in the country into trying to change their food culture, and for good food to be made a standard part of the educating of children, which it should be. Is it too much for school meals to be an occasion to look forward to rather than an endurance test, a mere fuelling up with the least offensive dish on the menu? But at least I can give plaudits to the enlightened few who have already made good food a part of their educative purpose and pleasure.

Judging by my son Harry's comments on the food at his Oxford college, there is no reason to be optimistic. It is worse even than the food in his house at Eton he tells me, where there were only 50 boys to cook for, and he has a palate I can vouch for. As I vouch for my daughter Miranda's, who is a brilliant, natural cook and really knows about good ingredients, but spent her first year at Bristol University condemned to eat the food in her hall of residence or pay twice, not a rule that King's enforced with me when I explained that I would not be dining in hall again. When Miranda was interviewed about the standard of food in her halls of residence on local radio, having had her first book, on student food, published, she was hauled up in front of the college elders and lambasted for daring to be critical, a characteristic that is seen as a desirable quality in every other walk of academe. It was as though staff and students alike didn't expect anything better and were too apathetic or just plain uninterested to do anything about it.

We feed our children lousy food at school and at university, although we are beginning to accept the consequences of so doing, if only in health terms, and there is universal apathy from the people who run the nation's premier educational establishments. It's as though food is beneath their interest, inquiry or expectation. Barmy! It irks me immeasurably that we are finally acting on health grounds rather than on the grounds of good taste, not something that could ever happen in France, Spain, Italy or any of the Mediterranean countries where nobody appears to bother with the notion of healthy food. They KNOW that good food is good for you.

Many of our children are brought up as food faddists by being fed 'children's food', and these are the children who probably don't see anything wrong with school food; they don't know any better. Children who will eat almost everything at home, and have been brought up with the sort of richly ethnic, multi-culinary diet that we take for granted now, are the ones who hate school food because they know it's bad. It looks bad, it tastes bad and it does you bad. And your mother would never serve it at home.

As I said before, a week into my first term at King's College Cambridge I abandoned institutional food forever, never eating in hall apart from at Founder's feasts or on special occasions. After five years of boarding school life, my real culinary education was about to begin. I knew good food from bad. Now I just had to learn how to cook it. I am still learning. Even then, I sort of knew that the key to it all was learning how to shop. The market in the middle of Cambridge was brilliant for that. If I went just before closing time, my favourite greengrocer would fill up my bags with seasonal fruits and vegetables and, knowing that I was an impecunious student, charge me a knock-down rate. I was the only person to use the kitchen on my staircase on a daily basis that first year, apart from the fridge, which was always subject to late-night and dawn raids. It was safer to keep things cold on the windowsill or buy things fresh every day, which is the best possible training anyway. Soon I was cooking for a group that wavered between three and six people for supper every night and surviving on a diet of toasted sandwiches for lunch. I started off with not a lot of cooking equipment but a hunger to experiment and learn, so my range of dishes became impressive quite quickly. There are only so many things a student can afford: the staples of beans, pulses, flour, rice and pasta; the cheaper cuts of meat and organ meat; potatoes, eggs, root vegetables; mackerel, coley, herring and squid. All these became the prime ingredients for our nightly dinners. In the days before readymade heat-and-eat horrors and before the dawn of the microwave, learning how to cook was a fundamental necessity. There were no short cuts.

Being starved of cash is really the only way to learn to cook, as is being pushed for space. The worse the kitchen, the smaller the budget, the more creative, organised and focussed the cook has to be. So I served up bubbling vats of belly pork and beans, lamb's livers roasted whole with root vegetables, pasta with ragù sauce, lasagne, the dread chilli con carne, fish pie and shepherd's pie, Irish stew, stew-like soups, soup-like stews and occasionally a full roast. Weekend brunches meant the full English, kidneys or chicken livers with eggs, rashers, mushrooms and tomatoes; otherwise I ploughed a deepening furrow through the pastures of Elizabeth David and Jane Grigson, who have remained my kitchen-shelf classics throughout my cooking life.

The excitement of trying new dishes, feeding armies of ravenous and seriously impressed fellow students, and experimenting with dishes and techniques that you've never tried before are part of the joy of student life, as is the knowledge that if you set yourself up as the cook, you've got devoted washers-up and admirers for life!

We have to return to that, to student life being as much about exploring and experimenting with food and wine as it is with the intellect. We must not lose another generation of potential good cooks like we did the last, whose mothers were too deep in work to bake a biscuit, too pushed for time to cook a proper supper; where grazing bred households for whom the ritual of sitting round the table with food, drink and conversation – the greatest act of civilisation in a civilised world – has been replaced by a solitary, silent supper tray of zapped TV dinner balanced on the knees.

So, if you are a student, on a gap year, still treading that most difficult trail of teenagedom, or coming to being self-sufficient in your twenties, get cooking. It will give you confidence, pleasure, sustenance of body, mind and spirit and an inordinate degree of satisfaction. It will console and comfort you during exams, heartbreak, parental rows and in all the difficult times of your life. Cooking is a thing of such absorption that all the extraneous problems and irritants are quickly forgotten while you create something wonderful, however simple, to eat. And by that, it only takes the mechanical skills and concentration in making poached eggs on toast to fill you with a sense of pleasure and well-being. Some of the recipes may seem less than frugal, but then everyone has to indulge a little sometimes.

MEZZE, STARTERS OR LATE-NIGHT MUNCHIE THINGS

These are the sort of things that I expect you will cook and eat regularly, keeping some of the ingredients you need in your store cupboard or fridge at all times, and getting to make them from memory and taste as soon as you have the experience.

TARAMASALATA

SERVES 6

1 slice of stale white bread, crust removed
200g/7oz piece of smoked cod's roe, soaked and then removed from its skin with a spoon
1 large clove of garlic, chopped finely
240ml/8fl oz extra virgin olive oil
juice of 1–2 organic lemons
black pepper

I lived on this when I first left home and boarding school after A Levels and was cramming for Oxbridge entrance in London. There was a wonderful Greek deli in Holland Park where the tarama was freshly made, not the evil, beetroot-dyed, sticky paste that seems to have more potato and inferior oil and less smoky roe, olive oil and fresh lemon juice than could ever make a good approximation of this classic mezze. We ate it with chunks of plaited Greek bread splattered with sesame seeds. It's also good with griddled pitta bread, toast and black olives. Tarama is traditionally made with the salted, pressed roe of the grey mullet or with smoked cod's roe. You can buy the cod's roe in its skin at good fishmongers, but leave it in water overnight to leach away some of its saltiness.

Wet the bread and squeeze it so it is damp rather than wringing wet and put it in a food processor with the pre-soaked cod's roe and the garlic. Blitz, adding a thin stream of olive oil. If the mixture over-thickens, slacken with a spoon or two of water. Add the lemon juice, season with pepper and taste to see if you need more lemon juice. Scoop into a bowl and pour a little more oil over the top.

Serve with a salad made from 2 tablespoons of salted capers that you have rinsed thoroughly under running water, some rocket leaves and a dressing made with extra virgin olive oil and sherry vinegar, and slices of griddled pitta bread.

HUMMUS BI TAHINI

225g/8oz chickpeas, soaked
    overnight in a bowl of water
1 onion spiked with a couple of
    cloves
2 sticks of celery
a couple of leek tops
a couple of chopped carrots
juice of up to 3 large lemons
2 tbsp organic tahini paste from dark
    or lightly roasted sesame seeds
3 cloves of garlic, peeled and
    chopped
olive oil
sea salt and black pepper
1 tsp cumin seeds or paprika
    (optional)
fresh coriander or parsley, finely
    chopped

An earthy Middle Eastern dish, which everyone tinkers with to find the proportions they like: lemony, less lemony, garlicky, with more or less tahini, made with either dark roast sesame seeds or the lighter ones and so on. There are those of you who will want to make it with tinned chick peas or buy it in tubs from the deli or supermarket – which to my mind is a real travesty, it is like wallpaper paste – to whom I say, just make it the proper way once and you will be converted, all, or most of the time. Any moron can make hummus well and since when was soaking pulses overnight a major chore? You put them in a bowl of cold water, leave them, rinse them and cook them for eons, by just leaving them simmering on the stove top. Then you whizz them to a purée with the other ingredients to taste. Maybe pour a little green olive oil over the surface to look pretty and prevent it from drying out on top and maybe sprinkle roasted cumin seeds or a little paprika on top to bleed into the oil.

It is filling, delicious and lovely to bring out at any time of day with some slices of griddled pitta bread or a salad of any kind. If you soak enough chickpeas you will have extra for a soup, stew or tagine. Begin the night before you want the hummus by soaking the chickpeas.

Put the drained chickpeas and the vegetables in a large heavy-bottomed casserole and cover with cold water to half a thumb above them. Bring to the boil, scum rigorously with a slotted spoon and some kitchen paper, then reduce to a simmer and cook with the lid on. In my experience, depending on the age of the chickpeas, they will take 1½–2 hours to cook. Drain them, keeping a little of the cooking water, which you may want to use a little of to thin down the hummus.

Put the chickpeas in a food processor with the juice of 2 of the lemons, the tahini, the garlic, 3 tablespoons of olive oil and the seasoning. Blitz to a thick paste, then taste. It may need thinning down with a tablespoon or two of cooking liquor, it may need more oil, more garlic, more lemon, more tahini. There is no right way, except the way you like it. The consistency should be that of a creamy paste or mayonnaise.

Put into a serving dish or terrine before cooling and serving. Top with a good splosh of olive oil onto which you can scatter a teaspoon of cumin seeds roasted dry in a small frying pan for a minute, then crushed in a mortar or a teaspoon of paprika. Some finely chopped parsley or coriander is also good. Serve with griddled pitta bread or toast. Sourdough bread is delicious with hummus.

AUBERGINE PURÉE WITH TAHINI

SERVES 6–8

2 large aubergines
2–4 cloves of garlic, chopped
juice of up to 3 lemons
2 tbsp tahini, the dark roasted or
    light sesame paste
sea salt and black pepper
olive oil
1 tsp cumin seeds, dry roasted in a
    small frying pan for a minute then
    ground in a mortar
1 tbsp parsley
some pomegranate seeds (optional)

This is a creamy, smoky purée that you can make as part of a mezze or just eat on its own with griddled pitta bread. It is also delicious with lamb – roast leg or shoulder, chops or kebabs – the sweet meat and the smoky, lemony, garlicky flesh a perfect taste and texture partnership.

Preheat the oven to 180°C/350°F/Gas 4. If you have a grill or a gas flame, sear the aubergines until their skins begin to blacken and blister. Charcoal is the best for a smoky flavour, but unless you're having a barbie, hold each aubergine over the gas flame with a pair of tongs, turning it as it blackens, or put them under the grill turning them likewise. Then put the aubergines on a baking tray and finish the cooking process, about another 30 minutes, depending on their size, until they feel soft right the way through when pricked with a skewer.

Allow the aubergines to cool to the point where you can skin them, then put them in chunks in the blender or food processor. Add 2 cloves of garlic to begin with, the juice of 2 lemons, 2 tablespoons of tahini and the seasoning and blitz. Add olive oil until you have a creamy textured paste, but don't overdo it; start with around 2–4 tablespoons. Taste and adjust anything, the lemon, the seasoning, the tahini, the garlic, the oil. Pour into a serving bowl while still warm or spread on a plate, sprinkling with a little oil, the cumin seeds and, if you like some jewels of pomegranate, which always give colour and glamour to this grey but divine-tasting dish.

TZATZIKI

1 cucumber, peeled, halved
    lengthways and seeded with a
    sharp teaspoon (the seeds would
    make the finished dish watery)
225g/8oz thick Greek yoghurt
2 tbsp extra virgin olive oil
4 cloves of garlic, peeled then
    crushed in a mortar with a little
    sea salt
1 tbsp finely chopped fresh mint
black pepper

This lovely dish is simple to make and adds a cooling element to any mezze. It can also be something you might like to serve with griddled pitta bread, grilled meat or prawns, sticks of raw veg or with a curry or the Red Pepper, Roast Onion and Feta Purée opposite. Don't leave it in the fridge longer than a couple of days or the garlic will develop a somewhat rank and bitter flavour. Try to find good quality thick Greek yoghurt.

Mix the cucumber, yoghurt, olive oil, salty garlic paste and mint together in a bowl. Scrunch on some black pepper and check the seasoning. Refrigerate for at least half a day to let the flavours marry and deepen.

RED PEPPER, ROAST ONION AND FETA PURÉE

SERVES 4 WITH OTHER DISHES

110g/4oz onions
340g/12oz red peppers or piquillo
    peppers in a jar
285g/10oz sheep's milk feta
6 tbsp olive oil
2 tbsp sherry vinegar or aged red
    wine vinegar
1 tsp fresh thyme leaves
sea salt and black pepper

A relaxed and delicious dipping dish or mezze or a lovely light lunch. You may choose to make this with the lovely piquillo peppers that Brindisa sell in a jar, all smoky from beech wood, or you may scorch and char ordinary red peppers yourself. Adapted from Theodore Kyriakou's lovely book *Real Greek Food*.

Preheat the oven to 200°C/400°F/Gas 6. Roast the onions in their skins for about 45 minutes. They should be soft right the way through when spiked with a skewer. Meanwhile, char the red peppers all over on a barbecue, under a hot grill, or by holding them with a pair of tongs over a gas burner.

When the peppers are charred all over, put them in a bowl, cover with clingfilm and leave for 10 minutes or so. The skins will have wrinkled and be easy to peel. When they're peeled, cut around the stalk and remove it with the seeds and white core of the peppers. Peel the onions. Mash the two together on a large plate or in a shallow bowl with the crumbled feta before adding the oil, vinegar and thyme with some seasoning. The texture should be coarse, not smooth.

WELSH RAREBIT

SERVES 4

225g/8oz Caerphilly, Cheshire or
    Cheddar cheese, grated
30g/1oz unsalted butter
2 tbsp fresh breadcrumbs
1 tsp Colman's English mustard
    powder, mixed with 1 tsp water
1 egg, beaten
salt and pepper
4 slices of good bread, white or
    brown, lightly toasted and buttered
a few drops of Tabasco and
    Worcestershire sauce (optional)

A store cupboard standby for all times. You may as well learn to make this simple snack, breakfast, tea or lunch dish the best way to begin with. Just melting cheese on a piece of toast under a grill can render it stringy and oily, the solids separating into liquid under the blast of heat.

Heat the oven to 220°C/425°F/Gas 7. Mix the finely grated cheese with the butter, breadcrumbs, mustard and egg. Beat well, season with salt, pepper and both sauces to taste and spread thickly on buttered toast. Cook in the hot oven for 5–10 minutes until golden brown and bubbling.

GORGEOUS GRAIN

Rice, polenta, couscous and bulghur – no student cook, indeed no fully-fledged cook can live without these simple staples. No meal is more filling, more satisfying, more soothing, more digestible or easier to embellish with good things. Grain is such an amenable backdrop too, that you can, once you've got the hang of cooking it, spice it up or let it down in a million ways. Make it the main event if you've bought high-quality grain and other ingredients in the first place and are short of money, thus transmuting pauper's ingredients into a feast fit for friends, family, a king.

Your kitchen cupboard should never be without a stock of all four of the above, so at a moment's notice you can feed the five thousand. A lemon risotto with some tiny fried leaves of astringent rosemary enriched with butter and cream; a spiced chicken liver pilav scented with saffron; a simple slop of wet polenta with branches of roast tomatoes and blue cheese or mascarpone stirred into it; a tabbouleh made from the nibbed, cracked wheat grains of bulghur, fresh with a giant fist of parsley, chopped onion, a zing of lemon juice and flecks of fresh tomato – these are dishes for all times, all seasons, all guests, dishes you will never tire of cooking, never tire of eating. Forget lumpy couscous, clogged, stodgy, wet rice, flavourless quick-cook polenta. Follow the rules and the rest will follow.

RICE

To find rice boring and dull is to fail to see the point of it. Its very versatility, like pasta, is that of a blank canvas, lending itself to either taking the front seat, or to blending in with its accompaniments. And don't forget it's a textural thing too, complementing in its starchy nuttiness or its smooth softness, the different textures and liquids you are serving it with. It is the vehicle with which you show off your meat, fish or vegetables. You can keep it plain, utterly plain and boiled; you can spike it with tempered spices – cumin, cardamom, coriander, fennel, fenugreek, turmeric, allspice and cinnamon; you can add jewels of raisins, dried fruit, toasted pine kernels or flaked almonds; you can hit it with a shriek of hot harissa or chilli, or subdue it with peas, tiny shrimps, coconut cream, cream and butter, or tender herbs like tarragon, thyme, parsley and coriander.

Rice calms and it soothes and it fills. If you have a dodgy digestion, it helps, particularly with the digestifs of spices, fennel and fenugreek. If you actually have an upset tummy, I find the best thing is to cook some rice and then drink the starchy water that has been left behind. It works every time.

SHORT AND MEDIUM GRAIN

These are both traditionally used for the most English of puddings. The Japanese use medium rice for their sushi, the Chinese use it as their everyday rice. The slight stickiness to the grain makes it ideal to pick up with chopsticks.The Spanish use short-grain rice for their paellas. Look for the name 'Calasparra', a lovely rice that absorbs all the liquid and the flavour of the ingredients you are cooking it with while maintaining its texture.

LONG GRAIN

When cooked properly, long-grain rice separates into individual grains and should have that appealing light, fluffy quality. Thai Jasmine rice is a long-grain rice as is basmati, which you can buy white or brown. Both have a subtle fragrance to them.

BROWN RICE

You can buy brown long-grain and short-grain rice and brown rice flakes. Since the outer husk hasn't been polished away, thus losing its outer husk or bran, it is superior nutritionally to white rice. If you fear shades of the '60s I guess you won't buy it, but its nutty flavour goes well with all manner of things, it makes for a far better tasting rice salad and it is not to be sneered at as an old hippie ingredient. Brown rice takes about 40 minutes to cook, but doesn't lose its texture as white rice sometimes does.

RISOTTO RICE

You have to believe it, the elitist pronouncements on the different types of risotto rice are all, for once, true. You simply can't make a risotto, a REAL risotto, without risotto rice. To my mind, the king is Carnaroli, followed by Vialone Nano and in third place, Arborio. All three have a starchiness to them that, when released little by little as you stir and stir, delivers a finished dish that is at once chalky, creamy and has a bite.

WILD RICE

Wild rice isn't rice at all. It is the grain from a North American grass and comes in long black needles with a nutty flavour and more bite and chewiness than ordinary rice. It is expensive, but you can mix it with other rices so that you use less of it, and it adds colour, texture and flavour to hot and cold rice dishes. You may be wary of it on the designer-rice principle, but it is a very good occasional ingredient, rather like the chubby, nutty grains of Camargue red rice, a recent addition to the supermarket and deli shelves.

GLUTINOUS RICE

Glutinous rice has that sort of compulsive comfort quality to it, that tongue-sticking appeal that makes one always want to eat too much of it. It can be white or black, short or long, it is the staple rice of some Asian countries but otherwise is mainly used in puddings. It needs a long soaking if it is going to be steamed, but if you are cooking it in the normal way, you don't need to bother.

BROWN RICE FLAKES

When I was gradually weaning my three children, I don't know what I would have done without organic brown rice flakes. They cook quickly in a little water, then can be sieved into whatever purées you have got on the go until you find the right gloopiness and glutinousness for your baby at that stage. Mix the rice flake purée with puréed fruits, cooked or raw, with vegetables, puréed chicken, fish, stock or gravy, and if you have a baby who is desperate for a bit of bulk, particularly to help him/her sleep through the night, this is the answer to your prayers. You won't need to purée the flakes once the baby can swallow slightly coarser textured food. Keep a bowl of the rice flake purée in the fridge for several days to stir into whatever you are cooking. I hope this is not too crazy a thing to put in the student section of the book when books not babies are on the menu, but this is the section on cooking rice!

HOW TO COOK RICE

SERVES 4 AS AN ACCOMPANIMENT

225g/8oz long-grain white rice
1 tsp sea salt

Plain, long-grain white rice, fluffed up with a fork, served steaming hot, the grains separate and tender, is the most versatile of accompaniments. You can throw virtually anything at it or over it, make it the main or the added attraction. You can even steam it back to life the next day over a colander, adding what you will from your store cupboard, or turn it into a cold, spiced rice salad, lubricating it with a good glug of olive oil and some zingy raw spring onions, toasted pine nuts, sultanas, peas, ground roast spices and lemon zest. But you have to know how to cook it first and how not to turn it to porridge when it's cooked!

Tip the rice into a measuring jug, noting the plimsoll line that the rice comes up to. Then shute it into the pan you're going to cook it in with the sea salt. Measure twice the quantity of water to the rice you've measured in the jug, and pour it over the rice. Bring to the boil, turn the heat down to a simmer and cover with a lid. The rice should take 12 minutes to cook. There should be no water left at this point and when you lift the lid you should just see steam holes in the rice. Taste with a fork. Remove from the heat and leave for a further couple of minutes under the lid before serving. Never stir around with a spoon, this breaks the grains of rice down into a porridgy pulp. Always use a fork to taste or fluff up and separate the grains of rice.

BASMATI OR THAI FRAGRANT RICE

SERVES 4

400g/14oz white basmati or Thai fragrant rice

Tip the rice into a saucepan with a tight-fitting lid and cover it by about 2.5cm/1in with cold water. Add salt, cover the pan and bring to the boil, boiling it fiercely for just under a minute before turning it down to a simmer. Continue to cook for 10 minutes, then remove from the heat with the lid still on and leave for 5 minutes. Gently fluff up the steaming rice with a fork. It will be rather stickier if you are cooking Thai rice, but should be dry with tender, separate grains.

DELICIOUS TITBITS TO ADD TO YOUR RICE

If you are feeling poor, lazy, like you need the comfort of serious white starch or all three, here are some suggestions that you can elaborate on and vary to add to a dish of steaming pure white rice, or fragrant brown or white basmati, or scented Thai rice.

- Fork in a large pat of butter with a handful of Parmesan and another of chopped tarragon or chives.
- Add some tiny cubes of bacon frazzled in a pan and their fat into which you've tossed a bundle of chopped spring onions at the last moment. Perhaps a handful of chopped parsley or snipped chives if you have them.
- Stir a tablespoon of spicy hot harissa into 4–5 tablespoons of olive oil and stir it into the rice. Add fresh coriander if you have it.
- Stir in a couple of large spoons of mascarpone and crushed garlic when the rice is piping hot with some butter and black pepper.
- Sauté some mushrooms in butter with some ground coriander and stir them in hot with black pepper.
- Add a handful of toasted pine nuts, the same of raisins, a handful of cooked peas and a teaspoon each of roasted crushed cumin seeds and coriander, plus a knife end of ground cloves, half a dozen crushed cardamom seeds and, if you feel like it, some thinly sliced onions fried in olive oil until they are brown and crispy piled on top.
- Butter, lemon juice and a quantity of chopped herbs such as basil, chervil, tarragon, parsley, coriander and chives.
- A handful of fresh chopped mint with half a peeled, seeded cucumber chopped into small dice, 3–4 tomatoes, peeled, seeded and finely chopped, some crushed garlic, olive oil and lemon juice all stirred in to the warm rice.
- A couple of finely chopped chilli peppers, seeded, stirred in with a finely chopped raw onion, a handful of coriander leaves and the Asian dressing on page 77.
- A whole mozzarella di bufala cut into small cubes and stirred into the hot rice with 3–4 skinned, seeded, chopped tomatoes and a handful of torn basil leaves, dressed with olive oil and balsamic vinegar.
- Wafer-thin slices of raw fennel and shavings of Pecorino dressed with olive oil, lemon juice and black pepper.
- A handful of cooked, shelled prawns, a handful of cooked peas, the zest of a lemon, a finely chopped, seeded chilli, a bunch of chopped spring onions, a bunch of coriander and a dressing of olive oil and lime juice.
- Cubes of oozingly ripe Taleggio or Fontina d'Aosta with slivers of raw fennel, torn basil leaves and olive oil.
- A good pinch of saffron stamens soaked in warm water and poured into the rice with little bits of chopped chorizo, prawns, a handful of peas, a few finely chopped piquillo peppers from a jar (Navarrico make the best ones) and a good glug of olive oil.

RICE COOKED IN THE EGYPTIAN WAY/SAFFRON RICE

This is a very good way of cooking plain, long-grain rice, particularly if you have chicken or meat stock rather than water to cook it in.

SERVES 6

2 teacups long-grain rice (about 450g/1lb)
3–4 tbsp olive oil
2 teacups water of water or chicken stock (see page 80)
sea salt

Wash the rice by putting it in a bowl and covering it with boiling water. Stir it briefly, then pour it into a sieve and pour cold running water over it until the water is clear, not starchy looking. Drain well. Heat 3–4 tablespoons of olive oil in a saucepan and throw in the rice, sautéing it gently until the grains are translucent. Add the stock or water and salt, bring to the boil and let it bubble for a couple of minutes before turning it down to simmer and covering the pan tightly. Do not stir once you have put the water in. Cook for about 20 minutes before checking – you should see little steam holes in the surface. Remove from the heat and leave to rest for 10 minutes. For saffron rice, soak a generous pinch of saffron stamens in a little warm water for 20 minutes and add when you have stirred the rice in the oil and it is time to add the stock or water.

KEDGEREE

This classic dish is perfect for breakfast, brunch, lunch and supper and is a simple, one-pan meal that I've been making and tinkering with all my cooking life. I favour a warm whiff of spice to make it mildly curried and always use natural smoked haddock. It may cost a little more but the orange-dyed stuff is heinous and you really don't need that much fish to flavour the rice with. You can use half the quantity given here and it will still taste great. Fresh herbs, a splash of cream and good organic eggs with slightly runny yolks, make this dish sublime.

SERVES 6

450–675g/1–1½ lb natural smoked haddock
300ml/10fl oz or so of milk
a bay leaf
a knob of butter
black pepper
about 560g/1¼lb brown or white basmati rice, brown makes the dish lovely and nutty
3 tbsp olive oil
2 large onions, thinly sliced
2 tsp cumin seeds
2 tsp coriander seeds
1 tsp garam masala
½ tsp cayenne
9–12 organic eggs
225g/8oz fresh or frozen peas, shelled weight
4–6 tbsp double cream
a knob of butter
a bunch of flat-leaf parsley or coriander, to taste
mango chutney

Put the fish skin-side down in a shallow gratin dish with the milk, bay leaf and a knob of butter and warm over a gentle heat until the milk is at a bare simmer. Season with black pepper and continue to simmer for 10–15 minutes, making sure the fish is basted with the cooking liquor. When it is ready, it will pull easily away from the skin with a fork. Meanwhile, cook the rice according to the instructions on the packet, remembering to start the rice earlier if it is brown as it will take longer. Start the onions off at the same time. Heat the olive oil in a large heavy-bottomed frying pan, big enough to hold everything at the end, and gently sauté the onions for a couple of minutes.

Now add the spices. The cumin and coriander can be roasted in a small pan for a minute or until they smell toasty, then crushed in a mortar and added to the onions with the garam masala. Continue to cook until slightly softened and translucent, then turn down the heat, put a lid on them and cook more slowly until they have completely softened, about 20 minutes. Meanwhile boil a pan of water for the eggs and just before it reaches boiling point drop the eggs in and boil them for 5½ minutes. Plunge into cold water so you can peel them. Cook the peas in a little boiling water until tender. Remove the fish and any stray bones from the skin and pull it into large flakes with a fork. Remove the lid from the frying pan and add the drained rice. Then add the peas and fish, season with a little more pepper if it needs it and pour in the cream over a low heat. Add a generous extra knob of butter and the finely chopped parsley or coriander and stir briefly to amalgamate. Remove from the heat and place the halved eggs all around the edge of the pan. Serve straight from the pan with some good mango chutney and a green salad.

PILAV

A Middle Eastern pilav is another cheap and amazingly versatile dish that lends itself as well to the treasures of the store cupboard – dried apricots, raisins and prunes; pistachios, cashew nuts, almonds and pine nuts; coriander, cardamom, saffron and bay – as it does to meat, vegetables and fish. The nature of the dish is at once sweet and mildly spiced, one reason why the combined sweetness of lamb and apricots is so successful. A pilav is a much drier dish than a risotto and is made with long-grain basmati rice, either brown or white. This is a simple pilav to accompany a meat or vegetable stew.

SERVES 2

55g/2oz unsalted butter
1 medium onion, finely chopped
about 6 cardamom pods, lightly
    crushed
1 cinnamon stick
2 bay leaves
170g/6oz basmati rice
about 300ml/10fl oz chicken stock
    (see p. 80), vegetable stock
    (see p. 380) or water

Melt the butter in a pan and add the chopped onion. Sauté the onion until it is beginning to soften and turn translucent, about 5 minutes. Throw in the spices and stir for a minute or so until they release their heady scent, then pour in the rice. Stir until the rice is coated all over, then add enough stock or water to cover the grain by about 2.5cm/1in. Bring to the boil then reduce to a simmer and cover with a well-fitting lid. Continue to cook for 15 minutes. Keep the lid on but remove the pan from the heat and leave for 5 minutes.

You may eat the pilav on its own with just a knob of butter or with a gently spiced meat or vegetable stew or some lamb kebabs. If you want to add some toasted flaked almonds or pine nuts and stir them in, with or without a handful of raisins you've soaked in a bowl of warm water to plump up for 20 minutes, then drained, do. Or you can simply sauté some onions and pieces of chicken in butter and serve them with the pilav.

TOMATO PILAV

SERVES 6

3-4 tbsp olive oil
2 medium onions, finely chopped
2 cloves of garlic, peeled
about 900g/2lb tomatoes, seeded and
    skinned, or the equivalent of
    tinned tomatoes
sea salt and black pepper
1 tsp unrefined brown sugar
2 bay leaves
450g/1lb long-grain rice, washed and
    drained

Heat the olive oil in a large, heavy-bottomed pan, then fry the onions and garlic over a medium heat until the onions have softened and turned translucent. Throw in the chopped tomatoes with the seasoning, sugar, and bay leaves and sauté for a few minutes. Cover with water and simmer gently for about 45 minutes. You may need to add a little water as the sauce reduces to prevent it sticking or turning too jammy.

Pour in the rice and an equal quantity of water, bring to the boil, then simmer gently with a tight lid for about 20 minutes when the rice should be tender. Remove from the heat and leave covered for 5 minutes before serving. Very good with lamb, or eat it on its own if you are feeling impoverished but in need of comfort food.

LAMB AND APRICOT PILAV

SERVES 6

110g/4oz unsalted butter
1 onion, finely chopped
450g/1lb cubed lamb shoulder, the
    fat trimmed a little
sea salt and black pepper
1 tsp ground cinnamon
a handful raisins
110g/4oz dried unsulphured apricots
    or Hunza apricots, the tiny musky
    ones from Afghanistan
450g/1lb long-grain rice

I have always loved the affinity the sweet sharpness of apricots has for the meaty sweetness of lamb, although I combine fruit with meat sparingly and pickily. Duck doused in tinned cherries, and ham and pineapple are not combinations I'd give houseroom to.

Melt half the butter in a heavy-bottomed pot, then throw in the onions and sauté them until golden and softened. Add the meat and brown on all sides before seasoning with sea salt, black pepper and the cinnamon. Stir to coat. Add the raisins and apricots and coat with butter, then cover with water and bring to the boil. Cover and simmer gently for about an hour. Melt the rest of the butter in another pan, add the rice and stir to coat the grains before shuting the rice into the lamb pan and adding enough water to the meat juices to cover. Bring to the boil, cover the pan and simmer for 20 minutes. I like to keep this dish more liquid than a conventional pilav.

LAMB PILAV

SERVES 6

3–4 tbsp olive oil or 75g/2½oz
    unsalted butter
1 large onion, finely chopped
450g/1lb cubed lamb, trimmed, but
    not without fat
sea salt and black pepper
1 tsp ground cinnamon
3 tbsp tomato purée or a good pinch
    of saffron stamens soaked in hot
    water for 20 minutes. One would
    cancel out the other, but both are
    good for colouring and flavouring
    the rice
a handful of chopped parsley
2 large tomatoes, skinned, seeded
    and chopped
1 red pepper, seeded and sliced into
    long strips
2 tbsp pine nuts, toasted in a pan
    until they colour (optional, but I
    favour this)
a handful of raisins (again, optional,
    but delicious)
450g/1lb long-grain rice, washed and
    drained

Cubed lamb shoulder is best for this dish as it is slow cooked so tenderises beautifully and exudes enough fat to flavour the other ingredients. It is also much cheaper than buying a lean cut of lamb.

Heat the oil or butter in a large, heavy-bottomed saucepan and sauté the onion gently until golden and softened. Add the meat and brown it on all sides. Season and add the cinnamon. Cover the pan and continue to cook gently for 10 minutes. Add the tomato purée with a little water or the saffron in its water and add more water to cover the meat. Sprinkle over the parsley, throw in the tomatoes, pepper, pine nuts and raisins and bring to the boil. Then turn down to a simmer and cook slowly for 1½ hours until the meat is tender and the liquid thickened and reduced.

    Throw in the rice and just under 600ml/1 pint of water to cover, bring to a rolling boil, cover and simmer gently for 20 minutes when the rice should be tender. You may scatter over more parsley before you serve.

TURKISH AUBERGINE PILAV

SERVES 6

450g/1lb aubergines
sea salt
1 teacup of olive oil
450g/1lb long-grain rice
knob of butter
yoghurt (garlic and cumin optional)

This is a dish that I found in the wonderful Claudia Roden's classic book *Middle Eastern Food*, one of my bibles when I was at university. I have adapted it slightly by roasting the aubergine as it absorbs less oil that way and is therefore less oily in the finished dish. Claudia serves this dish cold with plain yoghurt. You may want to spice your yoghurt up a little with a minced clove of garlic and a teaspoon or two of cumin seeds put in a hot pan over the heat for a minute, then crushed once they've started to release their toasty, spicy aroma.

Preheat the oven to 200°C/400°F/Gas 6. Cut the aubergine into small cubes. You may put them in a colander and sprinkle them with salt at this stage, leaving them to drain for 30 minutes to an hour before pressing out as much of the juices as you can and rinsing them, before drying them on kitchen paper. I am not entirely convinced this is necessary, perhaps aubergines have less bitter juices than they used to, so I don't bother with this instruction, which always used to preface any aubergine recipe. I simply toss the aubergines in about half the oil, put them in a single layer on a baking tray and roast them in a hot oven until they've softened. Test them with a knife point after 15–20 minutes.

Wash and drain the rice well. Heat the rest of the oil in a pan, pour in the rice and stir to coat before adding two teacups of water. Bring it to the boil, reduce to a simmer, cover and cook for 15 minutes. Now bury the chunks of aubergine in the rice and add a couple of tablespoons of water and a large knob of butter. Cover the pan with a clean tea towel and press the lid on firmly so that the dish can steam gently for about 20 minutes. Serve cold with yoghurt, spiced up with garlic and cumin if you like, to accompany it.

BROAD BEAN PILAV

SERVES 6

3–4 tbsp olive oil or 75g/2½oz
    unsalted butter
1 large onion, finely chopped
450g/1lb fresh, podded broad beans
    or frozen out of season
sea salt and black pepper
2 cloves of garlic, finely minced
1 tsp coriander seeds, toasted in a
    hot pan for a minute, then crushed
    in a mortar
a handful each of fresh dill and flat-
    leaf parsley, chopped
450g/1lb long-grain rice, washed and
    drained

This is a delicious hot accompaniment to meat or it can be served cold like the aubergine pilav with yoghurt and salad.

Heat the oil or butter in a large, heavy-bottomed pan and sauté the onion over a medium heat until it has softened and turned translucent. Add the broad beans, seasoning, garlic, coriander seeds and half the fresh herbs, shute in the rice and turn to coat everything in oil. Cover the rice with water, bring to the boil, then cover with a lid and simmer gently for about 15–20 minutes or until the rice is tender.

Add the rest of the fresh herbs and serve right away if you are using this as a hot accompaniment, or cool and serve with the yoghurt as suggested in the recipe above for Turkish Aubergine Pilav.

Broad Bean Pilav

RISOTTO

Risotto is about texture almost more than taste, so that is the thing to work on. You want to end up with a bowl of almost chalky-textured rice with a bite and firmness to it that counterpoints the sloppiness of the soupy, thickened stock, the butter and the melted Parmesan, which when combined, give the dish a rich, satiny, creamy finish at the end of cooking. The quality of rice is of the essence, as you will see if you refer back to page 133.

Chicken risotto is as good a place to start for the risotto novitiate as any, but it is only a starting point; you will probably end up experimenting for the rest of your cooking life once you have the consistency to a tee. There is the creamy, astringent lemon risotto, which I make from Anna Del Conte's recipe; risotto primavera with the first small vegetables of early summer, tiny broad beans and peas, artichokes and asparagus; there are the lovely mushroom, porcini or chanterelles risottos which you can make with fresh or dried fungi; a classic seafood risotto made with tiny shells, clam and mussel, a breath of saffron and a stock made with the shells of the prawns that you then add to the risotto; the wicked black risotto nero made with baby squid or octopus and its fishy dark ink that stains the rice, the fish, your hands, your teeth; winter risottos of frazzled sage leaves and roasted red onion squash or pumpkin; fresh brown and white crabmeat risotto with coins of tiny courgette, or, if you grow your own, whole fingers of tiny courgettes, the flower still attached; a pure white risotto which I make with ivory leeks, flooding the rice with a spoonful of near-liquid Vacherin Mont d'Or when I serve it; chicken liver risotto with, perhaps, a few peas added to sweeten and give colour; fennel risotto, the bulb hearts sliced slim as a wafer and added with the onion, then splashed with Pernod or Ricard instead of white wine and finished with feathery fronds of fresh dill at the end and an extra-generous handful of Parmesan.

There are as many variations as you could think of, but it is important not just to hurl a cacophony of pick-and-mix flavours into the pan and expect something good to emerge. A few well chosen and well married ingredients, be they only fresh herbs like tarragon and parsley stirred into a basic risotto when you add the butter and Parmesan, make a perfect supper from the simplest and cheapest of ingredients.

LEMON RISOTTO

SERVES 4

55g/2oz unsalted butter
1 tbsp olive oil
2 shallots, very finely chopped
1 stick of celery, very finely chopped
285g/10oz risotto rice, such as
    Carnaroli, Vialone Nano or Arborio
    (see p. 133)
1 litre/1¾ pints homemade vegetable
    stock (see p. 380)
5 or 6 fresh sage leaves, chopped
a small sprig of fresh rosemary,
    chopped
1 organic lemon, zest and juice
1 organic egg yolk
4 tbsp freshly grated Parmesan
    cheese
4 tbsp double cream
salt and black pepper

Risotto slips easily into the category of food best described as soothing. Comforting as it is in the eating, it is the cooking, with the gradual, gentle application of hot stock and the repetitive, mesmeric stirring of the wooden spoon, that makes it a relaxing ritual which is also simplicity itself – IF you follow the rules. I had rather thought my leek and Vacherin Mont d'Or risotto was the pinnacle of my risotto making, but was overjoyed to be proved wrong when I encountered this recipe from the peerless Italian food writer Anna Del Conte. She, in turn, ascribes it to Giovanni Goria, of the Accademia Italiana della Cucina, via her friend Romana Bosco who runs a cookery school in Turin. Whenever I have empty fridge syndrome, this is one of the few dishes I can still conjure out of the ether for six, eight, ten, even twelve. A house without lemons, good olive oil, Parmesan cheese and risotto rice is an empty house indeed.

Heat half the butter, the oil, and the finely chopped shallots and celery in a heavy saucepan and cook until the soffritto of shallot and celery is softened, about 7 minutes. Mix in the rice and continue cooking and stirring until the rice is well coated in the fats and partly translucent.

While this is happening, heat the stock and keep it simmering all through the preparation of the dish. When the rice becomes shiny and partly translucent, after 2 or 3 minutes, pour in about 150ml/5fl oz of the stock. Stir very thoroughly and cook until the rice has absorbed most of the stock. Add another small ladleful of simmering stock and continue in this manner until the rice is ready. You may not need all the stock. Good-quality Italian rice takes about 20–22 minutes to cook.

Mix the herbs with the lemon zest, adding them to the risotto halfway through the cooking. In a small bowl, combine the egg yolk, the juice of half the lemon, the Parmesan cheese, cream and a very generous grinding of black pepper. Mix well with a fork.

When the risotto is al dente draw the pan off the heat and stir in the egg and cream mixture and the remaining butter. Cover the pan and leave to rest for 2 minutes or so off the heat. Check the seasoning, and that there is enough lemon juice, then give the risotto an energetic stir, transfer it to a heated dish or bowl and serve at once with more grated Parmesan in a bowl to pass round.

Anna suggests that this dish is also a good accompaniment to costolette alla milanese or chicken jointed, sautéed in butter and cooked in a casserole in the oven with 200ml/7fl oz of double cream poured over – an old Milanese recipe.

Be warned – RISOTTOS DO NOT STAND AROUND WELL, but I have found it absolutely fine to get the risotto to the halfway stage up to an hour before you want to serve it, then leave it with a ladleful of hot stock poured over it and a tight lid on the pan while you have your first course or drinks. Then carry on with another ladleful of stock, cooking the rice for its last 10 minutes. It is as good a first course as it is a main one if you are doing something more than a family lunch or supper.

CHICKEN RISOTTO

SERVES 4

a few tbsp extra virgin olive oil
1 medium onion, finely chopped
2 cloves of garlic, finely sliced
1 carrot, chopped into very small dice
1–2 sticks celery, strung with a potato peeler and chopped small
340g/12oz Carnaroli rice
a glass of white wine (optional) heated to simmering point
about 850ml/1½ pints well-flavoured chicken stock, heated to simmering point (see p. 80)
the remains of a chicken chopped into small pieces, white and brown meat; think no more than a slice per person
170g/6oz freshly grated Parmesan
a knob of butter
sea salt and black pepper
1 tbsp flat-leaf parsley or tarragon, chopped

This is a dish to make when you have the remains of a roasted or poached chicken. You can pick the flesh clean from the carcass before making your stock from the bones, a good stock being the base of the dish before you add your rice, vegetables, chicken, herbs, Parmesan and unsalted butter. If you insist on using stock cubes, there is no point in my trying to convert you, but I ALWAYS have a good chicken stock lurking in the fridge or freezer. Vegetarians can make their risotto with vegetable stock, the water they have cooked their vegetables in and simply omit the chicken and add a few extra vegetables, say a little sautéed leek or courgette to the basic mixture.

Heat 3–4 tablespoons of olive oil in a large, heavy-bottomed risotto or frying pan. Add all the chopped vegetables together and sauté them over a medium heat until they begin to soften and the onion takes on a translucent glow. Throw in the rice and stir, turning it to coat it all over in the oil, before throwing in the white wine and allowing it to fizz and splutter and begin to become absorbed by the grain. Never let risotto dry out and stick to the pan. You must constantly top it up with liquid, a ladle or two at a time, so that it isn't overwhelmed and submerged and so that you can stir the white stuff continuously while it releases its chalky-thick starch into the stock.

When the wine is almost absorbed, add a couple of ladles of stock and stir until that too has almost been absorbed, making sure that no grain escapes up the side of the pan. The rice will begin to swell and you must continue to add the stock, a ladle or two at a time, until the rice has swollen, lost its hard-textured edge but kept a degree of firmness that has bite when you test it. Stir frequently – the secret of all good risottos is the stirring as it releases the chalky starch from the grains of rice. This should take 20–22 minutes. At this point, add the bits of chicken and stir them in. Then add a couple of tablespoons of Parmesan, the butter (a large knob the size of a couple of walnuts), salt and pepper and the fresh herbs, a final ladle of stock and give the dish a last stir.

Remove from the heat and cover to allow all the flavours to marry and the butter and cheese to melt as the last of the stock is absorbed. After 5 minutes, serve the risotto straight from the pan, allowing everyone to help themselves to extra grated Parmesan from the bowl. A plain green or simple salad is the only accompaniment this dish needs.

RISOTTO PRIMAVERA

SERVES 4

4 leaf artichokes, put in cold water
   with the juice of a lemon to
   acidulate and stop them from
   turning black
a bundle of asparagus, the bottom of
   the stems snapped off where they
   are woody, then the bottom half of
   each stem peeled with a potato
   peeler
3–4 tbsp extra virgin olive oil
1 small onion finely chopped
340g/12oz Carnaroli rice
a glass of white wine heated to
   simmering point (optional)
about 850ml/1½ pints vegetable
   (see p. 380) or chicken stock
   (see p. 80) at simmering point
110g/4oz peas, shelled weight
   (frozen will do when they are out
   of season)
110g/4oz broad beans, shelled
   weight, as small as you can find
a knob of butter the size of a couple
   of walnuts
sea salt and black pepper
170g/6oz freshly grated Parmesan
1 tbsp each chopped mint, chervil
   and parsley (optional, or just use
   one or two herbs)

In late spring or early summer, this risotto, verdant with green vegetables, is one of the greats. You may add just the asparagus and perhaps some rosy pink flecks of frazzled bacon, or any combination of the vegetables mentioned, but the ultimate is a handful of all of them and no meat. I think Risotto Primavera is almost better made with the cooking water from the peas, asparagus, beans and artichokes than with the additional flavour of the chicken stock, but see how you feel. The quantities of vegetables are very much guidelines, as you may have only a couple of artichoke hearts or be able to afford only a few spears of asparagus at the beginning of the season when it is most expensive.

Bring a pan full of water to a rolling boil and throw in the acidulated artichokes. Depending on their size they will take 20–30 minutes to cook, but the best test is to try to pull a leaf away from the stem. If it comes away easily the artichoke is cooked. Steam the asparagus while the artichokes are cooking – the water beneath them will also contribute to the stock. When the spears are tender, remove from the steamer and chop into chunks, the tips twice the length of the stems.

Heat the oil in a large, heavy-based pan and add the finely chopped onion, stirring until it begins to soften and turn translucent. Pour in the rice and turn it in the oil until it is well coated all over, then add the hot white wine and let it bubble away until it is nearly all absorbed. Then start adding the vegetable stock, a little at a time, as described in the preceding recipe for chicken risotto. Keep adding ladles of hot stock as the rice begins to absorb it and stirring to release the chalky starch that gives the dish its characteristic creamy texture.

Meanwhile, cook the peas and broad beans separately in a little water just to cover them until tender. The peas will take about 5 minutes from when you bring them to the boil; the broad beans you can throw into boiling water and they will only take 2 minutes. Drain both, reserving the water for the vegetable stock but leaving a little in the bottom of each pan so the vegetables don't dry out. Remove the leaves from the artichokes so that all that you have left is the central soft leaves and the choke and the stem. Remove the central leaves in one go and then chop off the stem. Scoop or scrape out the woolly choke and then you have the best bit left, the heart, which you can cut into small pieces. This is a very easy process once you know what to do!

When the rice is cooked, gently fold in the artichoke, asparagus, peas and beans and add the butter, seasoning and a good handful of Parmesan. Add one more ladle of the vegetable stock, stir gently to amalgamate and leave covered off the heat for five minutes. Remove the lid, scatter over the herbs and serve, with a bowl of the rest of the grated Parmesan to hand round.

PAELLA

This is not a dish to stir like a risotto, you may shake the pan to stop it sticking once or twice, but that is all you need to do. It should not be sloppy or saucy when finished; the rice in a paella should glisten like a jewel but not appear greasy or wet. Calasparra is a short-grain rice that absorbs liquid and different flavours brilliantly without losing its texture. Paellas, like risottos, change with the seasons. In the spring they come decked out with new season's green vegetables – asparagus, green beans, broad beans, baby courgettes and peas or mangetout snapped in half. There is usually pig somewhere in a paella, be it gammon, bacon, chorizo or pork, but if you're a veggie just leave it out and add mushrooms for meatiness. You don't need a paella pan to cook a paella in. A shallow casserole or heavy-bottomed frying pan will do.

SERVES 4

4 tbsp olive oil
1 medium onion, finely chopped
1 carrot, diced
170g/6oz streaky bacon, snipped into small strips
2 cloves of garlic, finely chopped
4 tbsp flat-leaf parsley
225g/8oz Calasparra rice
a pinch of saffron stamens (optional)
850ml/1½ pints hot chicken stock (see p. 80)
150ml/5fl oz dry white wine, heated to simmering point
200g/7oz asparagus, the woody bottoms trimmed, the spears peeled with a potato peeler and chopped, the tips longer than the spears
a handful of green beans, chopped into short lengths
1 courgette, thinly sliced
2 tomatoes, skinned, seeded and chopped
a handful of mangetout, strung and snapped in half, or a handful of peas, fresh or frozen

SPRING VEGETABLE PAELLA

If your pockets aren't deep enough for a bundle of asparagus, just add extra of the vegetables that you're using, with perhaps some broad beans later in the season.

Heat the olive oil in a paella pan or heavy frying pan and fry the onion gently with the carrot and bacon. When it has begun to soften, after 10 minutes or so, add the garlic and cook for another 5 minutes. Add half the parsley and the rice and stir it briefly to coat it in oil.

Meanwhile infuse the saffron, if using, in the stock for 10 minutes. Pour the heated wine into the hot stock and add one-third of the liquid to the pan. Bring to a simmer and throw in the asparagus. The rice will take 20–25 minutes to cook from the moment you add the first of the stock to it. When it has almost been absorbed, add another third of the stock and wine with the beans, courgettes and tomato. Stir them in briefly, wait until most of the stock has been absorbed and add the last third with the mangetout or peas.

When the paella is done, cover the pan and let it stand off the heat for 5 minutes before adding the rest of the parsley.

PAELLA WITH MONKFISH AND SAFFRON

SERVES 4

7 tbsp olive oil
450g/1lb monkfish tails, removed
from their cartilaginous bone and
cut into 2–3cm/1in cubes
2 large onions finely chopped
2 green pepper, halved, seeded and
finely chopped
6 cloves of garlic, finely chopped
½ tsp fennel seeds
850ml/1½ pints hot fish stock
a good pinch of saffron stamens
225g/8oz Calasparra rice
90ml/3fl oz white wine or fino sherry
1 small bunch flat-leaf parsley, finely
chopped
½ tsp sweet smoked Spanish paprika
sea salt and black pepper
225g/8oz piquillo peppers, torn in
strips (Navarrico and Anko do jars
of them and the ones cooked over
beech wood are particularly good)
1 lemon, cut into wedges

This is a paella recipe from the Sams of the wonderful Moro restaurant in London. They advise that clams or prawns can be added. I would add, so can mussels, 450g/1lb/1 pint of them. I think this is a great way to use tails of monk, which exude copious amounts of fishy liquor to help flavour the rice.

Heat 2 tablespoons of the oil in a paella or frying pan over a medium heat. Add the monkfish and stir-fry until fractionally underdone, a couple of minutes. Pour the monkfish and its juices into a bowl. Wipe the pan clean with kitchen paper and put it back on the heat. Add the rest of the oil, heat it, then add the onions and peppers. Cook for 15–20 minutes, stirring occasionally. Turn the heat down and add the chopped garlic and fennel seeds. Cook for a further 10 minutes or until the mixture is sweet and has some colour. Meanwhile, bring the stock to the boil and infuse the saffron in it off the heat. Add the rice to the pan and stir for a minute to coat with the vegetables and oil. (The paella can be prepared in advance up to this point; there is a further 20 minutes of cooking time.)

Turn the heat up to high and add the white wine or sherry to the pan, followed by the stock. Now add half the parsley and the paprika and season with salt and pepper. Do not stir from this point. Simmer for 10 minutes or until there is just a little liquid above the rice. Spread the monkfish out evenly over the rice with its juices. Push the monkfish under the stock. Shake the pan to prevent sticking and turn the heat down to low. Cook for 5 more minutes or until there is just a little liquid left at the bottom of the rice. Turn off the heat and cover the pan tightly with foil. Let the rice sit for 5 minutes before serving. Decorate with strips of piquillo peppers, the rest of the chopped parsley and the lemon. Serve with a salad.

PAELLA WITH PORK, CHORIZO AND SPINACH

SERVES 4

7 tbsp olive oil
340g/12oz pork fillet, halved
lengthways and sliced into rough
7mm/¼in strips
sea salt and black pepper
110g/4oz mild chorizo, cut into small
pieces
2 large onions finely chopped
1 large green pepper, halved, seeded
and finely chopped
4 cloves of garlic, finely chopped
225g/8oz calasparra rice
1 tsp smoked Spanish paprika
4 piquillo peppers
850ml/1½ pints chicken stock, hot
500g/1lb 2oz spinach, washed and
drained
1 lemon, cut into wedges

This is my version of a lovely paella in Sam and Sam Clark's *Moro The Cookbook*. They describe it as complex and comforting. It is also straightforward to prepare and inexpensive.

Heat the olive oil over a high heat in a 30–40cm/12–16in paella pan or frying pan, then stir-fry the pork strips for a few seconds so that they are still undercooked. Season with salt and pepper. Remove from the pan with a slotted spoon to a plate. Lower the heat and fry the chorizo for a minute. Add the onion and green pepper and cook for 20 minutes. Add the garlic and cook for a further 5 minutes. At this point the mixture should have caramelised and taste sweet. Stir the rice into the pan to coat for a minute. (Up to this point you can prepare everything in advance if you wish. The next stage will take 20 minutes or so.)

Season the rice with salt and pepper, add the paprika and peppers followed by the hot stock. Simmer for 15 minutes or until there is just a thin layer of liquid around the rice. Meanwhile, wilt the spinach briefly in a pan, drain and remove it. Scatter the pork over the rice followed by the spinach and with the back of the spoon gently push them partly into the oily liquid at the bottom of the pan. Turn off the heat, cover the paella tightly with foil and let it sit for 5 minutes. Serve with lemon and a tomato salad.

BURGHUL, OR CRACKED WHEAT

Perfect student fodder, cracked wheat is wonderful with stews instead of rice, with skewers of pork, lamb kebabs, or minced, spiced lamb; it's great for picnics, good in a pilav or just plain wonderful the Lebanese way in a tabbouleh. Sharpened with lemon juice, green and bursting with parsley and mint, the wheat has a beautifully earthy flavour and texture and it's up to you how cheaply or richly you decorate it!

Burghul is the Arabic word for cracked wheat. The wheat has been boiled, dried and ground. When you are cooking it like rice as a pilav, use coarse- or medium-ground bulghur. You will need about one and a half times the amount of stock or water to bulghur to cook it, so 500g of burghul needs about 1 litre of liquid.

TABBOULEH

You may add chopped piquillo peppers, coriander instead of parsley if you prefer, a handful of pitted black olives or some crumbled feta, but this is a plain, good, everyday tabbouleh.

SERVES 6

225g/8oz burghul
a bunch of spring onions, finely
    chopped or a small red onion,
    finely chopped
sea salt and black pepper
a bunch of flat-leaf parsley, chopped
a bunch fresh mint leaves, chopped
6 tomatoes, skinned, seeded and
    chopped
half a cucumber, peeled, seeded, cut
    into small dice, salted and drained
    for 30 minutes in a colander
6 tbsp extra virgin olive oil
6 tbsp lemon juice

Soak the burghul in cold water to cover in a large bowl for 30 minutes or so, during which time it will expand and absorb a lot of the water. Drain it and squeeze out as much water as you can with your hands. Dry the burghul on a tea towel before mixing it with the chopped onion with your hands so the onion juice flavours the burghul. Season and add the parsley, mint, tomatoes and cucumber, then dress the dish with olive oil and lemon juice. You want a really lemony flavour, much more lemon in proportion to the olive oil than you would ever dream of in a salad dressing.

Traditionally, tabbouleh is served in a mound on a huge plate lined with vine leaves, lettuce leaves or cabbage leaves. You may like to add half a teaspoon each of cinnamon and allspice to the lemon juice before you dress the tabbouleh and a clove of garlic crushed with a little salt in a mortar. Then stir in the olive oil.

BURGHUL PILAV

SERVES 6

1 litre/1¾ pints stock or water
450g/1lb coarse burghul
sea salt and black pepper
85g/3oz blanched almonds
4–5 tbsp light olive oil
85g/3oz pine nuts
55g/2oz raisins, soaked in warm
    water for 20 minutes or so
a bunch of fresh coriander, washed
    and chopped
1½ tsp cumin seeds, roasted in a
    small frying pan for a minute then
    ground in a mortar (optional)

This is a great and simple accompaniment to chicken, guinea fowl, pigeon or turkey. It's very easy to make and as healthy for the student purse as for the constitution!

Bring the stock or water to the boil in a large, heavy-bottomed pan, then throw in the cracked wheat and stir. Cover, reduce the heat to very low and continue to cook for 10 minutes or until all the liquid has been absorbed. The cracked wheat should be tender and not have a hard bite to it when it is cooked. Season.

Fry the almonds in the olive oil, turning them until they turn golden brown. Add the pine nuts and stir until they are golden. Stir the nuts, drained raisins, coriander and the cumin, if you are using it, into the bulghur and heat through gently.

BAKED KIBBEH WITH ONION AND PINE NUT TOPPING

SERVES 6–12

110g/4oz fine-ground bulghur
1 medium onion, quartered
500g/1lb 2oz lean lamb
½ tsp salt
1 tsp cinnamon
2 tbsp vegetable oil

TOPPING
500g/1 lb 2oz onions, sliced
3 tbsp extra virgin olive oil
55g/2oz pine nuts
salt and pepper
½ tsp ground cinnamon
pinch of ground allspice
½–1 tbsp pomegranate molasses

This is a mezze dish from the Lebanon, one of several you could hand out with drinks, or you could eat it as a main course. Claudia Roden first came across it when she visited Zahle, the world capital of the Arab mezze.

Preheat the oven to 190°C/375°F/Gas 5. Rinse the bulghur for the kibbeh in a fine sieve under cold running water and drain well. Purée the onion in a food processor. Add the lamb, salt, pepper and cinnamon and blend to a paste. Add the bulghur and blend to a smooth, soft paste. With your hand, press the paste in the bottom of an oiled, round, shallow baking dish, about 10cm/4in in diameter. Flatten the top and rub with the oil. With a pointed knife, cut into 6 wedges through the centre, and run the knife round the edges of the dish. Bake for 30 minutes until browned.

For the topping, fry the onion in olive oil until golden brown. Add the pine nuts and stir until lightly coloured. Add salt and pepper, cinnamon and allspice and, if you like a slightly sweet and sour flavour, the pomegranate molasses. Cook for a minute or so. Serve the kibbeh hot or cold with the topping.

COUSCOUS

The national dish of the North African countries of Morocco, Tunisia and Algeria, couscous is a type of semolina made from wheat grain. It is served with bubbling stews of meat, game, vegetables or fish, sometimes sweetened with dried fruits, sometimes spiced with harissa, and there are as many ways to cook couscous as there are cooks to cook it. The whole idea of couscous is to cook it wrapped in muslin in a perforated pan or steamer above a pan of stew, whose bubbling vapours will rise and penetrate the swelling grain above with its flavour.

There is the easy way to cook couscous and the traditional way, no less easy, just longer. If you have bought the pre-cooked variety, this is all you need to do. Put 500g/1lb 2oz medium-ground couscous in a large bowl. Add 600ml/1 pint warm water and a little salt and stir so that the water is absorbed evenly. After 10 minutes or so the grain will have begun to soften and will have swollen a little. Add 4 tablespoons of light olive oil or vegetable oil and work the grain with your fingers to let air into it and stop it forming any lumps. You can break down the small lumps between your fingers quickly and gently. Now put the grain into a piece of muslin, tie it loosely and place it inside a steamer to steam it with the lid off. As soon as the steam passes up through the grain it is ready. Alternatively, you can put the grain in an earthenware pot in the oven under foil and heat it through until it is hot and steaming. Break up the lumps before serving. If you want saffron-scented couscous, add a good pinch of saffron stamens to the water you soak the couscous in.

Purists may tell you that the grain has to be steamed twice, but not the experts who manufacture it. The great Claudia Roden quotes a manufacturer who gave her this advice when she was on a gastronomic tour of Tunisia, 'Once the couscous has absorbed an equal volume of water, all you need really is to heat up the grain, in a saucepan, oven or microwave, and to break up any lumps. If people steam it, it is because they are used to doing that. It is a ritual – part of the culture.' So make life easy for yourself!

HARISSA

85g/3oz Navarrico piquillo peppers from Brindisa or 1 red pepper
225g/8oz red chillies, sliced in half, the seeds removed. Please do this wearing rubber gloves and never rub your eyes afterwards
3 tsp cumin seeds, roasted for 30 seconds to 1 minute in a small pan, then coarsely crushed in a mortar
4 cloves of garlic
1 tbsp tomato purée
1 dsrtsp red wine vinegar
2 tsp sweet smoked Spanish paprika
6 tbsp extra virgin olive oil
sea salt and black pepper

This keeps for a couple of weeks in the fridge and is well worth making as you can add it to so many dishes. It is good with chicken, with plain baked fish or steaming bowls of mussels, even to spice up fried eggs or late night Welsh Rarebit. I have adapted the recipe from Sam and Sam Clark's lovely book, *Moro*.

If you're not using piquillo peppers you'll need to start by cooking and peeling the red pepper. Place the pepper in a hot oven on a baking sheet, turning it every 10 minutes until it is softened all over, or place under a hot grill and char each side until it is softened. Put in a bowl covered with clingfilm while it cools, so it will be easy to peel, core and seed.

Chop the chillies and put them in the food processor, blending them with a little salt and half the spices with the garlic cloves until smooth. Then add the peppers and blend until really smooth. Remove to a bowl and add the remaining ingredients. Taste for seasoning; you may need more salt. If you are keeping the harissa in the fridge, cover it with a thin layer of olive oil to seal it from the air.

MOROCCAN COUSCOUS

SERVES 6–8

1kg/2¼lb stewing lamb like scrag, on the bone

2 medium onions, chopped

55g/2oz chickpeas soaked in cold water overnight, but do extra and make a hummus at the same time or keep the rest for a chickpea and tomato soup

2 turnips, quartered

2 large carrots, cut into slices about as thick as a £1 coin

2–3 tbsp olive oil

sea salt and black pepper

½ tsp ground ginger

a pinch saffron stamens soaked in a little warm water for 20 minutes

450g/1lb couscous

4 tbsp light olive oil or vegetable oil

a handful of raisins soaked in warm water for 20 minutes

4 smallish courgettes, sliced

110g/4oz frozen or fresh broad beans or green beans strung and cut in half

110g/4oz fresh or frozen peas instead of or as well as the broad or green beans

4 tomatoes, skinned seeded and quartered

a bunch of flat-leaf parsley or half parsley, half coriander

a little cayenne and paprika or a homemade harissa (see p. 150)
55g/2oz unsalted butter

This is a basic couscous to which you may add or subtract seasonal vegetables, or omit the meat altogether. The most famous vegetarian couscous is Couscous with Seven Vegetables from Fez, where the number seven is said to be lucky. Chickpeas, onions, tomatoes, carrots, turnips, courgettes and pumpkin are cooked in the broth under the couscous, the grain is moistened with the broth, the whole served with homemade harissa. Cheap, delicious, spiced up and nourishing. However, stewing lamb is a cheap cut so if you're not a veggie, try this simple, lovely Moroccan staple.

Put the scrag lamb chops in a heavy-bottomed casserole with the onions, chickpeas, turnips and carrots and cover with cold water. Pour over the oil and season with the salt, pepper, ginger and saffron. Bring slowly to the boil, then simmer gently for an hour and a half with the lid on. Ten minutes before the end of cooking time, cover the couscous with 600ml/1 pint of warm water and a little salt and allow it to swell and soften for 10 minutes or so. Then add the light olive oil and work the grain with your fingers to let air into it and rid it of lumps. Add the raisins and other vegetables to the stew with the tomatoes and parsley and put a large sieve over the stew into which you can sit the couscous in its muslin. Simmer for 30 minutes.

Remove a ladleful of the broth into a bowl and stir in cayenne and paprika to taste, a scant half teaspoon of cayenne for mild heat, a teaspoon for something more intense, and hand it round for people to ladle over their couscous on the plate. Or hand round a bowl of harissa instead. In both cases, mound the couscous up high on a large, warmed dish; earthenware is best. Add the butter and fork it into the grain, then arrange the meat and vegetables decoratively on top and pour the broth without the chilli over it.

POLENTA

Fashion never does food any favours. As soon as the food fashionistas discovered polenta, the most delectable of golden grains, its number was up – it was going to become ubiquitous first, passé second. I refuse to be swayed by that sort of food faddism. Polenta is a wonderful dish, a superb vehicle for strong flavours from salty blue cheese and Parmesan to casseroles, stews and braises of game with their dark, intense gravies and sauces. I am something of a purist on the subject though. The instant, quick-cook polentas are not very good. Their somewhat acid flavour and their texture are both wanting. There really is no substitute for stirring; for time, a little trouble and buying the best-tasting polenta you can. There is both yellow and white polenta, from the meal from yellow and white corn, but the yellow is more common. Il Saraceno is very good. Coarse-grained yellow cornmeal is, to my mind, the most satisfying in terms of its robust texture and flavour. If you are really not prepared to stir for 40 minutes or so, I am giving you an oven-cooked version of polenta too, but the best is the one that needs the wooden spoon.

STIRRED POLENTA

SERVES 4

1.5 litres/3 pints water
2 tsp salt
255g/9oz coarse-grain yellow polenta

Bring the water to the boil in a large, heavy-bottomed pot. Throw in the salt, then add the polenta in a thin stream through the nearly closed fist of one hand, stirring with a whisk and keeping the water boiling. Now start stirring the polenta over a medium heat with a long-handled spoon – the pot needs to be large because the grain will splutter like a Vesuvial eruption to begin with. Carry on cooking and stirring for 10 minutes. For the remaining 30 minutes, stir every minute or so. The polenta is cooked when it forms a single mass that pulls cleanly away from the sides of the pan

When it is ready, plop it into a large bowl moistened with a little water to rest for a few minutes. Now turn the bowl over onto a large serving plate or wooden board and serve it at once. If you are going to cool the polenta and firm it up so that you can slice it and then fry, bake or griddle it, do not pour it into a bowl. Spread it on a board about 7.5cm/3in thick. This stage should be achieved several hours before you want to use it. You may refrigerate it in a block in foil or clingfilm for a few days.

HOW TO SERVE POLENTA

When the polenta is cooked, piping hot and soft, you may stir in some butter and grated Parmesan cheese and serve it just as it is. Little lumps of Gorgonzola stirred and mashed into the polenta are also delicious.

Both these ways of serving polenta are good with a branch of roasted vine tomatoes added to the top of the mound of polenta in each bowl.

Stewed game birds, pigeon, quail, rabbit and hare are also great with polenta. Plop the meat on top of the puddle of polenta and ladle over a generous amount of the braising liquid.

Once it has cooled, polenta can be cut into wedges and fried like fried bread crisply in olive oil and served with anything from salad to calves' liver and onion.

Polenta makes a great starter with a little ragout of mixed fungi and their winey, garlicky juices poured over it in shallow bowls.

OVEN-BAKED POLENTA

SERVES 6

340g/12oz coarse yellow polenta
2 tsp salt

Preheat the oven to 190°C/375°F/Gas 5. Bring 2 litres/3½ pints of water to simmering point. Add the salt, then the coarse yellow polenta in a very thin stream through your almost closed fist, whisking while you do. Stir constantly for 5 minutes with a long-handled wooden spoon while the golden grain boils and bubbles and coughs and splutters in the pot. Now pour the polenta into a well-greased ovenproof dish and cover with buttered foil. Cook for an hour.

PASTA

Please refer back to the lowdown on pasta on page 62 until the rules are ingrained in your brain. That way you will never have trouble cooking pasta or marrying it with its sauce. It is much quicker to re-read the lowdown than to have to start again because you've got a pan of starchy, slimy pasta that's horribly over-cooked and you have no idea why.

PASTA PUTTANESCA

Tart's or whore's pasta to the Italians because it is clearly made of hot stuff, this is one of the great store cupboard dishes I can always cook if people turn up unexpectedly. Tinned tomatoes, good olives and anchovies, salted or brined capers, dried chillies or cayenne, onions, garlic and spaghetti; make sure you never run out of any of them as they are wonderful standbys and no good kitchen should be without them!

SERVES 4

3–4 tbsp olive oil
1 medium onion, chopped fine
2 cloves of garlic, finely chopped
3–4 anchovies in olive oil, or salted anchovies, well rinsed under the cold tap and finely chopped
1 hot dried chilli, chopped fine with its seeds, or cayenne to taste
2 x 400g/14oz tins organic plum tomatoes
450g/1lb spaghetti
1 heaped tbsp capers
16–20 good black olives, or half green, half black olives, pitted and halved
a bunch of fresh basil (optional)
a knob of unsalted butter

Bring a large pan of water to the boil. Meanwhile, heat the olive oil in a large, heavy-bottomed frying pan and throw in the chopped onion. Cook over a medium heat until it is beginning to soften, then add the finely chopped garlic, the chopped anchovies and the chopped chilli. The anchovies will begin to melt into the oil. Let the garlic begin to soften and turn pale gold, no more, then add the tinned tomatoes, chopping them down into the sauce with a knife and bringing them up to a bubble. Simmer for 10–15 minutes while you cook the pasta.

Meanwhile, put the brined or salted capers on a slotted spoon and run the cold tap over them to rid them of their saltiness. Throw the olives into the pan when the sauce has reduced, thickened and become quite jammy, then add the capers and heat them through. Remove the pan from the heat. Tear the basil, which is optional, and stir it into the sauce. Check the seasoning – you have chilli, salt anchovy and caper, so may need no more. Drain the pasta and add a knob of unsalted butter. Pour the sauce over the hot pasta in the pan or bowl, toss well and serve immediately in warmed bowls.

PESTO SAUCE

SERVES 6

100g/3½oz fresh basil leaves
8 tbsp best extra virgin olive oil
3 tbsp pine nuts
2 cloves of garlic, finely chopped
scant 55g/2oz freshly grated
   Parmesan cheese
2 tbsp freshly grated Pecorino Sardo
   cheese
45g/1½oz softened butter
whatever pasta you like
sea salt and black pepper to taste

Pesto has become ubiquitous. It has become over-used and abused. People call things that bear no approximation to a real pesto sauce pesto, even if they've never seen fresh basil, pine nuts or Parmesan. The Sicilians have their own version of pesto which the great Italian food writer Marcella Hazan alerted me to. It contains almonds, Pecorino, mint leaves, chilli pepper and tomatoes, so is hot and ripe rather than the cool, green classic we've come to know through inferior bottled versions and dull hothouse basil. Ligurian basil may be hard to come by here, but at least use a really good, fruity olive oil, fresh, oily pine nuts and the right cheese, half Parmesan, half Pecorino Sardo.

Traditionally, the Genoese serve their pesto with waxy new potatoes and green beans and even if you think potatoes and pasta is a strange, carbohydrate-charged mix, I urge you to at least try the real thing in spring with some Jersey Royal potatoes coated in pesto and beans. It is quite simply divine. Pesto is perfect with trofie, penne, tagliatelle, pappardelle, spaghettini, potato gnocchi. It can be used with lasagne and béchamel sauce or with crespelli, Italian pancakes with béchamel sauce and fresh mozzarella. Please refer to the pasta lowdown on page 62 if you are a pasta/pasta sauce novice.

Wash and dry the basil leaves in a tea towel, then put them in a food processor with the olive oil, pine nuts, chopped garlic and salt and process until you have a creamy purée. Transfer to a bowl and stir in the two cheeses, then carefully mix in the softened butter.

When your pasta is cooked, drain it, keeping back a couple of tablespoons of the cooking water, which you should stir into the pesto sauce. Then tip the sauce over the pasta in the warm bowl or pan you are going to serve it and toss together really thoroughly. Add salt and pepper to taste and pass round an extra bowl of Parmesan and Pecorino.

PASTA WITH CHICKEN LIVER SAUCE

SERVES 4

450g/1lb spaghetti, tagliatelle or
  pappardelle
1 shallot or small onion, finely
  chopped
1 tbsp olive oil
30g/1oz unsalted butter
1 small clove of garlic, finely minced
2 rashers of organic smoked back
  bacon or 2 slices Prosciutto
  (optional)
6 sage leaves or the same of basil
225g/8oz frozen petits pois
340g/12oz or so fresh chicken livers,
  any green patches, fatty bits or
  tubes carefully removed, then the
  livers soaked in milk for 20
  minutes in a small bowl
sea salt and black pepper
4 tbsp white wine or vermouth
a knob of unsalted butter
freshly grated Parmesan

Chicken livers are one of my absolutely favourite foods, whether served fried in butter until dark crusted with a full-fry of a breakfast; made into a smooth, suave pâté or parfait, all rosy middled and velvety; packed tightly into a spiced pilav or turned with crisp sage and peas into pasta. I cannot understand offal haters. It is perfectly understandable to blench at liver that has been cooked to a dark grey, crumby resistance that almost chokes you as you chew, but the soft pink nuggets of chicken liver in this dish or delicate, pink-fleshed slices of calves' liver should convert the unconvertible. Then it's time to be brave and try sweetbreads, brains, kidneys and the rest.

Always buy organic chicken livers. Any residue from any chemicals or drugs used in the rearing of animals collects in the organs; and the flavour of organic livers really IS better. This is an inexpensive dish even with organic livers. See page 64 for the pasta and pasta sauce golden rules if you are not a pasta expert!

Put a large pan of water on to come to the boil before adding your pasta.

Meanwhile, put the shallot or onion in a heavy-bottomed frying pan with the olive oil and butter and sauté over a medium heat until it begins to soften. Add the minced garlic and cook it for a couple of minutes; you don't want it to go brown. Then add the bacon or prosciutto cut or torn into strips and the sage or basil leaves. In another small pan, boil some water, throw in the peas and boil them for a couple of minutes. Drain. Cook the bacon or prosciutto for a minute before adding the chicken livers, which you have patted dry and cut in half. Season with salt and pepper and turn the livers as each side begins to colour and lose its raw look. When they are coloured all over, add the wine or vermouth and allow it to bubble before adding the peas. Check the livers, they MUST stay pink in the middle. The dish is completely cooked once they are rosy middled without looking raw inside, about 5 minutes after the wine has been introduced to the sauce. Check the seasoning.

Turn the pan out over the drained, cooked pasta to which you've added a lump of butter and toss well to coat it all in the sauce. Serve immediately with a bowl of freshly grated Parmesan on the side.

SPAGHETTI AIO E OIO

SERVES 4

450g/1lb spaghetti or spaghettini
6–8 tbsp best extra virgin olive oil
a large clove of garlic, very finely
    minced
red chilli, chopped and seeded, to
    taste. Bird's eye chillies are very
    hot. Try a slightly larger chilli and
    DON'T rub your eyes or any other
    sensitive bit of your anatomy once
    you've chopped it!
2 tbsp flat-leaf parsley, chopped

Spaghetti or the tinier spaghettini is the right pasta for this cheapest and most deliciously simple of sauces. Just don't stint on the best olive oil and good pasta. Even a dish such as this can only be as good as its raw ingredients and you need a peppery, grassy, fruity olive oil to come through the hit of chilli and garlic. Always use flat-leaf parsley for this dish.

Put the pasta in a large pan of salted, boiling water and while it is cooking, make the sauce. (Make sure you have salted the pan of water as salt does not dissolve well in olive oil, so you don't want to be adding extra salt when you sauce your spaghetti.)

Put the olive oil, garlic and chopped chilli in a small pan over a low heat and cook gently until the garlic turns a pale gold but does not brown. When the pasta is cooked and drained, toss it immediately with the sauce, making sure it is all coated evenly. Add the chopped parsley and serve. What could be easier?

BROCCOLI, ANCHOVY AND CHILLI SAUCE

SERVES 6

675g/1½ lb broccoli
8 tbsp extra virgin olive oil
1 whole peeled clove of garlic
6 anchovy fillets chopped small
fresh chilli, chopped and seeded to
    taste. Bird's eye are too hot for
    me, I use one larger, less fiery
    chilli
sea salt and black pepper, depending
    on the heat and the salt of the
    sauce
6 tbsp freshly grated Parmesan
    cheese
675g/1½lb fusilli or orecchiette

Quick, easy, cheap, healthy and delicious, this simple pasta sauce is perfect fodder whether you're a student or just plain hungry and in need of a good dinner. Refer to the pasta rules on page 64.

Bring the water up to the boil in a large pan. Meanwhile, separate the broccoli florets from the stalks, then peel the stalks and chop them into thick discs. Steam the two together until al dente, about 7 minutes, then cut the florets into smaller, bite-sized pieces.

Heat the olive oil gently in a heavy-bottomed frying pan with the garlic clove. Add the anchovies and mash them down into the oil until they turn to paste. Throw in the broccoli and the sliced chilli and stir to coat with olive oil. As soon as the chilli is softened, about 5 minutes, remove the garlic clove, which is only there to flavour the oil, season and pour the contents of the pan over your cooked, drained pasta. Add the cheese and toss everything together well. Serve immediately.

LASAGNE AL FORNO

SERVES 8

2–3 tbsp olive oil
a knob of butter
2 large onions, finely chopped
3 sticks celery, chopped
3 carrots, finely diced
3 or 4 cloves of garlic, finely chopped
1kg/2¼lb ground beef chuck, or
    similar, with plenty of fat, you can
    add one-third ground pork to the
    beef if you wish
salt and fresh black pepper
2 bay leaves
240ml/8fl oz milk
about ¼ tsp nutmeg
240ml/8fl oz white wine
2 x 400g/14oz tin of plum tomatoes
1.2 litre/2 pints of béchamel, made
    with a bay leaf and nutmeg
    (see p. 70)
2 boxes dried lasagne, you will
    probably need 1½ boxes, of the sort
    that needs no precooking
freshly grated Parmesan cheese

When it is made with the best ingredients, with a ragù simmered for hours until its oily, tomatoey juices part company with the exquisite winey, milky meat and vegetables; when the béchamel is scented with bay and nutmeg and is creamy, smooth, velvety, and the dish is assembled and gratinéed with handfuls of fresh Parmesan, this is one of the great dishes of the world and the greatest of comfort foods. You may make the ragù sauce a day or two in advance, even freeze it, then all you have to do is perfect your béchamel on the day. Please choose a good quality lasagne to make the dish with, not the cardboardy kind that will ruin your perfect sauce. This is a dish for all ages to make and eat and for all occasions.

Warm the oil and butter in a heavy cast-iron pot, add the onion, and sauté gently until softened and translucent. Add the celery, carrots and garlic, cook for another couple of minutes, stirring to coat well. Add the ground beef and a large pinch of salt, and grind over some pepper. Stir until the beef has lost its raw pink look. Add the bay leaves and milk, and simmer gently for about 10 minutes, until the meat has absorbed most of the milk. Add the nutmeg, then the wine and let it simmer until it has nearly evaporated. Add the cut-up tomatoes with their juice and stir thoroughly. Cook at a lazy simmer, uncovered and with just an intermittent bubble breaking through the surface, for 3 hours or more. Stir from time to time. The fat will eventually separate from the sauce, but the sauce will not be dry. Taste and check the seasoning.

Preheat the oven to 200°C/400°F/Gas 6. Pour just enough béchamel to cover the base of your greased baking dish. Add a layer of lasagne, followed by a layer of the ragù, a layer of béchamel, and a good handful of Parmesan. Continue with two or three more layers, until your sauces are both used up, add a final sprinkling of Parmesan, and bake in the oven for about 30 minutes, The dish should be bubbling all over, and the knife should slip easily through the layers of lasagne. The ragù is also great with spaghetti.

LASAGNE DI MAGRO

SERVES 6

3 medium courgettes, chopped
2 medium carrots, chopped
4 fennel bulbs (optional)
120ml/4fl oz best olive oil
2 medium onions, finely sliced
225g/8oz shelled or frozen peas
salt and fresh black pepper
850ml/1½ pints béchamel sauce
    (see p. 70)
1 box dried lasagne that needs no
    precooking
170g/6oz organic chestnut
    mushrooms, sliced
310g/11oz freshly grated Parmesan
8 tomatoes, skinned and seeded
4 packets of buffalo mozzarella

A deluxe vegetarian lasagne for which you can alter the combination of vegetables according to season and taste.

Preheat the oven to 200°C/400°F/Gas 6. If you are using fennel, remove the outer tough layers, quarter the bulbs, then steam until almost tender. Heat the olive oil in a heavy-bottomed pan, add the onions, and a bit of salt to release the juices. Fry gently until softened and translucent, then add the courgettes, carrots and peas. Season with salt and pepper. Cook until the carrots are al dente, but unbrowned, about 10 minutes.

Pour just enough béchamel sauce to cover the bottom of your greased baking dish, then add a layer of lasagne. Cover with a layer of the cooked vegetables, then a mantle of béchamel, followed by a handful of sliced raw mushrooms, one of Parmesan, and one of tomatoes. Repeat until you have used up all the ingredients.

Cover the top with slices of mozzarella, and bake for 25 minutes. Remove from the oven, and allow it to rest and cool for a few minutes before you serve it. As always, garlic bread and a plain green salad cannot be bettered as accompaniments.

Lasagne al Forno

A FEW UNFIDDLY FISHY THINGS

The aversion children have to eating fish and later, as teenagers, to cooking it themselves seems to spring from, among other things, a dislike of finding and having to wheedle away tiny bones. So, content with fish fingers and fillets and perhaps the odd treat of smoked salmon, the real joy of the best fish, be it oily, white, pink, shelled or tentacled, seems to be an undiscovered pleasure for many unadventurous young people. Then there is the disappearance of many of the good wet fish shops that used to be a part of every town or neighbourhood, so that all that's on offer is supermarket fillets, dyed or otherwise, served by sales assistants who usually don't know the first thing about what they're selling or how to cook it.

Fishcakes are a way to start. You can buy good haddock and natural smoked haddock by the fillet and only have to remove the odd, stray, whiskery bone. You can make the fishcake mixture in advance, with leftover mash if you have any, though lumpy-textured mash, believe it or not, is better for the texture of the fishcake. You may spruce up the taste with a little Tabasco, some celery salt or the addition of a wonderful cool bowl of crème fraîche tartare to accompany the crisply fried cakes with. Parsley or dill work. A spritz of lemon and you're away. Next stop fish pie!

Wild salmon fishcakes from the leftovers of a whole poached salmon when you can afford it are the best fishcakes of them all.

SMOKED HADDOCK FISHCAKES

A small piece of smoked haddock with the fresh lifts this dish transcendently. Too much would overwhelm.

SERVES 6

675g/1½lb fresh haddock fillet
340g/12oz natural smoked haddock
milk
butter
black pepper
3 medium potatoes, peeled, steamed
    and mashed
¼ tsp celery salt
a scant fork end of cayenne pepper
2 heaped tbsp flat-leaf parsley,
    chopped
1 beaten egg
flour, salt and pepper
olive oil

Preheat the oven to 180°C/350°F/Gas 4. Grease a gratin dish with butter and lay your fish fillets in it. Add a splosh of milk, dot with little pieces of butter, season with black pepper and cook in the oven for 15 minutes. With a spoon and fork, flake away the fish from the skin into large chunks, and pile it on the top of the mashed potato. Add the celery salt and smidgen of cayenne, then scatter on a confetti of parsley. Season, remembering that the smoked haddock is quite salt. Mash together lightly; you want the fish to be flaky, not pulverised to a paste.

Have three large plates in front of you, one empty, one with the beaten egg, and one with some seasoned flour. Flour your hands, grab a fishcake's worth of the mixture and mould it before dipping it in the egg, then coating in flour. Shake off the excess and place the cake on the clean plate. This quantity should make 12 fishcakes.

Heat a good quantity of olive oil, 6 tablespoons or so, until hot, and cook the fishcakes until well bronzed on both sides. About 5–6 minutes a side should do it. Serve with lemon wedges and a leafy vegetable like purple sprouting broccoli.

FISH PIE

The best nursery-cum-comfort food there is, this may be the most basic of fish pies, but none the worse for it. You can graduate onto scallops and mussels and exotica later on when you have the desire and the budget.

SERVES 6

1.4kg/3lb plain haddock, cod, coley
or pollack according to budget,
skinned and filleted
110g/4oz natural smoked haddock
300–425ml/10–15fl oz milk
30g/1oz butter
white parts of 2 leeks, chopped small
1kg/2¼ lb potatoes
30g/1oz plain flour
1 bay leaf
grated nutmeg
salt and pepper
a bunch of fresh dill, chopped
a bunch of flat-leaf parsley, chopped
110g/4oz prawns if feeling flush
2 softly hard-boiled eggs (optional)

Preheat the oven to 180°C/350°F/Gas 4. Put the piece of haddock, cod, coley or pollack in a gratin dish with the smoked haddock, 300ml/10fl oz of the milk and a knob of butter, and bake for 15 minutes. Turn the fish into a deeper baking dish, flaking it gently and extracting any bones, but keeping it in largish bits. Reserve the cooking liquid. Gently simmer the leeks in the cooking milk until soft. Boil the potatoes, and mash thoroughly.

Melt the rest of the butter in a saucepan, add the flour and cook, stirring, for 1 minute. Add the bay leaf and a good pinch of nutmeg, and gradually stir in the liquid from the fish to make a béchamel sauce. Taste and adjust the seasoning, add the dill and parsley, then pour the sauce over the fish. Add the prawns if you have them. You could also add a couple of quartered, softly hard-boiled eggs to the cooked fish before mixing with the béchamel

Top the pie with mashed potato and cook in the oven for 15–20 minutes, until browned and bubbling on top.

CRÈME FRAÎCHE TARTARE

Here is a stunning accompaniment to most fried or breaded fish, particularly firm-textured white fish.

MAKES ENOUGH FOR 6

1 organic egg yolk
1 tsp Dijon mustard
sea salt
Tabasco
3–4 heaped dsrtsp crème fraîche,
d'Isigny is one of the best
2 tsp tarragon vinegar
1 tsp tarragon, chopped
1 heaped tbsp flat-leaf parsley,
chopped
1 tsp chives, chopped
1 tbsp rinsed capers, chopped
1 tbsp finely chopped cornichons

Beat the egg yolk with the mustard, sea salt, and a few dashes of Tabasco until emulsified. Add the crème fraîche, a dessertspoon at a time, and one teaspoon of the tarragon vinegar, whisking well with a small balloon whisk. Whisk until thick, but pourable. Stir in the other ingredients with the second teaspoon of vinegar. Adjust the seasoning.

BAKED COD WITH STOVE-DRIED TOMATOES

SERVES 4

olive oil
4 good, thick pieces of cod
sea salt and black pepper
a sprig of thyme
a handful of stove-dried tomatoes for
    each piece of fish

This dish is another one that might well make you see the pleasure and ease with which you can cook a good piece of fish simply, successfully and succulently. It is fun drying the tomatoes too. Depending on how many you dry, you can use them with cheese on toast and with pasta over the next couple of days. An autumn dish, this is for when outdoor tomatoes are ripe and sweet and full of flavour or at least cheaper and better in the shops. Dry the tomatoes 24 hours before you want to cook the cod.

Preheat the oven to 200°C/400°F/Gas 6. Oil a shallow baking tray with a film of good olive oil. Place each piece of fish on the tray, add a few more drops of oil to the top of the cod, with your fingers over the neck of the bottle to prevent a gush. Season well and pull the thyme leaves off the sprig onto the pieces of fish. Bake for about 8 minutes, remove from the oven and put a handful of the stove-dried tomatoes on top of each chunk of cod.

Return to the oven for 4–7 minutes, testing after 4 minutes, with a skewer pushed right through the fish at its thickest part. If the skewer slips right down unresistingly, the fish is cooked through. It is as easy as that, but be alert! Overcook a fish by 2 minutes and it's ruined. Serve with oodles of mash and a raw fennel salad grated fine on a mandolin and spruced up with lemon juice and olive oil to taste and some black pepper, 20 minutes or so before you want to eat it to soften the fennel a little. Two slimly shaved bulbs should suffice for four people.

STOVE-DRIED TOMATOES

two handfuls of cherry tomatoes or
    4 large vine-ripened tomatoes,
    cut into quarters
1 clove of garlic
40ml/1½ fl oz olive oil
2 sprigs of thyme leaves

Lay the tomatoes on a baking tray. If you're using quartered large tomatoes, lay them skin-side down. Finely mince a clove of garlic and stir it into the olive oil, then dribble the garlicky oil over the tomatoes. Sprinkle over the thyme leaves. Leave on a warmed hot plate, on the Aga hot plate or on a pilot light until they are dried but not shrivelled — this will take 24–32 hours.

SUBSTANTIAL MEATY DISHES

Student grants and expensive cuts of meat don't go together unless your father happens to be a butcher. My daughter Miranda, who is at Bristol University, has just been lucky enough to have a housemate whose father was a Covent Garden fruit and veg man. The five students in her flat had permanent trays of avocados and oranges stacked up in the kitchen and an endless supply of great vegetables that meant they had a little more to spend on meat. Or they could do away with meat altogether and create exotic vegetarian dishes.

There are plenty of cuts of meat I remember cooking when I was up at Cambridge that people no longer seem in a hurry to put in their ovens, let alone on their plates any more. Shanks, hocks and belly pork; liver and kidneys and heart; spare ribs and scrag and breast; oxtail and trotters and tripe. These cuts are where my student cooking life began, from the simplicity of kidneys in grain mustard to the delicate fragility and sophistication of a timbale of poached sweetbreads and spinach, or the strength and depth of flavour of a whole smoked tongue I served with walnut sauce. I may not have realised it then, but what I was experimenting with all those years ago, and presuming to be part of the classic repertoire I would cook throughout my cooking life, would seem avant garde if not downright disgusting to the average student these days. Chicken or calves' feet, spleen, brains, tongue? Lungs, intestines, testicles, udders? I hardly dare mention these last four as the lily livered wouldn't give them houseroom or even the time to read about them; they've all but disappeared from our culture. The richer we've become, the more the cheaper cuts have been erased from our diets. It is almost as though we believe them unworthy of our taste or appetite, as though we have to prove to our families and friends that we can afford sirloin and legs of lamb now, so that is what we will eat.

I remember as a student eating a dish of 'kokoretsi' on Corfu, the meat wound round a great skewer and charcoaled to a crisp on a wood fire, strong flavoured, gutsy, tender, utterly irresistible. Discovering that it was sheep's intestines didn't detract; it rather enhanced the pleasure, but I guess my eating habits and desire to taste a native speciality wherever, whatever, is probably rather unusual!

We've become a nation of skinless chicken breast and fillet fanciers, and we're all the poorer for it in terms of our ability and imagination to cook the cheaper cuts or our desire to eat them. So I am going to encourage you to swallow your prejudices and at least try some of the cuts of meat and offal that will broaden your culinary life, amaze your taste buds and not leave a chasmic hole in your wallet.

CHINESE SPICED BELLY PORK AND HOCKS

SERVES 6

2 tbsp extra-virgin olive oil
1 tbsp sesame oil
2 star anise
3 onions, peeled and sliced
1 piece of belly pork with the rind
and bone, weighing about
900g/2lb
2 pork hocks
2 large thumbs of fresh ginger, grated
3–4 cloves of garlic, grated
4 tbsp sherry vinegar
3 heaped tbsp muscovado sugar
120ml/4fl oz organic shoyu or tamari
sauce
black pepper

If you've got work to do, an essay to write, you want to go to the movies or you just want to relax and gradually be made aware of the seeping scent of this most succulent, spicy and sugary of dishes with its back note of ginger and star anise, sherry and garlic, this is the dish to cook. It is one of those earthy, hearty pot-simmered dinners where the meat falls off the bone like a bad cowboy off a horse.

Heat the oven to 150°C/300°F/Gas 2. Heat the oils gently in a heavy-bottomed casserole and throw in the star anise and the onions. Sauté for 5–10 minutes. Put in the belly, rind down, to frizzle with the hocks, which you should turn until browned all over. Place the belly rind-side up, add the ginger and garlic and sauté for a minute.

Pour in the sherry vinegar and let it bubble, then add the remaining ingredients. Now add water to almost cover – you don't want the strong flavours to be diluted too much, but the meaty part of the belly should be submerged. Bring to the boil, cover with greaseproof paper and a lid, and braise in the oven for 3 hours or more. The meat should be just on the verge of falling away from the bone.

When it is cool enough to handle, slice off most of the thick layer of fat and rind, then cut the belly into large chunks, some of which will be on the bone. Cut the hocks into hunks, too, and put both back into the pot. Cool and refrigerate overnight.

Skim the fat from the top with a spoon, then gently heat the casserole through until piping hot. Serve with Thai jasmine rice and pak choi briefly sautéed in sesame and olive oil with a little slivered garlic

BRAISED LAMB SHANKS IN HARISSA AND TOMATO SAUCE

SERVES 4

flour and seasoning to coat
4 organic lamb shanks
olive oil
2 large onions, chopped
4 cloves of garlic, chopped
2 sticks of celery with the leaves,
chopped
2 heaped tsp harissa, plus extra for
when it is cooked
1 tbsp tomato purée
400g/14oz tin whole tomatoes
a couple of strips of orange peel

Make the harissa yourself (see page 150). It is so much better than the squeezy tube or tinned version and it will keep for a couple of weeks in the fridge.

Heat oven to 150°C/300°F/Gas 2. Put a handful of flour in a Ziploc bag with a little salt and a good scrunch of pepper, throw in the shanks, seal the bag and shake until the shanks are coated in seasoned flour.

Heat 3–4 tablespoons of olive oil in a heavy-bottomed casserole and gently brown the shanks on all sides. Remove to a plate.

Add a little more oil if needed, then throw in the chopped onions, garlic and celery and sauté gently until they begin to soften.

Put the shanks back in the pot and add the harissa, tomato purée and tinned tomatoes, and enough water to nearly reach the top of the shanks. Bring to the boil, add the orange peel, reduce the heat to a simmer and cover the pot with a layer of greaseproof paper and a lid. Place in the oven for 2–2½ hours – the shanks should be falling off the bone and sweetly tender. Add more harissa if you'd like this to be even hotter and serve it with black beans and rice.

BELLY OF PORK AND BEANS

I first cooked this when I left home and went up to university and I have held it in great esteem and affection ever since. Hearty it is. If you can afford to add some good sausages, say half a dozen organic pure pork ones, do, but the meat is not the central theme of the dish. It is there to flavour and make glutinous and stickily delicious the beans and tomatoes and onions. You need a mountain of mash with some grain mustard stirred into it to pep up the pork if you feel like it, otherwise this needs nothing but a green salad to start or finish with. It works as well with butter beans as it does with haricot beans.

SERVES 6

450g/1lb haricot or butter beans soaked overnight

2–3 tbsp olive oil

1 large onion, or 8 or 9 shallots which are good in spring

6–8 cloves of garlic, peeled and whole

the heart of a head of celery with its leaves, chopped

675g–900g/1½2lb belly pork

2 x 400g/14oz tins organic peeled tomatoes

¼ jar organic passata

3 bay leaves, a bunch of thyme and parsley stalks tied together, and a large handful of fresh, flat-leaf parsley

black pepper and salt

extra flat-leaf parsley

Bring the beans up to the boil in plenty of water, remove the scum and boil furiously for 10 minutes. Then simmer with a lid on for 50 minutes. Strain, reserving the water. The beans will be undercooked. Meanwhile, heat the oil in a large, heavy-bottomed pan and sauté the chopped onion or whole shallots, with the garlic and chopped celery until softened and translucent.

Add the belly pork in 2.5cm/1in wide pieces you've cut down to the bone, cutting the bony pieces along their length as you would spare ribs. Put them rind-side down and cook until browned. Turn them over for 2–3 minutes, then add the tins of tomatoes, chopping as you go, and the passata. Tuck the herbs in, and throw in all but a few ounces of the beans, which I then mouli through the medium-sized disc to thicken and enrich the tomato sauce. Season with plenty of coarse-ground pepper and salt.

Add a little of the bean liquor if the liquid doesn't come above the stew, bring to the boil, then turn down to a gentle simmer. Cover tightly with a lid and forget it for 1½–2 hours. Check that the beans are cooked through. You may purée a couple of cups of them with a ladle of the juice if you like the contrast in texture and a thicker sauce. Sprinkle with flat-leaf parsley and serve with lashings of mashed potato to soak up the juice.

SLOW-COOKED SHOULDER OF LAMB
WITH BLACK OLIVE PASTE

SERVES 4

1kg/2¼lb cubed organic or pasture-fed shoulder of lamb

200g/7oz Carluccio's crema di olive nere (black olive paste)

This is the ultimate recipe for the unconfident cook. If you can shop for it, you can cook it to perfection and everyone will be impressed by what seems such a deep and complex dish that they'll think you're a deep and complex person, or at least an extremely competent cook. I couldn't believe that the dish relied on only two ingredients when I first discovered it in Buoux, at a tiny village restaurant in the Luberon in Provence, but I came home, did what I was told, and, magically, it worked. The transference of oily bitter black olive to fatty, bloody sweet lamb is all in the mingling of both sets of juices and the alchemy that ensues. The fact is, their joint flavours and qualities merge into a spectacular fusion of a result that cannot be imagined prior to passing the lips. Just don't be tempted to buy inferior meat or olive paste. The best jars of olive paste come from Seggiano or Carluccio and are available at good delis. It may seem expensive, but you need no other ingredients to add to the lamb.

Preheat the oven to 150°C/300°F/Gas 2. Simply put the cubed lamb shoulder in the bottom of a heavy casserole, then tip in a whole jar of the crema di olive nere. Cover with greaseproof paper, then a lid, and abandon in the oven while you work or watch a movie for 2 hours. Then take out and eat.

The black oily, olivey juices mingle with the lamb, colouring, scenting and tenderising.

BRAISED LAMB SHANKS
WITH ROSEMARY AND BALSAMIC VINEGAR

SERVES 4

2 tbsp plain flour
sea salt and black pepper
4 organic lamb shanks
2–3 tbsp olive oil, possibly an extra
  couple of tbsp
1 tbsp rosemary leaves, finely
  chopped
1 dsrtsp thyme leaves, chopped
2 large onions, peeled and sliced
  thinly
6 cloves of garlic, roughly chopped
300ml/10fl oz white wine
150ml/5fl oz balsamic vinegar
a bouquet of 2 strips orange peel and
  a couple of bay leaves tied
  together with string

A hearty dish that will stew happily in its own juice for up to two and a half hours, until the meat is spoon tender and falling off the bone and the sharp rosemary leaves have softened and scented the meat. It is essential to buy a good balsamic vinegar but not one that is life-threateningly expensive. You need the velvet, rich grapey undertones without the sharpness. Seggiano sell a good, mellow, musty organic balsamic vinegar.

Put the flour and seasoning in a re-sealable plastic bag. Throw in the shanks, seal the bag and give the shanks a good shake to coat them in the seasoned flour. (That way you don't end up wearing it.) Shake off the excess flour and remove the meat.

Heat the oil in a large, heavy-bottomed casserole and brown the shanks on all sides over a medium heat. This should be done quickly, a couple of minutes a side until they begin to brown and crust. Scrape up any burnt bits of flour from the bottom of the pan and remove with a slotted spoon. If the pan looks like it needs more oil, add it. Then throw in the rosemary and let them fizz and hiss for a minute. This begins to tenderise them and draw out their astringent scent. Add the thyme, onions and garlic, stir and cook until softened and beginning to turn translucent. Raise the heat and add the wine and vinegar together, bubbling them furiously for a couple of minutes.

Return the shanks and their juice to the pot, lower the heat and add the bouquet tucked into the side and cover the pot with a layer of greaseproof paper and the lid. Simmer very gently for 2–2½ hours, turning the shanks in the chocolate-brown liquor every so often. You may add a little more wine if it looks like the sauce is reducing too much. Serve with champ, a wonderful Irish dish of mashed potato (see page 89).

LAMB'S LIVER WITH MELTING ONIONS

SERVES 2

3 large onions
2 tbsp olive oil
55g/2oz unsalted butter
salt
2 tbsp red wine vinegar
1 tsp sugar
a sprig of marjoram or oregano
   (optional)
340g/12oz or 2 decent slices of
   lamb's liver per person, thinly and
   evenly sliced

Please read on. Even the word 'liver' is enough to send a shiver through the kitchens of legions of committed offal haters, who vow they never touch anything organic and by that I mean in the 'organ meats' sense: liver, kidney, heart, tripe, brain, sweetbread. Now is the time to try these things. They are cheap, nourishing – though that may be of little concern to you – and, most importantly, can be sublime in the right hands. The quicker you cook the liver and the slower you cook the onions, the better and more irresistible the dish will be, both components meltingly softened and tender, the liver still pink but the onions a gooey brown spoon-soft mass.

Peel and slice the onions into thin moons and then again into half moons and cook them slowly and gently in the olive oil and half the butter. A little salt sprinkled over them when you put them into the pan hastens the juices beginning to run. Do not cover the onions, just stir them from time to time to stop them sticking while you let them soften and turn gold for 30 minutes or so. Add the vinegar and sugar with the stripped sprig of herbs halfway through cooking and let the vinegar bubble and reduce at a higher heat for a couple of minutes before slowing down the cooking again. Or just add the vinegar to the pan juices once you have removed the liver at the end of its cooking time and scrape all the crusty bits in as you stir over a high heat for a couple of minutes.

When the onions are cooked, scoop them to the sides of the pan and melt the rest of the butter. Add the liver when the butter is sizzling and cook for 1–2 minutes a side. A knife cut will ensure the middle is really rosy but not raw. Don't wait to poke or you'll be too late.

Put a couple of slices of liver on top of a pile of onions on a warmed plate and consume with fervour and much mash!

IRISH STEW

2 large onions, peeled and sliced
2 sticks of celery, strung with a
   potato peeler and chopped small
   with their leaves
6 decent-sized carrots, peeled and
   cut into 1cm/½in chunks
8 pieces of neck or scrag of lamb, on
   the bone
lamb stock (optional)
2 medium potatoes per person,
   peeled
110g/4oz organic barley
parsley
sea salt and black pepper

A great comforter of an easy, cheap dish to prepare and one that is even better if eaten the day after it has been cooked, which allows the pot time to cool down and chill and you to scum the lamb fat off the top before you heat up the stew. Barley and potato provide serious ballast, but should not be introduced at the beginning of cooking time. The starch in them also serves to thicken the juices delectably.

Throw the onions, celery and carrots into a heavy-bottomed pot, then lay the pieces of lamb on top of them. Season, cover with water or lamb stock and bring slowly to the boil. Put a sheet of greaseproof paper over the top, put the lid on and simmer at a gentle blip on top of the stove for the first hour to 1½ hours. If you prefer, you can put the stew in the oven at 150°C/300°F/Gas 2.

Remove the lid and tuck the potatoes into the stew with the barley. You may need a little more hot stock or water as the barley will swell. Bring back to the boil, then turn down the heat and continue to simmer for another hour or until the potatoes are cooked through when you test them with a skewer and the barley is tender. Serve immediately with a large handful of chopped parsley on top, or cool.

If you've made the stew the day before you need it, chill overnight. Next day, remove the solid white fat, bring the meat back to room temperature and heat gently through to scalding hot before serving. Best served in a wide soup bowl with plenty of juice ladled in with the stew. One of the great one-pot dishes.

ROBERT CARRIER'S CHILI CON CARNE

SERVES 6

340g/12oz kidney beans soaked in
plenty of cold water overnight
2 sticks of celery, 2 chopped carrots,
a large, unpeeled onion spiked
with a couple of cloves and a
couple of leeks to flavour the
beans
10 whole black peppercorns
1kg/2¼lb cubed lean beef
450g/1lb cubed pork
2 tbsp bacon fat or, failing that,
1 each of butter and olive oil
1 large onion, finely chopped
4 cloves of garlic, chopped
600ml/1 pint good stock, beef
preferably (see p. 376), if not
chicken (see p. 80)
4 tbsp chili powder or ½–1 tsp chilli
powder or to taste
1 tbsp flour
2 bay leaves
1 tsp cumin seeds, toasted in a dry
pan for a minute then ground
½ tsp oregano
sea salt and black pepper

This dish has a history that is not entirely salubrious, but that shouldn't surprise you, as it is the alma mater of student party foods. Everyone has a story, everyone has their own version of the dish.

One of my first cookery books was Robert Carrier's *Great Dishes of the World*. I had no idea of his reputation when I bought the book a decade after publication, and didn't know about his sumptuous hotel, Hintlesham Hall in Suffolk, or of the modish Robert Carrier 'cookery cards' that I imagine were quite avant garde for the time – as must have been all the recipes in the book which had first appeared in the *Sunday Times* colour magazine. The book just seemed to sophisticatedly sum up the spirit of the cooking times and be the sort of book a fledgling and inexperienced cook would want to buy into when he or she wanted to show a bit of form but really wasn't much of an expert. What Carrier calls the 'emergency shelf', our store cupboard, was full of things like turtle soup, tinned milk and tins of minced clams, so you can see how things have moved on.

I assembled the ingredients, thrilled at the idea that my chilli wasn't going to be the ghastly grey slop one associates with gristly mince whose fat leaks grimly into the hot chilli, chunks of indigestible green pepper and tinned kidney beans flung in to eke out the meat. Carrier's chilli contains pounds of lean cubed pork and beef, bacon fat, cumin and oregano and 4 tablespoons of chilli powder. Some of you will already know what must have happened. Others, like me at the time, will be unaware, would just do as they were told, as I did. How was I to know that 'chile' or 'chili' powder, was not the same thing as 'chilli' powder. 'Chilli' powder is made entirely from powdered chilli, while 'chili' or 'chile' is a delicate mix of hot peppers, paprika, cumin seed, dried garlic and oregano.

One tablespoon of the hot stuff, the chilli, would be enough to blow the pan-lid off the pan. Four tablespoons rendered the dish so hot that its even touching your lips was enough to send you into shock.

I have made it since and it has been delicious, both with the chili and the chilli. Just don't do what I did first time around.

You have been warned. If you don't read the above piece on chilli something terrible could happen! If you do, you're in for the only version of this dish that I would consider cooking, and very delicious it is too. I have adapted Carrier's original recipe. Remember to soak the kidney beans the night before in cold water.

Put the drained beans in the bottom of a large, heavy-bottomed pan with the celery, carrots, onion, leeks and peppercorns and cover with a thumbnail to spare of cold water. Never salt pulses until they are cooked. It toughens the exterior of them and stops them cooking through satisfactorily. Bring to the boil, scum with a slotted spoon and allow to boil hard for 10 minutes, skimming off the froth as necessary before turning the heat down to a simmer and covering the pot. Check the beans after 1½ hours, though they may take 2 hours to cook.

You may cook the beans in advance of making your chilli and just cool them and keep them in their cooking liquor in a covered bowl in the fridge. The other vegetables have given up their goodness and need to be chucked. Keep the bean stock for soup.

Trim the fat from the meat then brown it, a single layer at a time, in the hot bacon fat or oil and butter. A minute or two a side is all it needs at this stage. Remove the meat from the fat and throw in the onion and garlic, allowing it to just begin to soften and turn translucent before you put the meat and its juices back in. Add the stock, which should be boiling. Bring to the boil, cover the casserole with a sheet of greaseproof paper and a lid and simmer gently for an hour.

Blend the chili or chilli powder with flour in a few tablespoons of the hot pan juices and return to the pot. Go easily if you are using chilli and taste to get the heat you want. You may always add a little more at the end when you taste the finished dish, but there is no going back if you overdo it. Add the bay leaves, cumin, oregano and seasoning, taste and adjust. Continue to simmer the dish under the lid until the meat is completely tender. This could take another hour. Check the seasoning again, then add a sufficient quantity of beans, without their cooking liquor, to the pot, roughly a ladleful per person. You can always use the leftovers in a soup or add them to the remaining chilli and have a beanier version the next day. Serve with plain boiled rice.

SAUSAGE AND MASH

olive oil
2–3 top-quality sausages per person
butter
1 medium-to-large onion per person, thinly sliced into rings
sea salt
1 tsp molasses sugar
1 glass red wine, Madeira or Marsala
300ml/10fl oz chicken stock (see p. 80) or leftover gravy
dash of Worcestershire sauce
1 tsp seeded mustard
black pepper

Don't be seduced by a cheap, commercial sausage laden with nitrites and preservatives and rusk and salt. For very little more money you can grab yourself a good, porky banger that's never even seen a filler, so will be all the meatier and more filling. The salt is generally added with such liberal abandon to hide the tasteless, inferior meat and fat that have been thrown into the casing and to give flavour to something which only the lowest of low ingredients have been added. Please don't ask, though if you insist – fat, eyelids, snout, gristle, the bits not good enough to go into anything recognisable. The Well Hung Meat Company and Swaddles Farm (see list of suppliers at the back of this book for details) will send you organic pork sausages from old breeds that have flavour, fat and texture and will be judiciously spiced and not salt. The cost is not much more and you'll find that two per person is quite enough.

Preheat the oven to 180°C/350°F/Gas 4. Heat a little olive oil in a large gratin dish, then add the sausages and turn gently (don't break the skins) over a low heat for a few minutes. Remove the sausages to a plate. Add a lump of butter and a slug of olive oil to the gratin dish and add the sliced onion, coating well. Sprinkle with sea salt so that the onions release their juice and cook down gently for five minutes before adding the molasses sugar and stirring in well.

Next pour in the wine, allowing it to bubble away with the onions for a few minutes. If you have some gravy left over from a roast, you may add up to 300ml/10fl oz. If not, add the same quantity of chicken stock and a slug of Worcestershire sauce to brown it.

Cook gently for a further 20 minutes before dunking the sausages in the gravy, adding the mustard and a good scrunch of black pepper. Cook in the oven for about 30 minutes, turning the sausages every 10 minutes, or cook gently in the pan on top of the stove. Some claim that sausages cooked in the oven dry out, but with the onions and their buttery juices in this recipe, it can't happen. And the 'Frying Tonight' smell is avoided. Serve with mashed potato.

BOSTON BAKED BEANS

500g/1lb 2oz packet of haricot or cannellini beans, soaked overnight in cold water
ham or chicken stock (see p. 80), or water to cover
half a jar of Meridian blackstrap molasses
170g/6oz molasses sugar
4 tsp English mustard powder
4 large onions, each stuck with 3 or 4 cloves
3 star anise
12 white peppercorns
sausages (optional)

A treacly, molassesey deep dark beany dish perfect to serve with sausages and mash or on its own with mash or rice.

Preheat the oven to 150°C/300°F/Gas 2. Drain the beans and put them in a heavy-bottomed casserole pot with stock or water to cover. Bring to the boil, skim off the scum and simmer for 30 minutes. They will still be hard. Pour off some of the stock, so that the beans are just covered. Put a ladle or two of the hot stock from the pot into a bowl with the molasses, molasses sugar and mustard powder, and stir well until everything has dissolved. Put the clove-studded onions and star anise into the pot, then the treacly mixture. Add the peppercorns, bring just up to boiling point, then put the pot, covered with a lid, into the bottom of the oven for 4 hours. Then, either remove the lid and return to the oven for another hour or so, or bury the best pork sausages you can find — as many as your appetite dictates — before returning to the oven for another hour.

It all tastes just as good the next day. Large quantities of mashed potato to mop up the juice is just the thing, or some whole, red sweet potatoes roasted in the following way, one per person: heat a splash of olive oil in a shallow-sided roasting tin, and add 1 tablespoon of finely chopped rosemary until they begin to fizz. Roll the sweet potatoes in their skins in the oil, sprinkle with good, coarse sea salt, and roast in a hot oven for 30 minutes, or until soft right through when pierced with a skewer.

HOMEMADE BAKED BEANS WITH A GREEN HERB AND PARMESAN CRUST

SERVES 6–8

450g/1lb haricot beans soaked overnight in cold water
2 sticks of celery, a couple of leeks, the green and the white, cleaned and halved, 2 large carrots chopped into chunks and 1 onion, unpeeled, spiked with a couple of cloves
10 whole black peppercorns
a bouquet of fresh herbs, to include some or all of the following: rosemary, parsley, bay and thyme, tied together with string
3 ladlefuls of fresh tomato sauce (see p. 66)
a large mugful of white breadcrumbs made from a stale loaf
1 bunch flat-leaf parsley, chopped somewhere between roughly and finely
2–3 tbsp freshly grated Parmesan
45g/1½ oz unsalted butter

Yes it's quicker to open a tin, but this isn't a baked beans on toast kind of a dinner. It's a homemade casserole of haricot beans in fresh tomato sauce baked in the oven with a brilliant green crust of parsley, breadcrumbs and Parmesan. Just remember to soak the beans in cold water the night before.

Drain the haricot beans of their soaking water and throw them into a large, heavy-bottomed casserole. Add the vegetables and peppercorns to the beans with the bouquet and cover with cold water to a thumbnail above the top of the vegetable and beans. Do not add salt until the beans are cooked or you will toughen them irrevocably. Bring to the boil, skim with a slotted spoon and boil for 10 minutes, skimming again if needs be, before turning to a gentle simmer and covering the pot. The older the beans, the longer they will take to cook. I allow 1–1½ hours for haricot beans.

When they are tender right the way through, remove the vegetables and bouquet, which have given up their goodness and strain the bean stock into a jug, reserving the beans in the casserole. Preheat the oven to 180°C/350°F/Gas 4. Mouli the tomato sauce on the coarse disc of a mouli if you want a textured but less chunky sauce, or just stir it into the beans. Then decant the beans in their sauce into a small casserole into which they will come nearly to the top. Put the breadcrumbs, parsley and Parmesan into a bowl and mix together well, then put a layer of the mixture on top of the beans. Dot with little bits of butter and cook for 20–25 minutes or until the top has gratinéed to a beautiful bubbling brown without turning too dark.

Homemade Baked Beans with a Green Herb and Parmesan Crust

450g/1lb broccoli, broken into small
    florets
225g/8oz baby corn
2 tbsp groundnut oil
1 large carrot, peeled and sliced
    wafer thin
225g/8oz mangetout
a bunch of spring onions, tough
    exterior removed, split down the
    middle
sea salt
black pepper
1 clove of garlic, sliced
1 thumb fresh ginger, finely sliced or
    coarsely grated
1 tsp sugar
1 tbsp rice wine or dry sherry
1 tbsp light soy sauce
3 tbsp dark soy sauce
225–340g/8–12oz cubed pork or
    beef, cooked or raw, or the same
    of de-frosted, drained large
    prawns
2 tsp sesame oil

STIR-FRY

The whole point of a stir-fry is to do something quick, crisp, vibrant flavoured and last minute, with whatever is lurking in the back of your fridge, with the addition of maybe a couple of fresh vegetables and the soy sauce and rice wine in your store cupboard. If you have a leftover bit of roast pork or beef, all well and good, otherwise either buy some ready cubed or make it a veggie dish. Or add some prawns from the freezer. This is an eking out and making do meal, but if you follow the running order of the recipe instructions, all the vegetables will retain their flavour and texture and you will have a sizzling, spicy Chinese-style supper in record time. If you don't have a wok, a frying pan will do.

Do not worry if you don't have all the vegetables. Just the broccoli and mangetout and carrots work, with onion if you have no spring onions. You do want a range of texture, colour and flavour though.

Blanch the broccoli and corn in a large pan of boiling, salted water for 3 minutes and then drain them in a colander, pouring cold water over them to arrest the cooking process. Pat them dry in kitchen paper or they will not fry and maintain a peak of crispness when introduced to the hot oil. They will merely splutter and begin to steam.

Heat the wok or a large frying pan over a high heat until it is very hot, then add the groundnut oil and heat until it is smoking. Throw in the broccoli, corn and carrots and stir-fry for a couple of minutes. Throw in the mangetout and spring onions and stir-fry for another minute. Season, add garlic, ginger, sugar, rice wine or dry sherry and soy sauces, then the meat or prawns. Stir-fry for another couple of minutes at a high temperature, turning the meat or fish well to brown all over and cook through if it's been started from raw. Add the sesame oil, stir for another 30 seconds, then transfer the contents of the wok to a warmed serving plate or spoon it over bowls of boiled rice. Serve with a bottle of shoyu sauce to hand round.

GARLICKY STIR-FRIED CHICKEN WITH GINGER AND BASIL

Seared and smoky, this quick chicken stir-fry should only be made with organic or free-range chicken, whatever your budget. It has the pzazz of basil and a hit of chilli bean sauce.

SERVES 4

450g/1lb chicken breasts
2 tbsp groundnut oil
4–6 cloves of garlic, chopped
a finger of fresh ginger, thinly sliced
a ladleful of chicken stock (see p. 80)
1 tbsp light soy sauce
1–2 tsp sugar
1 dsrtsp chilli bean sauce
2 tsp sesame oil
a handful of fresh basil leaves,
    without their stalks

Remove the skin from the chicken breasts, and the bones if you have bought them on the bone. Cut them into long, thin strips, 4 x 1cm/1½ x ½ in. Heat a wok or frying pan over a high heat until it is really hot, then add the oil. Wait until it begins to smoke before throwing in the garlic and ginger and stir-frying them together for 30 seconds. Throw in the chicken pieces and stir-fry them for 2 minutes, turning them frequently.

Add the stock, soy sauce, sugar and chilli bean sauce, bring to boiling point, then turn down to a simmer for 5 minutes. Stir in the sesame oil and tear in the basil leaves and stir for a further 30 seconds before removing from the heat and serving with boiled rice and some stir-fried vegetables.

STIR-FRIED PORK WITH CASHEW NUTS AND CHILLI

You may wish to cook the last dish just as a vegetable accompaniment and make this the main man. Pork and cashew nuts are a great duo. All you have to do here is marinade the meat first for 15 minutes while you prepare everything else. You may use chicken if you'd rather.

SERVES 4

450g/1lb organic or free-range pork
    fillet
1 tsp grated fresh ginger
sea salt and black pepper
55g/2oz cashew nuts, unsalted
1 tbsp rice wine or dry sherry
1 tbsp light soy sauce
1 tbsp chilli bean sauce
2 tsp sugar
a handful of chopped spring onions

MARINADE

1 tbsp rice wine or dry sherry
1 dsrtsp light soy sauce
2 tsp sesame oil
1 tsp cornflour

Mix the marinade ingredients in a bowl. Cut the pork into thin slices about 5cm/2in long and plop into the marinade. Heat a wok or frying pan over a very high heat, add the oil and when it is smoking hot, add the ginger, then the pork 20 seconds or so later. Season it with salt and pepper and stir-fry for a couple of minutes.

Remove the meat, throw in the cashew nuts and stir-fry them for a minute. Add everything but the spring onions, including the pork, and stir-fry for another couple of minutes. Throw in the chopped spring onions and serve.

SHEPHERD'S PIE OR COTTAGE PIE

SERVES 6

3 tbsp olive oil
1 large onion, chopped
2 sticks of celery, strung and
    chopped small
2 medium carrots, chopped into dice
3 cloves of garlic, chopped
675g/1½ lb minced beef or lamb
1 tbsp tomato concentrate
a few shakes from the Worcestershire
    sauce bottle
a glass of dry white or red wine, or
    the equivalent of good gravy from
    the Sunday roast
300ml/10fl oz stock, beef (see p. 376)
    or chicken (see p. 80)
sea salt and black pepper
1.4kg/3lb potatoes, peeled, with
    butter and milk for mashing
    (see p. 89 for mashed potato)
2 tbsp strong, unpasteurised Cheddar
    (optional)
1 tbsp freshly grated Parmesan

After the roast comes shepherd's pie. Or cottage pie. I didn't realise there was any difference between them until well into my cooking life, despite it being glaringly obvious, lamb being the hungry shepherd's pie and beef the meat used for a cottage pie. Without a mincer to mince the remains of your Sunday roast for Monday night's dinner, you will be more likely to start from scratch with raw mince, but in the days when everyone had a roast for Sunday lunch and kitchens were better equipped, albeit with non-electrical gadgets, leftovers were used up in shepherd's pie. And in rissoles, though I suspect they've been out of culinary fashion for long enough to stage a comeback. Even the name seems like a quaint archaism to a generation who have been brought up on heat-and-eat dinners, boil-in-the-bag food, take-aways and ready-mades.

If you want a more richly Italian version of this classic, call it an Italian shepherd's or cottage pie and just make extra ragù sauce when you are making a Bolognese or a Lasagne (see page 158). Crown it with the very un-Italian mashed potato instead of pasta. And gratinée the top, which you have sprinkled with freshly grated Parmesan, to continue the theme.

Preheat the oven to 180°C/350°F/Gas 4. Heat the oil in a large, heavy-bottomed frying pan, then throw in the onion, celery and carrot, stirring them over a brisk heat but not allowing them to brown. After 5 minutes or so add the garlic, reduce the heat and soften everything together. Raise the heat again and add the mince, stirring until it has all lost its bloody colour. Add the tomato concentrate, Worcestershire sauce, wine and stock, season and simmer for 10 minutes covered. Boil the potatoes and mash them in the usual way until really creamy and well seasoned.

Put the contents of the frying pan into a gratin or baking dish and cover evenly and thickly with the mashed potato. Either dot with butter or sprinkle cheese over the top. Bake for 45–55 minutes until golden and bubbling. If it suits you to bake for longer at a lower temperature begin at 200°C/400°F/Gas 6 for 10 minutes to start browning the top, then turn down to 180°C/350°F/Gas 4.

MOUSSAKA

SERVES 6

3 aubergines, sliced 1cm/½in thick
olive oil
2 onions, chopped
2 cloves of garlic, chopped
675g/1½lb lamb mince
sea salt and black pepper
1 tsp cinnamon
1 skinned, seeded, chopped tomatoes
2–3 tbsp tomato concentrate
a bunch of flat-leaf parsley, chopped
a few tbsp dry white wine
béchamel sauce made with
    600ml/1 pint milk (see p. 70)
Parmesan cheese, freshly grated
    (optional)

Greek holidays, student food – there is really no reason for this dish to have got a bad name, other than its being badly cooked and fighting for its life in an ocean of olive oil. It is inexpensive to make, great for a party, served with just a good green salad and a bowl of tzatziki (see page 130), and if you roast the aubergines in the oven, there will be no lingering frying smells and oozy, oily aubergines. They do tend to absorb tankersful of oil if you fry them in a pan. You may use courgettes or half courgettes and half aubergines if you feel like it.

Preheat the oven to 180°C/350°F/Gas 4. Brush the aubergines with olive oil on both sides before putting them on a baking tray in a single layer and roasting in the oven in batches or on two trays if you have them. They are ready when you can prick them with a fork and they are soft right the way through. Don't let them brown too much. They should take 10–20 minutes.

Meanwhile, heat 2 tablespoons of oil in a heavy-bottomed frying pan and sauté the onions until softened and pale gold. Add the garlic, sauté for a few minutes, then add the mince and fry until it is well browned and has completely lost its raw look, about 5–10 minutes. Season and flavour with cinnamon before adding the chopped tomato, tomato concentrate and chopped parsley. Stir well, add the white wine and simmer for 15 minutes. The meat will be cooked and will have absorbed most of the wine.

While the meat is simmering, make the béchamel sauce. Make sure you add a suspicion of nutmeg. Put alternate layers of aubergine and meat sauce in a deep baking dish or roasting tin, starting and ending with a layer of aubergines. Pour a thick layer of béchamel over the top; you may have some left over. Bake the dish in the oven for about 45 minutes or until it has browned beautifully on top and the meat and aubergine layers have married together. Sprinkle Parmesan over the top of the béchamel before you bake it if you want a richer dish. Serve piping hot straight from the baking dish.

PASTRY – THE LOWDOWN

There are people who spend their whole life avoiding it, getting other people to make it for them, buying inferior, flabby grey or butterless apologies for it, or never even attempting the tarts and pies that are dependent upon the successful making of it. Why people get a thing about it I can't imagine. You can't pass your driving test the first time you take to the road, so why would you suddenly become a proficient pastry chef on your first attempt? What is wrong with things going wrong or not quite right? It is an important part of our cooking life. It is the part that makes us think about what we are doing and how we are doing it, instead of just following a recipe slavishly.

Perfectionism is something we only have a sense of depending on how far away from it we are at any one time, and in my experience, the more experienced we become as cooks, the higher the standards we perceive and aspire to. Pastry is something we should start working with early on, even if it only means punching out the circles for the jam tart tins or using up the spare edges of our mother's pie crust for our own concoctions. That is what both my daughters did when they were too small to even stand at the worktop and cook; they did it from a kitchen chair and never looked back. Confidence comes from not attempting the A–Z of pastry on the first outing. Just pressing it into the tins and plopping in the strawberry jam, then eating the result is enough to get the fledgling cook going.

I never made pastry until I left home and I certainly didn't have the golden rules at my elbow. I learned by trial but mainly error. I still find it exciting that each time I make a pastry case I have no real idea quite how it is going to turn out, although the method and quantities are frequently the same. The point is there are variables: the age of the flour; the type of flour; how dry or damp it is; the chill and type of the butter; the heat of the stove; the temperature of the kitchen; how little you work the dough; the amount and coldness of the liquid you add; the thickness of the crust you roll. That is what keeps it interesting.

I have known friends panic and put custard powder in their pastry on the grounds it might firm it up; others are terrified if it doesn't go into the tin in one piece – they feel they've failed if they have to patch it like a quilt. There are those who will only make it by hand and those who will only make it in a food processor. It is important to do both. Knowing how food should feel at each stage of its journey from raw to cooked is tremendously important. The reason for the technique only comes alive and becomes clear when you use your hands and feel the texture of what it is you are doing and understand the importance of the speed at which you should be doing it. Most of all, before you begin to think how complicated pastry making is, let me refine it a bit for you.

There is really only one rule to remember – KEEP EVERYTHING COLD. That inevitably means you have to work fast when you make pastry. If you don't, the butter won't stay cold and your pastry will enter the realms of play dough or sticky plasticine.

Taking it to extremes, I have actually grated or cubed butter straight from the freezer into my flour and the result is better, more buttery and light and like puff pastry than shortcrust pastry. So, if you suddenly have to knock up a pie or a tart and your butter is all in the deep freeze, don't worry, don't sit and wait, get to work.

SHORTCRUST PASTRY

QUANTITY FOR 23CM/9IN TART TIN

170g/6oz plain white (preferably
    organic) or wholemeal flour
pinch of sea salt
85g/3oz unsalted butter, fridge cold

The simplest pastry of all. These quantities will give you enough to line your tin with some left over if the pastry is rolled out thinly enough.

I sift the flour and a pinch of sea salt into the food processor, then cut the fridge-cold butter into cubes on top of it. Pulse several times for 3–4 seconds a time before adding a tablespoon of cold water through the feed tube. If the paste is still in crumbly little bits after a minute or two, add a tablespoon more of water, but remember, the more water you use, the more the pastry will shrink if you bake it blind. The moment it has cohered into a single ball, stop, remove it, wrap it in clingfilm and put it in the fridge for at least 30 minutes.

If you are making pastry by hand, sift the flour into a large bowl with the salt, add the chopped butter, and work as briskly as you can to rub the fat into the flour. Use the tips of your fingers only, rather like running grains of hot sand through your fingers. Add the water bit by bit as above; wrap and chill the pastry.

Now scatter a bit of flour on your work surface, roll your rolling pin in it, dust the palms of your hands, and start rolling. Always roll away from yourself, turning the pastry as you go, and keep the rolling pin and work surface floured to prevent sticking. Once it is rolled out, slip the rolling pin under the pastry, and pick it up, judging where to lie it in the greased tin. Again, never stretch it because it will shrink back. Try to leave at least 30 minutes for the unbaked tart case to commune with the inside of your fridge. Or put it in the fridge the night before you need it.

BAKING BLIND

If you are baking your pastry case blind, preheat the oven to 190–200°C/375–400°F/ Gas 5–6. Some recipes also tell you to put a baking sheet in the oven to heat up. This can be invaluable if you are using a porcelain or other non-metal tart dish, as the hot baking sheet gives it an initial burst of heat to crisp up the bottom of the pastry. I know that some cooks will be shocked that I could even think of using anything other than metal but, as well as the aesthetic advantage when it comes to serving, china dishes are guaranteed never to discolour the pastry in the way that some metal ones do. If you are using a tart tin with a removable base (my preference, as they are by far the easiest to turn out), placing the tart tin on a baking sheet makes it easier to slide in and out of the oven.

Tear off a piece of greaseproof paper a little larger than the tart tin and place it over the pastry. Cover the paper with a layer of dried beans; the idea is to prevent the pastry from rising up in the oven. When the pastry is nearly cooked (the timing depends on the rest of the recipe), remove the paper and beans and prick the base of the pastry to let out trapped air that would otherwise bubble up. Return the tart to the oven for about 5–10 minutes to dry the pastry base.

GLAZING

Brush the partly baked pastry case with a light coating of beaten egg or egg white to ensure a crisp, finished tart

PÂTE SUCRÉE

This pastry, enriched with egg yolks, is perfect for summer fruit and chocolate tarts. I normally make it like a standard shortcrust, with 170g/6oz flour to 85g/3oz unsalted butter, adding a tablespoon of sifted icing sugar and using 2 egg yolks instead of water. It is even more important to chill this pastry thoroughly.

Pâte sablée (sandy pastry) is even sweeter, and crumbly, like a buttery biscuit. I use 170g/6oz flour to 110g/4oz butter, 55g/2oz icing sugar and 2 egg yolks. I put the butter, sugar and egg yolks into the food processor and work them together quickly, then blend in the sifted flour and work it into a paste. This needs longer chilling, a minimum of an hour, before rolling out.

CLASSIC QUICHE LORRAINE

You have probably already eaten a hundred different quiches all masquerading as the real thing; not surprising since this is the tart that has probably been bastardised more than all others. It is a dish that goes back as least as far as the 16th century and one where cream, eggs and smoked bacon, the best you can find, are all you'll need for the filling. Make it the classic way and then start re-inventing the wheel with herbs, Gruyère, goat's cheese or Parmesan, but remember, it's no longer Quiche Lorraine!

SERVES 6

SHORTCRUST PASTRY
170g/6oz organic white flour
pinch of sea salt
85g/3oz unsalted butter

FILLING
6 rashers of organic smoked streaky
    bacon
300ml/10fl oz organic double cream,
    Jersey if you can get it
2 organic eggs and 2 yolks
black pepper

Make the pastry (see page 181). Preheat the oven to 200°C/400°F/Gas 6. After chilling, line a 23cm/9 inch tart tin and prick the base with a fork. Bake the pastry blind (see page 181) for 15 minutes. Remove the greaseproof paper and beans, prick the pastry base with a fork and put back in the oven for another 5 minutes to dry. Brush a little egg white onto the pastry base — you can just pull out the oven rack and do this without taking the pastry case out of the oven — and quickly add the rest of the ingredients which you have prepared as follows.

Snip the bacon into strips and cook them gently in a frying pan until the fat begins to run. They should remain pinkly soft, not crispened. Drain, cool slightly, then spread over the bottom of the pastry case. Whisk together the cream, egg, yolks and pepper, then pour into the pastry case and bake for 20 minutes. Turn the heat down to 180°C/350°F/Gas 4 for a further 10–15 minutes, until the filling is goldenly puffed up like a soufflé and tremblingly set.

Remove from the oven and leave for 10 minutes before serving. Scalding-hot tarts don't taste of anything.

TREACLE TART

The sweetest of them all, this is the divinely gloopy, gooky toothache of a tart that is impossible not to love and impossibly easy and quick to make. No student can not afford to eat it or make this pudding. Just sharpen it up with lemon zest and lash on the cream.

Preheat the oven to 190°C/375°F/Gas 5. Make the shortcrust pastry (see page 181.) Line a 23cm/9in tart tin and chill. Save the trimmings to make a lattice top if you like. Bake blind for 15 minutes, then remove the beans, prick the base with a fork and bake for 5 more minutes. Turn the heat down to 180°C/350°F/Gas 4.

Warm the syrup gently, then, off the heat, add the butter and stir until melted in. Beat together the egg and cream and add to the syrup, with the lemon zest and breadcrumbs. Stir to mix evenly. The syrup should be thick with breadcrumbs and not too liquid, then pour into the pastry case. Add a lattice top if you like and bake for 25–30 minutes. The filling will have set to a gel.

Leave for about 20–30 minutes before serving warm – there is nothing like hot treacle tart for taking the roof off your mouth. Dollop on some clotted cream, then go for a brisk artery-clearing walk afterwards.

SERVES 6–8

SHORTCRUST PASTRY
170g/6oz organic white flour
pinch of sea salt
85g/3oz unsalted butter

FILLING
up to 8 heaped tbsp golden syrup
30g/1oz unsalted butter, cut into small cubes
1 large egg, beaten
2–3 tbsp double cream
grated zest of 2 organic lemons
4 heaped tbsp brown breadcrumbs, preferably granary

LEMON MERINGUE PIE

This is a classic, great for Sunday lunch, great for a dinner for friends and something my daughter Miranda began to make when she was in her teens knowing all her friends would be terminally impressed. You have to have a crisp crackle of meringue, something that rustles magically when you tap it or break into it with a knife and the interior should be mallowy and soft. This pudding is all about contrasts. The lemon should make your tongue smart and the meringue should shock it back to life with sweetness.

Preheat the oven to 190°C/375°F/Gas 5. Make the shortcrust pastry (see page 181). Line a 23cm/9 inch tart tin and chill. Bake the pastry blind for 15 minutes, then remove the beans, brush the pastry with beaten egg white, and return to the oven for 5 minutes. Remove the pastry case from the oven and turn the heat down to 180°C/350°F/Gas 4.

For the filling, put the lemon zest and juice in the top of a double boiler. Add the cornflour and whisk in with 2 tablespoons of the water until you have a smooth paste. Bring the remaining water to the boil, add to the lemon mixture and keep whisking over simmering water until the mixture is thick and bubbling. Remove from the heat and whisk in the egg yolks, sugar and butter. Leave to cool slightly while you make the meringue.

Whisk the egg whites until stiff, scatter in one-third of the sugar, and whisk again until stiff. Fold in another third of the sugar with a metal spoon. Spread the lemon mixture over the pastry. Pile the meringue on top and sprinkle it with the remaining sugar. Bake for 15–20 minutes. Allow to cool slightly, then turn out. Best served with thin cream.

SERVES 6

SHORTCRUST PASTRY
170g/6oz organic white flour
pinch of sea salt
85g/3oz unsalted butter
beaten egg white, for brushing

LEMON FILLING
grated zest and juice of 3 organic lemons
45g/1½oz cornflour
300ml/10fl oz water
3 large egg yolks
85g/3oz vanilla caster sugar
55g/2oz unsalted butter, cut into small pieces

MERINGUE
3 large egg whites
110g/4oz vanilla caster sugar

SHORTCRUST PASTRY
325 g/12oz plain flour
pinch of sea salt
170g/6oz unsalted butter

FILLING
55g/2oz light muscovado sugar
55g/2oz dark molasses sugar
¼ tsp ground cloves
¼ tsp ground cinnamon
⅛ tsp grated nutmeg
1 tbsp plain flour
grated rind and juice of ½ a lemon
grated rind and juice of ½ an orange
675g/1½ lb Cox's apples, peeled and
   sliced
30–55g/1–2oz butter
1 small egg, beaten
granulated sugar for the top
   (optional)

SPICED APPLE PIE

This is the first apple pie I ever baked and although I have made scores of different ones since, the nostalgia factor seems to win each and every time I return to it. It was a stunning recipe in the first place, alerting me to the fact that although apple pie is all about apples cloaked and sealed in a crisp, buttery crust, releasing their sweet sharp juices only when you cut into the pie, it is important to know what helps bring out their flavour and complements it in such a way as to make an everyday dish something ultra special. Also delicious made with spelt flour, which gives nuttiness and texture to the pastry.

Preheat the oven to 200°C/400°F/Gas 6. Make the pastry (see page 181). Roll out half the pastry and use to line a greased large pie dish — the Irish usually use a shallow pie plate.

Combine the sugars, spices, flour and grated rinds and strew a little of the mixture on the pastry base. Cover with some of the sliced apples and some more of the sugar mixture. Repeat until the dish is densely filled. Add the lemon and orange juices and knobs of butter. Roll out the remaining pastry to make the top crust. Crimp and flute the pastry edges together with a fork. Decorate with an apple made from the pastry trimmings and make one or two slits in the top crust to let out the steam. Brush lightly with beaten egg.

Bake in the oven for 35–40 minutes. Leave to cool slightly, then strew granulated sugar over the top of the warm pie if you wish. Wrap in foil if you are taking it on a picnic.

PUDDINGS AND DINNER PARTY LORE

If you are beginning to give your first dinner parties, cooking Sunday lunches for friends and family, seducing a boyfriend — food, after all, is at least the second quickest way to a man's heart if not the first — you don't want to set yourself anything too time demanding, complicated or expensive. You also want a pudding you can prepare in advance. The worst problem for the novice at entertaining is to feel you are providing waitress service and are chief cook and bottle washer while your guests are in another room having a party. So don't be a martyr to the cause. Find dishes that can sit around, be re-heated, left in the oven for overtime and not come to harm when people are late; dishes that can be made an hour, a day before.

Fruit is always great, handled as simply as possible, as are syllabubs and fools and Eton Mess when summer berries are in season. Don't feel ashamed about putting a bowl of hulled strawberries or raspberries that you have thrown a little sugar and perhaps a slosh of Kirsch over until the fruit has started to bleed a little, then gently turned in their juice, on the table. Ambition is not the mother of invention, it is the scourge of it at this stage of your culinary life. It's always better to cook something basic well, than struggle to decipher something that you really don't understand the technique for, what it should end up looking and tasting like, or, indeed, why it isn't working.

You really can't go wrong with any of the following. Just think hard about your menu before you decide what to go for. If you have cooked a creamy pasta or meat dish, don't serve a fool, Eton Mess or syllabub. I have known people serve three courses in a row with cream in each; experienced cooks too. It always strikes me how crazy it is that so many perfectly competent cooks don't think about colours, the need for different textures both within a dish and over several courses, and how much cream and butter they are using throughout.

So, don't serve an apple crumble after a chicken pie, or chicken liver pâté before roast chicken. Remember how indigestible and rich red meat is at night and don't serve a heavy meat starter before it. If you are starting with soup, don't move onto anything sloppy textured for your main course or pudding. Don't make simple errors like having the same element, tomatoes for instance, in one course as in the next. These are all startlingly obvious points once you think about the why not of them, yet all things I've been confronted by and not just by novice cooks. Rich puddings after a light fish or chicken dish, yes. Though steamed treacle pudding at night is not likely to give you the most comfortable night's slumber afterwards. There's nothing quite like suet for expanding inside your insides!

And if you are desperate, short of time and inspiration, there is nothing wrong with a fresh fruit salad, made a little exotic with passion fruit perhaps, particularly if it is orange and pineapple based. Just don't put bananas in ahead of time or they will go soggy and brown. Get your guests to help you chop it if you feel like it, once they have a glass of wine in hand. It's a great way to feel convivial instantly and to start creating that lovely sense of preparing the best ritual in the world as it should be prepared, with friends and chat and a good glass of something.

POACHED PEARS IN RED WINE AND SPICES

SERVES 8–10

zest of 1 lemon and 1 orange, pared
    with a swivel-bladed potato peeler
    so it comes off thinly with no pith
85g/3oz unrefined granulated sugar
1 bottle of red wine
6 large, firm pears such as
    Conference, Anjou or Packham
a cinnamon stick and a star anise
    (optional)

A lovely way to poach a pear, they will end up ruby red from their poaching in the winey brew. There is something about the simple beauty of a pear standing to attention with its mates in a bowl, stalk up, that always looks festive and inviting and as though you have made an effort. Use the spices or not, depending on whether you like your pears spicy.

Put the lemon and orange peel in the bottom of a pot in which all the pears will sit upright comfortably. Pour in the sugar and wine and heat gently to allow the sugar to dissolve. When it gets to the boil, reduce to a simmer for 15 minutes. Peel the pears with the potato peeler, leaving the stalks on. You may remove the little knobble at the base with the end of the peeler and then core the pear with a sharp teaspoon, or you may prefer to be idle about it and let everyone core their pears on their plates. You may also take a slim slice from the underside of the pear if it won't sit up properly. Put the pears in the winey brew as you peel them so that they don't discolour or you may prefer just to squeeze a little lemon juice over them.

When all the pears are in the pot, add some water to cover them and bring to the boil. Turn down so that just a single bubble appears to be breaking through the top. Cut a circle of greaseproof paper to fit exactly in the inside of the pan on the surface of the liquid and cut a hole in the middle of it. Place the greaseproof over the pears and poach slowly until they are tender right through when pierced with a skewer. This takes 10–25 minutes depending on their firmness. They should then cool to tepid as they are, when you can transfer them to a bowl.

Boil the winey syrup hard and fast for 20–25 minutes, depending on how much water you added, until it becomes syrupy. You should have roughly 300ml/10fl oz of syrup left. Strain it over the pears and serve them hot, warm or chilled. That is the great thing about poached pears; they are good at all temperatures. Great with ice cream.

PEARS BAKED IN CIDER

SERVES 6

6 firm pears, preferably Conference,
    Anjou or Packham
140g/5oz unrefined caster sugar
300ml/10fl oz dry cider
zest of a lemon, pared with a swivel-
    bladed peeler so you get no pith
55g/2oz crushed roasted hazelnuts
    or almonds (optional)

If you can't afford a bottle of red wine for your pears, cider is a sharp and delectable, not a lesser, alternative. Just buy a good bottle of the real stuff, not the violently coloured fizzy commercial brew. The great thing about this dish is that the pears take so long to cook you can go away for the afternoon and forget about them, or cook them the day before you want them and then chill them ready to lash cold cream upon.

Preheat the oven to 150°C/300°F/Gas 2. Peel the pears, leaving the stalks on and stand them upright in an earthenware or deep casserole, packed tightly so that they stay standing. Sprinkle them all with sugar. Pour the cider over, then add the same amount of cold water. Put the lemon peel in the pot, cover with greaseproof paper and a lid and put in the oven for 3–4 hours. The pears should not have broken up but should be tender right through when pierced with a skewer. Carry on cooking them until they really are tender, even if it means another hour. Let them cool to tepid in their liquid.

Remove the pears to a bowl and simmer down the liquid to half its volume on top of the stove, by which time it should be a sticky-thick syrup. Put the hazelnuts or whole blanched almonds on a baking sheet and roast in a medium-hot oven until they brown. Check after 10 minutes, then check again every few minutes as they can over-brown quite suddenly. Crush in a plastic bag with a rolling pin or with a mezzaluna until nubbly and not too ground. Either let people sprinkle their own nuts over the pears or add to each pear yourself as you serve them. Serve chilled, with thick cream.

BAKED APPLES

SERVES 4

4 Bramley apples
75g/2½oz unsalted butter
1 tsp cinnamon, grind your own
   for a really cinnamony scent
85g/3oz, or to taste, light muscovado
   sugar
4 dates, chopped
4 dried unsulphured apricots or
   prunes, chopped

Connotations of school dinners when wrinkly old apples were served with toenails of core at their heart and you KNEW the buttery juices were margarine. In the autumn you can find an orchard of apples to pick somewhere. If not people are virtually giving them away when there is a glut. This is a cheap and homely pudding and dead easy to make. It makes itself. Great after something rich like pork. Get scrumping.

Preheat the oven to 180°C/350°F/Gas 4. Make sure the apples are clean, then core them very nearly to the bottom with a corer making sure that every suggestion of a toenail is removed. With a sharp knife, pierce a line around the circumference of their belly to stop them bursting in the oven; exploding apples are not a pretty mess to clear up.

Grease a shallow baking tray and stand the apples close to each other in the centre. Put a lump of butter in the base of each hollowed-out apple, followed by a pinch of cinnamon, then fill up the cavity with the chopped fruits you've stirred into the sugar. Add another piece of butter to the top. Bake for about 30 minutes or until soft right through when pierced with a skewer. They will be oozing the gooey toffeed sugar and butter. Serve bubbling hot with lashings of thin, cold cream.

ETON MESS

meringues
strawberries
cream, Jersey for preference

As English as trifle and summer pudding, Eton Mess is an impromptu pudding, one not to make to any specific ideas of quantity. It is about responding to greed and what you've got. If you've got some meringues left over from the Overnight Meringues on page 28 or some broken ones that aren't quite going to cut it; if you've got some punnets of English strawberries, preferably not the ubiquitous Elsanta; and if you've got some gorgeous Jersey cream or even something lesser, make an Eton mess.

Hull the pile of strawberries and slice the large ones down the middle. Whip the cream until it is softly held — over-whipped rigid cream is not on — and always stop beating just before you think you've got to. Break up a few gooey-crisp meringues into chunky shards. Stir them and the strawberries into the cream in a glass bowl and either serve it like that or in individual bowls.

TASMANIAN LEMON PIE

SERVES 4–6

110g/4oz butter, softened
285g/10oz vanilla caster sugar
    (sugar that has been stored
    with a vanilla pod)
4 eggs, separated
4 tbsp plain flour, sifted
400ml/14fl oz milk
grated rind and juice of 2 lemons

I first ate this pudding at Old Head Hotel in County Mayo in the west of Ireland, where our family holidayed for over a decade. I think I was 9 or 10 when I first went there and Ireland, ever since, has been the most important place in my life. It was one of the three puddings, the others being Canadian pie and butterscotch tart, that Mrs Wallace, who owned Old Head, served weekly; none of the guests, old or young, ever tired of them. Magical summers they were, ones that I have gone some way to re-creating for my children since buying my own house on that wild Irish coast. All three puddings have lived on since I procured the recipes for them many years later from Alec Wallace, Mrs Wallace's son, who took over the hotel and became a lifelong friend. And all three are things I go on cooking with joy, particularly when I am there. My two daughters make Tasmanian lemon too. It is a rite of passage; the first easy and perfectly tangy sharp pudding to get children, teenagers or students to make. It's something I always have the ingredients for and which graces any occasion in the way only the best unpretentious home food can.

Preheat the oven to 180°C/350°F/Gas 4. Cream the butter with the sugar until light and fluffy. Beat in the egg yolks, then the flour and milk, a little at a time. Add the grated rind and juice of the lemons. Whisk the egg whites until stiff and add to the mixture, stirring in the first spoonful, then folding each subsequent spoonful lightly and quickly into the mixture to incorporate it as you would a soufflé. Pour into a greased baking dish, so the mixture comes about 5cm/2in up the side of the dish. Cook in the oven for about 25–30 minutes, until slightly brown on top and obviously set but faintly shuddery. Serve warm with clotted cream. The pudding should boast two specific textures – the top a light sponge, the bottom a lemony, gloopy custard.

BUTTERSCOTCH BAKED BANANAS EN PAPILLOTE

SERVES 4

4 large bananas, not over-ripe,
butterscotch sauce (see p. 38)
a little rum if you have it

En papillote is a great way to seal in flavour. It only means making a sealed parcel of what you want to cook, be it fish, meat, vegetables or fruit. So easy, the preparation of this is child's play and you can make the butterscotch sauce on page 38 way in advance and just warm it to thin it down a little before using it.

Preheat the oven to 180°C/350°F/Gas 4. Split the bananas in two down their middles. Cut 4 sheets of foil or greaseproof paper big enough to make baggy parcels for the bananas. Place the two halves of banana on each one next to each other. Dribble over some sticky sauce and a few drops of rum if you feel like it. Pull the paper or foil up so that you can fold and pinch the edges tightly together yet leave the parcel baggy. Stand on a baking sheet and put in the oven for about 10 minutes or until the bananas have softened and the sauce coated, but they have not started to over-soften and lose their shape. You can do this with the chocolate sauce on page 38 too, or simply put the bananas en papillote with a sprinkling of light muscovado or demerara sugar, a splosh of cream, a shake of rum and a spritz of fresh lemon or orange juice.

Tasmanian Lemon Pie

STRAWBERRY OR RASPBERRY FOOL

SERVE 4–6

450g/1lb strawberries or raspberries
1–2 heaped tbsp or to taste
    unrefined caster sugar
300ml/10fl oz double or Jersey cream
a spritz of lemon juice

The essence of summer, these creamy fools are simplicity itself, and far less demanding to make than custard-based ones. Just allow chilling time!

Make sure the strawberries are ripe but not over-ripe. Keep 12–18 of the strawberries or raspberries back to decorate with. Blitz the rest in a food processor or blender, then sieve the fruit, adding sugar and a squeeze of lemon to bring out the flavour. Taste to make sure it is to your liking. Whisk the cream until it is softly whipped but firm enough to hold. Now fold all or some of the fruit purée into the cream. You may place a few whole or halved strawberries or whole raspberries at the bottom of the bowl or individual glasses, or in the middle of the fool or save one or all of them to decorate the top. If you have kept back some fruit purée without cream, you may like to run a thin seam or two of fruit with the layers of the creamy fool in the bowl. Chill in the fridge for several hours before serving and serve with little biscuits.

MANGO FOOL

SERVES 4–6

2 ripe mangoes
1 lime
1–2 tbsp unrefined caster sugar
300ml/10fl oz double or Jersey cream

The most luscious and scented fool of them all. Limes bring out the flavour of mangoes as they do melons and pawpaws, so use lime instead of lemon juice to sharpen things up in this recipe. Mangoes, being a tropical fruit, are available all the year round; just make sure you pick ripe ones.

First deal with your mango. Cut as close to the stone the length of one side and then the length of the other side to remove the two less-than-halves. The bit around the stone is always harder than you would expect so the knife won't be able to get in that close. Then cut away all the rest of the flesh that is biddable and remove it from the skin, cutting it in chunks and putting it straight in the blender with its juice.

Blitz, scrape into a bowl, then spritz with lime juice and stir in the sugar to taste. No need to sieve as there are no seeds. Whip the cream until it is softly held and fold in the fruit purée. You may want to serve some extra slices of mango at the bottom of the bowl or glass or sprinkle a few toasted slivered almonds on top.

RAW BLACKCURRANT FOOL

SERVES 4–6

450g/1lb blackcurrants, pulled from
their branches with the tines of a
fork
several tbsp unrefined caster sugar,
to taste
a spritz of lemon juice
300ml/10fl oz double or Jersey cream

Just as cooked blackcurrants make a great fool if you turn them into a homemade custard, so raw blackcurrants make a vibrant and utterly different tasting fool if teamed with whipped cream. It is extraordinary how different the taste is between raw and cooked. Raw is definitely my preference. It seems to be deeper and subtler, and the sharp, almost musky, vitamin C-rich juice seems almost to taste of the leaves and bush.

Blitz the blackcurrants well in a food processor or blender, then sieve the resulting purée into a bowl. It will be thick and brilliantly purple. Add sugar until you have the desired taste, keeping it on the sharp side – chilling things accentuates the flavour of the sugar rather than the fruit. Add a squeeze of lemon juice. Whisk the cream until softly holding, then fold the purple purée thoroughly into it for a purple cream, or not so thoroughly if you go for a striated look. Plop into glasses or a glass bowl to chill and serve on its own or with biscuits as for the strawberry fool.

HUNZA APRICOT AND ORANGE FOOL

SERVES 4–6

200g/7oz Hunza apricots
fresh orange juice to cover
unrefined icing sugar
a spritz of lemon juice
300ml/10fl oz double or Jersey cream

The first fool I ever made. Once I developed a passion for the little hard, wrinkly Afghani apricots from the Hunza valley, with their subtle dry fruitiness and strong almost ancient taste, I used them stewed, turned into ice cream and in a wonderfully moussey wet cake that Elizabeth David made with ordinary apricots. You can get them from delis, health food shops and good supermarkets. Remember to start this dish the night before by soaking the apricots.

Soak the apricots overnight in the fresh orange juice, then simmer them gently in the juice until they are soft. This should take 5–10 minutes. Remove the little kernels and blitz the apricots in the food processor or blender. Boil down the remaining juice until it is reduced by a half and is lovely and syrupy. Stir the juice into the fruit purée and add a little icing sugar to taste and a spritz of lemon. Whisk the cream until it holds but is not rigid and fold the purée into it thoroughly. Plop into glasses or a large glass bowl and serve with biscuits. Hazelnut and almond biscuits or macaroons are the best with this fool.

LEMON MOUSSE

SERVES 4–6

4 egg yolks
110g/4oz unrefined vanilla caster
    sugar
zest and juice of 2 organic lemons
1 packet gelatine or leaf gelatine
    according to packet instructions
200ml/7fl oz double cream

This is such an old-fashioned pudding. I don't think anyone has served me one for a decade or two and I haven't seen one on a restaurant menu either. It's about time it came back as far as I'm concerned. It's not a difficult thing to make, but you must allow time for it to chill and set in the fridge. What you don't want is one of those rigid creations that has set within an inch of its life. A mousse should be dense compared to an airy soufflé, but light at the same time and have the sharpness of the lemon to cut through the creamy richness. So you must keep tasting to check the sharpness isn't being drowned by the billows of cream. This is the same recipe, stained almost beyond reading, that I first made when I was 18 and wrote into a recipe diary where it was the third pudding I ever made, after Tasmanian lemon pie and apple crumble. It merely reads 'Lemon' with a picture of a mouse after it. I am surprised and quite proud to read that I put 'vanilla caster sugar,' so had already started using the good cook's habit of storing my vanilla pods in with my sugar.

Separate the eggs, putting the whites into a bowl large enough for them to bulk up into when you whisk them, and the yolks into a bowl with the sugar. Whisk the yolks and sugar together in a KitchenAid or with electric beaters until they become very pale and have turned very creamy. Zest the lemons into the mixture. Squeeze the juice of both lemons into a small pan, add the gelatine and melt thoroughly over a very gentle heat. You don't want to knock out the fresh lemony flavour so it should not get very hot. Cool slightly.

Whip the cream until it holds softly, not stiffly. Pour the lemony gelatine mixture into the creamed yolks and sugar and whisk lightly, then fold in the cream with a metal spoon, again, gently and lightly. A gentle touch is paramount with a mousse. Taste for sharpness, adding a spritz more lemon if need be. Whisk the egg whites to stiff peaks, stiff enough to hold over your head without them slipping an inch! Stir the first spoonful of white into the mousse mixture to slacken it, then fold the rest in very lightly, a tablespoon at a time, keeping everything light and lifted and letting the air get into it until you have used up all the mixture. If you are doing it correctly, the mixture will seem to softly sigh and heave and bubble as you fold.

Scrape into a soufflé dish with a rubber spatula and put in the fridge to chill for a few hours or overnight. Some people like to decorate with squirls of cream but that is a retro-step too far for me. Some long, skinny grated zesty bits of either lemon or lime for colour are really all the dish needs, but pour over some cold thin cream if you like.

ELIZABETH RAFFALD'S ORANGE CUSTARDS

SERVES 8–10

rind of half a Seville orange, or, out of
   season, use part orange part
   lemon
1 tbsp brandy or orange liqueur, I've
   used Cointreau and Grand Marnier
juice of 1 Seville orange or half sweet
   orange to half lemon
110g/4oz unrefined granulated sugar
4 large egg yolks
300ml/10fl oz double cream
300ml/10fl oz single cream
1 tsp or to taste orange flower water
   (optional)
a few drops sweet orange oil from
   Culpeper or good delis or
   supermarkets (optional)

The idea of a cooking continuum – that the writers of some of our seminal cookery books should have their dishes passed down through the generations in the same way as hand-written family recipes are, with little changed except the gadgetry and what was taken for granted then and now – always appeals to me.

Mrs Raffald's *The Experienced English Housekeeper* of 1769 was one of the greats, and many of the recipes are adaptable to the present time and kitchen. She married at 30 and only lived another 18 years, but in that time had 15 or 16 daughters, a cooked-food shop selling pies and brawns and pickles, a domestic servant's employment agency, a confectioner's shop, two Manchester inns – and she wrote her cookery book. I first came across this recipe in Jane Grigson's all-time classic *English Food* when I was a student and then managed to find a facsimile of Mrs Raffald's book. I don't use candied peel as suggested as it is not something I'm overly fond of, but add a little orange-flower water and a few drops of sweet orange oil to the cream to intensify the flavour, and a twist of blanched peel to the top. You may use either, both or neither, but I beg you to try this divinely unctuous recipe. This is a pudding you will go on cooking for ever. It is easy to make in advance, cheap and will make people believe you are a seriously good cook. That is half the battle.

Preheat the oven to 170°C/325°F/Gas 3. Remove the rind from the citrus fruit with a swivel-bladed potato peeler, making sure there is no pith on the inside. Simmer the peel in a little pan in water for 2 minutes. Drain and put it in the blender with the brandy, orange (and lemon) juice, sugar and egg yolks. Blend hard until the peel has become pulverised to a slight grittiness and there are no large bits of it floating around.

Bring the creams to scalding point (that is the point just before they boil and rise up dangerously), together in a pan. Pour slowly into the blender, whizzing as you go. Check the flavour and add the orange-flower water and sweet orange oil accordingly, or, if you have neither, extra orange or lemon juice or sugar.

Place 8–10 small ramekins in a roasting tin. Pour the orange custard into the ramekins and pour boiling water to come halfway up their sides. Place in the oven for about 30 minutes or until the custards are set with a slight shudder in the middle when gently joggled in the tin. Remove from the water to cool as custard goes on cooking outside the oven. Serve warm or chilled with a slice of orange or a squirl of peel on top if you like.

CHRISTMAS

COUNTDOWN

4

I COOKED MY FIRST Christmas dinner when I was a student. It was one of

those extraordinary rites of passage that somehow make you feel you have truly transgressed to the other side and become a grown-up, even though you know at the time that the whole performance is at once an experiment and like play-acting the thing for real. You have, like Alice, looked through the glass. Curiouser and curiouser, it appears that the far side is unmapped and that nobody will ever tell you that you will always feel a little like you are acting out this self-same sacred ritual, even after you've established your own 'house style' and have been playing the part for years.

The particular Christmas I am writing about I was not cooking for my family. I was cooking for a huge bunch of friends, and had never done anything on that scale before. The whole event brought with it that sense of the new; of excitement, nervousness, anticipation, yet without any sense of certainty that I would be able to pull it off or knowledge that I had planted the first seeds of tradition. It is only now, more than two decades later, that I can look back and think how that was my first attempt to re-invent the most important of all family celebrations and rituals. All I have really been doing since then is enriching the mix, stirring better and better ingredients into the proverbial pudding in order to put my stamp on the celebration and make it mine, make it ours. I wanted to give my three children that known, yet unknown feeling each time of new-wrought yet familiar magic, that sense of the 'hidden thing, the somewhere joy' that my father originally wrote about in his poem for me, 'Getting Warm-Getting Cold'.

The tiny bed-sit I lived in during university holidays was possessed of a kitchen that was painted pillar-box red and was not big enough for two people to stand in at the same time. You couldn't have swung a mouse in it. There was one tiny work surface, a small fridge, an old electric cooker and a couple of shelves of storage space. The few plates I had were mismatched and I was going to have to borrow china, glasses, cutlery and an extra table, and tell people to bring their own chairs. Sheets would have to pass muster as tablecloths. The holly would have to be 'lifted' from the nearby park at night. The main room had a platform bed up a ladder and a dining table that sat eight at a squeeze. There were 25 coming to dinner. Advance preparations were all very well, but there was nowhere to advance them nor to put them once advanced. I had got used to marinating haunches of venison in the bath for up to three days at a time and my then boyfriend was a good cook and knew more than most students about food and wine, but I was doing the cooking, decking the place out and martialling the props. It all needed a game plan.

The one thing I was determined about was that everything would be done properly, everything would be done from scratch. You are always going to create a different atmosphere, a greater sense of drama, of theatre, if you imbue a sense of expectation into the guests by letting them know this is an OCCASION, albeit on a student or limited budget; that you have invited them to a serious gastronomic event which needs to be approached with due gravitas and empty belly, and that their being complicit in the event and doing their share is what's going to make it all come together.

I had never cooked a turkey. I had never made mince pies with my own drunken mincemeat or Christmas pudding topped to the gills with dried fruit, oily nuts, sharp grated apple, penetratingly deep dark molasses sugar and Guinness. I had no idea how to make brandy butter and had never made a sparkling, citrus-sharp fresh orange jelly, but I had made the most delicious chestnut, walnut, celery and apple stuffing for my cousin David's wife, Serena, and honed my basic cooking skills to the point at which I was a master, or mistress, of the level of cooking I had got to: I was a good, basic cook.

Christmas dinner is not demanding in terms of technique, not that I knew it then. It just needs co-ordination. You may only get to practise it once a year, so you still need to rev up for it each time, but otherwise it is not much different to a standard Sunday lunch.

In the haze of memory surrounding this first Christmas dinner, I can remember only the good things. That everyone had enough. Food and drink, that is. That it all tasted as good as I could get at that stage of my cooking life. That the ingredients were all good enough in the first place to give the novice cook a head start. That even the pudding did as it was told, its blue, brandy-sodden flame glowing boldly and brightly. And that at the end of it all I realised I could do it and had done it. I could now make cranberry sauce and brandy butter. I could make mincemeat, mince pies and Christmas pudding. I could get it all to the table at roughly the same time. And it would be fun to do it all over again the following year.

COUNTDOWN TO CHRISTMAS...

There is nothing more annoying than cookery writers telling you to get ahead – to plan your Christmas food in mid July, buy your presents in the summer sales, and start making and freezing your Christmas to New Year dishes almost before the clocks have changed in the autumn. It is enough to inspire anger, apathy and inadequacy in equal measure. Only YOU know how busy you are, how last minute you are and quite how impossible it is to take things in your leisurely stride and actually make your Christmas pudding on Stir-up Sunday and your battalions of mince pies for the freezer weeks in advance. So I will presume willingness but resistance. You know your own mind and limitations of time and will do what you can whenever you can fit any of it into the tight corners of your life. That's how I do it.

I may, in my present incarnation, be a food writer, but I seem to have less time than most as a result to cook what I want when I want to cook it. I am always tied to a subject and a deadline for a column, so I'm often three or four weeks ahead of myself, which doesn't mean I cook the turkey in November! I still have to do it all on the day. And then there is the book to write, the presents to shop for and the fact that, try as I might, I never get to wrapping up my Father Christmas presents until midnight on Christmas Eve, usually finishing a couple of hours later and wilting like the tree at the very thought of pulling off the great day on the morrow. Except by then, oh-my-God, it is not on the morrow, it is today.

So I am offering my traditional Christmas dinner in the order in which you need to make it, even if you're not able to get significantly ahead. That goes for making the pudding in advance whether it be three months, three weeks, or at worst three days, but most importantly, gives you a realistic timetable for the big day. This is just what I needed the first time I did it, but all I had was individual recipes.

...OCTOBER, NOVEMBER, AS SOON AS YOU CAN

CHRISTMAS PUDDING

MAKES 2 PUDDINGS

200g/7oz wholemeal flour
1 tsp mixed spice
1 tsp grated nutmeg
1 tsp ground ginger
285g/10oz sultanas
285g/10oz currants
200g/7oz raisins
200g/7oz mixed candied peel,
    finely chopped
450g/1lb dark muscovado sugar
110g/4oz blanched almonds,
    chopped
200g/7oz fresh brown breadcrumbs
200g/7oz shredded suet
1 large carrot, grated
3 Cox's apples, grated with the skin
6 organic eggs
300ml/10fl oz Guinness
60ml/2fl oz brandy
juice and grated rind of 1 orange
milk to mix

This is the first Christmas pudding I ever made and I didn't bother tampering with it for at least a decade. It is black, rich and drunk on the black stuff, a good frothy measure of Guinness. I love the bitter note stout adds to the pudding, combined with the darkly treacled molasses back-note of the darkest muscovado sugar. And it is not just dried fruity, it has the addition of sweet, grated carrot and sharp, grated apple. You may make it with suet or vegetarian suet depending on your predilections. Neither seems to alter the essential taste and depth of flavours of this wonderful, moist pud. The further in advance you make it, the more time the flavours have to develop, but you mustn't forget to keep pouring brandy, whisky or rum down the little skewer holes you pierce through the pudding. Once a week will do. Try not to be tempted to buy a Christmas pudding. They are easy and tremendously satisfying to make and you will undoubtedly prefer the end result. I always make an extra one and give it away as a present. There is always a good-friend-cum-good-cook who has run seriously short of time and will be grateful forever. Or you can keep it a little longer.

Grease two 600ml/1 pint pudding basins. Sift the flour into a large bowl with the mixed spice, nutmeg and ginger. Add the dried fruit and peel, sugar, almonds, breadcrumbs and suet, then the grated carrot and apples.

Beat the eggs well and add the Guinness, whisking until frothy. Then add the brandy, orange juice and rind, and stir into the dry ingredients. Add enough milk to get to a soft, dropping consistency. Divide the mixture between the two basins, leaving room at the top of the basin for the pudding to rise. Cover with pleated greaseproof paper and foil, tie securely with string, then boil for 7 hours.

To store, remove the wrappings and cover with clean greaseproof paper and foil. Store in a cool dark place. The puddings will need a further 2–3 hours boiling on Christmas Day before serving.

EXTRAVAGANT CHRISTMAS PUDDING

MAKES THREE PUDDINGS

200g/7oz plain flour
1 tsp ground cinnamon bark
1 tsp ground mace blade
1 tsp ground cloves
1 tsp ground dried ginger root
1 tsp allspice
200g/7oz each of sultanas, raisins
    and currants
225g/8oz each of Agen prunes, dried
    apricots and stoned dates
450g/1lb molasses sugar
110g/4oz each of Brazil nuts and
    almonds, chopped
200g/7oz brown breadcrumbs
3 sharp eating apples, grated with
    their skin
1 large carrot, peeled and grated
170g/6oz beef or vegetarian suet, or
    tiny bits of cold butter
6 organic eggs
300ml/10fl oz Guinness
60ml/2fl oz Somerset cider brandy or
    Cognac
juice and grated zest of an orange
little milk to mix

I finally broke out. Last year I decided to make a fruitier, more exotic pudding than ever, while staying faithful to my balance of ingredients, nuts, fruits, spices, flour, fat, sugar and alcohol. This is the result, which my family pronounced the best ever and I believe they were right. Don't worry if you can't find all the dried fruits, an approximation will be fine. Little bursts of sour cherries or cranberries, the graininess of figs, the sweetness of dates, the deep, sharp, softness of prunes, the firm acidic bite of unsulphured apricots — all can add textures and contrasting flavours that put the pudding way ahead of the ordinary vine-fruits model. A few Brazil nuts are lovely too, with their oily hardness giving the pudding a crunch amid its more yielding softness.

Grease three 600ml/1 pint pudding basins. Sift the flour into an exceptionally large bowl. Add the spices and dried fruits, then the sugar, nuts, breadcrumbs, apple, carrot, chopped suet, eggs, Guinness and brandy. Add the orange zest and juice that you have beaten together with a whisk.

Stir the liquid thoroughly into the dry ingredients. Add a little milk, if you need to, to make a soft, dropping consistency. Fill the pudding basins to just over three-quarters full. Cover with a layer of greaseproof paper and put a layer of foil on top of it, both pleated in the middle to allow the pudding to rise. Tie securely with string, making a handle, and place the puddings in a large, heavy-bottomed casserole on a trivet or layer of foil. You may need to use more than one casserole.

Fill the casserole to halfway up the sides of the puddings with boiling water, cover with a lid and bring to the boil. Cook at a gentle simmer for 6–7 hours, topping up with water every couple of hours if you need to.

Take the puddings out of the water, remove the foil and greaseproof, and allow to cool. Re-cover. They can be fed with extra brandy through skewer holes if you have made them well in advance. The puddings will need 2–3 hours further cooking on Christmas Day.

...NOVEMBER, DECEMBER, AS SOON AS YOU CAN...

HOMEMADE MINCEMEAT

MAKES TWO BIG JARS

about 340g/12oz each of organic sultanas, raisins and currants
170g/6oz blanched almonds, finely chopped
3 Cox's apples, cut into dolls' size dice
400g/14oz dark muscovado sugar
200g/7oz organic mixed peel, finely chopped
grated zest and juice of 1½ organic lemons, and the zest of an organic orange
1 tsp nutmeg, finely grated
¼ tsp ground cloves and cinnamon
⅛ tsp ground mace and dried root ginger
170g/6oz beef or vegetarian suet
4 tbsp dark rum
120ml/4fl oz Cognac or Somerset Cider Brandy

It takes longer to buy, assemble and weigh the ingredients for mincemeat than to make it, which, after all, only involves a bowl, a large wooden spoon and a liberal hand with the booze. It always feels exciting to get the children stirring and weighing and chuting fruit into the most capacious bowl you have before they ladle the ingredients into the jars and label them in their best hand. This is a Christmas ritual that shouldn't be shortcut, even if you only get round to it a few days before D-Day.

Simply mix all the ingredients together really well in a colossal bowl. Decant into sterilised jars, cover and keep in a cool dark place. Turn the jars upside down every so often so that the liquid permeates the mixture constantly.

NIGEL SLATER'S BIG FRUIT CAKE

340g/12oz unsalted butter at room temperature

340g/12oz soft dark brown sugar

1kg/2¼lb in total ready-to-eat figs, prunes, apricots, candied peel, glacé cherries

5 large organic eggs

100g/3½ oz ground almonds

140g/5oz shelled hazelnuts

500g/1lb 2oz in total vine fruits (raisins, sultanas, and currants)

5 tbsp brandy

the zest and juice of an orange and a lemon

½ tsp baking powder

340g/12oz plain flour

There is no cook or food writer more in touch with what we want to cook, what we REALLY feel like eating, than Nigel Slater. And I've always thought that baking is where he is truly at home; it is one of his real strengths. So this cake, which is every bit as Christmassy as it should be whether you dress it up with marzipan and Royal icing or leave it plain, is just a wonderfully old-fashioned, moist and boozily fruity cake.

You will also need a 23cm/9in cake tin with a removable base. Line it with buttered greaseproof paper, which should come 5cm/2in above the top of the tin. Preheat the oven to 170°C/325°F/Gas 3.

Beat the butter and sugar until pale and fluffy. I needn't tell you that this is much easier in an electric mixer, but I have occasionally done it by hand. Don't forget to push the mixture down the sides of the bowl from time to time with a spatula. While the butter and sugar are beating to a cappuccino-coloured fluff, cut the figs, prunes, apricots, candied peel and cherries into small pieces, removing the hard stalks from the figs. Add the eggs to the mixture one at a time – it will curdle but don't worry – then slowly mix in the ground almonds, hazelnuts, all the dried fruit, the brandy and the citrus zest and juice.

Now mix the baking powder and flour together and fold them lightly into the mix. Scrape the mixture into the prepared tin, smoothing the top gently, and put it in the oven. Leave it for an hour, then, without opening the oven door, turn down the heat to 150°C/300°F/Gas 2 and continue baking for 2 hours. Check whether the cake is done by inserting a skewer into the centre. It should come out with just a few crumbs attached but no trace of raw cake mixture. Take the cake out of the oven and leave to cool before removing from the tin.

To make the cake boozier, pierce holes in it and pour a little brandy into the holes every 3–4 days for a fortnight. Wrap the cake tightly in greaseproof paper, then in foil or clingfilm and lower it into a tin. Covered, it will be fine for several weeks.

EARLY DECEMBER, OR AT LEAST A WEEK BEFORE CHRISTMAS

CHRISTMAS CAKE, OR RICH PLUM CAKE

Here is a straightforward, honest and good Christmas cake, sans marzipan, icing or any adornment. I have to declare myself fruit-cake shy at this point, but I can appreciate the point and the quality of a good fruit cake and know what it should taste like. Do try to make your Christmas cake a couple of weeks ahead of Christmas, so that it may mature and flower at the right time.

MAKES A 18CM/7IN CAKE

225g/8oz unsalted butter, softened
225g/8oz light muscovado sugar
6 organic eggs
grated zest and juice of a lemon
½ tsp each of ground cinnamon,
   cloves, mixed spice and nutmeg
½ teacup black treacle
340g/12oz plain flour
340g/12oz currants
225g/8oz sultanas
55g/2oz glacé cherries, the undyed
   ones
55g/2oz candied orange peel
1 teacup strong, dry cider
1 level tsp bicarbonate of soda
¼ teacup dark rum

Preheat the oven 150–170°C/300–325°F/Gas 2–3. Line an 18cm/7in cake tin with three layers of greaseproof paper and a final layer of Bakewell paper.

Cream the softened butter and sugar together well until pale and fluffy. Separate the eggs and beat the egg yolks into the creamed butter and sugar one by one. Add the lemon zest and juice, the spices and the treacle. Work in half the flour and fruit and pour over enough cider to moisten the mixture. Mix the bicarbonate of soda with the rest of the flour and add it with the remaining fruit. Whisk the egg whites to stiff peaks, stir the first spoonful into the mixture, then quickly and lightly fold in the rest, a large tablespoon at a time. Add the alcohol and gently fold it in.

Pour into the lined tin and bake in the centre of the oven for 2–3 hours, until a skewer comes out clean when sunk into the cake. Leave the cake to cool in its tin. Keep in a tin with a lid on it for a couple of weeks.

...AT LEAST A MONTH BEFORE YOU WANT TO EAT IT

COUNTRY CHRISTMAS CAKE

MAKES A 20–23CM/8–9IN CAKE

FIRST LIST
1.2kg/2lb 8 oz mixed dried fruit
55g/2oz chopped candied peel
55g/2oz glacé cherries, halved
85g/3oz preserved ginger, drained
    and chopped
grated zest and juice of 1 large
    orange and 1 large lemon
1 tbsp bitter orange marmalade
1 tbsp apricot jam
225g/8oz stewed apple

SECOND LIST
225g/8oz lightly salted butter,
    softened
225g/8oz soft dark brown sugar
4 organic eggs
1 tsp pure vanilla extract
few drops almond essence

THIRD LIST
340g/12oz plain flour, sifted
1 tsp each ground cinnamon, ginger,
    nutmeg, cloves, mixed spice
1 tsp baking powder
enough blanched almonds to
    decorate the top of the cake with

AFTER BAKING
1 tbsp whisky or brandy

The fruit and spices for this cake need to sit and commune with the juice overnight before you actually make and bake, so plan accordingly. The recipe comes from one of my cooking heroines, Jane Grigson, from whose books I largely taught myself to cook. Elizabeth David was another inspiration, but it was always Jane's scholarly approach and accuracy that gave me the confidence to try things I didn't think I was up to. When I met her, I was struck by how closely she resembled the character of her recipes and writing: warm hearted, good humoured and generous spirited, dependable, accurate, scholarly and precise. The definition of a great cook. Start the night before you want to bake the cake.

Mix all the ingredients on the first list in a large basin. Turn them over thoroughly. Cover and leave overnight.

The following day, preheat the oven to 170°C/325°F/Gas 3. Gather the ingredients from the second list. Cream the butter and sugar until light and fluffy. Beat in the eggs one by one and add the vanilla extract and almond essence.

Put the flour, spices and baking powder from the third list in a bowl and stir them together. Mix the fruit and flour mixture alternately into the creamed butter and sugar, a little at a time. Line a 20–23cm/8–9in cake tin with three layers of greaseproof paper and a final layer of Bakewell paper. Pour in the mixture and decorate with blanched almonds, unless you intend to cover the cake eventually with marzipan and icing.

Bake for 2 hours before turning down the heat to 150°C/300°F/Gas 2 for a further 2 hours. Remove the cake from the oven, puncture it with a few holes with a skewer and pour in the booze; an extra tablespoon or two won't hurt. Leave the cake to cool in its tin.

Next day, remove the cake and peel off the greaseproof and Bakewell paper. Wrap it in fresh greaseproof paper and keep it in an airtight tin or in firmly sealed foil for at least a month before using it. If you want to finish the cake with marzipan and icing, make your own. The readymade stuff is never very good. Homemade is easy and tastes much better.

MARZIPAN

225g/8oz unrefined icing sugar
450g/1lb ground almonds
1 large organic egg
3–4 tsp lemon juice
1 tbsp apricot jam
1 tbsp water

Sift the icing sugar and mix it with the ground almonds. Beat the egg thoroughly, add the lemon juice and mix with the dry ingredients. Use a wooden spoon to beat everything to a firm paste, then knead it on a board or marble which has been sprinkled with icing sugar. Slice the top from the cake to make it even, then turn it upside down and put on a wire rack. Boil the jam and water in a small pan, sieve it into a bowl and while still hot brush it over what was the bottom of the cake and is now the top.

Set aside one-third of the almond paste and roll out the rest to a circle just a little larger than the cake. Do this on a sheet of clean greaseproof paper and use the cake tin as a guide. Press the glazed side of the cake down on to the circle of almond marzipan: reverse it so that you now have the greaseproof paper on top, then the marzipan and then the cake. Remove the paper and smooth the marzipan down over the sides. Measure the depth of the cake and its circumference. Roll out the remaining marzipan to these measurements, again on a sheet of greaseproof paper. Brush the cake sides with apricot glaze and roll the cake slowly along the strip of marzipan. Pat everything into place, closing the cracks and so on, and replace the cake on its rack. Leave for 2 days before icing.

ROYAL ICING

2 small egg whites
2 tsp lemon juice
450g/1lb icing sugar, sieved
(I use unrefined)

Whisk the egg whites until they are white and foamy but not stiff. Stir in the lemon juice, then the sieved icing sugar. Do this bit by bit, using a wooden spoon. When everything is mixed together, continue to beat the mixture until it is a dazzling white — although it will not be dazzling white with unrefined icing sugar! Cover the basin and leave it for an hour or so before using it.

Place a bowl of hot water beside the cake. Put about half the icing on the cake and spread it out with a palette knife which you have dipped in the water. The knife should be hot and wet, but not wet enough to soak the cake and ruin the icing. Cover the cake all over, then put on the remaining icing, either roughly to make a snowy effect, or in an elegant design with the aid of a forcing bag and nozzles.

3-2-1 DAYS BEFORE CHRISTMAS

MINCE PIES

Mincemeat (see p. 203)

SHORTCRUST PASTRY
450g/1lb flour
pinch of sea salt
225g/8oz unsalted butter
beaten egg for glaze

There are no mince pies as good as homemade ones, so even if you cheat and don't make my mincemeat (see page 203), do go the final furlong with the pastry. I am not a great one for flavoured pastry, but I rather feel Christmas is an exception. You may add the zest of an orange, a handful of near-crushed hazelnuts or almonds, a couple of tablespoons of ground almonds minus the equivalent of flour, even a tablespoon of brandy or orange liqueur to your pastry. Or just make your favourite shortcrust with either all butter or half butter, half lard. If you are tired of pie-shaped pies, buy a dozen little boat-shaped moulds from your kitchen shop; they look very good as flotillas floating on a large blue plate. I usually make a couple of dozen mince pies a day or two before Christmas, then start again on Boxing Day if they've all gone. They keep well stored in layers on greaseproof paper in a box with a good sealed lid, and they crisp up well when warmed through.

Make the pastry (see pages 180–181). To make the mince pies, fill the little patty tins with pastry and spoon in mincemeat generously. Brush the pastry rims with water and stick the pastry hats on, pressing down firmly all round the edges. Brush with beaten egg, prick a cross in the tops for the steam to escape through and cook in a hot oven, 200°C/400°F/Gas 6, for 15–20 minutes. Turn out on to racks to cool. Serve hot, warm or cold with brandy butter, cream or cream with some Cider Brandy or the like whisked into it.

MINCEMEAT AND APPLE TART

SERVES 6–8

SHORTCRUST PASTRY
170g/6oz organic white flour
pinch of sea salt
85g/3oz unsalted butter

FILLING
6 tbsp mincemeat
1 large Bramley apple, peeled, coarsely grated and stirred into the mincemeat
a beaten egg
unrefined icing sugar

A classic alternative for using up your mincemeat in something a little lighter. The tart apple cuts the brandied richness of the mincemeat too, but you can always restore it by lashing on the brandy butter (see page 210). You don't have to put a criss-cross lattice of pastry over the mincemeat, but the sticky, toffeed crust that attaches itself to the pastry strips as a result is pretty irresistible.

Make the shortcrust pastry (see pages 180–181). Line a 23cm/9 inch tart tin and chill. Save the pastry trimmings to make a lattice top if you like. Preheat the oven to 190°C/375°F/Gas 5. Bake the pastry case blind for 15 minutes (see page 181), then remove the beans, prick the base with a fork and bake for 5 more minutes.

Plop the mincemeat and apple into a pastry case. If you want to make a lattice top, hold the strips of pastry at each end and twirl them to get a rope-like effect before placing them over the filling.

Brush a little beaten egg over the pastry and bake until the filling is molten and erupting in between the lattice strips, and the pastry is golden brown. Remove and leave to cool for a while before serving warm with a scattering of icing sugar over the top.

Mince Pies

BRANDY, SOMERSET CIDER BRANDY OR RUM BUTTER

MAKES A GOOD BOWLFUL

225g/8oz best unsalted butter, softened
110g/4oz unrefined icing sugar for brandy butter, or half unrefined icing sugar, half light muscovado sugar for rum butter, sifted
2–3 tbsp Cognac, Somerset Cider Brandy or dark rum
grated zest of an orange
a small grating of nutmeg
a squeeze of lemon juice

Always best when made, or rather squelched, by hand. I'm sure the warmth of one's hands begins to activate the spice and alcohol and marry them to the butter and sugar. I love Julian Temperley's Somerset Cider Brandy. It is as good, if not better than, any Calvados from Normandy, but he's just not allowed to call it that. Its apple nose is lovely with the mincemeat.

Start with soft butter, which you can cream further in a bowl with a wooden spoon, before adding the sifted sugar and all the other ingredients. A suspicion of nutmeg only. Now work everything together with your fingers, the aim being to incorporate all the liquid and end up with a slushy alcoholic mixture. It will firm up in the fridge. Good with the pud and the mince pies.

CRANBERRY SAUCE

SERVES 8–10

340g/12oz cranberries
170g/6oz or to taste caster sugar
juice and zest of an orange

Make more if you're worried about not having enough for cold turkey and turkey sandwiches, which my children add stuffing and bread sauce to as well if there's anything left by then.

Weed out the squishy or bruised berries first, then put the good berries into a pan with the sugar and orange juice. Bring to the boil and bubble away until the berries begin to pop, about 7–10 minutes. Remove immediately so that they hold their shape. Taste for sweetness; you may need to add a little more sugar. Gently turn the zest into the sauce so that you don't break the berries up. Pour into a bowl and leave to cool then, cover with clingfilm and keep in the fridge.

CUMBERLAND SAUCE

1 orange
1 lemon
225g/8oz redcurrant jelly
1 tsp French mustard
60ml/2fl oz port
salt and pepper
ground cloves, nutmeg or ginger (optional)

This delectably sticky sweet sauce, underscored with spices and mustard and zinging with soft shards of citrus, is the perfect sweet-sour accompaniment to your Christmas ham. It can be made several days in advance and kept in a screw-top jar in the fridge for several weeks, so I like to make it just before Christmas and add to it if I need to when we eat the ham. Great in ham sandwiches too. If you can get Seville oranges during their short season do, but pre-Christmas you'll have to make do with oranges and lemons.

First comes the time-consuming part. Peel the orange and lemon with a potato peeler so there is virtually no bitter pith on the strips of peel. Shred the peel with a fine-bladed knife into long, impossibly skinny lengths and blanch in boiling water for a couple of minutes. Drain and set aside.

In a saucepan, heat the jelly and mustard together until well melted, add the port, and whisk until hot. Add the orange and lemon juice, season to taste, and if you feel like a bit of spice add a pinch of ground cloves, nutmeg or ginger. Stir in the peel and simmer for 5 minutes. Pour into a bowl or jar and keep in the fridge until you want to use it; it will keep for several weeks.

CHRISTMAS EVE

CHESTNUT, APPLE, WALNUT AND CELERY STUFFING

3 tbsp olive oil
1 large onion, finely chopped
½ a head of celery, finely chopped
110g/4oz walnuts, finely chopped
2 tart dessert apples, cored,
    unpeeled and finely chopped
450g/1lb tin chestnut purée
450g/1lb organic sausagemeat
225g/8oz wholemeal breadcrumbs
2 organic eggs, beaten
2 tbsp flat-leaf parsley, finely
    chopped
salt and pepper
450g/1lb vacuum-packed chestnuts

This makes enough stuffing to fill the cavity of a large Bronze turkey and a small roasting tin as well. There are lots of very good jars or vacuum packs of organic chestnuts on the market now and that's what I use for flavour and ease. You may wish to stuff each end of the turkey with a different stuffing, for example, the following lemon and thyme one, in which case make the same amount of the chestnut one. Use a larger roasting tin or gratin dish and you will have plenty left for your cold turkey and sandwiches. This is the stuffing I've been making for 20 years. There would be a mutiny if I changed it. Certain things in life are immutable, to one's children, that is.

Heat the oil gently in a frying pan, and fry together the onion, celery, walnuts and apple until golden and softened. Turn into a huge bowl and add all the remaining ingredients, mixing well. Add the whole chestnuts last, chopped in quarters so that they don't break up during the mixing. Stuff the bird. Put the rest in a roasting tin and cook separately.

LEMON, THYME AND PARSLEY STUFFING

225g/8oz stale white bread
grated zest of 2 lemons and the juice
    of 1
a large bunch of flat-leaf parsley
2 tsp fresh thyme, chopped a little to
    release the oils
110g/4oz butter, softened
3 organic eggs
sea salt and black pepper

Turn the bread to crumbs in a food processor. (If you only have newer bread, toast it in a slow oven until dry on both sides before making into crumbs.) Put the breadcrumbs in a large bowl and add the zest and juice. Add the roughly chopped parsley and thyme, amalgamate with the softened butter with a wooden spoon, then beat in the eggs and add the seasoning. A very good contrast to the richer, porkier chestnut stuffing. It works well made with sage instead of thyme if you are cooking a boned loin of pork. Stuff the bird, ready for Christmas morning/afternoon.

POTATO, SAGE, PRUNE AND GOOSE LIVER STUFFING

450–675g/1–1½ lb potatoes,
    depending on the size of the goose
85–110g/3–4oz unsalted butter
salt and pepper, grated nutmeg
3–4 onions, chopped
12–14 fresh sage leaves
2 tbsp olive oil
goose liver and heart
225g/8oz Agen prunes, soaked
    overnight in tea, then stoned and
    chopped

A stuffing for goose. If you are going to make this the night before, don't put it in the fridge. Mashed potatoes and fridges do not get on together. Just keep it somewhere cool overnight and don't add the goose liver until the morning, when you can fry it and the heart up with the sage leaves in a couple of minutes.

Peel and boil the potatoes, then drain and mash them, or put them through a mouli-légumes. Add butter, salt, pepper and nutmeg to taste.

   Cook the chopped onions in boiling water for 10 minutes. Drain and stir into the potato mixture. Tear the sage leaves into small pieces and stew in the olive oil over a low heat until the scent really comes out of them. Trim any green bits from the goose liver and heart and slice into thin strips. Add them to the pan and cook until pink, with the blood still running. Add the prunes. Tip the contents of the pan into the potato and onion mixture, stir gently and stuff the body of the goose.

CORNBREAD

285g/10oz smoked streaky bacon
2 red, or 1 red and 1 green chilli,
    seeded, cored and finely sliced
225g/8oz coarse cornmeal
75g/2½oz plain flour
3 tsp baking powder
1½ tsp bicarbonate of soda
285g/10oz sweetcorn kernels
600ml/1 pint buttermilk
2 large organic eggs
flat-leaf parsley, chopped

I know this is something of an American Thanksgiving thing rather than one of our indigenous traditions, but you may want to offer something different with your turkey and break with tradition just a little. A heavy, cast-iron skillet or Le Creuset-style frying pan that you can put in the oven is the tool to use for this.

Preheat the oven to 180°C/350°F/Gas 4. Take the rind off the bacon and snip into strips with a pair of scissors, then put it into a 30cm/12in heavy-bottomed frying pan to fry. Cook until the fat has run and the little snippets have started to brown and crisp, then remove them with a slotted spoon and place them on some kitchen paper.

   Fry the chillies gently in the bacon fat while you mix all the dry ingredients together. Add the bacon, corn and then the softened chillies. Whisk the buttermilk and eggs together and pour them into the bowl of dry ingredients. Heat the bacon fat to smoking and pour the mixture into the pan. Put the pan into the preheated oven. The cornbread will take about 30 minutes to cook and should look crisp and golden brown on top when it is ready. A skewer should come out clean in the usual way. Sprinkle with a little parsley and serve cut into triangular wedges.

Cornbread

CHRISTMAS DAY – THE LOWDOWN

Work everything backwards from the time you want to eat, making sure you allow 20–30 minutes for the turkey to rest after it has come out of the oven. My turkey usually takes 3½ hours to cook, so I put it in the oven at 10.30 am to be ready and rested by 2.30 pm. None of this slow-cooked, start-at-dawn malarkey when the martyred cook has to rise in the dark to switch on the oven and heave the poor benighted bird into it. So here is a rough schedule, assuming you are cooking a turkey, which you can adapt to your size of bird and the time you want to eat. This will work for a goose as well, though the average goose takes 2½ hours to cook, so count accordingly. Don't forget to lay the table. I'm sure efficient people do it the night before.

- 10.00 am: Preheat the oven to 190°C/375°F/Gas 5. Remove the stuffed turkey from the fridge – all meat should be cooked from room temperature. Remove the butter from the fridge and the extra tin of stuffing.

- 10.15 am: Peel and slice the onions for under the turkey and slap the softened butter onto the turkey.

- 10.30 am: Put the turkey in the oven as instructed in the recipe below.

- Now prepare the vegetables. I know some people swear by peeling their potatoes and parsnips the night before, but it really isn't much work, particularly if you've got a friend or child to help, and the veg do lose starch, vitamins and flavour overnight.

- Peel everything peelable, prepare your sprouts and any other vegetables and put them in cold water.

- 12.00 midday: Put your Christmas pudding into a large heavy-bottomed saucepan. Add boiling water from the kettle to come halfway up the sides of the pudding. Bring to the boil, turn down to a simmer and cover with the lid. It will steam happily for 3 hours, but you need to check and top up the water from time to time. This timing assumes you have made your own pudding and cooked it already.

- 12.15 pm: Start your bread sauce (see page 95) by tearing up the bread and assembling the milk, onion, cloves, etc.

- Cover the extra tin of stuffing tightly with foil and put in the oven.

- 1 pm: Put the potatoes and parsnips on in the same pan to parboil. They need to go into the oven for 1.15.

- Make your bread sauce and keep it warm under a lid ready to heat through. It will need extra milk and a little butter or cream if you want to make it a little richer.

- 1.10 pm: Heat the fat in the tin for roasting the potatoes and parsnips.

- 1.15 pm: Coat potatoes and parsnips all over in fat, ruffle the potatoes with a fork and put the tin on the top shelf of the oven.

- Remove bacon and chipolatas from the fridge. Turn oven up (see turkey recipe on page 216).

- 2.00 pm: Remove turkey and check it is cooked. Place it covered with foil and a tea towel on the carving board.

- Wrap the bacon round the chipolatas, plop them into the roasting tin and put in the oven.

- Put the turkey neck and giblets in a small pan and just cover with water. Bring to the boil, scum and simmer gently until you are ready to make your gravy.

- Remove the cranberry sauce from the fridge.

- Turn the potatoes.

- Re-heat the bread sauce gently with the extra milk.

- Put the other vegetables on to cook. Put some serving dishes to warm.

- 2.25 pm: Check the chipolatas and bacon and the potatoes. If they are ready, put into warmed serving dishes and keep hot. Likewise, transfer your cooked vegetables to warm serving dishes.

- Make the gravy (see page 216) and add the giblet gravy after you have removed the bacon and chipolatas from the roasting tin and heated the juices already in the tin with the addition of a glass of red wine. Add some of the parboiling water from your potatoes and parsnips in the usual way, to help thicken the gravy (see page 94).

- 2.30 pm: Carve the turkey and don't forget to serve the stuffing with it.

HOW TO ROAST A TURKEY

Bronze organic or free-range turkey
stuffing (see p. 211)
large onion, peeled and sliced
200g/7oz butter, softened and well-
    seasoned
coarse sea salt
pepper

First and all important is to buy a really good turkey and by that, I mean a Bronze organic or free-range bird that has been properly reared, slaughtered and hung. The gamier flavour and firmer-fleshed, less pappy meat of any bird that has been reared as a free-range or organic bird – one has to remember that turkeys refuse to go out on a bad day, they hate bad weather – make these the only birds to buy. Intensively reared turkeys are not worth paying less for. By cooking the turkey on its sides before you turn it breast up you will silence the critics who plead the impossibility of cooking this most delicately delicious of fowl through at the leg/thigh end without cremating and drying out the breast.

Preheat your oven to 190°C/375°F/Gas Mark 5. Then weigh your stuffed bird, and calculate the cooking time: 33 minutes per kilo or 15 minutes to the pound applies up to a 6.5kg/14lb bird. So, a 6.5kg/14lb bird will take 3½ hours. Always calculate like this up to this weight, even if the bird is bigger. For each extra pound allow 10 minutes, so, for a 8.7kg/20lb bird, your total cooking time will be 4½ hours. Still not worth getting out of bed early for.

Place the bird on its side, on a layer of peeled, sliced onions, and slap the well-seasoned butter on its skin. Shroud the bird in foil, a double layer, clinching it tightly around the roasting tin, so the bird is sealed in. Just before half time, turn the bird on to its other side, baste it with the buttery juices, seal it inside the foil, and continue to cook. About 30–40 minutes before it should be ready, remove the foil, turn the bird breast up and baste it. Season the skin well with coarse sea salt and pepper, hit the 200°C/400°F/Gas 6 button and allow the bird to crisp up.

Rest the turkey, covered with foil and a tea towel, for 20 minutes in a warm place while you make gravy. I simmer the giblets for 30 minutes with the vegetable water from parboiling my potatoes and parsnips, adding the liver towards the end. I sieve this mixture into the roasting pan with the onion and meat juices, add a splosh of red wine and more meat juices from the carving board as frequently as they exude, and stir while they bubble away for a few minutes. I strain the lot into a jug, and then into a dégraisseur.

large onion, peeled and sliced
4.8–6 kg/10–12lb goose, add the
    liver and heart to the stuffing
stuffing (see p. 212)
salt and pepper

HOW TO ROAST A GOOSE

I hate to think that the goose has been relegated to a low second in the Christmas stakes. It is such a marvellous fowl, but many are put off by its apparent richness, fatness, expense and low proportion of meat per pound, or per carcass, so to speak, compared with turkey. I find that you don't need a lot of goose precisely because its succulent richness is a thing to savour sparingly. If you slice it thinly, a goose will easily feed 8–10 people with leftovers for goose and apple sauce sandwiches. And you'll have fantastic stock and fat to cook your roast potatoes in over the winter months. So I buy a goose for New Year's Eve and a turkey for Christmas. That way I don't have to make a painful or unpopular decision with the children.

Place the onions in a layer in your roasting tin. Stuff the goose and place it, breast down, in the pan and roast for 1–1½ hours. Turn the bird breast side up, scatter with salt and pepper, and roast for another hour or so, spiking with a thin skewer every 20 minutes. Drain off the fat at intervals and keep it to make the most delicious roast potatoes

joint of ham
cider (optional)
onion, carrot, celery, chopped
bouquet of parsley, bay leaves and
thyme, tied together

HAM GLAZE

1 tbsp French or grain mustard or
Colman's mustard powder (my
preference)
1 tbsp dark muscovado or molasses
sugar
1 tbsp strong runny honey like
chestnut
1 tbsp marmalade or redcurrant jelly
zest of 1 organic orange
1 tbsp double cream
cloves to stud or 1 tsp ground cloves
1 tbsp cracked black peppercorns,
coarsely cracked in a mortar
1 tsp crushed juniper berries
(optional)
1 orange, thinly sliced (optional)

HOW TO COOK A HAM

Calculate the cooking time in the following way. Up to 2kg/4½lb in weight, 30 minutes to the pound and an extra 15–30 minutes depending on the cut. Test for doneness in the usual way. From 2–4.8kg/4½–10lb; 20 minutes per pound plus an extra 20 minutes. Once you are cooking a really large ham, the times are roughly as follows: for a 5.5kg/12lb ham, 3½ hours; for a 7kg/16lb ham, 4 hours; 8.7kg/20lb, 4½ hours; 11kg/24lb, 5 hours.

Put the ham into a huge pan or kettle, cover it with cold water and bring it to the boil. When it has simmered for 5 minutes, taste the water for saltiness; if it is too salty, throw it away. I do this anyway, adding dry local cider at this stage, but if you are happy with the water, just add the vegetables and bouquet garni you would to a stock pot at this stage and calculate your cooking once you've got them all going together. Ham stock with little pink shards of meat, with or without cider, is wonderful for lentil, split pea or pea soup (with frozen peas at this time of year).

I tend not to serve my ham hot. If you want to, remove the skin with a long, sharp-bladed knife when the ham is cooked and serve it with an onion or apple and onion sauce or with a mustardy gravy made with some of the stock, some Madeira or Marsala, a little grain mustard and some cream.

I prefer a glazed ham for serving cold. Take the ham out of its cooking liquor about 30 minutes before it is fully cooked, remove the skin and carve a diamond pattern with a sharp knife point into, but not right through the fat. Preheat the oven to 190°C/375°F/Gas 5. Mix the glaze ingredients together and spoon and press them onto the fat and into the channels you have cut into it. You may stud the diamonds with whole cloves the old-fashioned way if you like or just use ground cloves in your glaze. Or add some slices of orange, spearing them with cloves so they stick to the ham fat.

Glaze the ham in the oven until the glaze has bubbled up and made molten crust on the fat. You may have to keep spooning the brown goo back onto the fat as it does tend to slide off. When the glaze has welded itself to the ham, remove the beast from the tin and leave to cool. Serve with Cumberland Sauce (see page 210).

THE VEGETABLES

Turn to pages 94–95 for the roast potato and roast parsnip recipes if you need to. Otherwise, the following are a brief selection of the vegetables you may want to cook on the day or over the Christmas period for serving with your bird, game or joint.

SPICED RED CABBAGE WITH APPLE, MOLASSES AND CIDER VINEGAR

SERVES 10–12

1 large red cabbage, halved, cored and very thinly sliced
2 tbsp olive oil
3 medium cooking apples, peeled, quartered and cut unto chunks
molasses sugar
cider vinegar
apple juice or the Somerset Cider Brandy Company's Kingston Black Apple Aperitif, or some dry cider
6 cloves (or juniper berries)
salt and black pepper

It's worth cooking a whole cabbage, however many of you there are, as it's great cold with cold pork, ham or goose, good in a sandwich of these, or just as delicious, if not better, heated through the next day. Everyone has a favourite recipe for red cabbage. Mine changes a little each time I make it. The principle is long, slow cooking to leach out all the cabbagey juices. Some sort of agro/dolce or sweet/sour combination shows the cabbage off to best effect and some spice and fruit enhance it yet further.

Put a layer of cabbage in the bottom of a large, heavy-bottomed pot with the olive oil. Throw on one-third of the apple chunks, followed by about a dessertspoon of little lumps of dark brown molasses sugar, a sprinkle of cider vinegar with your thumb half covering the neck of the bottle, around 4 tablespoons of apple juice or apple alcohol, a good splosh, and a couple of cloves. Season. Repeat with another two layers of everything.

Bring to a gentle simmer on top of the stove, cover with a layer of greaseproof paper and a tight-fitting lid and simmer on. After an hour, check and stir the cabbage thoroughly so that the top layer cooks through in the liquid beneath and doesn't dry out. Repeat once more. It will be ready 2–2½ hours after the start of cooking time. Taste the cooking juices to make sure you have the right balance between acidic and sweet and adjust accordingly. If at any time the liquid level looks like it's too low to protect the cabbage and lubricate it, add some more apple juice or apple alcohol.

You can prepare and cook the whole dish a day ahead if you want and just heat it through really slowly the day you want to use it.

A few crushed juniper berries work well if you feel like scenting the cabbage with them rather than with cloves. You may wish to add red wine vinegar and red wine instead of the apple element, in which case onion instead of apple works best and you may like to throw in a few whole chestnuts at the same time.

Red cabbage is also delicious if you cook it with 450g/1lb cranberries and a large, chopped cooking apple in the same way as for this recipe, but with a cinnamon stick instead of the cloves. You will need to add extra sugar as the cranberries are sharper than sharp.

GREEN CABBAGE WITH CHESTNUTS, BACON AND JUNIPER

If you only have half an hour to play with and want to serve a cabbage dish worthy of your Christmas meats, use green cabbage instead of red and try this milder, creamier dish.

SERVES 6

organic green cabbage
salt
3 rashers organic smoked streaky
    bacon, snipped into strips
olive oil and butter
6 juniper berries, crushed in a pestle
    and mortar
18–20 chestnuts, cooked and peeled,
    or ½ packet Merchant Gourmet
    chestnuts
150ml/5fl oz double cream
salt and freshly ground pepper

Core the cabbage thoroughly, remove the tough stalky bits and shred finely. Blanch for a minute in plenty of boiling salted water, then drain and refresh in cold water to arrest the cooking.

In a heavy-bottomed pot, gently fry the bacon rashers in their own fat, then add a little olive oil and butter, the crushed juniper berries, and the cabbage. Stir well to coat the cabbage, season, put on the lid, and cook very gently for 15 minutes or so. This is a very good-tempered dish so a few minutes either way won't hurt. Stir in the halved chestnuts and the double cream and heat through. Check the seasoning and serve.

BRUSSELS SPROUTS WITH CHESTNUTS AND FRAZZLED BACON

Allow 10–12 sprouts per person. Any that don't get eaten can have a second chance in a gratin or bubble and squeak the following day. You may want to leave out the chestnuts or bacon on the grounds that if you are serving rolls of bacon with your turkey or a chestnutty stuffing, once is enough.

SERVES 8–10

1kg/2¼1b Brussels sprouts
6 rashers organic smoked streaky
    bacon, the rind snipped off
1 x 200g/7oz jar organic chestnuts or
    the vacuum packed ones
a little unsalted butter (optional)
a handful of flat-leaf parsley,
    chopped
a suspicion of grated nutmeg
black pepper

Remove the outside leaves from the sprouts and cut a cross in the base, though heaven quite knows why. Bring a large pan of water to the boil, salt it and throw in the sprouts. They will take 4–5 minutes to be firm but yielding to a knifepoint stuck right through them. Drain and refresh under cold water so they keep their colour and don't continue to cook. You can do this an hour ahead of needing them and keep them in the colander.

Fifteen minutes before serving, snip the bacon into small, slim strips and cook it in a heavy-bottomed frying pan, slowly, until it begins to release all its fat into the pan. Cook it further until it begins to brown and crisp, then throw in the roughly chopped chestnuts and sprouts and coat them in the bacon fat for a few minutes. You may need to add a walnut-sized lump of butter, or you may not want to. Remove from the heat, scatter over the parsley and season with nutmeg, sparingly, and a little black pepper.

HOT GRATED BEETROOT AND APPLE SALAD
WITH A WARM HORSERADISH DRESSING

The earthy-sweet acidity of the beetroot is a great match for white fish, white meat or even your cold Christmas ham. This is a lovely hot salad to give a pickle-sharpness to your cold meat and jacket potato.

SERVES 4

4 medium beetroots, skins on but
    cleaned, their whiskers intact
2 small sharp eating apples like
    Cox's
olive oil
red wine vinegar
2 tsp grated fresh horseradish or
    grated hot horseradish, or to taste
sea salt and black pepper
fresh dill or parsley

Preheat the oven to 190°C/375°F/Gas 5. Bake the beetroots whole and wrapped tightly in foil in the oven. This will take about 40–50 minutes.

Five minutes before they are ready, grate the apple. Warm the olive oil and wine vinegar, around 4:1 ratio in tablespoons, and stir in the horseradish to taste and the seasoning. Pour over the apple to stop discolouration. Remove the beetroot from the foil and peel it with a knife, holding the hot beetroot on the prongs of a fork to make it easier. Grate the beetroot on the large grater holes onto the pile of apple, toss it all together, scatter over your herbs and serve.

GRATIN OF BRUSSELS SPROUTS

A lovely, soothingly creamy, day-after sort of a dish to serve with cold turkey and all the trimmings, even cold bread sauce, which I love.

SERVES 4–6

450g/1lb cooked sprouts, or cook
    them as above, drain and cut in
    half roughly
150–300ml/5–10fl oz double cream
a clove of garlic
butter to grease the gratin dish
salt, pepper, nutmeg
a handful of brown or white stale
    breadcrumbs
2 tbsp freshly grated Parmesan
    (optional)

Preheat the oven to 200°C/400°F/Gas 6. Rub the garlic clove over the greased gratin dish while you are bringing the cream up to scald point, i.e. just short of boiling point. Place the Brussels sprouts in the gratin dish and season. Pour the cream over them then shake over the breadcrumbs and the Parmesan if you're using it. Gratinée for 20–25 minutes in the oven or until crusty, browned and bubbling furiously.

THINGS TO COOK OVER CHRISTMAS AND NEW YEAR

It is often difficult to know just when to stop trying to please everyone over Christmas, the pressure is so great. The time and the inclination to produce an endless succession of new, delicious, special treaty things dwindles and can end in exhaustion, resentment and the feeling that you've pulled out all the stops, but not really known where or quite how to call a halt. Menu planning and advance preparation are all very well if you have the time to do either, but sometimes you just need to have a couple of tricks up your sleeve, an alternative to a big bird, or a little digressive dish or two away from the main repertoire that will solicit awe and delight without costing you your time and your sanity.

These recipes are all about that. You may have the ingredients already since they are, generally speaking, the ones you'll have bought for your feasting, so this is a dip-into and dip-out-of section where you may just glean an idea or a little inspiration to try a new dish you can prepare or freeze in advance or steam straight into once the big day is over.

I do find myself desperate for fish over Christmas, maybe because it's the time of year when oily, smoky fish are what the hibernating energy levels are signalling a craving for; maybe partly because smoked salmon and eel are the things we give as presents or feed our loved ones with as treats. Christmas Eve is a great time to serve fish, a fish pie stuffed with prawns and nuggets of scallop, or nutty buckwheat blinis with smoked salmon and horseradish cream. Or just a pile of fresh langoustines from the east coast of Scotland, bound with a light lemony mayonnaise and sharp with apple, raw fennel and celery.

ROAST GUINEA FOWL WITH A CHESTNUT, BACON, THYME AND WILD RICE STUFFING

SERVES 6

85g/3oz mixed basmati and wild rice (Merchant Gourmet)
1 small onion
55g/2oz unsalted butter
2 rashers organic smoked back bacon, cut into small strips
1 tbsp fresh thyme leaves, chopped
6 juniper berries, gently crushed
1 x 200g/7oz jar organic peeled, cooked chestnuts (Sierra Rica from Waitrose or good delis)
1 egg, beaten
2 guinea fowl, they are small birds generally 1–1.2kg/2¼–2½ lb
1 onion, peeled and sliced
sea salt and black pepper
extra unsalted butter

If you are eschewing a great bird this Christmas or simply have a smaller family to feed, this is a good and special enough alternative to feel festive about and dress up accordingly. It won't leave you feeling short-changed or uncelebratory.

Cook the rice according to the instructions on the packet. Meanwhile, chop the onion finely and sauté in the melted butter over a medium heat for a few minutes until it begins to soften. Add the bacon strips and sauté them until their fat begins to run. Add the thyme leaves and juniper berries, then the roughly chopped chestnuts and continue to cook for a few minutes before adding the rice and stirring everything to amalgamate. You may not need all the rice. Judge the quantity as best you can from the cooked mixture and the size of the birds' cavities. Season, remove from the heat and stir in the beaten egg to bind the mixture together.

Preheat the oven to 200°C/400°F/Gas 6. Stuff the insides of both birds and set them on their sides on top of the sliced onion in the roasting tin. Season the butter and rub over the leg and breast uppermost of each bird. Cook for 20 minutes like this before putting the birds on their other side and rubbing with more seasoned butter. For the final 20 minutes, turn the birds breast up, baste them well with the buttery juices and season. The skin should be crisped by then and the birds ready to rest for 10 minutes while you make gravy and finish off your vegetables. Port or Madeira added to the pan juices for your gravy goes very well with guinea fowl, as does Marsala. Roast potatoes and parsnips, Brussels sprouts and bread sauce are a must.

CLAUDIA RODEN'S CHICKEN WITH ALMONDS AND HONEY

SERVES 8

2 large onions, chopped
4 tbsp sunflower oil
1 tsp ground ginger
1½ tsp cinnamon
2 chickens, cut into quarters
salt and pepper
½ tsp saffron stamens
juice of ½–1 lemon
225g/8oz blanched almonds
1 tbsp rosewater
4–5 tbsp honey

In a large saucepan, cook the onions with the oil until they soften. Stir in the ginger and cinnamon and put in the chicken pieces. Cover with water, add salt and pepper, saffron and lemon juice and simmer, covered, for 30 minutes. Taste and adjust the seasonings.

Heat the oven to 180°C/350°F/Gas 4. Lift the chicken pieces out of the saucepan and arrange them in a large, shallow baking dish. Pour over enough of the poaching liquid to make sauce for everyone and keep the rest for stock.

Grind the almonds coarsely in the food processor and mix with the rosewater and honey. Spread this paste over the chicken pieces and place in the oven. They will need about 30 minutes, but check after 20 — you want the crust golden and crisp, not brown.

Serve with spiced couscous. I add a cinnamon stick and a few cardamom pods while I am steaming it.

Claudia Roden's Chicken with Almonds and Honey

LANGOUSTINE SALAD

SERVES 4

16 large langoustines (Dublin Bay
    prawns), or more if you are feeling
    greedy
2 egg yolks
1 tsp Dijon mustard
1 clove garlic, pounded with a little
    salt in a mortar
150ml/5fl oz vegetable oil
150ml/5fl oz olive oil
live yoghurt to taste
juice of 1 lemon
black pepper
1 tsp Pernod (optional)
2 bulbs fennel with their fronds
2 sharp eating apples
the heart of a bunch of celery

A perfect Christmas-time starter, or lunch or supper dish. Marks and Spencer have started selling these noble little creatures caught off the east coast of Scotland, which are better known in Ireland as Dublin Bay prawns. They would be heading Spain-wards if M and S hadn't decided to coax us into buying them, like so much other good fish. You can just toss them in hot olive-oily butter with a clove of garlic and a chopped red chilli for 3–4 minutes a side and scatter parsley and crisp shards of bacon over them with a spritz of lemon while they are hot. However, here's a more sophisticated take on the sweet-fleshed creatures.

Put 12 of the langoustines belly down on your chopping board and run a knife down through the middle of them lengthways. Scoop out the flesh, including the delicious dark meat from the head, which you should keep separate from the white flesh.

Now make your mayonnaise. Stir the egg yolks together in a bowl with a wooden spoon before stirring in the Dijon mustard and salty garlic. Then begin to add the oils, mixed together, drip by drip to begin with, then in a steady stream, stirring constantly. (See page 255 for more on mayonnaise.) When you have used all the oil and have a thick, yellow emulsion, add a tablespoon of yoghurt followed by a spritz of lemon. Continue adding the two until you have the desired flavour and texture, which should be pouring consistency rather like double cream. Add pepper and Pernod if you have some to hand, then the chopped fronds from your fennel bulbs and the brown meat from the langoustines.

Remove the tough outer leaves of the fennel before slicing the bulbs wafer thin on your mandolin. Now peel, quarter and core the apples and slice them thinly, squirting a little lemon juice over them to stop discolouration. Peel the celery heart with a potato peeler before slicing it equally thinly on the mandolin.

Combine the vegetables and fruit with the 12 chopped langoustines. Spoon over some mayonnaise, turning the ingredients in it well. You may not need all the mayonnaise, but keep it for later. Place a pile of the salad on each plate, on some green leaves if you like, placing the final langoustine on top or on the side.

If you prefer, add the fruit and vegetables in thin layers and keep the langoustines for the top, instead of making a mélange.

SMOKED BUCKLING PÂTÉ

SERVES 4

2 buckling
unsalted butter, softened
lemon juice
1–2 tsp black peppercorns, cracked
     with a rolling pin or in a mortar

Do you remember the horrors of kipper pâté – the way it repeated on you for hours and the smell that permeated everything? Buckling are hot-smoked Atlantic herrings eaten cold, rather than cold-smoked like kippers, and they make a wonderful dish for a brunch party. They have a milder, subtler flavour that is really brought out by the smoke.

Eat the pâté cold with hot toast. It is particularly good with a walnut and rye loaf or with sourdough rye. Or you can spread the pâté on toasted bagels and fill them with peppery fresh watercress. Make this 2–3 hours before you need it or the night before.

Skin and fillet the fish. This is easy and quick, though the tiny bones can be a bit fiddly. The hair's breadth ones you can leave in as you won't notice them.

Gently mash the flesh on a plate with a fork, removing any further bones. Add about a tablespoon of butter to start with, mashing it in well to amalgamate but not crushing the fish to a paste. Now add another tablespoon of butter and repeat.

Squeeze over the juice of half a lemon and add a teaspoon of coarsely cracked peppercorns. Taste and add more lemon juice, peppercorns and even butter if you feel it needs it – this is a dish to make to your own taste. Put in a pot, press down, cover with clingfilm and refrigerate. Simple.

POTTED CRAB

MAKES 12 RAMEKINS

85g/3oz crabmeat per person; if you
    have a good fishmonger, he will
    pick the crab for you, and divide
    it into light and dark
about 400g/14oz best unsalted butter
a blade or good pinch mace
a good pinch nutmeg
⅓ tsp cayenne
salt and pepper
lemon juice

Classic potted crab is only made with the white meat of the crab, probably
because the brown doesn't have such good keeping quality, but why worry about
that? The brown meat deepens and intensifies the flavour and gives you the softer-
textured stratum to alternate with the white meat top and bottom. This warm-
spiced dish is something you'll only need a small, chilled pot of with some hot
brown toast. It is meltingly rich and delicious.

Preheat the oven to 150°C/300°F/Gas 2. Melt 225g/8oz butter gently, then pour it carefully
into another pan, leaving behind the milky, curd-like solids. Add the spices, then turn the
white meat into the spiced butter, amalgamate well and taste. You should have a breath of
spiced warmth, but not full-scale heat from the cayenne. Adjust accordingly, then add
salt, pepper and a squeeze of lemon juice to taste.

    Boil a kettle, and in the meantime fill each ramekin with a layer of the buttered white
crabmeat, followed by a layer of brown meat. Finish with a layer of the white meat. You will
just have enough room at the top of the ramekin for the final layer of clarified butter, which
you add after poaching the crab. Place the ramekins in a roasting tin, pour boiling water to
come halfway up their sides, and place in the oven for 25 minutes.

    Remove, cool, then clarify the rest of the butter and pour over each ramekin like sealing
wax. Place in the fridge. The ramekins should be removed 20 minutes or so before you
make your brown toast so that they are cold, but not fridge cold. Then slip a slim knife
blade all the way around the girth of each ramekin right to the bottom, turn them out on to
the palm of your hand, and put each one, butter-side up, on individual plates. The ones I
served on Saturday night tasted as good as when I had made them the previous
Wednesday night, but my fishmonger is very good.

SMOKED TROUT AND HORSERADISH CREAM PÂTÉ

SERVES 6–8 AS A SMALL STARTER

2 fillets smoked trout
1 tsp freshly grated horseradish
    mixed with 1 tbsp crème fraîche, a
    spritz of lemon and a scrunch of
    black pepper
1 tbsp best full-fat soft cream cheese
juice of half a lemon, or to taste
1 tbsp crème fraîche to slacken
black pepper

Another great idea to pass round with drinks on little squares or triangles of hot
toast or serve as a light lunch or supper with a salad.

Mash the fillets of trout on a plate. Transfer to a bowl and add the remaining ingredients,
stirring them in, in the order given. Taste and adjust lemon juice and seasoning. Serve cool
on hot toast cut into squares.

SMOKED SALMON PÂTÉ WITH LEMON

smoked salmon trimmings
equal amount of unsalted butter
lemon juice
knifepoint of cayenne

This is a delicious bonne bouche or starter and a great way to use up all your trimmings, or, indeed, if you can't afford a side or whole slices of smoked salmon, just buy trimmings in the first place. No one is going to know.

Weigh the top layer of crust from the side of smoked salmon, then pound it with an equal amount of unsalted butter. (You can use a food processor if the butter is not fridge cold.) The main seasoning is lemon juice, with a knifepoint of cayenne to pep it up.

You can use whipped cream instead of half the butter, which lightens the paste. If you use only butter, add a layer of clarified butter to seal the top, cover with foil and keep the pot in the fridge for up to 10 days.

The pâté makes a perfect Sunday supper with hot brown toast and runny scrambled eggs.

SMOKED SALMON PÂTÉ WITH CREAM CHEESE

This is a coarser textured pâté, with the addition of cream cheese. The following proportions work best: 50 per cent smoked salmon crust, roughly blitzed, to which you add 40 per cent softened unsalted best butter and 10 per cent good full-fat cream cheese. Work everything together with some cracked black pepper and lemon juice. Refrigerate until cold.

BLINIS WITH SMOKED FISH AND HORSERADISH CREAM

SERVES 6

BLINIS
30g/1oz fresh or 15g/½oz dry yeast
6 tbsp lukewarm water
215g/7½oz plain flour
110g/4oz buckwheat flour
240ml/8fl oz lukewarm milk
3 organic eggs, separated
1 tsp unrefined sugar
sea salt
3 tbsp sour cream
110g/4oz unsalted butter, melted

SERVING
smoked salmon
smoked eel fillets
cream, lightly whipped
grated horseradish
lemon juice
black pepper

These blinis need a little long-term planning, but no more than that. Think about them in the morning, whisk them into life and leave them. Think about them briefly in the afternoon, stir in the flour and leave them again. Then cook them in no time in the evening for your drinks or supper and let everyone pile their own goodies on top. Any smoked fish works well though salmon is the classic.

Whisk the yeast into the lukewarm water and leave it to froth for 10 minutes. Put the plain flour and half the buckwheat flour into a large bowl, make a well in the centre and add the yeast mixture and all the milk.

Whisk into a batter, cover with a tea towel and leave in a warm place for 3 hours. Stir in the remaining buckwheat flour and leave for a further 2 hours.

Beat the egg yolks, sugar, salt, cream and 3 tablespoons of melted butter together lightly and mix into the dough. Whisk the egg whites stiffly and fold them in. Leave for an hour. Brush a heavy frying pan with melted butter, warm the pan over a medium heat and cook the mixture, a small ladleful at a time. Cook on each side until small bubbles appear on the surface (about 2 minutes a side). Wrap them in a tea towel or napkin and put them in a warm oven while you make the rest.

Let everyone assemble their own blinis by passing round a plate of smoked salmon (one slice per person should be enough) and a plate of smoked eel fillets (one fillet per person as it is very rich). Have ready a bowl of lightly whipped cream into which you have stirred grated horseradish to taste, a squeeze of lemon juice and a scrunch of black pepper. Or use sour cream and horseradish with black pepper stirred in.

PULLED AND DEVILLED TURKEY

SERVES 6

450g/1lb cooked turkey breast
1 leg and 1 thigh from the cooked
  turkey

DEVIL SAUCE
1 tbsp Dijon mustard
2 tbsp hot mango chutney
1 tbsp Worcestershire sauce
$\frac{1}{2}$ tsp cayenne, or to taste
sea salt
2 tbsp olive oil

PULLED SAUCE
85g/3oz butter
170ml/6fl oz double cream
lemon juice
sea salt and black pepper
a handful of flat-leaf parsley, freshly
  chopped

What I love about this dish, almost more than the Christmas roast turkey, is the total contrast between the white meat with its soothing, creamy, bland sauce and the spicy-hot mustardy devil of the sticky brown meat. I have adapted the recipe from Jane Grigson, the late, great scholar-cook. It is just the thing to revive your interest in the kitchen after Christmas.

First, pull the breast meat apart with your fingers into pieces about 4cm/1$\frac{1}{2}$in long and the thickness of a large quill. Follow the grain of the meat so that the pieces look somewhat thready. Take the brown meat from the bone and divide it into larger pieces. Slash each two or three times.

Mix the devil sauce ingredients together, chopping up any large pieces of fruit in the chutney. Dip the brown meat pieces into it and spoon as much as you can into the slashes. Arrange in a single layer on the rack of a foil-lined grill and grill under a high heat until the pieces are crusted.

Meanwhile, melt the butter in a wide frying pan and stir in the cream. Let it boil for a couple of minutes and keep stirring until it thickens. Add the pieces of breast and any clinging jelly, and stir until very hot. Spritz with lemon juice and season with salt and pepper. Put the white meat in the centre of a serving dish and surround it with the brown. Sprinkle with the parsley. Serve with rice, watercress and wedges of lemon

TURKEY OR TURKEY AND HAM PIE

I'm a sucker for a good pie. In my mind, turkey and chicken are right up there as joint ultimate savoury pies, with their nutmeggy, silken béchamel sauce, jewels of meat and earthy sweet vegetables cloaked in crisp buttery pastry. The definition of comfort food. Mostly when making chicken pie I start from scratch by poaching the chicken first. For this, you just need the last of your brown and the last of your white meat, with, perhaps, a few good chunks of leftover ham and your turkey stock already made. Turn to page 272 and use the recipe for chicken pie with turkey.

CORIANDER CHUTNEY

a bunch of fresh coriander
half a bunch of fresh mint
4 cloves of garlic, peeled
1 tbsp sugar
juice of 1 lemon
3 green chillies (including seeds)
1 tsp sea salt

Great with your turkey curry, this is also wonderful on any meaty sandwich of Christmas leftovers that needs kick-starting with vibrant, spicy flavour.

Simply blend all the ingredients together and season to taste. That's all.

Pulled and Devilled Turkey

TURKEY TIKKA ON CIABATTA

A post-Christmas spice fest to freshen and enliven the jaded palate.

SERVES 4

450g/1lb small pieces of
   cooked turkey
3 tbsp Greek yoghurt
2 tsp sea salt
1 tsp chilli powder
1 tsp garam masala
1 lemon
1 tbsp olive oil
½ tsp dry fenugreek powder
   (optional)
4 tomatoes
½ cucumber
1 red onion
1 Romaine lettuce
4 baby ciabattas
butter
110g/4oz coriander chutney
   (see page 230)
200g/7oz mayonnaise

Mix the turkey with all the ingredients for the tikka (down to and including the fenugreek) and leave covered in the fridge for at least 2 hours. Heat the oven to 230°C/450°F/Gas 8. Place the turkey in a single layer on a baking tray and roast for about 5 minutes.

Slice the tomatoes and cucumber, chop the onion and shred the lettuce. Spread the ciabattas with butter and warm them on a hot pan or under the grill. Spread coriander chutney on one half of the ciabatta and mayonnaise on the other. Layer with shredded lettuce, tomatoes, cucumber, onion and turkey tikka and close the sandwich.

BOMBAY VEGETABLE SANDWICH

This is a must – a stunning hangover cure, brunch, lunch, supper or even, astonishing though it may sound, hoovered up at breakfast time. This is what we did when we made these sandwiches for the picture opposite, and everybody adored them.

SERVES 4

8 slices medium white bread
unsalted butter
coriander chutney (see page 230)
225g/8oz spicy mashed potatoes
   (made by mashing boiled potatoes
   with 1 tsp chilli powder, ½ tsp
   turmeric, 1 tbsp lemon juice, 1
   pinch cumin seed and sea salt)
4 tomatoes, finely sliced
1 red onion, finely sliced
sandwich masala (made with 1 tsp
   each ground cumin, ground ginger,
   chilli powder and ground black
   pepper, all mixed together)
sea salt
225g/8oz grated Gruyère

Make the spicy mashed potatoes or add spices to some leftover mash. Butter the bread and then turn the slices over so they are butter-side down on your work surface – messy but worth it.

Spread the chutney on the unbuttered side of the bread. Then, on four of the slices, spread the spiced potato, before piling on the tomatoes, onion slices, a sprinkling of sandwich masala, salt and finally the grated cheese.

Close the sandwiches with the other 4 slices of bread – chutney inside, butter out. Put the complete sandwiches on a greased baking tray in a hot oven until the butter is bubbling but not browned. Move to a preheated grill and toast until the tops are golden brown. Cut and serve as you wish – with or without crisps, salad and ketchup.

Bombay Vegetable Sandwich

SOUPS

SMOKED HADDOCK SOUP

A lovely winter warmer of a smoky, fishy soup, this may be all you can face making and all you really feel like eating.

Put the smoked haddock in a gratin dish, cover it with boiling water and leave for 10 minutes. Cut the white fish into cubes. Melt the butter in a large pan and sauté the onion gently, adding the flour when the onion has softened. Cook for a minute or two, then add about 150ml/5fl oz of the haddock-soaking liquor and the milk.

Put the cubes of white fish in the pan with the haddock, skin, bone and all, and simmer for 10 minutes. Remove the bones, then liquidise the soup. Throw in the prawns, add the cream and bring the soup to just below boiling point. Season cautiously – it may not need extra salt – and squeeze on a little lemon juice before adding the parsley and serving.

SERVES 4

225g/8oz natural smoked haddock
225g/8oz cod, hake or haddock
55g/2oz butter
1 large onion, chopped
1 tbsp flour
600ml/1 pint milk
225g/8oz large cooked prawns
150ml/5fl oz double cream
salt, pepper
1 lemon
handful of flat-leaf parsley, chopped

OYSTER SOUP

This is the time of year for good, native oysters and this is a lovely light, fishy soup, perfect for smarter or familial Christmas gatherings.

First, shuck your oysters. It is a murderous procedure for the beginner, but it gets easier, and the satisfaction of accomplishing the task is high. If you don't have an oyster knife with a protective shield, use a short, fat knife such as a penknife blade.

If you are right-handed, wrap your left hand in a tea towel, pick up the oyster, flat side up, and curl your fingers over it. Push the knife blade between the two shells at the hinge end and twist to lever open. Free the oyster from the shell with the knife tip, and remove any shell particles. Do this over a bowl to catch the juice.

Sauté the shallots, leek and celery gently in the butter until they are soft and beginning to turn golden. Sprinkle in the flour and cook for 30 seconds or so before adding the hot stock and turning up the heat. Strain the oyster juice into the pan through a sieve and season, going easy on the cayenne. Bring just short of boiling point and leave to simmer for about 20 minutes with the lid on.

Just before serving, pour in the cream and scatter in the chives. Remove from the heat and add the oysters and a spritz of lemon juice.

SERVES 6

2 dozen large oysters
2 shallots, chopped
1 leek, the white part, well cleaned
  and chopped
1 stick celery, destrung with a potato
  peeler and finely chopped
85g/3oz butter
2 tbsp flour
600ml/1 pint light beef stock
sea salt, pepper, cayenne and nutmeg
150ml/5fl oz double cream
a handful of chives, chopped
1 lemon

TURKEY SOUP

turkey carcass, with a handful each of dark and light meat stripped off to add at the end of cooking
2 or 3 onions, halved, in their skins
2 or 3 sticks of celery, broken in two, with the leaves
3 or 4 carrots, chopped in chunks
2 or 3 leeks, cleaned and trimmed, use green and white parts
a small bunch of parsley
6–8 peppercorns
two large handfuls of frozen or fresh petits pois
110–170g/4–6oz dark and light turkey meat, cut small along the grain of the flesh
2 tbsp cornflour (optional)
150ml/5fl oz double cream
sea salt and black pepper
parsley

Chicken soup is more than a soup, it's a symbol, and I don't just mean in its obvious sense as part of the Jewish tradition. Considered a cure-all and better known as Jewish penicillin, there is no dish as nourishing to the soul or, I suspect, medicinally to the body, as a proper chicken soup. This is the same recipe I use for my chicken soup but is, if you like, the Christmas edition made with the turkey. I try to leave the meat on the carcass for as long as I can so that it doesn't dry out. I wait until it is nearly picked clean but there is just enough left to add to the soup at the end. I am not starting from scratch here as I would with my chicken soup by poaching it gently with the vegetables before stripping off the meat and intensifying the flavour with the carcass and a fresh load of vegetables. This soup is easier, quicker and just as delicious. You may add or subtract vermicelli, pasta, dried morels, more tarragon, cream or what you will. There are surely as many recipes for it as there are cooks.

Break the carcass into two or three bits with your fingers and put them with any leftover bones and skin in a huge, heavy-bottomed pot. Heat gently, until the bones begin to brown and the skin starts to release its fat, then add the vegetables, parsley, peppercorns and enough water to cover. Bring to the boil slowly, then skim. Turn down to a simmer, put the lid on and bubble for a couple of hours.

Add the pieces of turkey now. Put the cornflour into a bowl and pour in a couple of ladles of the hot stock from the pan. Stir with a small whisk until free of lumps. Not everyone likes their turkey or chicken soup thickened so ignore this if you wish.

Return to the pan, add the cream, season and bring to boiling point. Serve with a scattering of parsley.

CHESTNUT AND THYME SOUP WITH JUNIPER

SERVES 4

1 tbsp olive oil
30g/1oz unsalted butter
1 small onion, finely chopped
1 good sprig of thyme, leaves stripped from the stem and chopped
4–6 juniper berries, crushed in a mortar
1 x 200g/7oz jar or equivalent vacuum pack of chestnuts, roughly chopped
850ml/1½ pints pheasant, turkey, goose or chicken stock (see p. 80)
sea salt and black pepper
crème fraîche (optional)

Not that one wants to turn Christmas into one long theme night, but this really is the time of year to use these deliciously mealy sweet nuts. They are often used as a sort of Cinderella ingredient, not allowed to the ball in the best gown, so to speak. Here they are the party piece and it is the back note of thyme, such an undervalued herb, and the scented muskiness of the juniper that play second fiddle. I use a jar of Sierra Rica organic chestnuts for this, which good delis, supermarkets and organic stores sell. The French or Italian vacuum-packed ones are very good too, and so little trouble.

Heat the olive oil and butter together in a heavy-bottomed pan and add the onion, stirring to coat. Cook over a medium heat until it softens and begins to turn golden. Add the thyme, which will release its astringent oily scent almost immediately, then add 4 of the crushed juniper berries and stir them in with the thyme. Add the chestnuts, followed by the hot stock. Bring to the boil, season and turn to a mere burble of a simmer for 15–20 minutes. Liquidise until smooth. Test the seasoning and juniper, which needs to be a background hint only, adding more if you need. Serve with a spoon of crème fraîche if you like, but I prefer to keep this soup light. Delicate, restorative and fragrant.

CHRISTMAS BRUNCH

To be taken any time between Christmas and the New Year when serial feasting fatigue has set in. Or at any other time of year when you're in the mood for a treat. When you're feeling seriously mutinous and bloated out, have gone to brandy butter hell, OD'd on Christmas pudding fried in butter — well, it had to be eaten up — and plunged headlong into the remains of the trifle, you won't feel much like eating or cooking any more rich and serious food for a while. Might just want to get the elasticated waistband into gear and run it all off while your children or house guests take over. Just might want a meal that is all about being relaxed and informal, not formal and filling. Brunch is your answer, American brunch. Here are a few dishes that might send you heading for the hills, but only so as you can run it off before you come back and enjoy them. Great breakfast or supper food dressed down and delicious for brunch, you can pick and swap, mix and graze and feel comforted all in one.

LOX AND BAGELS

SERVES 4

4 onion bagels (I think onion works best with smoked salmon)
225g/8oz fresh cream cheese, the best you can find
4 large slices smoked wild salmon
2 tomatoes (I know it's the wrong time of year, but try to find tomatoes with flavour and sweetness)
black pepper

The original, old-style Brooklyn smoked salmon is known as lox, after the Yiddish word for salmon, lachs, Claudia Roden tells us in *The Book of Jewish Food*. In the days before refrigeration, Brooklyn salmon was pickled in brine, then desalted and lightly smoked. It would have been much saltier than the smoked salmon we are used to, so it was paired with cream cheese to counteract the salt. This is the favourite American brunch food.

Split the bagels in half horizontally around their middles and grill them on both sides. Spread one half thickly with cream cheese before adding slices of smoked salmon.

Top with tomato and scrunch over some black pepper. Lightly spread cream cheese over the top half of each bagel and slam them together.

TUMBLED CRACKED BLACK PEPPERCORN EGGS AND HAM IN TOASTED BAGUETTES

SERVES 4

olive oil
large baguette, cut in 4 and sliced in half
1 clove garlic, peeled and whole
55g/2oz unsalted butter
8–12 large organic eggs
1 tbsp black peppercorns, cracked
salt
a handful of basil leaves
4 slices of really good ham or prosciutto
2 large tomatoes, cored and sliced

Half scramble, half omelette, these runny eggs are tumbled on to garlicky toasted baguette with basil and ham. This is also delicious with prosciutto. The cracked black peppercorns make it. I crack mine in a mortar, but a rolling pin works.

Scoop out some of the dough from the slices of baguette to make room for the filling. Pour best olive oil over each slice and rub over the garlic clove to scent the bread and oil. Put the 8 slices on a tray in a hot oven to toast or grill them on both sides.

Meanwhile, melt the butter in a frying pan and whisk the eggs well. Pour in the peppercorns and then tip the mixture into the pan. You want to tumble and push the eggs with a flat wooden spatula; worry them rather than wait and fold as you would for an omelette and don't stir to small lumps as you would for scrambled. The end result should be large waves of runny eggs punctuated by tweedy flecks of peppercorn.

Remove when still soft as they will keep cooking, and season with a little salt. Put a few basil leaves on the base of 4 baguette slices, then add the ham, the tomato and finally the egg, finishing with the top piece of baguette. Then try to get your mouth round it.

CELERIAC AND POTATO BUBBLE AND SQUEAK

2 tbsp olive oil
1 medium onion, peeled and chopped
leftover celeriac and potato mash
1 tbsp grain mustard
leftover cabbage (or, if you don't have any, very thinly slice a quarter cabbage and fry it quickly in oil first)
sea salt and black pepper
55g/2oz unsalted butter

Quantities are not helpful here as this is a leftovers dish, but one that is perfect for brunch, served with frazzled rashers of smoked bacon and a fried egg on top. Serve Bloody Marys on the side. If you have only leftover mash, just steam and mash about a third quantity of celeriac to mash and mix the two.

Gently heat 1 tablespoon of olive oil in a large, heavy-bottomed frying-pan, add the onion and fry until softened and golden. Tip the cooked onion into the cold celeriac and potato, add the grain mustard and shredded cooked cabbage and stir to amalgamate. Season and check it is mustardy enough.

Add the rest of the olive oil and the butter to the frying pan and press your large potato cake down to fry. Make individual cakes if you prefer, but I like to bring a whole panful to the table. Fry on one side until browned, then turn it over and fry the other side — you may need extra butter and a little oil when you turn the cake over. Serve piping hot from the pan with bacon and eggs.

Tumbled Cracked Black Peppercorn Eggs and Ham in Toasted Baguettes

CHRISTMAS AND NEW YEAR PUDDINGS

There has to be chocolate. You may wish to adulterate its simple black or white purity or you may be horrified at the mere notion of, as it were, diluting the drug. Chocolate arouses these strong feelings in people. There are those who hate chocolate punctuated with fruit, which they see as a travesty of good taste, and those who love it; those who despise or delight in chocolate being tainted with alcohol; those who love the nut and chocolate combo, and those who believe white chocolate shouldn't even bear the sobriquet chocolate. The following should give all chocolate fascists and all chocolate pluralists a run for their money.

CHOCOLATE AND CHESTNUT TERRINE

SERVES 10

200g/7oz best bitter chocolate, minimum 70% cocoa solids
1 tbsp Cognac
1 tbsp water
110g/4oz unsalted butter, melted in a pan
110g/4oz unrefined vanilla sugar
4 organic eggs, separated
3 x 200g/7oz packs of vacuum-packed chestnuts, the best you can find, chopped
almond oil or similar for greasing tin

You can make this well in advance and really quickly, then whack it in the fridge for a few hours or even days. You may process the chestnuts with the melted butter and all but a tablespoon of the sugar if you want a satin-smooth terrine, or follow the recipe and end up with nuggets of chopped chestnut in the chocolate for a more textured version.

Melt the chocolate in a double boiler with the brandy and water. Add the melted butter and all but a tablespoon of the sugar. Stir in the egg yolks one by one, then whisk the egg whites to soft peak stage. Add the remaining tablespoon of sugar and whisk until stiff. Fold in the chopped chestnuts as well as you can; the mixture will be very thick and sludgy at this stage. Plop it into a loaf tin, which you have greased lightly with an unobtrusive oil such as almond oil, and smooth down the surface. Leave to cool and put it in the fridge when cold.

I think this is best eaten after a day or two, so make it in advance. It will turn out beautifully on to a flat dish. Serve with pouring cream, to which you can add a tablespoon of freshly made coffee if you like. A couple of slices each are all you will want. Killer.

a little vegetable oil that doesn't taste
    to oil the loaf tin with
340g/12oz bitter chocolate, 64–70%
    cocoa solids
225g/8oz unsalted butter, cubed
4 organic eggs, separated, plus 4
    yolks
170g/6oz unrefined icing sugar
45g/1½oz Green and Black's organic
    cocoa powder
130m/4½fl oz double cream

MARQUISE AU CHOCOLAT

A densely rich chocolate terrine, this needs making a good half day before you want to eat it but can be made up to 3 days in advance.

Lightly oil a loaf tin or long terrine, 30 x 10 x 7.5cm/12 x 4 x 3in and line it with clingfilm. Melt the chocolate with the cubed butter in a double saucepan over, but not touching, barely simmering water or in a bowl placed in a pan over, not touching, simmering water. Stir until glossy and velvety and completely smooth. Cool to warm, then stir in the yolks one at a time. Sift the icing sugar and cocoa powder together into the chocolate mixture .

Whisk the egg whites to soft peaks. Stir the first tablespoon into the chocolate mixture, then lightly fold in the rest. Whisk the cream until it holds, but be careful not to whisk it rigid. Fold the cream into the mixture and pour it into the tin or terrine. Refrigerate covered with clingfilm overnight or for half a day at least before turning it out onto a plate when you are ready to serve it. Dip the knife blade into hot water to slice.

Restaurants do the whole crème Anglaise number with this sort of pudding, but I think thin cream or cream whisked with a little rum, a tablespoon or so, and a little icing sugar is perfect.

WHITE CHOCOLATE AND CRANBERRY TART

You can't get more Christmassy than this tart, with its white skating-rink surface and the gaudy crimson jewels of cranberry like baubles on the tree. Sharp and sickly sweet with a suspicion of cinnamon, this is a rich but not cloying alternative to mince pies after the turkey or after feasting on the ham or leftovers or partying after Christmas when everyone will have seen enough of the pudding and pies. Note: you need to prepare the filling 2–3 hours ahead and refrigerate the tart for at least an hour when it is ready, though you can leave it much longer in the fridge, so plan accordingly. You will need a 23cm/9in tart tin for the pastry.

SERVES 6

PASTRY
170g/6oz plain flour
2 tsp Green and Black's organic
    cocoa powder
1 heaped dsrtsp unrefined icing
    sugar
85g/3oz unsalted butter, fridge cold,
    cut into cubes
1 egg yolk

FILLING
200ml/7fl oz crème fraîche
240ml/8fl oz double cream
170g/6oz Green and Black's organic
    white chocolate
200g/7oz fresh cranberries
2 tbsp unrefined caster sugar
½ tsp cinnamon

Sift the flour, cocoa and sugar into the bowl of a food processor, add the cubed butter and pulse several times for 3–4 seconds a time. Add the egg yolk and a tablespoon of chilled water and pulse until the pastry coheres into a ball. Wrap the ball in clingfilm and refrigerate for an hour.

Preheat the oven to 200°C/400°F/Gas 6. Roll the pastry out on some flour mixed with a little more cocoa, line the tart tin and bake the pastry blind for 20 minutes (see page 181). Remove the foil and beans, prick with a fork and return to the oven for 5–10 minutes to finish cooking. Leave to cool.

For the filling, heat the crème fraîche with 100ml/3½ fl oz of the double cream. Break the chocolate into a bowl, pour the hot cream over it and leave for a minute, then stir until the chocolate dissolves. Cover with clingfilm, prick some air holes into it with a skewer and put in the fridge for 2–3 hours.

Meanwhile, toss the cranberries in the sugar and cinnamon in a pan and cook until they just begin to pop. Test for sugar, then allow to cool. Put a single layer of cranberries on the base of the tart tin. Whisk the remaining double cream until thick but still soft, not rigid, and fold it into the chocolate mixture. Smooth this over the cranberries with a rubber spatula. Refrigerate for at least another hour or overnight, in which case remove from the fridge 20 minutes before you want to eat it.

CHOCOLATE PROFITEROLES

MAKES 18–24

A mountain of airy light choux pastry, a thick slick of crème pâtissière or double cream, and a flood of sticky, syrupy bitter chocolate sauce flooding over each ball. Is any pudding such a man pleaser, boy pleaser, crowd puller? It may be old fashioned, but it shouldn't be confined to the chariot des desserts as it is a surprisingly easy and pleasing pudding to make. Choux paste is a knack, but a child could get it right. Splitting the little weightless buns to let the air out and stuff their middles is a pleasurably repetitive task.

CHOUX PASTE
85g/3oz unsalted butter
a pinch of salt
270ml/9fl oz water
140g/5oz plain flour, sifted into
  a bowl
4 organic eggs, three kept whole,
  one whisked

FILLING
300ml/10fl oz double cream, Jersey if
  possible

CHOCOLATE SAUCE
200g/7oz bar of good dark chocolate,
  Valrhona 64% cocoa solids
55g/2oz butter
4 tsp golden syrup
3 tbsp Jersey cream

Heat the oven to 200°C/400°F/Gas 6 . Line a baking tray with silicone paper and set aside. To make the choux paste, put the butter, salt and water in a pan and bring to the boil. Just as it comes to the boil, remove the pan from the heat and quickly add the flour. Stir with a wooden spoon until it coheres, then return to a low heat and cook for a minute until it comes away from the side of the pan.

Remove from the heat again and leave to cool for a couple of minutes – you don't want the eggs to cook when you add them. Break the first egg into the pan and whisk it vigorously in with a fork. Add the next 2 eggs one at a time. Then, depending on how resistant the mixture is, slowly add the final whisked egg a bit at a time until the mixture is a little easier to work and looks glossy.

Choux will solidify if you leave it, so immediately place teaspoons of the mixture on the baking tray and bake in the preheated oven for 15 minutes. Reduce the temperature to 150°C/300°F/Gas 2 and cook for a further 15–20 minutes or until crisp and brown. Remove and pierce the side of each profiterole to let out the steam. Cool on a rack.

Whisk the Jersey cream for the filling until slackly stiffened. Just before you are ready to serve the profiteroles, slit them, add a good spoonful of cream to the middles, re-splice and then pour over the warm chocolate sauce, as thickly as you dare.

Alternatively, fill the profiteroles with crème pâtissière. Follow the recipe on page 358, but stir in a teaspoon of espresso coffee or ordinary coffee granules into the milk.

CHOCOLATE SAUCE
Melt the chocolate in a double boiler with the butter, golden syrup and 3 tablespoons of Jersey cream. At no stage should the top pan or bowl touch the water, nor should the water boil, or your cocoa solids will separate. You can make this in advance and reheat it.

CRANBERRY AND APPLE PIE

A sharp-fruited pie to cut the Christmas richness, listen for the cranberries popping like bubble-wrap in the pan, their crimson juices leaking out as they burst. But let them hold their shape – remove them from the heat instantly!

Make a shortcrust-type pastry in the normal way (see pages 180–181) and chill.
Roll out the pastry and line a 23cm/9in tart tin, reserving some pastry to cut into strips for a lattice top. Chill the pastry case for at least 30 minutes. Preheat the oven to 190°C/375°F/Gas 5.

Put the cranberries and sliced apples in a saucepan and squeeze enough orange juice over them to almost cover. Simmer, uncovered, until the berries have all popped, the apple is cooked and and you have a thickly bubbling red brew. Add most of the muscovado sugar, stirring it in and tasting for sweetness; add a little more if necessary.

Stir half the mixture into the mascarpone or cream cheese. Spread this over the pastry base, then cover with the remainder of the cranberry mixture. Decorate with the pastry lattice, brush with beaten egg, and bake for about 35 minutes. Best eaten warm.

SERVES 6–8

SHORTCRUST PASTRY
110g/4oz flour
110g/4oz ground almonds
a pinch of sea salt
110g/4oz unsalted butter

FILLING
200g/7oz cranberries
200g/7oz apples, peeled, cored and thinly sliced
juice of 1 orange
170g/6oz light muscovado sugar
200g/7oz mascarpone or cream cheese, sieved
1 small egg, beaten

ST CLEMENT'S AND MARMALADE TART

This is the sort of dish to eat after roast goose, when something citrussy sharp is a must – if you can pick your head up off the table. If you can lay your hands on the lusciously bitter marmalade orange from Seville, do, but the season is short. If not, it's an oranges and lemons sort of a tart, a tart tart with a layer of bitter orange marmalade under the shudderingly set filling.

Preheat the oven to 180°C/350°F/Gas 4. Make the pastry (see pages 180–181) and chill. Roll out and use to line a 23cm/9in tart tin. Bake blind for 15 minutes (see page 181), then remove the greaseproof paper and beans and bake for a further 5 minutes. Spread the marmalade over the bottom of the tart.

Put the grated orange and lemon rind in a bowl. Beat in the butter and sugar, then add the beaten eggs and whisk everything together. Place the bowl over a saucepan of simmering water and stir until the mixture has melted and dissolved. Remove from the heat and stir in the orange and lemon juice. Test the sharpness and adjust if necessary. Pour over the marmalade-lined tart and return to the oven for 15–20 minutes, or until barely set. Serve warm, with thick cream if you like.

SERVES 6–8

SHORTCRUST PASTRY
170g/6oz plain white flour
pinch of salt
85g/3oz butter, chilled

FILLING
2–3 tbsp tart orange marmalade
grated rind and juice of 3 oranges and 1 lemon
125g/4oz butter, softened
225g/8oz vanilla caster sugar
4 large organic eggs, beaten

RASPBERRY CHRISTMAS TRIFLE

SERVES 6

5 macaroons
240ml/8fl oz white wine
4–6 tbsp raspberry liqueur
300ml/10fl oz pint milk
600ml/1 pint organic double cream
2 organic eggs and 2 yolks
1 tbsp cornflour, sifted
vanilla caster sugar to taste
340g/12oz raw raspberries
icing sugar to taste
juice of a lemon
lemon zest
toasted slivered almonds

This is a rich but softly delicious pudding that slips down surreptitiously, despite your misgivings on the calorific front. It is almost incomprehensible that tradition allows for such sweet richness after all the rest. Make your trifle the day before you want to eat it, but if you want to scoff it on Boxing Day, make it on Christmas Eve for obvious reasons. If it is impossible to find raspberries out of season, use raspberry jam. Pace yourself. This is no mere trifle and it is full of hidden depths.

Put the macaroons into a large glass bowl and pour over half the white wine and 2–3 tablespoons of raspberry liqueur. Beat the 2 eggs and 2 yolks with the sifted cornflour. Now bring the milk and 300ml/10fl oz of the double cream to scalding point, and pour over the egg mixture. Return to the pan and whisk until thickened. Add vanilla caster sugar to taste, and pour over the macaroons.

Purée the raw raspberries in a food processor, sieve and add icing sugar to taste. Pour this mixture over the cooled custard.

In a bowl, put the juice of a lemon, the rest of the white wine and raspberry liqueur, and stir in 30g/1oz sugar until dissolved. Taste for sweetness. Pour over the remaining 300ml/10fl oz organic double cream and whisk with a wire whisk until thickened but not stiff. Pour this over the raspberry mixture and decorate with lemon zest and toasted slivered almonds.

JELLY

Christmas has to have a fresh, citrus jelly of one sort or another after the riches, creams and fats of everything else. It unjades and enlivens the palate instantly and cuts feasting fatigue the moment it hits the tongue. We always had fresh orange jelly at home and, defeated by the mince pies and iffy about Christmas pudding when we were small, this is what we looked forward to.

Jellies are easy to make. Spare 10 minutes and you will be thrilled that you did. If you don't have a jelly mould, a glass bowl or individual glasses are just fine. Don't attempt to be clever and make a pineapple jelly. There is an enzyme in the fruit that prevents it from setting.

BUCK'S FIZZ JELLY

SERVES 6–8

8 leaves of gelatine
600ml/1 pint of Champagne
just under 600ml/1 pint of freshly
    squeezed organic orange juice

Collect the dregs, use Prosecco or sparkling wine like Spanish Cava if you can't afford real bubbles, but this IS the season to add pzazz to a fresh orange jelly if you don't have toddlers or very young children to please. The jelly is best with Champagne! Think of it this way – there are no other ingredients to speak of and you don't even need cream. And if you earmark a bottle for the jelly, you can always drink the rest.

Break the leaves of gelatine in half and soak them in 2–3 tablespoons of cold water for 10 minutes. Measure the Champagne and pour it into a bowl. Put the orange juice into a small saucepan with the leaves of soaked gelatine and their water – 8 sheets should set 1.2 litres/2 pints of liquid, but check the packet.

Gently heat the orange juice, stirring as you go with a wooden spoon to dissolve the gelatine completely. You do not want the liquid to become very hot or it won't taste so fresh, but make sure that there isn't a stringy trace of gelatine to be seen. Pour the orange and gelatine mixture into the Champagne and stir it all together. It will fizz as you do. Pour everything through a sieve into a jelly mould. Mine is big enough for 1.5 litres/3 pints, but I never seem to make a jelly quite that big. Leave to cool before putting it in the fridge to set.

You can make a jelly from 2 days to 4 hours before you want to eat it. It will keep for longer in the fridge, but the freshness of the fruit starts to diminish. Turn out by dunking the base half of the mould briefly in boiling water and inverting the jelly on to a plate, or serve from the mould.

FRESH GRAPEFRUIT JELLY

SERVES 6

juice of half a lemon
pared rind of a grapefruit
pared rind of an orange
85–110g/3–4oz caster sugar
300ml/10fl oz water
6 or 7 leaves leaf gelatine, but check
    the packet
600ml/1 pint freshly squeezed
    grapefruit juice

The astringence of this lovely sharp jelly is just what you need after the rigours of the roast, particularly if you have had a rich, fat goose or duck. If you can find pink grapefruits the colour will be a dreamy, dusty pink.

Put the lemon juice and grapefruit and orange rind into a saucepan with the sugar and 150ml/5fl oz of the water. Place over a low heat and leave to infuse for 10–15 minutes. Soak the gelatine (read the instructions for how much to use first) for 10 minutes in the other 150ml/5fl oz of water. Add the soaked gelatine with its water to the saucepan, stir to melt, then strain and leave to cool.

Add the gelatine liquid to the freshly squeezed grapefruit juice, stir well, and pour into a mould or into individual long-stemmed glasses. Leave to cool completely, then refrigerate to set further. The jelly will keep well for several days.

ORANGE, GRENADILLO AND MUSCAT JELLY

SERVES 6–8

2 grenadillos
8 sheets of gelatine, soaked in 2–3
    tbsp of cold water for 10 minutes
the juice of 8–10 organic oranges
    to make up just under 1.2 litres/
    2 pints of liquid
a half bottle of Bonterra organic
    Muscat, or something similar

These tangerine-coloured shelled fruits with their milky, moonstone interiors and jet-black seeds are exotic and scented and perfect in a sweet boozy jelly.

Halve the grenadillos and scoop out the innards and seeds. Heat them gently in a pan and sieve into a jug – it is easier to separate seed from fruit if it is warm.

Put the gelatine and its soaking liquid into a small saucepan with the orange juice. Heat through gently, stirring as you go. Make sure the gelatine is completely dissolved and then pour the contents of the pan into the jug with the grenadillo fruit, add the wine and stir everything together.

Pour the mixture through a sieve into a jelly mould, leave to cool, then set in the fridge for 4 hours or up to 2 days.

CLEMENTINE, PASSION FRUIT AND MUSCAT JELLY

SERVES 6–8

3 large, underripe passion fruit
a half bottle of Bonterra organic
    Muscat, or something similar
about 20 organic clementines
8 sheets of gelatine soaked for 10
    minutes in 2–3 tbsp cold water

It doesn't matter if you buy the passion fruit unwrinkly, which means they are under-ripe, as the sharpness is just what the jelly needs, contrasting as it does with the sweet clementines and Muscat. This is utterly divine.

Scoop the insides of the passion fruit into a small saucepan and warm over a gentle heat so that the seeds will separate more easily from the fruit. Sieve them into a jug with the wine. Squeeze the clementines until the jug has just under 1.2 litres/2 pints of liquid in it. Stir in the gelatine, and pour the liquid into the saucepan, heating it through very gently to just warm enough to dissolve the gelatine completely. Pour the mixture through a sieve into the jelly mould, cool and then put in the fridge.

The jelly will be ready to eat after just 4 hours or up to 2 days later, depending on when you want it. Serve with some thinly sliced oranges.

ICE IS NICE

A Christmas ice and a Christmas jelly, at some stage of the proceedings, add cool, light and fruity relief. Serve together if you are feeling nostalgic for the parties of your childhood. Ice cream is THE perfect pudding for any extended period of indulgence and entertaining. You can make an ice cream 2 or 3 days in advance and then just keep bringing it out in the pail or the box you've set it in. At this time of year, echoes of the other Christmas fruits, spices, alcohol and nuts are all things you can play around with, creating ices to match your jellies, your cakes, your mince pies and Christmas pudding, and your tarts.

ZABAGLIONE ICE CREAM

SERVES 4

5 organic eggs
110g/4oz unrefined vanilla caster
  sugar
a pinch of ground cinnamon
120ml/4fl oz Marsala
2 tbsp dark rum
300ml/10fl oz double cream,
  preferably Jersey

I have never cooked anything from one of Anna Del Conte's books and not been ravished by the result and this is no exception. Food historian and writer, Anna also believes that the emperor's new clothes are not for wearing or even getting seduced by. It can take a lifetime to perfect six of her native Italian dishes, she believes. I have always believed that innovation for the sake of it, in culinary terms, is a hiding to nothing. We tinker, we add and subtract a little, we learn what the great flavour marriages are and then we subtract again, trying to get to the heart and essence of a dish. Good ingredients are more important than a belief that imagination is the key to being a good cook. This is just an exceptionally fine ice cream and it needs no tinkering at all.

Separate the eggs, putting the yolks in one bowl and 3 of the whites in another. Add the sugar and cinnamon to the yolks and beat hard until you can leave a ribbon trail. Add the Marsala and rum while still beating.

Put the bowl over a pan of hot, not boiling, water and whisk constantly, using electric beaters if you have them, until the mixture is foamy and has doubled in volume. This will take about 10–15 minutes. Plunge the bowl into cold water and carry on beating every so often until the mixture is cool.

Whip the cream until it has slackly stiffened and fold it in, then whisk the whites to stiff peaks and fold them into the mixture a spoonful at a time. Churn in an ice cream machine if you have one, or freeze (see pages 334–335 for more on making ice cream).

LEMON ICE CREAM

SERVES 6

4 organic, unwaxed lemons
170g/6oz unrefined icing sugar
240ml/8fl oz water
300ml/10fl oz double cream, Jersey
    if possible

Pair this with the St Clement's tart or a citrus jelly or just scoop it out and serve it with a little Florentine or sweet orange and walnut biscuit.

Peel the lemons with a potato peeler and put the strips in a pan with the icing sugar and water. Simmer for about 20 minutes. Leave to cool, strain and add to the juice of the lemons. Whip the cream until it is softly stiff, not beyond, and gently fold in the cooled syrup. Taste for sweetness – you need it to taste slightly sharper than you think you need. Churn in an ice cream maker.

QUINCE AND PRALINÉED ALMOND ICE CREAM

SERVES 4–6

225g/8oz quince paste (membrillo)
2 tbsp lemon juice
1 tbsp water
1 tbsp Oloroso or another sherry
300ml/10fl oz double cream, Jersey if
    possible
140g/5oz almonds (ideally Valencia),
    whole but blanched (sold in good
    supermarkets)
55–85g/2–3oz unrefined caster sugar

I dreamt up this pudding with George, my friend and cooking companion. The recipe evolved when I couldn't be bothered to make a torta de Santiago with quince paste and almonds, and George suggested an ice cream instead. We had the membrillo, I suggested the pralinéed almonds, sherry seemed to enhance the flavours – we experimented.

Melt the membrillo gently in a pan with the lemon juice, water and sherry. Whisk the cream until it holds softly, but is not stiff.

In a non-stick frying pan over a gentle heat, scatter the almonds in a single layer, and pour the sugar over them. Stir as the sugar melts and the brittle turns the colour of butterscotch, but not dark brown. Remove from the heat instantly and pour on to a greased baking tray. Leave to solidify, then bash into small chunks and little shards.

Fold the cream into the membrillo mixture, then fold about one-third of the brittle into it, and freeze. Refrigerate for 30 minutes before serving and offer a bowl of the remaining brittle to scatter sparingly over the top.

STEM GINGER AND SPICE ICE CREAM

SERVES 6–8

450ml/16fl oz Jersey milk
2 vanilla pods, split and the insides
    scraped out
6 organic egg yolks
170g/6oz unrefined caster sugar or
    2 tbsp of runny honey
300ml/10fl oz double cream and
    300ml/10fl oz crème fraîche, or all
    double cream
6–8 globes of stem ginger,
    put 6 in the blender to begin with
1 tbsp ginger syrup
2 very finely chopped globes
    of stem ginger
6 or 7 cloves and a few little bits
    of cinnamon bark crushed
    together in a mortar

This feels fresh and Christmassy at the same time and is utterly delicious. You may use two large tablespoons of runny honey – a strong-tasting one such as chestnut – instead of the sugar if you prefer.

Scald the milk with the split vanilla pods and their innards. Whisk it into the egg yolks and sugar or honey that you have put into a bowl. Return the mixture to the pan, and cook it over a low heat, whisking as you go, until it thickens perceptibly. Do not allow the mixture to boil. You do not want it to curdle into scrambled egg.

Immediately the mixture has thickened, remove from the heat and whisk in the creams thoroughly. Whizz in the blender with the whole globes of ginger, ginger syrup and half a teaspoon of the spice mixture and taste until you have the right strength. The ginger should predominate, but you want a musky breath of spice.

Churn in the ice cream maker for 30 minutes and then add the tiny ginger bits to the setting mixture. You can put the mixture in a ice tray and freeze, but remember to stir the setting walls of the ice cream into the middle of the tray after the first hour, and then again an hour or two later, to prevent crystals forming.

FISH AND SHELLFISH
POULTRY AND GAME
OFFAL AND VEAL
BEEF, PORK, LAMB
BREAD-BASED PUDDINGS
CUSTARDS, FOOLS, ICE CREAMS, SORBETS
CHOCOLATE PUDDINGS
STEAMED AND SPONGE PUDDINGS
SOUFFLÉS

CLASSIC

RECIPES

5

SO WHAT ARE THE classics, the recipes from which you can begin to build and hone a repertoire? Is there even such a thing as a classic repertoire now, with every chef, food writer and cook eating and experiencing more ingredients and dishes from other countries and continents than from their own? Added to which we have more of a global cuisine now than at any other time in our culinary history. Traditional regional cuisine might still be vibrant in parts of the world like China, India, Italy and to a diminishing degree in France, but here we hardly have any indigenous regional dishes to our name any more, certainly not a nucleus of them big enough to constitute a cuisine. Instead, we have embraced other cuisines from all over the world, and, I might add, far more amorously than they have embraced ours.

Where once we could have said that things like mutton in caper sauce, steak and kidney pudding, steamed puddings, sweet and savoury, creams, possets and junket were all solid, British fare, what on earth are the modern equivalents? Pizza? Chicken tikka masala? Spaghetti bolognese?

It is a question I have continually asked myself through the writing of this book, feeling that at some point a kitchen bible has to offer a present-day view of all the dishes that could be said to constitute the classic repertoire. The things that at some stage in your cooking life you want to get under your belt and know you have accomplished. Great dishes which, once you have mastered them, you can feel confident enough with to experiment and make your own.

By this, I don't mean adding lemongrass to boeuf bourguignonne or preserved lemons to a blanquette de veau. I mean in the sense of refining and finessing your technique; reaching a deeper understanding of textures, flavours, colours, amounts and ingredients, and of their handling and buying; of paying attention to detail that you didn't even know existed, such as the thickness, smoothness, roughness or silkiness of a sauce or the length of time you cook a soffritto, sautéing each vegetable one by one to deepen its flavour and thus deepen the flavour of the whole dish when it has been pulled together.

Béarnaise sauce, ossobuco, pheasant à la Normande, custard, cassoulet and toad in the hole are all dishes that any competent cook can cook, but are they are also things that I know I now cook entirely differently to how I made them 20 years ago. I may not cook them every season, nor every year, but they are the things I always come back to, never really leave; they have perched in my culinary memory. I liken this process to the re-reading of a poem or the complete works of Jane Austen. You get something from these classics at every age and stage of life. They are always accessible, but your experience brings new rewards and unperceived revelations each and every time you come to them.

I am usually reminded of some long-lost dish from my past when I chance upon, say, a great veal butcher who understands how to prepare ossobuci; when there's a glut of apples lying under my tree, some spare cream in the fridge and the farmer's market has a brace of well-hung pheasants just waiting to be bought. I might go out to dinner and find someone has cooked something so retro that it just HAS to be rediscovered. Thus, with the apples and cream and pheasant I think back to the simple comfort of that perfect trinity of ingredients in the classic Normandy dish and wonder why I haven't re-visited it for so long, remembering the last occasion on which I cooked it and exactly how the dish turned out, critically speaking.

Without these dishes having worked their way into my kitchen over years of reading the great food writers like Elizabeth David, Jane Grigson, Richard Olney, Anna Del Conte and Marcella Hazan, Claudia Roden, Nigel Slater and Simon Hopkinson, I wouldn't have begun the lifetime exploration of what has become the somewhat polyglot cuisine that we have come to accept as our own, as modern cuisine. So what this section offers is a selection of both old and new classics, with, perhaps, some newer ways of cooking up the old. It is a personal choice, so it is not attempting to be all things to all people, but each dish is one that has given me pleasure in the past and present and will continue to do so in the future — when I remember it!

FISH AND SHELLFISH

POACHED SALMON

1 wild salmon
a glass of white wine
a lump of butter or splosh of olive oil
dill, fennel, parsley and chervil
salt and pepper

I don't have a fish-poaching kettle, never have and probably never will, but this en papillote method does the same job just as effectively and the low cooking temperature retains all the moisture and vibrant flamingo-pink colour of the fish. Most people lose their nerve with fish, particularly with a whole, large fish, and overcook them. It only takes a few extra minutes to turn juicy succulence to dry desiccation, so please don't! Use this method for sea trout too, which I favour even above salmon. A sea trout is to my mind the king of the river fish.

Hollandaise for hot and mayonnaise for cold, all quite within your grasp if you read the rules. I would always prefer to spend my money on one wild salmon once a year than eat the farmed stuff regardless of the season. Its flesh is palely greasy, its flavour not in the same league, its texture flabby and soft and I know enough about how they are reared to know I'd rather live without them.

Preheat the oven to 150°C/300°F/Gas 2. Put the fish on a large piece of foil on a baking sheet, raising the edges of the foil a bit so you can anoint the fish with a glass of white wine. Add a splash of olive oil if the fish is to be eaten cold, or a lump of butter for hot. A few branches of any combination of dill, fennel, parsley and chervil stuffed into the cavity will add to the flavour. Scrunch over some salt and pepper, and seal your fish into its baggy parcel. Make two foil straps and put them underneath the parcel at each end so you can left the fish out more easily when it is cooked.

Up to 2 and a bit kilos or 5lb, the fish will take an hour. If it is any larger, allow 12 minutes to the 450g/1lb. Leave the fish to cool to tepid in its parcel, when you can skin it most successfully.

HOLLANDAISE SAUCE

3 tbsp white wine vinegar
2 tbsp water
10 white peppercorns, bruised
3 organic egg yolks
170g/6oz best unsalted butter, cut into cubes
sea salt
lemon juice

An unctuous rich yellow ointment of a sauce, this is the perfect accompaniment to hot salmon or sea trout, or fresh asparagus (see page 426 for an alternative method of making hollandaise).

Put the wine vinegar, water and peppercorns in a small pan and bring to the boil. Bubble hard to reduce until there is only a tablespoon left. Strain it into a heatproof bowl and let it cool. Beat in the egg yolks and place the bowl over a pan of very hot, but not quite simmering water. Gradually whisk in the butter with a small balloon whisk, a couple of cubes at a time, making sure the pan of water underneath still doesn't actually simmer.

If the sauce gets too hot it will scramble like eggs and you will have to rescue it by beating another egg yolk, then gradually adding the curdled sauce, a drop at a time to begin with, until it thickens and coheres. Season with salt and a spritz of lemon to taste.

MAYONNAISE — THE LOWDOWN

People live in fear and terror of making mayonnaise, custard, soufflés and pastry — these four things more than anything else in my experience. The weird thing is, even mayonnaise that curdles is eminently easy to rescue. You just need a bit of patience and confidence. Remember the following:

- Mayonnaise is tremendously soothing and satisfying to make.
- It can be made in a matter of minutes.
- It tastes so much better than any commercial version that, unless you specifically want a Hellmann's sandwich there really isn't a substitute.
- Once you've got the hang of what is a very easy process for a very wonderful result, you'll wonder why you made such a big girl's handbag about it in the first place.
- Mayonnaise should be made with olive oil. Some people use half olive oil and half a tasteless vegetable oil, but really that misses the point. If you want a blander, less fruity mayonnaise, simply use a blander olive oil.
- The more egg yolks you use the easier and quicker it is to make the mayonnaise and the less likely it is to curdle, but you want a balanced flavour and that doesn't mean an eggy-tasting mayo.
- The French stir a little mustard into their yolks at the start.
- The Italians don't; they make it without.
- Don't overdo the lemon. The flavour should be of oil and eggs with a sharpening note of lemon, no more.
- If everything is warm when you start, the mayonnaise always seems to work much better. Have the eggs, oil and lemon at room temperature and don't make it in a cold bowl.

BASIC MAYONNAISE

People will always eat as much mayonnaise as you make, so the quantity here is more a guide than an instruction.

SERVES 4

200ml/7fl oz good, heavy yet not intrusively bitter, fruity or peppery extra virgin olive oil
2 large egg yolks, organic, free-range, fresh, the best, naturally!
1 teaspoon Dijon mustard (optional)
1 lemon, halved
a little salt and pepper

Measure the olive oil into a small jug. Break the egg yolks into a warm glass or china bowl and stir them in one direction with a wooden spoon. They will thicken in a matter of seconds. Either add the teaspoon of Dijon mustard now and continue to stir and thicken, or begin to pour in the olive oil, no more than a drop at a time to begin with. Keep stirring with your wooden spoon as you start to pour the oil a thin trickle now, speeding up the stirring so that the oil is taken up by the yolks instantly without any danger of separating.

As the mayonnaise begins to stiffen, rather than thicken, the trickle can become a thin stream, but do not get trigger happy. Even mayonnaise that looks too thick to do anything aberrant can curdle before your eyes at the last moment. Every so often you may add a tiny squeeze of juice from the halved lemon. Once you have used up all the oil, season, add a spritz of lemon, taste and adjust.

If by any chance you've taken your eye off the bowl and have a curdled mass before you, simply do the following: break an egg yolk into another bowl and stir it to thicken. Now add the curdled mayonnaise, a drip at a time to begin with, stirring defiantly as you go until you can begin to add it in a steady stream. The new yolk will absorb the whole mass of curdled mayonnaise and that will be that.

If you are planning on amalgamating the yellow ointment with your potato salad rather than serving it in a bowl with your salmon, I would suggest thinning it down with some of the lovely gluey, fishy, winey juices from the papillote. Add a spoonful at a time until the mayonnaise is more the consistency of double cream than of thick gloop.

If you are ever making a potato mayonnaise without the fish, thin it down bit by bit with milk instead of fish juices.

GREEN MAYONNAISE

To make a green mayonnaise for your fish, simply add a chopped tablespoon each of dill, parsley, chervil and tarragon or whichever combination of them you have to hand once the mayonnaise is made. Watercress is good too, particularly with cold, white fish.

HORSERADISH MAYONNAISE

A couple of teaspoons of grated horseradish stirred into mayonnaise is very good with smoked eel.

AÏOLI

Fish or chicken bourride, bacalao, even some raw vegetables all work well with a pungent hit of this classic Provençal sauce. It should ward off more than the devil if you make it strong enough. Simply pound 2, 3, more if you dare, cloves of garlic in a mortar with a little salt until they are crushed to a juicy purée, then continue as for a classic mayonnaise by stirring in the egg yolks.

MAYONNAISE MOUSSEUSE

This is good for cold chicken, salmon or asparagus. Simply whisk 150ml/5fl oz double cream until it holds in soft folds and stir it into your homemade mayonnaise just before amalgamating it with the chicken or serving it alongside the salmon or asparagus. It is also good with a combination of lobster, Jersey Royal new potatoes and avocado – impossibly rich, improbably delicious.

SAUCE RÉMOULADE

This creamier, more mustardy version of mayonnaise is the perfect, piquant sauce for a classic céleri rémoulade, made with celeriac, which is thickly grated, then blanched briefly in boiling water. The sauce is also good with any raw vegetables that need pepping up.

2 hard-boiled organic eggs, yolks only
a few drops of tarragon vinegar
1 raw egg yolk
1 dsrtsp grain mustard
200ml/7fl oz olive oil
a lemon
1 dsrtsp each chives and tarragon, finely chopped
1 dsrtsp capers, finely chopped
salt and pepper

Pound the hard-boiled egg yolks to a paste with a few drops of tarragon vinegar. Stir the raw yolk into the pounded hard-boiled ones with a wooden spoon before adding the grain mustard and continuing to stir. Now stir in the olive oil in the usual way, adding a spritz of lemon juice every so often. Add the chopped herbs and capers, season, taste and adjust with more mustard, lemon, herbs, capers or seasoning as you see fit until the sauce has a powerful flavour. It will coat the celeriac and be a foil to its earthy crunchiness.

LOBSTER

The best tasting lobsters weigh between 675g–900g/1½–2lb so don't be cajoled into buying a large brute and assume you'll get more or better for your money. You won't. In fact, the best thing to do is buy a whole lobster per person if they weigh around the 500g/1lb 2oz mark and you want to serve them for a main course.

Killing a lobster is as emotive to the Crustacean Liberation Front, as I have christened the brigade who write to me every time I publish a lobster recipe, as foie gras and battery hens. The truth, as always, lies somewhere in between. Let's face it, line-caught fish have a better death than most fish, who effectively die by drowning in nets. Abbatoirs, however quickly and efficiently they dispatch their beasts, and I speak as one who's watched, can't do it in a nanosecond or get each hit right. What worries me far more than a few seconds of pain at the end – far worse is endured by the human race – is the terrible life suffered by some animals, reared in boxes, crates or cages in fish farms; tethered immobile in their sties; kept in obscene quantities in chicken houses and fast bred with such ergonomic design faults that they can neither support their fast-growing breasts with their ulcerated legs nor grow without heart attacks or disease. Their lives are so unnatural as to make their very existence and justification shameful. And this is all in the name of factory farming, which we don't actually need. I'd better not go any further.

To my mind, the method of plunging the creatures into fast-boiling water is as acceptably brief as possible, but you do have a choice. If you don't like the thought of it, don't do it and don't eat lobster. I'd rather eat lobster than an intensively reared chicken or pig or a farmed salmon any day. A lifetime of cruelty for a paucity of flavour – what's the point?

There is another method for those who feel confident enough about the creature's anatomy to perform it accurately. At the top of the shell where the two side pieces of shell and the head intersect, there is the pattern of a cross. You may spear a thin but firm-bladed sharp knife down through the middle of the cross where the lines meet, which will sever the lobster's central nervous system instantly. Death, therefore, is also instantaneous.

HOW TO COOK A LOBSTER

A lobster is best cooked in seawater, the water it came from. Failing that, use a heavy hand with the salt. Bring a very large pan of salted water up to a rolling boil, then drop in the lobsters. A 500g/1 and a bit pounder should take 10 minutes, add another 10 minutes for each further 500g/1lb or so. The spiny lobster or crawfish, to my mind sweeter, subtler and better textured than the lobster, should be cooked in the same way.

COLD LOBSTER

If you are going to eat your lobster cold with mayonnaise, take it out of the water it has cooked in and let it cool before serving. Present it whole on a plate or large serving dish with any other shellfish you are serving or with any salad things that you feel suitably dressy to show off the vibrant colour and beauty of the cooked creature. You may split the lobster lengthwise if you like, starting at the head with a sharp knife point and cutting straight down through the middle of the shell to the end of the tail. Then pull out the black intestine that runs down the back. Crack the claws if you like. Otherwise, let people tackle their lobster with crackers and picks.

DRESSING FOR A COLD LOBSTER

SERVES 6

5 tbsp olive oil
1 tbsp Dijon mustard
a handful of parsley, tarragon and
   chives, chopped
1 heaped tbsp shallot, finely chopped
12 drops soya sauce
freshly ground white pepper
small glass of anisette, Pastis or
   Pernod

Simon Hopkinson in *Gammon and Spinach* gives the recipe for this sauce from the Comte de Courchamp's book of 1839, which he found in Elizabeth David's book, *An Omelette and a Glass of Wine*. In Jane Grigson's *Fish Cookery* an almost identical recipe is given, which she attributes to Alexandre Dumas in his *Grand Dictionnaire de Cuisine*, good also, she says, for crab, prawns and other shellfish. Dumas doesn't have any lemon juice in his dressing, otherwise both dressings use the same ingredients just in different proportions. This is Dumas's version of the dressing.

Simply mix together all the dressing ingredients. Fold diced lobster into the dressing.

HOT GRILLED LOBSTER WITH PIQUANT CREAM SAUCE

SERVES 6

cooked lobster
2 shallots, finely minced
45g/1½oz unsalted butter
1 glass Madeira or Fino (dry sherry)
600ml/1 pint béchamel sauce
   (see p. 70)
either 1 dsrtsp Dijon mustard or 3
   chopped anchovies or a handful
   mixed Gruyère and Parmesan
sea salt, pepper and cayenne
a handful each breadcrumbs and
   grated Gruyère for the top
30g/1oz melted butter

Rich though it is, the strange thing is that hot lobster is best set off with a rich sauce, even if it is the simplest of them all — melted hot butter with a spritz of lemon and black pepper.

First remove the meat from the cooked lobsters and dice. Sweat the shallots in the melted butter gently until softened, before adding the Madeira or sherry and reducing it to 1 tablespoon. Add the hot béchamel sauce and either the mustard, anchovies or cheese to taste. Season, going easy on the cayenne (add only a knife tip first) and tasting as you go.

Put a little sauce in the base of the shells then add the lobster meat and more sauce. Put the mixed breadcrumbs and cheese on top and dribble over the melted butter. Put the lobster shells on a baking tray under a hot grill and let them bubble and brown — keep a close watch on them. Take the lobsters out from under the grill and serve.

MOULES MARINIÈRE

SERVES 4

2 medium onions or 4 shallots, finely
    chopped
3–4 cloves of garlic, finely minced
a large handful of parsley, chopped
300ml/10fl oz dry white wine
2kg/4½lb cleaned mussels
extra parsley
55g/2oz unsalted butter, cubed
sea salt and black pepper

There is nothing difficult or time consuming about making this dish, which is really a garlicky mussel soup. I make it most in the late summer when the mussels have recovered their vim and vigour after spawning in Killary Bay near my house in County Mayo. In early summer the flesh is too soft and roe-like and the flavour isn't there. My friend John Kilcoyne, who has mussel rafts in the Killary, brings a sack of mussels straight off the ropes they're attached to over to the house and we set to work cleaning, de-bearding and de-barnacling the little violet blue shells. Then it's plain sailing straight to the bowl.

Put the onions or shallots, garlic, parsley and white wine into a large heavy-bottomed pan and bring to the boil. Simmer for 5 minutes. Now slosh in all the mussels, turning up the heat to full blast and stirring the mussels around a bit. Put the lid on and let the steam force the shells open. Check after a couple of minutes and stir the ones that haven't yet opened closer to the heat source, putting the lid back on until they have. Remove and discard any mussels whose shells don't open.

Put the opened mussels and the onion, garlic and parsley into a warmed serving bowl with a slotted spoon and keep them warm. Carefully strain the fish liquor into a pan to remove the grit and bring it to the boil. Now reduce the heat and whisk in little cubes of butter until you have a glossy sauce. Sprinkle over the extra parsley, season and return the liquor to the mussels. Serve with crusty bread and more butter and some chilled white wine.

900g/2lb white fish, cut into bite-
    sized chunks

COURT BOUILLON
2 tbsp white wine vinegar
300ml/10fl oz white wine
1 onion
1 bay leaf
a strip of orange peel
fennel
2 or 3 fish heads; any fishmonger
    should give you these
1 carrot, chopped
1 stick of celery, chopped
1 onion, quartered in its skin

AÏOLI
6–12 cloves of fresh garlic
sea salt and black pepper
3 organic egg yolks
up to 425ml/15fl oz best Provençal
    olive oil
juice of half a lemon

LA BOURRIDE

A Provençal bourride of gently poached white fish, with a pungent, heaving-with-garlic aïoli stirred into it, is superb. Use up to three of the following fish: hake, cod, bass, bream, John Dory, monkfish. Or serve the aïoli separately with poached salt cod, surrounded by French beans, boiled potatoes and carrots, steamed fennel, artichokes and softly hard-boiled eggs.

To make the court bouillon, bring a pan of water to the boil with the white wine vinegar, white wine, onion, bay leaf, orange peel, fennel and fish heads. Add the carrot, celery and onion. Simmer for about 30 minutes, then let it cool. Strain.

For the fish bourride, proceed as follows. Bring the strained court bouillon to the boil, then add bite-sized chunks of fish, allowing 225g/8oz per person, in order of thickness. Monkfish is chunkier and will take a little longer to cook (3–4 minutes), thinner slices will take 2–3 minutes, small hake steaks on the bone 5–6 minutes. The bouillon should be at a gentle simmer.

Remove the pan from the heat. Gently place the pieces of fish in a warm tureen with a couple of ladles of court bouillon. Put a tablespoon of the aïoli into a bowl and stir a ladleful of the bouillon into it, before returning the mixture to the tureen with the fish. Sprinkle with parsley. Serve the rest of the aïoli separately.

AÏOLI
Crush the garlic with a little sea salt in a mortar until it is a creamy paste. Beat in the egg yolks. Whisk in the olive oil, first drip by drip, then in a thin, steady stream when you have an emulsion. Add the lemon juice and season.

BREADED PLAICE

SERVES 2

flour
sea salt and black pepper
1 organic egg, beaten
a plateful of brown breadcrumbs
2 tbsp parsley, finely chopped
the zest of a lemon and some
    quartered wedges
2 large fillets of plaice, skinned

A simple supper and a lovely one when this milky-fleshed fish is in its prime, particularly when it comes with a fat slick of grainy roe to contrast with the soft, sweet white flesh.

Preheat the oven to 180°C/350°F/Gas 4. Put some flour on a large flat plate and season. Whisk the egg in a separate wide flat dish. Mix the breadcrumbs with the parsley and lemon zest and put them on another plate.

Dip the fish into the flour, shake the residue off and then dip each plaice fillet into the beaten egg, then into the breadcrumb mixture, coating thoroughly on both sides. Place the fillets on a buttered baking tray and put in the oven for 12–15 minutes or until soft right through when pierced with a skewer.

GOUJONS OF PLAICE

SERVES 2 AS A STARTER

2 large fillets of plaice, skinned
flour
sea salt and black pepper
1 organic egg, beaten
brown or white breadcrumbs made
    from stale bread, finely ground in
    the food processor
1 lemon

Cut the plaice fillets into ribbon strips and dip them in the seasoned flour, then in the beaten egg and finally in the breadcrumbs. If you have a deep-fryer, pour in some groundnut oil and bring it slowly up to 190°C. I don't have a thermometer, so I watch for the oil to start moving, then drop in a large crumb. If it seizes and starts to fry instantly, the temperature is hot enough for the fish. Put the goujons in the basket and lower them into the hot oil for 3–4 minutes until they are beautifully browned. Drain them on kitchen paper and season with a little salt.

Delicious served with the Thai dipping sauce on page 268 or the crème fraîche tartare on page 160.

Breaded Plaice

FISH AND CHIPS

Deep-frying is a once-a-year thing in my house and then it is not about rock and chips straight out of the paper. Fish and chips are what fish and chip shops are for, hot, crisp burn-the-roof-of-the-mouth batter with slippery white fish inside, and a rake of fat, hand-cut chips with as much sog as crunch and good shakings of malt vinegar and salt. However, even if you don't want to produce the nation's favourite dinner at home, you might want to make the best chips to go with your steak or steak tartare, and you might want to deep-fry fish or beignets or prawns in tempura.

LAGER BATTER

225g/8oz flour, plus extra for flouring the fish
240ml/8fl oz lager
1 tbsp olive oil

This is my favourite batter for fish on the rare occasions I get the deep-fryer out of hibernation. Its light acidity and flavour really complement the fish. Particularly good with a firm white chunk of huss or haddock.

Always flour the fish first if you are going to batter it, shaking off the excess before dunking in the batter brew.

Sift the flour into a bowl containing the beer, add the olive oil and whisk well. Flour the fish and dunk it in the batter. Put it into the basket of the fryer and lower it into the vegetable oil which should be at 180–190°C. Test with a piece of bread if you don't have a thermometer. It should fizz and splutter and brown within 30 seconds. Do not put too much into a deep-fryer at one time as it will lower the temperature of the bubbling oil and your food will start to absorb a lot more oil and won't fry properly.

Fry until golden, then remove the fish to some kitchen paper and drain thoroughly before serving. If you have to keep the fish warm, don't cover it or the batter will lose its crunch. Put it on some kitchen paper in a medium oven and leave the door open.

YEAST BATTER

4g/¼oz quick-acting yeast
240ml/8fl oz milk, plus extra for dissolving the yeast
225g/8oz plain flour
75g/2½oz potato flour
1 organic egg, separated
salt

This is a thicker batter than the lager batter but works very well if you are deep-frying vegetables like courgettes or making beignets.

Dissolve the yeast in a bit of milk and leave in a warm place for 10–15 minutes. Mix the plain flour and potato flour, both sifted into a large bowl, with the milk, an egg yolk (reserving the egg white) and a pinch of salt. Cover with a damp cloth and leave somewhere warm in the kitchen for a couple of hours. Whisk the egg white until stiff and fold it into the batter before using.

A SIMPLE FRITTER BATTER

This is great for mussels, clams and scallops.

110g/4oz plain flour
a pinch of salt
3 tbsp olive oil
about 150ml/5fl oz water
1 egg white

Sieve the flour and salt into a bowl and whisk in the olive oil and water. Continue whisking for a few minutes. Leave the batter to rest for a couple of hours, then whisk the egg white stiffly and fold it in. Dip the fish into the batter and fry briefly until delectably bronzed. Drain on kitchen paper and serve with the Asian dressing on page 77 or the crème fraîche tartare on page 160.

TEMPURA BATTER

200ml/7fl oz chilled water
55g/2oz plain flour
55g/2oz potato flour
salt

Whisk the chilled water with both flours and a pinch of salt until light and frothy. Despite its lumpy appearance, this makes a light, crisp, coating batter for things like prawns.

CHIPS

SERVES 2

2 large, floury winter potatoes; new
    potatoes simply won't do
groundnut oil for frying
sea salt

Remember, not to over-fill the fryer or the chips will stick to each other, absorb far too much oil and not crisp up. Make them in batches and keep them warm in a warmed dish on kitchen paper in a medium oven with the door open. There are no shortcuts to making the best most burnished, bronzed, crisp chips. They simply HAVE to be fried twice or you may as well forget it and go down to the chippy. I like my chips thick, but not so thick that the floury innard overwhelms the crisp outside. Skinny chips seem rather to defeat the object!

Peel the potatoes and cut them however thickly or thinly you like your chips. Wash the chips in a colander under cold running water until you can't see any milky starch, then pat them dry in a tea towel.

Half fill your deep-fryer with oil in the normal way and heat it to 180–190°C. Test with a thermometer or throw in a little bit of bread – if it sizzles and browns the oil is ready. Place as many chips as will fit the basket without crowding. Lower the basket into the bubbling oil and cook the chips for about 7 minutes. They will be cooked through but a pale gold, not darker. Remove and drain that batch on kitchen paper. Do the same with the next batch. You may leave the chips for a couple of hours at this stage if you need to.

Return the oil to the same dizzy height of temperature and dunk the basket of chips once again, this time for about 3 minutes until they bronze all over. If they haven't bronzed successfully with this second cooking, a third will do it.

Finally put some kitchen paper on top of the chips so the tops will also lose some grease. Shake over a little salt and serve with ketchup, malt or white wine vinegar or garlic mayonnaise.

SOLE DUGLÈRE

SERVES 2

1 sole weighing about 675g/1½lb,
   skinned and filleted
30g/1oz unsalted butter
25g/scant oz flour
90ml/3fl oz double cream
1 dsrtsp parsley, finely chopped
2 tomatoes, skinned, seeded and
   chopped
sea salt and black pepper

FISH STOCK

head, bones and skin of sole plus any
   extra bones from your fishmonger
1 onion, sliced
parsley stalks
fennel
chervil
tarragon
half white wine, half water

This was a dish that the late, greatest-of-them-all George Perry-Smith used to serve at Riverside in Helford, Cornwall. For all I know, he may have served it at his legendary Hole-in-the-Wall in Bath too, but that was before my time. It is all about refined simplicity, of which George was the master – not one ingredient too many or too few, and all of unimpeachable quality. His cooking, his understanding of how little one had to do to make good food taste superlative was unequalled. He may have cooked largely from Elizabeth David, but all of us who really who knew his cooking, knew how far beyond any one author or cuisine his food really went. His signature dish, salmon baked in pastry with currants and ginger, served with a sauce messine, was only one of many, many dishes that George delighted his guests with. I suspect it became the one most associated with George – more perhaps than his much copied fish soup with aïoli and rouille, and his chocolate St Emilion – because, on the face of it, it was such an unlikely marriage of flavours. Here is something simpler, more quickly realisable, though I don't have George's own recipe for this dish.

Make the fish stock. Put all the ingredients in a large pan and simmer for 30–40 minutes.

Preheat the oven to 180°C/350°F/Gas 4. Butter a gratin dish that will hold the fillets in a single layer, put them in and season. Pour over 200–300ml/7–10fl oz of hot fish stock and poach in the oven for 10 minutes. Pour the fish stock into a jug and keep the fish warm under a piece of butter paper in the warming oven.

Melt the butter, add the flour to make a roux and whisk in the strained fish liquor from cooking the fish. Whisk until smooth and keep simmering for a few minutes before adding the cream and letting it bubble hard for 2–3 minutes. Take off the heat and add the parsley and tomatoes. Correct the seasoning, put the fillets on individual plates and pour some sauce over them.

SKATE WITH CAPERS

SERVES 2

1 tbsp cider or white wine vinegar
675g/1½lb wing of skate
30g/1oz unsalted butter
2 tbsp white wine
2 tbsp salted capers, rinsed on a
   slotted spoon under cold running
   water
black pepper
spritz of lemon juice
1 tbsp flat-leaf parsley or chervil,
   chopped

Bring a large pan of water to the boil and add the vinegar. Drop in the skate and let it poach gently until cooked. This will take about 9–12 minutes, depending on its thickness. Test the thick part by the cartilaginous bone with a skewer.

Meanwhile, melt the butter, add the white wine and let it bubble up and reduce a little. Throw in the capers, stir, season with black pepper (the capers should provide enough salt) and remove from the heat, adding a spritz of lemon juice. Halve the skate wing and place each half on a warmed plate. Pour the sauce over the top and add a scattering of parsley. Serve with mashed potatoes and a green vegetable.

Skate with Capers

GRILLED DOVER SOLE

SERVES 2

2 Dover soles, each about
    285–340g/10–12oz weight
55g/2oz unsalted butter, clarified
parsley butter (optional), merely a
    tbsp chopped parsley mashed into
    55g/2oz unsalted softened butter
    and put into the fridge to firm up
1 lemon

This could be the simplest recipe in the book, but it is undoubtedly one of the finest when the sole is fresh, but not cooked, straight from the sea. The flesh needs a day or two out of the water to firm up to its lovely firm but yielding, juicy texture. We get Torbay soles from Brixham in Devon down here, at the fishmonger in Taunton. They are paler skinned, smaller in size and cheaper but a very good substitute for the Dover beauties.

The sole should be skinned on both sides, the head left on and the roe in if there is any. Your fishmonger will do this for you.

Clarify the butter. Heat it in a small pan and skim the milky residue from the surface before pouring the butter into a bowl, leaving the white solids at the bottom of the pan. Brush the sole with butter on both sides and put them under the grill for about 5 minutes a side or until a skewer slips easily through the flesh and to the backbone .

Serve with a couple of knobs of parsley butter placed on the fish and a wedge of lemon at the side.

CODCAKES WITH KAFFIR LIME LEAVES AND THAI DIPPING SAUCE

SERVES 2

1 shallot, peeled and chopped
2 garlic cloves, peeled and crushed
2 small hot red chillies, seeded and
    chopped
a handful of fresh coriander leaves,
    coarsely chopped
8 kaffir lime leaves, cut into strips
1 tbsp Thai fish sauce (nam pla)
sea salt
450g/1lb cod fillet
groundnut or grapeseed oil

DIPPING SAUCE
6 tbsp rice vinegar
4 tbsp light muscovado sugar
1 tbsp organic shoyu sauce
1 small red and 1 small green chilli,
    seeded and finely chopped
1 tbsp coriander leaves, very finely
    chopped
juice of 2 kaffir limes or 1 lime

The poor, exotically Oriental codcake served with Thai dipping sauce became a mantra of the trendy, fusion restaurant kitchen a decade ago, overworked, overdone and just plain over. It is a classic, though, I feel, and its brief fall from grace should eventually bring it back to non-ubiquitous but rightful place status. It is just a really good dish that you can serve as an appetiser, starter or main course and is really no more pretentious than our English version, a fishcake served with tartare sauce. You can make the codcake mixture in advance and keep it covered in the fridge until frying time. The dipping sauce keeps equally well and should be served cold. These cod cakes also make a sensational first course, in which case they will feed four.

Place the shallot, garlic, chillies and coriander in a food processor with the lime leaves and fish sauce and blitz. Scrape into a bowl and season with sea salt. Throw chunks of cod into the processor and blitz to a paste, not a sludge. Tip the fish into the other ingredients and mix everything together thoroughly.

Flour your hands a little to prevent sticking and form the mixture into 8 flat patties. Cover the patties and put them in the fridge until an hour before you want to use them.

Heat about 6 tablespoons of oil in a frying pan. Fry the codcakes until golden on each side (about 4 minutes). Drain on kitchen paper and serve with the sauce.

DIPPING SAUCE

Heat the vinegar and sugar in a small pan until the sugar has dissolved and the mixture is syrupy. Stir in the shoyu sauce. Leave to cool before adding the chillies, coriander and lime juice. Chill.

SALMON FISHCAKES

SERVES 6

about 600g/1lb 4oz wild salmon, cooked

about 285g/10oz cooked potato, mashed without milk and butter

sea salt and freshly ground black pepper

a handful of flat-leaf parsley, chopped

2 organic eggs

85g/3oz stale wholemeal bread, baked in small squares in a slow oven to dry out for 15 minutes, then whizzed to crumbs

vegetable or olive oil for frying

When I was a child it seemed extraordinarily glamorous to eat salmon fishcakes for breakfast and that is what my grandfather did, sitting at the head of an immaculately gleaming 18th-century oak refectory table. For a special treat, Rhoda, my grandmother's cook, would make a couple for me too. They are still a treat, and will always remain so. I would not, however, be interested in eating them if they were made with farmed salmon. Salmon fishcakes should be made with the leftovers from a perfectly moist, wild salmon whose flesh has slightly gelled overnight, been flaked but not crushed to a pulp, and bound with some dry, smooth, unbuttery mashed potato and a healthy seasoning of flat-leaf parsley, coarsely ground pepper and sea salt. These fishcakes are one of the small, select band of dishes that one can feel an urge for at any hour, breakfast, lunch or supper. Vary their accompaniment to suit the time of day; even I could not envisage sauce tartare for breakfast. If you don't have the amount of salmon listed here, the fishcakes are still delicious with half potato, half salmon.

Mash the salmon into the potato roughly so it still has coarse-textured flakes and is not a homogenous purée. Season and throw in the parsley, then shape the mixture into 12 2.5cm/1in thick cakes and place them on a large flat plate. Keep covered in the fridge for an hour or two to firm up, or longer if it is convenient.

Whisk the eggs and pour onto a large flat plate, and spread the dried breadcrumbs on another. Dip the fishcakes first in the egg on both sides, then turn them in the breadcrumbs, making sure the sides are well crumbed too. Place them on a third large plate. Heat a shallow film of oil, about 60ml/2fl oz, in a frying pan over a medium heat. Put the fishcakes in and fry for 4 minutes or so a side until golden brown. Drain on kitchen paper and serve with a dollop of crème fraîche tartare (see page 160).

POULTRY AND GAME

COQ AU VIN

SERVES 6

85g/3oz unsalted butter
3 tbsp olive oil
110g/4oz organic green back bacon,
    diced
18 shallots, but who's counting,
    peeled and left whole
4 whole cloves of garlic
18 organic mushrooms, halved
a large organic chicken, jointed or 6
    good-sized legs
flour
salt and pepper
a bouquet of fresh thyme, flat-leaf
    parsley and bay tied together
4 tbsp Cognac
1 bottle full-bodied red wine
1 tsp molasses sugar
1 tbsp each of butter and flour
1 handful of flat-leaf parsley

The classic of classics, this is an old-fashioned '70s bistro dish. But the great joy of that particular ilk and era of restaurant food is that it's the sort you always want to eat and the kind you want to cook at home. This dish is straight out of the bonne maman school of cookery. Make sure your fowl is the best you can afford, preferably a slow-grown, organically reared, free-range bird. Don't imagine, either, that there is cooking wine and drinking wine. There isn't. What's fit for the bird is only fit for it if it's drinkable. The sauce should coat the bird with a gluey, ruby-red richness and depth of flavour. You may use the whole bird or just legs, the bones of which will make the sauce even more delectably gluey.

Preheat the oven to 180°C/350°F/Gas 4. Heat the butter and olive oil in a heavy-bottomed casserole, and throw in the bacon. Sauté briefly, then add the shallots, garlic and mushrooms and cook gently until the shallots are beginning to turn opaque and pale gold. Remove with a slotted spoon. Shake the chicken pieces with some seasoned flour in a Ziploc bag, then shake off any excess flour. Add them to the pan and brown first on one side then the other, for 5 minutes a side. Return the bacon and vegetables to the pot, add the bouquet of herbs and season. Cover the pot with a lid and cook until tender, about 25 minutes.

   Set a saucepan on top of the stove on a moderate heat, warm the Cognac in a ladle, then pour it into the pan and set it alight. Let the alcohol burn off before adding the heated red wine and a teaspoon of molasses sugar. Reduce by about one-third, then thicken with some old-fashioned beurre manié. (Simply work together a tablespoon each of butter and flour until you have a paste, then break off pea-sized bits and whisk them into a ladle of the hot liquid and add to the sauce.)

   Strain the sauce into the coq and keep hot until ready to serve. Scatter with the chopped parsley.

1.5–2kg/3¼–4½lb organic free-range
    chicken
1 organic lemon
1 onion, stuck with 3 cloves
some leek tops
2 carrots, chopped
2 sticks of celery, chopped with their
    leaves
a bouquet of thyme, parsley,
    rosemary and bay tied together
12 peppercorns
½ bottle white wine
1 litre/1¾ pints or so chicken stock
    (see p. 80) if you have it; if not
    use water

SAUCE
55g/2oz unsalted butter
2 tbsp flour
300ml/10fl oz chicken stock
    (see p. 80)
240ml/8fl oz double cream
2 organic egg yolks
squeeze of lemon juice
sea salt and black pepper
1–2 tbsp tarragon (optional; it then
    becomes tarragon cream sauce)

CHICKEN IN A CREAM SAUCE

Sometimes simple, soothing dishes are the only thing that appeals and chicken in cream sauce (poulet à la crème) is one of them. Its ivory, creamy tones, rich, smooth softness of flesh and plush velvet sauce somehow defy the word bland that may spring to mind. The flavours may not be strong in the sense that they would be with the addition of herbs, spices, garlic, tomatoes, vinegar or red wine, but that is not the point of this dish. I believe it should be served with as snowy a heap of rice as the dish itself, with, perhaps, the addition of a pale winter root purée like parsnip, some braised fennel or some steamed celery. White on white on white. If you feel like a speckle of green though and want to add the herb that surely complements chicken better than all others, finish the sauce with some finely chopped tarragon stirred in at the last minute before serving.

Rub the chicken inside and out with the cut side of a lemon, then put the chicken breast up in a large, heavy-bottomed pot. Add all the vegetables, bouquet of herbs and peppercorns, followed by the white wine and enough stock or water just to cover the breast. Bring slowly to the boil and remove the scum. Turn down to the gentlest blip of a simmer, then cover with greaseproof paper and a lid and poach. If it's a small bird, turn it breast down after 45 minutes for the last 15 minutes; if it's a large bird do the same after an hour for the last 15 minutes.

Start making the sauce 30 minutes or so before the chicken is going to be ready. Melt the butter in a heavy-bottomed pan. When it begins to bubble, add the flour and stir it well in until it is a blond roux, pale golden and bubbling. Add the hot chicken stock, a ladle at a time, stirring well over a medium heat and making sure there are no lumps. You may wish to do this with a balloon whisk. Now add the cream and stir it in. The sauce will be quite thin at this point, but keep cooking it over a gentle heat for about 20 minutes, as it will thicken slowly. You don't have to stir it constantly, but regularly stirring will stop it sticking or forming a skin on top.

Just before you are ready to serve, remove the chicken to a carving dish and joint it, putting the pieces on a large warmed serving dish. Beat the egg yolks with a squeeze of lemon juice and add them to the cream sauce, stirring it in but keeping it just under boiling point so that it doesn't curdle. Season, taste – you may need more seasoning or lemon juice – and add the herbs if you wish before pouring it over the chicken. You may prefer to add parsley instead.

Serve with plain basmati rice and some vegetables as above or with a plain, green salad. The somewhat sumptuous plainness of the dish should be preserved throughout.

1.5kg/3¼lb organic free-range chicken and some leek tops, extra carrots, celery, onions and herbs
2 medium carrots, sliced into thick discs
2 sticks of celery, chopped
2 fat white wands of leeks, sliced into discs (use tops when poaching chicken)
2 medium onions, peeled and quartered
55g/2oz unsalted butter
55g/2oz flour
150ml/5fl oz full-cream milk
150ml/5fl oz chicken stock from poaching the bird, reduced by half by boiling
150ml/5fl oz double cream
sprigs of tarragon and flat-leaf parsley, chopped
sea salt and black pepper

SHORTCRUST PASTRY
340g/12oz plain flour
a pinch of salt
either 170g/6oz unsalted butter or lard, or half butter and half lard
beaten egg for glaze

CHICKEN PIE

Is this English? Well, the Americans have their chicken pot pie and who knows whether the French or the Italians would shroud a plump chicken in flaky, lardy-crisp pastry. This, to my mind, is the ultimate savoury pie, a dish that deserves serenading for its comfort and homeliness and hidden depths; for its golden crust concealing jewels of vegetables and chicken; and its creamy, satin mantle of a béchamel sauce made slightly aniseedy with tarragon. My children all love it, but it is good enough to produce at the smartest of dinners, not just for a family lunch. You can always add a few dried, soaked morels and their liquor to the sauce if you feel it does need a little dressing up.

Put the chicken breast up in a tightish-fitting pot with some leek tops, carrot, celery, onion, a few peppercorns and a bouquet of fresh herbs. Just cover with water, bring to the boil slowly and skim. Cover the pan and poach the chicken for 45–60 minutes.

Make the pastry (see page 181), working it quickly into a ball, then wrap it in clingfilm and chill it in the fridge for half an hour. Steam the vegetables by throwing them into the steamer in the order in which they cook, carrots first, celery next, then the onion and leek for the last 5 minutes.

Preheat the oven to 180°C/350°F/Gas 4 and place a baking sheet on the middle shelf of the oven to heat up. When the bird has cooled down sufficiently to handle, remove all the flesh you can from the bones, peeling off the skin as you go to use with the carcass to make more intensely flavoured stock the second time around. Tear the flesh along the grain, almost pulling it into long bite-sized pieces.

Make a roux with the butter and flour, then add the milk and reduced chicken stock, both hot, alternately, until you have a satin-thick sauce. Stirring as you go, cook the sauce long enough to get rid of the flouriness, then stir in the cream. Remove from the heat, season and add the chopped fresh herbs, a couple of tablespoons of each. Stir in the chicken and vegetables and leave to cool.

Line your buttered pastry tin or pie dish with two-thirds of the rolled-out pastry, then scrape in the filling and spread it out evenly over the pastry base. Cover with the remaining third of the pastry, and crimp the edges together with the tines of a fork dipped in cold water. Brush the top with beaten egg. Cut a cross in the middle of the pie right through the pastry to allow the steam to escape as the pie cooks. If your pie is deep rather than shallow, a china bird placed in the middle of the pie under the slashes is a good idea.

Bake for about an hour, then check. If the pastry is beautifully bronzed, cover the top with a sheet of greaseproof paper and cook for about another 15 minutes, or until your nose tells you that it is ready. Pastry does smell ready when it is! Don't cut into the pie for at least 10 minutes after taking it out of the oven.

COLD CHICKEN IN A TARRAGON CREAM SAUCE

SERVES 6

1.5kg/3¼lb organic, free-range
  chicken and some leek tops,
  carrots, celery, onions,
  peppercorns and herbs
600ml/1 pint of the stock you've
  cooked the bird in
150ml/5fl oz double cream
6 organic egg yolks, well beaten
a little lemon juice
a little white wine
sea salt and black pepper
a handful of fresh tarragon

This is a lovely summer lunch dish, the cream sauce set and languishing on the poached chicken and a pattern of long, aniseedy tarragon leaves climbing up the snowy slope of sauce like green branches. Make it in advance and eat it cold with an old-fashioned rice salad dressed with a good vinaigrette – sherry vinegar works well with tarragon – and jewelled with fresh young peas.

Put the chicken in a tightish-fitting pot with some leek tops, carrot, celery, onion, a few peppercorns and a bouquet of fresh herbs. Just cover with water, bring to the boil slowly and skim. Cover the pan and poach the chicken for 45–60 minutes, turning it over at half time.

Remove the bird from its stock once it is cooked. Carve when it is cool enough, the breasts each into two good, thick pieces, the legs into two pieces each and the wings. Remove every last bit of skin.

Mix the hot stock with the cream and the well beaten yolks. Pour into a wide-bottomed pan and stir or whisk constantly over a gentle heat. Since you are in effect making a custard, there is the danger of its scrambling if you allow it to hit boiling point. You must just have patience and keep whisking until the mixture, all of a sudden, has the consistency of thick cream and coats the whisk or wooden spoon. This usually takes between 10–20 minutes. If you get frightened and feel nothing much is happening, place your pan inside a larger pan containing hot water just under simmering point and leave the sauce, apart from the odd whisk or stir, for 20–30 minutes. It will thicken all by itself and have the added advantage of an even better flavour.

Once you have the desirable thick cream texture, season, add a squeeze of lemon juice and a tablespoon of white wine and a tablespoon of chopped tarragon. Keep the rest of the leaves whole for decorating. Stir off the heat until the sauce has cooled a little – it will go on thickening off the heat as all custards do as they are cooling – and pour it over the skinned pieces of chicken on a large serving dish. Dip whole leaves of tarragon in the stock and put them, Jack and the beanstalk-like, up either side of the dish on top of the sauce, say a thumbnail in from the edge of the chicken on each side. Serve cold.

SOUTHERN-STYLE FRIED CHICKEN

SERVES 4

flour
salt and pepper
celery salt
2 tsp paprika
2 tsp cayenne
8 organic chicken thighs, skinned
2 organic eggs, beaten
110g/4oz lard or 85g/3oz butter and
150ml/5fl oz olive oil

Classically cooked in bacon fat or lard, and served with sweetcorn fritters, this is a perfect autumn dish. It is here for the divine Rob, though it will never, I am sure, attain the heights of the childhood version he remembers made by Cora, the family cook. You need to serve the thighs hot from the pan, so make the sweetcorn fritters while the chicken is frying and keep them warm in the oven.

Season the flour and add a knifetip of celery salt and the paprika and cayenne. Put the seasoned flour in a Ziploc bag, throw in the thighs, seal and shake. Remove the floured thighs, shaking off any excess flour, and place them on a plate.

Turn each thigh in beaten egg before placing it on a rack for a minute. Repeat with more flour and beaten egg, before a final flouring. Place on the rack while you heat the lard or butter and oil in a heavy-bottomed frying pan.

When the fat starts smoking, put the thighs in with a slotted spoon and fry gently for about 10 minutes a side or until bronzed and crisped. You could serve this with a couple of rashers of well-crisped streaky bacon per person.

SWEETCORN FRITTERS

170g/6oz cooked sweetcorn, the
kernels cut from the cobs
55g/2oz flour
2 tbsp milk
1 pinch paprika
1 pinch cayenne
1 organic egg plus one egg white
sea salt
a knob of unsalted butter

Mix the sweetcorn, flour, milk, paprika, cayenne and egg together in a bowl. Whisk the egg white until stiff and fold it into the mixture, adding a little salt. Heat the butter in a pan and drop tablespoons of the thick batter into it, frying them on both sides until golden.

VIETNAMESE DIPPING SAUCE

2–4 tbsp water
1–2 tsp sugar
1 red chilli, seeds removed,
finely chopped
1 clove of garlic, smashed with the
back of a knife and finely chopped
juice of a lime
1 tsp rice vinegar
2–4 tbsp nam pla (Thai fish sauce),
available in supermarkets
2 tsp finely grated raw carrot

Heat the water and sugar until the sugar dissolves, then cool. Pound the chilli and garlic together in a mortar, then add the sugared water. Mix together, adding the lime juice, vinegar and nam pla to taste. Mix, and add the carrot before serving. You could add a spoonful of finely chopped coriander, mint or both.

1.5kg/3¼lb organic free-range
    chicken and some leek tops,
    carrots, celery, onions,
    peppercorns and herbs

CREAM OF CURRY SAUCE
55g/2oz onion, chopped
1 tbsp light olive oil
1 dsrtsp fresh Madras curry powder
1 tsp tomato purée
150ml/5fl oz red wine
120ml/4fl oz water
1 bay leaf
salt, pepper, a pinch of sugar
a slice or two of lemon and a
    squeeze or more of lemon juice
1–2 tbsp sieved apricot jam, apricot
    purée or mango chutney
400ml/14fl oz homemade
    mayonnaise (see p. 256)
about 4 tbsp double cream, lightly
    whipped

CORONATION CHICKEN

One of the first cookery books I was ever given as a teenager was *The Constance Spry Cookery Book*. It is still something I turn to, less for complete recipes, more to remind me of a cooking method or to compare her version of a technique with someone else's, who is perhaps more in touch with the zeitgeist. She is probably more famous for her coronation chicken with its cream of curry sauce than for anything else. Easy to laugh at what became a stock Sloane party or wedding dish and became mongrelised with a certain proprietary brand of mayonnaise, but when made properly it is a really lovely summer dish. It just needs to lose its Cordon Bleu connotations and be made with the right ingredients.

Put the chicken in a tightish-fitting pot with some leek tops, carrot, celery, onion, a few peppercorns and a bouquet of fresh herbs. Just cover with water, bring to the boil slowly and skim. Cover the pan and poach the chicken for 45–60 minutes, turning it over at half time. Remove the fowl from its bath of stock when the stock has cooled and joint it Remove the flesh from the bones and the skin from the flesh. Prepare the sauce.

Gently stew the chopped onion in the olive oil until translucent. Add the curry powder and stir to coat the onion. Cook for another couple of minutes. Add the tomato purée, the wine, water and bay leaf and bring to the boil. Add the seasoning, sugar and the lemon slices and juice. Simmer uncovered for 5–10 minutes. Strain thoroughly through a sieve, pressing down on it hard with a wooden spoon to extract the maximum flavour and cool. Add by degrees to the mayonnaise with the apricot jam, purée or mango chutney. Adjust seasoning, adding more lemon juice to taste. Obviously, fresh apricot purée will be sweeter than jam or chutney. Fold in the whipped cream.

Tear the chicken into pieces along the grain of the meat, the sort you could consider bite sized, and mix half the sauce in with the chicken. If you are following Constance Spry, arrange at one end of the serving dish with a rice salad of cooked peas, diced cucumber and finely chopped mixed herbs mixed in a well seasoned French dressing at the other end. Now coat the chicken with the rest of the curry cream sauce. Serve cold.

The sauce is also good served with cold lobster or, dare I say it, prawns, if you don't think that a blast from the '70s too far. If you weren't around then in cooking terms it could, of course, all be new to you.

4 tbsp sel de Guerande or coarse sea
   salt like Maldon
3–4 sprigs thyme leaves stripped
   from their stems
6–8 juniper berries
2 dried bay leaves
1 tsp sugar
12 black peppercorns
freshly grated nutmeg
4 free-range duck legs
600–700ml/1–1¼ pint duck
   or goose fat
half a head of garlic

CONFIT OF DUCK

This is resoundingly a mid-winter dish, the sort of thing you want to cook after Christmas when you have a giant bowl of goose fat left over, or after you have been roasting a duck and have the duck fat. Traditionally it is made with the legs of the duck or goose; the breast doesn't stand up so well to the salting and cooking ritual, becoming stringy and dry. You may want to eschew all things rich after Christmas, but think of it like this: it is something to sit in its snowy fat for a month until, in the depressingly dark, damp cold of February you think I MUST have a confit or a cassoulet.

Grind the first 6 ingredients together in a mortar with a little freshly grated nutmeg. Put half the mixture on a plate and put the duck legs flesh-side down on the mixture. Sprinkle the rest over the top, cover with clingfilm and put in the fridge for 24 hours, turning the legs over once at roughly half time.

   Preheat the oven to 130°C/250°F/Gas ½. Melt the goose or duck fat very slowly in a heavy-bottomed pan. Wash the brew off the duck legs and pat dry before putting them gently into the warm fat with the garlic, slightly bruised with the back of a knife but not peeled. Cook in the oven for 2 hours or until a skewer slides easily right into the flesh.

   Let the legs cool in the fat before putting them in a bowl or jar. Strain the cold fat over them to cover the legs completely, then keep them in the fridge for at least a month but up to 3 months. Serve with potatoes browned in goose fat.

POTATOES BROWNED IN GOOSE FAT

When you want to eat the duck confit, put the contents of the bowl or jar in a large pan and melt all the fat slowly. Remove the duck legs and sauté them slowly until hot in the fat that's clinging to them.

   Meanwhile, cook some whole small potatoes in stock just to cover with a couple of cloves of garlic. When they are done and the stock is syrupy and reduced, transfer them to a frying pan with a couple of tablespoons of the melted duck or goose fat, throw in the garlic cloves and brown on all sides in the fat.

6 duck legs
1 box of Maldon salt
pepper
a few cloves of peeled garlic, bay
  leaves and sprigs of thyme
225g/8oz duck or goose fat
white wine

BEANS
900g/2lb long white haricot beans or
  cannellini beans, soaked overnight
  in plenty of water, then drained
2 pig's trotters, salted, or 450g/1lb
  salt pork if you can't cope with
  trotters
225g/8oz pork rind, cut in squares
3 onions, peeled, and each stuck with
  a clove
1 clove of garlic
3 sticks of celery with the leaves,
  peeled
2 carrots
the white of a fat leek
1 bouquet of fresh herbs tied
  together (bay, thyme, rosemary
  and parsley)

PORK AND LAMB
450g/1lb or more shoulder of mutton
  or mature lamb
450g/1lb boned loin of pork
1 onion
450g/1lb Toulouse sausage, or any
  other coarse-cut pure pork
  sausage
450g/1lb garlicky boiling sausage
6 tomatoes
dry white wine

CRUST
225g/8oz breadcrumbs
a large handful of flat-leaf parsley,
  chopped

CASSOULET DE TOULOUSE

This recipe includes preserved duck. You could just roast a duck and then joint it, but this is the classic method for preserved duck or goose. You will need to leave the duck legs in the brine for 36 hours, so plan accordingly.

Begin with the duck. Shake a layer of salt on to a plate, pepper the duck legs, then place them on the salt with the garlic and herbs and cover with the rest of the salt. Cover with clingfilm and refrigerate for 36 hours.

Remove the duck from the brine and place in a casserole with the duck fat, a glass of dry white wine and one of water. Cover with a layer of greaseproof and a lid and cook gently, at 150°C/300°F/Gas 2 for 2½–3 hours. Leave to cool in the fat.

Put the beans in a large casserole with enough water to just cover, bring to the boil, cover, remove from the heat and leave for 40 minutes or so. This helps make them more digestible. Drain and cover them again with the same amount of cold water. Meanwhile, bring the trotters to the boil in plenty of water and drain immediately. Add them to the beans along with the pork rind, onions, garlic, celery, carrots, leek and bouquet of herbs. Bring to the boil, skim, then cover and cook for 2 hours.

Meanwhile, roast the lamb and pork on a sliced onion in a roasting tin for 1½ hours in a slow oven, adding the Toulouse and garlic sausages, whole tomatoes and a glass of dry white wine for the last 20 minutes. Remove from the oven.

Cut the meats and sausages into hearty chunks, similarly the trotters if you have used them. Remove the duck legs from their fat and brown them on a roasting tray in the hot oven for 10 minutes. Cool slightly before halving each leg at the joint. Remove the vegetables and the bouquet from the beans and discard.

Add the meats, rind, sausage and duck legs to the beans and the sticky tomato juices, without the onions, from the roasting tin. Make sure the meats are in the middle of the dish and the beans on top, before sprinkling some of the breadcrumbs and parsley over.

You can add a little of the duck fat over the crumbs if you like, then return the casserole to the slow oven for a further hour or longer. Serve as is, or break the crust and push it in. Pour in a little water if the cassoulet is drying out, add a second crust and return to the oven until it is golden before serving.

PHEASANT À LA NORMANDE

Sharp apples and quince cut the richness of meat like duck or pork admirably but they are also wonderful paired with the sweeter, less fat gameyness of pheasant, partridge or guinea fowl. You may cook the pheasant whole in the pot or joint them first into whole breasts and legs, leaving the wings and the carcass for stock. This is a particularly good way of cooking birds that have got a little long in the beak and would not be tender if roasted.

SERVES 4

a cock and a hen pheasant if you can get one of each, and their giblets; the cock pheasant is larger and slightly less tender and sweet,
85g/3oz unsalted butter
6 sharp eating apples like Cox's
a little cinnamon
300ml/10fl oz double cream
sea salt and black pepper
a brandy glass of Somerset Cider Brandy or Calvados

Brown the pheasant on all sides in half the butter over a medium heat. Meanwhile, peel, core and slice the apples and fry them in the other half of the butter, with a little smidgen of cinnamon sprinkled over them, for a few minutes. They should still be crisp.

Throw a layer of apples into the bottom of the deep, heavy casserole and add the pheasants, breast down. Put the giblets – heart, liver and neck – in the pot, then make a nest of the rest of the apples around the birds. Pour in half the cream, cover with greaseproof paper and the lid and cook over a gentle heat for 30 minutes before turning the birds breast up to finish them. Season, cover and cook for a further 20–30 minutes depending on how rare you like your pheasant. I like mine pink, so if the juices flow pink when the birds are spiked through the leg with a skewer and there is no resistance from the flesh, they are cooked. The cock, being bigger, will take a little longer than the hen.

If you prefer, cook the pheasants in the oven at about 170°C/350°F/Gas 4. Remove the birds from the pot and leave them to rest for 10 minutes lightly covered with foil while you add the rest of the cream to the apples and heat it through.

Remove the giblets, sieving the liver into the sauce. Now pour all the juices from the birds into a frying pan and heat them, adding the glass of Cider Brandy or Calvados and setting light to it. Let the flames burn off the alcohol before pouring the liquor into the pot with the cream and apples. Check the seasoning. Joint the birds and heat them through gently in the sauce before putting the whole of the contents of the pot into a warmed serving dish.

BRAISED PARTRIDGE WITH PUY LENTILS, LARDONS AND SHALLOTS

A lovely earthy dish for older birds at the end of the season, this is also delicious made with pigeon, guinea fowl or pheasant.

SERVES 4

55g/2oz unsalted butter
4 rashers unsmoked streaky bacon,
    snipped into small dice
4 partridges
a glass of brandy
a large glass of white wine
150ml/5fl oz pint game or chicken
    stock (see p. 80), heated
a bouquet of thyme, rosemary,
    parsley and bay tied together
225g/8oz Puy lentils
1 onion stuck with a couple of cloves
1 large carrot chopped in 3 or 4
    pieces
2 sticks of celery, broken in pieces
a few leek tops
a bay leaf
12 black peppercorns
butter and olive oil
12–18 shallots, peeled and left whole
a little molasses or dark muscovado
    sugar

Preheat the oven to 170°C/325°F/Gas 3. Melt the butter in a heavy-bottomed pan with the diced bacon and fry gently until the fat begins to run from the bacon. Put the partridges breast down in the pot to brown for a couple of minutes, then pour in the brandy and set light to it. When the alcohol has burned off, add the white wine which you have heated first in a small pan. Now add the hot stock and the bouquet of herbs, then cover with greaseproof paper and a lid. Put in the oven for 1½ hours to cook.

Meanwhile, rinse the lentils under running water (they do not need soaking first), and put them in another large heavy-bottomed pot with the onion, carrot, celery, leek tops, bay leaf and peppercorns. Just cover with water, bring to the boil and skim. Cover with a lid and simmer for 35–40 minutes or until the lentils are cooked but maintain their shape.

Fifteen minutes before the partridges are due to come out of the oven, put a tablespoon of olive oil and 30g/1oz unsalted butter in a heavy frying pan. When they are foaming add the whole shallots. Sprinkle over a teaspoon of sugar and cook on all sides until softened, well browned and glazed with sugar.

Remove the birds and all the bits from the pot and keep hot on a warmed dish while you reduce the cooking juices by boiling them down to half their original amount. Meanwhile, remove the vegetables you've cooked with the lentils and spread the lentils with the bits of bacon and the shallots over the bottom of the serving dish. Place the birds on top and pour over the sauce and serve with parsnip or potato and celeriac purée.

SERVES 6

HOT WATER CRUST
200ml/7fl oz water
170g/6oz lard
450g/1lb plain flour
½ tsp sea salt
1 organic egg (optional)
beaten egg for glaze

JELLIED STOCK
bones from the meat used to make
    the filling
2 split pig's trotters or a knuckle of
    veal
2 carrots, chopped
2 sticks of celery, chopped
2 onions, halved but still in their
    skins
a dozen peppercorns
a bouquet of fresh herbs tied
    together
water to cover

FILLING
450g/1lb game, well hung
225g/8oz pork back fat, minced
340g/12oz lean pork, minced
225g/8oz lean veal, minced
225g/8oz thin rashers green back
    bacon, 3 of them minced (the
    butcher will do this for you if you
    ask nicely)
a few tbsp Marsala, Madeira or dry
    white wine
grated nutmeg, cinnamon, cloves,
    half a dozen juniper berries
a handful of flat-leaf parsley,
    chopped
sea salt, black pepper

COLD RAISED GAME PIE

You may use any combination of game for this glorious cold raised pie, pheasant, partridge, grouse, woodcock, wild duck, pigeon. Raised pies are not the big girl's handbags they're cracked up to be. In fact, hot water crust pastry is far more difficult to ruin than ordinary pastry and is curiously satisfying to make as you work it up the pie mould or tin. The rewards of serving a dish like this far outweigh the effort which, though you need never confess it, is really not that great when you think of the result. A hinged mould, even if it only comes out of the back of the cupboard once a year, is a bit of a pièce de résistance.

To make the crust, bring the water and lard to the boil in a small pan. Tip them into the middle of the flour and salt in a large bowl and swiftly work together with a wooden spoon. You can also do this in a food processor. Add the egg for colour and richness if you like, but it is not essential. Leave the dough until it has cooled to the stage at which you can handle it, but not so long that it is actually cool.

Break off a quarter for the lid and put the rest into the base of a hinged pie mould, or a cake tin if you don't have a mould. Push the pastry up the sides with your hands as quickly as you can, sealing any cracks. If the paste collapses as you are working, never fear, it just means it is a little too hot, so squidge it back into a ball, wait and start again. You can shape small pies around jam jars, but you have to be really careful prising the jars out so the pastry stands proud on its own. It is not impossible, I have done it, and manual dexterity isn't my middle name. If you are going to use this method, I would place a strip of brown paper around the pastry and tie string around the circumference so that the pies keep their shape during the cooking.

To make the jellied stock, put all the ingredients into a large pan, bring to the boil, skim, then simmer for 3 hours. Strain and boil down the stock until you have about 425ml/15fl oz. Set aside to cool. It will set to a solid jelly and is incomparably better than adding gelatine to your stock, but if needs must, go ahead.

Remove the game from the bone, cut into small strips, season and set aside. Put the pork, veal and minced bacon in a bowl and splash with the alcohol. Season, add the spices and parsley and mulch it all together with your fingers.

Line the pastry with the rashers, then add layers of game and minced meats, packing them in tightly. Roll out the lid and put it on top with the help of some beaten egg. Cut a central hole, through which the steam can escape, and decorate with pastry trimmings as you will. Brush egg all over the pie and start the cooking at 200°C/400°F/ Gas 6 for the first 30 minutes. Reduce the temperature to 170°C/325°F/Gas 3 and cook for a further hour for small pies, or 2 hours for large ones. Cover the top with greaseproof paper if it is darkening too much.

Remove the pie from the oven and take it out of its mould or paper. Brush the sides with beaten egg once more and return to the oven for 10 minutes for a little colour enhancement. Then pour the jellied stock through the hole with a small funnel; the meat will have shrunk considerably so there will be room. Abandon the pie for at least 24 hours before you tuck in, but longer won't hurt. The beauty of hot water crust pastry is that it absorbs the meat juices and fat on the inside while managing to stay crisp on the outside. Best eaten cold with cranberry sauce or a tart jelly, ideally crab apple (see page 480).

HOT GAME PIE

Another good way of using up the more geriatric game birds at the end of the season. Pheasant, grouse, wild duck, pigeon or partridge or a combination is the best, depending on what you can get hold of.

Make the shortcrust pastry and put it in the fridge to chill (see pages 180–181).

Put the birds in a large heavy-bottomed casserole with the usual stock vegetables and stock to cover if you have some; if not use cold water with one-third white wine. Bring to the boil slowly and skim. Cover and simmer at a mere blip until the meat is cooked and comes away from the bone easily. Remove the birds from the pot and when they are cool enough to handle, strip the meat from the carcasses and put in a pie dish.

Preheat the oven to 200°C/400°F/Gas 6. Melt the butter with the bacon and when the fat begins to run, add the vegetables and sauté gently until golden and the mushrooms have begun to exude their watery juices. Stir in the flour at this point, followed by a ladle or two of hot stock and continue to stir so that the sauce becomes silken and lump free. You want the sauce to remain thick, so don't add more stock than you need. Pour the sauce with the vegetables over the game in the pie dish and season well, adding the thyme and parsley.

Cover with the pastry, put into the preheated oven and bake for 30 minutes. Turn the heat down to 190°C/375°F/Gas 5 and continue to cook until the pastry is golden and the filling bubbling merrily beneath. Serve with redcurrant jelly, cabbage, red or green and plenty of mash.

SERVES 4

1 hare, jointed
flour, salt and pepper
goose fat or olive oil and butter
2 carrots, diced
2 onions, chopped
a few cloves of garlic
3 sticks of celery, strung and sliced

MARINADE

1 bottle robust red wine
1 tbsp Cognac
2 tbsp olive oil
1 onion, thinly sliced
a few cloves of garlic, bruised
a couple of strips of orange rind
a couple of bay leaves
about 12 juniper berries, bruised
　　rather than crushed
the same amount of peppercorns

AILLADE

liver and kidneys of the hare
4 rashers organic green streaky
　　bacon, finely snipped
6 or 7 cloves of garlic, chopped into
　　tiny dice
4 shallots, chopped into tiny dice
4 tbsp red wine vinegar
a blade of mace
a sprig of thyme
salt and pepper

JUGGED HARE

I feel much more protective of this wonderful creature since abiding beside a family of huge ginger hares in the west of Ireland in the summer. They are creatures of habit, the male taking a sauntering stroll directly past my open kitchen door at around the same time each morning, the family sitting taking in the salt evening sun from the sea every evening in my field at the front of the house. March is their time. The mad March hares are clearly mate-crazy and seem to lose their minds to the extent of there always being one dead but still warm on the road after their frolickings for me to sling over my handlebars for the pot. Skinning and paunching are easy, if a little saddening.

Hare used to be jugged by those with no ovens, in stone jugs sealed with foil in a pan of simmering water over a flame. Now we still use the delightfully anachronistic term when we really mean stewed hare. The flavour of a hare is one of the great tastes, richly gamey but not fat, its deep ruby flesh falling from the bone if you cook it long enough, adding the liver, heart and blood in an 'aillade' with garlic and red wine vinegar towards the end. Serve with forcemeat balls (see opposite) as well as or instead of the aillade.

Mix the marinade ingredients and marinate the jointed hare for as long as it suits you, anything from 1 to 3 days.

Preheat the oven to 130°C/250°F/Gas ½. Remove the hare from the marinade, dry the pieces thoroughly with kitchen paper, then roll them in seasoned flour. I find shaking a few tablespoons of flour with some salt and pepper into a Ziploc bag, and sealing the hare inside it while you briefly toss it around is the best way to do the job unmessily, and without a surfeit of flour adhering to the joints.

Heat some goose fat or olive oil and butter in a heavy-bottomed casserole. Brown the hind legs and the saddle jointed into 2 portions for a few minutes on each side, then remove them to a plate. Scrape up any crusty brown bits from the pan, add more fat if you need to and gently sauté the carrots, onions, garlic and celery together. When they have begun to soften, place the hare joints on the vegetables, season well with salt and pepper, strain the marinade over the meat and bring gently to a simmer. Cover with a layer of greaseproof paper and a lid and cook very gently for about two hours, either in the oven or on top of the stove.

Meanwhile, make your aillade. Chop the hare liver and kidneys and put them, with the bacon, garlic and shallots, in a small pan with 4 tablespoons of red wine vinegar, the blood of the hare, mace and thyme and seasoning. Simmer at a whisper for a couple of hours, stirring occasionally to prevent anything from sticking. Pour the contents of the pan over the hare before serving. You may feel like offering a tart jelly as an accompaniment – rowan or crab apple (see page 480) work well.

The following day, you can add the ribs and fore legs to the pot of hare bones and remaining sauce, cover with water and add the usual stock vegetables. Simmer for a couple of hours until you have the base for a wonderfully gamey hare soup.

FORCEMEAT BALLS

SERVES 6

110g/4oz stale white bread turned
   into breadcrumbs
55g/2oz suet
1 tbsp parsley, chopped
2 tsp thyme
grated zest of an organic lemon
2 rashers fat bacon, finely snipped
sea salt and black pepper
1 organic egg, beaten

If you like the old-fashioned notion of serving forcemeat balls with your hare – or your venison or rabbit – this is a very good recipe.

Mix all the ingredients together in a large bowl then form the mixture into walnut-sized balls. Fry them in bacon fat or lard until they are browned all over and serve them round the hare, with more parsley on top.

RABBIT WITH MUSTARD SAUCE

SERVES 4

450g/1lb piece unsmoked fat bacon,
   cubed
1 large onion, chopped
3 sticks celery, strung and chopped
6 small carrots, sliced
3 cloves of garlic, sliced in half
2 bay leaves
6 sprigs of thyme, leaves stripped
   from their stems
salt and pepper
1 wild rabbit, jointed into 2 back legs
   and the saddle split in 2. Keep the
   carcass and forelegs for stock
150ml/5fl oz dry cider
2 glasses of Cider Brandy or
   Calvados, or brandy
2 organic egg yolks
6 tbsp double cream
2 tbsp mustard, 1 of Dijon and 1 of
   Moutarde de Meaux
handful of parsley and chives,
   chopped

Rabbits are an emotive subject in our house. Both my daughters, Miranda and Charissa, have kept pet rabbits, so I knew I was on dangerous territory bringing them to the table. In fact, I remember telling Charissa we were eating chicken the day I first served up a braised bunny to her. She was not deceived and, despite the fact that we were eating a wild rabbit, not one of the tasteless pappy-boned farmed ones that are much easier to lay your hands on, she remained mutinous and untemptable. I feel that the rabbit has been almost written off the culinary ledgers for far too long. It started with an outbreak of mixamatosis and then a snobbery – rabbit considered to be poor man's food. A whole generation became used to existing without it, didn't know how to cook it; were more content with chicken breasts and boned everything. The bones might be sharp, but the flavour is worth it, and the famous pairing of sweet, mild meat with sharp mustard is one of those great taste contrasts. Serve with some forcemeat balls (see recipe above) if you like.

Preheat the oven to 150°C/300°F/Gas 2. Mix the bacon, vegetables, garlic, bay and thyme and put half the mixture in the bottom of a heavy-bottomed casserole. Season. Lay the rabbit joints on top and cover them with the next half of the mixture. Pour over the cider and serious alcohol, cover with greaseproof paper and a lid and put in the oven. Braise for 2½–3 hours or until the rabbit is in danger of falling from the bone with very little provocation.

Remove the joints and all the vegetables and bacon to a warm serving dish and keep hot while you make the sauce. Beat the yolks and the cream together and add a ladle of the juices, whisking them together. Return to the casserole and cook at a bare simmer, not letting it come to the boil, until it thickens. Stir in the first tablespoon of mustard and taste. Add the second if it needs it. Adjust the seasoning. You need to add mustard late to dishes as it tends to make them bitter the longer it is cooked. Pour the sauce over the rabbit, sprinkle over the mixed parsley and chives and serve. Mashed or boiled buttery potatoes and some extra braised celery are the tops with this earthy dish.

OFFAL AND VEAL

CALVES' LIVER WITH ONIONS

SERVES 4

55g/2oz unsalted butter
4 tbsp light olive oil
675g/1½lb onions, sliced into very
    fine circles
sea salt
675g/1½ lb calves liver, very finely
    sliced
black pepper
1 tbsp flat-leaf parsley, chopped
2 tbsp red wine vinegar

The delicately flavoured calves' liver should be very finely sliced for this dish. You must stew the onions for as long as possible to a soft, sweet tangle, but pay careful attention to the liver. It will be cooked and pink middled in a matter of seconds. If you're cooking the liver alla Veneziana, cut it into strips first, then proceed as below.

Heat half the butter with the olive oil in a large, heavy-bottomed frying pan. Cook the onions over a gentle heat for 30 minutes, adding the salt at the beginning of cooking to draw out the moisture. Stir from time to time. The onions shouldn't go more than a biscuity gold, certainly not brown, as they wilt down and soften. When they are cooked, remove them from the pan with a slotted spoon and set aside.

Throw the rest of the butter into the pan and turn up the heat. Add the liver in a single layer and fry for about 30 seconds a side, or until pink but not raw in the middle. Transfer the liver to a warm plate and add the vinegar to the frying pan with the onions. Toss quickly together, season, add the liver and parsley and serve immediately.

CALVES' KIDNEYS IN A DEVILLED MUSTARD CREAM SAUCE

SERVES 4

2 veal kidneys, the suet removed and
    trimmed of their core of fat and
    membrane
55g/2oz unsalted butter
1 tbsp olive oil
sea salt and black pepper
3 shallots, finely minced
1 glass white wine or dry sherry, my
    preference
2 anchovies, chopped
150ml/5fl oz double cream
a few shakes of the Tabasco bottle or
    a pinch of cayenne
1 tbsp Worcestershire sauce
1 dsrtsp grain mustard

Calves' and lambs' kidneys have equally good flavour and a lovely texture, but I prefer the more delicate flavour of the calves' kidneys whenever I can get them. My grandfather often had kidneys for breakfast, which I remember thinking a supremely strange yet glamorous way to start the day. I think brunch, lunch or supper for me, not the early morning.

Cut the veal kidneys into small pieces according to their natural divisions. Heat half the butter with the olive oil. Drop in the kidneys, season, then sear them briefly until the outsides have coloured a little but the middles remain raw looking. Transfer to a warm plate. Lob in the extra butter and when it is foaming, put in the finely minced shallots and cook until softened over a moderate heat. Remove from the pan onto the plate with the kidneys.

Pour the juice from the kidneys into the buttery pan, add the white wine and let them bubble away together before adding the chopped anchovies and turning the heat down. Crush the anchovies into the liquid so they melt into it before pouring over the cream, Tabasco and Worcestershire sauce and plopping in the mustard. Stir and let everything bubble together. Add the kidneys and shallots to the pan over a gentle heat and turn the kidneys in the sauce until coated and cooked – that is, still pink in the middle. Serve on toast if for breakfast or with rice or mashed potato at any other time.

Calves' Liver with Onions

CALVES' SWEETBREADS IN A CREAM SAUCE

Sweetbreads are the thymus gland and pancreas of a young animal. Calves' sweetbreads, rather than lamb's are, to my mind, the most delicious and the most delicately flavoured and textured, which must be partially responsible for them being considered historically as food fit for invalids. They need to be very fresh when you buy them as they deteriorate very quickly and although they are a bit of a fiddly job to prepare the results are oh so worth it. Insipidity is a danger, so they can be served classically with a sharp, lemony sorrel purée, a sauce Gribiche, in a timbale with iron-leafed spinach, or with some bosky mushrooms — in this recipe, the prized morels. Start this dish the day before you want it, or in the morning if you want the sweetbreads for dinner.

SERVES 2

sweetbreads
wine vinegar
20–24 dried morels soaked in warm
    water to cover for 30 minutes
55g/2oz unsalted butter
3 shallots, finely minced
1 glass Marsala
300ml/10fl oz double cream
a little lemon juice

First prepare the sweetbreads. Steep them in a bowl of cold water, changing the water several times, for 2–3 hours. Now put them in a large pan, cover them well with cold water and a couple of teaspoons of wine vinegar and bring to the boil at a snail's pace. Let them boil for 2 minutes, then plunge the sweetbreads directly into cold water, replenishing it so that they cool really quickly. Now pull off and trim the little fatty, gristly bits, keeping the thin membrane that holds them together intact. Put the sweetbreads in a single layer on a plate, cover with another plate and some weights and put in the fridge for at least 2 hours but overnight if it is more convenient. This way they will all be the same thickness when you come to cook them. Lambs' sweetbreads are prepared in exactly the same way.

Remove the morels from their soaking water and reduce the scented water in a small pan by half to intensify the flavour. Melt the butter in a pan and when it begins to foam, fry the minced shallots over a medium heat until softened before adding the morels and seasoning. Fry for a further 5 minutes without browning; the shallots should be pale gold. Then splosh in the Marsala and let it bubble and cook down until only a tablespoon or so is left. Add the reduced liquid from the morels and continue to cook until the mixture is syrupy in appearance.

Add the cream, bring to a simmer, then add the sweetbreads in a single layer. Cook gently, stirring a little until the sauce has thickened. Adjust the seasoning, add a spritz of lemon juice and serve with mashed or boiled potatoes.

BLANQUETTE DE VEAU

SERVES 4

170g/6oz small whole button
    mushrooms, wiped clean
1 lemon
55g/2oz unsalted butter
1kg/2¼ lb breast and shoulder of
    veal, cut into 4 slices
2 large carrots, cut into small chunks
2 medium onions, each stuck with a
    clove
a bouquet of thyme, parsley,
    rosemary and bay, tied together
18–24 small shallots
1 tbsp flour
3 organic egg yolks
6–8 tbsp double cream
sea salt and black pepper
a little nutmeg
a handful of curly parsley, chopped

Best made with breast and shoulder, and, most importantly, with properly reared veal. This is pinker than the wan, white veal, reared inhumanely in crates, that we used to be able to buy from here or Holland, but that the Compassion in World Farming Trust have managed to get banned. An unctuously gluey, creamy-sauced mild dish, which is best served with an unassertive plain pilav of rice and some fresh peas cooked à la Française with lettuce, baby onions, sugar, butter and very little water as the lettuce and onion will release enough juice. Or you may serve it with the good tinned petits pois à l'etuvée.

Put the mushrooms in a small pan with a squeeze of lemon, a tablespoon of water, half a walnut-sized piece of butter, and cook over a high heat with a lid on for a minute. Put the slices of veal in a heavy-bottomed saucepan. Add the mushroom cooking liquor (but set the mushrooms aside) and enough water to cover by about a finger. Bring to the boil, skim, then add the carrots, onions and herbs. Bring back to a bare simmer, cover again and cook at this gentle heat for 1½ hours on top of the stove.

Towards the end of the meat's cooking time, cook the shallots in a little butter, turning them gently for about 15 minutes until softened and golden, not brown. When the meat is cooked, take out the 2 whole onions and discard them, then remove the meat and vegetables to a large dish or bowl and cover.

In another saucepan make a roux with the flour and 30g/1oz of the butter. Add the braising liquid and whisk well so there are no lumps and the sauce thickens to a smooth richness. Simmer on a very low heat for about 15 minutes, stirring occasionally. Pour the sauce back into the main pan and add the meat, vegetables and mushrooms. Cover and simmer gently for another 15 minutes.

Whisk the egg yolks in a bowl and add the cream and a few drops of lemon juice. Add this to the blanquette off the heat and then heat through without letting it reach boiling point. Season and add a suspicion of nutmeg. The sauce should have a wooden-spoon-coating consistency like custard. Remove from the heat and sprinkle with some chopped parsley.

OSSOBUCO ALLA MILANESE

SERVES 4

4 ossobuci, about 255g/9oz each
flour for coating them, seasoned and
    put into a resealable plastic bag
2–4 tbsp olive oil
45g/1½oz unsalted butter
1 small onion, finely chopped
1 small celery stick and its leaves,
    strung and finely chopped
150ml/5fl oz dry white wine
300ml/10fl oz meat stock

GREMOLADA

1 tsp grated zest from an organic
    lemon
1 small garlic clove, finely minced
2 tbsp flat-leaf parsley, chopped

Ossobuco is 'the bone with a hole' from the hind shin of a milk-fed calf. You get the meat around the bone and the marrow in the hole, the pieces of shin being tied so that they don't lose their shape during cooking. Purists do not cook ossobuco with tomato, though this is a classic dish of Emilia-Romagna. It is served with a risotto Milanese, dyed crocus yellow with saffron stamens. Without doubt this is one of the finest traditional dishes of Italy, which I feel would make the pantheon of classics anywhere in the world. I steer as close to the great Anna Del Conte's recipe as possible, right down to the garlicky gremolada of lemon zest and parsley sprinkled on top.

Tie a piece of string around the circumference of each shin. I promise you if you don't they will lose their shape. Throw the bones into the bag of flour, seal the bag, give it a shake and remove the shins. Shake off any excess flour and put the shins on a plate. Heat the olive oil in a large heavy-bottomed pan and brown the shins in a single layer. Remove them and put them on a plate.

Add 30g/1oz butter to the olive oil and throw in the onion and celery, sprinkling them with a little salt to encourage the onion to release its juice. When the vegetables are soft but uncoloured, after about 10 minutes, return the meat and its juices to the pan. Heat the wine in a pan and pour it over the meat. Turn up the heat and boil until the liquid is reduced by a half; keep scraping the bottom of a pan with a metal spoon. Heat the stock and pour half of it over the meat. Turn down the heat to a bare simmer, cover the pan first with a close-fitting circle of greaseproof paper, then with a lid and cook for 1½–2 hours, until the meat has begun to come away from the bone. Turn the shins every 20 minutes or so. You may need to add a few more tablespoons of stock during the cooking. If the sauce looks thin, remove the shins when they are cooked and boil it down a bit. Transfer the shins to a heated serving dish and keep warm.

Cut the remaining butter up small and add gradually to the sauce. Remove from the heat the moment the butter has melted and before the sauce comes to the boil. The sauce will now be shiny and delicate tasting.

Mix the gremolada ingredients together, stir into the sauce and leave for a minute to bring out the perfume. Spoon over the ossobuci and serve with risotto Milanese below.

RISOTTO MILANESE

SERVES 4

a generous pinch of saffron threads
2 shallots, peeled and chopped
1 tbsp olive oil
30g/1oz unsalted butter
340/12oz Carnaroli rice
150ml/5fl oz red wine
about 850ml/1½ pints well flavoured
    chicken stock (see p. 80)
55g/2oz Parmesan, freshly grated
salt and pepper

Soak the saffron threads in 1 tablespoon of hot water for an hour. Sauté the shallots in the heated oil and half the butter until softened and translucent. Add the rice, stirring to coat it well. Pour over the wine, keep stirring furiously, then add the saffron and half the stock (heated to simmering point) and stir for 3–4 minutes. Cover tightly and switch off until 15 minutes before you want to serve it. Continue cooking as below if you are not staggering the process.

Add the rest of the stock bit by bit until the rice is creamily soft, but not porridgy. Add the rest of the butter and the Parmesan, and stir it in. Season and serve the risotto under the ossobuco. For more detail on cooking risotto, see page 142.

VITELLO TONNATO

SERVES 10

1.5kg/3¼lb boned rolled loin of veal
1 large carrot, chopped
1 stick celery with its leaves,
    chopped
1 onion, stuck with a couple of cloves
a bay leaf, sprig of parsley and one of
    rosemary tied together
6–8 bruised peppercorns
150ml/5fl oz dry white wine
300ml/10fl oz chicken stock
    (see p. 80)
225g/8oz best tuna from Ortiz
    (Brindisa are the stockists)
6 anchovy fillets
6 tbsp double cream
1 tsp caster sugar
the juice of 1 lemon
4 tbsp extra virgin olive oil
salt and pepper
2 tbsp fresh tarragon

TO DECORATE
2 lemons
a few cornichons

This is a party dish to grace any alfresco or cold summer lunch. It is one of my great favourites when well made and the joy of it is that it is all the better prepared a couple of days in advance so that the flavours can gradually steep and permeate to perfection. Best veal is essential and albacore tuna as well as the very best olive oil to make the creamy, fishy mayonnaise that seeps into the sweet meat. I used to make a standard mayonnaise for the tuna until Anna Del Conte alerted me to this more intense yet less rich variation.

Put the joint of veal into a snug heavy casserole with the chopped chunks of carrot and celery, the whole onion, bouquet of herbs and peppercorns. Pour in the wine and half the stock and bring to the boil very slowly. Cover the pan with greaseproof paper and a lid, then cook at a bare simmer for about 1½ hours. Take off the heat and leave the meat cool in the casserole. When it is quite cold, remove the joint, take off the string and cut the veal into slices about 1cm/½ in thick. Lay them slightly overlapping on a large serving dish. Remove the herbs and liquidise the vegetables from the pan with the cooking juices.

Put the tuna and anchovies in a food processor, add a few tablespoons of the remaining stock and process for a minute. Add a few tablespoons of the vegetable purée, the cream and the sugar. Process again and continue to do so while gradually adding the juice of a lemon and the olive oil. Taste as you go and add more or less lemon as you like. Add some pepper and salt to taste. The finished sauce should be the consistency of thin cream, so add more stock if you need to. Coat the veal with a few tablespoons of the sauce, cover with clingfilm and refrigerate. Keep the rest of the sauce in the fridge.

When you are about to eat, spoon over a little more of the sauce and put the rest in a bowl to bring to the table. Scatter chopped tarragon and a few cornichons over the glorious pink dish and the lemons cut into wedges.

Serve with a cold rice salad doused in olive oil and some young broad beans, artichokes, asparagus and peas stirred into it – any combination you fancy.

BEEF

BOEUF BOURGUIGNONNE

SERVES 6

1.5kg/3¼ lb chuck steak or stewing
    steak
225g/8oz piece of unsmoked streaky
    bacon
1 tbsp each of rosemary, thyme and
    parsley, finely chopped
4 tbsp olive oil
1 bottle red wine
2 large onions, chopped
2–3 carrots, diced
2 sticks celery, strung and chopped
3–4 tbsp flour
4 tbsp Cognac or Armagnac
2 bay leaves
4 cloves of garlic
stock to cover
45g/1½oz unsalted butter
225g/8oz button mushrooms, wiped
    and left whole
24 small shallots
a bunch of parsley, chopped

The better the beef the better the taste. I made this classic recently with Longhorn beef, an ancient breed with wonderful marbling and fat from Richard Vaughan's herd in Herefordshire (see the list of suppliers at the back of the book for details). Hung for 33 days, the meat has an incomparable flavour and even the lesser stewing cuts taste like rump but cut like butter.

Cube the meat into large chunks, a good mouthful each. Chop the bacon into lardons. Roll the meat in the finely chopped herbs in a bowl and pour over half the olive oil and the red wine. Leave to marinate for 4–6 hours, turning the meat over a couple of times.

Pour the marinade into a jug through a sieve, leaving the meat to drain in the sieve. Add the remaining 2 tablespoons of olive oil and sauté the bacon lardons over a medium heat, turning them as they brown and begin to crisp. Remove with a slotted spoon and throw in the onions, carrots and celery. Stir them to coat with oil and bacon fat and cook for about 20 minutes until they begin to soften. Remove the vegetables to the plate with the bacon. Pat the meat dry with kitchen paper. Turn up the heat, adding a little more olive oil if you need to, and throw in the meat. Turn it to brown on all sides, then spoon over the flour and continue to turn the meat for the next 5 minutes.

Return the bacon and vegetables to the pot, pour in the Cognac and the marinade and stir everything in together well so nothing sticks to the bottom of the pan. Add the bay leaves, the whole cloves of garlic and just enough stock to cover and return to a simmer. Then cover with a layer of greaseproof paper and a lid and cook on top of the stove at a bare blip of a simmer for 2½–3 hours or until the meat is tender enough to cut with a spoon. Every so often give the pot a stir and make sure the meat isn't sticking to the bottom.

Heat half the butter in a pan and add the mushrooms, turning them over a high heat until their moisture begins to exude. Gently cook the button onions in the rest of the butter in another pan until they've softened and turned golden. Drain the cooking liquor through a sieve into a pan and return all the ingredients, including the mushrooms and shallots, to the big pot and keep them warm under a lid. Now reduce the cooking liquor by boiling it down, not too hard, for as long as it takes to reduce it by a half. Return the sauce to the pot and reheat gently until piping hot.

POT-ROAST BRISKET WITH ROOT VEGETABLES

A perfect cut to slow roast with all the vegetables and serve with proper English mustard and a potato and celeriac purée.

1kg/2¼lb brisket of beef
a selection of root vegetables; I used
   1 large parsnip, 1 swede, and
   3 carrots, onions and sticks of
   celery
olive oil
sea salt and pepper
bouquet of bay, parsley, thyme and
   orange peel, tied together
about 700ml/1¼ pint of robust red
   wine

Preheat the oven to 150°C/300°F/Gas 2. Assemble a selection of root vegetables. Cube the roots into 2.5cm/1in squares, quarter the onions, or halve them if they are small, and cut the celery, carefully strung, into 2.5cm/1in pieces.

Heat a little olive oil in a heavy-bottomed pot into which the brisket should fit snugly. Brown the brisket on all sides. Throw in the vegetables with a bit more olive oil and brown. Strew on some sea salt and pepper, tuck in a bouquet of bay, parsley, thyme and orange peel, then splosh on the red wine.

Cover with a sheet of greaseproof paper and cook in the oven for 2 hours, but another half hour won't hurt. If the red wine is reducing too much, pour on the same again. The vegetables should be tender when the dish is cooked, but if they are still a bit firm, keep the meat warm for 20 minutes while you finish cooking them separately. Serve this with lashings of buttery mashed potatoes. Good cold for sandwiches the next day.

75g/2½oz unsalted butter
2 onions, chopped
2 carrots, chopped
3 sticks celery, chopped
100g/3½oz button mushrooms
4 peeled tomatoes, chopped
100ml/3½fl oz tarragon vinegar
200ml/7fl oz white wine
200ml/7fl oz strong, well-jellied
    stock, beef (see p. 376) or chicken
    (see p. 80)
thyme, bay, parsley stalks
1 salt ox tongue prepared as
    described (see right)

CAPER SAUCE
the braising liquor
30g/1oz flour
1–2 tbsp vinegar decanted from the
    capers
sea salt and black pepper
1 tsp Dijon mustard
1 tsp redcurrant jelly
75ml/2½fl oz double cream
1 tbsp capers
1 tbsp parsley, chopped

BRAISED SALT OX TONGUE WITH CAPER SAUCE

There are people who are as squeamish about tongue as they are about blood, guts and offal and it is a sad state of affairs. After all, even the amorphous-looking lumps of meat that come plastic packeted and boneless emanate from something that once lived and breathed and moved. And though they choose to ignore it, the sausages and faggots and other made-up meats they buy are likely to contain eyelids, snouts, ears and innards and all the extremities and excrescences that these lily-livered people supposedly haven't the stomach to contemplate. I was reared to believe brains in black butter sauce were as choice a treat as a rump steak, and not to distinguish between the organ and the muscle in terms of the one being disgusting and the other desirable. I defer to Simon Hopkinson in the preparation of this particular meaty treat. He serves his with a robust caper sauce, I serve mine with a walnut sauce. Whichever appeals, the tongue needs something to kick against!

First rinse the tongue well in warm water, pat it dry and put it in a large, heavy-bottomed pot. Cover it with cold water and slowly bring it to a simmer. Once a layer of scum has formed, lift out the tongue and rinse it under cold running water. Throw out the water, clean out the pot and now you're ready to begin.

Preheat the oven to 130°C/250°F/Gas ½. Melt the butter in the pot, then add the vegetables and the tomatoes, cover and stew them gently for 20 minutes until lightly coloured. Add the vinegar, turn up the heat and reduce the vinegar to nothing, stirring frequently; the result should be a sticky mess. Add the wine and stock and stir in the herbs. Bring up to a simmer and bury the tongue (prepared as above) in the aromatic braising liquid. Turn it in the mixture a few times before covering it with a sheet of greaseproof paper to fit the interior of the pot and the lid. Cook in the oven for at least 2 hours, turning the tongue over from time to time. The tongue is cooked when a skewer pushed right through the thickest part shows no resistance.

When the tongue is cooked, scrape off the vegetables and herbs and leave to cool. Once the tongue is cool enough to handle, peel off the skin and discard it. Return the tongue to the dish, cover with foil and keep warm in the oven.

CAPER SAUCE

Strain the braising liquor through a fine sieve into a bowl. Leave to settle for 10 minutes. Discard the solids, spoon off the fat that has collected on the surface and add 2 tablespoons of it to a small pan. Pour away the rest of the fat. Add the flour to the fat and cook over a low heat, stirring for a couple of minutes until lightly coloured. Stir in the braising liquor slowly until the sauce is smooth and lightly thickened, I use a whisk for this. Add the vinegar, seasoning, mustard and redcurrant jelly. Simmer gently for 10 minutes. Whisk in the double cream, add the capers and stir in the parsley. Simmer for a couple of minutes and spoon over the tongue, which should be served cut into thick, juicy slices. Serve with mashed potato.

L'AILLADE TOULOUSAINE

This walnut sauce is also good with braised ox tongue.

85g/3oz walnuts
2–3 cloves of garlic
sea salt
150ml/5fl oz extra virgin olive oil
black pepper

Pound the walnuts in a mortar with the garlic, then season them with salt. Start adding the olive oil drop by drop as you would for mayonnaise (see page 256), stirring it with a wooden spoon, then begin to add it more quickly until you have a thick oily sauce. Season to taste and serve in a bowl alongside the tongue. Alternatively, spread the sauce onto bread with slices of tongue to make the most exotic tongue sandwich.

BRAISED OXTAIL

If you have an Aga, this is the dish to cook overnight in the slow oven until the meat drops from the gluey bones and the dish is braised to deep, dark perfection. There is no other flavour nor texture so redolent of icy winter, sustenance, ballast and succulence. You need to have made a good potful of veal, oxtail or beef stock before you begin (see page 376).

SERVES 6

2 large tbsp dripping or butter and
    olive oil
4 oxtails, ready jointed
sea salt and black pepper
2 onions, chopped
2 carrots, diced
3 sticks celery, strung and chopped
the white parts of 2 fat leeks,
    chopped
600ml/1 pint robust red wine
450g/1lb tomatoes, peeled and
    chopped or tinned plum tomatoes
a bouquet of fresh bay, thyme,
    rosemary and parsley and 2 strips
    orange peel, tied together
4 cloves of garlic
1.5–2.5 litres/3–4 pints veal, beef or
    oxtail stock
2 tbsp flat-leaf parsley, chopped

Preheat the oven to 190°C/375°F/Gas 5. Heat the dripping or oil and butter in a large, heavy-bottomed pot. Season the oxtails, then fry them, a single layer at a time, until browned on both sides. Remove to a plate as you go. Scrape all the crusty bits into the fat and add the onions, carrots, celery and leeks, turning them in the dripping and allowing them to soften but not brown over a medium heat. Lift them out with a slotted spoon, pour the wine into the pan and turn the heat up so that it boils fiercely and reduces by three quarters.

Now tip the oxtails and vegetables back into the pot, turning the heat down to medium. Add the tomatoes, bouquet of herbs tucked down the side of the pot, whole bruised cloves of garlic and stock to cover. Bring to boiling point, cover with a layer of greaseproof paper and a lid and braise in the oven until the meat is so tender it is ready to drop from the bone, about 2 hours.

Remove the bones from the pot and keep warm. Remove the bouquet and discard it. Now put all the vegetables and sauce through the coarse disc of a mouli so that you have a rough-textured purée – this works extremely well with oxtail. Check the seasoning and return the meat to the pan with the purée. Simmer gently together for a few minutes.

Serve in bowls with plenty of mashed potato, some root vegetable like parsnip or swede roasted in honey, and parsley scattered over the oxtails. There should be 3–4 decent-sized bones per person.

BOILED SALT BEEF AND PARSLEY AND HORSERADISH DUMPLINGS

SERVES 6

1.5 kg/3¼ lb salted silverside or brisket, ask the butcher if it needs soaking
2 large onions, unpeeled, each stuck with 2–3 cloves
a blade of mace
a suspicion of nutmeg
12 bruised black peppercorns

DUMPLINGS
110g/4oz self-raising flour
55g/2oz suet
2 tbsp parsley, chopped
a tsp tip of hot horseradish per dumpling
sea salt and black pepper

Has anybody even heard of this dish any more? Do people fear dumplings and steamed suet, treating them as the enemy, rather than as the potentially delicious ballast that any cold winter snap would inspire as the source of heat and joy and satisfaction? Get to it. Just the floury, slippery-edged circle of dumpling, enclosing the heat of the horseradish and the green freshness of parsley pushed into the beefy juices, should be enough to convert the carb-shy back to sanity.

Find a pot that the beef will fit into snugly, with the onions tucked in on either side. Put in the spices and peppercorns and cover the beef with half a fingernail to spare of warm water. Bring to simmer point, then cook at a bare blip for 3½ hours, skimming as and when you need to. If the cooking water tastes really salty after the first 10 minutes, drain it and start again. The water should not boil at any stage, so cover the pot only when you are happy the pot is burbling not bubbling.

Remove the meat to a warmed serving dish and keep it hot. Boil down half the beef juices in a separate pan while you poach the dumplings for 10–20 minutes with the rest of the cooking liquor. Remember, they will expand; suet does! And they are filling. Reheat the meat with the dumplings briefly and gently before serving. Serve the reduced sauce separately.

Do not cook vegetables with the beef. They will end up like soggy bedclothes and there is enough flavour in the meat and its juices to cook it with nothing but the spices. Serve with carrots Vichy (see page 420), or stew some leeks in butter to accompany the beef, dumplings and mashed potato, to which you can add some grain mustard if you like.

PARSLEY AND HORSERADISH DUMPLINGS
Sieve the flour into a bowl and mix in the suet. Throw in the herbs and season. Stir to mix together. Slowly add cold water and mix with a spoon to a slightly sticky but not too wet dough, finishing it off by hand to make it cohere properly. Flour your hands before pulling bits of the dough away and forming it into walnut-sized balls, into which you push a little horseradish before you start rolling.

STEAK

Steak is food for when you've been getting physical – and I'm not just talking leisurely strokes on the tennis court. First, find your appetite; second, sort out your technique; and third, remember that if it's not well hung, it won't do it for you. So what should you buy and how should you cook it? Fillet is flavourless, but people buy it because they know they can't go wrong with it. It's hard to make it tough, because it comes from a muscle underneath the ribcage that never does any work. It has neither the fat nor the flavour, which develop when the muscle is used.

What about rib-eye? Charlotte Reynolds, of Swaddles Green Farm, at Chard in Somerset, thinks it's as good as rump. 'It's a continuation of the sirloin', she says. 'Where the sirloin ends, it becomes fore-rib; and the rib-eye is the core of the fore-rib. It's where the weight of the animal is carried and where the legs work. It's very well marbled – the most marbled of all the steaks.' This is the steak best suited to barbecuing, because the marbling acts like a baster. 'The fibres lie the same way as on a fillet steak, so you can cut straight across it', Reynolds adds. 'Rib-eye is loose-textured compared to rump, so it's more tender, but equals it in flavour. In the rump there are several muscles going in different directions, so you always have to cut at right angles to the direction of the grain. Sirloin steak is dense, muscley and full of flavour. It's more tender than rump, but similar in flavour – and with more marbling.'

Breeding is important. Reynolds's beef is from native British breeds: Red Devons, Galloways, Shorthorns and Sussex. Hanging is critical, too: ask your butcher for a three-week minimum. This is something you're unlikely to find in a supermarket, where animals are cut into 'primals', the big main joints, then matured in vacuum packs. Without hanging and drying on the bone, the meat is bound not to taste so good. The darker hued and more marbled the meat, the better, because it is older and has been hung longer.

Steak is expensive, but there are some great cuts of beef that are both cheap and tender. What we call skirt (the French call it 'onglet' or 'bavette') is wonderful if cooked briefly at a high temperature and sliced paper-thin across the grain (long cooking renders it tough). Or a joint of rolled brisket can be slow-roasted in a pot with white wine and herbs. Eat it hot from the pot or cool it, slice and serve with a green sauce of summer herbs, cornichons, vinegar and horseradish.

Cooking steak is all about going against the grain, perfecting your technique, and buying the right meat for the job. Top rump or back rib are not equal to it. They will give you serious grief if you whack them, short-order style, on a hot griddle or barbecue. If you must use top rump, bash it senseless into minute steaks. Otherwise go for rib-eye, rump or sirloin.

Don't spike the meat with a meat blade. This sends a rush of blood to the surface, drying the meat and making you think your steak is undercooked. Touch is the answer when cooking steak. As the heat penetrates the meat, the muscles stiffen; so if you lay a finger on the surface of rare meat, it will feel soft, because the fibres haven't fused yet. As you cook the meat longer, it will become firmer. Medium rare will be slightly resistant to the touch; well done will feel quite hard.

STEAK WITH BÉARNAISE SAUCE

SERVES 6

1 steak per person, 2cm/¾in thick
sea salt
black pepper
olive oil

BÉARNAISE SAUCE

2 tbsp white wine vinegar (or
    tarragon vinegar)
3 tbsp French tarragon, finely
    snipped
30g/1oz shallot, finely chopped
10 peppercorns, crushed
4 organic egg yolks
3 tbsp cold water
225g/8oz clarified unsalted butter
sea salt and freshly ground black
    pepper
2 tbsp chervil, finely chopped
    (optional)
juice of half a lemon

If you like your meat blue, don't rest it. It will merely need a minute a side at a very high temperature to char the outside. (The interior will not be cooked, however, so make sure to start with the meat at room temperature.) Otherwise, it is extremely important to rest the meat to allow the heat to warm the blood in the middle of the steak. A good butcher will cut a steak about 2cm/¾in thick.

To cook the steak, first season the meat with sea salt and cracked black pepper. If you are using a griddle or pan, rather than a barbecue, brush it with a little olive oil as it gets hot. Heat until smoking before adding the meat. For a rare steak, cook for 2 minutes a side, then rest it for 6 minutes. For medium rare, cook for 2½ minutes a side, then rest it for 5 minutes. For well done, cook for 5 minutes a side and don't rest it at all.

BÉARNAISE SAUCE

Put the vinegar, 2 tablespoons of the tarragon, the shallot and crushed peppercorns in a small, heavy-bottomed saucepan and reduce gently by a half.

Let it cool, add the egg yolks and cold water and set the pan over a low heat, whisking continuously. The sauce will gradually emulsify. Be patient; it will take about 10 minutes. Do not allow it to reach boiling point.

Remove from the heat and whisk in the butter a little at a time. Season, then sieve the sauce and stir in the rest of the tarragon, the chervil if using, and the lemon juice to taste. Serve immediately. Good crusty bread is also delicious dipped into Bearnaise sauce.

STEAK TARTARE

SERVES 6

450g/1lb rump or fillet steak
sea salt and black pepper
4 tbsp or so of olive oil
Worcestershire sauce
2–3 tbsp minced onion
1–2 tbsp cornichons, finely diced
1 tbsp parsley, chopped
4 small organic eggs
a Little Gem lettuce
4 anchovy fillets (optional)

This is one of those dishes that you are more likely to order in a French brasserie than make at home, but if you have some good beef and serious carnivores to feed, it is simple to make. The ultimate protein hit, with a dash of piquancy, this is the thing to eat when only the raw red stuff is going to do it for you.

Chop the steak very small or mince it coarsely if you have a mincer. Mix it with the seasoning, olive oil (start with 3 tablespoons), Worcestershire sauce to taste, minced onion, cornichons and parsley. Then make patties or hamburger shapes with your hands and put them on a plate with some leaves of lettuce around them.

Separate the yolks from the whites of the eggs, putting a half shell with a yolk in it on top of each steak tartare and an anchovy on top of the meat if you like the salt-fish combination. It does give further depth to this all-meaty treat. Serve with chips or sauté potatoes; the hot and the cold go surprisingly well together.

Steak Tartare

STEAK AND KIDNEY PIE

SERVES 6

900g/2lb rump steak, cut into bite-
    sized pieces
450g/1lb ox kidney, cut similarly
2 tbsp flour
sea salt and black pepper
85g/3oz butter
1 large onion, chopped
600ml/1 pint beef stock, or half
    stock, half red wine
225g/8oz chestnut or portobello
    mushrooms, sliced
a bouquet made from 2 bay leaves
    and a bunch each of fresh thyme,
    rosemary and parsley tied together

PASTRY
340g/12oz shortcrust pastry made
    with 225g/8oz plain white flour, a
    pinch of sea salt and 170g/6oz
    unsalted butter, fridge cold (see
    pp. 180–181), or you can use puff
    pastry (see p. 301)
beaten egg for glaze

I hate those individual, flobby-pastried pub pretenders to the throne of the great steak and kidney, with their inferior, gristly, tinned meat and thin gravy, none of which approximate to what is surely one of the great British dishes of all time. Steak and kidney pies should be made in a proper deep dish, filled with rump, kidney and mushroom, red wine and stock, with a golden crust of lardy or buttery shortcrust pastry cloaking the handsome jewels of meat and offal and rich meaty gravy beneath. You may add 2 dozen oysters once you have cooked and cooled the filling if you want to be seriously retro and true, but whatever you decide, rump steak is the thing to go for here. Chuck steak will work if it's from a lovely well-hung bit of Longhorn, but for flavour it should be rump.

You may cook the filling a day or two in advance if you like, so all you need to do on the day is bake the pie.

Carefully trim the fat and skin from the meat, then toss it and the kidneys in a Ziploc bag containing the flour and some salt and pepper. Add two-thirds of the butter to a frying pan and gently sauté the onion, then remove it with a slotted spoon. Add the meat in batches in a single layer, letting it colour briefly on all sides. Transfer the meat to a casserole as you go. Pour the stock, with or without red wine, into the frying pan and bring it to the boil, scraping in any crusty bits from the sides of the pan, then pour it over the meat. Fry the mushrooms in the rest of the butter and add them to the casserole, tucking in the herbs. Cover with a lid and cook in the oven at 150°C/300°F/Gas 2 until the steak and kidney is almost cooked. This should take about 1½ hours. Cool and leave until you want to make the pie.

Preheat the oven to 220°C/425°F/Gas 7. Roll out the pastry and cut off strips to fit around the edges of the pie dish. Brush the rim of the dish with water first so that the strips will adhere. Spoon the filling into the pie dish and cover the whole with a sheet of pastry, pressing the edges together firmly. Decorate with pastry leaves or the like if the mood takes you. Cut a cross in the middle of the pastry through which the steam can escape. Brush the pastry with beaten egg. Bake for 15 minutes, then lower the oven temperature to 170°C/325°F/Gas 3 and cook for a further 45 minutes.

Best served with snowy mountains of buttery mashed potato or colcannon (see page 89), and buttered carrots or cabbage.

filling as for the steak and kidney
  pie, cooked and cooled (see
  opposite)

SUET CRUST
285g/10oz self-raising flour
110g/4oz beef suet
1 tsp baking powder
sea salt and black pepper
½ tsp fresh thyme

STEAK AND KIDNEY PUDDING

This is the rib-sticking reminder of times past, but with a thin, crisp crust. Cooking and cooling the filling in advance is the secret to perfect suet crust. It reduces the steaming time, thus making the pastry crisper and less damply heavy. I think the sealing in of all the meat and its fine juices in the suet coat makes this one of the great winter dishes. When the spoon sinks through the crust and into the spoon-soft meat and its gluey-dark, thickened juices, you smell heaven on a plate.

Mix all the dry ingredients for the suet crust together in a big bowl, working the suet in well. Stir in some cold water – as little as possible – and work it into a firm dough. Roll the dough out into a large circle on a floured surface and cut away one-quarter of it to use for the lid of the pudding. Butter a 1.5 litre/3 pint pudding basin and line it with the larger piece of dough, allowing a little to overhang the rim of the basin. Roll out the quarter piece into a circle big enough for the lid.

Spoon the filling into the basin, making sure it comes no higher than 2.5cm/1in below the rim. Brush the overhang with water, then put the lid on and press the edges together, sealing them tightly.

Cover the pudding with a sheet of pleated foil and tie string around it, making a handle at the same time. Lower the basin onto a trivet or some folded foil at the bottom of a pan of boiling water. The water should come two-thirds of the way up the sides of the bowl. Keep at a gentle boil for 1½ hours, checking the water level after an hour. Don't worry if the pudding is left to steam an extra half hour; it will not spoil.

Remove the pudding and cut off the string. Take off the foil and serve the pudding piping hot with good English mustard, Brussels sprouts and pommes Anna (see page 421) or mashed potato (see page 89).

FILLET OF BEEF EN CROÛTE

SERVES 8–10

1.8–2kg/4–4½lb piece of fillet from
   the thick part of the fillet
sea salt and black pepper
30g/1oz beef dripping or 2 tbsp light
   olive oil
puff pastry, bought or homemade
   (see opposite)
110g/4oz Portobello mushrooms
   chopped very finely
30g/1oz unsalted butter
110g/4oz chicken liver pâté
   (see p. 86)
1 organic egg, beaten

If you happen upon the silk purse of a large piece of good fillet this really is the
way to use it, and a far swifter and less difficult dish than you might imagine. If
you are not prepared to make your own puff pastry, and most people aren't, do,
I beg you, buy all-butter pastry. It's not worth cloaking a fillet in a grey fleece
when you can cloak it in a satin mantle. If you are making the puff yourself, you
may add 30g/1oz lard to the butter to make it more malleable. You can prepare
the fillet right up to cooking point in advance, as long as you make sure the
mushrooms, pâté and fillet are all cold when you put them together, and keep
loosely covered in clingfilm in the fridge.

Preheat the oven to 230°C/450°F/Gas 8. Trim the fillet of any fatty or sinewy bits and
season it well. Some people shake over a little Worcestershire sauce at this point too.
Heat the dripping or olive oil in a roasting tin and when it begins to smoke, put in the fillet
and brown it all over. Then place in the oven and roast it for 20 minutes. Remove to a plate
and let it cool.

Take your homemade or bought puff pastry. Divide the ball of dough into a one-third
and two-thirds. Roll out the one-third piece to just bigger than the length and breadth of
the fillet. Put the oblong of pastry on a baking sheet, prick it all over with the tines of a fork
and bake it for 15 minutes until golden. Place it on a rack to cool. Fry the mushrooms
briefly in butter in a small pan, stir them into the pâté and leave to cool. Put the pastry
back on the baking sheet and spread it carefully all over with the chicken liver and
mushroom mixture. Plop the fillet on top and cut away any pastry that peeps out from
the side of the meat.

Roll out the big piece of dough so that it is large enough to cover the fillet and tuck
underneath it. Pick the sheet up with the rolling pin and place it over the meat. Lift up the
underside at one end and brush it with the beaten egg, then lift the base edge of cooked
pastry up with a palette knife and tuck the top side of pastry underneath it. Work your way
round the other 3 sides doing the same. If there are any spare bits of pastry, use them to
make leaves for the top. Brush the top with beaten egg and put the baking dish in the
fridge. Leave for at least an hour but if you are going to leave it longer, cover loosely in
clingfilm until you want to use it.

Bake for 20 minutes if you like your meat rare, by which time the pastry should be
browned. If it is not, allow another 5 minutes. If you like your beef cooked medium, bake
for 30 minutes in total; if well cooked, 35 minutes in total.

Fillet of beef en croûte is delicious hot or cold. If you are eating it hot, don't carve it
until you bring it to the table so that the pieces are still rosy and juicy when people are
given their plates.

PUFF PASTRY

340g/12oz plain flour
a pinch of salt
225g/8oz unsalted butter
1–2 tbsp cold water

Sift the flour and salt into a mixing bowl, then rub in 25g/1oz of the butter, as for shortcrust pastry, or use a food processor. Mix in the water, using as little as possible, and gently knead the dough on a floured surface, preferably marble. Wrap it in clingfilm and refrigerate for 30 minutes.

Keep the rest of the butter out so that it softens, then flatten it into a rectangle 2.5cm/1in thick. On a lightly floured surface, roll out the dough into a rectangle 3 times the length and 2.5cm/1in wider than the rectangle of butter. Place the butter in the centre of the pastry, then fold over the top and bottom of the pastry to cover the butter.

With the rolling pin, press down on the edges to seal in the butter, then give the dough a quarter turn clockwise. Now roll the dough out so that it returns to its original length. Fold over the ends again, press them together with the rolling pin, and give a further quarter turn clockwise. Repeat the process once more, then rest the dough in the fridge for at least 30 minutes, remembering which way it is facing.

Repeat the rolling and turning process twice more, then refrigerate for a final 30 minutes before using or freezing. If the pastry gets warm and buttery at any stage during the process, put it in the fridge to chill.

PORK

PORK EN PAPILLOTE WITH PRUNES AND CREAM AND ARMAGNAC

SERVES 4

4 thick pieces of organic pork fillet weighing about 170g/6oz each
16 prunes, Agen if possible, soaked in tea or apple juice for a few hours
2 tbsp olive oil
45g/1½oz unsalted butter
a glass of Armagnac or Cognac
sea salt and black pepper
150ml/5fl oz or so double cream

Cooking en papillote is a wonderful way of sealing in all the flavours and juices of meat, fish or vegetables. You need good, thick fillets of organic, free-range pork for this dish, and as fillet isn't intrinsically a fatty cut, the tight parcel prevents the meat from drying out. Anyway, prunes and pork are a classic combination, as are prunes and Armagnac. With the slick of cream to lubricate, this is a lovely, easy recipe that's full of depth and flavour.

Preheat the oven to 180°C/350°F/Gas 4. Remove any sinewy bits from the meat and trim off any thin edges which would over-cook. Remove the prunes from their soaking liquor.

Heat the olive oil and butter until it begins to foam, then put the pork fillets in the pan and sear them on all sides until they have browned. Remove the meat from the pan to a plate and slosh in the Armagnac. Light it with a taper and let the alcohol burn off. Add the cream and stir until the mixture coheres.

Cut 4 oblongs of foil, which will contain the fillets in baggy but tightly sealed parcels. Put the fillets on the four sheets and season, then pull the sides of the foil up so that the liquid won't flow away when you add it. Put 4 prunes on each fillet and pour the sauce over them equally. Scrunch the parcels so that each edge of each one is tightly sealed and put them on a baking tray. Put in the oven for 30 minutes or until the pork is cooked right through and tender. To check, open up a parcel and test the fillet with a skewer – the juices should not run bloody. If the juices look quite thin when the pork is ready, pour them from each parcel into a pan and reduce them by boiling hard, perhaps adding a little more cream. Check the seasoning and return the sauce to each parcel.

Seal back up to serve so that everyone opens their own parcel at the table. Serve with mashed potatoes (see page 89) and something a little bitter, perhaps braised endives.

BOILED BACON AND CABBAGE

1.8–2.2kg/4–5lb unsmoked collar of
   bacon, without the rind
a selection of chopped vegetables
   (for example 3 onions, 6 carrots,
   2 leeks, 3–4 sticks of celery)
bunch of fresh herbs, tied in a bundle
1.5–2.5 litres/3–4 pints chicken
   stock (see p. 80) or water
1 large green cabbage, chopped and
   cored

The association of place and dish here is paramount for me. This is THE dish if I want to think of summers in the west of Ireland. It's the one I come home to each summer when I've made the trek across land and inhospitable sea and alighted on the doorstep of my marvellous neighbour Mary Gallagher in Mayo. She has it ready for us. We ring her with progress reports across Ireland and somehow, the 13-hour journey is made bearable in the knowledge that we're getting ever closer to this inimitable Irish dinner, the country's best known and best loved.

Soak the bacon in cold water for 24 hours, changing the water several times. Put the soaked bacon in a large casserole with the vegetables, herbs and stock or water. Bring just to the boil, skim, turn the heat right down and keep it simmering at a mere bubble, with the lid on, for about 30 minutes.

Add the cabbage and continue to simmer for a further 1 hour. This sounds like a long time, but you are not looking for a crisply al dente result; quite the reverse. The slow cooking will soften the cabbage completely. Turn off the heat and allow the meat to 'settle' for 20 minutes, then remove it from the pot, transfer it to a carving board and keep it hot for a further 10 minutes under a tight layer of foil and a cloth.

Using a slotted spoon, lift out the cabbage and discard as much as you can of the other vegetables. Lay a bed of cabbage on each plate, put a couple of thick slices of bacon on top, and serve the cooking liquor in a jug. All you need now is some good mustard and some champ (see page 89) to soak up the juices.

2 tbsp lard
2 best pure pork sausages per
    person; good ones are so meaty
    without rusk that 2 are enough
grain or honeycup mustard

BATTER
225g/8oz plain organic flour
a pinch of sea salt
2 large organic eggs
600ml/1 pint milk
enough hot dripping from the beef to
    cover the floor of the roasting tin

TOAD IN THE HOLE

It may not be a culinary peak, but this dish is as much a part of the nation's psyche as eggs and bacon, fish and chips and the Sunday roast. You must get the best bangers for this. The Well Hung Meat Company (see the list of suppliers at the back of this book for details) make marvellous organic bangers that have a coarser texture than the sort of industrial slurry that comes laden with rusk and nitrites from the commercial sausage companies. Their balance of spices, herbs and garlic, and their refusal to over-salt, make their sausages some of the best you can buy. You want a crisp crunchy Yorkshire with a contrastingly soggy middle to my way of thinking, and the mustardy sausages to have leached a bit of their tasty fat into the puffed-up swollen cloud of batter.

To make the batter, sift the flour and salt into a large bowl. Make a well in the centre with a wooden spoon and break the eggs into it. Add a little of the milk and whisk with a balloon whisk, gradually drawing down the flour from the sides of the bowl and adding more milk when the mixture becomes too thick to work. You should finally have a stiff batter which you should then whisk for as long as your arm will hold out for, up to 5 minutes. Add the remaining milk, whisk it in and leave to stand. (See page 40 for more on making batter.)

Preheat the oven to 220°C/425°F/Gas 7. Heat half the lard in a frying pan and cook the sausages briefly all over, 5 minutes will do it. Pour the hot fat into the roasting tin and add the rest of it. Put the tin in the oven for up to 5 minutes or until the fat starts smoking. Meanwhile, roll the sausages in enough grain or honeycup mustard to coat them. Pour the batter into the smoking fat and place the sausages at intervals across the tin. Bake for 30–35 minutes or until the batter has puffed right up and browned.

Serve hot straight from the tin with a couple of green vegetables and some buttery boiled potatoes.

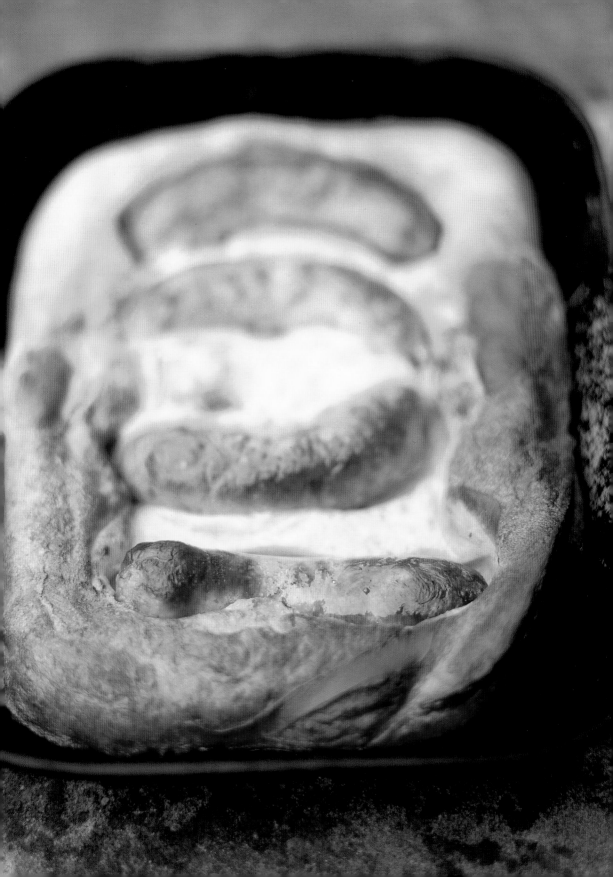

GAMMON AND PARSLEY SAUCE

My mother always serves her gammon with butter beans in parsley sauce. There are really few things finer than the simple, earthy flavour of the floury textured beans, the jewelled green béchamel spiked with nutmeg and the juicy tranches of gammon served with a little of its cooking liquor as a separate sauce.

SERVES 6

900g/2lb boneless tied piece of
    gammon
3 carrots, chopped
2 sticks celery, chopped
2 onions, peeled and chopped
2 bay leaves
a bouquet of fresh thyme and parsley
    with their stalks tied together
12 bruised peppercorns

PARSLEY SAUCE
600ml/1 pint milk
1 small onion stuck with 2 cloves
1 bay leaf
sea salt, black pepper and nutmeg
55g/2oz unsalted butter
55g/2oz flour
150–300ml/5–10fl oz cooking liquor
    from the gammon
a large bunch of curly or flat-leaf
    parsley, chopped

Put the gammon in a large, heavy-bottomed pot and cover with cold water before bringing it just to the boil and draining it. Put the gammon back in the pan and add the vegetables, 2 bay leaves, the bouquet of herbs and the peppercorns. Cover with cold water. Bring up to simmering and cook at this point for 1½ hours with the lid on. Have a look every so often to make sure that the water is murmuring, not bubbling. Check that the gammon is cooked by piercing a skewer right down deep into the gammon – it should be tender right through.

Start the sauce about 40 minutes in advance of this by putting the milk in a small pan with the onion stuck with cloves and a bay leaf. Bring to the boil, then simmer gently for a few minutes. Season with salt, pepper and nutmeg and put the lid on to let the milk draw the flavours into it. Melt the butter and add the flour to make a roux, then make a béchamel in the normal way (see page 70). Add as much cooking liquor to the milk as you need to get a silky sauce that is about the texture of double cream. Adjust the seasoning, take off the heat and stir in the parsley, which should not lose its rawness, but look like emerald flecks.

Slice the gammon thickly, add a little of the poaching liquid to each plate and pass round the parsley sauce. Mash is a must and butter beans or split peas – anything leguminous really. There's something about gammon and pulses!

LAMB

LANCASHIRE HOT-POT

This is the English version of the French lamb boulangère and the Emerald Islanders' Irish stew. Even the name 'hot-pot' evokes cosiness. A bastion-against-the-cold kind of a dish with its meatily browned potatoes and meat falling from the bone. If you like kidneys, put some into the pot too. They give great depth of flavour and texture to the dish and its cooking liquor.

SERVES 6

1.4kg/3lb scrag or best end of lamb neck chops
6 lamb's kidneys (optional), the membrane and any suetty fat removed
3 large onions thinly sliced
sea salt and black pepper
900g/2lb potatoes, peeled and thinly sliced into discs
sea salt and black pepper
about 55g/2oz unsalted butter

Preheat the oven to 200°C/400°F/Gas 6. Put a layer of chops in the bottom of a large heavy casserole, followed by a layer of onions, seasoning both as you go. If you are using kidneys, add them with the chops. Build up layers like this, ending with overlapping slices of potato on top. Pour in water to come halfway up the contents of the pot, then melt the butter and brush it lavishly over the potatoes.

   Cover the pot with greaseproof paper and a lid and put in the oven on the middle shelf. After 30 minutes reduce the temperature to 130°C/250°F/Gas ½ and cook for 2 hours. Remove the lid and greaseproof and cook for a final 30 minutes to brown the potatoes. Serve with something green like kale or cabbage.

NAVARIN OF LAMB

SERVES 6–8

1.4kg/3lb cubed shoulder of lamb
30g/1oz butter
2 tbsp olive oil
1 large onion, sliced
2 tbsp flour
600ml/1 pint lamb stock, heated
sea salt and black pepper
2 cloves of garlic, bruised
a sprig each of rosemary and thyme
 and a bay leaf
450g/1lb small waxy new potatoes
 like Jersey Royals
225g/8oz baby carrots
12 baby turnips, peeled
225g/8oz shelled weight broad beans
225g/8oz shelled weight peas
a bundle of asparagus (18–24
 spears)
6 artichoke hearts
a little parsley to finish

This is an early summer dish and one of the great one-pot dinners. I never think lamb really tastes at Easter when people traditionally eat the first of the spring lamb; it is too young. I'd rather eat hogget, its age gives it flavour and a better covering of fat. By May or June, when the best of the early summer vegetables are at their peak, it is a glorious dish to serve. You may include any combination of good new potatoes like Jersey Royals, artichoke hearts, asparagus, baby broad beans, tiny lanterns of turnip and baby's fingers of carrots. Later there will be squeaky sweet tiny peas, or you can cheat and add a few frozen ones. With the array of fresh veg no one will notice a single aberrant interloper. The kind of dish that gladdens the heart and makes you feel the sun is beginning to warm itself in readiness for summer.

Trim any large bits of fat from the meat. Melt the butter with the olive oil over a medium heat in a large, heavy-bottomed casserole. Throw in the onion and the meat together and stir to brown the meat and turn the onions golden. Remove both, adding a little extra butter and oil if you need to the pan. Stir in the flour and let it bubble into a blonde, biscuity-smelling roux before adding the hot stock, a couple of ladles at a time, stirring or whisking it to smoothness as you add more. Return the meat and onions to the pot with the seasoning, garlic and herbs. Put a sheet of greaseproof under the lid and simmer everything for an hour at a very gentle blip.

Add the new potatoes, whole carrots and the whole, peeled turnips and continue to simmer until they are only just resistant, about 40 minutes. Now add whichever of the other vegetables you are using – the broad beans, peas, peeled chopped asparagus, the spears kept longer than the stalks, and the whole hearts of artichoke. Cook for about 20 minutes or so, until you can pierce the asparagus and artichokes and they are tender right the way through.

If the sauce has become too reduced at any stage of the cooking process, just top it up with a couple more ladles of hot stock. Remove the pot from the heat, skim off any fat from the surface that offends you and scatter fresh chopped parsley over everything.

GIGOT D'AGNEAU WITH FLAGEOLETS

SERVES 8

FLAGEOLETS
450g/1lb flageolets, soaked overnight
    in plenty of cold water, then
    drained and picked
2 carrots, chopped into large chunks
2 sticks celery, broken into lengths
1 large onion, skin on, stuck with
    2 cloves
a leek top or two if you have them
12 peppercorns, bruised
2 fresh bay leaves
2 large sprigs rosemary and a few of
    thyme and parsley tied together

MEAT
1 leg of lamb about 2–2.3kg/4½-5lb
    in weight (or a shoulder of lamb
    for épaule d'agneau)
6 cloves of garlic
2 sprigs rosemary
3–4 tbsp olive oil
sea salt and black pepper
a glass of dry white wine
a knob of butter
3–4 tbsp double cream (optional)

There is something about the marriage of palely green leguminous flageolets and rosily bloody and garlicked leg of lamb that spells harmony and deep satisfaction. This is a king of a dish, scented with rosemary and bay and with some of the flageolets puréed and dosed with cream and butter to give a change of texture. It is just as successful a dish made with shoulder of lamb, which is my preferred cut. I like the more muttony strong flavour of the fuller fatted meat. Remember to soak the beans the night before you need them.

Put the soaked beans in a large heavy-bottomed pot with all the other ingredients for the flageolets and cover with water to 2cm/1in above the vegetables. Bring to the boil and scum rigorously with a slotted spoon. Lower to a simmer, put the lid on and cook at a bare bubble for about 1½–2½ hours, until the beans are tender right through but not beginning to break up.

Preheat the oven to 200°C/400°F/Gas 6. While the beans are coming to the boil, spike incisions into the fat and right down into the flesh of the lamb wherever there is no bone. Push a sliver of garlic and a little sprig of rosemary into each fissure. Pour the olive oil over the meat and season, before putting it at the bottom of the hot oven to roast for about 1½–1¾ hours.

When the meat is cooked but still deliciously pink in the middle – the juices run pink rather than bloody when pierced into the deepest part with a skewer and there is no resistance – remove from the pan to a carving board. Cover with a tight layer of foil and a tea towel. Skim off the fat from the juices in the roasting tin and put the tin on a high heat on top of the stove. Add the white wine and let it bubble.

Remove a large ladle of beans from the pot and liquidise them with about half a ladle of the pot juices. Put the remaining beans in a large warmed dish with a slotted spoon and stir in the puréed flageolets, a large knob of butter and some cream if you feel like it. Season to taste. Serve with the beans and some mashed potatoes (see page 89).

BRAISED MUTTON AND CAPER SAUCE

SERVES 8

2 tbsp olive oil
1.8–2kg/4–4½lb leg of mutton
    or lamb
large measure of brandy
2–3 cloves of garlic per person
300ml/10fl oz dry white wine
3–4 sprigs of thyme

CAPER SAUCE
45g/1½oz unsalted butter
45g/1½oz flour
the cooking juices, wine and brandy
    and stock to make it up to
    600ml/1 pint
sea salt and black pepper
1 organic egg yolk, beaten with 4
    tbsp double cream
1 heaped tbsp capers, drained and
    rinsed
1 tbsp flat-leaf parsley, chopped

Traditionally, mutton was boiled and often served with boiled onions, as well as the caper sauce, and perhaps a turnip purée. I favour a winey braise, some whole baby steamed turnips and a piquant caper sauce.

Heat the oil in a heavy-bottomed casserole and gently brown the meat all over. Add the brandy and set light to it with a taper. Wait until it has finished crackling and the flames have died down, then add the garlic and wine. Strew the thyme on top of the joint, cover with greaseproof paper and a tight lid, and simmer very gently for 2–2½ hours. Serve with caper sauce.

CAPER SAUCE
Melt the butter in with the winey juices when you have removed the meat to rest. Sprinkle in the flour and allow it to turn biscuit coloured and begin to cook, before adding ladles of hot stock, whisking as you go, until the sauce has the texture of thin cream. Keep cooking and occasionally stirring for 15 minutes. Then season and whisk in the egg yolk and cream off the heat. Put back on a low heat and whisk, but do not allow the sauce to bubble or boil at this stage. Throw in the capers and parsley, stir and serve.

LAMB STEAKS WITH GREEN PEPPERCORNS

SERVES 2

2 lamb steaks
30g/1oz green peppercorns
1 tbsp parsley, chopped
2 tsp homemade English mustard
1 egg white
30g/1oz breadcrumbs

Green peppercorn sauce had its short-lived day in the 1980s, so it must be due for a comeback. This combines the muskiness of the crushed spice with heat from the mustard and a souffléed top. It was inspired by a long-forgotten dish by the French chef Roger Vergé.

Take the meat out of the fridge an hour before you want to use it. Cook on a griddle or barbecue until browned, about 2 minutes a side. Keep any juices from the meat. While the meat is cooking, crush the green peppercorns finely (leave some texture) and stir in the parsley and mustard. Whisk the egg white until stiff, then fold it into the peppercorn mixture.

Heat the grill. Spread the mixture thickly over the two steaks on the uppermost side, sprinkle with breadcrumbs, pour over the fatty cooking juices and grill for 3-4 minutes until golden brown. Serve immediately with new potatoes and green beans.

LAMB STEAKS WITH SAUCE PALOISE

These need to be cut as thickly as a rump steak. Rub olive oil, thyme, rosemary and minced garlic into the flesh and griddle until cooked as you like – rare, medium rare, medium or well done. Sauce paloise is the ultimate sauce for lamb, particularly if you've barbecued the meat and want the simple, unctuous tones of butter and mint to accompany lamb and charcoal.

SERVES 6

lamb steaks
olive oil
thyme, rosemary
minced garlic

SAUCE PALOISE
2 tbsp white wine vinegar
3 tbsp mint, finely chopped
30g/1oz shallot, finely minced
10 peppercorns, crushed in a mortar
4 organic egg yolks
3 tbsp cold water
225g/8oz clarified unsalted butter
sea salt and black pepper
juice of half a lemon

Lamb of this quality and cut doesn't need marinating before you barbecue it, neither do you want to mask its intense flavour and sweetness with barbecue sauce. Make the herbed oil a few hours in advance so the herb oils are released into the olive oil. Take the meat out of the fridge an hour before you want to use it. When you're ready to cook, rub in the herbed oil.

If you like rare lamb, cook the meat for 2 minutes a side, then rest it for 6 minutes; if you like it medium rare, cook for 2.5 minutes a side and rest for 5 minutes; medium: 3 minutes a side and rest for 4 minutes; well done: 5 minutes a side and no resting time.

SAUCE PALOISE

Put the vinegar, 2 tablespoons of the mint, the shallot and crushed peppercorns in a small, heavy-bottomed saucepan and reduce gently by a half. Let it cool, add the egg yolks and cold water, and set the pan over a low heat, whisking continuously. Alternatively, make this stage of the sauce in a double boiler over gently simmering water (the pan must not touch the water beneath it). The sauce will gradually begin to emulsify (allow up to 10 minutes). Do not allow it to come to the boil.

Remove from the heat and whisk in the butter a little at a time. Season, then sieve the sauce and stir in the remaining tablespoon of chopped mint. Squeeze in the lemon juice to taste. Serve immediately.

BREAD-BASED PUDDINGS

BREAD AND BUTTER PUDDING

SERVES 6–8

10–12 slices of white bread, or chollah if you like sweet bread, crusts cut off

enough unsalted softened butter to butter all the bread

8 organic egg yolks

170g/6oz unrefined caster sugar

1 vanilla pod

300ml/10fl oz Jersey full-cream milk

300ml/10fl oz double cream

a handful of sultanas, soaked in warm water or warmed sherry or rum for 20 minutes or so until they plump up

extra caster sugar for the top or 3 heaped tbsp Seville orange marmalade

Given the ancient tradition we have of basing fruit and custard puddings on stale bread to use it up, these first few puddings, jewels in our pudding crown, are all bread based. This classic defines everything that is best about English puddings. It is incredibly cheap to make. You probably always have the ingredients in your store cupboard or the sort of approximations that will make a different version of it. It is simple and comforting while also something you can spruce up and decorate like a Christmas tree for special occasions – try soaking your sultanas in sherry, using panettone instead of bread, adding candied fruit or little jewels of prune and apricot. You can make bread and butter pudding with cream or milk, spread the bread with marmalade or leave it buttered, make it with teacakes or give it a dark mantle of chocolate custard.

Preheat oven to 180°C/350°F/Gas 4. Butter the slices of bread. Whisk the egg yolks and caster sugar together thoroughly in a bowl. Split the vanilla pod down the middle and extract the black seeds by running a sharp pointed teaspoon down the middle of the pod. Put the seeds and the pod into a pan with the milk and cream and bring them to simmering point. Then pour the contents through a sieve onto the egg yolk and sugar mixture. Whisk a little until frothy.

Grease a shallow pudding basin. Cut the buttered bread into triangles and arrange them in overlapping layers in the basin, throwing over the sultanas as you go. Pour the egg custard over the bread and allow it to soak in for a few minutes. Put the pudding dish inside a roasting tin with boiling water halfway up its sides.

Poach for about 20–30 minutes. The custard will have thickened considerably but not set as there are only egg yolks in it. Remove the dish from the roasting tin and either scatter caster sugar over the surface in a thin layer and caramelise it briefly under the grill or melt the marmalade with a dessertspoon of water and brush it over the surface of the pudding.

If you want a firmer set to the pudding, use three whole eggs and three yolks whisked together. You may put marmalade on the buttered slices of bread before you cook the pudding, in which case leave the top layer of bread just buttered so the marmalade doesn't burn on top. Add a top coat of marmalade or of caster sugar as described.

SUMMER PUDDING

SERVES 6

750g/1lb 10oz raspberries
200g/7oz redcurrants
110g/4oz vanilla caster sugar
day-old loaf of good white bread cut
    into slices, the crusts removed
1–2 tbsp raspberry liqueur

I happen to believe that Elizabeth David and Jane Grigson got it right – the best summer pudding is made with raspberries and redcurrants only, at a ratio of about 4:1 raspberries to redcurrants. Blackcurrants tend to overpower, though a few whole strawberries put into the pan when you have finished bleeding the other fruit briefly – soggy strawberries are not a texture to inspire the palate – and perhaps some good cherries, stoned, do add different notes and acidity and texture. I also tried a white summer pudding, which was a wonderful departure from the original, full of gooseberries, whitecurrants and white Napoleon cherries. Or in the autumn, you could use blackberries, plums and blueberries. This dish is the definition of the perfect pudding for the English summer; our soft fruits are peerless. Don't worry about the raspberry liqueur if you don't keep it. Just make sure there is enough juice left over to pour over the crown of the pudding and render it thoroughly bloodied with trickling pink fruit. Serve with clotted cream.

Put the raspberries and redcurrants in a heavy pot with the vanilla caster sugar. Heat gently and briefly until the fruit begins to bleed and the sugar is dissolved, no more than about 3–4 minutes. The fruit must not cook or lose its shape.

Line a pudding basin with slices of bread. There should be no gaps. With a slotted spoon, pile in the fruit, leaving some of the juice in the pot. Sprinkle a tablespoon or two of raspberry liqueur over the pudding before finishing with a top layer of bread.

Cover with a plate that just fits, add some heavy weights on top, and put the basin in the fridge overnight. Just before you serve the pudding, turn it out onto a not completely flat plate that can hold the juice, and pour over the rest of the juice to which you've added more raspberry liqueur to taste. You should still pass round the bottle too!

APPLE CHARLOTTE

This is a classic pudding, as virtuous for its cheapness as for its scrumptiousness. There is something about crisp, warm, buttery bread and a tart apple purée that can only be topped one way: with the best Jersey cream. You may cook the apple, cool it and add the egg in advance. I make this in a 23cm/9in springform tin.

SERVES 8

225g/8oz unsalted butter (you may not need it all)
8–10 Granny Smiths or firm, tart eating apples such as Cox's, peeled, quartered and thinly sliced
110g/4oz unrefined caster sugar
2 organic eggs, separated
half a large loaf of good white bread
1 tbsp demerara sugar

Preheat the oven to 200°C/400°F/Gas 6. Put a knob of the butter in a saucepan with enough water just to cover the base of the pan and add the apples and the caster sugar. Cover and bring to the boil, then remove the lid and bubble furiously until the apple is cooked but maintains some of its shape and texture. Remove from the heat, beat the egg yolks and stir them in.

Cut the crusts off the loaf and cut into slices 1cm/½in thick, 3cm/1¼in wide and the height of the tin. Melt the remaining butter gently in a small pan, then skim off the curdy white solids and froth, leaving the yellow, oily mass. Brush a little of the butter on the base and sides of the tin, then add the demerara sugar and turn the tin so that the sides and base are sugar-coated. Dip the bread in the butter and press the slices gently against the sides and base of the tin. Brush the joins with lightly beaten egg white to act as mortar and fill the tin with the apple mixture.

Cover the top with more butter-soaked bread and bake for about an hour, reducing the temperature to 190°C/375°F/Gas 5 after 20 minutes. The charlotte will look gloriously browned. Remove from the oven, snap open the spring and turn out on to a large plate.

PAIN PERDU WITH JAM SAUCE

Also known as Poor Knights of Windsor, this lovely medieval dish was eaten in both England and France. It was originally made from bread baked with the finest flour, which was dipped in beaten egg before frying, spicing and sugaring. Today, the Americans call this French toast, but the original names have the romantic edge.

SERVES 4–6

6 slices of day-old good bread
4 tbsp single cream
3 organic eggs
1 tbsp sherry or Madeira
unsalted butter
caster sugar
cinnamon

JAM SAUCE
1 x 225g/8oz jar raspberry jam
1–2 tbsp water
spritz of lemon juice
1 tbsp Cognac (optional)

Remove or leave the crusts on the bread, according to your preference and cut each slice diagonally into two triangles. Whisk the cream, eggs and sherry thoroughly in a bowl, then soak the bread in the mixture on each side.

Melt the butter in a frying pan, and slip in the slices of egged bread before the butter browns. Fry them on both sides until they are browned and crisp. Put them into a warmed serving dish, and sprinkle with a little sugar and cinnamon.

JAM SAUCE
Slowly melt the jam in a small pan with 1 tablespoon of water and the lemon juice. Judge whether it needs slackening a little with more water. Add the alcohol if you are using it. When the sauce is hot, pour into a jug to pour over the pain perdu. Strawberry, cherry, blackberry, blackcurrant or apricot jams all work equally well as do compotes of the same.

Apple Charlotte

SERVES 6

TOPPING
55g/2oz unsalted butter
140g/5oz bread, torn to crumbs
55g/2oz light muscovado sugar
2 tsp cinnamon ground from
    cinnamon sticks in a mortar with
    1 tsp allspice

APPLE PURÉE
6 large Bramley apples, peeled,
    cored and chopped
110–140g/4–5oz unrefined vanilla
    caster sugar
30g/1oz unsalted butter

APPLE BROWN BETTY

What a lovely autumnal pudding, homely in the best sense of the word without being dowdy or frumpy or plain Jane-ish. There are versions where the crumb is cooked like a crumble, but I prefer it like this, scattered over all crisp and cinnamony and buttery crumbed at the last minute when the apple purée has been dolloped onto the plate. This is the sort of pudding which can easily be forgotten, but once remembered never disappoints. Make it with apricots, plums, damsons, blackberry and apple, or prunes if you like, turning the fruit into a rich purée first.

Melt the butter in a heavy-bottomed frying pan and when it begins to bubble, throw in the breadcrumbs and stir to coat them in the butter. You will need to go on stirring every so often for much longer than you think to get the breadcrumbs really crisp.

While that's happening, cook the apples with the sugar and a couple of tablespoons of water in a covered pan. Stir every so often as the chunks at the bottom soften so that the rest of the apples get near the heat source. After about 10 minutes you should have a coherent purée, but if the apples still look too watery, just cook them down a little longer with the lid off the pan. They should taste sharp, not too sweet. Remove the apples from the heat and stir in the butter.

Once the crumbs have crisped, remove them from the heat and stir in the sugar, ground cinnamon and allspice. Taste — you want a harmonious hit of spice with the cinnamon's warm tones coming through clearly. Spoon the apple purée into bowls and let everyone sprinkle over their own crumbs. Pouring cream, clotted cream or crème fraîche needed.

MILK AND CREAM PUDDINGS

Puddings made with milk or cream have their own repertoire, like those made with bread in the last few recipes. Junkets, rice pudding, trifles and creams have been part of the English pudding landscape for centuries. The cheaper, more everyday ones rely on good, creamy milk. If you can get Jersey milk, so much the better. Do not use semi-skimmed – the flavour and texture will never be as good.

CRÈME CARAMEL WITH HAZELNUT BRITTLE

SERVES 4–6

85g/3oz vanilla caster sugar
1 tbsp cold water
2 whole organic eggs and 2 yolks
2 tbsp vanilla sugar
1 vanilla pod, insides scraped out
600ml/1 pint milk

HAZELNUT BRITTLE
85g/3oz vanilla caster sugar
100g/3½oz whole, skinned hazelnuts

This soft, bittersweet pudding with its toffeed sheen and satiny feel is the simplest and cheapest of all. I first made it as an impecunious student, but the attraction has never waned. The bitter molten sugar contrasting with the creamy, vanilla-ey depths is true inspiration and pure simplicity. The hazelnut brittle turns it into a party piece but is an optional extra.

Preheat the oven to 150°C/300°F/Gas 2. Gently melt the 85g/3oz caster sugar in a saucepan, until it is liquid and has turned a burnished mahogany colour. Just as it starts to bubble, throw on the cold water and quickly pour the mixture into the base of a soufflé dish, rolling it slightly up the sides until it sets.

Break the eggs and yolks into a bowl, add the sugar and the innards from the vanilla pod, and whisk. Scald the milk in the sugar pan, and pour it over the egg mixture. Once the caramel has set pour the egg and milk mixture over it. Set the soufflé dish in a roasting tin and pour boiling water to come two-thirds of the way up the dish. Cook for 1½–2 hours, making sure that the custard is still trembling slightly in the middle when you remove the dish from the oven. Leave it in the tin of water until the set is complete, then take it out, cool, and finally chill it in the fridge for a few hours. It should be served cold.

To turn the crème caramel out, run a palette knife cautiously around the edge of the dish, place a plate with enough of a lip to hold the caramel over the top and invert it carefully onto the plate.

HAZELNUT BRITTLE
Scatter the vanilla sugar in the base of a saucepan, and heat it to the same point as the caramel. Throw in the chopped hazelnuts, stir briefly, and spread on a buttered baking tray. Leave to cool and set, then bash the brittle up a bit to serve alongside the crème caramel.

BAKED RICE PUDDING

75g/2½oz short-grain pudding rice
850ml–1.2 litres/1½-2 pints Jersey
  milk
30g/1oz butter
2 tbsp sugar
1 vanilla pod, split, or 1 cinnamon
  stick

Unlike the American food writer Jeffrey Steingarten, whose formidable reputation was ultimately endorsed when he became 'the man who ate everything', this is the point at which I have to confess to falling short. I have hated milk with a passion all my life. At school, those warm bottles clinking in the crate with their cloggy thick creamy tops made me heave just to look at them, and rice pudding meant an excuse note; for God's sake, I could barely be in the same room, let alone stick a spoon in it. The way some girls stirred their raspberry jam into it, pinkening the white horror with its skein of throat-gagging skin, not to mention the smell itself left me certain if there was one food I would never grow into, this would be the one. I haven't disappointed on that score. I take my tea black and the idea of junket, rice pudding, semolina or tapioca are all still very much on a par. So the only person I can turn to with this shortcoming is Jane Grigson. She had a similar phobia, but got out of it, citing three conclusions that tipped the balance and without which, rice pudding is still the mean, slimy, inedible excuse of a pudding to her that it still is with me! The three conclusions are: a rice pudding must be flavoured with a vanilla pod or a cinnamon stick; it must be cooked long and slowly; it must be eaten with plenty of double cream. I wouldn't believe anyone else on the subject.

Put the rice with 600ml/1 pint of the milk and the remaining ingredients into a heatproof stoneware or glass dish. Leave in a gentle oven, 140°C/275°F/Gas 1, for 3 hours. After an hour, stir up the pudding and add more milk to slacken the mixture. After 2 hours, do the same thing again, and, if you like, add some single cream. The butter and the cream are what form the delicious skin. Serve with a jug of double cream.

If you reduce the heat, say, to 130°C/250°F/Gas ½ or even lower, you can leave the rice pudding in the oven for twice as long. Add more milk occasionally; you may need some extra if you cook it for this long. Beneath the crust, the rice will caramelise slightly to an appetising brown. Rice pudding is the definition of slow food; don't try to speed it up.

TRINITY BURNT CREAM, OR CRÈME BRÛLÉE

MAKES 8 RAMEKINS

1 vanilla pod
850ml/1½ pints organic double
    cream, Jersey if you can get it
7 large organic egg yolks
3 dsrtsp vanilla caster sugar
demerara sugar

Whatever anyone says, this is easy to make as long as you have the patience to keep stirring. I feel it needs a good 8 hours in the fridge, and that on no account should it be made in the oven in a bain-marie. The consistency will never have that satiny finish of a properly stirred, all-cream custard. The other mistake is to over-sweeten; remember, the top is pure caramel. Some people like to tinker with this dish, adding a few raspberries or strawberries at the bottom of the ramekins, a little alcohol or fruit purée to the custard. Experiment by all means, but I think the original is the best.

Chill the ramekins in the freezer while you make the custard. Split the vanilla pod, extract the seeds, and put them in a pan with the cream and the pod. Bring the cream to scalding point, then remove from the heat and leave to infuse for 10 minutes. Whisk together the egg yolks and caster sugar, then strain in the cream through a sieve, and return to the pan.

On a low heat, stir the mixture continuously, until you can feel it thickening. This takes 10–15 minutes. On no account be tempted to turn up the heat or you will end up with scrambled eggs. Eventually you will find that a trail is left behind by your spoon as you stir. I use a little balloon whisk as the custard begins to thicken, which I sort of worry quickly across the custard.

Remove from the heat, and pour into the chilled ramekins. Place in the fridge for a good 8 hours. Remove half an hour before you want them, scatter a thin layer of demerara over the surface with your fingers, followed by a tiny sprinkle of water. Blast with a blowtorch or under a very hot grill until the sugar has caramelised. Return to the fridge for 30 minutes before serving.

WHIM WHAM

SERVES 6

600ml/1 pint double cream
150ml/5fl oz muscatel dessert wine
    or sweet sherry
55g/2oz unrefined caster sugar
grated zest of a lemon
6 pieces of sponge cake or 2 boudoir
    or amaretti biscuits per person
1 tsp roasted flaked almonds or
    chopped hazelnuts
or
blanched lemon or orange peel

The word whim wham means a little trifle, or something trifling and this recipe was a popular emergency pudding in the 18th century – something people could conjure up from the store cupboard. It can be made with slices of plain sponge cake, or boudoir or amaretti biscuits. Make it either in individual glasses or in one large glass bowl.

Pour the cream and wine into a bowl with the caster sugar and lemon zest and whisk with a balloon whisk until the cream holds in soft folds but is not whisked to rigidity. Break up each slice of cake or biscuit and put half in the bottom of each glass followed by half the cream. Repeat the layers, ending with a snowy layer of cream on top.

Decorate with the roasted nuts and a little blanched lemon or orange peel if you like. A sprig of rosemary would do if your cupboard is bare!

Whim Wham

CRÈME ANGLAISE

1 litre/1¾ pints Jersey or full cream
    milk
170g/6oz vanilla caster sugar
1 vanilla pod, split down the middle,
    the seeds scooped out with a
    teaspoon
10 organic egg yolks

MERINGUE

4 egg whites
a pinch of salt
140g/5oz unrefined icing sugar, sifted

OEUFS À LA NEIGE

There is something magical and ethereal about this whisper of a light pudding, with its sea of eggy, vanilla-rich custard beneath the clouds of snowy, poached meringue.

Bring the milk to scalding point in a pan with the vanilla caster sugar and the vanilla pod and scooped-out seeds. Remove from the heat, cover and leave to infuse while you start on the meringues.

Add a tiny pinch of salt to the egg whites and whisk them until they reach stiff peaks. Sift over the icing sugar, then whisk again thoroughly.

Remove the pod from the milk and heat it through again to just below simmer point. Now plop in heaped teaspoons of the meringue mixture, only about 5 or 6 at a time as they need room to swell. Turn them carefully after a couple of minutes and poach the other sides for another couple of minutes. Lift them out with a slotted spoon and put them on a mesh rack with a bowl underneath for them to drain into.

When you have finished poaching all the meringues, put them onto a large serving dish and make the crème anglaise. Add the drained milk from the meringues to the rest of the milk. Beat the yolks before adding them to the milk and whisking them together. Now heat and make in the same way as for the custard recipe on page 332. When the custard has thickened, remove the pan from the heat and carefully pour it around, but not over the poached meringues. Cool first, then chill in the fridge and serve cold.

LEMON CREAM POTS

SERVES 8

120ml/4fl oz lemon juice, about
  3½ organic lemons' worth
a few drops of pure lemon oil,
  Boyajian do one that is available
  in supermarkets (optional)
85g/3oz vanilla caster sugar
6 large organic egg yolks
375ml/13fl oz organic double cream

Bring back the ramekin! Individual creams, brûlées and custards are a lovely way to end dinner, as are little chocolate pots and the like. They are symphonies of measured richness – you get one, and it is rich and profound enough for you not to need more. The most you may do is pour a slick of cold, thin cream over it if you want to go too far.

Preheat the oven to 170°C/325°F/Gas 3. Combine the lemon juice, lemon oil if using, and sugar in a bowl and stir well to dissolve thoroughly. Test for sweetness. In a separate bowl whisk the egg yolks, then add the cream. Whisk the lemon juice mixture into the eggs and cream, then strain through a sieve into a jug.

   Boil a kettle. Set 8 ramekins in a roasting tin and pour the cream mixture into them. Pour boiling water into the tin to reach halfway up the sides of the ramekins. Cover the ramekins with a sheet of greaseproof to prevent a skin from forming and bake in the middle of the oven for about 30 minutes until tremblingly set. They will carry on cooking once removed from the oven. Take the ramekins out of the water and cool on a rack. Refrigerate for at least 2 hours or overnight before serving.

GERANIUM CREAM

300ml/10fl oz double cream
75g/2½oz caster sugar
2 rose-geranium leaves
140g/5oz cream cheese

Picking the leaves of flowers or currant bushes and steeping them in sugar syrup to use in ices or in scalded cream for creams is an old tradition. Petals are good, too. Rose petals make a delicious cream and a soft-set jelly for toast, and rosewater is used in many Middle Eastern and North African puddings as a flavouring. I always use a handful of blackcurrant leaves in the summer to make the best sorbet of them all, and it is surprising just how intense the flavour is and just how unguessable to the uninitiated. It has a blackcurrant note to it that is somehow purer and more true than the fruit itself, but the sorbet is white! Geranium and lemon verbena creams also used to be popular. I found this cream in Mary Norwak's lovely book, *English Puddings Sweet and Savoury*. She also refers to rose-geranium leaves being used to flavour sponge cakes and crab apple jelly. Make this pudding the day before you want to eat it.

Put the cream into a bowl with the sugar and rose-geranium leaves. Put the bowl over a pan of hot water and heat gently until the cream is hot but not boiling. Remove from the heat and leave until just cold. Gradually add the cream to the cheese, mixing together until smooth and creamy. Put into a bowl, cover and leave in a cool place, not the fridge, for 12 hours. Take out the leaves and put the mixture into a serving bowl. This is delicious with fresh raspberries or blackberries.

PANNACOTTA

SERVES 6

425ml/15fl oz double cream
150ml/5fl oz Jersey milk from the top
of the bottle
a small piece of vanilla pod, split and
the seeds scraped out
85–100g/3–3½ oz vanilla caster sugar
a leaf of gelatine (consult the packet)

Here is an Italian pudding that slips down with cool, elegant ease. It could take a lifetime of experimenting with, as you must get that magical, barely set texture that doesn't smack of a heavy hand with the gelatine, and you need to develop your own ideas as to how creamy and rich or milky and mild you like it. Cinnamon, rosewater, a few berries, a note of vanilla, some eau de vie or rum are all variations and embellishments to the main theme, but I am of the mind that the pudding should be innocent of all extras, particularly if you have the best ingredients to show off. It should be as light and angelically set as a thing of feathers and as slippery as can be. If you can get unpasteurised Jersey cream you are more than halfway to pannacotta heaven.

Heat the cream, milk, vanilla seeds and pod in a pan. Add the sugar, bring to the boil and boil for a minute. Take the pan off the heat, cover and leave to infuse for an hour. Remove the piece of pod. Soften the gelatine in cold water, squeeze and dissolve in 4 tablespoons of hot water.

Strain the cream mixture and add a couple of tablespoons to the gelatine, stirring rapidly. Add the gelatine to the cream mixture, stirring thoroughly to dissolve it. Pour into dariole moulds or ramekins and allow to cool. Cover with clingfilm and chill in the fridge for at least 2 hours. Run a palette knife around the side of the ramekins or moulds to turn the pannacotta out on to individual plates.

Some people like to eat pannacotta with a fruit purée or compote. I love the simple purity of the dish on its own.

FROMAGE BLANC

SERVES 6

150ml/5fl oz double cream
90ml/3fl oz thick yoghurt
1 large organic egg white
1 tbsp unrefined icing sugar

Here is a light cream to serve with summer berries or layer inside a sponge, Genoise or otherwise, with raspberries or strawberries.

Pour the cream into a cold bowl and beat it into soft billows so that it just holds its shape. Fold in the yoghurt. Beat the egg white to stiff peaks, then gently fold it into the cream. Add a little sprinkle of icing sugar to taste, folding it in briefly and gently.

LES CREMETS

285g/10oz fromage frais
150ml/5fl oz crème fraîche
2 egg whites

This is a lovely light, lactic, cool accompaniment to soft summer fruits. Fraises de bois if you can lay your hands on them are the best.

Remember to make this the night before you want it and check you have the muslin before you start. It's the same process as draining yoghurt for labneh, so at a pinch you could use a j-cloth.

Line your sieve with clean muslin, sparing enough to fold over the top later. Mix the fromage frais and crème fraîche together well in a cold bowl. In a separate bowl, whisk the egg whites until they form stiff peaks, then fold them lightly but thoroughly into the creams. Do not knock the air out; be brief. Spoon the mixture into the muslin and fold the extra muslin over the top. Put the sieve over a pudding basin in the fridge overnight.

The following day, unmould it. The cream will have shrunk and lost a lot of its moisture as it solidified. Serve in a bowl with a separate bowl of soft fruit to hand round. Delicious with cold, thin cream poured over it.

COEUR À LA CRÈME

225g/8oz curd cheese
2 organic eggs, separated
55g/2oz vanilla caster sugar
1 packet gelatine
240ml/8fl oz whipping cream

This is a firmer cream than the cremet above because of the gelatine. It is best set in a heart-shaped mould, the kind with holes in the bottom. Wonderful with soft summer fruit and berries or with a fruit compote in the winter.

Put the curd cheese through the coarse disc of a mouli-légumes to aerate it. This improves the texture, so if you don't have a mouli, push it through a sieve. Stir in the egg yolks and sugar. Dissolve the gelatine in 6 tablespoons of very hot water in a bowl and set aside. When it is almost cold and smooth, stir in the cream and whip until stiff. Fold in the curd cheese mixture thoroughly but lightly. Whisk the egg whites until they form stiff peaks and fold them into the mixture.

Line a large mould or several little heart-shaped moulds with muslin and spoon in the cream, folding the muslin over the top. Put the moulds in the fridge until they set. Turn out onto plates or a large serving dish and pile mounds of soft fruit, sugared until it bleeds a little, around them.

LEMON POSSET

SERVES 6–8

600ml/1 pint double cream,
   Jersey if possible
140g/5oz vanilla caster sugar
juice of 2 lemons

So simple it's almost inconceivable, but utterly delicious. Seventeenth-century recipe books were full of possets, the name of a medicinal drink of milk, curdled with wine or ale and spices, which was said to be good for colds. There is nothing curdled about this sharp, delectable cream.

Put the cream and sugar in a pan large enough to allow it room to boil. Bring to the boil and boil for 3 minutes. Remove from the heat and whisk in the lemon juice. Strain the mixture into a jug before pouring into the ramekins. Let them cool, then leave them into the fridge for 4–6 hours before serving. Serve with almond and orange florentines or macaroons.

ALMOND AND ORANGE FLORENTINES

MAKES ABOUT 16

3 organic egg whites
140g/5oz unrefined icing sugar
400g/14oz flaked almonds
grated zest of 2 oranges

Another gooey delight from the Ottolenghi brethren (see list of suppliers at the back of the book), these golden, chewy florentines are great on their own or served with fools, creams, sorbets and ice creams.

Preheat the oven to 150°C/300°F/Gas 2. Line a baking tray with silicone paper and brush lightly with vegetable oil. Mix all the ingredients together by hand. Using a wet hand, make little mounds of the almond mix on the tray, spaced well apart. Dip a fork in water and flatten each biscuit until very thin.

   Place in the oven and bake for about 12 minutes, until the florentines are golden brown. Leave them to cool and harden before removing from the tray.

Lemon Posset with Almond and Orange Florentines

CHOCOLATE POTS

MAKES 5 LITTLE RAMEKINS

170ml/6fl oz good double cream
a heaped tsp freshly ground coffee
140g/5oz good dark chocolate,
    Valrhona or similar
90ml/3fl oz Jersey milk
2 organic egg yolks
I heaped tbsp unrefined icing sugar

Bitter, black and velvety rich, you can plunge a spoon into one of these little pots and it will remain standing. The scent of coffee spiking best Valrhona chocolate is irresistible. You can make the pots the day before you need them and keep them in the fridge. Cold, thin cream can be poured over the top by those who are seriously over the top.

Heat the cream with the coffee until just below boiling. Remove from the heat, cover and leave to infuse for an hour.

Preheat the oven to 140°C/275°F/Gas 1. Melt the chocolate very gently in the milk. Beat the egg yolks with the sugar, then add the chocolate milk. Sieve the coffee and cream, add to the chocolate mixture and and beat together until blended. Pour into the ramekins and put them in a roasting tin with scalding water to reach halfway up the sides of the ramekins. Bake for 45 minutes, remove from their bain-marie and let them cool. Put them in the fridge for a few hours before serving. You can omit the coffee and use half a vanilla pod split, with the black grains extracted and used too, if you prefer.

CHOCOLATE BAVAROIS

SERVES 4

3½ gelatine leaves
600ml/1 pint milk
340g/12oz dark, bitter chocolate,
    broken into pieces
5 organic egg yolks
300ml/10fl oz double cream

This recipe comes from one of the all-time great chefs and food writers Simon Hopkinson, who has hung up his kitchen clogs professionally speaking, thus robbing me and many others of his inspired and bossily definitive recipes in *The Independent*. We have plenty of his books to turn to when we want to make sure we're doing things properly, knowing that Simon's taste is as good as it gets and as rich as it gets and that the recipes don't fail. And by that I mean don't fail to excite, not just don't fail to work. This is from his classic, *Roast Chicken and Other Stories*.

Put the gelatine leaves in a bowl, cover with cold water and leave to soften. Heat the milk and melt the chocolate in it. Gently whisk together until smooth. Whisk the egg yolks and add them to the milk chocolate mixture. Cook over a gentle heat until thickened, like custard. Drain the gelatine and add it to the chocolate mixture while it is still hot. Whisk together well.

Pass the mixture through a sieve into a cold bowl. Place over crushed ice and stir with a wooden spoon until starting to set. Lightly whip the cream until holding soft peaks, then carefully but quickly fold it into the chocolate. Pour into individual ramekins or a soufflé dish and refrigerate for at least 2 hours before serving with cold crème Anglaise (see page 332).

SYLLABUS

SERVES 6

4 tbsp Oloroso or good dry sherry
2 tbsp Cognac
finely grated zest and juice of a
    lemon
2 tbsp vanilla caster sugar
425ml/15fl oz double cream, Jersey if
    possible
a suspicion of nutmeg
blanched lemon peel or a sprig of
    bruised rosemary to decorate each
    glass

SYLLABUB

In *The Closet of the Eminently Learned Sir Kenelme Digby Kt Opened* published in 1669, the Prospect Books facsimile of which I have a copy, the distinguished knight offers several recipes and quite a discourse on the subject of the syllabub, a light, liquor-laden cream that goes back to at least the mid-17th century.

The texture we expect today is a little heavier than it was then, and we glean why from 'my Lady Middlesex' whose recipe Sir Kenelme gives. She beats her cream, her wine and her Sack together with fine sugar powder 'till all appeareth converted into froth'. Then it is poured into syllabub glasses and let stand all night: 'The next day the Curd will be thick and firm above, and the drink clear under it.' Sir Kenelme also recommends decorating the glass with a sprig of rosemary, bruised, or a little lemon peel to 'quicken the taste' or amber sugar, spirit of cinnamon, nutmeg, mace or cloves, a very little. Later in the book, his syllabub recipe uses the syrup from making 'dryed plums', which he describes as less sweet than fruity. I like the idea of boiling this syrup up and reducing it a little, like intensely sticky prune juice, and perhaps adding eau de vie de prune to the wine instead of brandy.

Nowadays we beat everything together until it hangs suspended in soft waves, the liquor incorporated beyond separation or froth point.

Syllabubs are best left overnight at the stage before you beat them with the cream, so that the lemon juice, zest and liquor – brandy and white wine or sherry being the usual combination – macerate thoroughly. However, I often make an instant syllabub and add soft summer berries, peaches or nectarines and the like in strata between the billowing folds of cream and can't say that I am unduly worried by the diminution of depth of flavour.

Keep the syllabub for a day or two before serving it if you have the time to make it that far in advance.

Put the first three ingredients in a bowl, cover and leave overnight if you have time, or for as long as you can.

Strain the liquid into a bowl and stir in the sugar until it has completely dissolved. Pour in the cream, grate over a tiny bit of nutmeg and begin to beat with a balloon whisk. It seems hard to imagine that the liquid will be taken up and absorbed by the cream, but it does happen and it doesn't take forever. Keep whisking until the syllabub holds in soft folds, then spoon it into glasses. Keep cool but not very cold or the cream will harden too much. Decorate and serve with little biscuits such as macaroons or the almond and orange florentines on page 328.

CUSTARDS, FOOLS AND ICE CREAMS

CUSTARD OR CRÈME ANGLAISE

600ml/1 pint Jersey full-cream milk
1 vanilla pod, split down the middle, and the seeds extracted with the point of a teaspoon
6 large organic egg yolks
110g/4oz vanilla caster sugar

This is another rite of passage, one that takes nerve and practice and eventually allows you to join the exclusive club of passing for a serious cook. Along with pastry, soufflés, mayonnaise, hollandaise and béarnaise, custard is one of those things that can't be hurried or short cut, short of buying the ready made which will never, ever, be as good in terms of texture or ingredients. If it goes wrong and turns to scrambled eggs, you will learn a valuable lesson: cook it more slowly over less heat, stir constantly, pay attention. It isn't difficult if you follow the rules. This is a recipe you will use for ever, for ice creams and fools, as a sauce on its own, or spruced up with chocolate, coffee, alcohol. Its heftier cousin, crème pâtissière (see page 358), is made with the addition of cornflour. Crème pâtissière is perfect for your summer fruit tarts, which need a custard that sets and won't scramble, but is ultimately not such a test of a cook. It's more a half marathon of a challenge.

Put the milk with the pod and the seeds in a pan with a good heavy base and bring slowly to scalding point, whisking the seeds to break them up. Remove from the heat, cover and leave to infuse for 30 minutes if you have time. This is not essential but does intensify the vanilla flavour.

Whisk the egg yolks with the vanilla caster sugar until pale and thick. Strain the milk mixture over them, whisking as you go and forcing the little beads of vanilla through the sieve with a wooden spoon. Return the mixture to the pan over a low heat and stir or whisk continuously – don't let it get to simmer point. The mixture will begin to look frothy, but make sure the underneath isn't beginning to stick to the base of the pan. Whisk all over the pan right down to the bottom.

Eventually – it may take 15 minutes – the custard will have thickened perceptibly. Take off the heat and test with your finger – you will be able to feel and see whether it has the texture of a proper custard. When it is ready, whisk a little longer off the heat as the base of the pan will still be hot and you don't want any scrambly bits.

When cooled, this is your base for all the best ice creams and fools. It can also be served hot, warm or cold as a pouring custard for puddings.

GOOSEBERRY FOOL

SERVES 4–6

about 450g/1lb tart gooseberries,
   topped and tailed
4 tbsp or so muscovado sugar
55g/2oz unsalted butter
240ml/8fl oz single cream, or half
   each single and double
3 organic egg yolks, beaten
2–3 tbsp elderflower syrup (optional)

ELDERFLOWER SYRUP
6 heads of elderflower
3 tbsp vanilla caster sugar

The fool of fools. There is something about the gooseberry – the splurting of the sharp seeds; the pale green, golden or deep pink hairy orbs which hang like miniature lanterns with an armoury of spikes to contend with as you pull them from the branch; the way the berries collapse and yield when cooked; the network of veiny channels on their translucent skins. Paired with elderflower they are a classic combination, the scented sweetness matching the acid sharpness to perfection.

Stew the gooseberries gently in the melted butter and sugar in a heavy-bottomed frying pan. Turn frequently as the sugar begins to coat and caramelise and do not allow them to overcook. The berries are cooked when you can crush them with a fork without resistance. Leave them to cool.

Scald the cream in a small pan. Pour it over the beaten egg yolks, whisking as you go, then return the mixture to the pan. Continue to cook and stir or whisk over a gentle heat until the custard has thickened. Pay attention at this stage or the mixture will scramble.

If you are using elderflower syrup, stir that into the fruit purée first, then fold the fruit into the custard. Cool and spoon into glasses or a glass bowl. Top with a sprig of redcurrants or a twist of lemon peel to add colour.

ELDERFLOWER SYRUP

Simmer the elderflower heads with 240ml/8fl oz water and the vanilla caster sugar for 15 minutes. Leave to infuse under a lid before straining through a sieve.

GOOSEBERRY ICE CREAM

SERVES 6

gooseberry fool (see above)
300ml/10fl oz double cream

A delicious frozen version of the preceding fool, with added cream, naturally.

You do not want frozen lumps of gooseberry in this deliciously acidic, delicate concoction, so sieve the fruit mixture from the above recipe. Fold it into the custard and add the floppily whipped double cream, folding it well into the gooseberry custard. Freeze. See page 334 for more on making ice cream.

VANILLA ICE CREAM

MAKES JUST OVER 1 LITRE/2 PINTS

6 large organic egg yolks
140g/5oz vanilla caster sugar
2 vanilla pods, split down the middle
   and the seeds scooped out with a
   sharp pointed teaspoon
500ml/18fl oz Jersey milk
600ml/1 pint double cream, Jersey if
   possible

There are many recipes for the supposedly best vanilla ice cream, a lot of which use far more egg yolks than the six I always use, or a higher proportion of milk for a more Italian soft-ice texture. I like this one precisely because it is rich without tasting eggy and the vanilla shines through. Only good, sticky-fresh vanilla pods will do, from Madagascar if possible. The dried ones don't cut it any more than does vanilla extract or, God forbid, vanilla essence. How many things does vanilla ice cream go with? It is perfect with apple pie, cherry pie, gooseberry pie; it works well with rich chocolate cakes of the pudding kind and it is great with crumbles. It laps up chocolate or butterscotch sauce, which freeze to its edges in the most beguiling way, the warm puddle of sauce trickling off in its black wake. It is great with a pile of raw summer berries, with poached peaches or with a compote of spiced winter fruit.

Separate the eggs, putting the whites in one bowl and the yolks in another bowl with the vanilla sugar and the vanilla seeds. Whisk the yolks, sugar and vanilla seeds together until they amalgamate. Heat the milk with the split pods slowly until it reaches scalding point. Pour it straight over the yolk and sugar mixture through a sieve, whisking as you go. Return the mixture to the pan over a very gentle heat and continue to whisk, watching carefully so that no bits of the mixture overheat and scramble at the edges of the pan — the mixture should not get to simmer point. This should take 10–15 minutes, whisking continuously. Once the mixture has thickened, remove the pan from the heat and stir in the double cream.

Leave to cool until it is warm rather than hot, stirring every so often so a skin doesn't form on top. Churn in an ice-cream machine and finish freezing in the freezer in its pail.

If you are making the ice cream by hand, put the mixture in a sealable plastic container once it has cooled completely and put it in the freezer. Every 30 minutes, remove and whisk the ice cream to stop crystals forming and ruining the smooth, velvety texture. When the ice cream has set enough to be difficult to whisk, even in the middle, just leave it in the freezer until it has set completely.

The ice cream can be made a day or two in advance, but the flavour does tend to diminish quite quickly, particularly once you have opened the lid and started eating the ice cream. This is the base for many fruit, spice and other ice creams.

BROWN BREAD AND BRANDY ICE CREAM

300ml/10fl oz double cream
300ml/10fl oz single cream
170g/6oz vanilla caster sugar
2 tbsp Cognac, or use rum or whisky
170g/6oz granary breadcrumbs
55g/2oz unrefined granulated sugar
4 tbsp water
1 organic egg white (optional)

This was the first ice cream I ever made. I'm including it in the classics chapter because I rather feel that is what it has become. It is cream, rather than custard based, so gave confidence to an inexperienced cook. I have seen many recipes for it since but none with granary bread, which gives a better texture than wholemeal and a slightly malty flavour to the ice cream.

Whisk the creams together with the vanilla sugar and Cognac until they have turned to a light, thick cream. Chill in something shallow in the freezer while you toast the breadcrumbs in a hot oven until golden brown. Keep checking and turning them so that they don't burn.

Put the granulated sugar and water in a pan and boil them hard for a few minutes before leaving them to cool. When cool, mix the breadcrumbs into the syrup and stir it into the chilled creams, which you have scraped into a bowl. Fold all together then beat well, before putting in an ice cream maker to churn, or freeze as for vanilla ice cream opposite.

To make a lighter textured ice cream, beat an egg white to stiff peaks, then fold it into the ice cream after the breadcrumb and syrup mixture.

STRAWBERRY ICE CREAM

225g/8oz strawberries
110g/4oz unrefined icing sugar
juice of half a lemon and half an
    orange
300ml/10fl oz double cream

This is another classic ice cream that doesn't need to have the full custard treatment, just the full cream. It is good for turning raw soft summer fruits into ice cream before they over-ripen. Just make sure you adjust the sugar to the acidity of the fruit, always leaving it a little sharper than you think you need to. That way, when you add the cream, the fruit will retain more of its flavour.

Blitz the strawberries in a food processor, then put them through a nylon sieve, pushing through as much of the pulp as you can. Stir in the sugar and the lemon and orange juice. Whisk the cream until it holds in soft folds and fold the strawberry mixture into it. Churn or freeze in a container (see opposite for more details).

I like to serve fresh raspberries with strawberry ice cream and vice versa.

SORBETS

BASIC SORBET

STOCK SYRUP
225g/8oz vanilla caster sugar
300ml/10fl oz water

Sorbets are a light alternative to cream ices. They really show off the fruit, they are immensely easy to make and ideal if you've had a rich main course such as pork, duck or anything creamy and buttery. It is no more difficult to make two or three sorbets at a time, particularly in mid-summer with all the berries and currants available, since all you have to do is make a larger quantity of stock syrup. Just remember to add the same amount of fruit purée as stock syrup, with a spritz of lemon juice to bring out the flavour of the fruit.

Bring the sugar and water to the boil in a pan and boil for a further 3 minutes until you have a thick, sweet syrup. Leave to cool.

When it is cold, mix the stock syrup with sieved fruit purée and a matching slug of alcohol if you like – Calvados for an apple sorbet, eau de vie de poires for pear, framboise for raspberry, kirsch with almost any scented fruit. Go easy; a couple of tablespoons should be enough flavour-wise and too much alcohol inhibits the freezing process. Add a spritz of lemon, or lime if it's a mango or melon ice, and it's ready for the freezer. See the lemon sorbet recipe below for the next stage.

LEMON SORBET

300ml/10fl oz freshly squeezed
    lemon juice
285g/10oz vanilla caster sugar
600ml/1 pint water
2 organic egg whites

Bring the sugar and water to the boil in a pan and simmer together for 5 minutes. Cool, then add the fresh lemon juice, tasting to make sure you have the right strength and sharpness.

Strain into ice trays, cover and put into the freezer or churn in a sorbetière. Freeze the mixture for 3–4 hours or until you have a firm block of lemon water ice. Whisk the egg whites to stiff peaks. Fold the lemon ice into the egg whites a spoonful at a time until the mixture has bulked up to a foamy mass. Re-freeze in a larger container until the sorbet is firm and snowy.

RASPBERRY SORBET

450g/1lb raspberries, blitzed in a
    food processor and sieved
450ml/16fl oz water
285g/10oz vanilla caster sugar
juice of 1 lemon
juice of 1 orange
2–3 tbsp framboise or kirsch,
    (optional)
2 organic egg whites (optional)

You don't have to add egg whites when you are making a sorbet. I prefer the foamy light texture they give, but you may wish for the purer, iced fruit-water flavour or choose to add just a single whisked egg white.

Purée and sieve the raspberries. Simmer the water and sugar together for 5 minutes. Let it cool and add the lemon and orange juice. Fold in the raspberry purée and add the alcohol if you're using it. Freeze as for the lemon sorbet. Whisk the egg whites if you are using them and the raspberry ice into the whites a spoonful at a time. Re-freeze.

Raspberry Sorbet

LEMON GRANITA

285g/10oz vanilla caster sugar
600ml/1 pint water
300ml/10fl oz freshly squeezed
lemon juice

Bring the sugar and water to the boil in a pan then simmer together for 5 minutes. Cool before adding the fresh lemon juice, tasting to make sure you have the right strength and sharpness. Strain into ice trays, cover and put into the freezer or churn in a sorbetière.

Every 30 minutes stir the frozen edges of the mixture from the side to the middle of the ice trays. Depending on how deep your freezing tray or box is, the mixture should be ready in 2–3 hours, by which time it will be like slushy granules; a granita to the Italians. Serve it scooped into tall glasses with soft amaretti or any sweet pudding biscuit.

COFFEE GRANITA

12 tbsp ground espresso coffee
1.2 litres/2 pints water
55–85g/2–3oz sugar

I remember my first coffee granita, and my second. Both were seminal experiences which countered the mid-afternoon heat of the places I was in – the caffeine hit of the icy granules freezing the throat as they slid down, the feeling of quietly sophisticated sheer pleasure, and the heat being sloughed off by the cold. The first experience was in a famous ice cream shop in Florence called Vivoli's, which I first went to when I was a student. The other great discovery in this wonderful establishment, where I would have happily spent every afternoon trying every ice, was the grapefruit sorbet. We are all used to lemon and orange sorbet, but grapefruit was another orbit; unexpected, unusual, miraculous.

The second granita experience was on my first trip to New York, also as a student. I found myself at a small café in Greenwich Village and simply ordered what everyone else was having in that swampy, breathless heat of an August afternoon. The tall, black glass came with a cloud of whipped chantilly cream at its summit, and all the better for it. I went back every afternoon until I left.

Put the coffee into a tall, warmed jug and pour the boiling water over it. Stir with a wooden spoon and leave to brew. After 10 minutes, strain it and stir in the sugar. When it is cold, pour through a double sheet of muslin into freezing trays. Taste for sugar. Freeze, stirring the sides away from the edge of the container every 30 minutes until it is the texture of slushy granules. Serve in tall glasses with a cloud of crème chantilly – whipped cream sweetened with a little sugar.

CLASSIC FAVOURITES

PAVLOVA

SERVES 6

6 organic egg whites
a pinch of salt
½ tsp cream of tartar
400g/14oz vanilla caster sugar
2 tsp distilled white vinegar

FILLING

300ml/10fl oz double cream
1 tbsp raspberry eau de vie
   (optional)
255g/9oz raspberries
6 wrinkly passion fruit, the flesh and
   seeds scooped out

The essence of this pudding, with its sweeter-than-sweet meringue, is to pair it with a sharp fruit and to make the meringue as gooey and marshmallowy middled as possible in contrast to its shatteringly crunchy exterior. The soft folds of cream complete the picture. So go for raspberries with either redcurrants, bananas or passion fruit. Try cranberries or jewels of pomegranate at Christmas. I have even made a pavlova with caramelised Bramley apples, which my best cooking friend George Morley insisted would make me overcome my pavlova phobia. She was right. Up to a point! In Simon Hopkinson's retro-tome *The Prawn Cocktail Years*, written with Lindsey Bareham, he explains that it is the chemical reaction of vinegar with cream of tartar that produces the magical marshmallowy texture. Simon also says 'don't overdo the fruit' and what Simon says, like the game, we all have to do.

Preheat the oven to 140°C/275°F/Gas 1. Whisk the egg whites with the salt and cream of tartar until frothy. Incorporate three-quarters of the sugar, beating until glossy, very firm and holding stiff peaks. Fold in the remaining sugar and the vinegar.

Cut out a sheet of parchment paper to fit a heavy, flat baking sheet. Draw a 25cm/10in circle on the paper, dampen it with a little water and place it on the baking sheet. Spoon the egg whites onto the circle and smooth and shape into a nest, making sweeping, scalloped edges with a damp tablespoon. Bake in the bottom of the preheated oven for 1–1½ hours until the meringue is crusty on the outside and just set on the inside. Allow it to cool, then carefully peel off the paper and transfer the meringue to a serving plate.

Just before serving, lightly whip the cream, with the eau de vie if you are using it, to form soft peaks. Spoon it into the middle of the meringue, spreading it out towards the edges. Decorate the pavlova with raspberries and passion fruit.

ZABAGLIONE

4 organic egg yolks
80g/scant 3oz unrefined caster sugar
80g/scant 3oz Vin Santo

Ethereal, foamy, this is a whisper of a pudding with its gentle warmth and heady scent of Vin Santo. It comes from my favourite Italian chef Francesco Zanchetta at Riva, Andrea Riva's wonderful restaurant in Barnes. I have never eaten less than superlatively well here and have long since stopped asking for the menu, preferring to let Andrea ask Francesco just to cook something we'll like. I have also been making Francesco's zabaglione-based tiramisu ever since he gave me the recipe, and his budino, which is unequalled. In season, his homemade taglierini with a snowstorm of fresh white truffles grated over it is the best I've ever had and that includes some in Alba, the home of the truffle.

Place the egg yolks, sugar and Vin Santo in a copper or stainless steel bowl and put it over a pan of gently simmering water. Beat the mixture with a whisk, increasing the speed and circular motion as it becomes paler, light and fluffy. The zabaglione is ready when, lifting the whisk from the bowl, the mixture peaks and floats a little before melting in again with the bulk of it. Pour into stemmed glasses and serve with boudoir biscuits.

POACHED PEACHES IN AN ORANGE-FLOWER SABAYON

SERVES 6–8

8–10 peaches
500ml/18fl oz water
500ml/18fl oz white wine
200g/7oz caster sugar
1 orange, sliced
½ a lemon, sliced
1 vanilla pod

SABAYON
6 organic egg yolks
100g/3½oz caster sugar
pinch of salt
120ml/4fl oz sweet white wine
4 tbsp fresh lime juice
3 tbsp fresh orange juice
1 tbsp orange-flower water

The sabayon is just the French version of the Italian zabaglione and makes a wonderfully light sauce, less rich than cream or custard, for any poached fruit. It's particularly good with the summer scented fruits like peaches, nectarines and apricots. You don't have to use sweet white wine, you may use framboise instead if you are making the sabayon for peaches, but 3–4 tablespoons is enough. Use kirsch for poached cherries. White peaches are the ones to go for flavour-wise and be sure they are ripe. Unlike plums, under-ripe peaches are not improved by poaching; they remain acidic and hard, not juicy fleshed and with the right balance of acid to sweetness. This is a sublime recipe of which I am both fond and proud; it never fails to elicit a gasp.

Put the peaches in a saucepan with the water, wine, sugar, orange, lemon and vanilla pod. Bring to the boil, skim, then cover with a circle of greaseproof paper cut to fit inside the pan with a little air hole snipped into the middle of it. Simmer very gently for 15–20 minutes. Let the peaches cool in the syrup, then peel off the skins, halve and remove the stones. Reserve the syrup.

For the sabayon, put the egg yolks, caster sugar and salt into a bowl and whisk. Add the wine and 120ml/4fl oz of the poaching syrup and whisk in a double boiler over simmering water for about 10 minutes or until the mixture leaves a ribbon trail when the whisk is lifted. Whisk in the lime juice, orange juice and orange-flower water. Spoon the sabayon generously over the peach halves.

PASSION FRUIT ROULADE

This was a recent Christmas offering from the incomparable Nigel Slater, and it would whet the appetite of even the most doubtful of rouladers.

SERVES 8–10

6 large organic eggs
100g/3½oz vanilla caster sugar
2 lemons
2 heaped tbsp plain flour

FILLING
12 wrinkled passion fruits
340g/12oz lemon or orange curd (to
    make your own see p. 488)
270–300ml/9–10fl oz double cream
unrefined icing sugar

Preheat the oven to 180°C/350°F/Gas 4. You will need a baking tray measuring roughly 36 x 30cm/14 x 12in with shallow sides. Line the tray with a piece of baking parchment making sure it comes up the sides of the tray.

Separate the eggs. Whisk the yolks with the sugar until thick and pale. Grate the zest of both lemons, making sure there is no pith, and squeeze the juice of one of them. Beat the egg whites until they are thick and just capable of standing in soft peaks. Fold the juice and zest into the egg yolk and sugar mixture, followed by the sieved flour. Then add the egg whites slowly and gently so the air is not knocked out of them. It is crucial not to over-mix. Scoop the mixture into the lined baking tin, smoothing it gently out to the edges.

Bake for about 10 minutes until the top is very lightly coloured and it feels softly set. It should barely colour. Let it cool for a few minutes.

Put a large piece of greaseproof paper on the work surface and turn the roulade out onto it. Be fairly forthright: just tip the roulade out in one swift movement. The cake should be crust-side down. Carefully peel away the paper and cover the roulade with a damp tea towel. It will be fine like this for an hour or so, or even overnight.

When you are ready to roll, remove the towel and spread the curd over the surface. Whip the cream to soft peaks and spread it over the curd. Cut 8 of the passion fruits in half and spread the juice and seeds over the cream. Now take one short end of the greaseproof paper and use it to help you roll up the roulade. If the surface cracks, then all to the good. Dust with icing sugar and serve cut into thick slices, with the remaining passion fruit juice and seeds squeezed over each slice.

CHOCOLATE PUDDINGS

CHOCOLATE ROULADE

SERVES 6–8

6 large organic eggs
75g/2½oz vanilla caster sugar
55g/2oz dark cocoa powder,
   Green and Black's organic
   if possible
200ml/7fl oz double cream
unrefined icing sugar

CHOCOLATE SAUCE
140g/5oz best bitter chocolate,
   70% or more cocoa solids
1 tbsp golden syrup
45g/1½oz unsalted butter
1 tsp espresso coffee powder stirred
   into 1 tbsp hot brandy or hot
   double cream

It always amazes me that this pudding has never fallen from grace, or at least from the tables of the food fashionistas, when so many joys like lemon mousse and steamed puddings largely have. Roulades and pavlovas have to be the Sloanie puddings of all time. However good or bad the cook, whatever the occasion, the answer always seems to be to serve up a tooth-achingly sweet meringue, with a main artery of cream whipped to within an inch of its life and squozen into its buxom bosom. Either that or a dried up, over-sweet roulade oozing, yet again, a plethora of over-whipped cream. No matter what has gone before, the theme is cream on cream on cream. Here is a positively scrumptious rendering of this well known pudding, one that might whet your appetite for the joys of dark chocolate and cream.

Preheat the oven to 180°C/350°F/Gas 4. Butter and line a 30 x 20cm/12 x 8in shallow-sided baking tray with greaseproof paper. Separate the eggs and beat the yolks with the caster sugar until pale and thick. Sift in the cocoa powder and whisk them together. Whisk the egg whites to stiff peaks, stir a couple of spoonfuls into the chocolate mixture, then cut and fold in the rest lightly and quickly. Pour onto the greaseproof in the baking tray and cook for 15 minutes in the centre of the oven.

Take the roulade out of the oven and let it cool for a few minutes before covering it with a damp tea towel to stop it cracking. Meanwhile, make the sauce. Put the broken squares of chocolate, syrup, butter and the coffee in its hot liquid into the top of a double boiler or in a bowl over a pan of barely simmering water, the bowl not touching the water. Stir over a gentle heat while the chocolate melts.

Whip the cream so that it just holds soft folds. Put a large piece of greaseproof paper down onto the work surface and sift icing sugar over it. Turn the cake upside down onto it in one fell swoop and remove the top layer of greaseproof. Spread the chocolate sauce over it with a palette knife up to 2cm/¾in away from the edges, then cover the sauce with whipped cream. Use the greaseproof to help you roll the roulade into shape. It is bound to crack a little at this point, but that's just how it should look. Put the roulade onto a large serving dish and slice.

COFFEE CRÈME ANGLAISE

MAKES 850ML/1½ PINTS

8 organic egg yolks
75g/2½oz vanilla caster sugar
2 tsp fresh ground coffee
300ml/10fl oz Jersey milk
300ml/10fl oz double cream

This is made with a rich custard, half milk and half cream. It can be flavoured with other ingredients depending on what you are serving it with. For example, try infusing a couple of cardamom pods in the milk and cream for 30 minutes after it has come to the boil. You may do the same with strips of orange peel and sweet orange oil; orange-flower water or rosewater and cinnamon; rosemary or bay; grated ginger and the syrup from the stem ginger jar; rum or Baileys; or chocolate.

Whisk the egg yolks and sugar together thoroughly until pale and creamy and well amalgamated. Put the teaspoons of coffee into the milk and cream in a pan and bring slowly to scald point. Put the bowl with the yolks and sugar over a pan of barely simmering water, the base of the bowl not touching the water, or scrape the egg and yolk mixture into the top of a double boiler. Whisk the coffee-flavoured cream and milk into the yolk and sugar mixture over the hot water and stir or whisk continuously until it thickens. Pour through a fine sieve to remove any coarse coffee granules. When it has cooled, pour a puddle of sauce onto each plate and top with a slice of chocolate parfait (see below).

CHOCOLATE PARFAIT

SERVES 8

7 organic egg yolks
110g/4oz vanilla caster sugar
200g/7oz best bitter chocolate, chopped
1 tbsp amaretto, brandy or strong freshly made black coffee
600ml/1 pint double cream

A parfait is like a light, almost moussey ice cream, lifted with a foam of beaten eggs and sugar. It can be made well in advance of when you want it and frozen. Turn it out of its loaf tin or terrine a couple of minutes after you take it out of the freezer and it's ready to eat. Make it with half chestnuts if you like, and serve it with the coffee crème Anglaise above or just with cold pouring cream.

Line a 25cm/10in long terrine or loaf tin with clingfilm. Whisk the egg yolks with the vanilla caster sugar over a double boiler in a bowl large enough for the ingredients to expand to well over double their original size; this will take 10–15 minutes. The more you beat, the more the eggs expand in volume, and the lighter the result.

In a separate bowl, melt the chocolate with the amaretto, brandy or coffee, then stir it into the egg and sugar mixture. Pour in the cream and whisk until the mixture forms soft peaks. Pour into the lined terrine and freeze until set.

When you are ready to serve the parfait, dip the terrine into boiling water for a few seconds, turn out on to a plate and peel away the clingfilm.

SIMPLE CHOCOLATE MOUSSE

SERVES 4

200g/7oz best bitter chocolate,
   70% cocoa solids
3 tbsp espresso coffee
30g/1oz unsalted butter
1 tbsp Cognac (optional)
3 large organic eggs, separated

The thrill of pushing the spoon into a dark, lightly airy, yet deeply rich ramekin of chocolate mousse is a constant. It is a perfect pudding, a simple pudding and one that wants no more than to be covered in chilled white pouring cream when you serve it – this has the curious effect of making it seem less rich. Or is this an illusion? The first chocolate mousse I made was a simple one, with far less good chocolate than the Callebaut and Valrhona we have now. I still make it like this sometimes, but try the rich version below, too, for special occasions.

Break the chocolate into squares and put it in a bowl with the coffee and butter. Place in the top of a double boiler or in a bowl over simmering water; the bottom of the bowl must not touch the water. The water must stay at a bare simmer throughout. Melt everything together, stirring gently, then remove from the heat and stir in the booze if you are using it. My children hate brandy, so I spurn it when they're going to be eating the mousse.

While the mixture is still hottish, stir in the yolks, one at a time. Whisk the egg whites to stiff peaks. Stir the first tablespoon into the chocolate to slacken the mixture, then fold in the rest in large spoonfuls. Work lightly and gently to keep the air in the mousse.

Scrape into ramekins or a single glass serving bowl and cover. Chill in the fridge for at least 6 hours but overnight if it suits you better. Serve with thin pouring cream, which you can pour over the top of the individual ramekins if you like before serving them.

MOUSSE AU CHOCOLAT, THE RICH VERSION

SERVES 8–10

140g/5oz vanilla caster sugar
3 whole organic eggs, separated
3 extra yolks
1 tbsp Green and Black's cocoa
   powder
200ml/7fl oz double cream
85g/3oz unsalted butter
225g/8oz best bitter chocolate,
   I use L'Atelier's 70% couverture
   chocolate or Valrhona 64%
1 tbsp Armagnac or Cognac
extra double cream and dark
   chocolate

This is the Ferrari of chocolate mousses, rich, velvety, louche and luxuriant. It will leave you in no doubt that there is a more breathtaking spoonful of deepest, darkest, butter-smooth chocolate pleasure than you had even considered possible when you made your first, simple version.

Put 55g/2oz of the sugar, all 6 egg yolks, the cocoa powder and the cream in the top of a double saucepan or a bowl over simmering water. Keep whisking it over a gentle heat until it thickens enough to coat a wooden spoon. Take off the heat, add small pieces of the butter and chocolate and stir until fully melted. Add the alcohol and stir it in.

Whisk the three egg whites with the rest of the sugar, adding the sugar as you whisk, not at the end. This method makes a thickly glossy meringue that you want to whisk to soft-peak stage. Decant the chocolate mixture into a bowl and lightly fold in the meringue. Pour into a large bowl or individual glasses and refrigerate before serving. When you're ready to eat, whisk some more double cream to hold soft peaks and spoon onto the mousse. Grate over a little dark chocolate.

Rich Chocolate Mousse

FRUIT

Fruit is at its best when ripe and raw and eaten at its prime — unadulterated, and in your fingers. To eat a warm-fleshed, scented-with-ripeness peach in the morning sun under the tree whose bough you have just plucked it from, is one of life's simple but unsurpassed pleasures. The trouble is, you have to head south to Nîmes, Valencia or Seville to do it!

What we have instead, in these colder, more northerly climes, are superlative raspberries and strawberries and ancient orchards of stoned, pipped and berried fruits. There are few dishes more redolent of perfect summers than a plate of brilliant, garnet-hued, glossy cherries, icy cold from the fridge or set over ice on a dish, served with an unpasteurised goat's cheese like the Irish beauty Mine-Gabhar or an unctuously creamy English sheep's milk cheese such as Wigmore. Little else is needed for an al fresco lunch other than a bowl of fresh raspberries or strawberries, warmed by our gentle sun and served with a dripping clot of thick, ivory cream.

I'm sure this is why so many of our puddings require no transmogrification of the fruit itself from raw to cooked. What they need, at most, is to be puréed or crushed raw into fools or creams or ice cream, or to bask in syrup heaven in a fruit salad, with perhaps some scented sweet Muscat or a nip of kirsch. Or, as with a summer pudding, the juices are bled from the fruit so that the fruit's raw flavour is kept intact but the essence of its fruitiness can be poured like a libation over the final creation at the table.

But sometimes only a pudding will do, a proper, more heavyweight pudding. We are lucky that our fruits don't all ripen in the warm season, and many of the best are great bottled or frozen. or stored through the autumn for the 'hungry gap' at the turn of the year.

There are still apples stored in my shed at the end of January as I write; there is the joy of jars of dark, almost sinister-looking bottled fruits, their semi-suspended shapes plumped and shoulder to shoulder in their sugary, spicy brews; and fruity alcohols like cherries in vodka, and damson or sloe gin. The Seville oranges are on their way. Cranberries offer tartness, blueberries their cloudy-skinned sweetness. There is still a kept quince or two in the bowl and some quince paste to turn into creams and ice creams.

Florida oranges and grapefruit will give a citrussy boost and freshness at this lean time, and at the fat time, over Christmas, where we eat them in jellies and fruit salads. There are sweet, sticky Medjool dates and glistening pomegranate seeds, pineapples, and mangos — the fruit for all seasons since they are tropical. There are the lovely gooey, mineral-rich, dried vine fruits; prunes and unsulphured, dark, sharp-tasting apricots, all of which lend themselves as well to tarts and pies and steamed puddings as they do to winter creams and baked custards. There are the warming, wintry spices to bake and scent them with and the tart, almost aggressive, mouthy sharpness of the wrinkly, crackle-skinned passion fruit that burst with flavour on the tongue and enliven Valentine's Day, if in name alone! There are the tender candy pink wands of Wakefield rhubarb grown in the dark and harvested by candlelight that make the New Year not just a time for conserved, pickled, bottled and stored fruits and for the flown-in exotica that now blur our seasonal boundaries. But somehow one is always brought back to the Garden of Eden, to the first and finest fruit of them all, the apple.

Baked, stewed, roasted, in compotes or salads, fruits are turned into delicious puddings in these simplest of ways through the changing seasons of the year. A light sugar syrup, a spice or two, a slug of alcohol, a strip of zest or bit of butter is all they need before they are softened or transformed by slow heat or chilling. Serve these simple fruit puddings on their own, with homemade ice cream or any of the pudding cakes that match the fruit: something almondy with apricots, plums, prunes or rhubarb; quince with apple or almond; peaches, nectarines or apricots with vanilla or orange scented things; figs with vanilla, thyme or orange, pears or rhubarb with ginger and so on.

FRUIT SALAD

A basic, every day fruit salad.

SERVES 4–6

2 apples
2 pears
the juice of a lemon
a small bunch of seedless green
    grapes
2 oranges
1 scented melon like Galia, Ogen or
    Charentais
1 small pineapple
1 quantity stock syrup (see p. 336),
    or the juice of two to three extra
    oranges
1–2 passion fruit, optional
a punnet of English strawberries if
    they are in season
1 banana
a few sgs of mint

Peel, core and quarter the apples and pears, cut them into smallish chunks and put them in a glass fruit bowl. Sprinkle over some lemon juice so that they don't discolour. Halve the grapes and add them to the bowl.

Now, here's how to cut the oranges into pithless slices that don't look as though they've been mugged: first cut the ends of the orange off with a small sharp knife so that you just see orange and no pith. Stand the orange up on one end and carve down, following its natural curve and removing the skin to leave just orange, no pith. Once the orange has been de-nuded of its skin, put the blade of the knife just inside the skin of one of the pegs and slice into it, repeat down the other side of the peg and extract it. Work your way round the orange like this, putting the pegs in the fruit salad as you go.

Cut the melon into slices, remove the seeds and cut into wedges, putting them in the bowl with the other fruit and as much juice as you can save. Remove the skin and little brown core-like bits from the pineapple and cut it into thick circles. Remove the core with the apple corer and cut the rest into chunks, adding them to the bowl. Hull the strawberries and split the big ones lengthways down the middle. Put them in the bowl up to 30 minutes before you are going to eat the fruit salad. Add the stock syrup or orange juice, then scoop out the middles of the passion fruit and add them as a decoration on top. Cover and chill for 30 minutes in the fridge and add the chopped banana just before serving. A few sprigs of mint put in at the end freshen up the look and the flavour.

You can make a good exotic fruit salad with mangoes, pineapple, passion fruit or grenadillos, scented melon, limes and pink grapefruit. A fresh berry salad is also good, made with whatever you can lay your hands on, such as raspberries, loganberries, strawberries, cherries and blueberries, with a few fresh peaches thrown in.

BAKED PLUMS WITH DARK RUM AND DEMERARA

A lovely late summer dish if you have your own plums. If not, use imported ones later in the year. Particularly good with homemade vanilla ice cream.

SERVES 6

12 plums
2 tbsp demerara sugar
2 tbsp dark rum
2 tbsp water
2 or 3 clementines
½ lemon

Preheat the oven to 180°C/350°F/Gas 4. Put the plums in an earthenware dish, sprinkle with a couple of tablespoons of demerara sugar, the same of dark rum, and the same of water. Place a sheet of greaseproof paper over the top, and bake for 20–25 minutes or until just tender when pierced with the point of a skewer.

Test the juice. It will be too sweet. Squeeze the clementines and half a lemon, and stir the juice into the syrup. Adjust if you need to. The plums will have burst out of their jackets revealing their pretty pomegranate-pink flesh. Cool them in the dish, then refrigerate.

BAKED BERRIED APPLES ROLLED IN CINNAMON SUGAR

SERVES 4

1 large apple per person, scored
   around its middle with the point of
   a knife and thoroughly cored
   nearly to the base
½ cinnamon stick crushed in a
   mortar to give 1 tsp cinnamon
2 tbsp unrefined granulated or
   demerara sugar
30g/1oz unsalted butter, melted
4 tbsp blackberries or blueberries
splosh of sloe gin (see p. 490)
double cream

Experiment with this simple, but delicious fruit pudding, more exotic than the version on page 189. Why not use prunes and sharp apricots with a few twists of nubbly walnut rather than just vine fruits? Or try an almond paste scented with orange zest, some blackberries with a little kirsch, a few chopped dates and almonds. The cinnamon-scented sugar was divine inspiration. I must have had it in my pudding memory from the very best crisp-fried doughnuts I ever ate in America. Always grind the cinnamon in the mortar yourself – very little extra effort for a very much muskier, sweeter, fresher whiff of the lovely bark.

Heat the oven to 180°C/350°F/Gas 4. Make sure the cavities of the apples are cleanly cored. Mix the cinnamon with the sugar, then brush each apple with the warm melted butter before rolling it all over in the cinnamon sugar.

Sit the apples on a baking tray, then plop a spoonful of berries into the cavity. Add a little extra melted butter and some sugar on top.

Bake until soft right through when spiked with a skewer. This should take about 25–30 minutes, unless the apples are enormous. Once they are crustily caramelised, put the apples in bowls and pour a splosh of sloe gin over them. Serve with a jug of cold, thick cream.

ROASTED PLUMS IN CINNAMON BUTTER SYRUP

SERVES 4

12 plums
55g/2oz butter
55g/2oz vanilla sugar
1 split vanilla pod
1 cinnamon stick

A real wintery taste, the plums caramelise in the dark sugary spiced juices and are delicious served with a spice ice cream like nutmeg, ginger or cinnamon (see page 452).

Heat the oven to 190°C/375°F/Gas 5. Halve and stone the plums and place them in a single layer in a large, heavy-bottomed casserole. Melt the butter in a small pan with the sugar, vanilla pod and cinnamon stick, then trickle it over the plums. Roast for 15 minutes, or until tender, basting every 5 minutes. Remove the vanilla pod and the cinnamon stick and cool the plums.

BLUEBERRY, RASPBERRY AND STRAWBERRY COBBLER

SERVES 4

900g/2lb berries (strawberries, raspberries, blackberries, blueberries)
2–3 tbsp light muscovado sugar
30g/1oz butter, cut into small pieces
100g/3½oz chilled unsalted butter
225g/8oz plain organic flour
2 tsp baking powder
3 tbsp unrefined caster sugar
170ml/6fl oz double cream

I suppose a cobbler is really a sort of pie with a scone-like crust and to my mind it is one of the finest puddings there is, with the purple juices bleeding through the crisp golden crust in between its gaps. I made this combination several times last summer in Ireland – keeping the strawberries whole so they didn't turn to pink cottonwool – and it was a triumph. Blueberries are much better flavoured when cooked, and the cobbler top is somehow lighter than a fruit pie. I also made a plum version which was delicious, as would be apple and blackberry. Serve with lots of Jersey cream.

Heat the oven to 200°C/400°F/Gas 6. Put the fruit into a baking dish and scatter over the muscovado sugar and little knobs of butter.

Rub the 100g/3½oz unsalted butter into the flour and baking powder in a large bowl. Don't over-mix it because this will make the cobbler too oily. When you have a fine breadcrumb texture, lightly and quickly stir in all but a tablespoon of the caster sugar and all the cream using a fork.

Shape the dough into little biscuits about 5cm/2in in diameter and about 1cm/½in thick, and place them on top of the fruit. Sprinkle the rest of the sugar over the top and bake for about 40 minutes. The fruit will peep through a little and bleed delectably into the dough as it bubbles up and bakes. Serve with plenty of double or clotted cream.

COMPOTE OF PEARS WITH QUINCE AND VANILLA

4 quinces
1 vanilla pod
225g/8oz sugar
8 large pears

This beguiling and beautiful dish becomes a deep garnet red as it cooks. The recipe comes from Jane Grigson's seminal *Fruit Book*.

Rub any fluff from the quinces. Wash them and remove the peel, then quarter and core. Put the vanilla pod and quince debris into a pan and cover generously with boiling water. Cover the pan and simmer steadily for 30 minutes. Strain off the liquid into another pan, take out the vanilla pod and put it into the pan with the liquid, plus the sliced quince and sugar. Simmer with a lid on the pan, until the fruit begins to become tender and the liquid looks deep pink.

Peel and core the pears, then cut them into wedges. Put them carefully into the pan, cover and leave to simmer until the pear slices are tender.

Remove the fruit to a bowl with a slotted spoon. Taste and consider the liquid: if it is copious and watery, boil it down hard. It should have a syrupy consistency. Pour over the fruit, putting the pod on top, and leave to chill. Serve with cream and little biscuits such as shortbread (see page 30).

Blueberry, Raspberry and Strawberry Cobbler

STEWED RHUBARB WITH HONEY AND ORANGE

SERVES 4

450g/1lb rhubarb (forced if possible)
juice and zest of an organic orange
2 heaped tbsp acacia or other mild-
   tasting runny honey
¼ tsp ground ginger

Cut the rhubarb into 4cm/1½in pieces and put them in a pan. Add the juice and zest of the orange and the honey and sprinkle over the ginger. Bring to simmering point, then cover and cook for 7–8 minutes. Don't cook it any more or it will turn to threads, unless it is of the older, fatter variety available later in the year. Instead, remove the pan from the heat and let the rhubarb cool with the lid on. It will continue to poach in the juice as it cools.

BAKED RHUBARB

450g/1lb young rhubarb
110g/4oz vanilla caster sugar

Choose the tender pink wands of early forced rhubarb that you don't even have to peel. The lower the temperature and the slower they are cooked, the more they will exude deliciously syrupy juices, so don't add any water. To each 450g/1lb of fruit add 110g/4oz vanilla sugar. Make more than you need as rhubarb is delicious cold with honey and yoghurt, with vanilla ice cream, or on its own for breakfast, lunch or supper.

Heat the oven to 130°C/250°F/Gas ½. Cut the rhubarb into 4cm/1½ in lengths, or double this if you like the idea of batons, and put it into an earthenware or ovenproof dish that has a lid. Scatter the sugar over the top of the rhubarb and cover it tightly with a layer of greaseproof paper and the lid. Bake for 20 minutes before checking, then subsequently every 10 minutes or so, until the rhubarb is tender and has stewed to softness in its own juice but not lost its shape.

SPICE-ROASTED FIGS WITH BALSAMIC VINEGAR

A mellow, spicy, delicious way of roasting figs.

SERVES 4

12 figs
3 tbsp mild honey like acacia
150ml/5fl oz stock syrup (see p. 336)
1 cinnamon stick
3 cloves
3 star anise
a thumb of root ginger
2 strips orange peel without the pith
1 split vanilla pod
3–4 bruised black peppercorns
3 tbsp aged balsamic vinegar

Heat the oven to 150°C/300°F/Gas 2. Cut off the tips of the figs and cut little crosses in the tops of them, as you do on Brussels sprouts. Put them upright, cheek by jowl and tightly packed, in an enamel baking dish.

Put all the other ingredients into a small pan, bring to the boil and boil hard for 3–4 minutes until reduced to a syrupy sauce. Brush the syrup over the figs and cook for about 30 minutes until soft, basting every few minutes. Serve them warm in their syrup or cold with pouring cream or a spice or vanilla ice cream.

Baked Rhubarb

QUINCES IN SYRUP

SERVES 4

juice of ½ a lemon
225g/8oz unrefined sugar
4 small quinces or 2 very large ones,
  weighing about 900g/2lb in total
clotted cream

Fill a pan with 1 litre/1¾ pints of boiling water and add the lemon juice and sugar.

Wash the quinces and scrub to remove the light down that covers their skin in patches. Cut them in half through the core but do not peel them. Quinces are extremely hard, so you will need a strong knife and a lot of strength. Do not core them. The pips are important as they produce a wonderful reddish-pink jelly.

Cook the quinces as soon as they are cut, as the flesh discolours quickly. Put them, cut side down, into the pan, adding more water if necessary to cover, and simmer until tender. This takes 20–60 minutes. Watch the fruit so that it doesn't fall apart.

As soon as the quinces are tender, lift them out. When they are cool enough to handle, cut out the cores with a pointed serrated knife and throw them back into the pan. Reduce the syrup by simmering, then return the fruit to the pan and cook until the syrup becomes reddish and thick. It can take more than an hour to turn into a reddish jelly.

Arrange the quince halves, cut-side up, on a serving dish and pour the syrup on top. It will turn into a jelly when it cools. Serve chilled or at room temperature with dollops of clotted cream.

ROASTED QUINCES

Baking the rock-hard fruit whole is a great way to cook a quince. Once they are soft, you can treat them in a number of ways.

SERVES 4

4 small quinces
4 tsp unsalted butter
8 tbsp unrefined sugar
clotted cream (optional)
seeds of a pomegranate

Heat the oven to 190°C/380°F/Gas 5. Roast the quinces whole on a baking tray until they feel soft. Depending on their size and ripeness, this can take 45 minutes to 2 hours, so watch them.

Cut the quinces in half down through the core and cut out the cores with a sharp paring knife. Put them cut-side up on a baking dish with a sliver of butter on top of each and sprinkle with sugar – 1 tablespoon on the smaller halves and 2 on the larger ones. Put the quinces back in the oven for about 30 minutes until they are very soft and have turned a rich burgundy colour. Alternatively, put them under the grill for a minute until the sugar has caramelised. Serve hot or cold with clotted cream. Strew with pomegranate seeds just before serving.

FRUIT TARTS

TARTE AUX POMMES

SERVES 6–8

450g/1lb cooking apples
170–200g/6–7oz vanilla sugar
1 vanilla pod, split lengthways
450g/1lb eating apples such as Cox's
45g/1½oz butter, melted

PÂTE SUCRÉE

170g/6oz flour
pinch of sea salt
85g/3oz unsalted butter
2 dsrtsp icing sugar
2 organic egg yolks

French apple tarts are legendary and there are many different versions. This one has an underbelly of sharp apple purée beneath the little buttery sugared crescents of apple. Pâte sucrée (sweet pastry) makes a good contrast with the tartness of the purée.

Make the pâte sucrée (see page 182). Chill, then roll out and and line a 23cm/9in tart tin.

Peel, core and roughly chop the cooking apples. Stew them very gently with 110g/4oz of the sugar and the vanilla pod and its scraped-out seeds in a covered saucepan until almost puréed. You can then sieve the apples if you wish, or merely leave them to cool, depending on whether you prefer a coarsely textured or smooth result. Taste for sharpness, and stir in a bit more sugar if you have a wickedly sweet tooth.

Preheat the oven to 200°C/400°F/Gas 6. When the apples are cold, fill the uncooked pastry case with your apple purée. Peel and slice the eating apples and arrange them over the purée as artistically as you like. Brush the slices with the melted butter and sprinkle over the remaining sugar. Bake for about 35 minutes.

Serve hot, with cold pouring cream. If you want to add a sophisticated note to what is essentially rustic food, make a sabayon (see page 340) with some Calvados or cider.

KEY LIME PIE

SERVES 6–8

4 organic egg yolks
1 x 400g/14oz can sweetened condensed milk
1 tsp finely grated lime zest
150ml/5fl oz freshly squeezed lime juice
fully baked shortcrust pastry case in a 23cm/9in tin (see p. 181)
240ml/8fl oz double cream
1 tbsp unrefined caster sugar

This is the all-American classic, but that's no reason for it not to be here. We love American pie: their pecan pie is already something of a classic here too, and we are becoming acquainted with their pumpkin pie, shoofly pie, black bottom cream pie and Mississippi mud pie. The names alone are enough to get me baking. If you can get your hands on a bottle of pure Key lime juice from Florida you're halfway there. If not, the ordinary kind will do.

Preheat the oven to 180°C/350°F/Gas 4. Whisk together the egg yolks, condensed milk and half the lime zest, then slowly stir in the lime juice. Pour the mixture into the pastry shell and bake for 20 minutes. Let the pie cool on a wire rack before refrigerating it for about 2 hours or until chilled.

Decorate the top with pinches of lime zest. If you want to go very rich, whip the double cream, fold in the sugar and the rest of the lime zest, then dollop it on top of the pie.

TARTE TATIN

The classic of classic French apple puddings, the one we remember when we think of long, languorous French lunches off some beaten track; the kind that begin at midday in those lovely provincial towns and villages throughout France, whose clocks chime to send their inhabitants to a well-prepared table, to a glass of the local wine, bread from the village bakery, cheese from down the road, and a chef who is probably following his father and his grandfather before him. Where most of the produce comes from within a ten-mile radius and the locals all meet as if by divination for Sunday lunch, fêtes, weddings and birthdays at the local restaurant's linen-clad tables. Before I am accused of film-score sentimentality, it is important that you know that this famous tart was invented by the Tatin sisters at the Hotel Terminus Tatin near Orléans. History does not relate whether this famous tarte renversée was then made with other fruits in the way we now do, even using the principle for savoury tarts such as shallot, endive or tomato, or whether the sisters held a torch for the purity of the original.

I have eaten and made many of these tarts over the years and believe that my Le Creuset tatin pan turns out the best ones and that it is important not to let the fruit juices leak into the pastry to such an extent that it becomes sodden. This happens more with juicy fruits like pears and plums and peaches than it does with apples. One solution is to cut the fruit into quarters, rub it with lemon juice and let it dry out in the fridge for a couple of days before making the tatin. Gordon Ramsay once told me that this is what his pâtissier did when I asked him how he coped with the problem. But we are home cooks and will probably not get round to doing it!

One other solution is to poach, say, the pears in sugar, cinnamon and red wine first, though this does mean the fruit is cooked twice. When they are cooked, decant the juice and boil it down, reducing it to a few tablespoons, which are then spooned like a sticky syrup back onto the pears before they are covered with their mantle of pastry. This way you will not get the bitter caramelised finish that I love in contrast to the sweet fruit, but it will sort out the pastry problem. Other than that, just remember not to turn the tart out until the moment you are going to serve it – that way your pastry will remain crisp.

If anyone thinks turning out a tatin is a feat, or sleight of hand only performable by a magician or Michelin-starred chef, please think again. It is a very easy turn-and-plonk operation and it ALWAYS turns out in one. The most important thing is to make sure that the plate you are turning it onto is bigger than the tatin and has enough of a lip to capture the moat of buttery, fruity, caramelised juices that will run from the tart when it has been renverséed.

SERVES 8

FILLING
85g/3oz vanilla caster sugar
55g/2oz unsalted butter
8–10 crisp, good-flavoured eating
   apples
juice of 1 lemon

SHORTCRUST PASTRY
180g/6oz flour
pinch of sea salt
85g/3oz unsalted butter

Make the pastry (see page 181) and chill while you prepare the apples. You can also use puff pastry (see page 301) instead.

Preheat the oven to 180°C/350°F/Gas 4. Put the sugar in the frying pan (one that can also be put in the oven, see opposite) in a thin layer and heat gently. Watch it all the time, as some bits will brown before others. You want the sugar to melt to a dark brown liquid all over without burning. On no account stir it. Just shake the pan and turn it as you need to redistribute the sugar. Remove from the heat and immediately add tiny bits of butter, about one-third of the 55g/2oz, over the sugar. It will bubble instantly.

Peel and slice all the apples into quarters except one, which you should peel and cut in half. Core them all. Squeeze some lemon juice over them to prevent them from discolouring. Put a half apple, cut-side up, in the middle of the pan, then a wheel of quarters around it, tightly packed. Dot with the remaining butter and place over a gentle heat to start it cooking. Remove from the heat.

Roll out the pastry to a circle just bigger than the frying pan. Roll it loosely over your rolling pin and use it to blanket the apples. Tuck the pastry down the sides of the pan like bedclothes to seal in all your apples, and bake in the middle of the oven for 25–30 minutes. Remove from the oven and leave to cool for 10 minutes. Cover the pan with a serving plate and flip the tart over on to it. Any stray fruit can be rearranged. The fruit should look glossily, gloopily burnished.

SERVES 8 GREEDY PEOPLE

about 1kg/2¼lb strawberries
about 4 tbsp redcurrant jelly

PÂTE SUCRÉE
225g/8oz flour
110g/4oz unsalted butter
3 dsrtsp unrefined icing sugar
the scooped out insides of a vanilla
    pod
2 organic egg yolks
a little cold water

CRÈME PÂTISSIÈRE
340ml/12fl oz Jersey milk
150ml/5fl oz double cream
1 vanilla pod, split lengthways, the
    seeds scooped out with the sharp
    tip of a teaspoon
1 large organic egg
3 large yolks
75g/2½oz vanilla caster sugar
45g/1½oz cornflour

STRAWBERRY TART

This is the spirit of summer, the tart that the first June strawberries are all about, set into the thickly creamy, vanilla-scented crème pâtissière right up to their middles and crowned with a sticky gloop of redcurrant. I make this every summer, at least once. My children all insist and vote it top of the summer pudding list, though Harry is its number one devotee. You may use raspberries instead, or a cornucopia of summer fruit, dangly branches of redcurrants and whitecurrants with strawberries, raspberries, blueberries, peaches and figs, glazing the paler fruits with apricot jam instead of redcurrant jelly. This is not a tart to be served up the following day; the crème pâtissière tends to soften and dampen the pastry within a few hours of making. No hardship there, just eat it all up at one sitting.

Make the pâte sucrée (page 182) and chill for at least an hour. Preheat the oven to 200°C/400°F/Gas 6. Line a 30cm/12in tart tin with the pastry and bake blind (see page 181), then remove the beans and return to the oven for 10–15 minutes, until golden and cooked. Watch closely: the edges burn swiftly, and you don't want scorch marks on the bottom. Leave to cool.

Turn the cold pastry case out on to a plate or bread board and scrape in the crème pâtissière (see below) with a rubber spatula. Hull the strawberries. Starting at the edge of the tart and with the largest strawberries, place them upright into the crème pâtissière in a circle. Work your way in, using smaller strawberries for each circle. Melt the redcurrant jelly with a tablespoon of water and brush it liberally over the strawberries and the custardy gaps. Stand back and admire before you cut into slices.

CRÈME PÂTISSIÈRE

This is a very amenable custard to make. The cornflour will stop it splitting and you just need to beat the hell out of it to get rid of the tiny, floury lumps. To avoid a skin forming on the top of the custard when it has been cooked and is cooling, rub a little butter over the surface with a knife.

Pour the milk and cream into a heavy-bottomed pan and throw in the vanilla pod and the scraped-out seeds. Bring to scald point over a gentle heat. Meanwhile, whisk the egg, egg yolks and sugar together with a balloon whisk until light, creamy and pale. Sift one-third of the cornflour into the bowl and whisk thoroughly until the mixture is smooth. Then do the same with the next third and the last third, making absolutely sure you have beaten out the lurking lumps.

Remove the vanilla pod from the hot milk and pour one-third of the milk into the egg and sugar mixture, whisking well. Pour this back into the rest of the milk in the pan, and continue to whisk as vigorously as you can over a gentle heat as the custard begins to thicken. Keep whisking as it simmers for another 5 minutes to cook out the floury taste, just as you do for a béchamel. Pour it into a bowl, cover and cool before using. Crème pâtissière can also be used for sweet soufflés and choux pastry, either as is or flavoured with chocolate.

BAKEWELL TART

SERVES 8

170g/6oz really good raspberry jam;
strawberry is good too
110g/4oz unsalted butter
110g/4oz vanilla sugar
110g/4oz ground almonds
4 organic egg yolks and 3 egg whites
1 tsp bitter almond extract (I use
Culpeper's)
a handful of flaked almonds

SHORTCRUST PASTRY
170g/6oz plain white flour
pinch of salt
85g/3oz unsalted butter

This is as classic a tart as lemon meringue or treacle and is a real old favourite that you will always have the ingredients for in your store cupboard. It really doesn't matter if you use raspberry, strawberry, apricot or blackcurrant jam for the middle or something more esoteric altogether like damson or rhubarb.

Make the shortcrust pastry in the usual way (see page 181) and use to line a 23cm/9in tart tin. Chill. Preheat the oven to 200°C/400°F/Gas 6. Spread a layer of the jam generously over the pastry base.

Melt the butter until it smells nutty. Whisk together the sugar, ground almonds, egg yolks and whites and almond extract, then pour in the hot butter and whisk to amalgamate. Pour this over the jam and bake for about 30 minutes until lightly browned and just set. After 25 minutes, strew the flaked almonds over the top of the tart, so they get a chance to brown slightly.

A tart to be eaten 20 minutes after it comes out of the oven, warm, with some cold, thin cream.

TARTE AU CITRON

SERVES 10

PASTRY
450g/1lb plain flour
140g/5oz unrefined icing sugar
225g/8oz best unsalted butter, cubed
    and cold
scooped-out seeds from a vanilla pod
2 organic egg yolks

FILLING
9 organic eggs
340g/12oz unrefined vanilla caster
    sugar
juice of 5 organic lemons and the
    zest of 2
270ml/9fl oz double cream
extra icing sugar to caramelise with a
    blow torch

Is there any greater test of a cook? I think not, though at each stage of one's cooking life one does what one is capable of doing, and there's nothing wrong with a journeyman tarte au citron. I just wish I had found a better recipe earlier in my cooking career so I didn't waste all those years turning out decent but dull lemon tarts, tarts that didn't quite have that right degree of rich, vanilla-ed crispness to their pastry, a yielding gel-like sad centre, or the sharpness verging on mouth-hurt of the lemon, brought back from the edge by the contrasting sweet crumbliness of the pastry and the bitter sweet caramelised top. I wish that I had known how to make a tart that had just the right amount of egg yolk and lemon to cream and just the right amount of zest to give that sherbety texture and feel to the gel-like custard. Well here it is, so hone those skills and fear not, I have given you all the help you need to know how to get it right, even if you aren't a serious cook!

These quantities are enough for a 30cm/12in tart ring, which I place directly on to a baking sheet, or the equivalent tart tin with a removable base. If you only have a smaller tart tin, make a few individual tarts with the remainder of the pastry and keep them uncooked in the fridge with the remaining lemon mixture in a jug until you want to use them.

Sieve the flour and icing sugar into a bowl and throw in the chilled, cubed butter. Work to a crumb as quickly as you can or pulse in the food processor. Add the sticky seeds from the vanilla pod and the egg yolks and work into a ball, adding a little ice cold water if you need to, a tablespoon at the most. Wrap in clingfilm and put in the fridge for 30 minutes.

Heat the oven to 180°C/350°F/Gas 4. Flour your marble or work surface and the rolling pin, then roll the pastry out to a circle just a little bigger than the ring or tart tin. Grease the tin or the inside of the ring and the baking tray. Gently ease the pastry over the back of the rolling pin and into the tin. It will shrink, so work it loosely into the tin and don't stretch it. Let the overhang remain at this stage. Bake blind for 15 minutes (see page 181), remove the foil and beans, cut off the shrunken overhang of pastry and prick the bottom and sides of the pastry with the tines of a fork to prevent them bubbling up before returning the tart base to the oven for 5 minutes.

Meanwhile make the filling. Whisk the eggs with the sugar and lemon zest, then stir in the lemon juice and fold in the cream. Put the mixture in a jug so it is easier to pour into the tart case.

Reduce the oven temperature to 130°C/250°F/Gas ½. Slide the tart case as far out of the oven as you dare and pour in the filling up to the top of the pastry. Gently push the tart back into the oven and cook for 30 minutes or until the centre is still juddery without being liquid. The custard will go on cooking out of the oven and you don't want it to set solid. Cool completely.

Heat the grill. Sieve a thin layer of icing sugar over the top of the tart and flash it under the grill briefly without letting the pastry edges burn. Cover the pastry edges with a strip of foil if necessary to stop them burning. Or get out your blowtorch and blow. Serve warm or cold. This tart has to be made only 3 or 4 hours at the most before you serve it. Pastry is never the same if left for a day or overnight.

SPONGE PUDDINGS

These used to be all about suet; about pudding basins, steam-drenched kitchens and welter-weight crusts enclosing murky, treacly depths; or the jammy, sticky, clotted strawberry heaven of guard's pudding, the burst lemon and brackish, buttery, molasses sugar lake of the Sussex pond pudding; or the black-pocked delight of the spotted Dick, moated with speckly homemade vanilla custard.

These are things we turn to more rarely nowadays, the gut and the girth resisting such delights unless a cold snap combined with fevered exercise nullifies the guilt factor. Instead there are lovely light tangy lemon sponges sitting atop their liquid lemon custards; apple or rhubarb sponges as fruity as they are spongy; gushing chocolate sponges whose sad centres pour molten black in sexy puddles on the plate; upside-down pear or pineapple or banana sponges caramelised away from pure sweetness. These are great British puddings, relying on lightness of touch and ingredient rather than Berlin Walls of suet and stodge and winter ballast.

Some suetless sponges are steamed while others are baked. Sponge puddings can be based upon the same weight of butter, sugar, flour and eggs, or, for economy, you may use up to half the weight of flour again. Milk is used to make a dropping consistency – this means the uncooked sponge mixture slides and plops willingly off the spoon.

EVE'S PUDDING

An apple sponge that can be made the plain, classic way as below or with half quince, half apple; with orange zest, cinnamon or cloves; with chopped walnuts turned into the apple purée; or ground almonds in place of half the flour.

SERVES 4

FRUIT
450g/1lb Bramley apples
85g/3oz unrefined granulated or light muscovado sugar, or to taste
4 cloves or 1 tsp cinnamon or allspice

SPONGE
140g/5oz unsalted butter, softened
110g/4oz vanilla caster sugar
2 organic eggs
grated zest of a lemon
110g/4oz plain flour
1 tsp baking powder
a little milk

Preheat oven to 180°C/350°F/Gas 4. Peel, core and slice the apples thinly, then put them in a heavy-bottomed pan with a couple of tablespoons of water, the granulated sugar and the cloves. If you are using ground spice, don't put it in at this stage. Put a lid on the pan and cook the apples slowly, stirring from time to time as the slices closest to the heat will soften first. When the apples have begun to lose their shape and are soft, take them off the heat, remove the cloves and stir in 30g/1oz of the butter with the ground spice if you are using it. Put the mixture in the bottom of a greased pie dish.

Cream together the butter and vanilla sugar until light and pale and fluffy. Beat the eggs in one at a time. Add the lemon zest and sift in the flour and baking powder, folding in well with a metal spoon. Mix to a soft dropping consistency with a little milk. Spread the sponge mix over the apple and bake for 40–45 minutes. Serve with cream or custard.

FRUIT SPONGE

Using the basic sponge mixture on page 361, you can make a fruit sponge with any whole fruit in the same way, apricots, peaches, gooseberries or plums being particularly good. The fruit doesn't need precooking, just sprinkle it with sugar in the pie dish. Small stoned fruit like apricots and plums should be halved and stoned first, peaches and nectarines should be scalded and peeled, then halved, stoned and each half sliced into 3 or 4 pieces. To skin the fruit, pour boiling water over it and spike a slit in the skin. Wait for a minute, then pour off the water and peel the fruit once it has cooled enough to handle.
This only works if the fruit is ripe. Unripe fruit isn't worth skinning, cooking or eating!

APPLE AND WALNUT SPONGE

A lovely autumnal dish, this is just a bit of a riff on the Eve version on the previous page.

SERVES 6

6 medium-sized apples that will purée
3 strips of organic orange peel and the juice of the orange
about 85g/3oz light muscovado sugar to taste

SPONGE

140g/5oz unsalted butter, softened
140g/5oz unrefined vanilla caster sugar
110g/4oz self-raising flour, sifted
1 tsp baking powder
55g/2oz walnuts, ground coarsely
2 large organic eggs

CRUMBLE TOP

55g/2oz plain flour
55g/2oz unrefined granulated sugar
55g/2oz unsalted butter
1 heaped tsp cinnamon (preferably ground in a mortar)

First prepare the apples. Peel and chop, then cook them uncovered in a heavy pan with the orange peel, juice and sugar until they have collapsed, but still have a little texture. Remove the orange peel and leave to cool,

Heat the oven to 190°C/375°F/Gas 5. The sponge can be made in a food mixer. Whizz the butter, sugar, sifted self-raising flour, baking powder, ground walnuts and eggs together until completely smooth. Spread on top of the apples in a greased 23–25cm/9–10in pudding dish.

Whizz the crumble ingredients in a food processor or by hand. Sprinkle a thin layer over the sponge (you do not want a thick, heavy top). If there is any left, keep it for another crumble or use it to top muffins.

Bake on the middle shelf of the oven for about 45 minutes until the topping and the sponge are well browned and risen, and the sponge is clearly set, even in the middle. Leave for 10 minutes before serving with clotted cream, or custard if you are feeling in school mode. Homemade, please.

STICKY TOFFEE BANANA UPSIDE-DOWN CAKE

Toffeed bananas are not just for children. Their soft sweetness lends itself brilliantly to upside-down cakes and they look stunning with the sticky dark lengths of the fruit curving round the cake top when they're turned out.

MAKES A 23CM/9IN CAKE

TOPPING
55g/2oz unsalted butter
55g/2oz light muscovado sugar
4 tbsp double cream
4 bananas sliced in half lengthways

CAKE
110g/4oz unsalted butter, softened
200g/7oz vanilla caster sugar
seeds scraped out of a vanilla pod
4 organic eggs
140g/5oz flour
1 tsp baking powder

Heat the oven to 180°C/350°F/Gas 4. Bubble the butter, sugar and cream for the topping together in a small pan, stirring to amalgamate. Pour the mixture into a 23cm/9in tin, spreading some up the sides as you go. Place the bananas, cut side down, over the topping, arranging them in a wheel or straight across, depending on how they fit best. You may have to cut and stitch.

Beat the butter and vanilla caster sugar with the vanilla seeds in a bowl or food processor until pale, smooth and creamy, then add the eggs, one at a time and continue to beat. Sift the flour and baking powder on to the mixture and fold it in. Scrape it over the bananas, smooth it down and bake for 40 minutes, or until a skewer comes out clean. (I put the tin on a baking tray as the butterscotch has a tendency to leak.)

Remove on to a rack and, after 10 minutes, turn upside down on to a plate if you are going to eat it hot. Otherwise leave it and turn it out when it is still warm. Serve with crème fraîche or vanilla ice cream.

RHUBARB, GINGER AND MUSCOVADO SPONGE

A lovely winter warming pudding with its spice and muscovado.

SERVES 4–6

450g/1lb or so rhubarb, cut into
    batons about 7.5cm/3in long
4 heaped tbsp muscovado sugar

SPONGE
110g/4oz unsalted butter, softened
110g/4oz muscovado sugar
2 organic eggs
110g/4oz plain flour
1 tsp baking powder
1 tsp ginger

Heat the oven to 180°C/350°F/Gas 4. Simmer the rhubarb and sugar together gently until the fruit is cooked through but just maintaining its shape. Drain off all the sticky pink juices and set aside for later. Grease a soufflé dish and put the rhubarb in a layer in the bottom of it.

Cream together the softened butter and sugar thoroughly. Add the eggs, sifted flour, baking powder and ginger a little at a time, scraping them from the sides of the bowl as you go. Smooth the mixture over the top of the fruit and bake for about 30–35 minutes. The sponge will emerge an almost treacly brown. Warm the rhubarb juice to serve from a jug, and offer double cream too.

STEAMED PUDDINGS

The welter weights. What do we think of when we think of steamed puddings? I think of the cannonball weight of the treacle pudding, its dense sweet syrup penetrating the spongy layers as they cook until, when you turn it out and cut into it, a slow, thick treacle puddle oozes out from beneath. This is the sort of pudding that can only be eaten in the middle of the day before enforced, serious exercise to counter the otherwise inevitable state of digestive torpor. Then there are the old school delights, re-fashioned with better ingredients — steamed chocolate pudding with chocolate sauce, steamed ginger pudding, dead man's arm and jam roly-poly. The more gastronomic delights of sticky toffee pudding were not something anyone had heard of until the legendary Francis Coulson of Sharrow Bay in Cumbria came up with his modern classic.

STEAMED TREACLE PUDDING

SERVES 4–6

225g/8oz flour
110g/4oz suet
½ tsp ginger
½ tsp bicarbonate of soda
200ml/7fl oz milk
170g/6oz light or dark muscovado sugar, depending on how molasses-ey you like the taste
225g/8oz golden syrup
zest of a lemon

Sift the flour into a large bowl, add all the other ingredients and mix them together well. Grease an 850ml/1½ pint pudding basin and add the mixture — make sure it has at least a thumb's width to spare at the top as the pudding will expand and rise. Cover the basin with a layer of greaseproof paper with a pleat in the middle of it and then a sheet of foil, also pleated, on top. This, too, leaves room for expansion. Tie string around the rim of the basin to keep the foil on and make a string lid over the top of the pudding so that it is easy to remove from its hot water bath. Put the pudding in a heavy-bottomed pan and pour boiling water halfway up the sides of the basin. Cover with a lid and keep the pudding at a steady simmer for 2 hours, topping up the pan with boiling water when necessary.

Remove the pudding from the water. Cut the string, remove the foil and greaseproof top and leave it for 5 minutes. Then slip a palette knife gently down the sides of the pudding. Put a plate over the top of the pudding basin and invert the pudding onto it. Serve, remembering that what looks like a small slice is actually as filling and as heavy as anything you're likely to eat! Serve with cream to complete the indulgence.

If you prefer, use individual plastic basins with snap-on lids, in which case eschew the greaseproof, foil and string. These little puddings will only take 1½ hours to steam.

LEMON BOMB OR SUSSEX POND PUDDING

SERVES 6

225g/8oz self-raising flour
110g/4oz suet
110g/4oz slightly salted butter
about 150ml/5fl oz milk and water
110g/4oz molasses or demerara
    sugar, depending on how black
    and how treacly you can take it
1 large organic lemon

You need a thin-skinned lemon for this. I guess the detonator doesn't work on a thick-skinned one. The boiling and roiling of the water obviously trigger the explosion and when you cut into the suet crust, a black sugar puddle pours forth with the remains of the exploded lemon to do battle with the richness. Who dreamt up this ribsticker of a pudding I wonder?

Mix the flour and suet together in a bowl. Add the half milk, half water to make a soft dough. Roll the dough out into a large circle, then remove one-quarter with a knife to use as a lid.

Butter a 1.5 litre/3 pint pudding basin. Drop the larger piece of dough into it and press it together to line the basin. Put half the chopped butter into the basin with half the sugar. Prick the lemon all over with a fine sharp skewer or larding needle to help the juices escape. Place the lemon on top of the butter and sugar and cover with the remaining butter and sugar. Roll out the remaining quarter of suet dough and lay it on top to seal the filling inside.

Cover with greaseproof paper and foil in the usual way (see steamed treacle pudding, page 364) and make a string handle. Lower the pudding into boiling water in a large saucepan, making sure the water comes halfway up the basin. Cover with a lid and steam for 3–4 hours. Slip a palette knife gently down the sides of the pudding, then turn the pudding out onto a large plate with plenty of room for the moat. Make sure everyone gets some of the lemon, all of which will be edible. Clotted or thick cream, naturally.

SPOTTED DICK

SERVES 6

225g/8oz self-raising flour
2 tbsp vanilla caster sugar
170g/6oz currants
110g/4oz suet or butter, cut into
    small cubes
2 organic eggs, beaten
a little milk

This school classic is not to be confused with spotted dog, which is the dead man's arm version. I imagine if you are French or Italian and reading this you will think I have left the planet, but these old-fangled English puddings are as well known for their names as for their taste. So, spotted dog is a long, steamed suet roll, dotted with currants like a Dalmatian. Spotted Dick is the pudding basin version, also known as plum bolster. Homemade custard is mandatory.

Grease a 850ml/1½ pint pudding basin. Sieve the flour into a large bowl and add the sugar and currants, stirring them in. Mix in the suet or if you are using butter, it will have to be rubbed in. Add the beaten eggs and mix, followed by enough milk to give a dropping consistency. Pour the mixture into the greased basin and cover as for treacle pudding (see page 364). Steam for 2 hours. Invert onto a plate and serve with homemade custard.

STEAMED GINGER PUDDING

SERVES 4–6

85g/3oz unsalted butter, softened
85g/3oz vanilla caster sugar
2 organic eggs, beaten
110g/4oz self-raising flour, sifted
110g/4oz preserved ginger, chopped
2 tbsp ginger syrup
½ tsp ground ginger
zest of a lemon
a little milk

Something of an adult taste compared to the treacle and jam varieties of steamed pudding, this is also somewhat lighter as it eschews the suet.

Cream the butter and sugar until light and fluffy, then add the beaten eggs, sifted flour, ginger, ginger syrup, ground ginger and lemon zest. Mix well and add enough milk to make a soft dropping consistency. Pour into a greased 850ml/1½ pint pudding basin, leaving room for it to rise. Cover and steam in the usual way for 2 hours (see page 364).

Turn the pudding out and serve with custard or cream. If you want yet more ginger, whip the cream with a couple more tablespoons of ginger syrup and about a tablespoon of preserved ginger chopped into tiny dice.

STICKY TOFFEE PUDDING WITH APRICOTS

SERVES 8–10

170g/6oz unsulphured dried apricots
1 tsp bicarbonate of soda
300ml/10fl oz boiling water
55g/2oz unsalted butter
150g/5oz vanilla caster sugar
1 organic egg, beaten
225g/8oz flour
1 tsp baking powder

TOPPING
200g/7oz dark muscovado sugar
110g/4oz unsalted butter
6 tbsp double cream

The famous Sharrow Bay Hotel version of sticky toffee pudding has become a national favourite. It is tooth-achingly sweet, what with its cascade of toffee sauce and addition of the sweetest fruit of all, dates. Joyce Molyneaux, the retired proprietor and chef of The Carved Angel in Dartmouth and another of the great George Perry-Smith's protégés, made her pudding with apricots instead and to my mind it is the version I would infinitely rather tuck into. The apricots' acidic sharpness more than stands up to and contrasts with the velvety thick toffee sauce. This pudding is steamed rather than baked, so turns out moister than the baked sponge version.

Place the ingredients for the topping in a small pan and stir over a gentle heat until the butter has melted and the sugar dissolved. Bring to the boil and simmer for 3 minutes. Pour into two buttered 850ml/1½ pint pudding basins.

Place the apricots in a bowl with the bicarbonate of soda and pour the boiling water over them. Leave to cool thoroughly. Cream the butter and sugar thoroughly until light and fluffy, then beat in the egg. Sift the flour and baking powder into the mixture and fold it in. Stir the apricot mixture into the batter and divide between the two pudding basins.

Cover each basin in the normal way (see page 364) and place the basins in heavy-bottomed pans, filling them halfway up the sides of the basins with boiling water. Cover the pans with lids and steam for 1½ hours. Check from time to time to see if the pans need more boiling water. Lift out of the water and turn the puddings out onto warmed serving dishes. Serve immediately. I think you might just find cream to be somewhat supererogatory at this point.

JAM ROLY-POLY

SERVES 6

170g/6oz self-raising flour
pinch of salt
75g/2½oz suet
150ml/5fl oz cold water
225g/8oz best strawberry jam with
    whole berries

Not for me the grey clods of pasty, damp suet like a pocked arm weeping inferior fruitless jam from its wounded length. They used to be turned out from their ancient, hinged roly-poly moulds – does anyone possess such a thing nowadays – and served in stodgy, steaming hefts. School jam roly-poly was enough to put you off suet for life, especially if you got the little snodgel at the end which, like the elbow joint, was a hard, lumpen ball the jam had somehow failed to trickle into.

A real roly-poly pudding, oozing whole fruit jam, its seeded crimson stickiness penetrating the layers of dense yet light suet, is a wonder to behold and to eat. You may pour more hot red liquid over it – melt another half pot of jam with a tablespoon of water and a squeeze of lemon juice – and serve with a jug of cold cream. Or eat it with a vanilla-scented custard. Just don't consign this pudding to the realms of school horrors best left behind with childhood.

Heat the oven to 220°C/425°F/Gas 7. Stir the flour, salt and suet together and mix them to a firm dough with the water. Flour a work surface and your rolling pin and roll out the dough lengthways to about 10 x 25cm/4 x 10in. Don't roll it too thinly, it should be about 1cm/½in thick. Spread a thick layer of jam over the surface, not going quite to the edges. Roll the dough up like a Swiss roll, tweaking the edges together. Place on a greased baking sheet and bake for 40 minutes until browned.

STEAMED MARMALADE ROLL OR PUDDING

Here is a sharper version of the sweet roly-poly.

SERVES 6–8

110g/4oz unsalted butter
110g/4oz vanilla caster sugar
2 organic eggs
110g/4oz self-raising flour, sifted
a little milk
1 pot bitter Seville orange
    marmalade
2 tbsp whisky

Cream the butter and sugar together thoroughly until light and fluffy. Beat in the eggs one by one, then fold in the sifted flour and add enough milk to make a soft, dropping consistency. Spoon about 225g/8oz of the marmalade into the bottom of the pudding basin. Add the sponge mixture on top and cover in the normal way (see page 364).

Place the basin in a heavy-bottomed pan, filling it halfway up the side of the basin with boiling water. Cover the pan with a lid and steam for 1½ hours. Check from time to time to see if the pan needs more boiling water. Lift out of the water and turn the pudding out onto a warmed serving dish.

To make the sauce, melt the rest of the marmalade with the whisky and serve it from a bowl or spoon it over the turned-out pudding.

Jam Roly-poly

SOUFFLÉS – THE LOWDOWN

Even some good, experienced cooks tremble at the thought of making soufflés, the way others do over custard, mayonnaise or pastry. But if you always run round your backhand it's never going to improve; you just have to leave it out of your repertoire. Soufflés really are all about technique, and if you learn the right technique to begin with you won't go wrong. They are not just for experienced, confident cooks to make. You should be able to whisk up a soufflé in a hurry if you suddenly want a good show-off special pudding – you'll always have the ingredients to hand. Or you can make a delicious savoury cheese, courgette or mushroom soufflé, topped with a golden crust of Parmesan. Again, no special ingredients needed, yet a soufflé warrants a flourish. It makes an occasion and something special of the humblest of ingredients as it is brought tremulously to the table before it sinks gracefully back into its dish.

- Always brush the insides of the ramekin or soufflé dish with softened butter. For savoury soufflés, add a mixture of breadcrumbs, grated Parmesan, or ground nuts. For sweet soufflés, add grated chocolate or a little caster sugar. The soufflé won't rise properly if you don't do this. Shake out any excess of the crumb/cheese/nut/chocolate/sugar mixture.

- When you beat the first spoonful of egg white into the base mixture you can be quite vigorous, as you are trying to slacken the mixture. With the rest of the egg white you must have a very light touch, folding it in carefully and deeply, right to the bottom of the bowl and trying to keep as much air in the mixture as possible.

- Running a sharp knife round the edge of the soufflé before you put it in to cook will help it rise evenly.

- Put the soufflé on a baking tray to cook.

- You may prepare the soufflé mix in advance, whether it is a fruit mix for sweet soufflés, or a vegetable or cheese and béchamel mix for savoury soufflés.

- To see if a soufflé is cooked, open the oven door and give the ramekin a nudge. If it is obviously very wobbly and unset, keep it in. If there is just a tremor, remove it.

HOT CHOCOLATE SOUFFLÉ

SERVES 8

450ml/16fl oz milk
1 vanilla pod, split
85g/3oz unsalted butter, softened
55g/2oz plain flour
20g/⅔oz unsweetened cocoa powder,
    plus some extra for sprinkling the
    soufflé dish
6 organic eggs, separated, plus
    6 extra whites
85g/3oz bitter chocolate
    (64–70% cocoa solids), chopped
1 tbsp rum or liqueur
    such as Grand Marnier
3 tbsp caster sugar

The best sweet soufflé I've ever eaten was Michel Roux's at Le Gavroche. A pale, fragile cloud of pistachio, it had a hole carved into its top and a scoop of pistachio ice cream sunk into its airy light depths. It doesn't get much better than that, though Michel's chocolate soufflé is divine and you really can make it at home.

For really stiff smooth egg whites, freeze them up to a week ahead and defrost on the day you want to use them.

Bring the milk to the boil with the vanilla. Beat the butter until smooth, sift in the flour and cocoa powder and pour in the hot milk. Bring back to the boil over high heat, whisking continuously. Remove from the heat and whisk in the egg yolks, chopped chocolate and rum or liqueur. Cover with buttered greaseproof paper and set aside.

Preheat the oven to 190°C/375°F/Gas 5. Butter 8 ramekins (9cm/3½in diameter x 6cm/2½in deep) and sprinkle with a little cocoa powder, tipping out any excess. Whisk the chocolate mixture until smooth. Whisk all the egg whites in an electric mixer until frothy. Add the caster sugar, 1 tablespoon at a time, and continue whisking until stiff yet still smooth. Beat one-third of the egg whites into the chocolate mixture until smooth, then gently fold in the rest. Pour the soufflé mixture into the ramekins, smooth the surface with a palette knife and then run the point of a knife around the rim: this helps the soufflé to rise evenly. Place in the oven for 11 minutes; the soufflés should still be creamy in the middle. Serve immediately, dusted with a little icing sugar, along with a jug of hot rich chocolate sauce.

RICH CHOCOLATE SAUCE

240ml/8fl oz single cream
25g/scant 1oz caster sugar
110g/4oz bitter chocolate, chopped
25g/1oz butter

Boil the cream with the sugar. Remove from the heat and beat in the chocolate and butter; keep warm but do not boil. This can be refrigerated and gently reheated in a double boiler.

FRUIT SOUFFLÉS

450g/1lb fruit such as strawberries
spritz of lemon juice
300ml crème pâtissière (see p. 358)
4 organic egg whites
55g/2oz sugar, plus extra for dusting
    the soufflé dish

Blitz and sieve the fruit and a spritz of lemon juice to bring out the fruit's flavour. Fold the fruit into the crème pâtissière. Whisk the egg whites with the sugar and fold into the fruit mixture (see opposite).

Preheat the oven to 190°C/375°F/Gas 5. Dust the ramekins with sugar. Pour the soufflé mixture into the ramekins, smooth the surface with a palette knife and then run the point of a knife around the rim: this helps the soufflé to rise evenly. Place in the oven for 11 minutes; the soufflés should still be creamy in the middle. Serve immediately.

FOOLPROOF

FAVOURITES

6

DO ANY OF WE COOKS or food writers ever really invent a new recipe? Is

that really what we're trying to do and is the next new dish, the next new idea what recipe junkies really want to read and to cook? Jane Grigson believed she only invented one recipe in the whole of her illustrious career, which included 22 years of writing about food for *The Observer.* Who are the rest of us to believe we can do better than that?

This book has been about giving you the best recipes and instructions for them that I know after cooking for three decades, and is as shamelessly subjective as any cookery book invariably is. Right down to my belief that the simplest food is the hardest food to cook well, but the most important; it is what we always come back to, even if we set ourselves the challenge of learning and incorporating the toughest of techniques into our repertoire.

At the bottom of the legendary Paul Bocuse's menus at his three Michelin star temple to gastronomy at Collonges-au-Mont-d'Or on the outskirts of Lyon, are the words of another great artist, Van Gogh: 'Comme il est difficile d'être simple.' It is, in fact, a lifetime challenge, and one which the great masters and mistresses of the kitchen are all too aware of. Nowhere are the virtues of classic technique and traditional food more apparent than at Bocuse. His Loup en Croûte Feuilletée arrives, a fish-shaped pastry coffin etched with the detail of each scale and fin. When it is cut into, its shiny mahogany crust lets out a steamy sigh before the whole fish is filleted before you with mesmerising skill and precision. The mousseline spiked with pistachios is laid along the fillets, the pastry shroud replaced, each leaf as light and crisp as autumn leaves in contrast to the firm, delicate-fleshed fish and its slippery silk mousseline. We can all cook a fish en croûte, but what Bocuse, at 79, shows us is what a lifetime of striving for absolute perfection can do: the dish is one of wonder, awe and beauty, while appearing a thing of perfect simplicity. It has taste, texture and appearance – a trinity of faultless skills and ethereal deliciousness. A dinner such as this inspires me to want to cook better, to hone my skills harder, to start again.

I think it takes 20 years to learn how to cook. That's assuming you are keen, you experiment, you don't give up on something when it doesn't work first time, and you don't get stuck in the groove of cooking something in one way just because that's how you've always done it. It then takes the rest of your life to learn how to cook better, assuming you are aware of better and interested and driven enough to want to. And it takes the rest of your life to refine your cooking so that when friends come to dinner it is no longer about the stressful business of cooking an impossibly difficult and time-consuming tableau of dishes. It is about presenting them with, say, the best lemon risotto they've ever tasted, made with intensely flavoured jellied chicken stock and Carnaroli rice stirred continuously to a starchy bite. The rosemary, parsley, sage and lemon zest is stirred in halfway through the proceedings, the stock added hot by the ladleful, and an emulsion of ivory Jersey cream and egg yolk, lemon juice and freshly grated Parmesan swirled in off the heat with fresh sweet butter and black pepper, then left for a couple of minutes to harmonise and become absorbed.

Should one serve one's guests the simplest of dishes, no meat or fish, just a tender Treviso bitter leaf salad with the best of aged balsamics and the new season's Seggiano olive oil, when they have come to the table expecting a special dinner? Well, I wouldn't have had the confidence to do it 20 years ago, but now it is the strongest statement I can make, and it is the one I happened to make last night. This is the way I like to cook, it says, with the best ingredients transformed with love and respect and good timing into the best of simple, peasant dishes. Refined peasant admittedly! And why can't simplicity be special?

So, the dishes in this chapter are not necessarily the culinary crucible on which you are going to cut a dash. Your skills should have evolved by now into an understanding of when to embellish and when to let well alone, when to provide succour, succulence and comfort, and when to go up a notch and feed the soul and the stomach with glamour, spectacle and brilliance.

The following are dishes that I love to cook, love to eat and can't imagine not being a part of my cooking life. I have tried to include as diverse a range as possible as that is how we all cook nowadays. We want the magpie thrill of stealing from all cuisines and adapting from one to another with the ease that the global shopping trolley and our travels have inspired us to do. These dishes reflect the age we live in, the absorbing of different cultures and methods alongside our narrower focus, tradition and skills. How long this approach to food and cooking will last is an imponderable, but once the genie is out it is difficult to put the stopper back in the bottle.

It is a hugely exciting age to be cooking in, barraged as we are by so many different vibrant influences, ancient traditions and accessible modern renditions of them. The thing to hang on to, though, with all good cooking, is the essential honesty and truth of the dish. There is nowhere to hide when you cook. All our senses eat the result before our eyes and criticise or applaud it. The saddest thing is not to cook at all. To be excluded from this whole world of joy and delight and study is unthinkable. Once you know how to scramble an egg or bake a cake you, too, are a part of it.

SPECIAL SOUPS

FRENCH ONION SOUP

The threads of gooey Gruyère pulled like skeins from the softened toasts, make this the homeliest and sexiest of soups. So typically French – it has to be done.

SERVES 6–8

55g/2oz unsalted butter
2 tbsp light olive oil
1kg/2¼lb onions, exceptionally thinly
    sliced; use a mandolin if you
    have one
sea salt
55g/2oz flour
1.5 litres/3 pints beef stock or half
    beef, half chicken stock; at worst,
    all chicken stock (see p. 80),
    heated
sea salt and fresh black pepper
1 baguette sliced into 12–16 slices,
    2.5cm/1in thick
olive oil to brush the bread with
a cut clove of garlic
110g/4oz Beaufort or other good
    Gruyère mixed with 55g/2oz of
    freshly grated Parmesan

Melt the butter and olive oil in a heavy-bottomed pan. Throw in the thinly sliced onions and sprinkle them with salt so that they start exuding their juices. Cook, stirring from time to time, over a low heat for about 20 minutes until they turn a gorgeous golden brown colour and are wilted. Scatter the flour over them and stir for a couple of minutes. Pour the hot stock over the onions and stir before partially covering the pan and letting it blip away at a low simmer for about 30–40 minutes. Season with salt and pepper to taste.

While the soup is simmering, preheat the oven to 170°C/325°F/Gas 3, put the slices of baguette on a baking tray and toast for 10–15 minutes on one side. Then brush both sides with olive oil and toast the other side. Rub the slices with the cut garlic.

When the soup is ready, you may either float a couple of slices of baguette in each filled bowl and pass the cheese round, or gratinée them the REAL onion soup way. To do this, place the slices of baguette in the pot of soup or individual bowls – you need ovenproof bowls for this – sprinkle cheese on top and sprinkle a few drops of olive oil onto each one. Turn up the oven temperature to 190°C/375°F/Gas 5. Put the pot or bowls in the oven for 10 minutes or until the cheese has melted, then slip under a hot grill to brown.

BEEF STOCK

1kg/2¼lb beef bones
usual stock vegetables – onion,
    celery, carrot, leek tops if you have
    some, roughly chopped
bouquet of bay leaves, parsley and
    thyme tied together

Brown the beef bones in a roasting tin, then transfer to a large pot. Add the vegetables and cover with water. Bring to the boil and skim, then simmer for 2 hours. Strain well.

MEAT STOCK

This is Matthew Fort's lovely slow-cooked meat stock, which you may use for the French onion soup above or for any other soup that needs a deep full flavour.

MAKES 6 LITRES/10½ PINTS
boil it down further if you want
a stronger stock.

1kg/2¼lb chicken bones and/or meat
1kg/2¼lb pork ribs and/or meat
1kg/2¼lb unsmoked bacon
6 litres/10½ pints water

Place all the ingredients in a big pot. Put the pot into the oven overnight, or for not less than 8 hours, on an 'S' for slow setting – about 110°C/225°F/Gas ¼. If you have an Aga, put the pot in the simmering oven overnight. That way, the contents come very slowly to the heat at which the flavours are leached from the meat and bones, so you're left with a naturally clear stock and don't have to do any skimming or clarifying.

Alternatively, bring the pan to the boil, boil vigorously while scum rises to the surface, and then skim it off. When the froth on top is white, turn down the heat to a gentle simmer and let it mutter away for 2 to 3 hours. Strain through a fine-mesh sieve or muslin and it's ready to use.

FENNEL AND WHITE BEAN SOUP

SERVES 4

3 bulbs fennel, remove fronds and
    set aside, discard tough outer
    leaves
30g/1oz butter
1 tbsp olive oil
300ml/10fl oz vegetable stock
    (see p. 380) or chicken stock
    (see p. 80)
110g/4oz haricot beans, soaked
    overnight, then cooked until
    tender; keep the cooking liquor
sea salt and white pepper
4 tbsp double cream

Mild and palely interesting, the slightly medicinal, aniseedy tones of fennel are not overwhelmed by the floury-textured beans. You may spruce this up a little by adding a handful of finely chopped fennel fronds to each bowl just before serving.

Finely slice the fennel and stew in the butter and olive oil until it softens. Add the chicken stock and simmer gently for 10 minutes. Liquidise and return to the pan.

Purée the haricot beans in a ladleful of their cooking liquor, then add to the pan. Season with sea salt and white pepper and add more of the bean liquor until you have the right consistency (the soup should not be too thick).

Before serving, stir in the cream which you have boiled and reduced slightly, and season. To serve, finely chop a tablespoon of the green fennel fronds set aside at the start, and add them to the soup.

POTAGE BONNE FEMME WITH CORNMEAL DUMPLINGS

45g/1½ oz butter
2 large leeks, cleaned and finely
    sliced
3 carrots, diced
450g/1lb potatoes, peeled and diced
sea salt and black pepper
1 tsp sugar
a little cream (optional)
flat-leaf parsley and chervil

DUMPLINGS
200g/7oz wholemeal bread, finely
    torn into pieces
2 organic eggs
2 tbsp duck fat (or melted butter)
55g/2oz minced smoked streaky
    bacon
2 heaped tbsp fresh horseradish,
    grated
85g/3oz polenta
sea salt and black pepper

A soup of substance and address that you may serve as a lunch or supper dish in its own right in the winter.

Melt the butter and add the leeks and carrots. Make sure they are coated in butter before adding the potatoes, 1.2 litres/2 pints of water, seasoning and sugar. Simmer for 20 minutes before adding the dumplings.

Mix the dumpling ingredients in a large bowl. Roll into about 12 balls and cook in the gently simmering soup for about 15 minutes. Remove and keep warm.

Adjust the seasoning to the soup, liquidise it, and add a little cream if you like. Put the dumplings back as you serve the soup and sprinkle with chopped chervil and flat-leaf parsley.

WALNUT SOUP

SERVES 6

170g/6oz shelled walnuts
a large clove of garlic
1.2 litres/2 pints chicken stock (see
    p. 80)
150ml/5fl oz cream
sea salt and freshly ground black
    pepper

This has to be included, favourite as it was of my two culinary heroines Elizabeth David and Jane Grigson. It is delicate and robust at the same time and highly unusual. You need to use very high-quality fresh walnuts.

Crush the walnuts and garlic to a paste with a little of the stock in a mortar or a liquidiser. Incorporate the rest of the stock slowly until the mixture has the consistency of single cream. If the walnuts have been liquidised they will probably take up most of the stock; if they've been pounded in a mortar they'll take about 850ml/1½ pints. Pour the soup through a sieve into a saucepan and bring to the boil. Add the cream and correct the seasoning with salt and pepper. Serve straight away.

SPLIT PEA SOUP

SERVES 4–6

450g/1lb green split peas, washed
    and picked clean of grit
1.5 litres/3 pints ham stock, chicken
    stock (see p. 80) or water
⅓ bottle white wine
2 onions, stuck with a couple of
    cloves each
a bouquet of fresh bay, thyme,
    parsley and rosemary, tied
    together
3 carrots, chopped into large chunks
2 sticks of celery, chopped
green tops of 3 leeks
12 peppercorns
a ham bone
225g/8oz or so chunks of good meaty
    ham with the fat on
fresh mint leaves
a little butter to stir in if the mood
    takes you

Pease pudding and split pea soup are the sine qua non of the Christmas ham, or any other time a hock or two come your way or you have a tender pink piece of organic gammon. Pea soup can be made with chicken stock, but the stock you cook a ham in is infinitely superior, with the little snippets of leftover meat pulled from it and thrown like pink jewels into a thick sea of green. So thick, the proverbial spoon should stand up in it. With a hunk of burnt-crusted white bread and some good butter, I can't think of a nicer way to beat the winter chill. Remember that pea soup, like treacle tart, has a way of staying nuclear hot longer than any other substance I know, and then welding itself to the roof of your mouth. Blow and beware.

Put the split peas in a large, heavy-bottomed casserole with the stock, wine, onions, bouquet of herbs, carrots, celery, leek tops, peppercorns and the ham bone and bring to the boil. Skim off the scum with a slotted spoon and some kitchen paper, then turn the heat down to a simmer and leave the pot on the stove for about an hour.

When the peas are cooked through, the other vegetables should be too. Remove the leek tops, bouquet and the cloves from the onions and purée all the rest together in a blender. Return to the pan and season to taste. You may not need salt as the ham bone and stock may be quite salty enough. Add the chopped mint, about 6 leaves, and a knob of butter if you like, 30g/1oz or so, stirring it in as the soup heats through. Throw in the little chunks of ham off the heat and serve.

1 tsp cumin seeds
1 tsp coriander seeds
1 tbsp sesame seeds
30g/1oz butter or
   1 tbsp light olive oil
1 medium red onion, finely chopped
2 cloves of garlic, finely chopped
a thumb of fresh ginger, peeled
   and chopped
1–2 green chillies, seeded
   and chopped
zest and juice of a lime
1.2 litres/2 pints vegetable stock
1 tsp honey
340g/12oz sweet potato,
   peeled and diced
340g/12oz pumpkin, peeled and
   diced
a handful of coriander leaves,
   roughly chopped

GARNISH

120ml/4fl oz live yoghurt or 1 tin
   coconut milk
olive oil

1.2 litres/2 pints water
250ml dry white wine
2 large carrots, cut into chunks
2 sticks of celery, cut in half
2 medium onions, unpeeled and
   stuck with 2 cloves each
4 shallots
green tops of 3 leeks
2 whole tomatoes
1 bulb fennel, chopped
a few whole mushrooms or
   mushroom peelings
bouquet of fresh thyme, rosemary,
   parsley and bay
1 tbsp white peppercorns

NELISHA'S SPICED SWEET POTATO AND PUMPKIN SOUP

There was an ingredient I couldn't detect when I tried this magical soup, cooked by Sri Lankan chef Nelisha Wickremasinghe. It was the roasted sesame seeds.

Lightly roast the cumin, coriander and sesame seeds separately for about one minute, then grind them together. Heat the oil or butter in a heavy-bottomed pan and cook the onion and garlic over a medium heat without browning, until they are softened.

Add the ground spices, ginger, chillies and lime zest and stir them in. Cook for a minute to amalgamate the flavours. Add the stock, half the lime juice, the honey, sweet potato and pumpkin and coriander leaves and bring to the boil.

Then reduce to a simmer and cook until the vegetables are tender (about 20 minutes). Liquidise until very smooth, adding more stock to achieve the right consistency if you need to. Add the rest of the lime juice and seasoning to taste.

Serve with a swirl of yoghurt or coconut milk and a few drops of olive oil.

VEGETABLE STOCK

Bring the water and wine to the boil. Add the vegetables and herbs and return to the boil. Skim off any grey froth. When the surface is clear, add the peppercorns: if you add them earlier, you'll skim most of them off. Simmer gently for 40 minutes, then strain.

LEEK, BROCCOLI AND STILTON SOUP

SERVES 4

1 small onion
2 tbsp olive oil
30g/1oz butter
3 finely chopped leeks, the whites only
a head of broccoli divided into florets, the stalks peeled and chopped into slices
1.2 litres/2 pints chicken stock (see p. 80)
150ml/5fl oz cream
up to 55g/2oz Stilton or other blue cheese
black pepper

I first made this great winter soup at Rob's new Murray's Cheese Shop on Bleecker Street in Greenwich Village as there was some crumbly, creamy Stilton from Cropwell Bishop on the counter. The important thing is to add the Stilton crumb by crumbled crumb at the end and to keep tasting. The cheese is very salt and very strong and you don't want it to overwhelm. If you don't have Stilton, use Roquefort, Cashel Blue, Beenleigh Blue, Fourme d'Ambert or any other good blue.

Chop the onion very finely and cook it gently in the oil and butter for a few minutes. Add the leeks and broccoli and turn to coat them. Let them sweat, cook down and begin to soften for about 5 minutes before you add the hot stock. Simmer very gently until the broccoli is cooked through but hasn't lost its colour and barely tender feel. Add the cream and blitz in the liquidiser.

Return to the pan and heat gently without boiling, slowly adding little crumbly bits of Stilton and some black pepper until you have the right balance of cheese and vegetable. You may not need any salt as the Stilton is very salty.

CREAM OF ASPARAGUS SOUP

SERVES 4

a bundle of asparagus (about 450g/1lb), well soaked in water to clean out any sand)
a small onion or shallot, finely chopped
55g/2oz unsalted butter
1 tbsp potato flour or flour
1.2 litres/2 pints water or chicken stock (see p. 80)
sea salt, black pepper
a little lemon juice
150ml/5fl oz double cream

Asparagus is a vegetable with a strong enough identity not to demand chicken stock when you turn it into soup. The cooking liquor takes on the scent of the asparagus and I would hardly want to diminish that so choose between chicken stock and water, depending on how purist you are feeling. When asparagus first comes into season I want nothing else but the frail green wands with their tight furled buds steamed and doused in a puddle of good French butter, with maybe a spritz of lemon and a good scrunch of pepper. But as the short season goes on, soups and tarts and salads and eggs also figure on my menu.

Cut the bottoms of the asparagus stems off if they look dry and peel the bottom third of each stem with a potato peeler. This really does make a difference to the texture of the asparagus. Now cut the stems into 4 and throw all the stems, keeping back the tips, into the boiling salted water or stock. Simmer them for about 15 minutes.

Meanwhile, melt the butter in a pan and gently soften the chopped onion. Throw the tips into the pan with the stems and simmer for a further 10 minutes until tender. Remove the stems and tips to a plate, separating them into two piles. Stir the flour into the buttery onion for a couple of minutes and add the asparagus liquor and stems. Simmer them together for a few more minutes. Blitz in the liquidiser, then sieve to get rid of any woody bits. Season, adding a little lemon juice. Stir in the cream and the asparagus tips and reheat to just under boiling point.

GAZPACHO

SERVES 6–8

450g/1lb tomatoes; use organic
    tinned tomatoes with their juice
    if you can't get good tomatoes
2 slices stale white bread, crusts
    removed
1 small onion, cut into chunks
2 cloves of garlic, chopped
2 tbsp best olive oil
sea salt and cayenne
1 cucumber, half-peeled, quartered
    lengthwise and seeded
1½ red peppers
2 tbsp best sherry vinegar
600–850ml/1–1½ pints very cold
    water straight from the fridge

Predating Roman times, this ancient soup is said to have as many versions as there are mortars and pestles. If you are making it at the last minute, it can be whacked into the freezer for a 30-minute freeze down. If you have time, make it the day before you need it, keep it in the fridge overnight and allow the intense flavours to mingle. On the day, just add a jug of cold water and stir to the desired texture and strength. I serve mine in glasses, but if you want to add little bits of chopped egg, olive, pepper, onions or jamón, serve the soup in bowls and let people spoon in the accompaniments. Do use organic vegetables if you can.

Chop the tomatoes. I don't bother to skin them – you may prefer to – but I do halve and seed. Hold the bread under the cold tap, then squeeze out the water and put it in the food processor with the onion, garlic, olive oil, a teaspoon of sea salt and the cayenne. The soup is meant to have warmth, not fire, so start with the tip of a teaspoon of cayenne, and correct at the end if it is not quite right. Blitz briefly to a pulp.

Add the cucumber, peppers, vinegar and tomato and blitz until liquid. The mixture will be coarse rather than puréed. Pour into a bowl, cover and chill as above. Just before serving, dilute with the fridge-cold water, stirring and tasting to the required texture and flavour. Adjust the seasoning and serve in tall glasses or bowls.

AVOCADO SOUP

SERVES 4

2 ripe avocados, stones removed
250ml/8½fl oz whipping cream
1.2 litres/2 pints chilled, gelled
    chicken stock (see p. 80)
lemon juice
Tabasco sauce
Worcestershire sauce
sea salt and black pepper
1 tbsp raw onion, very finely minced
1 tsp sugar
2 tbsp chives, chopped
crème fraîche (optional)

This soothing, cooling soup is thickly rich and creamy, with the oiliness of the avocado muted by lemon juice and a burst of chilli.

Put all the ingredients except the chives and crème fraîche into the blender – start with the juice of half a lemon until you have tasted the mixture. Go easy on the Tabasco and Worcestershire as you don't want either of them to take over, just to warm and deepen the flavours. When you have the right balance, pour the soup into a glass bowl and chill for a few hours. Finish with a sprinkle of chopped chives. If you are serving the soup in individual bowls, add a dollop of crème fraîche over which you may scatter the chives.

BRAZIL NUT AND LEMON SOUP

SERVES 6

30g/1oz unsalted butter
1 medium onion, sliced
1.2 litres/2 pints chicken stock
    (see p. 80)
110g/4oz Brazil nuts
zest of a lemon, cut into thick strips
sea salt and freshly ground black
    pepper
60ml/2fl oz single cream

Joyce Molyneaux, who was in partnership with the great George Perry-Smith of Hole in the Wall fame, was the joint proprietor and chef of The Carved Angel at Dartmouth for many golden years. Joyce clearly came from George's stable, as did a number of other great cooks who George's legacy left to West Country watering holes and pastures beyond. Joyce had her own style and her own dishes too, although their ethos was the same: the best local produce cooked in the Elizabeth David style with the minimum of fuss but the maximum of skill and attention to detail. I first cooked this soup from Joyce's lovely *The Carved Angel Cookery Book* years ago, and, as she cites, if you have any leftover Brazil nuts after Christmas, it's a good way to use them up. It is an unusual and delicately refreshing soup.

Melt the butter in a heavy-bottomed pan. Sweat the onion, covered, for 15 minutes. Add the hot stock, nuts and lemon zest, season, cover and simmer gently for a further 20 minutes. Process in a liquidiser until smooth. Return the soup to the pan and stir in the cream. Check the seasoning and reheat before serving.

SOUPE AU PISTOU

SERVES 8–10

225g/8oz dried cannellini or haricot
    beans, soaked overnight
4–5 tbsp olive oil
1 large onion, chopped
2.3–3 litres/4–5 pints chicken stock
    (see p. 80) or water
225g/8oz potatoes, cubed
225g/8oz carrots, cut into small
    cubes
1 fat leek, chopped
2 sticks of celery, chopped
salt and pepper
225g/8oz string beans, sliced
225g/8oz courgettes, chopped
450g/1lb tomatoes, skinned, seeded
    and chopped
55g/2oz macaroni
large pinch of saffron threads

PISTOU
6 cloves of garlic, finely chopped
a large handful of fresh basil
2 tbsp Parmesan cheese, grated
2 tbsp tomato purée
6 tbsp olive oil
extra Parmesan for serving

Drain and rinse the beans and put them in a saucepan with water to cover. Bring to the boil, cover and simmer for 1–1½ hours until tender.

Heat the oil in a large, heavy-bottomed casserole, add the onion and cook over a low heat until softened. Add the stock or water and bring to the boil. Add the potatoes, carrots, leek and celery, and some salt and pepper, and simmer together for about 15 minutes. Stir in the cooked dried beans in their cooking liquid, then add the string beans, courgettes, tomatoes, macaroni and saffron. Simmer until tender, about another 15 minutes.

Meanwhile, make the pistou. Put all the ingredients into a food processor or liquidiser and swirl together. Add a ladleful of the soup liquid to the pistou, stir, and pour it into the soup. Serve with a bowl of freshly grated Parmesan.

THYME SOUP

SERVES 4

a whole handful of thyme, as much
  as you can wrap your fist around
a knob of butter
olive oil
1 small onion, finely chopped
2 small new potatoes, washed and
  diced
700ml/1¼ pint strong chicken stock
  (see p. 80), i.e. strong enough to
  jellify in the fridge
450ml/16fl oz Jersey milk
salt and pepper

Fresh herb soups are a delight. You may make this soup with a couple of large sprigs of rosemary chopped with a mezzaluna instead if you like – fizz the tiny needles in a pan with a lump of butter for a minute before adding the onion and potato and proceeding in the normal way. Or try making it with an enormous bunch of flat-leaf parsley or several handfuls of lemony sorrel. Even onion and potato with some bay leaves steeped in hot milk first works well.

Strip half the thyme stalks, about 10 or 12 twigs, of their leaves and chop to release the oils. Melt a knob of butter and a couple of tablespoons of good olive oil in a heavy-bottomed casserole, then add the onion, diced potatoes and chopped thyme. Stir to coat for a few minutes, then ladle in the stock. Bring to the boil, add the milk and bring to the boil again. Turn down to a lazy simmer and add the rest of the thyme stalks, tied in a bundle like a bouquet garni, salt and pepper.

Put the lid on the pan and continue to simmer for about 20 minutes. Remove the bunch of thyme, check the seasoning and put the soup through the thinnest of the three discs of a mouli-légumes. The result is utterly white, with tiny flecks of thyme. Do not add cream, or you will dilute the magical flavour, the essence of the herb.

THAI LETTUCE AND PEA SOUP

SERVES 6

1 tsp coriander seeds
1 tsp cumin seeds
2 medium onions, roughly chopped
1 tbsp olive oil
2 cloves of garlic, peeled and
  chopped
1 thumb fresh ginger, peeled and
  chopped or grated
½ tsp fresh chilli paste, use Bart's
  Spices fresh hot chilli in sunflower
  oil, or some seeded red chilli
  crushed in the mortar with a bit
  of salt
1 medium potato,
peeled and cubed
850ml/1½ pints of vegetable stock
  (see p. 380)
400ml/14fl oz tin coconut milk
300g/10oz fresh or frozen peas
1 lettuce, roughly chopped

Roast the coriander and cumin seeds briefly in a frying pan for only 30 seconds or so until they exude their scent; any longer and they burn.

Sauté the onion gently in a little olive oil. Add the garlic, ginger, roasted spices and chilli and sauté for a few more minutes until softened and translucent. Add the potato and stock, then simmer together for 25–30 minutes. Proper vegetable stock is best, but you could use an organic stock cube if you are desperate.

Add the coconut milk and bring back to a simmer. Add the peas and lettuce and bring the soup back to a simmer once again before removing from the heat. Process in the blender, season and serve.

STARTERS

The thing about starters is that they set the tone and style of the meal. They are really there, in my view, to whet the appetite, act as something of an overture to the main event, and aid the passage of the digestion and the drink. I believe strongly in eating while you drink. There is nothing sorrier than a glass of good wine on an empty stomach, except a glass of bad wine, obviously. The Spanish have got it right with tapas – little salt, savoury, fishy, meaty, eggy or vegetable bites – but we often give no more than a crisp or peanut, or a wodge of pastry stodge that bears no relation to the main event and doesn't complement or look ahead to what's to come. A meal has to be thought of as a symphony or a picture. The different movements have each to provide colour, tone, texture and flavour. There has to be crescendo and diminuendo, surprise and repetition – you are, after all, going to eat more than one bite of each thing.

The days of the formal dinner party are dimming. Most of us prefer to do things informally, subtract a course or two and not eat so heavily as we used to. We have less time to prepare things than the generations of couples who didn't live such frenetic lives or have such demanding jobs. Pleasure has to be experienced by the giver as well as the guests, that is the thing that I think we have all come round to over the last decade. Dinner should not mean an ordeal of timing, pressure and struggle for perfection; it should be relaxed and communal and not about showing off. And if the cook is in the kitchen, the guests should be there too. After all, they are your friends and you are not just there as a hired hand.

So, you may eschew a starter altogether, though I favour keeping that course, however dinky and bite-sized, be it only a square of blackly salty, oily, olivey tapenade and toast. There is no need to serve pudding and cheese, one or the other will do fine, unless you are intent on competing with la grande bouffe and sending your guests home sated and torpid.

No dish is too homely or humble to feed yourself, your family and loved ones or your friends. That is the thing I think we have to unlearn more than anything. Cook what you feel like cooking with the best of ingredients and think carefully about the balance – the richness, the texture and the heaviness.

COUNTRY TERRINE WITH PRUNES, PISTACHIOS AND GREEN PEPPERCORNS

FILLS A 1.2 LITRE/2 PINT TERRINE

Ask the butcher to coarsely mince the following:
450g/1lb belly pork without the rind and small bones
340g/12oz unsmoked streaky organic bacon
450g/1lb pig's liver
170g/6oz pork back fat
half a pig's kidney

OTHER INGREDIENTS
75g/2½oz unsalted butter
450g/1lb onions, chopped
4 cloves of garlic, peeled and finely chopped
a bunch of flat-leaf parsley, finely chopped
3–4 sprigs thyme, chopped
a sprig of rosemary, very finely chopped
1 heaped dsrtsp green peppercorns, drained from their brine
6 juniper berries, crushed in a mortar
50g/scant 2oz whole pistachio nuts
100g/3½oz Merchant Gourmet mi-cuit Agen plums, stoned and quartered
1 organic egg, beaten
½ tsp each mace and nutmeg
a fresh bay leaf
60ml/2fl oz Calvados, Somerset Cider Brandy or Cognac
60ml/2fl oz Fino sherry
sea salt and freshly ground black pepper

This has guts, substance and depth and is remarkably easy to make. It is undoubtedly the best-tasting terrine I've yet made, so much so that I sat down to lunch with a friend on Monday and we polished off more than I dare relate. Why we no longer consider the homemade terrine a thing for the table I do not know. It is as quick as making mincemeat or a stew and your butcher does the work with his mincer. A great lunch with a few cornichons or some céleri-rémoulade (see page 257), or a wonderful starter, particularly before a fish or vegetarian main course. I served mine with the spelt flour, walnut and onion bread on page 476, toasted.

My meat came from my friend Peter Whiteman, from whom I bought one-quarter of a Middle White cross organic porker. Buy from a good old breed that lays down a lot of fat if you can and a pig that has been properly raised. The lean, mean, fast-bred modern pig doesn't lay down enough fat and the meat is tough and stringy because it doesn't get the marbling of fat it needs to give it flavour and texture. You may double up quantities and make a terrine for the freezer. Try to make the terrine at least a couple, it not four days before you need it so the flavours marry and develop.

Melt the butter in a heavy frying pan and gently sauté the onions, coating them in the fat, for about 25 minutes until softened and golden. Put all the other ingredients up to but not including the bay leaf into a huge bowl and mix well to amalgamate. Place the bay leaf in the middle of the bottom of the terrine, then turf in the buttery onions when they've cooled down a little. Put the liquor in the onion pan and warm before setting light to it and letting the alcohol burn off. When the flames have died down, pour the alcohol into the bowlful of mixture and add the seasoning, turning everything together well.

Preheat the oven to 150°C/300°F/Gas 2. Put the mixture into the terrine, cover it with foil and its lid and put it in a roasting tin with boiling water poured three-quarters up its sides. Cook on the middle shelf for an hour. Uncover and insert a skewer deep into the terrine, count to ten then see if it is hot on your tongue. The meat juices should be pink. Put back into the oven uncovered for 15–30 minutes, depending on whether the skewer was hot or warm and the juices bloody or pink after the first hour.

Take out of the oven and replace the foil while you let the terrine cool. Put in the fridge for a couple of days at least and remove it 30 minutes before you want to eat. Serve with toast or a good sourdough or crusty loaf and a few cornichons or green olives.

SCALLOPS WITH PARSNIP PURÉE

SERVES 2

1 medium parsnip, peeled and cut
    into chunks
55g/2oz unsalted butter
a knife point of cayenne and the
    same of cumin seeds, tempered
    and crushed (optional)
sea salt and black pepper
2 large scallops per person, cleaned
    and trimmed, the white sliced into
    3 discs, the coral kept whole
1 tsp flat-leaf parsley, chopped

There is no more perfectly pure, sweet, taste-of-the-sea starter than the scallop, with its disc of firm white flesh and its gaudy, soft coral comma. Sweet and sweet work beautifully together; you may serve scallops with a parsnip purée, a minted pea purée or a purée of Jerusalem artichokes. You may even hit a hot, sharp note and serve them with tomato chilli jam (see page 493) as Peter Gordon, the talented New Zealand chef, does. If you want to go simpler still, flash fry or griddle the scallops and dress them with a walnut or hazelnut vinaigrette with lots of parsley and a little minced garlic. Let the scallop speak for itself. Perhaps it is keeping it somewhat separate from the other tastes and not cooking them all in together that help it retain its identity.

Steam the parsnip. Mash it or put it through the smallest disc of your mouli-légumes, adding two-thirds of the butter, the spices if you are using them and the seasoning to taste. Keep warm.

Melt the rest of the butter in a pan and add the whites of the scallops when it is bubbling. Cook for about 30 seconds a side, or until the white turns opaque, then turn them over, add the corals, and cook for a further 30 seconds or so. Turn over the corals and continue cooking them until just set, about 30–45 seconds. Season, then put a little mound of parsnip on each plate, followed by the buttery scallops and parsley and serve.

Cooking the scallops on a griddle is just as good. Brush a griddle with olive oil, heat it to hot and put the scallops on it for the same amount of time as above, turning them over at half time. That way, less butter and a satisfying branding of black griddle stripes.

SCALLOPS WITH MINTED PEA PURÉE

SERVES 2

2 large scallops per person, cleaned
    and trimmed, the white sliced into
    3 discs, the coral kept whole
228g/8oz fresh or frozen peas or
    petits pois
a little chicken stock (see p. 80)
    to cover
a knob of butter
2 tbsp double cream
sea salt and black pepper
1 dsrtsp fresh mint, finely chopped

As far as I know, Rowley Leigh of Kensington Place takes credit for putting the pea with the scallop in such a simple and disarmingly delicious way.

Cook the scallops in a pan with butter or on a griddle as above. Cook the peas in simmering chicken stock. Drain, keeping the stock, and place in a food processor with the butter and cream and a tablespoon of chicken stock. Process roughly; I like texture not baby food. Add the seasoning and any more stock or butter or cream you think it needs to taste. Scrape out onto a plate and stir in the mint.

Make a mound of brilliant green pea purée on each plate, arrange the scallops and their brilliant corals as you like and serve.

SCALLOPS WITH JERUSALEM ARTICHOKE PURÉE

SERVES 2

2 large scallops per person, cleaned and trimmed, the white sliced into 3 discs, the coral kept whole
225g/8oz Jerusalem artichokes, scrubbed but not peeled
sea salt and black pepper
2 tbsp double cream
a knob of butter
1 tsp flat-leaf parsley, finely chopped

Again, cook the scallops in a pan or on a griddle (see opposite). Steam or boil the Jerusalem artichokes until tender. Allow them to cool a little, then remove their skins and mash or mouli, adding plenty of black pepper, some salt and some cream and butter. They are watery; don't let them get sloppy.

Re-heat the purée in a small pan, then scrape into a little mound on each plate. Add the scallops and inject a burst of colour with a little finely chopped parsley.

CEVICHE OF LEMON SOLE WITH TOMATO AND CHILLI SALSA

When you want light, quick, sharp, fresh, easy, fishy, this is the one. You may make a ceviche with all sorts of different fish, the lemon or lime juice do the job of cooking it. Use oily fish like salmon or mackerel, or white fish like scallops or lemon sole.

SERVES 2

225g/8oz boned, skinned lemon sole fillet
juice of a lemon
olive oil
a handful of flat-leaf parsley
salt and pepper

SALSA
½ small red onion, very finely chopped
1 red and 1 green chilli, very finely chopped
2 ripe tomatoes, skinned, seeded and diced
1 tbsp each of very, very finely diced yellow and red pepper
1 tsp very finely chopped garlic
1 tbsp chopped coriander
dash each of Tabasco and Worcestershire sauce
olive oil
sea salt and black pepper

Cut the fillet of sole on the diagonal into thin strips. Marinate for at least an hour in the lemon juice, drain well and dress with olive oil, parsley and seasoning. Serve with a spoonful of salsa.

SALSA

To make the salsa, mix the finely chopped onion and chilli, then add the tiny diced tomatoes and peppers. Add the garlic and coriander, Tabasco and Worcestershire and stir in enough good olive oil to loosen. Season to taste. You may wish to add a few thin slices of cooling avocado to the salsa.

CEVICHE OF WILD SALMON

SERVES 6–8

675g/1½ lb salmon, a skinned and
 filleted piece from the centre of
 the fish
170ml/6fl oz dry white wine
juice of 1 lime
juice of ½ an orange
juice of ½ a lemon
1 small onion, sliced in thin rings
1 small clove of garlic, sliced
salt and pepper
4 tbsp olive oil

This is a dish I have cooked, or should I say assembled, many times over the years, but always obeying one simple rule: use wild salmon. There are certain compromises I won't entertain and farmed salmon, even if it is organic, is one of them. The great wild fish, in season, is what I love, even if only once a year. The flavour and texture of the farmed stuff and the method of rearing it, poor, pale, greasy, flobby imitation that it is of the magnificent tail-thrashing wild specimen, is just not something I want anything to do with, or a dish I care to serve or eat.

Using a very sharp knife, slice the salmon, straight from the fridge, into 5mm/¼ in slices. Put into a container with a lid – an old plastic ice cream container is ideal. Add all the other ingredients, cover and refrigerate. Turn the salmon occasionally, or shake the container gently. The dish is ready to eat after about 8 hours. It will keep well for about 24 hours in a sealed container in the fridge, but remember to remove the onion and garlic after the first 8 hours so that they don't overwhelm the fish.

To serve, strain off the marinade and put a tablespoon of the cucumber and avocado sambal (below) alongside the fish, and some brown soda bread if you like.

CUCUMBER AND AVOCADO SAMBAL

½ a cucumber, skinned and seeded
1 red pepper, skinned and seeded
1 avocado
lemon juice, olive oil and balsamic
 vinegar, to taste
1 tbsp fresh dill, finely chopped

Chop the cucumber as finely as you can – into dice about 3mm/⅛in square. Do the same with the red pepper, and chop the avocado into slightly bigger cubes.

Sprinkle on some lemon juice, a little olive oil and balsamic vinegar, then add some black pepper and finely chopped dill. Perfect with the ceviche of salmon and with the soufflé opposite.

GRUYÈRE SOUFFLÉ

You may make this with a mature unpasteurised Cheddar or a lovely lactic Lancashire like Mrs Kirkham's if you'd rather, but a good Gruyère like Beaufort makes a stunning soufflé. Please don't turn the page in fear of the perils of the sunken, leathery soufflé, or the soufflé that failed to rise to your challenge. If you follow this simple method you will have a light, creamy, tremblingly perfect interior and a crisp, browned crust. See page 370 for more on soufflés.

SERVES 4

a knob of softened butter

1 tbsp each of breadcrumbs from a stale loaf and grated Parmesan, or ground walnuts instead of the breadcrumbs, mixed with 1 tsp chopped fresh thyme

55g/2oz unsalted butter

45g/1½oz flour

300ml/10fl oz full-cream milk

4 large organic egg yolks

85g/3oz Gruyère, Beaufort if possible

freshly ground black pepper

tsp tip of cayenne

6 large organic egg whites, room temperature

1 tbsp Parmesan, grated

The soufflé dish should be one that holds 750 ml/1½ pints, but it can be fun to make it with one that holds a little less, tying a strip of well buttered greaseproof paper like a collar around the top of the dish and securing it with a paper clip. That way the soufflé rises Vesuvially and when you rip off the collar it stands tremblingly proud, like a chef's toque, for a few seconds. Culinary fireworks.

Prepare the soufflé dish. Grease it well with the softened butter and sprinkle on the crumb, cheese and thyme mixture which should stick to the buttered edges; discard what doesn't.

Preheat the oven to 200°C/400°F/Gas 6. Place a baking sheet in the middle of the oven. Melt the butter in a small pan, add the flour and let it simmer for a minute or two into a blond roux before adding the hot milk at scalding point. Take off the heat and whisk fiercely until it becomes smooth, then add the egg yolks one by one, whisking them in. Throw in the cheese, pepper and cayenne and keep warm on a low heat nowhere near boiling point. Whisk the egg whites with a pinch of salt until they are at stiff peak stage. Stir a tablespoon of the whites into the cheese mixture to slacken it. Lightly fold in the rest, a spoon at a time, with a rubber spatula or metal spoon, keeping the mixture light and airy. Don't overwork it.

Scrape the mixture into the prepared soufflé dish. Sprinkle the Parmesan over the top and put the soufflé onto the baking tray in the middle of the oven. Check after 25 minutes by pushing the dish with your hand and seeing how shuddery it is. It will probably take another 5 minutes, but you need it trembling but not liquid-middled. The top should be lightly browned. Remove from the oven, rip the collar off if you've used one and set the soufflé on the table immediately.

1 tbsp butter
2–3 tbsp day-old brown
   breadcrumbs
1 tbsp Parmesan cheese, grated
pinch of cayenne pepper
1 small tsp curry powder (optional)
340g/12oz crab meat, brown and
   white
1 tsp French mustard
a few drops of Tabasco sauce
2 tsp dry sherry
salt and pepper
150ml/5fl oz béchamel sauce
(see below)
1–2 tbsp double cream
4 organic egg yolks
6 organic egg whites

BÉCHAMEL SAUCE
2 tsp butter
2 tsp plain flour
1 small bay leaf
150ml/5fl oz milk
salt and pepper

CRAB SOUFFLÉ

This is the king of the savoury soufflés and one instance when cheese and fish work together, so don't lose the Parmesan. See page 370 for more on soufflés.

Preheat the oven to 190°C/375°F/Gas 5. First make the béchamel sauce: melt the butter in a saucepan, add the flour and cook, stirring, for 1 minute. Add the bay leaf and gradually stir in the milk. Cook, stirring constantly, until the sauce is thick and smooth. Season to taste. (See page 70 for more on béchamel.)

Butter a soufflé dish generously, then roll the breadcrumbs and half the Parmesan around the inside of the dish, tipping out and reserving what doesn't adhere to the butter. Melt a knob of butter in a saucepan, add the cayenne and curry powder if you are using it, and cook for 1 minute. Remove from the heat and add the crab meat, mustard, Tabasco, sherry and salt and pepper to taste. Warm gently, then stir in the béchamel sauce and the cream. Remove from the heat and stir in the egg yolks. (The mixture can be prepared ahead up to this point.)

Whisk the egg whites until stiff. Fold them briskly but lightly into the mixture and turn into the soufflé dish. Sprinkle the remaining Parmesan and breadcrumbs over the top. Fix a piece of greaseproof paper around the dish, the top 5cm/2in buttered on the inside, and fasten with a paper clip. When the soufflé has risen and the paper is taken away, this looks spectacular. Bake in the oven for 20–25 minutes: the soufflé should be firm and well risen, with the barest hint of a shudder at the middle if you shake it gently. Bring it directly to the table as soon as you have taken off the greaseproof paper. This is good with the cucumber and avocado sambal on page 390.

OTHER SAVOURY SOUFFLÉS

Vegetables that make good, strongly flavoured purées also make good soufflés. Spinach, with a salty hit of a few anchovies, is fantastic; parsnip is good with a teaspoon each of cumin and coriander which has been tempered then ground; mushroom with some dried ceps and chanterelles and plenty of fresh parsley. Try fennel, 4–5 bulbs steamed, puréed and mixed into the béchamel made with a glug of Pernod or Anise and some fennel fronds and dill.

To start a vegetable soufflé, sweat a very finely chopped shallot or small onion with a finely minced clove of garlic in 55g/2oz butter. You then add 225g/8oz of cooked, puréed vegetable and turn this into the béchamel before proceeding in the normal way.

Fish soufflés are also good. Omit the garlic from the sweated onion mixture and add 225g/8oz of firm-textured white fish like sole or John Dory, or some quickly cooked discs of scallop, with the roes cooked whole even more briefly, a minute a side for the whites and 30 seconds a side for the corals. Omit the cheese with the fish, adding instead a good tablespoon of dill, chervil, parsley or chives according to the fish and 150ml/5fl oz white wine or Vermouth as half the liquid for the béchamel.

Smoked salmon also makes a good soufflé if you have some leftover bits. Just stir the same quantity as for the fish soufflé into the béchamel with some chopped dill.

SOUFFLÉS À LA SUISSESSE

These little soufflés are poached, more like quenelles, and gratinéed with cream and cheese to a delicate and rich deliciousness. They used to be on offer in many restaurants for the simple reason that they are cooked twice, so easy to hold and finish with the second cooking when they've been ordered. They are a lovely and easy starter and you can get ahead like the restaurants, too. Serve them with a small bitter salad of Treviso chicory or radicchio and a dressing of walnut or hazelnut oil.

240ml/8fl oz milk
55g/2oz flour
sea salt, black pepper and nutmeg
55g/2oz unsalted butter
110g/4oz Parmesan, freshly grated
3 organic egg yolks
2 organic egg whites
340ml/12fl oz double cream
a little chopped fresh thyme,
     (optional)

Bring the milk to scalding point in a pan. Let it cool to blood heat before pouring it into the flour and whisking to stop it going lumpy. Add the seasoning with a grating of nutmeg and cook over a gentle heat, stirring all the while until the mixture thickens. Let it cool a little, then add half the butter, a generous half of the Parmesan and the egg yolks, one at a time, whisking them in well. Whisk the egg whites to stiff peaks. Stir the first spoonful into the cheese mixture, then gently fold in the rest a tablespoonful at a time.

Preheat the oven to 180°C/350°F/Gas 4. Scrape the mixture into well-buttered ramekins filling them two-thirds full. Put the ramekins in a small roasting tin and add boiling water to come three-quarters of the way up their sides. Poach for 20 minutes or until set and slightly springy to the touch.

Butter a gratin dish and sprinkle in some of the remaining Parmesan. Remove the ramekins from their water bath. When they have cooled slightly, run a knife blade around each one, turn out onto your hand and plop into the buttered gratin dish. Pour the cream over the soufflés and sprinkle each one with Parmesan and a pinch of thyme. Put them back into the oven for 20 minutes until gratinéed, golden and bubbling, or hold them to finish off later.

PARMESAN OR MONTGOMERY CHEDDAR BISCUITS

The great thing about these flaky, cheesy-crisp biscuits, rolled in sesame and/or nigella (black onion) seeds, is that you can make a cylinder of the cheese pastry and freeze it, ready to cut and bake when you need a great bite for drinks. If you are going to make them with Cheddar cheese, please use a good, strong, nutty, unpasteurised one like the greatest of greats, Montgomery. They need a punch. Adapted from *Baking with Passion*.

310g/11oz plain flour
285g/10oz Parmesan or Montgomery's Cheddar, freshly grated
285g/10oz fridge-cold unsalted butter, cut into cubes
⅓ tsp cayenne pepper
1 tsp sea salt
1 tsp coarsely ground black pepper
1–2 tbsp water
1 organic egg, beaten
2 tbsp sesame seeds
2 tbsp nigella, black onion seeds

Shunt the flour, cheese and cubed butter into a food processor with the cayenne, salt and pepper. Pulse to crumbs, then slowly add the cold water down the feeder until the dough coheres into a ball. Roll it into a biscuit-sized cylinder on a lightly floured surface, wrap in clingfilm and put in the fridge for at least 4 hours or overnight. If you don't want to use all the dough at once, make two cylinders and freeze one of them.

Brush the cylinder with beaten egg all over. Either cut in half, rolling one half in the sesame seeds and the other in the nigella seeds, or roll the whole cylinder in a mixture of the seeds. Wrap and chill for a further hour.

Preheat the oven to 180°C/350°F/Gas 4. Using a sharp knife, cut the cylinder into 5mm/¼in thick biscuits and place them on non-stick baking trays. Leave some space between each one – they shouldn't touch each other. Bake for 20–25 minutes or until golden. Transfer to a wire rack to cool. The biscuits will feel soft when you lift them with a palette knife, but they firm up as they cool. Eat on the day you make them.

110g/4oz fine plain flour

a pinch of salt, black pepper and a knife tip of cayenne

1 tsp mustard powder (optional depending on your taste and the filling)

85g/3oz unsalted butter

240ml/8fl oz water

3 organic eggs, beaten

55g/2oz strong farmhouse Cheddar, an unpasteurised one like Montgomery's, Keen's or Quicke's, diced into small cubes

FILLING

30g/1oz unsalted butter

1 medium onion, finely chopped

a stick of celery, strung and finely chopped

110g/4oz Portobello mushrooms, sliced or 30g/1oz dried ceps or morels, soaked in warm water to re-hydrate

or 360g/12oz crab meat, half white, half brown

or 340g/12oz cooked chicken or pigeon or guinea fowl or pheasant, torn with the grain into thin strips

30g/1oz flour

300ml/10fl oz chicken stock, or fish stock for the crab recipe

sea salt and black pepper

1 tbsp chopped parsley for the mushroom or chicken recipe, 1 tbsp dill/chervil for the crab

4 tbsp double cream

TOPPING

2 tbsp Parmesan

2 tbsp dry breadcrumbs

GOUGÈRE

Think of this as a gorgeous empty vessel that you can fill with smoked fish like haddock or salmon, or with mushrooms, vegetables or chicken. It is made with a cheese choux paste and its golden, crisp crust is best offset by a lovely gloopy-sauced filling of old-fashioned comfort and simplicity.

Sift the flour, salt, pepper, cayenne and mustard powder if you're using it a couple of times from on high; they need to be sifted fine.

Put the butter and water in a large heavy-bottomed pan and heat them together slowly. When the butter has completely melted into the water let them come to a rolling boil and add the flour mixture. Remove from the heat and beat soundly with a wooden spoon until the mixture starts to leave the sides of the pan. Leave to cool.

Preheat the oven to 200°C/400°F/Gas 6. Once this mixture is warm rather than hot, beat in the lightly beaten eggs a little at a time until the mixture is glossy, shiny, and of a dropping consistency — this may be before you've used up all the egg. Stir in the cheese. Grease a baking tray and make a circle of spoonfuls of the gougère mixture around the edge of the tin, so that the ring can be filled with the filling later. Bake until puffed up and golden, about 25 minutes.

Meanwhile make the filling. Melt the butter in a pan and gently soften the onion and celery. Add the mushrooms, crab, chicken or game and cook for 5 minutes. (Dried fungi will take longer so if you are using it, allow 10–15 minutes.) Sprinkle over the flour and stir for 2–3 minutes before adding the hot stock. Bring to the boil, turn down the heat and simmer for 5 minutes, then season and stir. Add the herbs and the cream, check the seasoning, then turn the filling into the middle of the gougère ring.

Sprinkle the topping over the filling and return to the oven for 15 minutes until bubbling and golden on top.

FENNEL À LA GRECQUE

You may also use celery hearts or the whites of leek for this dish which is just a classic, simple starter or a side dish for grilled pork or fish.

SERVES 4

4 large fennel bulbs, the outer tough
   leaves ruthlessly pruned
6 tbsp olive oil
juice of 2 lemons
1 onion, sliced into thin rings
2 cloves of garlic, bruised
12 coriander seeds
1 tsp fennel seeds
a bouquet of thyme, bay, parsley and
   rosemary with a strip of orange
   peel, tied with string
sea salt and black pepper
chopped flat-leaf parsley

Quarter the fennel bulbs down through the core so that they don't break up. Lie them flat in one layer in a heavy-bottomed frying pan. Add all the other ingredients except the parsley and just cover with boiling water. Bring to the boil, turn down to a simmer and cover. Cook for about 20 minutes until tender right through the core.

Remove the herbs and spoon the fennel and its cooking liquor onto a deep serving dish. Leave to cool and serve at room temperature or cold with plenty of parsley.

MUSHROOMS À LA GRECQUE

SERVES 2–3

170g/6oz button or closed-cap
   mushrooms
lemon juice
olive oil
1 tsp coriander seeds, crushed
2 bay leaves
salt, pepper
3 large tomatoes, skinned, seeded
   and chopped (optional)

Clean the mushrooms, and halve them if they are on the large side. Brush a little lemon juice over them. Cover the bottom of a heavy pan with a film of olive oil and cook the coriander seeds for a few seconds over a low heat. Add the mushrooms and bay leaves. Season. If you are including tomatoes, add them now. After a minute, cover the pan and cook for another 3–5 minutes, but no longer.

Pour the mushrooms with their cooking juices into a serving dish and sprinkle them with fresh olive oil and lemon juice to taste. Serve chilled, or hot with veal or chicken.

SPICED CHICKEN LIVERS WITH WILTED ENDIVES

This is something of a rarity, a dish that I claim as entirely my own, even if someplace, sometime, someone else also believes they have invented it, which is also eminently possible. The curry-crusted, warm-spiced livers, blushing pink and oozingly buttery, are a great titbit to put in your mouth with a glass before dinner, but if you team them with the bitter sweetness of the endive you have a full-scale proper starter. Don't serve chicken afterwards though. Enough's enough.

Temper the cumin and coriander in a small frying pan over a gentle heat for 30 seconds to a minute, until the spices exude their scent. Tip into a mortar and crush with the sea salt and peppercorns. Add the cayenne, then the flour, and stir well together. Set aside.

Clean and de-vein the livers, keeping them whole, and removing any green patches. Pat them dry and leave in the fridge until about 30 minutes before you want to cook them.

Just before cooking, roll each liver in the spice mixture in the mortar and put on a plate. Heat a good knob of unsalted butter or olive oil, whichever you prefer, in a frying pan – I err on the side of butter, with a tiny addition of oil to discourage burning. Throw in the livers when the fat is hot. Allow one side to spit and crisp for a couple of minutes, turn over and repeat, then test with a knife point. When gorgeously oozily pink, shunt the contents of the pan on to a white plate with the endives.

WILTED ENDIVES

Cut the base off the endives, core them and strip them into leaves. Heat the olive oil gently in a pan with the molasses sugar, then throw in the endives and stir them in the warm oil. They will begin to wilt pretty quickly. Season, remove from the heat and spritz on the lemon to taste.

SERVES 4–6

as a starter with drinks, depending on greed and what's to follow

1½ heaped tsp cumin seeds
1 tsp coriander seeds
1 tsp sea salt crystals
1 tsp black peppercorns
the tip of a tsp of cayenne
1–1½ tbsp plain flour
450g/1lb organic chicken livers. I'm afraid I take a purist line here – only organic will do, since chemical residues collect in the liver and kidneys
olive oil or a good-sized knob of unsalted butter

WILTED ENDIVES

3 endives
4 tbsp best olive oil
1 tsp molasses sugar
sea salt and black pepper
lemon juice to taste

FALAFEL

340g/12oz chickpeas, soaked
    overnight
2 medium onions, finely chopped
4 cloves of garlic, chopped
2 green chillies, seeded and finely
    chopped
1 handful flat-leaf parsley
1 handful fresh coriander
2 tsp cumin seeds
2 tsp coriander seeds, ground with
    the cumin in a mortar
salt, pepper
600ml/1 pint ground nut or grape
    seed oil (double the quantity if
    deep-frying)

We've all eaten hummus, but that is as much as many of us know about the versatile chickpea. Usually chickpeas need soaking and long cooking, yet in this recipe they are used raw. I love these little fried balls of spicy chickpeas served with a sauce based on tahini, with the deliciously dense crushed sesame paste that comes in oily jars. Serve a tomato and cucumber salad on the side, too. A very good start if you have serious red meat or game to follow.

I soak the chickpeas for 24 hours since they are not being cooked before frying. Drain, dry them on a clean tea towel and place in a food processor with the onions, garlic, chillies, chopped herbs, ground spices and seasoning. Blitz to a pulp, but don't expect it to be smooth; the chickpeas will give it a grainy texture. Take walnut-sized quantities of the mixture and form it into little patties. You can use them immediately or keep them in the fridge until you want them. They are fine the next day.

Heat the oil and use a bit of the mixture to check it is hot enough. It will resurface instantly, bubbling furiously if the oil is hot enough. Don't put too many patties in the pan at once because they will lower the temperature of the oil. Cook until deep golden brown. If you are frying them in a shallow pan and not immersing them totally, about 2 minutes a side should do it. Remove to a plate and drain on kitchen paper.

Serve with yoghurt thinned with a spoon of milk and mixed with a teaspoon or so of tempered and ground cumin and a clove of crushed garlic, or with tahini cream sauce.

TAHINI CREAM SAUCE

2 cloves of garlic
sea salt
juice of 2½–3 lemons
150ml/5fl oz tahini paste
2 tbsp live sheep's or goat's yoghurt
1 tsp tempered, ground cumin seeds
a handful of flat-leaf parsley,
    chopped

Crush the garlic in a mortar with a little sea salt. Put it in a bowl with a tablespoon of the lemon juice and stir. Add the tahini and stir it in, followed by the rest of the lemon juice and the yoghurt. Add water, a spoonful at a time, to make it into a thick, smooth cream. Add the cumin and any more of the other flavours you need to keep it tart and strong – garlic, lemon juice or more salt or spice. Sprinkle over the parsley and serve cold in a bowl for people to spoon next to their hot, crisp falafel.

GNOCCHI

There are times when an Italian comfort blanket of warmth and security is all you want, and pasta doesn't always feel quite as right as starchy semolina or potato gnocchi. They really are not as much trouble to make as you might imagine and some recipes can be prepared well in advance, leaving just the finishing stages to do at the last minute. I think the simplest gnocchi are almost without equal — little soft, starchy pillows, dribbled with butter and salt Parmesan, with perhaps the crisp scrunch of a few frazzled sage leaves.

My mentor on the gnocchi front is the great Anna Del Conte whose books have graced my kitchen and my table constantly throughout my cooking life. I have even been lucky enough to eat Anna's homemade pumpkin gnocchi at her home in Dorset. She insists that if she didn't grow the pumpkins over here from Italian seeds she'd never consider making the dish. Our pumpkins are too watery and fibrous. How right she is, though red onion squash make a very good alternative as far as I'm concerned.

GNOCCHI ALLA ROMANA

SERVES 4

1 litre/1¾ pints milk
sea salt
225g/8oz ground semolina, (semolina flour)
3 large organic egg yolks
75g/2½ oz freshly grated Parmesan
¼ tsp grated nutmeg
75g/2½ oz unsalted butter

The easiest of all the gnocchi to make. Buy the coarse-ground Italian semolina in preference to the other types. You may finish the dish with a thin béchamel or with cream and Parmesan.

Heat the milk with a little salt in a heavy pan. When it begins to simmer, add the semolina in a thin stream, beating quickly to prevent any lumps from forming. Cook for about 15 minutes, beating constantly until the semolina has formed a thick paste and comes away from the sides of the pan. Remove the pan from the heat and allow the semolina to cool a little.

Add the egg yolks, one at a time, mixing them in thoroughly. Add all but 4 tablespoons of the Parmesan, the nutmeg, 30g/1oz of the butter and a pinch of salt. Incorporate everything thoroughly, then turn the mixture out onto a slab of marble or work surface previously moistened with cold water. Spread the semolina to a thickness of 1cm/ ½ in and cool it completely for about 2 hours.

Preheat the oven to 230°C/450°F/Gas 8. Cut the semolina into 4cm/1½ in rounds. Place a layer of rounds in the bottom of a buttered ovenproof dish, put the leftover scraps in between, then cover with another layer of the gnocchi rounds, slightly overlapping.

Melt the remaining butter and pour it over the gnocchi. Sprinkle with the remaining Parmesan and bake in the oven for about 15 minutes, until the gnocchi are heated through. Allow to cool for a few minutes before serving.

POTATO GNOCCHI

1kg/2¼lb floury potatoes, scrubbed
1 tsp sea salt
285g/10oz Italian 00 flour
1 large organic egg, beaten
75g/2½ oz unsalted butter
2 garlic cloves, lightly crushed
3–4 sage leaves, torn
75g/2½oz Parmesan, freshly grated

Another easy rendition of the classic, these starchy potato pillows are served with a trickle of garlicky butter and the musty, medicinal astringence of the sage leaf. Anna Del Conte cites these gnocchi as much easier to make than the Piedmont version, which do not contain any egg.

Boil the potatoes, drain, and peel them while still hot. Sieve them in a food mill or a potato ricer onto the worktop. Sprinkle a little salt onto the flour in a bowl and mix well. Add the beaten egg and half the flour to the potatoes. Knead, gradually adding more flour, until the mixture is soft, smooth and slightly sticky. Shape the mixture into rolls, about 2.5cm/1in in diameter, then cut into 2cm/¾in pieces.

To shape the gnocchi, take a fork and hold it with the tines resting on the worktop at an angle of 45 degrees. Take each piece of dough, dust it with flour, then press it lightly with the thumb of your other hand against the inner curve of the prongs. With a quick downwards movement, flip it towards the end of the tines. The gnocchi should be concave on the thumb side, and convex with ridges on the fork side.

Bring 5 litres/8–9 pints of water to the boil in a large pan. Do not put salt in the pan as this tends to make the gnocchi stick together.

Meanwhile, make the sauce. Put the butter, garlic and sage in a small, heavy pan and cook slowly. The sauce is ready when the foam has disappeared and the butter is light golden. Discard the garlic and keep the sauce warm.

Drop the gnocchi into the boiling water – you can cook about 30 at a time in a big pan. Cook for 20 seconds after they come to the surface, then lift out with a slotted spoon, pat dry with kitchen paper and transfer to a heated dish.

Pour over a little sauce, sprinkle with some Parmesan and keep warm. Repeat until all the gnocchi are cooked. Pour the remaining sauce over and sprinkle with Parmesan.

BUTTERNUT SQUASH GNOCCHI

SERVES 4

1 tbsp olive oil
500g/1lb 2oz butternut squash or red
    onion squash
500g/1lb 2oz sweet potatoes
200g/7oz Italian 00 flour
2 tsp baking powder
salt
2 large organic eggs
4 tbsp Parmesan, freshly grated
a generous grating of nutmeg

DRESS THE GNOCCHI WITH EITHER
OF THE FOLLOWING
75g/2½oz unsalted butter
30g/1oz Parmesan, freshly grated
1 tbsp sugar
1 tsp cinnamon

OR
75g/2½oz unsalted butter
6 fresh sage leaves, snipped
55g/2oz Parmesan, freshly grated

Preheat the oven to 180°C/350°F/Gas 4. Line a baking tray with foil and brush it with oil. Cut the squash in half, scoop out the seeds and fibrous bits and place cut-side down on the foil. Pierce the sweet potatoes with a skewer and put them on the foil with the squash. Bake for 40 minutes to an hour until both vegetables can be pierced easily with a fork.

Peel the sweet potatoes and scoop the flesh out of the squash. Using a mouli-légumes or potato ricer, purée both together into a bowl. Mix in the flour, baking powder and salt, then break in the eggs. Mix everything together well, add the Parmesan and season with nutmeg and more salt to taste.

Bring a large pan of salted water to the boil. Flour your hands and shape the gnocchi into small balls. Drop into simmering water and cook for 1–2 minutes after they have come to the surface of the water. If you prefer, you can use a piping bag and a large plain nozzle to shape the gnocchi. Fill the bag with the mixture and hold it over the pan, squeezing it with one hand and cutting the mixture as it comes out of the nozzle with the other. Cut short shapes, about 2cm/¾ in long, letting them drop straight into the simmering water.

Cook the gnocchi in 3 batches. Lift them out of the pan with a slotted spoon and place in a large shallow ovenproof dish. Dress each batch separately and keep the dish in a low oven. For the first dressing, melt the butter in a double boiler or a bowl over a pan of simmering water. Pour the butter over each batch of gnocchi and sprinkle with Parmesan, sugar and cinnamon.

For the second dressing, put the butter and sage leaves in a small pan and heat until the butter melts and begin to foam. Spoon the buttery sauce over each batch of gnocchi and sprinkle with the Parmesan.

SPINACH AND RICOTTA GNOCCHI

SERVES 4

500g/1lb 2oz cooked spinach
2 large organic eggs
200g/7oz ricotta
200g/7oz Italian 00 flour
½ tsp grated nutmeg
100g/3½oz Parmesan, freshly grated
sea salt and freshly ground black
   pepper
100g/3 ½oz unsalted butter

A perfect starter or main course. Try to get fresh ricotta if you can – the flavour and texture is so much better than the industrial version. If you are serving the gnocchi as a starter, remember not to serve anything too heavy afterwards, or anything with cheese for your main course. Some simply baked or grilled white fish with a lemony sauce and a green salad would be my preferred option.

Press all the water out of the spinach with a wooden spoon and a conical strainer if you have one; if not, press through a colander or sieve. Now chop the spinach or push it through the coarse disc of a mouli-légumes. Beat the eggs together in a bowl and mix in the ricotta, beating them both together. Mix in the flour, spinach, nutmeg and half the Parmesan. Taste and adjust the seasoning.

Dust your hands with flour and form the mixture into balls the size of large marbles. Place them on a baking tray and chill in the fridge for 30 minutes.

To cook the gnocchi, bring 5 litres/8–9 pints of salted water to the boil in a very large pan. Add the gnocchi, a dozen at a time, and cook them for 3–4 minutes after the water returns to the boil. Lift them out with a slotted spoon and transfer them to a dish. Dot with a little butter, sprinkle over a little Parmesan and keep them warm while cooking the rest.

Meanwhile, melt the remaining butter in a small pan. Just before serving, spoon the butter over the cooked gnocchi and sprinkle with the remaining Parmesan.

TARTS

Having written *The Art of the Tart* and *Tarts With Tops On*, it will be clear to you just how seriously I take the delectable self-contained joys of buttery pastry with a creamy-rich filling of eggs, cheese, fish, meat or vegetables. The following are a special selection of some of my favourite tarts, all of which make stunning starters, suppers or lunches. I prefer making large tarts to dinky ones, even for starters, but if you want to make some to eat with drinks, and they need to be collapse-proof, jam-tart sized are your answer. They are fiddly to make, but I made dozens for the opening of Rob's new Murray's cheese shop in Manhattan and still emerged sane.

ROASTED AUBERGINE, GOAT'S CHEESE AND SMOKED PAPRIKA TART

SERVES 6

1 aubergine
extra virgin olive oil
1 yellow pepper
1 Vulscombe or similar fresh goat's cheese
2 organic eggs and 2 extra yolks
about 200ml/8fl oz double cream and crème fraîche, half of each
1 small bunch coriander
1 small bunch mint
sea salt, black pepper and a pinch of smoked-pepper paprika, such as Bart's picante pimenton

SHORTCRUST PASTRY
170g/6oz flour
a pinch of salt
85g/3oz unsalted butter, chilled

This is a firecracker of a tart with the sharp, lactic cheese and musky, smoky paprika taking their place alongside the softened peppers and roasted aubergines. A hit of coriander leaves takes the provenance of this tart somewhere between Oriental and Mediterranean and it is quite simply delicious. It also makes a great lunch or supper if you want something vegetarian but special. Brushing discs of aubergine with olive oil and roasting them on a tray in the oven stops their natural tendency to soak up lots of oil. I use a whole, crumbled Vulscombe goat's cheese from Devon, but any fresh goat's cheese will do.

Heat oven to 190°C/375°F/Gas 5. Slice the aubergine into discs, brush with olive oil on both sides and place on a sheet of silicone paper. Halve, core and seed the yellow pepper, then cut into thin strips and place them on the same baking tray. Sprinkle over a little olive oil and turn the peppers in it. Roast for about 20 minutes until the aubergine slices and peppers are tender when pierced with a fork.

Make the shortcrust pastry, line a 23cm/9in tart tin and bake the pastry shell blind in the usual way for 15 minutes (see page 181). Remove the dried beans and greaseproof paper, prick the base with a fork and return to the oven for 5–10 minutes until lightly browned and cooked.

Crumble the goat's cheese. Whisk together the eggs, yolks and creams, then whisk in the chopped herbs. Season with salt and pepper.

As soon as the pastry shell is cooked, cover the base with slightly overlapping slices of aubergine, add spokes of yellow pepper, then scrape in the goat's cheese and distribute it evenly. Add the herby custard, then scatter over a pinch of smoked paprika.

Bake until the custard is browned and trembling (about 30 minutes). Leave to cool for at least 10 minutes before eating.

SPINACH AND ANCHOVY TART

SERVES 6

30g/1oz unsalted butter
1 tbsp olive oil
340g/12oz organic baby spinach
black pepper
200ml/7fl oz double cream
1 organic egg and 2 yolks
12 anchovy fillets

SHORTCRUST PASTRY
110g/4oz organic white flour
pinch of sea salt
55g/2oz unsalted butter
1 generous tbsp best olive oil

Perfect at any time of year, but plus-perfect in the spring, when you can buy or grow tiny pousse, the baby leaves of spinach that are gently, tenderly unferrous and don't exude copious amounts of liquid when you cook them. Spinach and anchovies: what can I say, other than that they are a heavenly marriage. Inspired by a soufflé, I set out to reproduce the taste in a tart. Curiously there is no battle, therefore no winner, no loser, between these two strong tastes when they're put together; the one doesn't cancel out the other, but enhances it. Just don't be tempted to add more anchovies than I've used in the recipe below. Don't add salt: the anchovies have it in spadefuls.

Make the shortcrust pastry (see page 181), but, instead of adding water, add a generous tablespoon of your best olive oil to the mixture before blitzing it all together. Chill, then roll out and line a 23cm/9 inch tart tin. Preheat the oven to 190°C/375°F/Gas 5. Bake the pastry blind for 15 minutes (see page 181), then remove the beans, prick the base with a fork, and return to the oven for a further 5 minutes.

While the pastry is in the oven, heat the butter and olive oil in a heavy-bottomed enamel saucepan. Add the spinach and pepper, and stir briefly for a couple of minutes until the spinach has wilted but not lost its shape.

Whisk the cream, egg and yolks together, then pour in any liquid from the spinach pan. Tip the spinach and anchovies into a food processor and process as briefly as you dare — you want to keep their texture and not reduce them to a slushy purée. Throw them into the bowl with the cream and eggs and stir with a fork. Pour the whole lot into the pastry case and cook for about 25 minutes.

Leave to cool for 10 minutes. Serve with something plain, like a cherry tomato salad, and good white country bread and butter.

SOUFFLÉD CRAB TART

SERVES 6

450g/1lb crab meat, brown and white
salt, black pepper, cayenne
3 organic eggs
1 tbsp each of grated Parmesan and
    Gruyère
240ml/8fl oz double cream
2 tsp French mustard

SHORTCRUST PASTRY
170g/6oz flour
85g/3oz unsalted butter

Make the shortcrust (see page 181) and line a 23cm/9in tart tin. Preheat the oven to 200°C/400°F/Gas 6. Bake the pastry blind for 10 minutes (see page 181), then remove the beans, prick the base with a fork, and return to the oven for 5 minutes. Remove the pastry case from the oven and turn the heat down to 190°C/375°F/Gas 5.

Season the crab, going carefully with the cayenne – you want a bit of heat, but nothing overwhelming. Beat in 1 whole egg and 2 yolks, and then the cheeses, cream and mustard. Whisk the 2 egg whites until stiff, and fold gently and quickly into the mixture. Pour the mixture into the pastry case, and cook for about 30–40 minutes. Check after 30; it should be puffed up but have a slightly wobbly centre, like a soufflé. Remove from the oven and leave to cool for 10 minutes before serving. A spoonful of cucumber and avocado sambal (see page 390) is a good accompaniment.

OATMEAL AND TOMATO TART

This tart is enough to convert even the most recidivist of meat and two veggers. It is one of the greats. I have served it at a 'big girls' lunch' and had everyone begging for the recipe. It is also a wonderful picnic tart, the sturdier pastry a better container than thin shortcrust.

SERVES 8–10

1 organic egg
150ml/5fl oz double cream
1 tbsp each of grated Parmesan and
    Gruyère
2 tbsp grated mature Cheddar
salt and black pepper
fresh thyme

OATMEAL SHORTCRUST
110g/4oz organic white flour
110g/4oz organic porridge oats
pinch of sea salt
110g/4oz unsalted butter

TOMATO SAUCE
3 tbsp olive oil
2 onions
2 sticks of celery
6 cloves of garlic, finely chopped
1kg/2¼lb ripe tomatoes, skinned,
    seeded and chopped
1 x 400g/14oz tin organic tomatoes
200g/7oz tomato passata
1 tbsp tomato purée
2 bay leaves
2 tsp molasses sugar
150ml/5fl oz red wine
salt and black pepper
basil leaves

Make shortcrust pastry in the normal way (see page 181), but using organic porridge oats as well as flour. Chill, then roll out just a little thicker than for normal shortcrust and line a 30cm/12in greased tart tin. Reserve the remaining pastry in strips for a lattice or, if you can't be bothered, save it for another tart.

Preheat the oven to 190°C/375°F/Gas 5. Bake the pastry blind for 10 minutes (see page 181), then remove the beans, prick the base with a fork, and return to the oven for 5 minutes.

Make the tomato sauce. Heat the oil in a large, heavy-bottomed pan and sauté the onions, celery and garlic until softened. Add the fresh and tinned tomatoes, passata, tomato purée, bay leaves, sugar and red wine, then season. Simmer for at least 30 minutes until the sauce is thick and jammy. Sprinkle with the torn basil when the sauce has cooled down a bit.

Whisk the egg and cream together, then whisk in the Parmesan, Gruyère and half the Cheddar. Season and scatter in a few thyme leaves. Spread a thick layer of tomato sauce over the pastry to come halfway up the pastry case, then pour over the custard. Arrange your pastry lattice over the top and sprinkle with the remaining Cheddar.

Bake for about 25 minutes, until set and palely browned. Leave to cool for about 10 minutes before serving.

CEP AND RED ONION TART

This is a wonderfully intense, musky-flavoured tart, perfect for the lean, wintery months when one turns more to the store cupboard and to dried foods than at any other time of year. The mascarpone, delicately enhanced by the cep liquor, makes it less rich than if the tart was full of cream, and it doesn't set in quite the same way as the eggier tarts; it rather slides slowly off its pastry base when sliced, like an earthy, densely flavoured ragout.

SERVES 10 AS A STARTER
6 AS A MAIN COURSE

55g/2oz dried ceps
2 medium-sized red onions
30g/1oz unsalted butter
255g/9oz mascarpone
1 large organic egg and 3 yolks
8–10 sage leaves, or the leaves from
    2–3 sprigs of thyme
salt and black pepper

SHORTCRUST PASTRY
110g/4oz wholemeal or organic white
    flour
pinch of sea salt
55g/2oz butter

Soak the ceps in 300ml/10fl oz of warm water for about an hour, turning them when you remember, to ensure they're all completely rehydrated.

Meanwhile, make the shortcrust pastry in the usual way (see page 181). A wholemeal crust is always delicious with fungi. Chill, then roll out and line a 23cm/9in tart tin – or a rectangular tin measuring 36 x 12.5cm/14 x 5in. Preheat the oven to 200°C/400°F/Gas 6. Bake the pastry blind for 10 minutes (see page 181), then remove the beans, prick the base with a fork, and return to the oven for 5 minutes. Remove from the oven and brush the pastry with a little beaten egg. Turn the oven down to 180°C/350°F/Gas 4.

Strain the ceps, pressing gently, and reserve the liquid. Slice the onions finely into rings, and sweat them gently in the butter for a few minutes until softened. Chop the ceps coarsely, add them to the onions and cook for a further few minutes. Strain the cep liquid into the pan and let it reduce completely, then tip the mixture into a bowl and leave until it is cold. You can complete the cooking to this stage several hours before serving if it is more convenient.

Whisk the mascarpone, egg and yolks together, then add the finely chopped sage or thyme and stir in the cep and onion mixture. Season, then spread the mixture over the bottom of the pastry case and cook for 10 minutes. Turn the heat down to 170°C/325°F/Gas 3 and cook for a further 25–30 minutes, but check after 25 minutes. Remove the tart from the oven while it is still obviously shuddery, and leave for 10 minutes before turning out and serving warm.

RED ONION PISSALADIÈRE

This is glorious picnic food, with a pungent, sweet onion and anchovy filling. It is best served warm.

SERVES 8–10 FOR A PICNIC
4–6 AS A LUNCH DISH

CRUST
55g/2oz butter
200g/7oz wholemeal or plain flour
salt
15g/½ oz fresh yeast
1 organic egg

FILLING
450g/1lb red onions, very finely
    sliced
3 tbsp olive oil
3–4 tomatoes, skinned, seeded and
    chopped
4 cloves of garlic, chopped
sprig of thyme
salt and pepper
small tin of anchovies, drained

Cut the butter into small pieces and rub it into the flour. Add a pinch of salt. Dissolve the yeast in 2 tablespoons of tepid water. Make a well in the centre of the flour and add the egg and yeast. Mix it all together and knead the mixture until it no longer sticks to the bowl. Put the mixture on a cloth in a warm place and leave it to rise for a couple of hours.

Preheat the oven to 200°C/400°F/Gas 6. Stew the onions very gently in the olive oil in a covered saucepan. They are ready when they are totally wilted and golden, after about 30 minutes. Add the tomatoes, half the garlic, and the leaves from the thyme. Season with salt and pepper and simmer until the mixture is quite thick. Pound the drained anchovies together with the remaining garlic and stir this into the mixture when you have taken it off the heat.

Sprinkle the dough with flour and knock it back, then knead it into a ball again. Press it into a well-oiled flan tin, working from the middle outwards until it rises up round the sides. Spread the filling over the dough and place the flan tin on a baking sheet in the oven for 20 minutes. Reduce the heat to 180°C/350°F/Gas 4 and cook for another 20 minutes.

SALADS

Embracing the exotic as we have, where no salad is considered worthy of the plate if it hasn't been primped and preened with noodles and lemongrass, sesame and galangal, preserved lemon or lime juice, pillow bags of mixed leaves, roasted vegetables or Parmesan and balsamic, we have almost lost sight of the simple, green, perfectly dressed leaf. Never be ashamed to serve a green salad made with a luscious cos lettuce with its milky, bitter heart chopped in with the leaves, or a floppy English round lettuce with its softer, wavy green leaves. A good dressing is what counts and that I have already discussed on pages 75–77. These salads on the following pages are more substantial. They can constitute a complete lunch or supper, a starter, part of a brunch, what you will.

GREEK SALAD

4 large, ripe tomatoes or two punnets of cherry tomatoes
1 cucumber
225g/8oz feta (make sure it is a good, pure sheep's milk cheese)
1 mild onion, or a bunch of spring onions, including the green tips
1 handful good, glossy black olives that have been kept in olive oil, not brine
1 handful fresh oregano or marjoram
black pepper
your best olive oil, a good fruity green one

What really makes this salad so good is the quality of the tomatoes, something we are never going to match in these northerly climes. Ours are thin and acidic rather than fat, meaty and luscious. But every so often we can get the real McCoy, or we can just make a tomato salad with what we've got and imagine the difference!

Core and slice the large tomatoes or halve the cherry tomatoes and spread them out, slightly overlapping, on a large plate. Peel alternate strips of the cucumber, then cut in half, remove the seeds and slice into coin-thick semi-circles. Lay them over the tomatoes.

Crumble the feta on top, or cut it into the thinnest slices you can. Finely sliced onions make the next layer, or scatter over the chopped spring onions and their greenery. Then sprinkle over the olives and oregano. Scrunch over some black pepper and pour on a generous libation of olive oil before serving with good, crusty bread. Salt is unnecessary – the feta is salty enough.

SPICED PEARS WITH GORGONZOLA, WATERCRESS AND SALTED WALNUT SALAD

These spiced pears are the most wonderful winter fruit dish and I use them with venison, guinea fowl, partridge and pheasant as well as in this salad. You may cook quinces in the same spice mix, too, to serve with game or pork. A lovely re-working of the classic combination of pears and blue cheese, this is luscious and creamy, salty and fresh tasting.

Put the chilli, herbs, spices, honey, lemon rind and most of the juice, Marsala and sugar in a pan just large enough to hold the pears as well and bring slowly to the boil. Simmer for 5 minutes.

Meanwhile, peel the pears, leaving the stalks on. Rub the pears with a little lemon juice so they don't discolour. Put the pears in the pan with the spicy liquid and add a little water to just cover if you need to. Bring back to the boil then simmer for 30–40 minutes or until soft right through when pierced with a skewer.

Let the pears cool, then cut them in half and remove the cores. Cream the Gorgonzola and cream cheese in a bowl with a fork. Stir in the spring onions and herbs and season. Spoon the mixture into the cavities of the pears and place them on a plate on top of the salad leaves.

Melt the butter in a pan and when it is foaming, throw in the walnuts. Add the maple syrup or sugar and turn the nuts to coat. Cook the halved walnuts until they are hot but not browned and add enough salt flakes to give them a deliciously buttery salt/sweet balance. Strew them on the salad when they are still warm. Add the salad dressing and serve.

SERVES 6

SPICED PEARS
1 red chilli, halved and seeded
1 sprig of rosemary
1 bay leaf
2 star anise
2 cinnamon sticks
2 tbsp honey
pared rind and juice of 2 lemons
600ml/1 pint Marsala
450g/1lb unrefined caster sugar
6 conference pears

FILLING
225g/8oz Gorgonzola
110g/4oz best cream cheese
1 tbsp spring onions, finely chopped
2 tsp chives, finely chopped
1 tsp thyme leaves, chopped
black pepper

SALAD
a handful of watercress for each
    plate, or rocket leaves – you need
    something peppery
a simple dressing of extra virgin olive
    oil and good balsamic vinegar

TOPPING
knob of butter
110g/4oz walnuts
1 dsrtsp maple syrup or sugar
good sea salt like sel de Guerande

ROASTED AUBERGINE, FENNEL AND ONION SALAD WITH CHICKPEAS, FETA AND SPINACH

SERVES 4

a handful of chickpeas
1 onion, stuck with cloves
1 carrot, chopped
1 stick of celery, chopped
thyme and bay leaves
1 aubergine
2 red onions
4 large tomatoes
2 fennel bulbs
4 or 5 cloves of garlic
a sprig of fresh thyme
olive oil
a well-aged balsamic vinegar; you
    need something mellow and
    velvety, not sharp and rough
a handful of baby spinach leaves
110g/4oz good sheep's milk feta
sea salt and black pepper

You may add or subtract from this with whatever seasonal vegetables are good for roasting and offer some contrast – colour, flavour and texture-wise – from each other. So, sweet potatoes, squash, pumpkin, courgettes and red or yellow peppers can all be thrown into the roasting tin in whatever quantities you happen to have.

Soak the chickpeas overnight in cold water. Next day, rinse them and just cover with fresh water in a large earthenware casserole. Add the onion, carrot, celery and herbs and bring to the boil. Skim, then cover and leave to simmer at a mere burble for 2 hours.

Preheat the oven to 220°C/425°F/Gas 7. Cube the aubergine, peel the onions and cut them into eighths, and halve the tomatoes. Remove the outer leaves of the fennel bulbs and cut them through their cores into quarters. Place all the vegetables on a roasting tray with the garlic and dribble olive oil over everything. Add the thyme and roast for 30–40 minutes until everything is cooked through. Remove from the oven and add a libation of olive oil and some balsamic vinegar to taste.

Place the roasted vegetables on a pretty, flat plate. Toss in the cooked chickpeas and the raw spinach, which will wilt gently in the warmth, and crumble over the feta. Season and serve.

POTATO SALAD

SERVES 4

675g/1½lb or so waxy new potatoes
    like Jersey Royal, Pink Fir Apples,
    Rattes or Anya
mint
1 tbsp Dijon mustard
2 tbsp red wine vinegar
90ml/3fl oz vegetable oil
2 tbsp extra virgin olive oil
a bunch of spring onions, finely
    chopped with a little bit of their
    green shoots, or a shallot or mild,
    small onion, finely chopped
a bunch of snipped chives
sea salt and freshly ground black
    pepper

Like all disarmingly simple things, this can be spoiled by not paying attention to detail and using inferior ingredients. As this is one of the most wonderful and versatile of dishes, as good with chicken or grilled meat as it is with baked fish or a raft of other different salads, it is worth getting right.

Scrape the potatoes if they are Jersey Royals. If they are Pink Fir Apples it is easier to take the skins off when they are boiled and still hot as they are so nubbly and knobbly. Boil them in salted water with a few sprigs of mint, then drain.

While the potatoes are cooking, make the dressing by whisking all the ingredients together and seasoning to taste. Skin and chop or just chop the potatoes when they are hot and dress them immediately, turning them well with the dressing, shallot or spring onion and the chives. Eat warm.

SPICY PRAWN NOODLE SALAD

This is a zingy, fragrant, oriental-inspired salad, full of great raw vegetables and vibrant tastes.

SERVES 4

1 clove of garlic, finely chopped
1 red chilli, seeded and diced
a finger of fresh ginger, grated
1 dsrtsp fresh coriander, chopped
4 tbsp organic shoyu sauce
olive oil
the juice of a lime
12 large raw prawns in their shells
255g/9oz packet of organic plain
　　or spinach egg noodles
1 large carrot
a handful of mangetout
a handful of beansprouts
5 or 6 raw chestnut mushrooms
a bunch each of fresh mint and fresh
　　coriander

DRESSING

3 organic lemons
3 organic limes
1 clove of garlic
a finger of fresh ginger, grated
1 dsrtsp runny honey
olive oil
a piece of stem ginger and 1 tbsp of
　　the syrup (optional)
salt and pepper

Mix together the garlic, chilli, ginger, coriander, shoyu sauce, olive oil and lime in a bowl, add the prawns and leave to marinate. Cook the noodles as per instructions for 4 minutes, then coat them lightly with sesame or olive oil so they won't stick.

Peel the carrot, then, using the peeler, ribbon it from top to bottom. Throw the ribbons into the bowl with the noodles. Thinly slice the mangetout into strips, throw them into the bowl and add the bean sprouts and mushrooms.

Remove the prawns from the marinade. Griddle the prawns until pink and cooked through on both sides, then shell them.

To make the dressing, peel the citrus fruits thinly with a potato peeler so that you have strips of peel with no pith. Put the slices of peel with the juice of the fruit in a pan with the garlic, fresh ginger and honey. Bring to the boil and reduce by a half until you have a lovely, syrupy sauce. Strain it into a bowl through a sieve, add the olive oil until you have a dressing you like the taste of, then add the finely chopped piece of stem ginger and its syrup. Season to taste.

Throw half the roughly chopped coriander and mint into the salad, add the dressing and toss with your fingers to amalgamate well. Add the rest of the herbs and serve.

SALADE NIÇOISE

It is always difficult to give a recipe for a dish about which people feel such national pride, subjective fervour and purist indignation. Irish stew and Caesar salad also spring immediately to mind. In France you wouldn't give a recipe for this salad because no one would read it anyway. They would just look in their fridge, their garden, their store cupboard, their leftover bowls and FIND the ingredients – I mean invent the ingredients for that particular night's rendition of La Niçoise. The attraction of the Niçoise is the combination of the cooked and the raw, the vibrant and the mild, the known and unexpected with the non-formulaic twist. Here is a little guidance on how I like to play with the theme and a purely personal one it is too. There are certain ingredients and ways of cooking them that I would always use, while others are a movable feast.

Scrape the Jersey Royals, or wash them and cook with their skins on, depending on how rustic you feel. Drain and slice when still hot. While the potatoes are cooking, throw the topped and tailed green beans into plenty of boiling, salted water – a handful at a time, so that the temperature doesn't fall below a rolling boil. That way, the beans retain their colour and don't turn khaki. Do not undercook. Al dente green beans are a fad of the food photographers who want their beans emerald green. They should be cooked to tender as the French do! Drain and refresh in cold water.

Throw the shelled broad beans into boiling water. If they are new season's and tiny, cook for no more than a minute, then pour cold water over them and drain thoroughly.

Boil the eggs for 6–7 minutes depending on their size, then pour cold water into the pan for a couple of minutes. I like softly hard-boiled eggs whose yolks still have a memory of crocus-coloured goo about them. Peel when you can stand the heat and slice in half.

Mix the first 4 dressing ingredients together well, then pour in the oil, whisking as you go, until you have the desired flavour.

Find a beautiful, shallow, earthenware dish and strew the washed, torn lettuce and its heart over the bottom of the dish. In the middle of the lettuce, pile a mound of the green and broad beans, potatoes, artichokes, cucumber and tomatoes, tuna and black olives. Artful arranging is fine at this stage. I like things not too regimented, but I always put the halves of egg around the edge with a cross of anchovies over them.

Dress the salad with the dressing and herbs, bring it to the table, and gently toss the central ingredients in front of the assembled company if you feel like it. A bit of a ritual is good with a dish such as this. Good French bread is a necessity.

SERVES 4

450g/1lb waxy new potatoes like Jersey Royals
450g/1lb green beans
450g/1lb shelled weight broad beans
6 organic eggs
1 cos lettuce
4 large, meaty, ripe tomatoes, skinned and quartered
a cucumber, skinned, split in half, seeded with a teaspoon and chopped into dice
8 small artichoke hearts, cut into chunks; I favour the charcoal-roasted ones in olive oil from Seggiano
1–2 tins best tuna or ventresca (belly of tuna) from Ortiz sold by Brindisa, or a couple of seared tuna steaks cooked rare and broken into chunks
a tin of anchovies in olive oil
16–20 black olives, the glossy Niçoise ones if you can get them
a little bunch of chives, snipped small
1–2 sprigs tarragon, chopped small

DRESSING

1 heaped tsp French mustard
sea salt and black pepper
2 tbsp tarragon vinegar
2 cloves of garlic, finely minced
6–8 tbsp best extra virgin olive oil

FRESH FIG AND MINT SALAD

SERVES 6

1kg/2¼lb ripe figs, freshly picked if
    possible
3 thin slices prosciutto, fat removed
12–15 fresh leaves of mint
juice of 1 lemon
salt
200ml/7fl oz Jersey cream

I have long been an admirer of the great food writer Richard Olney, an American who became an honorary Frenchman; he was so much more than a Francophile even before he moved to France. His writing is of the order of Elizabeth David, and this recipe, though more practicable in the south of France where you can pick a ripe fig straight from the tree, is nevertheless do-able and delectably so over here. Olney refers to the fact that 'French friends find the recipe bizarre, but all who have tasted it have been delighted by the clean, clear, surprising combination of flavours and fragrance.' How right he is.

Olney peels the figs, I do not, before cutting halfway down from the stem end, making two incisions in the form of a cross. Press gently from the sides to open them slightly. Arrange the figs closely packed on a serving dish and chill for about an hour in the coldest part of the fridge.

Cut the ham into fine julienne strips about 2.5cm/1in long and matchstick width. Crush about half of the mint leaves in the lemon juice, leave to macerate for 20–30 minutes, then discard them. Dissolve the salt into the lemon juice and slowly stir in the cream – the acid of the lemon will thicken it somewhat and adding the cream a little at a time while continuing to stir encourages the thickening. Taste for salt.

Sprinkle the figs with half the ham julienne and spoon over the cream sauce. Distribute the remaining ham on the surface and decorate with the remaining mint leaves.

AUBERGINE SALAD WITH A WILD ROCKET PURÉE

SERVES 2

1 large aubergine (the stripy purple
   and white kind if you can find
   them)
best extra-virgin olive oil to brush
   over the slices
1 bunch of rocket, torn to shreds
90–120ml/3–4fl oz best extra-virgin
   olive oil
lemon juice
55g/2oz pine nuts
black pepper
a small piece of sheep's milk feta
a sprig of mint

Aubergines are particularly good in salads if they haven't been subjected to the frying-in-oil treatment that makes them so oily and spongy you could positively wring them out. This method of brushing the aubergine slices with a little olive oil and roasting them solves both the oily and the textural problem. They soften uniformly and emerge quite, but not entirely, dry. This purée was, I have to admit, a stroke of genius. The sharply lemony, peppery vibrant green stuff is a perfect foil to the aubergine's gentle, smoky flavour.

Preheat the oven to 180°C/350°F/Gas 4. Slice the aubergine into discs, brush each side with olive oil and place them on non-stick paper on a baking tray. Roast for 15 minutes or so, the aubergines should be soft, but not browned and crisp. Place in a single layer on a plate, slightly overlapping.

Blend the rocket, olive oil, lemon juice and pine nuts with a good scrunch of black pepper, making sure you do not over-blend it to a sludge. Spread a little of the purée over each aubergine slice and keep the rest covered in the fridge to use another time.

Crumble a small lump of feta into little pieces over the salad, add some finely chopped mint leaves, and sprinkle over a little extra virgin olive oil and a spritz of lemon juice. Serve just warm, or at room temperature

WARM CHICKEN AND PUY LENTIL SALAD WITH STOVE-DRIED TOMATOES

SERVES 4

4 large vine-ripened tomatoes,
    stove-dried (see p. 162)
675g/1½lb chicken thighs
90ml/3fl oz lemon juice
9 cloves of garlic
90ml/3fl oz extra virgin olive oil
10 sprigs thyme
1 carrot, peeled and diced
1 stick celery, diced
1 white onion, peeled and diced
1 bay leaf
100g/3½oz Puy lentils, picked and
    washed thoroughly in a sieve
1 tbsp red wine vinegar
850ml/1½ pints chicken stock
    (see p. 80)
1 organic egg
170g/6oz Greek or Turkish yoghurt
sea salt and black pepper
140g/5oz rocket

This is a stunning salad, served at the healthiest fast-food joint I know – Leon's in Soho's Great Marlborough Street. Remember to start it ahead of time as the chicken needs marinating and the tomatoes need drying. I don't soak the lentils, I just clean them thoroughly. Stove-dried tomatoes are also fantastic in pasta with chunks of goat's cheese, sage leaves frazzled in olive oil, and crème fraîche and a little butter stirred in.

Start preparing the stove-dried tomatoes a day or so before you want to eat this salad (see page 162). Dice the chicken into chunky, bite-sized pieces and marinate overnight in 2 tablespoons of the lemon juice, 3 of the garlic cloves, finely chopped, and 1 tablespoon of olive oil. Cover with clingfilm and refrigerate overnight.

The next day, heat the oven to 150°C/300°F/Gas 2. Warm a generous tablespoon of oil in a heavy-based pan on a medium heat and throw in the carrot, celery and onion. Add a few sprigs of thyme, 2 chopped cloves of garlic and the bay leaf and sweat without colouring for about 10 minutes.

Add the drained lentils, pour in the red wine vinegar and reduce until the liquid has evaporated. Pour in the chicken stock, cover with a layer of greaseproof paper and foil and bake in the oven for 20 minutes, or until tender but with a slight bite. Season to taste and allow to cool.

Chop the remaining garlic and put it in the blender with the egg. Whizz for a few minutes until pale and fluffed up, then start pouring in the rest of the olive oil, a drop or two at a time to begin with. Add 40ml/1½fl oz of lemon juice, then turn out into a bowl and stir in the yoghurt. (If you prefer to make the sauce by hand with a wooden spoon as I do, use an egg yolk not the whole egg.)

Season the chicken and grill for about 10 minutes, turning halfway through. Meanwhile, put the rocket on a large serving dish, followed by the stove-dried tomatoes and half the lentils. Scatter the chicken over the top when it is cooked, then dress with more lemon juice and olive oil.

Spoon over as much of the garlic sauce as you like, but don't drown the salad – you can keep what remains and use it for crudités later. Add the rest of the lentils and thyme, and serve warm with wedges of lemon.

TOMATO SALAD

It is all very well thinking this is the easiest of salads to make, but it isn't. We can't even buy tomatoes worthy of it here; ours are acidic and watery and seedy and the skins are tough and unyielding. So, get Italian or Provençal tomatoes if you possibly can and organic ones whenever possible. The apologies that are grown hydroponically are tasteless and cotton woolly.

Always core tomatoes with a small sharp knife. To peel, blanch them in boiling water for 30 seconds and spike them with a knife to help the skin loosen and tear. Drain and refresh them briefly in cold water; you do not want the tomatoes to cook.

Slice the tomatoes and place them slightly overlapping on a large plate. Never dress them until just before serving. Allow a big tomato per person and a little extra for the dish. Strew with torn basil, finely chopped tarragon, parsley, chives, chervil or whichever herb is to hand, and season liberally with black pepper. You may add some very finely chopped garlic too, if you wish.

Just before serving, add a little salt – no earlier or it will encourage the tomatoes to water – and a liberal libation of the best extra virgin olive oil you have. You may wish to add a good teaspoon of Dijon mustard to the oil before you dress the salad. I like to take this dressing in a screw top jar on bracing Irish picnics!

CAESAR SALAD

2 cloves of garlic, crushed
170ml/6fl oz olive oil
6 tbsp cubed white bread – use good French-style sourdough
leaves from two heads of Romaine or a couple of small cos lettuces, washed and chilled
2 organic eggs
juice of 2 lemons
8 drops of Worcestershire sauce
6 tbsp freshly grated Parmesan cheese

This is the original Caesar salad recipe, as served by Caesar Cardini in Tijuana in Mexico. He didn't put anchovies in his, but I have to chop or pound a few into mine and add them with the oil.

The great American food writer Julia Child travelled to Tijuana in the 1920s to eat Cardini's famous salad with her parents, and wrote about it in *Julia Child's Kitchen*: 'Caesar rolled the big cart up to the table and tossed the Romaine in a great wooden bowl, and I wish I could say I remember his every move, but I don't. The only thing I see again clearly are the eggs. I can see him break two eggs over that Romaine and roll them in; the greens going all creamy as the eggs flowed over them.' People actually began to drive to Mexico to eat the famous salad and then it spread across the restaurant menus of the States to the point when it became the most famous recipe to originate there in years. The salad leaves should not be torn or cut, but plenty of restaurants take no notice of that detail.

Put the garlic in the olive oil and leave for an hour or more to infuse. Preheat the oven to 200°C/400°F/Gas 6. Brush the bread with some of the oil and bake until golden.

Put the lettuce leaves in a big bowl. Place the eggs in cold water, bring to the boil and boil for 1 minute. Break the eggs over the salad leaves and toss the salad slowly with your hands. Add the lemon juice, olive oil, Worcestershire sauce and seasoning, then toss the salad very well again. Add the cheese, toss one more time and serve.

Caesar Salad

MOROCCAN CARROT SALAD

SERVES 4

500g/1lb 2oz carrots, peeled and cut
    into sticks
4 cloves of garlic, peeled
4 tbsp olive oil
2 tbsp cider vinegar
1 tsp cumin, roasted in a pan then
    ground
1 tsp paprika
sea salt and black pepper
2 tbsp fresh coriander, chopped

This is one of the many wonderful dishes Sami cooks at Ottolenghi, my favourite traiteur/Viennoiserie/café, in London. The earthy, smoky flavours here work really well with red meat, lamb, beef or pork, the cider vinegar cutting the fat. It is also good if you are serving a chermoula with fish or meat (see page 433).

Put the carrots in a saucepan and cover with boiling, salted water. Add the garlic, and cook until tender but not soft. Drain, crush the garlic cloves and add them to the carrots with the remaining ingredients, leaving aside half the coriander.

Transfer to a serving dish while hot and sprinkle over the rest of the coriander. I serve this at room temperature, but it can be served hot or cold.

BAZARGAN OR CRACKED WHEAT AND NUT SALAD

SERVES 6–8

340g/12oz bulghur (cracked wheat)
6–8 tbsp extra virgin olive oil
3 tbsp pomegranate molasses or
    2 tbsp tamarind paste dissolved in
    4 tbsp boiling water
juice of a lemon
4 tbsp tomato paste
1 tsp ground cumin
1 tsp ground coriander
½ tsp ground allspice
½ tsp ground cayenne or chilli
    pepper, or to taste
140g/5oz walnuts, very coarsely
    chopped
100g/3½oz hazelnuts, very coarsely
    chopped
55g/2oz pine nuts, lightly toasted
a large bunch flat-leaf parsley, finely
    chopped

This inspirational Syrian dish is from Claudia Roden's seminal *The Book of Jewish Food*. The sourness of the pomegranate molasses or tamarind gives the grain a delicious sharp-sweet flavour and colours the bulghur, which should be of the coarse kind.

Roden advises making it 4 hours before serving so that the wheat absorbs the dressing properly. I made mine with pomegranate molasses.

Put the bulghur into a large bowl and cover with plenty of cold, slightly salted water. Leave to soak for an hour or until tender (the coarse bulghur takes much longer). Drain in a sieve and press out the excess water.

In a serving bowl, beat the olive oil with the pomegranate molasses or dissolved tamarind paste. Add the lemon juice, tomato paste, cumin, coriander, allspice and cayenne and beat well. Pour over the cracked wheat and mix thoroughly. Add the nuts and flat-leaf parsley, mix again and adjust the seasoning if necessary.

SALADE CAUCHOISE

This amount is for one person. You don't need to be too precise about quantities – or even ingredients: if you don't have spring onions, use chives, shallots or onions.

Finely shred about 55 g/2oz cooked ham into long thin strips, and put in a bowl with a stick of finely chopped celery. Add 1 tablespoon of chopped spring onions, and another of well-broken walnuts, then season with salt, pepper and a clove of crushed garlic. Add a few boiled tiny new potatoes if you want to make the dish more substantial. Mix well, and bind with some homemade mayonnaise that you have thinned with cream or milk.

BROAD BEAN SALAD WITH PRESERVED LEMON, CORIANDER AND SPANISH PAPRIKA

SERVES 4

500g/1lb 2oz small broad beans (frozen are fine but thaw them first)
1 large onion, thinly sliced
1 tbsp Spanish paprika
1 tsp cumin, roasted in a pan then ground
4 tbsp extra virgin olive oil
6 tbsp water
sea salt and black pepper
1 medium bunch of coriander, coarsely chopped
half a preserved lemon, thinly sliced
juice of a lemon

This is another great Ottolenghi dish from Sami, one of the best cooks of vegetables I know. It is wonderful with the tiny, pale, nail-sized new season's beans in early summer, or make it with frozen broad beans after the season has finished.

Put the broad beans, onion, paprika, cumin, olive oil and water in a large saucepan. Season, cover and bring to the boil. Turn down the heat and simmer until the beans are just cooked (about 10 minutes if they are large, frozen beans; 1–3 minutes if they are baby, new season's beans). You may need to add a little more water during the cooking.

Add the chopped coriander, preserved lemon and lemon juice, then adjust the seasoning. Serve hot or warm.

VEGETABLES

What are worse, the sins of omission or the sins of commission?

This section will always feel incomplete because it could so easily be book length, so I can really only give recipes for a few special dishes that I return to time and time again. Some are the essence of simplicity, others a little more outré and complicated. I have gone for the classics wherever possible because a book such as this without a recipe for pommes dauphinois or Anna, carrots Vichy or creamed spinach, would deny you the pleasures that have fuelled more good dinners in my life than almost any others. They are the comfort foods of the root, shoot and leaf world, without which our daily bread would be all the more impoverished. They are the dishes we crave, in their appropriate season, when the body either needs the depths of ivory, garlicky, creamy carbohydrate of the dauphinois, or the oily-rich, thyme-scented fragrance of a summer ratatouille, served warm with a hunk of bread and a glass of rosé.

I have huge nostalgia for carrots Vichy, too. It was the first vegetable I cooked for a grown-up dinner, having learned how to make them under the tutelage of my cousin David's wife Serena, a stunningly good cook. Until then I had not even known that there was a way of cooking vegetables that didn't just involve boiling water. At that time, roasted vegetables, other than the potato, hadn't been invented, so the vegetable kingdom was somewhat limited to steaming, boiling and the odd blanket of béchamel or cheese sauce being thrown over the greenery.

CARROTS VICHY

SERVES 4

450g/1lb organic carrots
30g/1oz unsalted butter
1 tsp molasses or muscovado sugar
water or chicken stock (see p. 80)
sea salt and black pepper
a little chopped mint, parsley, chervil
    or chives

This classic dish makes sweet carrots sweeter. If you make it with chicken stock it is even better. The best thing to serve with a Sunday roast and with so many different meat and fish dishes, it is a way of cooking carrots that I expect you will use all your cooking life. I have.

If the carrots are young and small they won't need cutting or peeling, merely washing; if they are somewhat long in the tooth, peel them and slice them into long, chunky strips.

Place them in a heavy-bottomed pan with a wide surface area and throw on the butter and sugar. Half cover with cold water or chicken stock. Bring to the boil and cook at a brisk boil with no lid on until the water or stock has all but evaporated. Then get in there quick and toss the carrots to coat and caramelise them in the sugary, buttery juices. Do not let them burn. Remove them from the heat the moment they've begun to caramelise and there is no longer any liquid.

Season and add chopped herbs. Do not salt before cooking as the salt will intensify as the liquid reduces.

POMMES ANNA

SERVES 3–4

675g/1½lb potatoes, peeled and
    thinly sliced
85–110g/3–4oz unsalted butter,
    melted
sea salt
black pepper

I cook this deliciously simple dish in a cast-iron, heavy-bottomed, stubby-handled frying pan that can go in the oven. Traditionally the pan should be lidded but mine isn't, so I use greased greaseproof paper.

Preheat the oven to 200°C/400°F/Gas 6. Wash the starch out of the potatoes in a colander, pat dry in a cloth, and place the slices in overlapping circles on the well buttered base of the pan. Brush butter over each layer as you go, and season. Cover with greaseproof paper or a lid and cook in the oven. Check with a skewer after 45 minutes, but the potatoes can take up to an hour.

SAFFRON-STEWED JERSEY NEW POTATOES WITH CHICKEN STOCK AND THYME

SERVE 4

675g/1½ lb Jersey new potatoes,
    skins on but scrubbed
30g/1oz butter
a good pinch of saffron threads
1 bay leaf
a sprig of thyme
120ml/4fl oz of hot chicken stock
    (see p. 80)
1 spring onion, finely chopped
knob of butter (optional)

These are a marvellous accompaniment to grilled or baked white fish, intensely flavoured with the reduced stock and saffron and the scent of bay and thyme. A lovely early summer way to cook the little pebbles of Jersey New at the start of their season.

Sweat the potatoes in the butter in a heavy-bottomed casserole for a couple of minutes. Add the saffron threads, bay leaf and thyme and shake the pan. Add the hot chicken stock, cover the pan and simmer gently for about 15 minutes.

Remove the lid and boil to reduce the liquid until it is a syrupy glaze. Remove the thyme and the bay leaf, add the finely chopped spring onion and another knob of butter if you like, and cook the potatoes a couple of minutes longer.

POMMES DAUPHINOIS

SERVES 4–6

900g/2lb potatoes, peeled, sliced
  about 5 mm/¼ in thick on a
  mandolin or a Magimix slicing disc
  into cold water
600ml/1 pint double cream, Jersey if
  possible
150ml/5fl oz full-cream milk, Jersey
  if possible
1 fat clove of garlic, finely chopped
nutmeg
sea salt and black pepper
unsalted butter for greasing the
  gratin dish

The thing that many people get wrong when they cook this dish is the oven temperature. If you nuke the potatoes, the cream will curdle; inexorable fact. There are those who grate Gruyère into their Dauphinois, but the classic way, the best way, to my mind, is the simplest of all: potatoes, a suspicion of garlic, cream, milk and seasoning. Extraordinary that a dish of such succulence, its layers almost meltingly fondant, the cream bubbling and scented with the faintest whiff of the allium and nutmeg, should be so unsurpassably wonderful.

Peel the potatoes and slice them about 5mm/¼in thick on a mandolin or with a Magimix slicing disc. Put them in cold water.

Preheat the oven to 140°C/275°F/Gas 1. Pour the cream and milk into a pan and add the chopped garlic, a good grating of nutmeg and the seasoning. Warm through to hot on a low heat.

Meanwhile, drain the potatoes, dry them on kitchen paper or a clean tea towel and throw them back in the bowl. Pour the cream mixture over them and turn to coat. Scrape the creamy potatoes into a well-buttered gratin dish and push them well down into the dish. Bake in the middle of the oven for an hour before inserting a skewer right down deep. If the potatoes are still resistant, and not golden and bubbling on top, give them a little longer until they are and flash them briefly under a hot grill to brown. If, on the other hand, you find the potatoes are browning too quickly, cover with a sheet of greaseproof.

Gratins of vegetables are a lovely accompaniment to roast meat or baked chops and the dauphinois can be adapted to the time of year and what's in season so that you have your vegetables and potatoes in one dish. Use Jerusalem artichokes with the potatoes, in equal proportion, or celeriac – I favour one-third of artichokes or celeriac to two-thirds potato. Parsnips are lovely too, with crème fraîche and a tablespoon of grain mustard added in lieu of ordinary cream. Turnips are good, half and half, or you may leave the rooty theme and add sliced fennel in between the layers of potato.

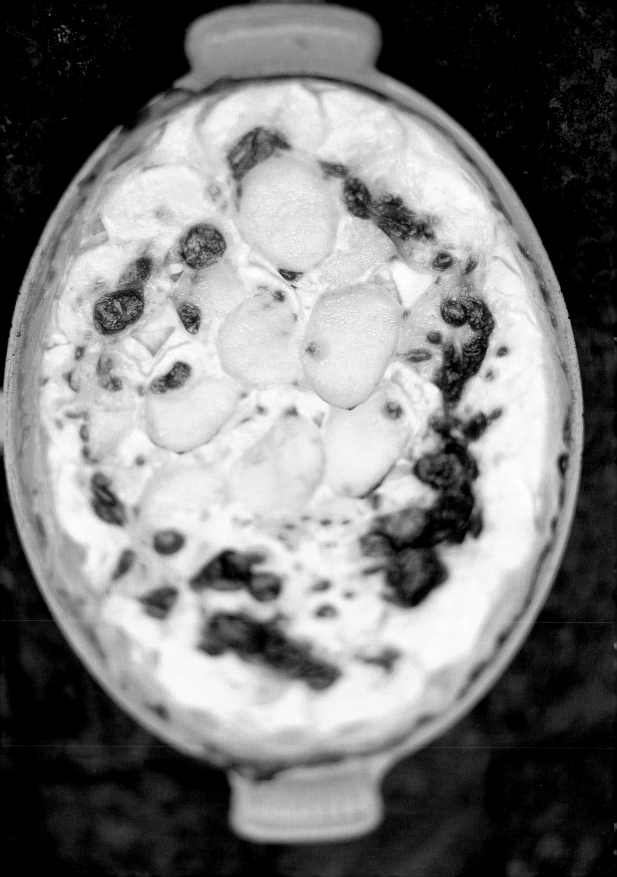

BAKED BEETROOT

The sweet earthiness of the beetroot is inimitable but it is an acquired taste. Not many children can cope, and the bleeding of the ruby juices into their surrounding companions can be off-puttingly institutional, but persevere. Here's how to do it.

Wash, but do not peel the beetroot. Do not disturb the wispy rooty bits by cutting them as the beetroot will instantly start secreting its dark juices. Wrap each beetroot separately and tightly in foil and bake in a medium oven until tender when pierced with a skewer.

Peel when you can bear to and serve the beetroot as they are, or chopped into cubes with a dollop of crème fraîche spritzed with a little lemon juice, some black pepper and a tablespoon of dill or chives.

SERVES 4

8 small or 4 medium beetroot

OPTIONAL
crème fraîche
lemon juice
black pepper
dill or chives

CABBAGE WITH GRAIN MUSTARD AND LARDONS

A good winter way with a white cabbage, especially if you are serving something porky or beefy.

Halve the cabbage, removing any tough, outer leaves and remove the core before slicing as slimly as you can into long shreds. Snip the rashers into strips and put them in a large, heavy-bottomed pot over a medium heat, allowing them to begin to release their fat. Add the clove of garlic when the rashers are beginning to brown. Stir it around, then turn up the heat, add the olive oil and heat it through.

Hurl in the cabbage and stir to coat it in oil. Cook for a matter of a few minutes until the cabbage is no longer raw but has crunch and has turned opaque. Stir in the mustard – it turns bitter if it goes in any earlier – and add the pepper, any salt you think it needs and a knob of butter if you like.

SERVES 6–8

1 cabbage
4 rashers organic streaky bacon
2–3 tbsp olive oil
a fat clove of garlic
2 dsrtsp or to taste grain mustard
black pepper
30g/1oz unsalted butter

COURGETTE GRATIN

This is as good served with fresh tomato sauce as it is with grilled meat or fish. A little tarragon can be added as well as the parsley. Serve warm rather than hot.

Heat the oven to 180°C/350°F/Gas 4. Gently sauté the onion in the oil until softened and translucent, adding the garlic midway through the process.

Toss in the courgettes and chopped parsley (and some tarragon, if you like) and continue to cook gently until the courgettes have softened but still retain some texture.

Throw in the rice and stir, allowing it to absorb the liquid, and cook for 10 minutes. Season. Beat the eggs with the cheese, add to the courgettes and turn into an oiled earthenware dish. Bake in the oven for about 30 minutes until bronzed and bubbling. Serve warm rather than hot.

SERVES 4

1 large onion, chopped
3 tbsp olive oil
3 cloves of garlic, finely chopped
450g/1lb small courgettes, cut coin thin
handful of flat-leaf parsley
55g/2oz long-grain rice
sea salt and black pepper
3 organic eggs
2 handfuls freshly grated Parmesan or Gruyère

STUFFED COURGETTES OR TOMATOES

SERVES 4

1 medium onion, finely chopped
olive oil for sautéeing and dribbling
    over the courgettes
2 cloves of garlic, finely chopped
110g/4oz each pork and veal mince
55g/2oz cooked ham, diced
1 large tomato, peeled, seeded and
    chopped
handful of parsley
110g/4oz spinach, briefly cooked and
    thoroughly drained and chopped
handful of breadcrumbs
1 organic egg
sea salt and black pepper
a couple of handfuls of freshly grated
    Parmesan
4 round courgettes with the tops
    removed and the inner flesh
    scooped out to leave a strong wall;
    or if unavailable use long ones

Think in terms of leftovers, rather than specific quantities, and which flavour you would like to be predominant in this dish. You may use less meat, only one kind of meat, or olives or spinach in the farci. If you have some cooked beef, chicken or lamb, simply omit the browning stage. Onion, garlic and herbs are a must, as is the binding force of the cheese.

Heat oven to 200°C/400°F/Gas 6. Sauté the onion gently in olive oil for 15 minutes, adding the garlic and the minced meat when the onion has softened. Cook until the meat has lost its raw colour.

In a bowl, mix the remaining ingredients, except the cheese and courgettes, and season. Pack the courgettes with the stuffing and top with their 'hats'. Place the courgettes in a gratin dish, sprinkle with Parmesan and drizzle with olive oil.

Bake for about 40 minutes, then check with a skewer that the courgettes are cooked right through. Remove from the oven to cool and eat while still warm.

ENDIVES AU BEURRE

SERVES 4

4 Belgian endives or Treviso chicory
45–55g/1½–2oz unsalted butter
black pepper
lemon juice

As underused in salads as they are as a cooked vegetable, endives enhance fish and meat equally well. I serve mine alongside a chined loin of pork.

The most important thing to remember is not to cut the bottoms off the endives, which will lead to the release of bitter juices. Leave them whole, and complement their mildly bitter flavour with lemon at the end. I added no salt to the dish.

Heat oven to 150°C/300°F/Gas 2. Pack the endives tightly into a small earthenware or glass casserole, adding knobs of butter and fresh black pepper. Cover and place in the oven for 1–1½ hours until cooked (the base should be tender when pierced with a skewer). Add a good squeeze of lemon juice and serve.

450g/1lb asparagus

HOLLANDAISE SAUCE
170g/6oz best unsalted butter
2 organic egg yolks
sea salt and black pepper
juice of ½ a lemon

ASPARAGUS WITH HOLLANDAISE

I am of the firm opinion that asparagus needs dressing down rather than dressing up, and that its most compatible partners are butter and eggs. Choose the freshest asparagus you can lay your hands on; any sign of dried, withering, scaly stalks and it's not worth buying. Simply dressed, with butter, vinaigrette or hollandaise, asparagus should be eaten warm, and in the fingers. You'll find one method of making hollandaise on page 254. This is an alternative.

Trim the bases if the spears need it. Either stand the bundles upright, tied with string, in a lidded pan with 8cm/3in of boiling, salted water, or lower them diagonally into a steamer, leaving the tips to just poke out from the semi-closed lid so they don't overcook. Check with the point of a knife after 5 minutes, and if it slips in unresisted, the asparagus is cooked. The fattest stems will take up to 5 minutes longer.

Drain well and put on the plate with a deep yellow puddle of hollandaise. If you're having the new potatoes for your next course, cook them around the asparagus; it will scent them deliciously.

HOLLANDAISE

Melt the butter in a small pan, take it off the heat and after a minute or so skim the white frothy solids from the top with a spoon and some kitchen paper. Whisk the egg yolks with a dessertspoon of water in a small pan over a very low heat until thick. Add the melted butter bit by bit, whisking as you go. Do not use the milky curd-like solids at the bottom of the pan and remove from the heat before there is any danger of the mixture simmering and curdling. Season and add lemon juice.

CELERY COOKED WITH CREAM

1 head of celery
150ml/5fl oz double cream
2 organic egg yolks
sea salt and black pepper

This is a perfect accompaniment to plainly grilled lamb cutlets or French-trimmed rack of lamb.

Wash and trim the celery and peel each stalk with a potato peeler – this simple process makes all the difference. Chop the pieces into 7.5cm/3in lengths on the diagonal, and steam until tender when pierced.

Transfer the celery to a pan. Whisk the cream with the eggs, pour over the celery and heat gently so the sauce thickens without boiling. Season and serve immediately.

BAKED ONIONS WITH PORCINI

SERVES 4

4 medium-to-large onions, peeled
4 slices pancetta or organic oak-
    smoked bacon (omit if cooking for
    vegetarians)
15g/½oz porcini, reconstituted in hot
    water
1 clove of garlic, finely minced
olive oil
2–3 sprigs each of thyme and
    rosemary
200ml/7fl oz double cream
sea salt and black pepper
a large handful of freshly grated
    Parmesan

Heat the oven to 200°C/400°F/Gas 6. Cook the onions in plenty of fast-boiling salted water until tender (25–30 minutes) and drain. Slice off the tops and scoop out a little of the middles to set aside. Place the onions in a gratin dish so that they just fit.

Dice the pancetta or bacon and strain the soaked porcini. Chop the onion that you have set aside and gently fry it with the garlic in a little olive oil. Add the diced pancetta, porcini, herbs and cream. Season, then stir in most of the Parmesan and pour the mixture over the onions. Sprinkle with the remaining Parmesan and bake for about 20 minutes until molten and bubbling.

RATATOUILLE

SERVES 4–6

2 large aubergines
2 red peppers
1 large onion, finely sliced
3 cloves of garlic, chopped
olive oil
4 courgettes, sliced
a sprig of thyme and a couple of bay
    leaves
sea salt and black pepper
1 x 400g/14oz tin plum tomatoes or
    450g/1lb fresh tomatoes, skinned,
    seeded and chopped
a handful of fresh basil

There are no short cuts for this classic-for-all-seasons. The secret of the best ratatouille is simple: the vegetables have to be cooked separately before they are married. That way they retain their individual flavour, texture and character. You do not, after all, want an amorphous swamp of bland, over-stewed, oily-puddle-on-a-plate apology for this Mediterranean joy. Ratatouille is particularly good with plain roast meat or grilled fish, or as part of a summer lunch with salads and cold meat. Otherwise, just serve it for lunch with some good country sourdough bread to mop up the juices.

Slice the aubergines into discs, brush them with olive oil and place on silicone paper on a baking sheet. Roast them in a hot oven, 200°C/400°F/Gas 6 for 15–20 minutes until tender. This is quite the best way to cook aubergines without them absorbing barrels of oil.

Meanwhile, put the red peppers on a baking sheet in the oven and turn them every time a side chars, or hold them with a pair of tongs over a naked flame. Put the charred peppers into a plastic bag or a bowl covered with clingfilm for 20 minutes until they are cool enough to handle and the steam has eased the skin from the flesh. Peel, core, seed and cut them into strips or larger pieces, depending on your preference.

Sauté the onion and garlic gently in a little olive oil until softened. Add the courgettes, thyme, bay leaves and black pepper and a little more oil if necessary. When the courgettes have begun to soften, add the tomatoes and bring to a bubble before adding the aubergines and red peppers. Stew everything gently for a further 5 –10 minutes. Check the seasoning and leave to cool. Ratatouille is best eaten warm or cold rather than hot. Strew the torn basil leaves over the top before serving.

WARM BROAD BEAN AND PEA PURÉE WITH VINAIGRETTE

SERVES 4–6

1lb/450g broad beans (shelled
    weight)
1lb/450g fresh peas, but frozen will
    do (shelled weight)
chicken stock (see p. 80) or water
handful of fresh mint

VINAIGRETTE
1 clove of garlic
sea salt
1 tsp Dijon mustard
½ tbsp white wine vinegar
juice of half a lemon
black pepper
4–5 tbsp best olive oil

First make the vinaigrette by crushing the garlic with the sea salt in a mortar, then adding the rest of the ingredients. Add the olive oil last and whisk into an emulsion as you go. Check the seasoning.

You need baby broad beans, unless you are prepared to take off the leathery jackets from older ones when they're cooked. Throw the beans and peas into boiling stock or water and cook for 5 minutes. Drain, purée in a food processor and stir in the chopped mint. Dress the purée with vinaigrette when still warm. Good served with pork chops.

SPINACH

Spinach can be tough, spinach can be watery, spinach can be teeth-furringly ferrous with its oxalic acid, but it can also be one of the most wonderful vegetables to eat. It can be served raw or cooked and is good with gammon, fish or steak or just about anything. When it is young, tender and tiny-leaved spinach is known as pousse. Stir it raw into hot lentils or chickpeas for a salad where it will immediately wilt, but lose none of its flavour. A few spices, cumin and cayenne, a spritz of lemon juice, a dollop of crème fraîche or a mustardy dressing and you have it – a great one-plate lunch. A spinach salad served with some sliced raw mushrooms, frazzled bacon, avocado and toasted sesame seeds in a garlicky dressing is also a great lunch dish.

CREAMED SPINACH

30g/1oz unsalted butter
30g/1oz plain flour
300ml/10fl oz milk
sea salt, black pepper, nutmeg
3–4 tbsp double cream (optional)
900g/2lb spinach leaves, washed, tough stalks removed, some water left clinging to the leaves

This is the perfect thing with a piece of aged rump steak, a veal or pork chop or any meat or fish cooked without a sauce. The secret is not to make too much béchamel sauce and to make the sauce slightly thicker than normal, so any juices from the spinach will not thin it down too much. The cream is not essential, but you might like to enrich the sauce with it. A larger grating of nutmeg than the usual suspicion is good, as the spinach is quite strident and needs standing up to.

Make the béchamel in the normal way, but rather thicker, as mentioned above (see page 70). While the sauce is simmering and losing its flouriness, put the spinach in a large pot over a high heat and stir to make sure it doesn't stick to the bottom. There should be some water clinging to the leaves, but they should not be sodden; you just want to cook the spinach until the leaves wilt and begin to exude their juices. This takes a matter of minutes. Now drain the spinach, pressing it in a conical strainer or colander. Keep some juice in case the sauce needs thinning. Put the spinach back in the pan.

Add cream to the sauce if you like and thin with the spinach sauces if necessary. Check the seasoning and pour the sauce over the spinach.

COLD SPINACH WITH CRÈME FRAÎCHE

SERVES 4

4 tbsp olive oil
2 small cloves of garlic, peeled and finely chopped
1.8kg/4lb spinach, trimmed and thoroughly washed
grated zest of 1 large lemon
juice of half a lemon
3 tbsp crème fraîche
coarsely ground black pepper
Maldon sea salt

This is a perfect dish to eat with cold poached salmon or cold rare beef on a summer's day. It comes from one of my great food heroes, Simon Hopkinson.

Heat the olive oil. Add the garlic, stir briefly and put in the spinach. Stir-fry together, being careful not to allow the garlic to brown. Tip onto a large plate and spread out to cool.

When cold, pick up the spinach with your fingers and arrange in loose mounds on individual serving plates. Sprinkle with the lemon zest. Add the lemon juice to the crème fraîche and stir to thin slightly. Spoon the cream over the spinach, grind over plenty of black pepper and add a pinch of Maldon sea salt.

Cold Spinach with Crème Fraîche

FENNEL BRAISED WITH THYME, OLIVES AND CARDAMOM

SERVES 4

4 bulbs fennel
2 tbsp olive oil
2 cloves of garlic
8 black olives, stoned
3 cardamom pods, crushed
a bunch of thyme
a scant 600ml/1 pint chicken stock
    (see p. 80) or half water, half
    white wine
salt and pepper

This gently aniseedy braised dish is brought to life with salty olives, thyme, garlic and a breath of fragrant cardamom. It is something I always go back to when I am cooking a special fish or pork dish, as it exudes quiet sophistication and good taste. What's more, you can abandon it while you concentrate on cooking the rest of the dinner.

Preheat the oven to 180°C/350°F/Gas 4. Once you have removed the tough outer layer of the fennel bulbs, cut vertically down and quarter each one. Sweat them gently in the olive oil in a heavy-bottomed casserole.

Add the garlic, olives, cardamom, thyme and liquid, season, and bring to the boil. Cover with the pan with greaseproof paper and then with a lid, and bake in the oven for $1\frac{1}{4}$–$1\frac{1}{2}$ hours. Particularly delicious with pork or fish.

ROAST RED ONION SQUASH OR PUMPKIN WITH CHILLI, ROSEMARY AND THYME

SERVES 4

1 red onion squash
sprigs of rosemary and thyme,
    exceedingly finely chopped
2 cloves of garlic, finely chopped
1 red chilli, seeded and finely
    chopped
good olive oil
sea salt and black pepper
butter or balsamic vinegar (optional

The people of Italy and the Middle East all knew eons ago what we now know — just how easy and delicious it is to roast a vegetable. When the roast vegetable came into fashion here, a new world opened up. Sogginess, water, bleached-out colour and flavour were replaced by vibrant, rich, oily, roasty, herby tastes and robust texture. We haven't let it go for the next new thing and have developed the roast vegetable into something that makes as great a pasta sauce as it does a salad. I find the red onion squash as intensely flavoured as the best Italian or French pumpkin. It has yielding, mealy textured flesh and skin that softens to the point where you can eat it.

Preheat the oven to 200°C/400°F/Gas 6. Scoop the seeds out of the squash and cut it in melon-like slices. Put the finely chopped rosemary, thyme, garlic and chilli into a little bowl of good olive oil, sea salt and pepper to macerate, then spoon a little into the boat of each squash. You could use sage instead of rosemary and thyme for a change.

Bake the squash for about 30–40 minutes until cooked through, basting the slices a couple of times. You can add a knob of butter at the end if you feel like it or sprinkle over a little balsamic vinegar before serving.

MAIN COURSES

These are the special things that don't exactly fit into the 'classics' section of this book but are more my own, personal classics, the things I turn to, return to, tinker with, forget, abandon, but always come back to with the same degree of enthusiasm, desire, remembered and renewed pleasure and hunger. Many of them are dishes my children have been brought up with and begged for over the years. They have become family classics that unfailingly comfort and delight, and which friends have loved and gone on to cook for themselves. You will have seen some of them in my previous books and I make no apologies for that. This, after all, is the bible whose ceiling has to be a little higher, more vaulted and a lot more all encompassing.

ROAST LOIN OF COD WITH GREEN OLIVE CHERMOULA

The chermoula is an exotic species, a musky, chunky, Moroccan spice rub that I use with chicken, lamb or fish. The olives and preserved lemons give it a sharp, sherbety fragrance and acidity and the cod carries robust flavours with fortitude. A powerful and specially good dish.

SERVES 4

2 tsp cumin seeds
1 tsp coriander seeds
1 onion, peeled and cut into chunks
3 cloves of garlic, peeled and chopped
a bunch each of fresh flat-leaf parsley and coriander
a finger of fresh ginger, peeled and chopped
1 tsp paprika
6 large Cerignola or similar green olives
1 preserved lemon
4 tbsp olive oil
sea salt, black pepper and cayenne
2 thick pieces of cod loin, about 600g/1lb 4oz each

Heat the oven to 200°C/400°F/Gas 6. Dry-roast the cumin and coriander seeds briefly in a small pan for 30–60 seconds, then crush them to powder in a mortar. Put the onion, garlic, herbs, ginger, paprika and dry-roasted spices in the food processor and blitz until they look finely chopped (but don't overdo it).

Chop the olives and lemon together coarsely, discarding the pips. Stir them into the spice mixture, adding olive oil to make a paste. You may not need all the oil. Season to taste, adding a teaspoon tip of cayenne, and slap the paste over the fish. Cover with clingfilm and refrigerate for a couple of hours.

Remove an hour before cooking. I cooked my cod in an oiled gratin dish for 15 minutes.

STEWED SQUID WITH LEEKS, FENNEL, ORANGE, CHILLI AND RED WINE

SERVES 4

1kg/2¼lb squid, innards removed and the tentacles left whole
1 onion, peeled and sliced
4 cloves of garlic, peeled and sliced
1 leek, trimmed, sliced and well washed
1 small bulb of fennel, sliced
2–3 tbsp olive oil
equal quantities of fennel seeds, dill seeds and coriander seeds, ground together to make 1 tbsp in all
2 small hot chillies, chopped
zest and juice of 2 oranges
½ bottle red wine
110g/4 oz fresh or frozen peas
a small handful of mint leaves, chopped
a little extra grated orange zest and chopped garlic mixed together

The extraordinarily talented Stephen Markwick, chef/proprietor of what was Bristol's best restaurant Markwick's, and ex-pupil of the great George Perry-Smith, is now at Culinaria in Bristol. Stephen was cooking this dish last time I steamed into his kitchen to watch him at work and write about him. He has been quietly going about his business for several decades, but his dedication to the kitchen and the pursuit of good cooking is as fresh as it is unfaltering. I have never tasted anything less than excellent when dining with him, and have always been impressed by the way in which he has ploughed his own furrow. Elizabeth David is an influence without being obtrusively and obviously so, Stephen is too creative for that, and times, after all, have moved on. Stephen serves this lovely dish as a first course, with a few croutons of thinly sliced baguette brushed with a little olive oil and crisped in the oven. I think it is as successful as a main course served with plainly cooked rice. Slow braising renders the squid softly succulent, as does cooking it in a flash. Anything in between and you end up with something chewy and rubbery. It will wait around in the pot for you if need be, and it is as delectable warm as it is brought straight from the stove.

Stephen throws chopped coriander over his finished dish. I use mint because I add peas to the dish and prefer the marriage of the twain.

First prepare the squid. Cut the body into rings, the wings into strips and leave the tentacles whole.

Preheat the oven to 140°C/275°F/Gas 1. In a heavy-bottomed casserole, gently fry the onion, garlic, leek and fennel together in the olive oil until softened. Add the ground seed mixture and the chillies, then stir in the squid. Stir around a little until the squid has stiffened and then introduce the zest and juice of 2 oranges and the red wine. Season well – squid absorbs a great deal of salt – and bring everything to a simmer. Cover and braise slowly in the oven for about 2 hours. Add the peas for the last 20 minutes of the cooking time. Stir in the chopped mint, sprinkle over the extra orange zest and garlic, and serve directly from the pot in one of the ways suggested above.

ROAST STUFFED MONKFISH WITH A LEMON AND CAPER SAUCE

SERVES 10

1 tbsp each of thyme, black
    peppercorns and sea salt
2.3kg/5lb monkfish, a single tail if
    possible. Ask your fishmonger to
    remove the bone, leaving the fillets
    on either side still attached
55g/2oz tin of anchovies in olive oil,
    drained, or 55g/2oz salted
    anchovies washed and de-spined
    under the cold tap
2 red peppers, roasted, peeled and
    seeded; or buy the wood-roasted
    piquillo peppers, Brindisa if you
    can get them
a pinch of saffron threads, soaked in
    a tablespoon or two of warm water
    for 10 minutes
3–4 tbsp best olive oil
1 lemon
55g/2oz unsalted butter
2 tbsp capers, drained then rinsed in
    a slotted spoon under the cold tap
a handful of flat-leaf parsley,
    chopped

A summer feast, this is an abstract splash of colour of a dish that you can either prepare or actually cook in advance if you decide to serve it cold. Monkfish weep juice like no other fish (bar the odd mollusc like mussels and oysters), scenting the sauce for you to finish it with substance and strength. The cracked black peppercorns, lemons, thyme, saffron, peppers and anchovies perform this with brio. The finished dish will look like a picture, yet presents no challenge to assemble and cook despite its seeming complexity.

Put the thyme, peppercorns and salt in a mortar and crush until coarsely ground. Open the fish out like a book and spread the anchovies and red peppers evenly over both surfaces. Pour over the saffrony liquor, then half the olive oil. Close the fish together, and hold it while a friend or child ties string around it at 2.5cm/1in intervals, to make 10 portions.

Preheat the oven to 200°C/400°F/Gas 6. Scatter the thyme mixture in a roasting tin, roll the fish in it to coat, then pour on the rest of the olive oil. Put the fish in the middle of the oven to roast for about 35 minutes. Check with the point of a skewer that it has cooked right through and is not resistant in the middle. Remove it to a warm serving dish if you are going to serve it hot and rest it, shrouded in foil, while you make the sauce.

Boil the remaining liquor from the roasting tin down to about half the quantity you started with. Meanwhile, peel the lemon, removing all the pith with the blade of a sharp knife, and divide the fruit into segments. In a small frying pan, melt the butter gently until it begins to turn brown and nutty, add the pieces of lemon, then throw in the drained capers. Add the fish liquor and stir it in, then pour it over the fish. Strew over the parsley and carve the fish into tranches 2.5cm/1in thick. Remember to remove the string before serving.

If you are serving the fish cold, do not offer the butter sauce. Make the sauce with olive oil instead or omit it, merely pouring over the reduced liquor while the fish is cooling.

4 hake steaks or cutlets, on the bone,
    4cm/1½ in thick
olive oil to brush
sea salt and black pepper
1 tsp fresh thyme, chopped

ROMESCO SAUCE
30g/1oz whole blanched almonds
6 tbsp best olive oil
2 cloves of garlic, finely chopped
a slice of stale bread, brown or white
225g/8oz skinned and seeded
    tomatoes, or the equivalent from a
    tin, with juice
1 red chilli, seeded and finely
    chopped, or cayenne to taste
30g/1oz whole roasted hazelnuts
2 tbsp red wine vinegar
4 tbsp fino sherry

GRILLED HAKE STEAKS WITH ROMESCO SAUCE

Hake is a fish I associate with Spain, where I have eaten it more often than any other fish. The Spaniards really revere the hake, though it has never really caught on here. I know not why. It has perfect firmness and bite for a fish stew, a lovely delicate flavour, a flakiness that doesn't collapse on cooking, and it doesn't dry out if you anoint it with oil and show it to the grill or the griddle, either of which works for this recipe.

If you are going to grill your fish, line the grill pan with foil and preheat. If you are using a griddle, brush it quickly with a little olive oil when it is hot, trying not to frazzle your pastry brush. Brush the hake with olive oil on both sides, season and add a pinch of thyme to the uppermost side. Place under the grill or on the griddle and watch like a hawk. You will see the heat cook down through the fish under the grill, or work its way up the flesh if it's on the griddle. You will also see the pearly juices begin to collect.

When the fish looks cooked halfway through, after about 5 minutes or even less, turn it over gently with a slice, season again and continue to cook. This side might take a little less time. Poke a skewer gently down through the fish – it should not be resistant.

Remove the fish from the grill or griddle and pour over the fishy, oily juices. Serve with the Romesco sauce, as powerful a piece of work as a sauce gets.

ROMESCO SAUCE

Roast the almonds briefly in a moderate oven until pale gold. Slowly heat 4 tablespoons of the olive oil in a pan with the chopped garlic. When the oil is hot, remove and reserve the garlic and fry the bread briefly on both sides until crisp and golden. Remove the bread from the pan, add 2 more tablespoons of oil, then the tomatoes and chilli and stir until they are reduced and jammily thickened. This will take about 10–15 minutes.

Grind the nuts in a food processor, or a mortar for a better texture, then add the bread and garlic and continue to pound with the vinegar and sherry. Stir in the cooled tomato sauce and serve in the mortar.

FISH STEW WITH A ROUILLE

Not la vraie bouillabaisse, but a delicious, simple-to-make stew on the same principles.

SERVES 8

FISH STOCK
1.5–1.8kg/3¼–4lb fish bones
3.5 litres/6½ pints water
2 fennel bulbs, chopped
2 sticks of celery, chopped
with leaves
2 onions, chopped
6 quartered tomatoes and 1 tbsp
tomato purée
saffron and a splash of Pernod
(optional)

ROUILLE
140g/5oz roasted, peeled peppers
1 seeded red chilli
1 slice of day-old bread, crusts
removed
5 small cloves garlic, peeled
120–170ml/4–6fl oz olive oil

FISH STEW
675g/1½lb filleted, boned weight of
red mullet
675g/1½lb boned monkfish tail
675g/1½lb squid, cleaned and cut
into rings
675g/1½lb large prawns in shells

First make an intensely flavoured fish stock with the fish bones. Sole and turbot are good, and I add prawn or crab shells to enhance the flavour and colour. Add the water, bring to the boil, remove scum and simmer for 30 minutes. Sieve and discard the bones. Simmer for a further 30 minutes.

Add the other ingredients. Simmer until softened, press through a sieve and season. You can refrigerate this overnight, then the stew will take a mere 3 minutes to cook after reheating the stock.

ROUILLE
Process together the roasted, peeled peppers with the chilli, bread that you have soaked in water and wrung out, and the garlic. Pour the olive oil in a steady stream into the processor until you have a sumptuously thickened, vermillion ointment. Taste and season.

FISH STEW
I used the fish listed, but you can improvise. Cut the fish into generous 5cm/2in chunks and throw them into the barely simmering pot of fish stock. They are ready as soon as they lose their translucence, about 3 minutes. Put in the peeled prawns, and serve with toasted slices of baguette spread with rouille.

BAKED TURBOT WITH SAUCE BRETONNE

Sauce Bretonne is great with any firm, white fish, or you may even serve it with wild salmon or sea trout. It has peppery watercress, mustard, the mild aniseed of chervil and the buttery vinegar to give it body, acidity and richness. Turbot is the king of the white fish to my mind, and a real treat that benefits from simple baking in a hot oven.

Preheat the oven to 200°C/400°F/Gas 6. Stuff the fish with the herbs. Grease a large roasting tin with butter, and place the fish in it. Pour over the white wine, dot the fish with butter and season. Cover the fish with a sheet of greaseproof paper and cook it for about 25 minutes before testing it with a skewer right the way through. How long the fish will take depends on the thickness, so if it is only a tiny bit resistant at its thickest point, check it again in 5 minutes. It is not difficult – fish are not temperamental or more difficult to master than meat, but there is less leeway between being cooked and overcooked. Roughly 10 minutes before you are going to test the fish, start making your sauce.

SAUCE BRETONNE

Stir together the egg yolks, salt and pepper with the Dijon mustard. Add a few drops of the tarragon vinegar, then the watercress and chervil and slowly stir in the melted butter, a few drops at a time to start with, as you would for mayonnaise. The sauce will hold if you place it over a bowl of hot water, but do not make it in advance – you want the herbs to be green and fresh tasting.

Experiment with other herbs like chives, flat-leaf parsley and dill, the best herb if you want to try the sauce with a piece of poached wild salmon or sea trout.

SERVES 6

1 x 2.3–3kg/5–6½lb turbot
a small bunch of chervil and flat-leaf
    parsley, chopped
50g/2oz unsalted butter
150ml/5fl oz white wine

sea salt and black pepper

SAUCE BRETONNE
4 organic egg yolks
sea salt and pepper
2 tsp Dijon mustard
a few drops of tarragon vinegar, if
    you don't have any, use white wine
    vinegar with 1 tsp of fresh
    tarragon
2 tbsp watercress, chopped
2 tbsp chopped chervil, chopped
110g/4oz melted unsalted butter, the
    creamy solids removed

CHICKEN BAKED WITH 40 CLOVES OF GARLIC, POULET À L'AIL

SERVES 6

1 large chicken, 1.8–2.3kg/4–5 lb,
   with its liver and giblets
1 lemon, halved
3 tbsp olive oil
40–50 cloves of garlic, peeled or
   unpeeled as you prefer
salt and pepper
2–3 sprigs of thyme

There are two ways of preparing this daunting-sounding dish, and both are equally pleasurable. In the first, the garlic cloves are peeled and stewed in an ivory nest around the bird. In the second, the cloves are put in unpeeled and served with toasted baguette so they can be popped out of their skins and eaten on the toast with hunks of oily, herbed chicken.

Preheat the oven to 150°C/300°F/Gas 2. Remove and reserve the liver and giblets and tuck the lemon halves inside the chicken. Heat the oil in a casserole and gently brown the chicken on all sides. Add the garlic cloves and turn them to coat with oil. Turn the bird breast down, season, add the giblets (not the liver) and thyme and put on the lid. Cook in the oven for 1½ hours, then turn the bird breast up, put the lid back on and cook for another 30 minutes.

Lift the chicken out of the casserole, holding it on end so all the delicious juices run into the pot, then put it on a carving board and wrap in foil. Discard the giblets and add the liver to the casserole to cook briefly, either cut in thin strips, or mash it as you go. Add the juices from the resting bird to the pot, carve, and serve with some of the cloves of garlic on each plate, along with a moat of golden juice.

Mashed potato or rice should be served with the chicken, and a couple of contrastingly coloured vegetables, say carrots and spinach or courgettes.

2 tsp coriander seeds
12 cardamom pods
1 finger of root ginger, cut into small
 dice
6 cloves
sea salt and 6 black peppercorns
3–4 tbsp olive oil
55g/2oz unsalted butter
1 medium-sized organic chicken,
 around 2kg/4½lb, jointed into 2
 breasts and the legs jointed into
 2 pieces each. Keep the thighs and
 carcass for stock
1 organic lemon
a bunch of watercress or mustard
 and cress
mango chutney

SAUCE
olive oil
butter
2 medium onions, peeled and sliced
½ tsp turmeric
1 tsp grated root ginger
salt and pepper
a small pot of live yoghurt, goat's or
 sheep's
2 tbsp double cream
a handful of currants
a bunch of coriander

SPICED POT-ROASTED CHICKEN

This is a dish I first adapted from a recipe for spiced grilled chicken and cooked two decades ago as an enduring fan of the greatest of food writers, Elizabeth David. It is from her classic book *Summer Cooking*, which like all her books is always on the shelf of my most important cookbooks in my kitchen. The dish is a variation of an Indian kubab chicken, which, Mrs David suggests can be fried in butter rather than grilled, or pot roasted, my preferred cooking method. The spices need to penetrate the chicken for 2 hours before cooking, so heat up the oven accordingly.

Heat the coriander seeds in a small pan on a high heat for 30 seconds or so to temper them. Pound the cardamom pods in a mortar, removing the husks and leaving the seeds. Add the coriander seeds, diced ginger, cloves, a little salt and the black peppercorns. Pound them together with a pestle before adding about 1 tablespoon of the olive oil and butter and working it into a paste.

Gently lift the skins of each bit of chicken by pushing your fingers between the skin and the flesh, without tearing. Score the flesh a little with the sharp point of a knife. Put a teaspoon of paste onto each bit of flesh and spread it across as far as you can go and as evenly as you can. Put the skin back and rub some of the paste onto the cut sides of the chicken too. Leave for 2 hours for the spices to penetrate.

Preheat the oven to 180°C/350°F/Gas 4. Heat the olive oil in a large, heavy-bottomed pot that the chicken will fit into in a single layer. Brown the chicken briefly on both sides, ending up with it cut side down. Cover with a sheet of greaseproof paper and a lid and pot roast in the oven for 30–40 minutes, checking with a skewer that the juices do not run bloody but are milky pink when it is cooked through.

Meanwhile, as the chicken goes into the oven, start on the sauce. Melt 30g/1oz of butter and a tablespoon of olive oil in a frying pan and fry the onions gently for about 20 minutes, until they soften and turn translucent. Shake over the turmeric and the grated ginger and season. Stir and cook for another 5 minutes. Then add the yoghurt and stir until it thickens. Add the cream and currants. You may make the sauce in advance and heat it through, without bringing it to the boil, when you need it.

Put the watercress or mustard and cress on a serving dish and put the pieces of chicken in their juices on top. Add quartered lemons to the dish. Sprinkle chopped coriander lightly over the sauce and serve it in a bowl alongside a bowl of mango chutney.

SERVES 6

1 x 2kg/4½lb organic chicken
2 onions, peeled and one of them
    stuck with 2 cloves
2 carrots, peeled and sliced in half
    lengthways
3 sticks of celery, chopped in half
2 leeks, trimmed and well washed
2 bay leaves and 2 sprigs of thyme
salt

SAUCE

55g/2oz butter
55g/2oz flour
400ml/14fl oz poaching stock
300ml/10fl oz dry white wine
240ml/8fl oz double cream
100g/3½oz Gruyère cheese, grated
1tbsp Dijon mustard
55g/2oz tarragon leaves, chopped
salt and pepper

TOPPING

55g/2oz breadcrumbs
30g/1oz Parmesan cheese, grated

CHICKEN SAVOYARDE

I have to include this as it is the single dish that has given more pleasure to those I truly love than any other I can think of. It is disarmingly simple; rich, old-fashioned, rooted in place, the Savoie, obviously, and entirely dependant on the absolute best ingredients for its being so good. Anything less than the best organic, free-range, properly reared bird, gentle poaching with fine vegetables and herbs, a good Gruyère like Beaufort, careful simmering of the stock and white wine and cream with the addition of mustard and an absurd amount of tarragon, will render the dish pedestrian rather than great, sumptuous, special. There is nothing difficult about this dish; attention to detail is all. You may poach and cool the chicken the day before you need it if you want to get ahead and make life simple on the night.

Put the chicken in a large pot, add the vegetables and herbs and salt. Poach very gently for around an hour and a half, skimming off any scum that comes to the surface. Once cooked, lift out the bird and allow to cool. Strain the stock through a fine sieve and discard all solids. Leave to settle and lift off any surface fat with several sheets of absorbent kitchen paper. Set aside until you are ready to make the sauce.

Remove all the meat from the chicken carcass (discarding skin and also removing all sinews from the drumsticks) and cut into large, bite-sized pieces.

To make the sauce, melt the butter in a pan, add the flour and cook for 3 minutes without browning. Gradually add the hot poaching stock, white wine and cream and stir until thickened. Stir in the cheese, mustard and tarragon, correct the seasoning and simmer all together for about 20 minutes.

Preheat the oven to 230°C/450°F/Gas 8. Put the chicken in a buttered gratin dish, pour over the sauce and sprinkle with the breadcrumbs and Parmesan cheese. Bake in the preheated oven for 20–25 minutes until the dish is golden brown and bubbling well around the edges. Eat with buttered new potatoes and a crisp green salad.

MANTUAN CHICKEN

SERVES 12

10 large organic chicken breasts, in
    fact, mine were so large that 8
    would still have been generous
1 litre/1¾ pints chicken stock
300ml/10fl oz dry white wine

SAUCE
5 level tbsp light muscovado sugar
120ml/4fl oz dry white wine
85g/3oz sultanas
grated zest of 2½ lemons
5 tbsp best balsamic vinegar, choose
    a well-aged, velvety 4-star
    vinegar; you want rich, mellow
    velvet not sharp, thin acid
2 tsp sea salt
freshly ground black pepper
120ml/4fl oz best olive oil

A glorious cold dish for the summer months, this is a 17th-century Mantuan recipe dug out by the great Italian food writer Anna Del Conte. It is the perfect dish to make if you have a huge party of people to feed – it is festive, beautiful and can be prepared in advance. I have only altered the recipe in one small way, as I feel it needs rather more sauce than in the original.

Put the breasts in a single layer in as many heavy-bottomed pans as you need (I used three), and cover each with some of the stock and white wine mixture. Poach at a mere burble, turning every 5 minutes, until cooked through, with only a faint pink in the liquid when pierced with a skewer; 20–25 minutes should do large chicken breasts and they will continue to cook as the liquid cools. When cool, transfer to one pan with their liquid, cover and keep in the fridge overnight.

Just over 3 hours before you want to eat, take the chicken out of the fridge and make the sauce. Put the sugar and wine in a small pan and bring it very slowly to the boil, stirring to dissolve the sugar completely. Take off the heat, and add the sultanas and lemon zest to infuse. Leave to cool, while you cut each breast downwards into 1cm/½in slices, re-assembling them on a large serving dish.

Strain the sauce, reserving the zest and sultanas in the sieve. Add the vinegar to the sauce, and the salt and pepper, then start adding the oil in a trickle, whisking as you go to form an emulsion. Return the zest and sultanas to the sauce, taste, adjust the seasoning, and pour over the centre of the breasts. Cover with clingfilm and keep at room temperature for 3 hours. Serve with new potatoes or plain rice and some cold white wands of leeks.

GUINEA FOWL STEWED WITH TREVISO CHICORY

SERVES 6

3 tbsp olive oil
55g/2oz unsalted butter
3 jointed guinea fowl, leg and breast
   in one large piece
7 or 8 heads of chicory
1 finely chopped onion
3 tsp molasses sugar
juice of 1½ lemons
200ml/7fl oz white wine
240ml/8fl oz crème fraîche
salt, pepper
a handful of flat-leaf parsley,
   chopped

You may use Belgian endives instead of the lovely garnet-coloured Treviso if you like and you may also make this dish with pheasant or chicken. The juices are at once caramelly, unctuous and sweetly sharp; it is one hell of a good dish. Serve with mashed potato.

Heat the oil and butter together in a heavy-bottomed casserole, then add the joints of guinea fowl, skin side down, and fry for a few minutes until golden and crispened. Turn over and repeat, then move to a plate with a slotted spoon.

Halve the chicory vertically and put with the onion and sugar in the casserole. Cook for about 5 minutes until the chicory begins to caramelise. Add the lemon juice, return the guinea fowl to the casserole, and pour in the wine. Bring to the boil, then simmer gently for a few minutes.

Pour in the crème fraîche, stir it in thoroughly, season, and cover the pot with a lid. Cook at a bare simmer for 35–40 minutes, then test that the meat juices run clear when pierced with a skewer. Pour the sauce into a saucepan, putting the lid back on the guinea fowl and chicory, and bubble the buttery, creamy juices until they're thickened and amalgamated. Pour over the casserole, add parsley and serve.

CHICKEN OR PHEASANT COOKED WITH RED WINE VINEGAR AND HERBS

SERVES 4

1 organic chicken or pheasant, about 1.4kg/3lb in weight

55g/2oz organic smoked streaky bacon (I use Swaddles Green Farm's because they cure without nitrites)

a sprig of rosemary, 4 sage leaves, 2 fresh bay leaves and a little bunch of thyme

olive oil and unsalted butter

1 dried chilli (optional)

2 large cloves of garlic, peeled and bruised with the back of a knife

4 or 5 Navarrico piquillo peppers, cut in strips

100ml/3½fl oz good red wine vinegar

1 tsp sugar

55g/2oz butter

sea salt and pepper

The sharp whiff of vinegar is boiled away to mellowness and sweetened with molasses sugar in this recipe. This is a classic Italian dish – Pollo alla Cacciatore – and is imbibed with a completely different, less rich flavour than if the liquid had been red wine. Do finish the sauce with little bits of butter to turn it to red velvet gloss.

Joint the bird so that you have 4 pieces of leg, 4 pieces of breast and 2 wings. Snip the bacon into small strips. With a mezzaluna or sharp knife, chop all the herbs together really finely and roll them into the bacon.

In a large, heavy-bottomed casserole that will fit all the chicken pieces in a single layer, heat a generous splosh of good olive oil with about 55g/2oz of butter. Gently sauté the bacon and herb mixture with the dried chilli if you are using it, and the cloves of garlic. Remove the chilli and garlic once you sense the aroma of them has been released into the dish. Add the pieces of chicken, season and brown properly on both sides for a total of 15 minutes. Add the strips of piquillo pepper. Raise the heat, add the red wine vinegar, then let it bubble furiously for a minute or so before adding 150ml/5fl oz of hot water.

Reduce the temperature to a gentle simmer, cover the pot with a lid and cook the chicken for a further 30 minutes. It should be tender when pierced with a skewer. Remove the chicken with all the herbs, peppers and bacon to a heated dish and keep warm.

Boil down the juices for a few minutes with a teaspoon of sugar until they become more syrupy. Add some small pieces of butter to make the sauce glossy, check the seasoning and pour the sauce over the chicken. Everyone can have half a breast and a piece of leg, and you still have the wings to suck on. I serve this with brown jasmine rice.

SLOW-STEWED DUCK'S LEGS WITH CELERY, GINGER AND STAR ANISE

A lovely winter's dish of warming spice and fat duck.

SERVES 2

2 duck legs
a little olive oil and butter
1 head of celery, using all but the
    outside stalks, strung with a
    potato peeler and sliced
    crossways
4 cloves of garlic, thinly sliced
2 glasses of full-bodied red wine
2 star anise
2 knobs of stem ginger, finely diced,
    with 2 tbsp of the syrup
2 pieces of orange peel, stripped of
    their pith
sea salt and black pepper

Warm the oven to 130°C/250°F/Gas ½. Sauté the duck legs over a high heat in a little heated olive oil, skin-side down, so that they begin to crisp and release their fat. Lower the heat, turn the legs over and give them a minute on their flesh side before removing them to a plate.

Add a knob of butter to the pan and throw in the celery and garlic. Cook for a few minutes, turning them gently to coat, then add the wine and bubble it for a few minutes. Throw in the star anise, ginger, syrup and orange peel. Season, then cover with a layer of greaseproof paper and a lid, and put in the oven.

Leave to stew for 3 hours or so, before skimming off the duck fat from the surface. Serve with mash or pommes Anna (see page 421).

BREAST OF VEAL STUFFED WITH OLIVES

SERVES 8

a thick slice of white bread, crusts
    removed
a little milk
2 cloves of garlic
a bunch of flat-leaf parsley
fresh basil
110g/4oz lean minced pork
12 black olives, stoned
black pepper and nutmeg
1 organic egg, beaten
1 breast of veal, about 1.8kg/4lb
    before it is boned (keep the bones)
olive oil
1 onion, sliced
2 tomatoes, skinned and chopped
170ml/6fl oz white wine
170ml/6fl oz meat stock or water
salt

Heat the oven to 170°C/325°F/Gas 3. Soak the bread in the milk, squeeze it out and chop it with the garlic, parsley and a few basil leaves. Add the pork and chopped olives. Season with pepper and nutmeg and add the egg.

Spread the stuffing in a layer over the boned, flattened veal, then roll it up like a sausage. Tie securely at 5cm/2in intervals. Heat 2 tablespoons of olive oil in a heavy-bottomed pan and gently cook the sliced onion, until wilted and golden, with a little extra garlic if you like.

Add the meat and brown lightly on all sides, then add the skinned, chopped tomatoes and wine, and reduce a little. Add the stock or water, a little salt, and the meat bones. Cover with greased greaseproof paper and the lid, and cook for 3 hours.

This dish is great eaten cold, the meat sliced thinly and served with a salad. The sauce needs to be strained and left to set. Skim off the fat, then spoon the jelly around the meat.

LAMB AND APRICOT TAGINE

SERVES 4

340g/12oz unsulphured apricots,
  soaked in half fresh orange juice,
  half water overnight
olive oil
1kg/2¼lb shoulder of lamb, cut into
  5cm/2in cubes
2–3 tbsp flour
sea salt and black pepper
4 medium onions, finely sliced
3 fat cloves of garlic, finely sliced
3 sticks of celery from the heart,
  strung with a potato peeler and
  finely sliced
1 tsp coriander seeds
1 tsp cumin seeds
1 tsp cinnamon bark
1 tsp ground dried ginger root
½–1 tsp cayenne
2 fresh bay leaves
chicken stock or water
a handful of fresh coriander, chopped

The natural affinity betwixt apricot and lamb is a known, surprising sharpness on the palate mollified by the sweet meat. The plush, spiced undertones of this Moroccan dish are mildly subtle and absolutely delicious. Serve with couscous and make the harissa on page 150, unless you are feeling too lazy to make it yourself and want to buy a jar.

Soak the apricots in the orange juice and water the night before you want to cook this dish.

While you warm 2–3 tablespoons of olive oil in a heavy-bottomed casserole, dry the meat with a piece of kitchen paper and put it into a Ziploc bag with the flour, sea salt and black pepper. Shake the bag until all the meat is lightly covered with flour but not clogged. Put the meat straight into the pan, in a single layer, while it is still dry. Brown on all sides for a few minutes, then lift out the meat with a slotted spoon and put it on a plate.

Add a little more oil to the pan, throw in the vegetables and sweat them gently. Temper the coriander and cumin seeds in a small frying pan for a minute or so, until they exude their toasted spice smell, then crush them in a mortar with the cinnamon bark. Add them with the other spices to the vegetables when they have softened, after about 10 minutes, then add the bay leaves and apricots, without their soaking liquid, a couple of minutes later. Return the lamb to the pan, and just cover with stock or water. Bring to the boil, cover, then simmer at a mere blip for about 1½ hours until really tender. Check the seasoning and, if possible, cool and refrigerate for a day or two before reheating and serving. Sprinkle with chopped fresh coriander before serving.

SPICED SHOULDER OR LEG OF LAMB IN A GINGERED, CURRIED YOGHURT PASTE

SERVES 8

1 shoulder or leg of lamb, about
   2–2.5 kg/4 ½–5½ lb
3 onions, chopped
a piece of fresh ginger, cut into 5
   2.5cm/1in cubes, then peeled and
   chopped
12 cloves of garlic, roughly chopped
2–3 green chillies, seeded and finely
   chopped
55g/2oz blanched almonds, roughly
   chopped
500–600ml/18–1 pint live natural
   yoghurt
1 tbsp ground cumin
1 tbsp ground coriander seeds
½ tsp cayenne pepper
1 tsp seeds from cardamom pods
1 tsp garam masala
1 tsp salt
3 tbsp olive oil
4–5 cloves
a cinnamon stick
4–5 peppercorns
a handful each of sultanas and flaked
   almonds
fresh coriander, chopped

This dish is a stunner and one you need to get marinating 24 hours before you want to cook it to tenderise the meat and almost suffocate it with the infusion of spice and yoghurt. I find even children who believe they don't like curry adore this. Marinate the meat in a Pyrex or enamel dish that you can then cook it in. A roasting tin is not the thing; it would taint the flavour.

Cut the lamb into 3 or 4 large pieces on the bone or get your butcher to do this for you. Put the onions, ginger, garlic, chillies, blanched almonds and one-third of the yoghurt in a food processor and blend to make a smoothish paste. Pour the rest of the yoghurt into a bowl, add the onion paste, cumin, ground coriander, cayenne, cardamom, garam masala and salt and whisk lightly to amalgamate.

Make slashes in the lamb flesh and push in as much of the spicy paste as you can, then pour all the remaining paste over the pieces of lamb. Cover the dish with clingfilm and refrigerate, ideally for 24 hours.

Take the dish out of the fridge an hour or so before you intend to cook it. Preheat the oven to 190°C/375°F/Gas 5. Heat the oil in a small frying pan. When it's hot, drop in the cloves, cinnamon and peppercorns, then pour the whole lot over the lamb.

Cover the dish with foil or a lid and bake for about 30 minutes. Remove the lid, sprinkle on the sultanas and flaked almonds, and put back into the oven, uncovered, for 10 minutes longer. Test that the lamb is cooked – it might need a few more minutes if the legs are huge. Sprinkle with chopped coriander and serve with rice and poppadums and one or two vegetables. A real feast of a dish, not too highly spiced for children.

MEDALLIONS OF VENISON WITH SPICED BEETROOT, CORNICHONS, TARRAGON AND SOUR CREAM

2 shallots
butter
6 juniper berries, crushed
1 heaped tsp redcurrant jelly
60ml/2fl oz port
120ml/4fl oz red wine
300ml/10fl oz game or chicken stock
    (see p. 80)
675g/1½lb or so medallions of
    venison, at least 1cm/½in thick
60ml/2fl oz sour cream
4 or 5 cornichons
fresh tarragon, finely chopped
2 or 3 medium beetroot, scrubbed,
    whiskers still attached, wrapped in
    foil and baked in a medium oven
30g/1oz unsalted butter
salt and pepper
aged balsamic vinegar

Wild roe deer have an incomparable flavour, particularly when the meat has been well hung, but they are not always easy to find. You may use loin of venison for this dish if you prefer, in which case, take it off the bone and marinate it in red wine, a little olive oil and Cognac, a bouquet of thyme, rosemary and bay and some sliced onions and peppercorns for a couple of days. There is no fat to speak of on venison, so go gently with the heat and don't let it overcook and dry out.

Chop the shallots finely and sweat them in a little butter with the crushed juniper berries until softened, before adding the redcurrant jelly, port and red wine. Reduce them by about a half, then add the stock and again reduce by a half.

While this is happening, cook the medallions in a pan with a little melted butter, turning them frequently and making absolutely sure that you don't overcook them. Dried-out venison is not one of the great pleasures of life; tender, pink, stickily oozing venison is. Check with the point of a skewer — you want a little blood, but the meat should feel soft right through, after about 3 minutes a side. Season.

When the stock has reduced, finish it with sour cream, some finely sliced cornichons and a little finely chopped tarragon. The beetroot you can cook in advance, peel when it is not too hot, and grate. Then all you need to do is heat it through in a bit of butter, salt and pepper and a little aged balsamic vinegar.

PASTA CON LE SARDE

SERVES 4

a handful of pine nuts and sultanas
1 onion, peeled and chopped
good olive oil (I use Sicilian Ravida)
2 fennel bulbs, finely chopped
4 anchovies, chopped
225g/8oz fresh sardines, chopped
225g/8oz fresh sardines, filleted
1 tsp of fennel seeds
pepper
450g/1lb penne

This is another of the lovely Italian food writer Anna Del Conte's recipes, which I have cooked for summer lunches and suppers for the last three or four years. It is very hard to get really fresh sardines here, but I find the Portuguese frozen ones that are sold by the box in my fishmongers are probably better tasting than the fresh. They have been frozen so soon after being caught that they haven't lost the oily fresh flavour that turns to rancid so quickly with all the oily fish like sardines, mackerel and herring. My children raved about this dish when I first cooked it, so it has become part of the regular repertoire.

Soak the sultanas in warm water for 10 minutes and drain, and toast the pine nuts. Lightly fry the onion in olive oil and add the pine nuts and sultanas. Blanch the fennel for 1 minute, before adding to the onion for another 15 minutes. Add a little of the blanching liquor liquid if the mixture is too dry.

Add the anchovies to the pan, with the chopped fresh sardines. Scatter over 1 teaspoon of fennel seeds, season with pepper and cook for a further 10 minutes.

Preheat the oven to 200°C/400°F/Gas 6. Meanwhile, cook the penne until it is al dente. Drain, turn into the sauce and transfer to an oiled gratin dish. Add the fillets of sardines and a further libation of olive oil. Cover with foil and bake in a hot oven for 15 minutes.

SICILIAN PESTO

SERVES 4

55g/2oz blanched almonds
1 garlic clove, peeled
4 tbsp extra virgin olive oil
2 tbsp grated Pecorino cheese
a handful of tightly packed, washed
   fresh mint leaves
½ tsp dried red chilli pepper, or more
   to taste
3 or 4 ripe, firm, fresh plum
   tomatoes, peeled, seeded and
   chopped
1 tsp sea salt

This lovely riff on a well-known theme comes from the mysterious mountain town of Erice, high above Trapani in Sicily. I was there for a conference on molecular gastronomy a few years ago. Erice is perched high above the sea, but the skeins of swirling mist conceal the views a lot of the time, revealing snatches of them every so often as you walk through the medieval streets around the town. This recipe is by the other doyenne of Italian cookery writing, Marcella Hazan. It is a southern red rather than a northern green sauce. The Genoese pesto is herbal and cool; this Sicilian version warmer, feistier, riper. This quantity makes enough for 450g/1lb of pasta.

Put all the ingredients in a food processor and process to a creamy consistency. Taste and correct for salt. Toss with pasta that has just been drained and is still piping hot. Serve at once. The sauce may be refrigerated in a tightly sealed container for up to a week.

Pasta con le Sarde

PUDDINGS AND CAKES

Difficult to be concise here, particularly since I, like my father and my youngest daughter, Charissa, seem to have a pudding gene that defies any kind of re-routing or self-control. We simply love puddings. It is not that I have a preternaturally sweet tooth, I don't. I HATE meringues, pavlovas, sweetened cream squelching out of puddings dusted with a snowstorm of icing sugar. Dark chocolate, yes, the richer, more buttery and eggier the better. Ice creams and fruit pies burnished with leaves of golden pastry and steaming with sharp fruit, yes. Comforting sponges, airy mousses with their contradictory lightness of being and deep-down heavy richness. Bring them on.

It is not the butter-cream cakes, the finger-thick whipped cream lurking mid sponge sandwich, the iced tops or the frosted layers I go for. It is the simple, sticky-sweet treacliness of a ginger cake, the scent of oily almonds in a damp macaroon cake, the bitter, near-to-burnt shock of a rich caramel ice cream, the heady, perfumed sherbetty snow of a lemon and basil sorbet. Here they all are, the things I find as irresistible as sleep, love, sex and good wine — the permanent seducers.

CINNAMON ICE CREAM

2 whole cinnamon sticks
700ml/1¼ pints full-cream milk, Jersey if possible
10 organic egg yolks
170g/6oz unrefined vanilla caster sugar
250ml/8½fl oz double cream

There is something wintery, even Christmassy, about this musky, warming ice cream, if warming is a word that can be applied to an ice. But I always think of cinnamon, ginger and cloves as the warming spices that the body seems to hanker after in the cold months. This is a subtle and special ice that is particularly good with Sally Clarke's buttermilk, cinnamon and pecan cake on page 457.

Snap the cinnamon sticks in half and put them in a pan with the milk. Bring slowly to scald point, remove from the heat, cover and leave to infuse for 20–30 minutes. Beat the egg yolks thoroughly with the vanilla caster sugar.

Warm the cinnamon milk to scald point again, then pour it into the egg yolk and sugar mixture, whisking as you go, before returning the whole bowlful to the pan. Cook over a gentle heat (see custard making page 332), stirring constantly with a wooden spoon and making absolutely sure the mixture never reaches boiling point, until you have a custard that coats the back of the spoon and has visibly thickened. Remove from the heat and strain through a sieve into a glass bowl. You may speed up the cooling process at this point if you need to by putting the bowl into a sink full of ice.

Whisk the cream until it is softly held but not rigid. Fold it into the custard, a large spoonful at a time, until the two are as one. Pour into an ice cream machine or freeze in the usual way (see page 334).

2 tbsp sugar
1 cup double cream
1 cup full-cream milk
2 tbsp grated orange zest
2 cups freshly squeezed orange
    juice; George has also made it
    with blood oranges
¼ cup + 1 tbsp Cointreau
¼ cup + 2 tbsp sugar for the
    caramel
¼ cup organic egg yolks, about 10
    large ones

BURNT ORANGE ICE CREAM

My great culinary partner-in-greed George Morley originally found this recipe in an American book, *Walking on Walnuts*, by Nancy Ring and she made it for me one memorable weekend. The caramel matches the reduced, intensified orange juice and Cointreau taste for taste and is strong enough to withstand the freezing process without losing its strength and subtlety. Serve with orange and almond florentines (see page 328).

Place the 2 tablespoons of sugar in a mixing bowl. In a medium saucepan, scald the cream and milk with the orange zest. Take off the heat and leave them to steep together with a lid on the pan for about 30 minutes.

Simmer the orange juice and Cointreau until reduced to 1 cup. Whisk into the cream mixture and strain, then return it to the pan and keep warm over a very gentle heat. In another pan caramelise the ¼ cup plus 2 tablespoons of sugar until very dark (just past the colour of an Irish setter). Do not stir at any time. Swirl gently in the pan if necessary to ensure even colour. Remove from the heat, protecting your stirring hand with an oven glove, and immediately temper the caramel with a small amount of the warm orange cream while stirring vigorously. Keep adding cream slowly until the caramel stops bubbling violently. Whisk all of the tempered caramel back into the remaining cream and place on the stove over medium heat to scald once more.

Add the yolks to the sugar in a mixing bowl and whisk together when the cream scalds, but not before. Temper the yolks with the scalded cream by pouring a small stream of the hot cream into the yolks while whisking continuously. Pour back into the pan and return to the stove over medium heat. Stir continuously with a spatula until the mixture thickens to a perceptible custard and a line can be drawn through it with your finger. Cook only until it is just thickened or it will curdle.

Immediately strain the finished ice cream base and stir to cool, then churn in an ice cream machine or put into a freezer tray. If you use a tray, remember to stir the setting walls of the ice cream into the middle of the tray after the first hour, and then again an hour or two later, to prevent crystals forming.

LEMON AND BASIL SORBET

8 good lemons
2 oranges
340g/12oz unrefined caster sugar
2 dozen large basil leaves, chopped
fine

Herbs and spices may seem unusual paired with fruit in ice creams and sorbets, but think, for example, how they have been seen as partners to chocolate by the South Americans for centuries. Star anise and chilli, tonka beans and thyme, infusions of tea, geranium, roses and jasmine, ginger and pepper – the list is endless. I think orange and bay, lemon and basil or thyme, strawberries and black pepper or balsamic are all instances of the one enhancing and drawing out the best from the other.

Scrub, wash and dry the fruit. Remove the rind with a potato peeler so that you don't get any pith and put it in a saucepan. Add 600ml/1 pint water and the sugar and bring slowly to the boil. Simmer until the sugar has dissolved. Turn the heat up and boil rapidly for 3–4 minutes. Remove from the heat and allow the syrup to cool completely. Squeeze the lemons and oranges and strain the juice into the cold syrup together with the basil leaves. Pour the mixture into an ice cream maker and churn, or freeze in a metal bowl for a couple of hours before beating in the sink with a whisk to break down the crystals. Taste to check it is sharp enough. Add more lemon juice than you need as sorbet always tastes sweeter once it is frozen. Continue to freeze and whisk until it is ready. Transfer the sorbet to the fridge about 30 minutes before serving. See page 336 for more on sorbets.

PASSION FRUIT AND LIME SORBET

SERVES 8

2 cups of sugar
8 wrinkly passion fruit
2 limes

Limes bring out the flavour of melons, mangoes and passion fruit, a point well worth remembering. They have the ability to make the fruit taste more itself than it does without them, so always squeeze on a little lime juice even if you are just eating a plain wedge of cut melon. This sorbet is stunning, a real refresher if you have had a heavy rich main course like duck or pork or shoulder of lamb. It breezes in and blasts the fat away leaving you feeling almost virtuous.

Measure 2 cups of water and 2 cups of sugar into a pan; each cup should be about 240ml/8fl oz in volume. Dissolve them together, bring them to the boil and simmer for 5 minutes.

Scoop the pulp from the passion fruits into another pan, pour over half the hot syrup and set over a gentle heat until the flesh starts to loosen from the seeds. Sieve into a bowl and press through as much of the pulp as you can with a wooden spoon. Reserve half the seeds.

Zest the limes onto a small plate and squeeze the juice. Add the lime juice and the remaining syrup alternately to the passion fruit until you have the right tang to sweet balance for your taste. Mix in the reserved seeds bar one teaspoonful. Freeze in your ice cream machine or in the usual way (see page 336). You may add a whisked egg white to the mixture before you freeze it if you like the lighter, airier sorbet it makes. Serve in glasses with a little zest and a few seeds on top.

Lemon and Basil Sorbet

SWEET CRUST PASTRY
225g/8oz plain flour, sifted
110g/4oz unsalted butter,
    chilled and cut into cubes
2 tbsp unrefined icing sugar, sifted
the seeds of a vanilla pod
the zest of a lemon
2 organic egg yolks
cold water if needed
a little egg white for brushing

CURD FILLING
10 large or 14 small, wrinkly
    passion fruit
2 large organic eggs
3 large organic egg yolks
110g/4oz unrefined caster sugar,
    or to taste
110g/4oz unsalted butter

PASSION FRUIT CURD TART

This is something I feel inordinately proud of. I am not claiming it as my own invention as I'm sure I'm not the first person to have ever made a passion fruit curd tart, but I did conceive and work up the idea, tweak and tinker and sharpen and make several curds before hitting the high note and getting the timing accurate for that sublimely semi-set wobble that the curd has to shake and salsa with. This version is as triumphant as I think I can produce. It is a show-stopper of a tart.

Make the pastry in the usual way (see page 181), adding the sifted icing sugar to the sifted flour and cubed butter, vanilla seeds and lemon zest before pulsing briefly to a crumb. Add the egg yolks and pulse, adding a tablespoon of cold water if you need more liquid to make the paste cohere. Wrap and chill. You may make the pastry a little less rich by just adding 2 tablespoons or so of iced water and not using the egg yolks.

Preheat the oven to 200°C/400°F/Gas 6. Roll out the pastry and line your greased tart tin. Bake blind for 15 minutes (see page 181). Remove the beans and greaseproof or foil, prick the bottom and sides of the tart case and brush it with a little egg white. Put it back in the oven for 10 minutes or until cooked and a pale biscuit colour.

While the pastry is in the oven, scoop the flesh out of the passion fruits into a sieve over a bowl. Using as much muscle power as you can, stir and push the juice and some of the pulp through the sieve, then transfer the flesh and seeds still in the sieve to a small pan. Warm gently and stir so flesh parts company more easily from seed.

Beat the eggs together with the yolks and the sugar. I make my curd in a large, enamel heavy-bottomed Le Creuset pan; you need as wide a surface area as possible as this speeds up the time the mixture takes to come together to a shockingly day-glo beauteous curd. Melt the butter in the pan over a very gentle heat, then stir in the egg and sugar mixture and the sieved juice of the passion fruit. Keep cooking and stirring until the curd is ready, about 5 minutes with my pan. Add the rest of the pulp that you warmed and pressed through the sieve, and a tablespoon or so of seeds, then remove from the heat. You may want to add a few more seeds, I prefer the crunch to be restrained amid the unctuous yellow ointment of passion fruit curd.

When the tart shell comes out of the oven and has cooled a little, pour the glorious curd into it and leave to cool until the curd is set. Refrigerate for at least 2 hours, the pastry will be spectacularly crisp. A few raspberries bled with sugar and framboise and left to cool in the fridge or a raspberry sorbet can be served with the tart if you like.

225g/8oz flour
salt
1 tsp ground cinnamon
140g/5oz sugar
140g/5oz light muscovado sugar
55g/2oz pecans, chopped
150ml/5fl oz vegetable oil
½ tsp each baking powder and
    bicarbonate of soda
1 small egg
240ml/8fl oz buttermilk

SALLY CLARKE'S BUTTERMILK, CINNAMON AND PECAN CAKE

It may seem overtly American, but I do believe a good cake is as good a vehicle for sharing with a bowl of ice cream as is a pie or tart, and this mildly spicy, nutty cake is good for tea or with a creamy ice. You may want to make a cinnamon ice cream (see page 452) to echo the theme or venture off into something fruity instead like a damson or blackcurrant sorbet to get sharp with. Sally Clarke has been a landmark of a cook with a landmark of a restaurant, her eponymous hostelry at the upper end of Kensington Church Street, for over two decades. Here, next door to her food shop, a treasure trove of good things, she has espoused clean, simple, magnificently sourced ingredients with a pure vision of how the food should speak for itself and really taste. Her no-choice menu makes dining with her just like going to a really good dinner party.

Heat the oven to 170°C/325°F/Gas 3. Mix the flour with the salt, cinnamon, sugars, pecans and oil. Mix the raising agents with the egg and the buttermilk and mix into the flour until smooth.

Pour into a greased and lined cake tin and bake for about 40 minutes. Test with a skewer before cooling on a rack.

HONEY AND WALNUT CAKE

225/8oz lightly flavoured honey, such
   as a flower honey
6 organic eggs, separated
a teacup of sifted flour
a teacup of walnuts pounded in a
   mortar with a tablespoon of caster
   sugar
½ teacup cream

This is more a heavy, sticky sort of soufflé than a cake. Elizabeth David made this cake with honey and hazelnuts, but it is every bit as good with walnuts. Serve it with raspberries and cream, or blackberries bled with caster sugar and Mûre in the autumn.

Preheat the oven to 180°C/350°F/Gas 4. Put the jar of honey in a pan of boiling water so that it is workable. Beat the egg yolks in a large bowl, then pour the honey over them. Gradually add the sifted flour and the walnuts and sugar, then bind the mixture with the cream, stirring it all together thoroughly. Whisk the egg whites stiffly. Stir the first tablespoon into the mixture, then lightly fold in the rest with a metal spoon.

   Butter and line a soufflé dish or cake tin and coat the buttered sides with a few extra ground walnuts. Pour in the mixture and cook for about 40 minutes. Cool before turning out on to a rack.

SOMERSET APPLE CAKE

SERVES 6

170g/6oz sultanas
150ml/5fl oz good, dry cider
225g/8oz unrefined caster sugar
170g/6oz unsalted butter
2 organic eggs
285g/10oz plain flour
1½ tsp baking powder
1 tsp cinnamon
zest of 1 lemon
2 large Bramley apples, peeled and
   thinly sliced

The best cakes to my mind are always the ones that double up as teatime treats or are good enough for pud, which this one, laced with a lovely dollop of sweetened, cider-brandied crème fraîche, certainly is.

Soak the sultanas in the cider for 30 minutes.

   Preheat the oven to 170°C/325°F/Gas 3. Cream the sugar and butter thoroughly, then add the eggs, one at a time, beating as you go. Fold in the dry ingredients, the lemon zest and the thinly sliced apples.

   Add the sultanas soaked in cider, along with any remaining cider. Bake in a greased, lined 20cm/8in springform tin for 45–50 minutes, or until a skewer comes out clean. Cool in the tin, then remove the cake to a rack. Reheat it if you are going to eat it as a pudding and serve with crème fraîche. Lace the crème fraîche with a little Calvados or Somerset cider brandy if you like.

Somerset Apple Cake

BLUEBERRY AND CINNAMON FRIANDS

MAKES 10–12

170g/6oz unsalted butter
140g/5oz ground almonds
1 tbsp grated organic lemon zest
1 tsp ground cinnamon
285g/10oz unrefined icing sugar
5 tbsp organic plain flour
5 organic egg whites
200g/7oz punnet blueberries

These charming little friands are good with coffee or at tea time and for pudding, with ice cream or a bowl of chilled fresh berries. Make them in the same tins you would use for jam tarts or individual Yorkshire puds. Great made with blackcurrants or cranberries too.

Heat the oven to 200°C/400°F/Gas 6. Melt the butter gently in a pan and cook it until it is golden, not brown. Put the ground almonds, lemon zest, cinnamon, sifted icing sugar and flour into a bowl and mix together, then stir in the egg whites and combine. Stir in the melted butter, then pour the mixture into the greased tins and scatter over the blueberries.

Bake for about 15 minutes or until light and springy to the touch, then leave to cool on a rack. Serve with a little extra icing sugar sifted on to them.

COCONUT AND VANILLA CREAMS WITH A MANGO, LIME AND PINK GRAPEFRUIT SALAD

SERVES 4

150ml/5fl oz full cream milk
60g/2fl oz single cream
30g/1oz organic creamed coconut from a block (sold in supermarkets)
20g/⅔oz unrefined granulated sugar
1 vanilla pod, seeds scraped out
2 leaves of gelatine soaked until soft in a few tbsp cold water
150ml/5fl oz double cream

FRUIT SALAD
1 mango
2 limes
1 pink grapefruit
1 tsp Billington's light muscovado sugar

I was looking through my old *Carved Angel Cookery Book*, by the wonderful Joyce Molyneaux, and found a pudding that she claimed to have adapted from Jane Grigson, and which I, in turn, am adapting from her. Its tropical, creamy, fruity ingredients are just what is needed to brighten the mid-winter months, when the store cupboard is dull.

In a small saucepan, warm the milk, single cream, coconut, sugar and scraped-out vanilla seeds over a gentle heat, whisking to dissolve the coconut. Remove from the heat and add the soaked gelatine. Stir until it has dissolved. Add a squirt of juice from one of the limes for the fruit salad to taste, then pour the mixture into a bowl and refrigerate for an hour until it has begun to set. Whip the double cream lightly and fold it into the coconut mixture.

Line four pudding basins, dariole moulds or ramekins with clingfilm and pour in the mixture, then refrigerate. Turn them out and serve with the fruit salad.

Slice the mango in half lengthways, peel and slice into long pieces and put into a glass bowl. Peel the lime with a potato peeler so that you have only the zest in strips – no pith – then blanch slices in simmering water for 2 minutes.

When the slices of peel are warm, cut them into fine shreds. Cut the peel and pith off the remaining lime and grapefruit with a sharp knife, and slice out the segments so that you have no skin or innards. Add to the mango, which you have spritzed with a little extra lime juice. Add the sugar, then toss the fruit in the sugar and juice. Scatter over the zest. Cover and keep in the fridge until you are ready to serve it with the creams.

BAKED STUFFED NECTARINES OR PEACHES

SERVES 4

4 nectarines or peaches, steeped in boiling water for a minute, then skinned and halved
75g/2½oz amarettini de Saronno or amaretti biscuits
1–2 tbsp vanilla sugar
1 organic egg yolk
butter

White nectarines are the best, or white peaches, with their more delicate, ethereal flavour, but the most important thing is to make sure the fruit is ripe. Stoned fruit in this country is often sold disgracefully under-ripe. Some supermarkets clearly have no notion of the simple fact that if the fruit is picked from the branch really under-ripe without the right acid/sugar balance, it will never complete the ripening process. And cooking it won't help either: it will not soften the bullet, juice up the fruit or get rid of a cotton woolly texture. This dish marries the almondy flavour of the amaretti with the fruit and you may go further with a raw raspberry sauce if you feel like the whole Nellie Melba combination.

Preheat the oven to 170°C/325°F/Gas 3. Enlarge the stone cavities of the nectarines or peaches, keeping the extra pulp and juice in a bowl. Crush the amarettini in a pestle and mortar, or in a plastic bag with a rolling pin. Tip the crumbs into the bowl with the extra fruit pulp, add the sugar and egg yolk, and pound together until it is a damp, coherent mass of stuffing.

Heap the stuffing generously into the nectarine or peach cavities so that it mounds over the fruit, then set the fruit halves in a greased gratin dish and bake for 30–40 minutes. Serve warm or cold. I serve mine warm with some cold raw raspberry sauce dribbled over the summit.

RASPBERRY GENOISE

MAKES A 23CM/9IN CAKE

55g/2oz melted butter
4 organic eggs
110g/4oz vanilla caster sugar
rind of an orange
110g/4oz organic flour and a pinch of
    salt
285g/10oz raspberries, and 1 dsrtsp
    or so of sugar
raspberry liqueur

A Genoise is a rich, firm, buttery yet light sponge for which the whole eggs and sugar are beaten together over a pan of barely simmering water until thickened. I like to cook my genoises with berried fruits, blackberries, blueberries, strawberries or raspberries, all bleeding beautifully into the sponge so that it turns out delectably mottled and juicy.

Preheat the oven to 180°C/350°F/Gas 4. Brush a little of the melted butter over the base and sides of a 23cm/9in springform cake tin. Cover the base with a circle of baking parchment, also buttered, and sprinkle flour over it, shaking off the excess.

Beat the eggs, sugar and rind together until trebled in volume, light and foamy. The beaters will leave a trail. You can do this in a KitchenAid if you have one; otherwise beat over a pan of barely simmering water, and when expanded, remove and beat until cool. Sift half the flour on to the egg mixture, and fold it in gently with a metal spoon. Sift over the rest and the salt, then pour in the rest of the warm butter, without its white sediment, around the side, and fold them both in thoroughly but lightly.

Pour half the mixture into the tin, throw in the raspberries and sprinkle them with a dessertspoon of sugar. Cover with the other half of the mixture. Bake for about 40 minutes. The top should spring back to the touch when cooked. Cool for 10 minutes, then turn out onto a wire rack. The raspberries will be uppermost. While still warm, brush with raspberry liqueur and serve. Pass the bottle around for people to pour on more liqueur.

CHOCOLATE PUDDING CAKE WITH CHOCOLATE GANACHE

SERVES 8–10

4 organic eggs, separated, plus one
    whole egg
170g/6oz vanilla caster sugar
225g/8oz best bitter chocolate,
    Valrhona 64% or Green and Black
    70% cocoa solids
140g/5oz blanched almonds, freshly
    ground
1 heaped tsp ground coffee

GANACHE
225g/8oz dark chocolate
120ml/4fl oz double cream

The marvellous thing about this most sumptuous of cakes is that it can be made well in advance and kept in a tin or sealed container before you adorn it with a rich chocolate ganache. A truly special chocolate cake. Serve with the homemade vanilla ice cream on page 334.

Preheat the oven to 170°C/325°F/Gas 3. Whisk the egg yolks and egg together with half the sugar, until pale and doubled in volume. Melt the chocolate in a double saucepan or in a bowl over simmering water. Whisk the egg whites, adding the rest of the sugar a bit at a time, until they are at the satiny, soft peak stage. Add half of them to the egg and sugar mixture, folding them in gently. Add the chocolate and the rest of the whites, folding as you go. Then do likewise with the almonds and coffee.

Grease and flour a 20cm/8in springform tin and line the base with a circle of greased greaseproof paper. Scrape the mixture into the tin and bake for 30 minutes. Then turn the oven off and leave the cake in for another 15 minutes or until a skewer comes out clean from the centre. Remove from the oven and leave to cool in the tin.

Scald the cream in a small pan, remove from the heat and stir in the broken up chocolate. Cover the cake with the ganache and leave to cool.

PASTRY

8 amaretti bicuits
170g/6oz plain flour, sifted
85g/3oz unsalted butter, cut into
    pieces
2–3 tbsp iced water

TOPPING

8 ripe peaches (white are the
    absolute best, but yellow-fleshed
    are fine)
juice of 1 lemon
1 vanilla pod
85g/3oz caster sugar
55g/2oz unsalted butter

PEACH, VANILLA AND AMARETTI TARTE TATIN

This is another of those rare occasions on which I do feel somewhat proud of making a dish I feel I can call my own. It's not the first time amaretti and peaches or peaches and vanilla have become bedfellows, but I did dream up this tart, with its amber peaches speckled in vanilla caramel and the sandy, almondy amaretti pastry that shrouds the fruit until it is upturned to serve. A holy trinity of ingredients and a simple, true taste. Use nectarines if you would rather.

To make the pastry, crush the amaretti in a food processor, add the flour and butter and process briefly to combine. Add 2–3 tablespoons iced water and process until the mixture comes together. Wrap in greaseproof paper and chill for at least 20 minutes.

Preheat the oven to 190°C/375°F/Gas 5. Roll out the pastry to 1cm/½in more than the circumference of the pan – I use a heavy, 25cm/10in diameter Cousances enamelled cast-iron frying pan with a metal handle that I can put in the oven. Set the pastry to one side.

Scald the peaches in boiling water for 30 seconds. Peel, and sprinkle them with lemon juice to prevent discolouration.

Split the vanilla pod and scrape the seeds out into the sugar. Warm the sugar in the frying pan until it is a deep, dark brown and totally liquid. Do not stir, but move the pan around to prevent burning. Remove from the heat and dot with half of the butter. Put half a peach in the middle of the sugar mixture, cut-side up. Quarter the rest, and, starting at the outside of the pan, lay them next to each other in a tightly packed wheel. Arrange the remaining quarters in an inside wheel. Dot with the rest of the butter and put the pan back over the heat for 2–3 minutes to gently start the cooking.

Remove from the heat, cover with a mantle of pastry that you tuck down round the edges, and bake for 25–30 minutes. Remove from the oven and leave for 10 minutes before inverting on to a plate. Delicious with crème fraîche.

STICKY BLACK GINGERBREAD

SERVES 8–10

110g/4oz butter
55g/2oz molasses sugar
55g/2oz demerara sugar
2 organic eggs
two-thirds of a 450g/1lb jar
    blackstrap molasses (Meridian
    make a good one you can buy in
    healthfood shops)
1 tsp grated dried ginger root or
    powder if you can't get it
225g/8oz plain flour, sifted
5 knobs stem ginger and 2 tbsp
    of the syrup
2 tbsp milk
scant ½ tsp bicarbonate of soda

This is my absolute favourite recipe for that most palate-clinging of sticky cakes, the molasses-rich treacly gingerbread. This is hardly the rather sedate version I remember as a child, which was paler and drier and had certainly not been introduced to blackstrap molasses, dried ginger root and ginger in syrup. Serve this as a glorious pudding with poached pears, turn it into gingerbread ice cream, a gingerbread bread and butter pudding, or toast it and serve it buttered with a blueberry compote. Or just lash on some clotted cream dribbled with more ginger syrup and some grated stem ginger, a sort of gingerbread pain perdu.

Preheat the oven to 170°C/325°F/Gas 3. Grease and flour an 18cm/7in loaf tin.

Cream the butter and sugars thoroughly, then mix in the eggs one at a time, followed by the blackstrap molasses. Add the dry ginger root with the sifted flour, finely chopped stem ginger and syrup to the cake mixture. Warm the milk slightly and stir it into the bicarb until dissolved, then add to the mixture and fold in. Pour the mixture into the loaf tin, and bake for about 1½ hours. Check with a skewer. I favour a sticky, gooey cake, slightly sunken in the middle, so when you turn it out to cool on a rack, it looks like a depressed, blackened brick. When cool, wrap it up in greaseproof paper and foil. It keeps very well for a few days.

CHOCOLATE ESPRESSO CAKE

SERVES 8–10

185g/6½oz unsalted butter, diced,
    plus extra for greasing the tin
185g/6½oz best dark chocolate,
    broken into pieces
60ml/2fl oz very strong freshly
    brewed coffee
6 organic eggs, separated
185g/6½oz unrefined caster sugar
185g/6½oz almonds, blanched,
    roasted and coarsely ground

Simply one of the best pudding cakes I have ever come across with its deep, rich, undertones of coffee under the black velvet chocolate. Sally Edwards used to serve this cake every day at her café in Taunton. There would have been a riot if she hadn't and now she's gone we have to make our own.

Preheat the oven to 190°C/375°F/Gas 5. Melt the butter and chocolate together with the coffee in a bowl over a pan of barely simmering water.

While they are melting, cream the egg yolks and sugar in an electric mixer for 8–10 minutes, until pale and light. Continue to whisk, adding the melted chocolate and butter. Stop the machine, remove the whisk and fold in the almonds with a metal spoon. In a clean glass or metal bowl, whisk the egg whites to stiff peaks. Stir a spoonful of egg white into the chocolate mixture to lighten it before folding in the rest.

Grease the sides of a 25cm/10in springform tin and line the base with a circle of buttered greaseproof paper. Pour in the mixture and bake for 20 minutes. Turn the oven down to 170°C/325°F/Gas 3 and continue cooking for a further 40 minutes.

Remove the cake and leave in the tin set on a rack until completely cool. Turn out of the tin and remove the greaseproof paper. Delicious served with crème fraîche or ice cream as a cake or pudding.

VESUVIAL CHOCOLATE COOKIES ROLLED IN ICING SUGAR

MAKES DOZENS

340g/12oz butter, unsalted
340g/12oz good-quality chocolate,
    70% cocoa solids
3 organic eggs
450g/1lb light muscovado sugar
1 double espresso
500g/1lb 2 oz self-raising flour
1½ tsp baking powder
unrefined icing sugar to roll the
    cookies in

These are the best ever, the recipe imparted by the brilliant cooks at Ottolenghi in Notting Hill, the most Zen traiteur and food emporium around in my opinion. You may keep some of the dough in the deep freeze if you make enough. The end result is a pile of oozing, dark chocolate cookies, risen until they crack like parched earth and sweetly crisped by their crackly coat of icing sugar. Serve with tea, coffee or ice cream, or just pile into them as you work, play or watch the television.

Gently melt the butter and chocolate together in a double boiler or in a bowl over, but not touching, hot water. Whisk the eggs and sugar in a KitchenAid or with electric beaters for 3 minutes, then add the warm chocolate mix and the espresso. Sift the flour and baking powder and fold them into the mixture by hand. Wrap the dough in clingfilm and leave it to cool for a couple of hours before baking or put it in the fridge overnight.

When you are ready to bake the cookies, preheat the oven to 180°C/350°F/Gas 4. Take the dough and roll walnut-sized balls in your hand. Roll them in icing sugar and put on silicone paper with some space between each one. Bake for 10–12 minutes and allow to cool on a rack.

LUSCIOUS CHOCOLATE PUDDINGS

MAKES 6

5 organic eggs, plus 5 extra yolks
110g/4oz vanilla caster sugar
225g/8oz best bitter chocolate
225g/8oz unsalted butter
55g/2oz plain flour, sifted
cocoa powder and icing sugar
    (optional)

Everyone has their own version of these dense, dark chocolate puddings, which pour out a river of runny chocolate sauce when spoon sinks into sponge. You can make the pudding mixture the day before if you like, fill the ramekins and put them to bed in the fridge until you want them. Cold pouring cream is needed to add an ivory wave to the hot chocolate lake.

Beat the eggs, yolks and sugar together until pale. Melt the chocolate and butter in a bowl over, but not touching, simmering water. Remove from the heat and add to the egg mixture, beating as you go. Fold in the flour. Pour into the buttered moulds immediately. Cool, then refrigerate for a couple of hours.

Preheat the oven to 180°C/350°F/Gas 4. Bake the puddings for about 12 minutes; the tops will have risen and feel dry to the touch. Turn out with a bendy palette knife and serve. You can sprinkle a bit of cocoa powder and icing sugar over the top if you are feeling decorative.

STEAMED LEMON CURD PUDDING

SERVES 6

170g/6oz caster sugar
110g/4oz butter
2 organic eggs
juice and rind of 2 lemons
110g/4oz flour
1 tsp baking powder
a bit of milk to slacken
1 x 310g/11oz jar lemon curd or
    make your own (see p. 488)

I have made this stunning steamed pudding with lime and blood orange curd as well. Curds are simple and satisfying to make and will always taste better than jarred ones, but if you can't be bothered, reach for a top notch brand like Duchy. My lemon curd recipe is on page 488 or if you want to be even more exotic, make this with my passion fruit curd on page 456.

What you want is a molten-thick golden puddle seeping slowly out of the spongy depths, giving tang to the sweetness.

Cream the sugar and butter together thoroughly, then beat in the eggs. Add the juice and rind of the lemons, then sprinkle over the sifted flour and baking powder. Add a bit of milk to slacken to a dropping consistency, but don't let the mixture become sloppy.

Scrape the lemon curd from the jar into the bottom of your pudding basin, a snap-on lidded plastic one is fine if you don't want to cover and tie an old-fashioned pudding basin (see page 364 for how to do this). Spoon the pudding mixture over the curd, cover, set on a trivet in a large pan, and pour boiling water to come halfway up the sides of the basin. Simmer for about 1½ hours, then turn out on to a large dish; remember there will be a lake of sauce.

CHOCOLATE AND PRALINÉED NUT NO-PASTRY TART

SERVES 10–12

55g/2oz almonds, skinned and
    chopped
55g/2oz walnuts, chopped
1 tbsp unrefined icing sugar
140g/5oz best bitter chocolate
55g/2oz unsalted butter, cut into
    small pieces
60ml/2fl oz double cream
5 organic egg yolks and 7 egg whites
55g/2oz caster sugar
55g/2oz ground almonds
1 heaped tsp ground coffee
30g/1oz Green and Black's organic
    cocoa powder

TOP
140g/5oz best bitter chocolate
about 90ml/3fl oz milk

This is a great show-off of a pudding and perfect for pastry-phobes who fight shy of the dough and believe they will never be able to master it. I don't have much sympathy on that front – pastry just needs practice – but here is a pudding that will work whatever level of cook you are and will be admired by all.

Put the chopped nuts in a gratin dish, throw the icing sugar over them and place under a hot grill, turning the dish every so often. You want the sugar to dissolve and adhere to the browning nuts. Watch carefully: the nuts should be brown, not black.

Preheat the oven to 180°C/350°F/Gas 4. Butter and flour a 30cm/12in tart tin. Melt the chocolate in the top of a double boiler. Stir the butter into it, then the cream and remove from the heat.

In a large bowl, whisk the egg whites with the caster sugar until stiff, then gently fold in the yolks, followed by the ground almonds, coffee and cocoa. Then fold in the chocolate, butter and cream mixture and mix gently to incorporate. Pour half the mixture into the tart tin, add the pralinéed nuts to cover the surface, then pour on the rest of the mixture. Cook for 15 minutes. Remove from the oven and leave to cool slightly before turning out on to a wire rack. Leave until completely cold.

For the top, melt the chocolate and milk together in a double boiler and spread over the tart. When cool, you could gently sieve on a touch more cocoa, but don't be heavy handed; cocoa is bitter, with 70 per cent cocoa solids. I am anti the current trend of dredging everything in icing sugar, which is for sponge cakes or for brûléed tart tops as far as I'm concerned.

BREAD
PRESERVATION!
JAMS
PICKLES
CHUTNEYS

SERIOUS

SKILLS

7

JUST AS THERE ARE SEASONS for making jams and chutneys,

for bottling and preserving fruits, for pickling and for potting, and those seasons are an integral part of the turning year if you live in the country, so there are seasons in one's cooking life when one wants to master a new technique, experiment with a culinary ritual. If you grow your own or at least pick your own, the glut or the crop, its ripeness or readiness dictate your work.

I say this staring out at the heavy hedges laden with accusatory elderflowers which I haven't as yet turned into cordial, although we are approaching Midsummer's day and another week will put paid to their creamy, lacey blooms. But I have been pickling cucumbers to eat with the fine sea trout from the River Dart which I have been poaching over the last week.

Preserving and pickling speak of home and hearth, gathering and preparing good food for your table, and are two of the most satisfying branches of the great tree of life you will ever engage in. It may take you some time to bring this particular root and branch into your life, but once you have made your first soot-black currant jelly, or glowing amber pot of crab apple or quince jelly; your first sharp Seville marmalade or bread and butter pickle; your first sticky golden ointment of lemon curd or deep purple jar of damson gin, you will find the seasons speaking to you in a more personal way. 'Now is the time', they will say, and each year you will add to or change your range of the lovely store cupboard jars and bottles that glow proud with handwritten labels and speak of foraging, forays, fruit soaking and simmering; of the sharp, clean smell as the scent of vinegar for your chutney fills the kitchen, or the oranges stew down languorously for your marmalade. The sentries of old jam jars standing to attention on your shelves will make wonderful repasts and last-minute presents of the kind that money just can't buy, but time and care can transform into something special. I would rather a pot of a friend's spiced redcurrant or quince jelly or a jar of rumtopf than anything bought from a shop with a mobcap and a printed label. Get started.

Bread is another of these accomplishments that you really need to work at over months and then years, even if breadmaking doesn't become a regular part of your cooking life. You will learn more by making batches of different loaves over a period than by making the odd one as and when the mood descends upon you. The best time to start is an autumnal or wintery weekend afternoon as the dark days take over, when you have got time and need the comfort of wonderful yeasty smells invading your kitchen.

This chapter is not just for the serious cook, but it is about the serious skills that will make you feel you are beginning to master what makes a true cook and gives most pleasure in the kitchen. The seasonal rituals of picking and washing fruit, particularly if you have grown it yourself, of watching pale orbs of currants darken on the bush before you fill your jam pan with them and bubble them to delectable jams and jellies, is a pleasure that it is never too early or too late to indulge in. Can anything taste better than a sharp-fruited, soft-set jelly plopping off the spoon onto thickly buttered homemade bread? I think not.

There is nothing intrinsically difficult about making anything in this chapter. The rewards are far greater than the effort involved in picking up and preserving a few of life's serious culinary skills.

BREAD

Bread making can be a way of life or an occasional pleasure and is, I think, the most rewarding of kitchen pleasures in the most atavistic, primitive way. The pleasure is not dependant upon the success of the end result, for bread is the least likely thing you will ever cook to turn out tasting or looking the same twice. The flour, the water, the yeast, the warmth, damp and atmosphere, your hands, the stove – there are so many factors that determine the difference, rather than the similarity, of the loaf you happen to be baking.

If the loaf doesn't rise as much as it should, is too damp or close textured, the crust too soft, or too hard and dry, somehow just the smell of the raw dough, the rising dough, the baking bread, the loaf on the rack, the butter melting on the slice, still creates the same effect and the world feels like a better place. Nobody is immune to walking into a kitchen and scenting the mealy, yeasty smells of the sweet, freshly baked loaf and, like pastry or any other kitchen art, even a string of failures or less than successes should lead you to knocking out and kneading good bread with a bit of patience and practice.

The following loaves are only blueprints. Experiment with different flours – you can use any combination of flour and seeds that thrill you, just exercise caution and restraint. Nine seeds is at least half a dozen too many in a loaf, sun-dried tomatoes are rarely the answer, and apricots and figs have to be seen in context, not as things you throw in with a load of different nuts and seeds to try to create something original. A loaf of spelt or rye, plainly and properly executed, is better any day.

The best flour and toasted wheatgerm I have found is from John Lister's Shipton Mill in Gloucestershire (see the list of suppliers at the back of the book for details). They sell more than 20 different kinds. You must remember that flour changes character every day, and the longer it is kept, the less it will give to that extraordinary staff of life creation – the loaf. If you want to remind yourself of the real joy of the kitchen, making bread is the single most evocative and life-enhancing way to do it.

MALTED GRAIN LOAF

I leave it to you to vary the flavour with the different flours and seeds.

MAKES 3 LOAVES

1kg/2¼lb Shipton Mill or Dove's Farm organic malted grain flour
500g/lb 2oz strong organic wholemeal flour, again Shipton Mill or Dove's Farm
3 heaped tsp sea salt
45g/1½oz fresh yeast
3 heaped tsp molasses sugar
850ml/1½ pints hand-hot water; it should neither feel boiling, nor tepid
3 tbsp extra virgin olive oil
sesame, sunflower or poppyseeds and a little milk for the top of the loaves

Tip the flours out into a very large mixing bowl and add the salt. Boil a kettle, and put about 200ml/7fl oz of boiling water in a measuring jug, topping up to the 425ml/15fl oz mark with water from the cold tap. The water should now feel hand hot. Drop in the molasses sugar and fresh yeast and stir vigorously for a few seconds until the liquid looks creamy. Leave it for 15 minutes to rise. I still find this as absorbing as I did when I baked my first loaf, the living organism fizzing, popping, bubbling, and the sudden rush and rise in volume like a geyser with a will of its own inhabiting the jug.

Pour the contents of the jug into the flour, and then another 425ml/15fl oz of hand-hot water immediately afterwards, then pour in the three tablespoons of olive oil. With one hand, start working the wet dough together until it coheres completely into a ball. Remove it from the bowl on to the work surface and start kneading it. Sometimes the dough will appear too dry to work, sometimes too wet and claggy. Simply add a little more water for the former, and sprinkle with a little more flour for the latter; the dough should not feel sticky. After you have started working the dough vigorously with both hands on the work surface, you will, from time to time, probably need to shake a little more flour on to the work surface. The dough will elongate into a sausage each time you work it, which you need to furl back into a ball shape each time before repeating the process.

After 10 minutes, place the ball back in the bowl and cover the top with a clean linen tea towel, which you have wetted under the hot tap and wrung out. Leave at the side of the stove for about an hour, or until it has swollen to about twice its original volume and appears light and spongy.

Turn the oven to 230°C/450°F/Gas 8 to warm up. Brush the insides of your bread tins with olive oil. Turn the dough out on to the work surface, and divide it into 3 pieces with a sharp knife. Knock the air out of each loaf for 3 or 4 minutes, without kneading it, and place each loaf in its tin.

Re-cover with a hot, damp cloth, and leave in the warmth close by or on top of the oven for 20–25 minutes. Brush the top of each loaf with a little milk, and sprinkle over a handful of seeds. Put 2 loaves together on a higher shelf and one on a lower. Set the timer for 35 minutes, but they could take 40. You want a distinctive hollow sound when you tap the base of the bread while turning it out on to a rack with a palate knife. Allow the loaves to cool for at least 40 minutes; bread is steamy, doughy and indigestible if you eat it too soon after coming out of the oven.

These principles apply to all the other types of loaves I listed, and to rolls, which naturally take less long to cook. When you are using a plain flour and wish to add seeds to the actual bread mix, throwing in a handful of all three types of seeds – sunflower, sesame and poppy – seems to work beautifully.

WHITE LOAF

MAKES 2 LOAVES

1kg/2¼lb Shipton Mill traditional organic strong white flour
45g/1½oz fresh yeast (you can buy it at the bread counter of your supermarket IF they have a bakery in the store)
3 tsp fine sea salt
600ml/1 pint warm water at 30°C in summer, 40°C in winter. To guess it, it needs to be hand-hot, not boiling

Here is a sensationally good white loaf made with Shipton Mill's strong white flour, a handful of their newly toasted, deliciously oily wheatgerm, and an overnight or overday rise to maximise the fermentation. I now make bread on a terracotta stone. It should be a thick one according to John of Shipton Mill, but my pizza stone does two loaves beautifully. It radiates the heat evenly and there are no tin sides to give you a less crusty crust. Heat transfer is critical during baking and stones radiate heat in a totally different way to a metal tin. I also throw in a splash of water or squirt it into the oven with my iron spray — the steam helps to caramelise the surface of the loaf. I think it works best after the loaf has been in the oven for 10 minutes, but see what you think.

Allow approximately 14½ hours from the time you start the dough to cooking your bread. Dissolve a piece of yeast the size of a pea in 120ml/4fl oz of warm water. I stir the yeast in with a tiny whisk in a jug. Leave it for 10 minutes, then add it to 200g/7oz of the flour to which you have added half a teaspoonful of fine sea salt. Mix the dough a little with your fingers until it just coheres, then cover it with a tea towel soaked in cold water and wrung out — this prevents a skin forming on the dough. Leave it for 12 hours at room temperature in the kitchen. I have left it a couple of hours longer when convenient and it has not come to any harm.

Twelve hours later, dissolve the remaining yeast in 120ml/4fl oz of warm water, whisking it as before. Leave it for 10–15 minutes in the warmth of the kitchen. It won't froth up as it does with a quick-rise bread when you add sugar to the yeast and water at this stage.

Mix the rest of the bag of flour with the remaining salt and throw in a handful of wheatgerm. Add the starter dough, which will be spongy, to the mixture, then the yeasty liquid followed by the remaining 340ml/12fl oz of warm water. Work it in the bowl with your fingers until it coheres, then remove it to the work surface and knead energetically for 8–10 minutes.

Put it back in the large bowl, cover with the damp cloth again, and leave it for an hour to rise; it will double in volume. Put the dough back on the work surface. Seize it, and bash the air out of it, then leave it uncovered for 15 minutes.

Preheat the oven to 220°C/425°F/Gas 7 and put the baking stone on the middle shelf to heat up. Divide the dough into two pieces with a knife and bash out the air again. Form each piece into a ball and cover with a damp cloth for 50 minutes. It will double in size again. Snip a little decorative hole or two in the middle of the top, scatter a tiny bit of flour over and, with a flat spatula, plop the loaves on to the hot stone. After 10 minutes, spray or throw a little water into the oven until the steam hisses. The loaves will need 35–40 minutes. Check that the bottoms sound hollow before leaving them to cool for an hour on a rack.

ERIC TREUILLE'S FOCACCIA

Eric Treuille and his wife Rosie Kindersley are the owner-managers of my favourite playing-truant shop, Books for Cooks in Notting Hill, London. Eric has a lovely version of focaccia with thyme, Gruyère and crème fraîche, that makes the centrepiece of a light lunch, needing no more than a Provençal tomato salad or roasted tomato soup alongside. Eric suggests making and kneading the dough and leaving it to rise in the fridge all day or all night, for 8–12 hours, before letting it stand at room temperature, knocking it back and shaping it.

MAKES 1 LARGE LOAF

DOUGH
500g/1lb 2oz strong white flour
2 tsp sea salt
325ml/11fl oz tepid water
2 tsp dried yeast

TOPPING
500g/1lb 2oz baby potatoes
110g/4oz grated Gruyère
2 tsp fresh thyme leaves
sea salt and black pepper
4 tbsp crème fraîche
coarse salt to sprinkle

Put the flour in a bowl, make a well in the middle and put the salt on the raised ridge of flour around the sides. Pour the water into the well and sprinkle over the yeast. Leave for 5 minutes to soften, then stir to dissolve. Draw in enough of the flour to make a soft paste. Cover with a cloth and leave to sponge for 20 minutes until bubbly and slightly puffed up. Draw in the rest of the flour to make a rough, sticky dough. Turn out on to a lightly floured surface and knead for 10 minutes until smooth, light and elastic. Put back into the bowl, cover with a cloth and leave until doubled in size, about 1½ hours.

Preheat oven to 220°C/425°F/Gas 6. Cut the potatoes into 5mm/¼in slices. Bring a pan of salted water to the boil, add the potatoes and bring back to the boil. Cook for about 5 minutes until the centres are just tender when pricked with the tip of a knife. Drain well and cool.

Deflate the dough by pressing down with the palm of your hand. Roll out into a flat round, about 23cm/9in across, and place on an oiled baking sheet. Spread about half the cheese evenly on top of the bread dough, arrange the potatoes on top, scatter with thyme and sprinkle with a little salt and pepper. Cover with a cloth and leave until risen, about 30 minutes. Dot teaspoons of crème fraîche over the potatoes and scatter on the remaining cheese.

Bake for about 30 minutes or until the potato topping is crisp and golden and the bread sounds hollow when tapped underneath. Cool on a wire rack. Serve warm or at room temperature, sprinkled with coarse salt and cut into wedges.

WALNUT AND ONION SPELT LOAF

MAKES 2 LOAVES

675g/1½lb spelt flour (you can use
   ⅓ white flour to ⅔ spelt)
1 tsp sea salt
1 heaped tsp dark molasses sugar
1 x 7g/¼oz sachet easybake yeast
425ml/15fl oz tepid milk
150ml/5fl oz walnut oil
110g/4oz good, fresh, oily walnuts,
   chopped, but not too small
1 medium onion, finely chopped
a little egg white and a handful of
   sesame seeds (optional)

Eat this delicious bread toasted with the terrine on page 386. The walnuts and onions work beautifully with the pork and the spelt flour gives it a lovely coarse, branny nuttiness.

Sift the flour and salt into a bowl and add the sugar. Empty the yeast into the milk and pour it straight into the flour, then pour in the walnut oil. Knead well for 10 minutes, adding extra milk if you need to, to obtain a springy dough.

Put back in the mixing bowl, cover with a damp cloth and leave to rise for 2 hours. When the dough is about 3 times its original size, take it out of the bowl and knock it back, throwing in the nuts and onion and working them in briefly. Divide into 2 with a sharp knife and form into balls.

Leave to prove on a greased baking tray in the warm for 45 minutes. Preheat the oven to 190°C/375°F/Gas 5. Brush with a little egg white and throw a handful of seeds over the top of the loaves. Bake in the centre of the oven for 40–45 minutes or until the crust is brown and the loaves sound hollow when you tap their underside. Leave to cool on a rack.

A SIMPLE FLATBREAD

MAKES 6

500g/1lb 2oz strong, white plain flour
½ tsp sea salt
1 x 7g/¼oz sachet dried yeast
300ml/10fl oz warm water
a glug or tbsp olive oil

From the divine Nigel Slater, a must for the mezze.

Put the flour into the bowl of a food mixer with a beater attachment and add the salt. Empty the yeast into a small glass, pour on enough water to make a thin paste, then stir in the rest of the warm water. Pour the water onto the flour and turn the mixer on slow. Introduce the olive oil, mixing until you have a stiffish dough. Tip it out onto a floured board and knead with your hands, pushing and folding the dough until it feels springy and elastic to the touch. Set aside in a warm place in a bowl covered with a clean tea towel and leave to rise for an hour or so.

Heat the oven to 230°C/450°F/Gas 8. When your dough is about 4 times the size it was, break it into 6 pieces and push each one into a slipper shape. Dust with flour and put them flat on a baking sheet. Bake for 5 minutes then turn the temperature down to 220°C/425°F/Gas 7 and continue baking for a further 5 minutes or so until the underside of the bread sounds hollow when you tap it.

Walnut and Onion Spelt Loaf

PARMESAN GRISSINI

110g/4oz full-cream milk
1 tsp dry active yeast
55g/2oz unsalted butter
55g/2oz fresh Parmesan, grated
200g/7oz strong white flour
½ tsp fine sea salt

This is bread guru Dan Lepard's version of the chef Giorgio Locatelli's Parmesan grissini.

Heat oven to 180°C/350°F/Gas 4. Warm the milk until tepid, then whisk in the dried yeast. Melt the butter in a small saucepan over a low heat and pour the butter into the warm milk. Add the grated Parmesan and stir together, then add the flour and salt and work the mixture until a dough is formed.

Knead lightly for 10–15 seconds, then wrap the dough in a damp tea towel and leave for 10 minutes. Knead the dough once more for a further 10–15 seconds, cover again, and leave for 30 minutes. Knead a final time for 10–15 seconds, cover and leave for 45 minutes. Lightly flour the work surface and roll the dough until it's about 1cm/½in thick. With a sharp knife or pizza cutter and a ruler, cut strips of dough about 1cm/½in wide. Roll each strip into grissini and place them on a non-stick baking sheet.

Bake for 15–20 minutes until crisp and lightly golden. Remove from the oven and cool on a wire rack, and continue with the remaining dough until it is finished.

PANE PUGLIESE

½ tsp easy-blend yeast
140g/5oz strong white flour
200g/7oz sparkling bottled water, warmed
1 tsp honey
1 tsp chickpea flour, available from health-food stores (optional)
340g/12oz Italian '00' flour or 85g/3oz strong white flour and 255g/9oz semolina
110g/4oz sparkling water
2 tsp fine salt
1 tbsp extra virgin olive oil
1 tbsp chickpea flour (optional)

Whisk together the yeast, strong white flour, 200g/7oz warm sparkling bottled water, honey and teaspoon of chickpea flour until smooth. Cover the bowl with clingfilm and leave in a warm place for an hour. This is called the 'sponge' and it will be the ferment that aerates the final dough.

To this sponge, add the Italian flour or flour and semolina, 110g/4oz of sparkling water, salt, olive oil and tablespoon of chickpea flour. Mix until you have a soft, slightly sticky dough. Tip an extra teaspoon of olive oil on to the palms of your hands and knead the dough 12 times (20 seconds). Cover with clingfilm for 10 minutes. Knead another 12 times and cover again for 10 minutes. Repeat and leave to prove for 30 minutes.

Take a small bowl and line it with a tea towel. Dust lightly with flour, then knead the dough into a ball and place it seam-side up in the cloth-lined bowl.

Lightly fold the corners of the cloth over the top of the dough, and leave in a warm place for 45 minutes. Heat the oven to 230°C/450°F/Gas 8.

Dust a metal tray with semolina or polenta. Peel back the cloth and upturn the dough on to your hand, placing the dough seam-side up in the centre of the tray. Place the tray on the centre rack of the oven and bake for 45–55 minutes, or until the loaf is dark golden brown and sounds hollow when tapped underneath. Leave to cool on a wire rack before serving.

POTATO AND PORCINI FOCACCIA

340g/12oz sparkling bottled water, warmed (the increased bi-soda content gives a lighter, crisper loaf)

1 tsp easy-blend yeast

1 tsp runny honey

480g/1lb 1oz strong white flour

1 tsp malt extract (you can buy it at health-food shops)

2 tsp fine sea salt

10 tbsp extra virgin olive oil

TOPPING

1 large potato, washed, unpeeled and finely sliced on a mandoline if you have one

1 small onion, finely sliced

2 fresh porcini mushrooms, or a handful of sliced dried porcini

2 tbsp extra virgin olive oil

2 tsp Maldon salt

Dan Lepard writes: 'I know of a town in Italy where every loaf contains a little pork lard, giving the dough a strange richness.' I've removed it from this recipe, adding a little honey to help speed the dried yeast. If you're using fresh yeast, there is no need to add the honey.

In a small bowl, mix together 200g/7oz of the water with the yeast and the honey. Whisk together until the yeast has dissolved, then whisk in 140g/5oz of the flour. Cover the bowl with clingfilm and leave in a warm place for 2 hours, giving the mixture a stir after the first hour. By this time it should be bubbling and have risen to double its original height.

Scrape the sponge into another larger bowl, then add the remaining water and the malt extract and whisk together until the sponge has combined roughly with the water. Add the remaining flour and the salt and squidge the mixture together with your hand (try to do this with one hand to keep the other clean and dry). The mixture will be very soft, slightly lumpy and very sticky. This is good.

Scrape the dough down from around the sides of the bowl, then give your hands a good wash to remove any excess dough. Tip 1 tablespoon of the olive oil on to your hands, remove the dough from the bowl and rub the oil all over the surface of the dough.

Place the oiled dough on the worktop and knead 5 times (about 10 seconds). Cover with clingfilm and leave for 10 minutes. Rub another tablespoon of oil over the surface and knead 12 times (about 20 seconds). Cover and leave to prove for 30 minutes.

Knead a further 12 times, then cover and leave for 30 minutes. Heat the oven to 230°C/450°F/Gas 8. Take two 30 x 40cm/12 x 16in trays and rub the insides liberally with olive oil. In a bowl mix together the thinly sliced potatoes, onions and mushrooms with 2 tablespoons of olive oil and a pinch of salt. Stir until the potato slices are well coated with the oil.

Divide the dough in two and knead each piece into a ball. Place each ball on a tray and lightly flatten with a rolling pin. Don't worry if the dough springs back. Cover with clingfilm and leave in a warm place for 20–30 minutes.

Pick up the corners of the dough and stretch them out until they reach the corners of the tray. Tip the potato mixture evenly on top of each sheet of dough. Cover with clingfilm and leave a further 15 minutes. Remove the clingfilm, dimple the surface of the dough with your fingers, add a little extra salt if you wish and bake for 30–45 minutes, until the surface is golden brown and the potatoes tender. Remove from the oven and slide the focaccia on to a cooling rack.

PRESERVATION!

A dying art? The province of gnarled Women's Institute ladies in the shires? Of the Aga-owning, stay-at-home classes, who have the time to raid hedge and tree, then to bottle, pickle and preserve? Absolutely not. This is the sort of communal activity which any family should, could do together, be they city, town or country people. Children are happy to hull strawberries, men are happy to splurt blackberries into baskets from autumnal hedges, even happier to pick sloes and damsons if they are going to get a glug of fruited gin at the end of it; well, two years down the line.

CRAB APPLE JELLY

as much fruit as you can pick
water
unrefined sugar, 450g/1lb for each
    600ml/1 pint of juice

My affection for crab apple jelly is a deep and enduring one. This was my father's favourite breakfast treat, so it has to be mine. On odd years I feel cheated, the tree just doesn't rise to it. On the even years the boughs bend with the rosy-cheeked squat fruit, their waxen crimson and yellow an invitation to pick and pot. I drape muslin from a beam in the kitchen, letting the amber juice drip till its last drop. A sprig of lemon peel at the summit of each jar is a kind of elegant closure. The labels are written in my customary purple ink. Then the spoon-soft jelly drops onto my toast until it is no more and I have to move on to the next, the quince, the marmalade, whatever else is in store. These are the rituals of the cooking year that somehow, somewhere, have to be preserved.

Wash the fruit, put it in a huge preserving pan and just cover with water. Bring to the boil and simmer slowly, covered, until the apples are softened to a pulp. Put this into a jelly bag or piece of muslin and suspend it above a bowl so the juice can strain through. Leave it to drip overnight. You do not want to squeeze or hurry any of the juice through; this will make your jelly cloudy instead of sparkling.

Measure the beautiful pink juice in a jug, and add 450g/1lb of unrefined sugar to each 600ml/1 pint of juice. Bring to the boil, scum and keep boiling until you reach setting point. I start testing after 10 minutes. Put a small saucer in the fridge to cool, then place a teaspoon of boiling juice on the saucer, and put it in the freezer for a couple of minutes. If the liquid on the saucer wrinkles when you push it with a finger, the jelly has reached the setting point.

I scald the jars with boiling water in the sink as I wait for the setting point. Ladle the jelly through a funnel into the jars as soon as you have reached setting point. Cover immediately with cellophane and an elastic band.

...gle Jelly
october '03

SPICED REDCURRANT JELLY

MAKES 3 OR 4 JARS

1.5kg/3¼lb redcurrants
850ml/1½ pints water
3 cloves
a short length of cinnamon bark
240ml/8fl oz cider vinegar
1.5kg/3¼lb unrefined granulated
    sugar

I have a particular affection for this lovely glowing ruby jelly as it was the first jelly I ever attempted a couple of decades ago. Not only did it work, I found its cider-vinegar sharpness and musky spiciness far preferable to the commercial over-sweet confections or even the homemade sugary jellies I had been used to. I have stuck with it and it's great for lamb, venison, hare and grouse.

Throw the redcurrants into a large preserving or enamel pan as they are, with their stalks. Add the water and spices, bring to the boil and simmer until the redcurrants are soft. Strain the juice by putting the fruit into a muslin or jelly bag and leaving it suspended above a bowl to drip through overnight. Do not squeeze or hurry any of the juice through; this will make your jelly cloudy instead of sparkling.

Add the vinegar and sugar to the liquid in the pan, and boil until it reaches setting point. To test for the setting point, put a small saucer in the fridge to cool, then place a teaspoon of boiling juice on the saucer, and put it in the freezer for a couple of minutes. If the liquid on the saucer wrinkles when you push it with a finger, you have reached the setting point. Pour into warm jam jars and cover while the jelly is still very hot.

BLACKCURRANT OR WHITECURRANT JELLY

340g/12oz granulated sugar to each
    450g/1lb of blackcurrants or
    whitecurrants

The most intense and scented fruit of them all, the blackcurrant makes a jelly so highly flavoured and strong that it is the perfect one to use in a queen of puddings or with a branny damp slab of homemade soda bread.

Put the currants, along with their stalks and leaves, into a large pan. Add the sugar. Bring to the boil, skimming off the scum as it comes to the surface, then boil fast for 10 minutes. Pour into a bowl through a hair or nylon sieve. Press the fruit down lightly – not firmly, or the jelly will cloud. Test for setting as in the recipe above. Pour it warm into warm jam jars and seal. The blackcurrant jelly is wonderful in puddings.

BLACKCURRANT JAM

1kg/2¼lb black currants
850ml/1½ pints water
1.4kg/3lb unrefined granulated sugar

Simmer the fruit with the water until it is soft right through, about 45–50 minutes, then add the warmed sugar, bring to the boil and boil until setting point has been reached. Test after 10 minutes – see spiced redcurrant jelly above for wrinkle test.

UNCOOKED REDCURRANT JELLY

I first discovered this in Jane Grigson's seminal *Fruit Book*, where she quotes its origins in Joseph Favre's *Dictionnaire Universel de Cuisine Pratique* of the late 19th century as follows: 'The nomads of Arabia and Indo-China have their own way of making a currant jelly without fire which is as good as any made in Europe, both for its transparency and its delicacy.' Her more modern methodology works beautifully. Uncooked raspberry jelly can be made in the same way.

For every litre/1¾ pints of juice, warm 1kg/2¼lb of sugar in a heavy bowl in the oven until it is really hot. Put the bowl on the table and stir in the juice until the sugar has dissolved. Strain and pour into little jars. Leave them in an airy place for 12 hours, and then cover them. Best stored in the freezer.

The best way to extract the juice, which Jane Grigson doesn't bother to go into, is to pull the currants from their stems with the tines of a fork and throw them into the food processor. Process until they turn to liquid slush, then force the juice through a nylon sieve with a wooden spoon extracting as much as you possibly can. The same applies to raspberries, loganberries, blackcurrants and whitecurrants.

STRAWBERRY JAM

340g/12oz unrefined granulated sugar to every 450g/1lb strawberries
juice of a lemon for every 1.4kg/3lb fruit

Crush a large spoonful of berries with a fork and put them in a preserving pan with an equal amount of sugar. Warm gently until the sugar has dissolved, then add the rest of the hulled fruit and bring slowly to the boil, giving it an occasional stir.

Warm the sugar in a low oven (this stops the temperature in the pan from lowering), and add it to the fruit with the lemon juice – the lemon provides extra pectin. Boil rapidly for 10–12 minutes, or until setting point has been reached. (See redcurrant jelly recipe opposite for how to do the wrinkle test.)

Sometimes the fruit rises to the top of the pot (this happens with strawberries and cherries particularly), but if you leave the fruit in the pot after it has finished cooking for about 30 minutes, then stir and pot the jam, all should be well.

1kg/2 ¼lb strawberries
1kg/2¼lb unrefined granulated sugar
300ml/10fl oz redcurrant juice

STRAWBERRY JAM WITH REDCURRANT

The fruits stay whole exceptionally well in this jam and the syrup is really good. There is a lot of pectin in the currants to help the set.

Pour the sugar over the hulled berries in a large bowl and leave them overnight so that the juice starts to bleed from the fruit. Tip the contents of the bowl into a large preserving pan with the redcurrant juice. Bring to the boil slowly, then boil until setting point is reached. See the spiced redcurrant jelly recipe on page 482 for details of setting test.

RASPBERRY JAM

Allow equal weight of raspberries to sugar. Tip the sugar in an ovenproof dish and warm it through in a moderate oven for 15 minutes. Heat the fruit slowly in the preserving pan until the juices begin to bleed, then add the warm sugar and bring to the boil. This jam shouldn't take longer than 3 minutes to cook if the fruit is fresh and ripe. You don't want it to collapse too much. Test and pot in the usual way.

UNCOOKED RASPBERRY JAM

Again, allow equal quantities of fruit to sugar, unrefined caster sugar in this case. Put the sugar in one ovenproof dish and the raspberries in another and place in a moderate oven for 15 minutes. Remove from the oven and scrape the warmed sugar into the raspberries, stirring the two together for 10 minutes. Leave them to stand for 20 minutes. Repeat the stirring and standing a further couple of times each and then pot the jam. Put the pots uncovered into a cool oven for 1 hour, then cover them.

LOGANBERRY JAM

Whenever possible I prefer not to boil berries for fools, ice creams and, in this case, jam. The minimal cooking naturally results in a wonderfully intense flavour. It works just as well for raspberries.

Preheat the oven to 180°C/350°F/Gas 4. Put equal weights of loganberries and granulated sugar in a large dish in the oven. Let them get very hot, but do not allow to boil. Check after 20 minutes, although it could take 30 minutes.

Turn the fruit and sugar into a bowl and mix together thoroughly with a wooden spoon. Pour warm into warm jam jars and cover with discs of paper that you have first dipped in brandy, then seal. If mould forms on top of the jam, don't worry; the jam underneath will be fine, and it keeps extremely well.

PLUM JAM

2kg/4½lb plums
300–600ml/10fl oz–1 pint water, depending on the juiciness of the plums
2kg/4½lb unrefined granulated sugar

Halve the plums to remove the stones, then bash about half the stones with a hammer or rolling pin to extract the kernels. The French believe the secret heart of the fruit is contained in the kernels and their best apricot jams always contain little halves of kernel, adding the most intensely almondy, scented taste to the jam. Blanch the kernels in boiling water then set aside on a plate.

Tie the plum stones in muslin to cook with the jam. Simmer the fruit with the water and stones until soft. Meanwhile, warm the sugar in an ovenproof bowl in a moderate oven, then add to the softened fruit and continue to simmer. Test after 15 minutes (see page 482), although the jam will probably take 15–20 minutes to set. Add the kernels before you pot the jam.

GOOSEBERRY JAM

1.4kg/3lb under-ripe green gooseberries
600ml/1 pint water
1.8kg/4lb sugar
2–3 heads elderflower tied in a muslin (optional) or 2 tbsp Rock's organic elderflower cordial

Simmer the fruit with the water until it is soft, about 20 minutes. Warm the sugar as above and add it to the pan. Let the sugar dissolve, add the elderflowers or cordial, then bring the jam to the boil. Test after 10 minutes for setting point (see page 482), though it may take as long as 20 minutes. Remove the elderflowers if using and pot the jam.

ORGANIC SEVILLE ORANGE MARMALADE

ENOUGH FOR 17 POTS OF
VARYING SIZES

2kg/4½lb organic Seville oranges
3 organic lemons
3.2kg/7lb organic unrefined
    granulated sugar
5 litres/9 pints water

This has become an enshrined ritual in my kitchen every January, which my great friend and superlative marmalade-maker Gale partners me in. It was she, after all, who got me going, disabusing me of my prejudice against the glowing amber pots of bitter orange that I had previously managed to burn or cook to rigidity, setting them in stone rather than soft, golden gel.

Wash the oranges and lemons, halve and squeeze them, reserving the juice and the pips from the squeezing separately. Extract the remains of the pulp, pith and pips from the orange halves with your fingers and put them into a muslin bag with the other pips. Halve the halves, and pile the quarters into a tight stack that you can feed down the feeder tube of a food processor through the slicer disc. Trim any bits of peel that have not been properly shredded.

Put the sliced peel into a large preserving pan with the squeezed juice, water and the muslin bag tied to the side and bring gently to the boil. Cover with a lid and put into the simmering oven of an Aga, or continue to simmer very gently on top of the stove. It will take about 2½ hours inside the Aga or rather less, about 2 hours, on top of the stove, for the peel to have absolutely no bite to it right the way through.

Remove the jelly bag and suspend it over a bowl for the juice to drain through for about 30 minutes, then add the juice to the liquid in the pan. Now divide the mixture accurately into three batches for the next stage, because it sets better in small quantities. Put one-third of the mixture back into the preserving pan, with one-third of the sugar, and heat gently, stirring to dissolve the sugar completely. The mixture mustn't boil until the sugar has completely dissolved. Now boil hard until you reach setting point; ours took about 15 minutes, but start testing after 10. Put a small saucer in the fridge to cool, then place a teaspoon of boiling juice on the saucer, and put it in the freezer for a couple of minutes. While you do this, remove the marmalade from the heat so that it doesn't cook any further. If the liquid on the saucer wrinkles when you push it gently with a finger, it has reached setting point.

Now leave the pan off the heat for 30 minutes before you ladle the marmalade into warm clean jars, otherwise the shreds will rise up the jar to the top, and you'll have half-overshredded, half-gel marmalade. Don't fall at the last fence. Be patient, the waiting is all. Repeat with the remaining two-thirds of ingredients.

LEMON, LIME OR ORANGE CURD

2 large, organic lemons
85g/3oz unsalted butter cut into
    cubes
225g/8oz unrefined granulated sugar
3 large organic eggs

I make my curd in a heavy-bottomed, wide-based pan. The wide surface area speeds up the gelling of the curd. Grate the zest from both lemons into the pan with a zester and add the juice of the lemons, the butter and the sugar. Stir over a gentle heat until the sugar is dissolved, making sure the mixture doesn't come to the boil. Beat the eggs and add them to the mixture, then keep stirring and watching like a hawk until the curd thickens. Remove from the heat instantly and pot.

You may make lime and orange curds in the same way, altering the sugar balance to taste. Seville oranges make a lovely curd for a tart.

QUINCE PASTE, OR MEMBRILLO

2kg/4½ lb quinces
300ml/10fl oz water
granulated sugar

This scented, deep amber paste is one of the great treats of life, perfect eaten with Manchego or an English sheep's milk cheese like the blessed Wigmore, my own and my son Harry's favourite. A perfect pudding partnership, it takes care of the cheese or pudding debate as it does both things at once.

Remove the bloom from the quince skins with a cloth. Wash them, cut into quarters and stew them in the water until they're soft. Sieve them and weigh the purée, then return it to the pan with an equal amount of unrefined granulated sugar. Boil slowly until the mixture comes away from the sides of the pan, like polenta, stirring constantly and carefully so as not to get splattered, with a wooden spoon.

Pour into metal trays lined with Bakewell paper and dry out for a few days in the airing cupboard or on top of the Aga if you have one. Store in a sealed container somewhere cool.

Lemon Curd

RUMTOPF

1kg/2¼lb strawberries, hulled
500g/1lb 2oz sugar
1 litre/1¾ pints rum, the French use
    brandy
other fruits such as cherries,
    raspberries, loganberries,
    blackberries, peaches, pears,
    plums, apricots as and when they
    come into season

Around Christmas time, my Swedish friend Kristina von Wrede always presented a giant jar of rumtopf and a glass ladle to guests at dinner along with a homemade ice cream or just with whipped cream. Rumtopf is a lovely thing to make in the strawberry season and dispense in cold times, an Austrian tradition that her husband's family must have taught her about. This has to be started in June or July when strawberries are in season.

Once the strawberries are hulled, put them in a bowl, sprinkle them with the sugar and leave them overnight. The next day, tip the entire contents of the bowl into a rumtopf and pour over the booze. Put a saucer down onto the fruit so that it can't float above the surface of the liquor, cover the jar with clingfilm and the corked lid and keep it in a cool dark place like a larder or outhouse. Keep on adding more fruit and sugar prepared in the same way in whatever quantities you have as the summer fruits season progresses and keep on topping up the booze in proportion to it.

Once the rumtopf is full, add a final slug of booze and hide it until around Christmas. You may serve it straight from the jar, ladling it into glasses and topping them with cream, or pour it lusciously over ice cream, pannacotta, creams or possets.

DAMSON, SLOE OR MULBERRY GIN

MAKES A LARGE JAR

850ml/1½ pints of damsons or sloes;
    put them in a measuring jug as
    you pick, or, if you make mulberry
    gin, use equal measures of
    mulberries and gin
340g/12oz unrefined sugar
1.2 litres/2 pints good gin
either half a dozen kernels from
    inside the damson stones, which
    you crack open with a hammer, or
    a few drops of Culpeper's bitter
    almond essence

After the autumnal hedgerow foraging, the dark staining of fingers, the pricking of the fruit with a fork or silver pin to get the juices flowing, the cracking of the kernels and jarring and sealing of the wine-coloured brew, there is the waiting, turning and shaking as alcohol, sugar and fruit turn to a perfect purple linctus.

Prick the damsons, sloes or mulberries and put them into a large Kilner jar. Add all the other ingredients, seal the jar and give it a good shake. Shake every week until Christmas, when you may strain and bottle the gin. The fruit will be delicious with a bit of the sticky purple linctus eaten with some homemade vanilla ice cream.

This recipe also works well for 'moonshine', which Stephen Markwick, brilliant chef at the restaurant Culinaria in Bristol, makes. Moonshine is vodka based, filled with cherries and a lot of the kernels from the cracked cherry stones.

Sloe Gin

APRICOT OR PLUM CHUTNEY

1kg/2¼lb apricots or plums, halved
and stoned
225g/8oz sharp apple, chopped
225g/8oz onion, sliced
110g/4oz carrot, coarsely grated
110g/4oz raisins
225g/8oz light muscovado sugar
1 dsrtsp sea salt
1 star anise
1 tsp ground cloves
1 tsp ground dried ginger root
1 tsp ground allspice
1 small dried red chilli
600ml/1 pint white wine vinegar

This is a lovely spicy chutney, all the better for using proper white wine vinegar instead of the throat-wrenching malt vinegar.

Put the fruit in a large bowl with the onion, carrot, raisins and sugar and mix it all together. Put the salt, spices and vinegar into a pan and bring slowly to the boil. Add the fruity mixture, stirring it all in together and bringing it back up to the boil. Let it simmer away steadily until the mixture is thick and gloopy and has turned to chutney. Pot into warmed jars, cover and keep somewhere cool and dark for at least 6 weeks before using.

COURGETTE CHUTNEY

MAKES 900G/2LB

2 small lemons
3 medium courgettes
2 onions, peeled and thinly sliced
100ml/3½fl oz Riesling or other dry
white wine
2 tsp brown sugar
24 black peppercorns,
coarsely crushed
2.5cm/1in piece of fresh ginger,
peeled and finely chopped
sea salt

Peel the lemons, cutting away all the pith, then slice them thinly and discard the pips. Cut the courgettes in half length-wise, then across into 2.5cm/1in pieces. Combine all the ingredients in a saucepan, adding a little sea salt. Cover and cook over a moderate heat for 1 hour, stirring from time to time. There will be quite a bit of liquid at the end of the cooking time, but once the chutney has cooled, the consistency will be perfect.

Either bottle, or put in a bowl to serve. It will keep in the fridge for 4—5 days.

TOMATO CHILLI JAM

MAKES TWO LARGE JARS

750g/1lb 10oz very ripe organic tomatoes
4 red chillies, with their seeds
6 fat cloves of garlic, peeled
3 thumbs of fresh ginger, peeled and roughly chopped
40ml/1½fl oz Thai fish sauce (nam pla)
450g/1lb unrefined golden caster sugar
150ml/5fl oz red wine vinegar

Quite simply, your kitchen should never be without this jam, and it keeps in the fridge for weeks if it is allowed the chance to do so. Great with a Montgomery Cheddar sandwich, in a toasted sandwich or slicked onto bruschetta under a row of slices of Ragstone or Golden Cross goat cheese; serve it with cold pork, on griddled scallops, or come up with your own idea. Versatile it is. I have upped the quantity from Peter Gordon's original recipe and this quantity of ingredients make enough for two outsize jars. Mine took double the cooking time he suggested, nearly an hour and a half, so don't panic if nothing seems to be happening after an hour.

Blend half the tomatoes, the chillies, garlic, ginger and fish sauce to a fine purée in a blender. You need the chilli seeds for the heat, which is not intense, and the tomato seeds for the pectin, which will make the jam set.

Put the purée, sugar and vinegar into a deep pan and bring to the boil slowly, stirring all the time. When it reaches the boil, turn down to a gentle simmer and add the remaining tomatoes cut into tiny dice, about 5mm/¼in, skin and all. Skim off the foam and cook gently for 1¼–1½ hours, stirring every so often to release the solids that settle on the bottom and prevent them from burning. Be sure to scrape the sides of the pot too, so the entire mass cooks evenly.

When the jam is done, pour it into warmed glass jars. Allow it to cool to room temperature before storing in the fridge or a cold larder for later use.

PICKLED CUCUMBER

SERVES 4

½ tbsp caster sugar
3 tbsp tarragon white wine vinegar
1 cucumber, peeled and finely sliced on a mandolin or by hand
1 tbsp dill, finely chopped
black pepper

This is perfect served as a vegetable with a cold poached salmon or sea trout (see page 254). Its sharpness, with a hint of a sweet note, perfectly complements the rich oily flesh of the fish.

In a bowl, stir the sugar into the wine vinegar until it has dissolved. Throw in the cucumber slices and dill, and scrunch over a goodly amount of black pepper. Leave to macerate for at least an hour before serving, turning the slices 2 or 3 times in the liquor; the cucumber will continue to exude juice as it macerates. Serve straight from the bowl, with as little of the liquid as possible.

SUPPLIERS

The Ark Chicken Company
Top quality, organic guinea fowl, quail and several kinds of chicken

Roosters of Babylon
Silverton, Exeter, Devon EX5 4DT
Tel/Fax: 01392 860430
Web: www.arkchicken.co.uk
Email: info@arkchicken.co.uk

L'Artisan du Chocolat
Gerard Coleman is arguably the finest chocolatier in England. He sells to the best restaurants and has a shop in Lower Sloane Street in London and a stall in Borough Market

89 Lower Sloane Street, London SW1W 8DA
Tel: 020 7824 8365
Web: www.artisanduchocolat.com
Email: order@artisanduchocolat.com

Baker and Spice
Bread, cakes, wonderful puff pastry, traiteur
Web: www.bakerandspice.co.uk

54–56 Elizabeth Street, London SW1W 9PB
Tel: 020 7730 3033
Fax: 020 7730 3188
Email: belgravia@bakerandspice.com

47 Denyer Street, London SW3 2LX
Tel: 020 7589 4734
Fax: 020 7823 9148
Email: chelsea@bakerandspice.com

75 Salusbury Road, Queen's Park,
London NW6 6NH
Tel: 020 7604 3636
Fax: 020 7604 3646
Email: queenspark@bakerandspice.com

The Bay Tree Food Company
Jams, jellies, chutneys and relishes

Lower Westcombe Farm, Evercreech, Shepton Mallet, Somerset BA4 6ER
Tel: 01749 831300
Fax: 01749 831233
Web: www.thebaytree.co.uk

Phil Bowditch
Excellent fishmonger

7 Bath Place, Taunton, Somerset, TA1 4ER
Tel: 01823 253500
www.philbowditch.co.uk

Bramley and Gage's
Gorgeously sticky, fruity liqueurs, and sloe and damson gins

4 Longmeadow, South Brent,
South Devon TQ10 9YT
Tel/Fax: 01364 73722
Web: www.bramleyandgage.co.uk

Brindisa
All things Spanish, the best of the best

32 Exmouth Market, Clerkenwell,
London EC1R 4QE
Tel/Fax: 020 7713 1666
Email: retail@brindisa.com
Web: www.brindisa.com

Brown and Forrest
Huge range of smoked foods, including the best smoked eel

The Smokery, Bowdens Farm, Hambridge,
Somerset TA10 0BP
Tel: 01458 250875
Fax: 01458 253475
Web: www.smokedeel.co.uk
Email: info@smokedeel.co.uk

Carluccio's
Italian deli, plus cafés and restaurants. Visit website for all locations

28A Neal Street, London WC2H 9QT
Tel: 020 7240 1487
Fax: 020 7497 1361
Web: www.carluccios.com

Clarence Court eggs
The best eggs, available at Tesco, Sainsbury's and most Waitrose stores

Coach House Farm, Cheltenham Road,
Broadway, Worcestershire WR12 7BY
Tel: 01386 858007
Fax: 01386 858009
Web: www.clarencecourt.co.uk
Email: info@clarencecourt.co.uk

Sally Clarke
Restaurant and shop with homemade bread, cookies, soups and tarts

122 & 124 Kensington Church Street,
London W8 4BH
Tel: 020 7221 9225
Web: www.sallyclarke.com
Email:
restaurant/bakery/shop @sallyclarke.com

Dove's Farm
Organic and gluten-free bread, flours, cookies and cereals

Salisbury Road, Hungerford,
Berkshire RG17 0RF
Tel: 01488 684880
Fax: 01488 685235
Web: www.dovesfarm.co.uk
Email: portenquiry@dovesfarm.co.uk

The Fine Cheese Company
Wide range of British, Irish, French and Italian cheeses, biscuits, chutneys, jams, relishes and wine. Also agents for Seggiano products

29–31 Walcot Street, Bath BA1 5BN
Tel: 01225 448748
Web: www.finecheese.co.uk
Email: sales@finecheese.co.uk

H. Forman and Son
Britain's oldest established salmon smokers, sell wonderful wild smoked salmon. They also sell smoked marlin, sturgeon and swordfish, and caviars Beluga, Oscietra and Sevruga

6 Queens Yard, Whitepost Lane, London E9 5EN
Tel: 020 8985 0378
Fax: 020 8985 0180
Web: www.formans.co.uk
Email: sales@formans.co.uk

Le Fromagerie
The best French cheeses
Web: www.lafromagerie.co.uk

30 Highbury Park, London N5 2AA
Tel/Fax: 020 7359 7440
Email: highbury@lafromagerie.co.uk

2–4 Moxon Street, London W1U 4EW
Tel/Fax 020 7935 0341
Email: moxon@lafromagerie.co.uk

Furness Fish, Poultry and Game Supplies
Brown shrimps, fish, smoked fish and meats

Stockbridge Lane, Ulverston, Cumbria LA12 7BG
Tel: 01229 585037
Fax: 01229 582485
Web: www.morecambebayshrimps.com
Email: orders@morecambebayshrimps.com

Hill Station
Excellent ice creams and sorbets

Stanier Road, Calne, Wiltshire SN11 9PX
Tel: 01249 816596
Fax: 01249 816597
Email: info@hillstation.co.uk
Web: www.hillstation.co.uk

Huntsam Farm Pedigree Meats (Richard Vaughan)
Longhorn beef, the finest in the land from our oldest breed, and Middle White pigs

Goodrich, Ross on Wye, Herefordshire, HR9 6JN
Tel: 01600 890 296
Fax: 01600 890 390
Web: www.huntsham.com
Email: Richard@huntsham.com

Lighthouse Bakery
Exceptional bread

64 Northcote Road, London SW11 6QL
Tel: 020 7228 4537
Fax: 020 7223 7315
Web: www.lighthousebakery.co.uk
Email: info@lighthousebakery.co.uk

Lina Stores
Homemade fresh pasta and a wide range of Italian food

18 Brewer Street, London W1R 3FS
Tel: 020 7437 6482

Ottolenghi
Traiteur, café, wonderful salads, tarts, croissants and cakes. Will cook for your party
Web: www.ottolenghi.co.uk

63 Ledbury Road, London W11 2AD
Tel: 020 7727 1121
ledbury@ottolenghi.co.uk

287 Upper Street, London N1 2TZ
Tel: 020 772881454
upper@ottolenghi.co.uk

Poilâne
The famous Poilâne loaf

46 Elizabeth Street, London SW1W 9PA
Tel: 020 7808 4910
Web: www.poilane.fr
Email: info@poilane.fr

Rocombe Farm Fresh Ice Cream Ltd
Delicious organic Jersey cream and ice creams

Middle Rocombe Farm, Stoke in Teignhead, Newton Abbot, Devon TQ12 4QL
Tel: 01626 872291
Fax: 01626 835777
Email: sales@rocombefarm.co.uk
Web: www.rocombefarm.co.uk

Seggiano
Olive oil and all things Italian

Tel: 020 7272 5588
All products are available by mail order from The Fine Cheese Company,
Tel: 01225 448748, or online at
www.finecheese.co.uk

Shipton Mill Ltd
Stock more than 20 kinds of flour, including organic Irish soda, three malts and sunflower, spelt and rye, and can supply by mail order

Long Newnton, Tetbury, Glos GL8 8RP
Tel: 01666 505050
Fax: 01666 504666
Email: enquiries@shipton-mill.com

Somerset Cider Brandy Company
Somerset Cider Brandy, single-variety cider, Stoke Red and Kingston Black

Pass Vale Farm, Burrow Hill, Kingsbury Episcopi, Martock, Somerset TA12 5BU
Tel: 01460 240782
Fax: 01460 249220
Web: www.ciderbrandy.co.uk

Somerset Lamb Direct
Traditionally reared, properly hung lamb and mutton as well as beef, pork and poultry; game in season

Bittescombe Manor, Upton, Wiveliscombe, Taunton, Somerset TA4 2DA
Tel: 01398 371387
Fax: 01398 371413
Web: www.somersetfarmdirect.co.uk
Email: deawood@btinternet.com

Swaddles Green Organic Farm
Wonderful meat, poultry, hams, sausages, and a range of cooked dishes, including puddings, cakes and pies

Hare Lane, Buckland St Mary, Chard, Somerset TA20 3JR
Tel: 0845 456 1768
Fax: 01460 234591
Email: info@swaddles.co.uk
Web: www.swaddles.co.uk

Vegetables
If you are interested in joining a box scheme, call the Soil Association on 0117 9290661
They also have an organic directory

The Village Bakery
The organic Village Bakery at Melmerby will send the best raspberry jam or Seville orange marmalade and loaves of wonderful bread, including a naturally leavened Campagne and Hadrian, a spelt bread made with raisin pulp, and inspired by the Romans.

Melmerby, Penrith, Cumbria CA10 1HE
Tel: 01768 881811
Fax: 01768 881848
Web: www.village-bakery.com
Email: info@village-bakery.com

Graeme Wallace
The best of the farmed venison

Wallace's, Hill Farm, Hemyock, Devon EX15 3UZ
Tel: 01823 680307
Fax: 01823 680329
Web: www.welcometowallaces.co.uk
Email: info@welcometowallaces.co.uk

Well Hung Meat Company
Geoff Sayers's farm produces the best coarse-textured organic pork and Toulouse sausages. He also sells beef, lamb, chicken and local oysters.

Tordean Farm, Dean Prior, Buckfastleigh, Devon TQ11 0LY
Tel: 0845 230 3131
Web: www.wellhungmeat.com
Email: sales@wellhungmeat.com

INDEX

DEDICATION

Tamasin's Kitchen Bible is dedicated to the three G's, who have kept me sane and insane serially as I have struggled to complete this mighty tome over the last two years. Their friendship, advice and addiction to good food have kept the keel if not even, at least afloat over a period in which it would have been all too easy to abandon ship. In fact, the three G's have undertaken the task for rather longer than the gestation of this book, they have all been wonderful friends for two decades.

For Gale, Georgie and Gladys with my love and thanks.

ACKNOWLEDGEMENTS

It seems unbelievable that as I write this in late June we almost have closure on a book which was conceived nearly three years ago and written over the course of the last two. The thinking, the structuring and the writing have moved gently, yet inexorably towards their final soldering; to being joined to the other elements. To those elements that are needed to make the jewel shine; that give polish, finish, style and poise and turn base metal to diamond. The cutters and polishers of *Tamasin's Kitchen Bible* have now worked together for nine years, over which period they have produced eight cabochons, this bible being the eighth in the series.

This time we wanted to do something different and although you, the reader, will be the judge of whether or not we have succeeded, I as the author am convinced that the team have contributed exceptional skill and artistry in producing and refining what I hope will become a dog-eared, stained and splashed, enduring and favourite companion on your cookery shelves and the shelves of your children and grandchildren.

Lippa Pearce has changed our look from aspirational pretty to bold, vibrant, arresting, sexy. David Rowley, our art director, has had the colossal task of initiating the new look and making it homogenous, beautiful and different. Nigel Soper has made the design simple, elegant, intelligible in a world where some cookery books have are almost impossible to read, so over-stylised and complicated have they become. Susan Haynes has offered her usual quiet, undogmatic, understated encouragement and total support as she has with each and every previous volume. Jinny Johnson has been a powerhouse and sounding board, involved at each stage, and my 'reader in the kitchen' as we shoot the photographs. If she doesn't understand my instructions then I know I have to re-write. To her a great debt of gratitude. Michael Dover, as publisher, is my backroom guru, pulling the invisible threads together like a puppet master but also being the best fun to work with, eat with, drink with and climb with. Whenever the mountain is showing through the cloud, that is.

David Loftus is unarguably — and yes, I am biased and subjective on the matter — the best food photographer there is. And that is because he doesn't think, approach or look at food as a food photographer. He is far more than that: his pictures are the pictures of an artist, they are the pictures of dreams; he interprets the way I see my food in my head and exactly how I think it should look. He is a master of composition and simplicity. He doesn't do cheffy or unattainable, nor do I. And Rosie Scott, his assistant, finds the look, the props, the plates with consummate style. Thanks to all of you.

Also thanks to Anthony Cheetham for commissioning *Tamasin's Kitchen Bible* in the first place and for continuing to be my disinterested, yet most valued and astute critic, and to George Capel for smoothing the path and always understanding the troughs and setbacks and wildernesses that writers get into unwittingly and unwillingly as they struggle to their conclusions!

Tamasin Day-Lewis
June 2005
Somerset

First published in Great Britain in 2005
by Weidenfeld & Nicolson

This paperback edition first published in 2007
by Weidenfeld & Nicolson
10 9 8 7 6 5 4 3 2

Photography by David Loftus
Styling by Rosie Scott

A CIP catalogue record for this book
is available from the British Library.

ISBN 13: 978 0 297 85357 2
ISBN 10: 0 297 84363 X

Design director David Rowley
Editorial director Susan Haynes
Designed by Nigel Soper and Lippa Pearce
Edited by Jinny Johnson
Proofread by Constance Novis
Index by Elizabeth Wiggans

Printed in Italy

Weidenfeld & Nicolson
The Orion Publishing Group Ltd
Orion House
5 Upper Saint Martin's Lane
London, WC2H 9EA
www.orionbooks.co.uk

Next page: Oeufs en Cocotte (p56)